A MODERN HISTORY
OF THE KURDS

A MODERN HISTORY OF
THE KURDS

DAVID McDOWALL

I.B.Tauris *Publishers*
LONDON • NEW YORK

Second revised and updated edition published in 2000 by I.B.Tauris & Co Ltd
Victoria House, Bloomsbury Square, London WC1B 4DZ
175 Fifth Avenue, New York NY 10010
Website: http://www.ibtauris.com

In the United States of America and in Canada distributed by
St. Martin's Press, 175 Fifth Avenue, New York NY 10010

First published in 1996 by I.B.Tauris & Co Ltd
Revised and updated edition published in 1997

ISBN 1 86064 535 6
A full CIP record for this book is available from the British Library
A full CIP record for this book is available from the Library of Congress

Library of Congress catalog card: available

Typeset by the Midlands Book Typesetting Company, Loughborough
Printed and bound in Great Britain

CONTENTS

MAPS

SOURCES

A few books have been used in many chapters. Rather than cite them repeatedly in the list of sources for each chapter, they are listed here:

Published

Martin van Bruinessen, *Agha, Shaikh and State: the Social and Political Structure of Kurdistan* (London, 1992).
Gerard Chaliand (ed.), *A People without a Country: The Kurds and Kurdistan* (London, 1980).
Abdal Rahman Ghassemlou, *Kurdistan and the Kurds* (Prague and London, 1965).
Chris Kutschera, *Le Mouvement National Kurde* (Paris, 1979).
Basil Nikitine, *Les Kurdes: Étude Sociologique et Historique* (Paris 1956).
Arshak Safrastian, *The Kurds and Kurdistan* (London, 1948).
Muhammad Amin Zaki, *Khulasa tarikh al Kurd wa'l Kurdistan,* vol. i: *Min aqdam al usur al tarikhiya hatta alan* (Cairo, 1939/Beirut 1961/London 1986) vol. ii: *Tarikh al dual wa'l amarat al Kurdiya fi'l ahd al Islamiya* (Cairo, 1948/London 1986).

Unpublished

Wadie Jwaideh, 'The Kurdish national movement: its origins and development' (PhD diss., Syracuse, 1960).

ACKNOWLEDGEMENT

Writing this book proved a greater undertaking than I had anticipated at the outset, largely because I found myself drawn into detailed research particularly of the archival material available in the Public Record Office. As a consequence I owe a considerable debt to a number of institutions and their staff: the Public Record Office, the India Office Library, the British Library, the London Library, l'Institut Kurde, the Kurdish Students Aid Committee, the Kurdish Information Centre, the Kurdish Advice Centre, the Kurdish Cultural Centre, the Kurdish Workers' Association, the School of Oriental and African Studies, Chatham House Press Library and my local reference library in Richmond. The staff of all these archives, libraries and centres have been both efficient and helpful, and I am most grateful.

As any researcher knows, nothing can substitute for the advice and information provided by others who have laboured in the same or neighbouring fields. Both in Kurdistan and in Europe I have met with nothing but helpfulness from those who had some experience or knowledge of the Kurdish question. These include many who corrected wild misconceptions or errors of fact, some who did translation work for me, and others who went out of their way to explain or elucidate points which had left me perplexed.

I should apologize for omissions from my list of thanks, the result of forgetfulness or, in the case of Turkey, a deliberate decision not to cite any names in case it should incur state retribution. There are a few names I may cite safely in the Turkish case because they have already been penalized: Musa Anter and Meded Serhat, both of whom were assassinated as a result of their views in September 1992 and November 1994 respectively; Serhat Bucak and Ismet Imset, whose lives were both threatened by the state in 1993 and 1994 respectively and who sought asylum in Britain; Ismail Besikci, a Turkish professor of anthropology whose steadfast and courageous insistence on Kurdish identity and rights has led him back to yet another heavy prison sentence, and Hatib Dicle, who was stripped of his parliamentary immunity and in December 1994 sentenced to 15 years' imprisonment for exercising the right and – in a democracy – duty of free speech.

Those I can name are Sami Abd al Rahman, Ibrahim Ahmad, Dlaweh Alaaldin, Hama Ali, Nawshirwan Mustafa Amin, Sarbast Aram, Sedaat Aybar, Maia Muhammad Ismail Bilbas, Hamit Bozarslan, Martin van Bruinessen, Sami Coskun, Kemal Davoudi, Mehmet Ali Kikerdem, Shirwan Dizai, Rebwar Fatah, Hassan Ghazi, Tom Hardie-Forsyth, Salah al Din Hafidh, Muhammed Hawar, Mustafa Hijri, Jane Howard, Ziba Mir Hosseini, Shaikh Izz al Din Husayni, Kamran Adnan Mufti, Adil Murad, Hoshmand Othman, Mahmud Othman, Siyamand Bayan Rezannezada, Mansur Ssajjadil Barham Salih, Estella Schmidt, David Shankland, Sami Shoresh, Robert Soeterek, Jawhaar Surchi, Umar Surchi, Jalal Talaabani, Abbas Vali, Lale Yalchin-Heckmann and Hoshyar Zibari. Of these I owe a very special debt to Adnan Mufti who took me under his wing in Iraqi Kurdistan and introduced me to people he shrewdly realized would answer questions that were still forming in my mind; to his friend Adil Murad who spent hours explaining in great detail particular events over the past two decades in Iraqi Kurdistan; to Hassan Ghazi who spent much time digging out information on events in Iranian Khurdistan and correcting my many misunderstandings; and Maia Balcioglu-Brisley and Estella Schmidt who arranged a wide range of contacts and hospitality on my first visit to Turkey. Needless to say, I remain responsible for any errors of judgment or fact.

I owe a particular debt of gratitude to the Author's Foundation which provided a generous grant that enabled me to visit Kurdistan to talk with a wide variety of people. All I can say is that their money was extremely well spent.

I owe special thanks to Anna Enayat, my editor, who as ever read the text with a critical and informed eye, questioning things that either did not make sense or which contradicted her own considerable knowledge of the region, and to Anne Rodford who prepared the text for publication quickly and very efficiently.

I am most grateful to the following for their assistance with advice, comment and material for the second edition:

Martin van Bruinessen, Julie Flint, Nelida Fuccaro, Lokman Meho, Estella Schmidt, The International Association of Human Rights for the Kurds for its excellent weekly bulletins, The Kurdish Human Rights Project, which kindly permitted me to reproduce much of *The Kurds of Syria* (KHRP, 1999); and the Washington Kurdish Institute for its comprehensive press service.

Finally, my greatest thanks must be to my family – my sons, Angus and William, who had to live with my fixation, – and above all to my wife Elizabeth. She maintained me for four years in every sense, earning enough for us to live on and raising my spirits when they were low. To her, true love and helpmeet, I offer this book with all my love and thanks.

David McDowall

FOREWORD

The Kurds number at least 25 million, yet there is only modest information available about them. There is probably a larger literature available on Kuwait, a state with barely half a million citizens. The reason is obvious: the Kurds inhabit a marginal zone between the power centres of the Mesopotamian plain and the Iranian and Anatolian plateaux. They remain marginalized geographically, politically, and economically.

However, during the past decade the Kurds have steadily grown in importance. It is difficult to imagine they will sink again into the relative obscurity of the middle years of this century. Today they have emerged, not quite yet as a coherent nation, nevertheless as an ethnic community that can no longer be ignored. For that reason alone, they deserve to be much better understood.

Because so little has been written about Kurdish history, I have written in greater detail than would be necessary were the context better known. Even so, it must be tentative since English, French and Arabic provide only a limited basis. A working knowledge of Persian, Turkish and Russian, let alone Kurdish, is also needed to fill out the picture.

I have devoted considerable space to the years 1918–25. The reason is simple: during this narrow period the Kurds lost their one great opportunity for statehood, and found themselves apportioned as minorities in the new state system that replaced the Ottoman and Qajar empires. It was a defining moment for the Kurdish people. Understanding how and why the contestants behaved then is critical for understanding later developments.

I have also concentrated particularly on the Kurdish struggle in Turkey and Iraq, since it is in these two countries that Kurds constitute 20 per cent or more of the population and the broad implication of this should be self-evident. This is also where Kurds have been most active. I have in addition tried to cover the Kurdish story in western Iran, since here they number over five million and constitute approximately 10 per cent of Iran's population, although the national movement has achieved much less than in Iraq or Turkey. My canvass was already so broad that I baulked at discussing the Kurdish question in either Syria or the former Soviet Union except as appendices to this new edition.

I regret I have found it almost impossible to achieve consistency in nomencalature and transliteration. Latinized script in Turkey changed conventional European spellings of place and proper names. In Turkey, Iran and Iraq, names have been changed, or conventional spellings altered over the years. Furthermore, Kurdish spelling itself is often unrecognizable except to Kurds, for example Wirmi (for Urumiya), and Shnu (for Ushnaviya). In other cases it has changed for one reason or another, for example Sawj Bulaq became Mahabad, Sinna became Sanandaj and Julamirk became Hakkari. Consequently I have tried to use the name appropriate to the era and I hope that by cross-referencing in the index, readers will not encounter any difficulty. Regarding transliteration, the simplest solution seemed to adopt simplified standard Arabic transliterations wherever possible, except for post-1923 Turkey. For example, Ghazi and Ghassemlou, two important Iranian names, appear as Qazi and Qasimlu.

The term Kurdistan is controversial. I use it simply to indicate the region where the majority of people are Kurds, not to peddle any particular political views. In the case of Turkey, therefore, it means the same as the euphemistic 'East' or 'South East', in the case of Iran it implies more than the province of Kurdistan (except where that is clearly the sense) to include the Kurdish parts of West Azarbaijan and Kirmanshah, and in Iran it means more than the autonomous region.

Finally, I have resisted the temptation to provide a reference for every little-known fact, since this would have made the book unacceptably long. Instead, I have tried to confine endnotes to points of elucidation or references to a quotation. My primary sources have been twofold. A substantial number of people, almost entirely Kurds, have been very generous with their time and understanding to explain aspects of their history or the contemporary situation; their contribution has been invaluable. My other primary source has been the archives of the Public Record Office; that has both advantages and disadvantages. British diplomats reported regularly on events in different parts of Kurdistan from the 1870s through to 1945. These reports are probably the single most important historical archive on Kurdistan and as such are invaluable. But they must be treated with caution. This is not because the motives of an imperial power are suspect; that may be true, but diplomats still sought to understand and report faithfully what was taking place. The reason is that British diplomats saw events in Kurdistan through a prism of British interests. There must have been any number of things happening in Kurdistan which did not attract their attention. Of these perhaps the most important were the processes of economic and social change. I cannot help feeling that if these were better documented and understood, many of the events we do know about in Kurdistan would undergo re-evaluation.

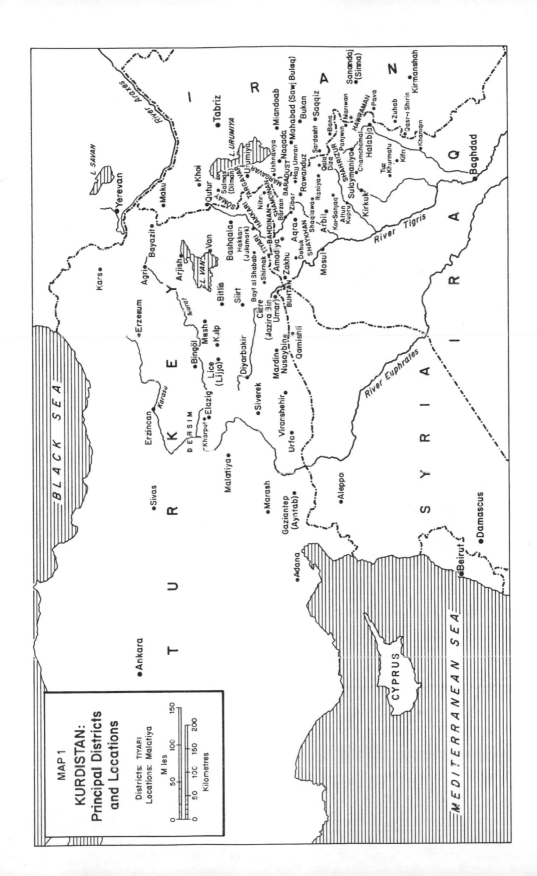

MAP 1
KURDISTAN:
Principal Districts
and Locations

Districts: TIYARI
Locations: Malatiya

Miles
0   50   100   150

Kilometres
0   50   100   150   200

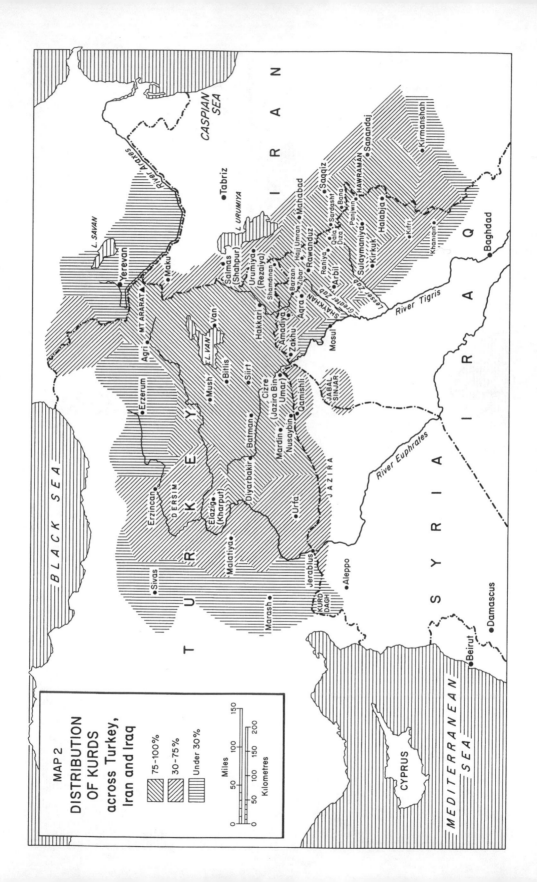

MAP 2

DISTRIBUTION
OF KURDS
across Turkey,
Iran and Iraq

75-100%

30-75%

Under 30%

Miles

Kilometres

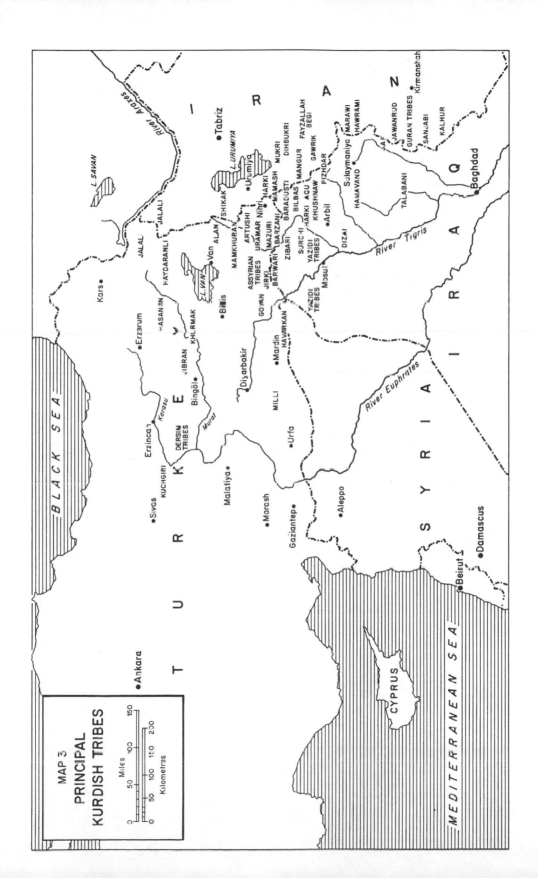

MAP 3
PRINCIPAL
KURDISH TRIBES

Miles
0   50   100   150
Kilometres
0   50   100   150   200

BLACK SEA

MEDITERRANEAN SEA

CYPRUS

I R A N

I R A Q

S Y R I A

T U R K E Y

River Araxes

L. SAVAN

L. URUMIYA

L. VAN

River Tigris

River Euphrates

Korasu

Murat

•Tabriz
•Urumiya
•Kars
•Erzurum
•Erzincan
•Sivas
•Ankara
•Bitlis
•Van
•Diyarbakir
•Mardin
•Urfa
•Malatiya
•Marash
•Gaziantep
•Aleppo
•Mosul
•Arbil
•Baghdad
•Kirmanshah
•Beirut
•Damascus
•Bingöl

JALALI
JALAL
HAYDARANLI
HASANLI
JALALI
MAMKHURAN
KHLRMAK
JIBRAN
DERSIN TRIBES
KUCHGIRI
ALAN
ISHIKAK
ARTUSHI
URAMAR Nihri
ASSYRIAN TRIBES
GOYAN
JIRKI
BARWARI
MAZURI
HAVERKAN
MILLI
HARKI
MAMASH
MUKRI
DIHBUKRI
BARADUSTI
BILBAS AQU
MANGUR
ZIBARI
BAZRANI
SURC-I
HARKI
YAZIDI TRIBES
YAZIDI TRIBES
KHUSHNAW
GAWRIK
BEGI
PIZHDAR
DIZAI
FAYZALLAH
HAMAVAND
TALABANI
Sulaymaniya
JAWANRUD
JAF
MARAWI
HAWRAMI
GURAN TRIBES
SANJABI
KALHUR

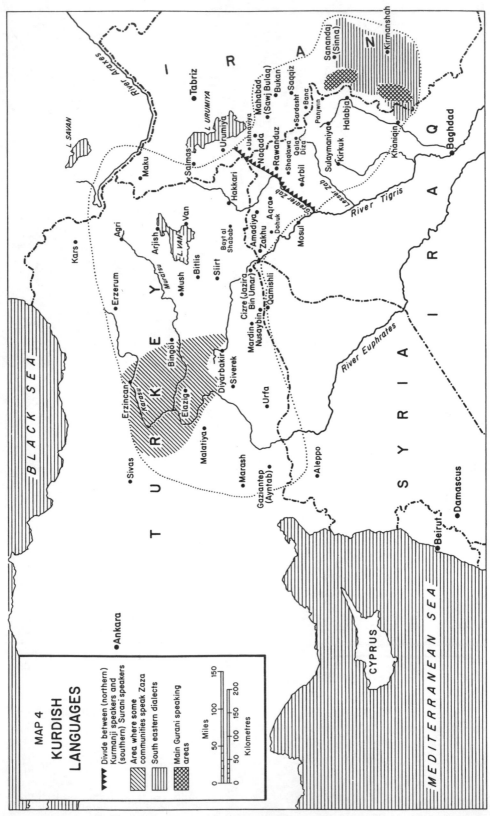

MAP 4

KURDISH LANGUAGES

Divide between (northern) Kurmanji speakers and (southern) Surani speakers

Area where some communities speak Zaza

South eastern dialects

Main Gurani speaking areas

Miles
0   50   100   150

Kilometres
0   50 100 150 200

CHAPTER 1

INTRODUCTION: KURDISH IDENTITY AND SOCIAL FORMATION

Following his conviction in a Turkish court on 29 June 1999, the PKK leader, Abdullah Ocalan declared:

'I have no doubt that I will be acquitted morally and politically by history."

Ocalan's expectation depends partly on whether and how the Kurds of Turkey advance their cause for political and cultural rights, and partly on his contribution to the emergence of the Kurdish people during the twentieth century.

Any modern history of the Kurds must examine two inter-related questions. The first is the struggle between the Kurdish people and the governments to which they are subject for control of the lands they inhabit. Until the nineteenth century that struggle was largely between two contestants. There were states that wished to control the Kurdish territory they considered theirs but that had neither ideological nor practical ambitions to assimilate Kurds into some kind of homogeneous entity. The Ottoman, Safavid and Qajar empires were all noted for their ethnic pluralism, and sought solely the acknowledgement of sultan or shah as suzerain. Ideologically the furthest these states went was to persecute those who did not subscribe to the same religious tradition. Pitted against them were an array of local rulers, many either tribal or presiding over primarily tribal communities, who sought to ensure their own position by co-operation with or defiance of the state, depending on the local balance of forces and on opportunity. These local rulers did not consider themselves as the representative leaders of a Kurdish people.

The second question concerns the struggle of the Kurds to move from being merely a people who happen to have the attributes commonly described as 'Kurdish' to being a coherent community with the essential characteristics of nationhood. With the exception of the seventeenth-century poet, Ahmad-i Khani, there is virtually no evidence that any Kurds thought in terms of a whole Kurdish people until the later years of the nineteenth century. There is no doubt that a

1

Kurdish people had existed as an identifiable group for possibly more than two thousand years, but it was only in the early years of the twentieth century that they acquired a sense of community as Kurds.

This sense of national community occurred at more or less the same time that Turks and Arabs also began to embrace an ethnic sense of identity in place of the two previous basic forms of solidarity – the idea of Ottoman citizenship and membership of a religious community, or *millet*. In both Turkey and Iran, *millet*, which once indicated religious identity, became in the twentieth century a term meaning nation. A consequence was that Kurds redefining themselves in terms of ethnicity found themselves competing against states intent on forging a new identity based upon an ethnicity they felt denied their own identity. Unlike the Turks and Arabs, the Kurds were fatally disadvantaged because they lacked both a civic culture and an established literature. In the case of modern Turkey the new identity was called Turkish, ideologically defined as those who, though not necessarily of Turkish ethnic origin, nevertheless were claimed as Turkish because of social conditioning. Such a definition was produced by the ideologue of the new Turkish republic, Ziya Gokalp, a man born and bred in Diyarbakir, a man who considered himself Turkish because it was in his view both his mother tongue and his culture, but who was arguably of Kurdish ethnicity. In Iran, the Kurds found themselves in a more complex situation; for the Iranian state was barely 50 per cent Persian, the balance being a mosaic of Azari Turk, Kurd, Arab, Baluch, Lur, Turkoman and other smaller groups. Yet Persian was imposed as a unifying language for all 'Iranians'. Unlike Turkey, there was no denial of Kurdish identity, merely an insistence that it be subordinated to the homogenizing ideology of Iranian national integration. In this context religious difference – Kurds being largely Sunni, Iranians being largely Shi'i – remained an important component of Kurdish distinctiveness. In Iraq the Kurds had to operate in a political climate that was, from the outset, overwhelmingly Arab in character and that moved progressively towards Arab nationalism as an ideology which, *in extremis*, considered Kurds to be inhabitants of part of the Arab patrimony.

Do the Kurds constitute a nation? If so, how did this nation come into being? What are the characteristics which distinguish a nation from either an ethnic category – certain people who happen to share a common ancestry, language or culture – or indeed from an ethnic community – people who think and act as Kurds rather than according to religious, social or political ideas of solidarity? Such issues pose difficult questions for a community that still does not enjoy international acceptance as a nation within a recognized territory. However, one might argue that essential characteristics of nationhood include common institutions, a widely acknowledged body of rights and duties for all members of the community, a common culture and a civic ideology, and possibly common aspirations and perception to bind them together in an acknowledged homeland. In the case of the Kurds, feelings of solidarity initially come through the (possibly fictive) idea of common ancestry. Another tool for attaining that collectivity is clearly a shared language. Here the Kurds face a practical difficulty based partly upon language differences, the very recent creation of a literature (since the 1920s) and the prevalence of different scripts – Latin in Turkey, Cyrillic in the ex-Soviet Union, and Persian in Iraq and Iran. They also face the twin irritants that while Iranians belittle Kurdish as merely a 'dialect' of Persian, linguists are often inclined to categorize the different forms of Kurdish as related languages rather than dialects, which implicitly casts doubt on the unity of the Kurdish people.

There is also the question of a recognized territory. While regional states may deny its existence, Kurdistan exists within relatively well defined limits in the minds of most Kurdish political groups. There is both a practical and a mythical interpretation of political Kurdistan. The former affords Kurdistan the borders its political leadership either hopes or believes it can achieve. In 1919 these included a narrow neck of land that gave access to the Mediterranean just north of Alexandretta, Mosul and the left bank of the Tigris as far south as Mandali, and the eastern side of Lake Urumiya. Few Kurds would claim quite as much today, but would still claim the city of Kirkuk, even though it had a larger Turkoman population as recently as 1958.

The mythical view of Kurdistan is equally important. Occupancy by the Kurds stretches back into the mists of time, 'from time immemorial' to use a resonant phrase, conferring on the Kurdish people a unique association with the land. Moreover, the idea of Kurdistan for many Kurds is also characterized by an almost mystical view of 'the mountain', an imaginary as well as a real place. Although an increasing proportion of Kurds leave the mountain valleys to live in towns or cities, the mountain image loses nothing of its potency, for nations are built in the imagination before they are built on the ground. The ambiguous ethnic status of Kirkuk exemplifies how contradictions between the practical and mythical view of a patrimony can co-exist.

The Kurdish Population

Today there are probably in the order of 24–27 million Kurds living in the Middle East. About half of these, at least 13 million, live in Turkey. In 1975 Martin van Bruinessen reckoned they constituted an estimated 19 per cent of the population.[2] But their reproductive rate is almost double that of Turks, and it is reasonable to suppose that during the past 20 years they have increased as a proportion of the republic to possibly about 23 per cent. In Iraq the reproductive rate is probably not dissimilar from the Arab population and if, as van Bruinessen suggests, Kurds are already 23 per cent of the population, they must now number about 4.2 million. They constitute probably about 10 per cent of the Iranian population, and therefore number about 5.7 million. More than 2 million Kurds live elsewhere: there are just over one million in Syria, mainly in the Jazira and along the Turkish frontier; most crossed the frontier to escape Turkish repression in the 1920s. Up to about 700,000 live in Europe, mainly in Germany, and up to another 400,000 are in the ex-Soviet republics, mainly Armenia and Azarbaijan.

How many of these disclaim their Kurdish identity is a moot point. Certainly in Turkey many Kurds were assimilated into the nation Ataturk sought to forge in the 1920s and 1930s. But they must to some extent be offset by those who have rediscovered their ethnic identity as a result of state oppression, particularly since the 1970s, and by others living in eastern Turkey who, though not of Kurdish ethnic origin, have nevertheless embraced Kurdish identity because it most closely approximates to how they feel about their socio-economic position in the Turkish state. I do not propose to discuss whether this last category are genuinely Kurds, except to make two points: it would not be the first time 'Kurdishness' has been defined in socio-economic rather than ethnic terms, and also that such a self-definition conforms with the principles enunciated by Ziya Gokalp. Nor should one forget those Kurds who consciously prefer another identity, the majority of whom are fervent Sunni Muslims. There are also Alevis and Zaza-speakers (see below) who identify with those Turks who also share and emphasize one of these two minority identities.

In my view the Kurds only really began to think and act as an ethnic community from 1918 onwards. Does that mean that a Kurdish nation did not exist previously? For Kurdish nationalists there can be no question that the nation has existed from time immemorial, long asleep but finally aroused during the course of the twentieth century. Kurdish nationalists are therefore likely to see the past in a particular light, with ancient myths and symbols that validate Kurdish identity.

Various myths exist concerning Kurdish origins. The myth that the Kurds are descended from children hidden in the mountains to escape Zahhak, a child-eating giant, links them mystically with 'the mountain' and also implies, since the myth refers to children rather than one couple, that they may not all be of one origin. A similar story suggests that they are descended from the children of slave girls of King Solomon, sired by a demon named Jasad, and driven by the angry king into the mountains. Another myth claims the Prophet Abraham's wife Sarah was a Kurd, a native of Harran, and thus validates Kurdish identity within the mainstream of monotheism. There is a danger of outsiders dismissing such myths as worthless; they are valuable tools in nation building, however dubious historically, because they offer a common mystical identity, exclusive to the Kurdish people.

History, as well as myth, plays an important part in nation building and it is no accident that history has been a major preoccupation of Kurdish nationalists. From the 1930s onwards a number of historical works appeared, written by Kurds who were clearly nationalist in their thinking. The most solid of these was Muhammad Amin Zaki's *Khulasat tarikh al Kurd wa'l Kurdistan* (*Excerpts from the*

History of the Kurds and Kurdistan), first published in Kurdish in 1936 and clearly intended to awaken the literate class to their national history.

There can be little doubt that throughout history periodic invasions, clashes or trade with peoples of a foreign tongue impressed upon Kurdish consciousness that they were distinct from their neighbours. However, that sense of ethnic distinctiveness did not find written expression until the late seventeenth century, in Ahmad-i Khani's poem, *Mem-u-Zin*:

> Look, from the Arabs to the Georgians,
> The Kurds have become like towers.
> The Turks and Persians are surrounded by them.
> The Kurds are on all four corners.
> Both sides have made the Kurdish people
> Targets for the arrows of fate.
> They are said to be keys to the borders
> Each tribe forming a formidable bulwark.
> Whenever the Ottoman Sea [Ottomans] and Tajik Sea [Persians]
> Flow out and agitate,
> The Kurds get soaked in blood
> Separating them [the Turks and Persians] like an isthmus.[3]

Ahmad-i Khani very clearly expresses a political point of view, one with which Kurds today can easily identify: a formidable yet oppressed people on account of their strategic location. It is unclear whether many of Ahmad-i Khani's contemporaries or indeed any Kurds prior to the late nineteenth century shared the feelings he expressed. Yet it is not surprising that nationalist Kurds seeking to trace a national continuity fixed upon 'heroes of the nation' across the centuries. This is something nation-builders do everywhere. For the Kurds the great heroes of national identity include Saladin, despite the fact that he acted essentially as an Islamic rather than Kurdish national leader, and certain more recent figures, for example the Amir Badr Khan, Shaykhs Ubayd Allah and Said and the tribal chief Ismail Simqu, all of whom are discussed in later chapters.

The nation-builder's task is to persuade members of an ethnic category to subordinate all other loyalties, be they social or religious, to the primacy of ethnic identity – one in which the nation must cast itself in secular terms not to be subsumed in the collectivity of religion. It also brings a conflict with primordial kinship identity, particularly in the case of tribes.

The Land

Although Kurds live in the republics of Armenia and Azarbaijan, in Syria and also in Khurasan in eastern Iran, or in cities like Istanbul, Ankara, Tabriz and Tehran, the majority still live in the mountains and plateau regions where the states of Turkey, Iraq and Iran meet. The heart of these mountains is formed by the Zagros range running in ridges north–west to south–east either side of Iran's border with its western neighbours. In places, for example Hakkari, these mountains are particularly precipitous, with villages clinging to steep slopes or perched on shelves. To the west the mountains give way to rolling hills and these in turn give way to the Mesopotamian plain. To the north-west the mountains give way to the Anatolian plateau, a vast area of sweeping steppes broken by yet more mountains. On the east side the mountains level out onto agricultural lands, while to the south the mountains continue, inhabited by the Kurds' cousins, the Lurs.

In the understated words of a Foreign Office handbook published in 1919, 'the climate of these mountains is bracing all the year round.'[4] In practice this means for many settlements a mean August temperature of 30°C and a mean January one of −5°C, temperatures which apply to Diyarbakir, the largest city in Kurdistan. Much of Kurdistan was once wooded. It lost its great trees as a result of the demand over several centuries for timber in the neighbouring region, the defoliant effect of modern war, and the stripping of the landscape either by humans for fuel or by goats killing shrubs and saplings.

Kurdistan remains an important region for agriculture and stockbreeding. It accounts for approximately 15 per cent of total cereal production in Turkey and 35 per cent and 30 per cent in Iran and Iraq respectively. Since the turn of the century the region has become a significant producer of two cash crops, cotton and tobacco. Until the end of the nineteenth century stockbreeding was the single most important economic activity in Kurdistan; large flocks of sheep and goats would be driven up to the higher summer pastures each year. These flocks would often belong to more than a single tribal community, and might include the livestock belonging to several peasant villages within a tribe's orbit of patronage. Such movements in spring and autumn tended to be moments of tension either between pastoralists and peasants − since pastoralists often led thousands of livestock through settled areas − or between one tribe and another because of competing territorial claims, or because their respective migrations perhaps by mischance clashed. In the nineteenth century Kurdistan provided much of the meat for Anatolia, Syria and Mesopotamia; large flocks would be driven to Istanbul, Baghdad, Aleppo or Damascus and sold. The journey from Van to Istanbul could take 18 months. Even with the virtual disappearance of nomadism in the second half of the twentieth century, settled people still stockbreed.

The term 'Kurdistan' was first used in the twelfth century as a geographical term by the Saljuqs. The geographical extent of this definition almost certainly grew during succeeding centuries as Kurds moved outwards: to the north beyond the Araxes river, to the west as far as Sivas, Erzerum and Marash and on to the Mesopotamian plain around Kirkuk; and to the east beyond the city of Kirmanshah. The majority of such Kurds were tribal, moving among and beyond what non-Kurdish peasant settlements already existed.

Except to its own inhabitants Kurdistan must be considered a peripheral region, lying along the geopolitical fault line between three power centres of the Middle East. Until the beginning of the twentieth century no one cared very much about the boundaries of Kurdistan, or the numbers of people who lived there. The only sensitive issue concerned the actual number of Muslims (largely Kurds) compared with (Christian) Armenians living in eastern Anatolia in the second half of the nineteenth century, and this was largely on account of the danger that Russia would use the Armenians as a pretext to seize the eastern marches of the Ottoman empire. Apart from that, it did not really matter how generously terms like Kurdistan or Armenia were scrawled across tracts of either the Ottoman or Qajar empires – all that changed in the twentieth century. One reason has already been given: the anxiety of the new states to impose their identity on all peoples within their territory. Another reason is strategic: the mountains certainly provide Iran and Iraq with a defensible strategic frontier; to move the boundary either west or east of Kurdistan would not make strategic sense to either state. Turkey's attitude to its frontiers in Kurdistan is special. It has an emotional and ideological view that its frontiers (except with Iraq) cannot be changed without threatening the foundations of the republic. This is partly because of the terms of the National Covenant of 1919 and the bitter war fought to achieve the aims of that covenant. The integrity of Turkey within its present borders has acquired an almost mystical quality for those faithful to the legacy of modern Turkey's founder, Mustafa Kamal Ataturk. As a result, the loss of Kurdistan, despite its great poverty, would be perceived as a grievous blow to the spatial identity of Turkey.

Another reason why control of Kurdistan has recently become more important is that its oil and water resources have grown in significance since the Second World War. No government will willingly surrender control of its oilfields in the Kurdish region, Rumaylan (Syria), Batman and Silvan (Turkey), or Kirkuk and Khaniqin (Iraq). With population growth and the increased demand for energy and more extensive irrigation, water is rapidly becoming more important than oil. Iraq has already exploited the waters that flow off the western slopes of the Zagros down the Lesser Zab and Diyala rivers, with the Dukan and Darbandikan dams respectively; and before the Kurdish uprising of 1991 it had begun work on a dam at Bakhma, high up the Greater Zab in the heart of Bahdinan. Turkey is currently developing a system of dams on the upper Tigris and Euphrates. These dam projects vitally affect the amount of water flowing across the Mesopotamian plain. Neither government will willingly surrender control of this water to the Kurds.

Nationalists clearly lament that the Kurdish people are divided by the international borders drawn across their community. It would be natural to infer that these borders represent a major impediment to the Kurdish people; but a few reservations should be made. It is important to remember that, apart from periodic variations, the border between Iran and its western neighbours is approximately 400 years old. For centuries this permeable frontier has provided

Kurdish society with opportunities in three respects. It has afforded economic opportunity, first for pastoral movement which was unrestrained by international frontiers until the 1920s. Several major tribes, notably the Harki and the Pizhdar, seasonally crossed the border with their flocks. During their migration the Harki took Iranian salt to sell on the Mesopotamian plain, and returned with wheat. The border was also increasingly used for smuggling, still an important source of income in impoverished areas like Van and Hakkari. Moreover, a permeable frontier has afforded a refuge for those who offend the state. Kurdish leaders have been seeking sanctuary in neighbouring states for hundreds of years. Most major Kurdish leaders have attempted to cross one of these borders when they have been defeated; some have been caught in the attempt, others have escaped to resume their rebellion under more propitious circumstances. Finally, Kurds have been able to exploit border tensions between adjoining states to advance their own cause. In the mid-nineteenth century, for example, a Shikak section was encouraged by Iran to undermine Ottoman suzerainty in Somay, the border district opposite the northern tip of Lake Urumiya. All three functions continue to this day. Frontiers have not been wholly disadvantageous to the Kurds.

However, there can be no doubt that today such borders are much less permeable. The use of wire-mesh fences, minefields and air surveillance makes it increasingly difficult for people to cross borders except through authorized crossing-points. This undoubtedly retards Kurdish national progress and has largely suffocated Kurdish cross-border trade (except for smuggling). Kurds are now drawn more closely into the fabric of the states in which they live. Moreover, these frontiers run across rather than along the linguistic–cultural divides in Kurdish society. There is, therefore, a tension between the 'imagined' community of the Kurdish nation and the practical requirements of economic survival which persuade large numbers of Kurds to seek employment in Istanbul, Tehran and so forth.

The People

It is extremely doubtful that the Kurds form an ethnically coherent whole in the sense that they have a common ancestry. The majority of Kurds are probably descended from waves of Indo-European tribes mainly moving westwards across Iran, probably in the middle of the second millenium BCE. But we know nothing of them. Long before any mention of Kurds as such, we know that Kurdistan was a troublesome zone on the edge of ancient polities. For a period during the twenty-first century BCE, Sumer sent almost annual expeditions against Kurdistan, burning Urbillum (Arbil). In the ninth century BCE Persians moved southwards, originally possibly from across the Caucasus, via Urumiya region towards Fars. By the end of the ninth century BCE the kingdom of Mannai existed in much of Kurdistan south and west of Lake Urumiya, a buffer between Assyria, its arch enemy Urartu to the north, and the Medes who established themselves between

Tehran and Hamadan. Both Shalmaneser III and Sargon marched across Kurdistan against Urartu, in the ninth and eighth centuries respectively. In the seventh century Saqqiz seems to have been the eponymous capital of the Scythians. In the sixth century Persia became a coherent empire. The population of the Zagros mountains can hardly have remained unaffected by such developments, but we know nothing of what these effects were.

By the time the Kurds were first clearly recorded, as 'Cyrtii' from the second century BCE onwards, they were almost certainly already an amalgam of Indo-European tribes that had made their way into the region by different routes and at different periods. Semitic tribes may also have inhabited the Zagros during this period. The term 'Cyrtii' was first applied to Seleucid or Parthian mercenary slingers dwelling in the Zagros and it is uncertain that it denoted a coherent linguistic or ethnic group at this juncture. Certainly by the time of the Islamic conquests a thousand years later, and probably for some time before, the term 'Kurd' had a socio-economic rather than ethnic meaning. It was used of nomads on the western edge of the Iranian plateau and probably also of the tribes that acknowledged the Sassanians in Mesopotamia, many of which must have been Semitic in origin.

There can be no doubt that at a later stage certain Arab and Turkoman tribes became Kurdish by culture. Kurdish and Turkoman tribes co-existed, or even melded in the same confederations, while Turkish chiefs often attracted Kurdish followers and *vice versa*. Two Turkoman dynasties in western Anatolia before the rise of the Ottomans are generally thought to be of mixed Turkoman and Kurdish origin. At the beginning of the present century there were Kurdish-Turkish tribes in Cilicia. A similar pattern probably occurred in northern Mesopotamia where Kurdish and Arab tribes mingled. For example, the Arab Rawadid tribe, which moved into Kurdistan at the beginning of the Abbasid era (750CE), was considered to be Kurdish within 200 years, although its Arab origin was well known. It was one of many. Likewise a substantial number of Kurds, more notably those who became professional soldiers in the Muslim armies, and also peasants and tribes who moved into predominantly Turkish- or Arabic-speaking areas, lost their Kurdish identity.

Finally, those who have investigated the physiognomy of the Kurds (shape of head, colour of eyes, hair, build, etc) have concluded that the most significant feature is their similarity with neighbouring non-Kurdish communities.

Language

Another indicator of varied origins lies with the linguistic variety of Kurdistan. Two major languages or dialects exist today, Kurmanji spoken by most northern Kurds, and Surani spoken by most southern Kurds. Grammatically, they differ from each other as much as English and German, although vocabulary differences are probably of the same order as those between Dutch and German. In both cases these two languages represent a standardized version of a multiplicity of local dialects, which still varied almost valley by valley a century ago. There are three other languages spoken by sizeable minorities. In the south-east from Sanandaj to Kirmanshah, most Kurds speak a dialect much closer to modern Persian than Surani. The other two are Gurani, spoken in certain enclaves of southern Kurdistan, and Zaza, spoken in north-western Kurdistan by both Sunni and Alevi Kurds and also by Alevi Turks. Zaza and Gurani are related, belonging to the north-western group of Iranian languages, while Kurmanji and Surani belong to the south-western group. This suggests that Zaza and Gurani speakers may be of distant common origin, probably from Daylam and Gilan on the south-west side of the Caspian. Up to the present century certain subject peasants in the Sulaymaniya area were known as *guran*, locally believed to be of different descent from tribal Kurds in the area. It is plausible to link the Guran tribespeople, who are also Gurani speakers, and *guran* peasantry as being probably of common origin.[5] It is also likely that the Zaza and Gurani speakers were already in the Zagros region when Kurmanji and Surani speakers entered it. During this population movement it is thought that the Zaza speakers may have been pushed westwards into Anatolia, while the *guran*/Gurani were enveloped, to become a distinct, and in places subject, community.

Religion

The vast majority of Kurds, approximately 75 per cent, follow Sunni Islam. But the religious particularism of the remaining Kurds may point to longstanding differences of origin. Take, for example, the Alevi religion which is strong in central Anatolia, particularly in the Dersim region. While claiming devotion to the Imam Ali, the Alevi (or Qizilbash) religion – like Baktashi beliefs – lies on the extreme edge of Shi'i Islam. It is a mixture of pre-Islamic, Zoroastrian, Turkoman shaman and Shi'i ideas that became the basis of a religious sect during the fifteeenth century CE. There is a large overlap between Zaza speakers and Alevis, and one must therefore suspect a connection. It is possible that the tribes that espoused Alevism had previously been Sunni, but it seems more likely that Sunni Zaza speakers were once either Alevi or of a related sect.

Likewise in southern Kurdistan it is probably no accident that the Ahl-i Haqq religious group uses Gurani as its sacred language. The Ahl-i Haqq religion bears many similarities to Alevi beliefs, quite apart from a common veneration of the Imam Ali. At the basis of both religions lies a body of Zoroastrian religious ideas. Although the Ahl-i Haqq are found mainly around Zuhab and Qasr-i Shirin, there are smaller colonies either side of the Zagros range, as far north as Urumiya in West Azarbaijan, and also around Sulaymaniya, Kirkuk and Mosul.[6] Neither the Alevis nor the Ahl-i Haqq are exclusively Kurdish. There are many Turkish Alevis and a smaller number of Turkoman Ahl-i Haqq, but both groups seem to have inherited an amalgam of beliefs built on Iranian religious ideas.

Alevis and the Ahl-i Haqq share a veneration for progenitors of the Safavid dynasty that rose to power on the basis of such heterodox beliefs.

One other important heterodox religious group requires mention, namely the Yazidis. The Yazidis, who are Kurmanji speakers, live chiefly in Jabal Sanjar and Shaykhan, west and east of Mosul respectively. Until very recently a substantial number lived in the Mardin-Midyat area of Turkey, but these have virtually all migrated to Germany to escape the oppressive circumstances of life in modern Turkey. Substantial numbers had already moved into Russia to escape the pan-Islamic movement at the end of the nineteenth century. The Yazidi religion is a synthesis of old pagan elements, Zoroastrian dualist elements, and Manichaean gnosis overlaid with Jewish, Christian and Muslim elements.

A significant feature of all these religious groups is that until very recently they were predominantly rural and subscribed to a tribal or kinship ideology (discussed below). In other words, religious particularism ran closely with tribal organization to form discrete communities.

Up to 15 per cent of Kurds are, like most Iranians, Ithna 'Ashari Shi'is. They live in the Kirmanshah (Bakhtiran) province of Iran, with a few living in the southern parts of Kurdistan province, and speak the south-eastern dialect. Another group of about 150,000 of Kirmanshahi origin, known as 'Fayli Kurds', were expelled to Iran from Iraq in the 1970s and 1980s. It is extremely difficult to know how long the Kurds have been Shi'a. Ithna 'Ashari Shi'ism became widely accepted in Iran in the sixteenth century and it is possible that before this time the Shi'i Kurds were mainly Ahl-i Haqq. There seems to have been a pattern more recently of chiefly families abandoning the Ahl-i Haqq in favour of the official state religion, presumably in order to improve their own political and social position in the state, with subsequent imitation by those placed lower in the social order. One may speculate that other tribes converted to Ithna 'Ashari Shi'ism at an earlier date. The main Ahl-i Haqq shrine at Baba Yadigar is venerated, as it has been for centuries, by a large number of Shi'i Kurds.

It might be thought that the majority of Kurds, being Sunni, conformed in religious matters with the majority of Arabs and Turks in neighbouring Kurdistan. Certainly religiously-minded Sunni Kurds have sided with non-Kurdish Sunnis against heterodox Kurds, and in parts of Turkey continue to do so. However, they differ from their non-Kurdish Sunni neighbours in two vital respects: most Turks and the Arabs of Mesopotamia accepted the official Hanafi school of jurisprudence following the establishment of Ottoman authority in the sixteenth century; the Kurds remained adherents of the Shafi'i school which had predominated in the region in preceding centuries – a testimony, presumably, to the independence their amirs enjoyed *vis-à-vis* the sultan.

Kurdish religious distinctiveness has also been expressed in the strength of Sufi brotherhoods (*tariqa*, pl. *turuq*) and their eccentric practices, which include ecstatic utterances, trances, fire-eating and self-mutilation. These practices are not peculiar to Kurdish society alone; they can be found among other communities which prefer 'folk' Islam to the formalized religion. But they are suggestive of pre-Islamic religious rites and exercises peculiar to the societies in which they take place, and may suggest some origins in common between Kurds belonging to different religious groups.

The Sufi brotherhoods served both to strengthen and divide society. Kurds of the same *tariqa* network felt a common bond, regardless of tribe. On the other hand, there was often a sense of tension with a rival *tariqa*. The shaykhs of different orders, or indeed, shaykhs within the same order but with their own followings, competed to build the client networks on which their authority would be based. A classic example is the conflict between two Naqshbandi dynasties, the Sayyids of Nihri and the Shaykhs of neighbouring Barzan in the second half of the nineteenth century.

Other religious communities exist in Kurdistan which, while claiming their own identity, might also arguably be considered part of a wider Kurdish cultural community. Jews have lived in Kurdistan for over two millenia; they have tended to be traders and artisans living mainly in larger settlements. In the early nineteenth century there were substantial communities, with synagogues, in places like Zakhu, Amadiya, Arbil and Sulaymaniya. Some were peasants and some were possibly affiliated as dependents of certain tribes. A few Jews remained in Kurdistan in spite of the Zionist exodus of 1948–52, and many of those who migrated to Israel still consider themselves Kurds.

There has always been a sizeable Christian community in Kurdistan. The largest concentration historically were the Armenians of eastern Anatolia, who were probably only slightly less numerous than the Kurds themselves in this region during the nineteenth century. The Armenians formed a substantial and largely non-tribal community to be found in both towns and villages mainly in eastern Anatolia and Cilicia, but they were virtually extinguished during the First World War (chapter 6).

The Armenians were established in the Van area by the sixth century BCE. It is difficult to say whether they are racially distinct from the Kurds. It is widely believed that since the sixteenth century or so some Kurdish tribes – the Alevi Mamakanli are the most frequently mentioned – are descended from Armenian converts. In the 1940s a shrinking Armenian but Kurdish-speaking tribe with a tenuous grasp of Christian doctrine was noticed in central Kurdistan, where it was progressively merging with a Kurdish tribe.

The other principal Christian community is Assyrian. At one time the Assyrian (Nestorian) Church, which broke theologically with the Western Church in 431CE, extended as far as China, Siberia, Turkestan and eastern Iran. But it never recovered from the depredations of the Mongols at the end of the fourteenth century, and shrank to a small community known as Assyrians concentrated in the mountain fastnesses of Hakkari and also on the hills and plain surrounding Urumiya. A monophysite Christian sect, the Syrian Orthodox (or Suryani, often known as Jacobite) Church has existed mainly in Tur Abdin and Mosul districts.

It had both tribal and non-tribal elements. The community in Tur Abdin has been virtually extinguished, like the Yazidis, by Sunni Muslim oppression.

Whatever their later status may have been, Christians were clearly included in the term 'Kurd' in the early Islamic period. In his *Muruj al Dhahab*, the mid-tenth century geographer al Masudi refers to 'Christian Kurds'. A substantial proportion of Assyrian and Syrian Orthodox may well be of the same racial stock as their Muslim neighbours.

Kurdish Society

At the time of the Islamic conquests, the term 'Kurd' had meant nomad. From the eleventh century onwards many travellers and historians treated the term 'Kurd' as synonymous with brigandage, a view echoed by nineteenth-century European travellers. By the middle years of the nineteenth century 'Kurd' was also used to mean tribespeople who spoke the Kurdish language. True, some Kurdish-speaking people had no tribal affiliation whatsoever, living as peasantry or town dwellers, but these were probably a minority and certainly were exceptional to the widely acknowledged image of Kurdishness. The dominant tribal image, even in an age in which nomadism was in sharp decline, indicated a society based upon kinship ideology. Such kinship ideology is usually rooted in a myth of common ancestry. Most Kurdish tribal groups have their own real or imagined ancestry which often harks back either to a hero of the early Islamic period, or even to descent from the Prophet himself. This was a particularly attractive form of legitimation during the period of Islamic empire. Several chiefly families claimed either descent or association with the great early Islamic general, Khalid ibn al Walid. Others invoked an Umayyad or Abbasid connection. The Jaf claimed a connection with Saladin.

The difficulty in discussing Kurdish tribal culture is that tribes are not easy to define since their size, structure and internal organization can vary from place to place and epoch to epoch. The imprecision implicit in the term 'tribe' is evident in the various words used by Kurds in different parts of Kurdistan, drawn from Arabic, Persian and Turkish, as well as Kurdish, to denote a tribal group: *il, ashira, qabila, taifa, tira, oba, hawz* and so forth. I have tried to list them in descending order of size, but different groups can use such terms differently. Very broadly, these terms range from tribal confederation down to clan, sept or section, and to a tented encampment of probably about 20 tents. The actual form taken by a tribal group may depend upon internal factors, such as the personality of its leaders, economic or kin relations with tribal or non-tribal neighbours, and upon external factors – relations with tribal or non-tribal neighbours and, most importantly, with neighbouring states.

It is often thought that tribes, not to mention tribal confederations, share a common imagined ancestry. This is not necessarily true. Tribes may be, and often are, an aggregate of different kinship groups, each aware of its distinct ancestry but forming a section of the tribal whole. The Shikak, a tribal confederation which coalesced to become important in the second half of the nineteenth century on both sides of the Ottoman–Qajar border, is a case in point. There were two main chiefly lineages competing for paramountcy, each commanding tribal formations which included kin and unrelated groups. Another case is the Havarkan, supposedly a confederation of 24 tribes, east of Mardin. Twice in the nineteenth century, one line of paramounts was displaced by another. The unity of the tribal group collapsed with the murder of the paramount in 1919, and a new power struggle ensued within the wider family between rival third cousins until one established undisputed control. In the cases of both the Shikak and the Havarkan, the majority of tribespeople had no kin relationship with the chiefs. It is only with the medium to small groups, the *taifa* and *tira*, that integral kinship is normally implicit. Yet even a small tented group may include people whose bond is not necessarily kinship but possibly clientship. This is particularly true of subordinate stockbreeders, who nevertheless live in the same encampment in the summer pastures, and who may even share the same winter quarters.

Almost every tribe or tribal section also possesses a strong sense of territorial identity alongside ideas of ancestry. This is primarily to do with any settled villages and recognized pasturages a tribe uses. But it also includes, in the mind of the tribe, the lands of subject peasant villages, and in the mind of a chief, any district where he is charged by government to maintain good order and possibly collect taxes. These three concepts need not be co-extensive, for the simple reason that a powerful chief, for example Ismail Simko of the Shikak (chapter 10), might well be vested by a weak government with territorial responsibilities far beyond the territory of the tribe. Inevitably, with the passage of time, a proprietorial sense extends, by dint of chiefly authority, to include these territories. In a similar fashion, religious shaykhs with temporal power will extend their realm of authority as this comes to be recognized over a widening area by both tribe and village. The Sayyids of Nihri, who saw the Shikak as potential regional rivals in 1880 (chapter 4), are a good case in point.

Such are the basic differences between state and tribe that the two systems seem fundamentally incompatible, their relations at best only temporarily symbiotic. States are static, intent on exercising a monopoly of power within a defined territory. They require an urban dimension which embodies a bureaucracy and culture based upon the written word. They comprise a multiplicity of economic, legal and administrative functions in town and country, and may include religious functions also. Tribes operate on kinship ideology and territoriality; the latter includes both established villages but also more fluid ideas that no state could entertain. Tribes can be territorial in two other senses: first, they insist on a basic right of passage for seasonal migration – for example, the case of the Pizhdar versus the Iranian state in the 1920s (chapter 10) – and second, certain pastures pertain to them, possibly shared with other tribes on a seasonal basis. For example

Kurdish Milli and Arab Shammar tribes – though enemies – shared certain pastoral areas of northern Jazira, used by the Milli escaping the frozen Anatolian plateau in winter, and the Shammar (and Tayy) tribe driven north by the heat of summer.

The fundamental reason, however, why states and tribes are incompatible lies with the whole reason for tribal hierarchy. Tribal chiefs at all levels are required to discharge certain functions. Within the group acknowledging their chiefship they act as arbitrators of disputes and allocators of resources, benefits and duties. Beyond the tribal group, the chief acts as mediator either with his peers and the paramount chief, or with the state. A chief jealously guards his monopoly of all relations with the outside world.

If a state exercises a monopoly of power, its authority regarding taxation and the administration of justice will extend to every individual within its territory, rendering the mediation of a tribal chief with the outside world, and thus the *raison d'être* of tribal existence, meaningless. One does not need the myth of common ancestry merely to take one's livestock to pasturage if the state, rather than one's own chief, will facilitate it. The tribe exists because it seems a preferable system for many pasturalists. The state, if it is able, will take every measure to bring tribespeople under its direct control. It is this conflict between the role of the tribe and that of the state which must make one sceptical about tribal chiefs whose utterances are apparently aimed at a Kurdish state, as opposed to an independent tribal entity.

In practice, of course, it is only since 1918 that states abutting Kurdistan have been able to crush tribes and erode the kinship ideology that underpins them. Even with those tribes that have abandoned stockbreeding and are entirely sedentary, even partly urban, mutual aid based on kinship ideology remains amazingly durable. It is a commentary on the failure of states to meet all the individual's needs – employment, fair allocation of resources, arbitration, health and welfare and so forth – that this kind of tribalism persists.

Until the present century, states have been unable to monopolize power in the marginal zones of their territory. In order to handle the defiance implicit in tribal groups in these areas, states have resorted to a variety of tactics, sowing dissension where they can, supporting pretenders to chiefships where this will either weaken a tribe or bring it into greater obedience, and most importantly seeking to co-opt and incorporate tribal chiefs into the ruling elite of the state. In this paradoxical way the state can validate and strengthen a chief in the eyes of his tribal group. This pattern has continued for centuries. Contemporary examples are given in chapters 17 and 20 of how the Turkish and Iraqi states continue to co-opt tribal chiefs to provide pro-government forces against rebellious Kurds.

It is easy to assume that tribes are necessarily inviolable loyalty groups. This is not so. Mention has been made of internal dissension where a chief may be challenged by a pretender and each may seek outside assistance in their struggle, possibly from neighbouring states. Struggles can also take place between rival sections of a tribe. In addition tribes or clans may decide to abandon one tribal grouping in favour of another, if this suits their situation. A large confederation comprising many client tribal groups may shrink to its core in a few years of adverse circumstances in which clients can do better elsewhere. This is what happened to the Havarkan, when a strong leader was murdered in 1919. Disintegration was only reversed when another dynamic leader emerged. Contemporary examples of shifting loyalties are not hard to find. In December 1994 a section of the Harki tribe shifted its allegiance from the Kurdistan Democratic Party (KDP) to the Patriotic Union of Kurdistan (PUK) in return for support of a territorial claim. These two political parties constitute contemporary neo-tribal confederations. Tribal groups remain in a permanent state of flux both internally and with regard to the outside world.

In addition a tribe may be no more than a ruling family that has attracted a very large number of clients. The Barzani family in the mid-nineteenth century is a good example, for the shaykhs of Barzan attracted a large following of non-tribal peasantry escaping the repressive regime of neighbouring tribes. In this manner the Barzanis created a tribe, 'tribalizing' non-tribal people. (One must assume that despite the one-time definition of Kurds as tribal nomads, there has been movement between nomad and settler, tribal and non-tribal throughout Kurdish history.)

The Barzani case is evidence of the important role religion can play in reinforcing group solidarity. The *tariqa* networks can be a force for enhancing group solidarity, though a chief must be careful that a religious shaykh does not usurp his position as the focus for group loyalty. In the past 150 years there have been numerous examples of religious shaykhs acquiring the role of a tribal chief. Successful ones, like the Barzanis or the Sayyids of Nihri, were able to achieve extensive followings of kinship groups unrelated to each other but embracing group solidarity.

Yet it does not necessarily follow that all members of one confederation belong to the same religion, or that those belonging to one particular sect will enjoy group solidarity. Yazidis, Suryani and Assyrian tribes or tribal sections belonged to predominantly Sunni confederations, for example in northern Jazira, Tur Abdin and in Hakkari, and there are a few cases where kinship exists across the religious divide. For example, although intermarriage ceased, courtesy visits are still exchanged between Yazidis and a tribal group in Shaykhan that converted to Sunni Islam.

An oppositional dichotomy exists in Kurdish society, often based on an imagined conflict harking back to imagined origins two or more millennia ago, between two ancient groups, called Zilan and Milan, an apparent equivalent to the Qays–Yamani dichotomy among Syrian Arab tribes. This dichotomy is not confined to Muslim Kurds. At the turn of the century, and possibly still today, Alevi tribes in Dersim recognized the Milan–Zilan dichotomy. Yazidis apparently divided between the tribes of the Jawana and those of the Khurkan. The Assyrian tribes were integrated into the amirate of Hakkari and followed the dichotomy that applied to the whole Hakkari confederation, between the tribes of the 'left' and those of the 'right'. These terms 'left' and 'right' had no connection with the 'left' and 'right' of the modern political spectrum. Loyalty to 'left' or 'right' preceded confessional loyalty. Even towns in the amirate had their 'left' and 'right' families. The Sunni Artushi and Pinyanish tribes of Hakkari continue this oppositional dichotomy within the political system of modern Turkey.

Finally, something more should be said about the non-tribal Kurds. The case of the *guran* suggests there may have been aboriginal inhabitants of Kurdistan who may not have been tribal. Whether this is true or not, non-tribal Kurds have always existed. Some have probably converted to Islam from other religions at times when the pressures to integrate have been great. Others undoubtedly are of Turkish, Turkoman or Kurdish tribal origin, who have become sedentary and for whom the purpose and value of kinship ideology has been lost. In some cases that has happened very rapidly, for example among many Sunni Kurdish tribes in Iran during the twentieth century. However, one must be cautious. In certain cases, particularly with tribespeople who may have moved to a large city but feel uncomfortable with other possible identities – either ones of ethnicity or citizenship – kinship ties remain important.

Many peasant Kurds have been subject to tribal rule and it is worth pointing out that the Assyrian tribes of Hakkari held subject Kurdish peasantry. In other words, the social and political hierarchy of Kurdistan could be defined as much by socio-economic as religious or ethnic identity. Other peasant Kurds had no connection with tribes, but were subject to Ottoman or Safavid (or Qajar) fiefholders; they lived in conditions of direct landlord–peasant relations that lacked any sense of group solidarity. Landlords often controlled the essentials of life: land, water, livestock and equipment, seed, and labour itself, a situation still true in parts of Kurdistan at the end of the 1970s. Peasants were often unable to move at will. As recently as the 1960s an Iranian Kurdish peasant had to obtain permission from the landlord or his agent to leave the village.

Until comparatively recently few urban Kurds would have described themselves as such. Until ethnicity became an issue this century, townspeople would have defined themselves in terms of their *millet*, or religious community, and their urban status which lifted them (in their view) above the rough-cut peasantry and ensured their antagonism to the tribes and their alien values.

The Kurdish struggle has been as much about the conflict of such urban Kurds with the class of chiefs, the *aghawat*, and the hierarchies of the tribe, or of landlord and peasant, as it has been about freedom from state control.

Sources

Published: Benedict Anderson, *Imagined Communities: Reflections on the Origin and Spread of Nationalism* (London, 1983); Peter Alford Andrews, *Ethnic Groups in the Republic of Turkey* (Wiesbaden, 1989); Ali Banuazizi and Myron Weiner (eds), *The State, Religion, and Ethnic Politics: Afghanistan, Iran and Pakistan* (Syracuse, 1986); Carleton Coon, *Caravan: The Story of the Middle East* (New York, 1958), G.R. Driver, 'Studies in Kurdish history' and 'The religion of the Kurds', *Bulletin of the School of Oriental and African Studies* (BSOAS), vol. ii, (London, 1922); Lescek Dziegel, *Rural Community of Contemporary Iraq: Kurdistan facing Modernization* (Krakow, 1981); *The Encyclopaedia of Islam*, 2nd edition, Leiden, 'Ahl-i Hakk', 'Kizilbash', 'Kurds'; R. Girshman, *Iran from Earliest Times to the Islamic Conquest* (London, 1954); Amir Hassanpour, *Nationalism and Language in Kurdistan, 1918–1985* (San Francisco, 1992); John Joseph, *The Nestorians and their Neighbours* (Princeton, 1961); Philip Khoury and Joseph Kostiner (eds), *Tribes and State Formation in the Middle East* (London and New York, 1991); Philip Kreyenbroek and Stefan Sperl, *The Kurds: A Contemporary Overview* (London, 1992); Roger Lescot, Enquête sur les Yezidis (Damascus, 1975); David McDowall, 'A briefing note on the Alevi Kurds' (Minority Rights Group, London, July 1989); Matti Moosa, *Extremist Shiites: The Ghulat Sects* (Sycracuse, 1988); Basil Nikitine, 'La féodalité kurde', Revue du Monde Musulman, vol. 60, 1925; Georges Roux, *Ancient Iraq* (London, 1964); Anthony Smith, *National Identity* (London, 1991); Mark Sykes, *The Caliph's Last Heritage* (London, 1915).

Notes

1. Abdullah Ocalan, *Declaration on the Democratic Solution of the Kurdish Question*, (London, July 1999) p. 6.
2. Van Bruinessen, *Agha, Shaikh and State*, p. 15.
3. This translation is from Hassanpour, *Nationalism and Language*, p. 53.
4. Great Britain, Foreign Office, *Armenia and Kurdistan* (London, May 1919), p. 3.
5. See van Bruinessen, Agha, Shaikh and State, pp. 107–113, and David MacKenzie, 'The role of the Kurdish language in ethnicity' in Andrews, *Ethnic Groups in Turkey*.
6. They are known in Iraq as Kakaiya (Kirkuk), or Sarliya and Bajwan/Bajilan in the environs of Mosul.

BOOK I

THE KURDS IN THE AGE OF TRIBE AND EMPIRE

CHAPTER 2

KURDISTAN BEFORE THE NINETEENTH CENTURY

Early History

It is not intended to burden the reader with much early history of Kurdistan, but there are some observations worth making since they indicate that many of the characteristics of the nineteenth and twentieth centuries are longstanding.

With the Arab conquests the Kurds emerged from historical obscurity, rapidly confirming the longevity of their reputation for political dissidence. They first came into contact with the Arab armies during the latter's conquest of Mesopotamia in 637. The Kurdish tribes had been an important element in the Sassanian empire, and initially gave it strong support as it tried to withstand the Muslim armies, between 639 and 644. Once it was clear that the empire was doomed, the Kurdish chiefs one by one submitted to the Arab armies and to the new religion.

The pattern of nominal submission to central government, be it Persian, Arab or subsequently Turkic, alongside the assertion of as much local independence as possible, became an enduring theme in Kurdish political life. Kurdish tribes sometimes supported government against rebels and external enemies, for example on behalf of the Caliph Marwan II against the challenge of his cousin in 746, in support of al Ma'mun's bid for the caliphate against his brother al Amin, and against Byzantium. Equally frequently such tribes were in rebellion, sometimes on their own, sometimes with other dissident groups. They rose in 645 and 659, and in 666 they revolted twice in Ahwaz and Fars. They rose against the Umayyads in 685, 702 and 708, and periodically rebelled during the Abbasid period, particularly in the second half of the ninth century when the Abbasids became progressively weaker: for example, in 840, 846 and 866 when they actually seized Mosul; in the years 869–883 when certain tribes supported the Zanj rebellion; and in 875 in support of the rebellion of Ba'qub al Saffar.

Even when they were not in a state of rebellion, many tribes were able to achieve functional independence, even if they were required to give formal recognition either to central government or to local government appointees. By the end of the Saljuq era, when many Kurdish rulers had been replaced by Turkish ones, many Kurdish tribes still lived relatively freely. Military officers, whether Turks or Kurds, were rewarded for their services with a grant of lands and absorbed into Kurdish culture as a new layer of local rulers.

These fiefholders stood at the apex of Kurdish society. Some were probably local chiefs who had rendered good service with their tribes as auxiliaries in Muslim armies. Others were professional officers who received land grants in Kurdistan in return for the readiness to provide troops in time of war. Beneath them were their soldiers who sometimes formed new tribal groups and the Kurdish tribes themselves. These tribes were predominantly pastoralist and transhumant. They all belonged to the warrior class, living by fighting in time of war and by stockbreeding in peace. Below these people of the sword was a non-tribal class of peasant cultivators (*rayyat*), and also townspeople.

The Kurds were famous for the provision of troops to the Islamic armies, fighting with distinction on the frontiers of Islam against Byzantium, Armenia, Persia's eastern marches and in the Crusades. Some almost certainly joined the caliphal armies because there was inadequate land to sustain more people in Kurdistan. Just as nomad areas, the Arabian peninsula and the central Assian steppes, forced tribes northwards out of the Arabian peninsula and westwards into Iran, so too some Kurdish tribes were almost certainly forced to find a new economic basis for existence.

The Kurds adjusted to the Arab invasion and, in spite of intermingling, were never swamped by Arab tribes. They had a much harder time, however, with the Turkomans, as wave after wave of Turkic bands entered the region. In spite of Saljuq efforts to keep these disruptive forces on the move into Asia Minor, Kurds found themselves displaced in northern Mesopotamia and in Azarbaijan. Efforts by local Kurdish rulers to incorporate Turkic tribesmen into their forces usually proved disastrous. Even when chiefly families intermarried, Kurds found these tribes anarchic and unreliable. In some cases it took over a century for Turkoman and Kurdish tribes to establish a *modus vivendi*.

Kurdish forces were deliberately recruited by the Abbasid caliphs to weaken the preponderant power of Turkish troops in the caliphal army; from the eleventh century they were likewise recruited by the Saljuqs. But relations between Turkish and Kurdish military formations remained highly explosive, even up to the end of the twelfth century.

Kurdish military bands, some as tribes from the outset and others forming themselves into military tribal groups, participated in campaigns and established military camps and colonies in various parts of the empire. Senior Kurdish officers were by no means a rarity in the Islamic army. For example, Acre was defended from the Crusaders by a Kurdish commander, and when he was appointed to govern Jerusalem he was succeeded in Acre by another Kurdish officer. Kurdistan had a reputation similar to Scotland as an acknowledged source of good officers and troops. The most illustrious of these was Saladin (Salah al Din) who decisively defeated the Crusaders and established the Ayyubid dynasty in Egypt, Syria and Iraq. Like many of his fellow Kurdish warriors, Saladin never lived in Kurdistan. He was born in Takrit. It is unlikely that he or his fellow Kurdish warriors ever thought of their political identity as Kurdish, but rather as soldiers of Islam. Had his Kurdish identity been relevant to him it is unlikely that he would have given the fertile Shahrizur plain in the heart of Kurdistan as a fiefdom to one of his Turkish mamluks.

One must in the same way be cautious about the 'Kurdishness' of the dynasties in Kurdistan that sprang up in the tenth and eleventh centuries. These seized as much territory as they were able while the power of the Abbasid caliphate declined, and were eliminated one by one as the Turkish dynasties, beginning with the Saljuqs, ruthlessly reasserted central authority over the regions. During this period a welter of petty principalities and dynasties emerged; some happened to be Kurdish – when a chiefly family managed to establish its writ through a relatively wide area and abandoned its tented encampment for the relative splendour of a regional capital. The most famous of these dynasties were the Shaddadids (951–1075) in east Transcaucasia between the Kur and Araxes rivers; the Marwanids (984–1083) in the land from Diyarbakir southwards into northern Jazira; and the Hasanwayhids (959–1095) who dominated the Zagros between Shahrizur and Khuzistan, on the east side of the Shatt al Arab.

In other places a recently arrived Turkoman family might establish control and slowly become absorbed into its cultural environment. As with Kurdish mercenary troops, it is unlikely these dynasties thought of themselves as essentially Kurdish or Turkish in political terms. Their identity was based upon family ties, ethnic cultural tradition and Islam.

Apart from its tribal society, there was another reason for the apparently high level of disturbance in Kurdistan. The region lay athwart the main highways running west–east. As a result, every raiding army that moved from Iran to Mesopotamia moved through some Kurdish area. Sometimes parts of Kurdistan suffered devastation, for example from the Khwarazmian nomads who came from east of the Aral Sea in central Asia in the eighth century and periodically made forays westwards, from Ghuzz raiders in the mid-eleventh century, and from the occasional Byzantine forays. On other occasions the tribes were able to submit peacefully, as they did to the great Saljuq warrior Alp Arslan after his victory over Armenia and Byzantium at Malazgirt in 1071. Malazgirt marked the end for the Kurdish dynasties and governorates, for the Saljuqs preferred to administer the new province of 'Kurdistan' through Turkoman officers.

The first half of the thirteenth century proved disastrous for Kurdistan. In 1217 the Khwarazmians began raiding the region and this continued intermittently until 1230. They abandoned the scene in 1231 only because, terrible though they had been, a yet more fearful threat appeared in the form of Mongol raiders. Before the year was out the Kurds had had their first taste of Mongol warfare:

Diyarbakir was sacked and not one inhabitant left alive; Mardin and Nusaybin fell victim next. In 1235–36 Mongol raiders cut fresh swathes through the region; Shahrizur was pillaged in 1247 and Diyarbakir suffered a second visit in 1252. After his sack of Baghdad in 1258 the Mongol leader, Hulagu, turned back towards Tabriz, sending his forces in another sweep through the lands of Diyarbakir, Jazira bin Umar, Mardin and Hakkari.

Once the Mongols were firmly established, some tribes served their new masters, for example helping Sultan Uljaytu take control of the province of Gilan on the edge of the Caspian Sea. But others remained in ferment, mainly because of the enormous economic disruption caused by the Mongols. The tribes around Diyarbakir, for example, almost all disintegrated, new ones emerging during the fourteenth century. By this time the economy had still not shown much sign of recovery, and Kurdistan produced only one tenth of the revenues normal in the pre-Mongol period. One reason for this, undoubtedly, was the widespread abandonment of cultivation; it was easier to survive as a pastoralist with mobile wealth, and this in turn ensured that the nomadic culture became the dominant one for centuries.

A century and a half after the Mongols, Kurdistan suffered another major devastation. In 1393 Tamerlaine captured Baghdad and moved northwards to Mosul. While he campaigned further west he left Kurdistan to the tender mercies of his son, Jalal al Din Miranshah, who proceeded to sack the major centres of the region: Diyarbakir, Mardin, Tur Abdin and Husn Kayf. In 1401, following a Kurdish revolt, Tamerlaine sacked Arbil, Mosul and Jazira bin Umar. It was said that only one Christian village was spared in the whole Jazira area.

The record of events leaves a picture of endemic conflict between warring tribes, with neighbouring governments or passing armies. But it must be assumed that historians recorded the exceptional rather than the norm and perhaps it is more prudent to view such periods of conflict as ones of disequilibrium in an otherwise balanced network of relationships. Political relationships were established which reflected the balance of power between one chief and another, or the degree and penetration of government writ into the countryside. Ordinary people, it should be remembered, wanted to get on with life in peace, producing the daily necessities and trading the surplus in local markets. Caravans moving from Isfahan or Tabriz westwards plied their way across the region, paying dues to the tribes through whose territory they passed. Tamerlaine's Turkoman appointee as governor of Hakkari, for example, in order to keep the trade route open between Aleppo and Tabriz, promptly married into the local ruling house, and was soon courted by both sultan and shah.

Disequilibrium occurred when a chief or group of chiefs sought to expand their area of control, when government endeavoured to extend its authority, or when either governmental or tribal authority perceptibly weakened, providing an opportunity for others. Most commonly of all, local conflicts arose periodically over pasturage rights, the succession to the chieftainship of a tribe, or some such issue. Generally speaking, a tribe's importance could be said to grow in inverse ratio to the strength and authority of government or of neighbouring tribes.

Chaldiran and the New Border Marches

In the sixteenth century, the equilibrium between the Ottoman and newly emergent Safavid empires created the conditions for a more stable political structure for Kurdistan than hitherto. Indeed, the conditions established at this time determined the general pattern of political relations between the state and the Kurdish periphery for the next three hundred years. At the beginning of this period, no such equilibrium could have been foreseen. By the mid-nineteenth century, it was already possible for Kurds to look back nostalgically on a 'golden age' of independent existence in a mosaic of Kurdish principalities. This was the mythical (and nationalist) view. The reality was more complicated and certainly fell short of the idealized image.

The Ottoman empire, in spite of its nomadic tribal origins, turned its back on tribalism and consciously created a highly centralized form of government along-side a civic and formal culture. It created a standing army, a large and relatively efficient bureaucracy, and incorporated and strengthened Sunni institutions within the establishment. Since its primary income derived from agriculture, it had no real place for nomadic tribes, except in nostalgia for the origins of the Ottoman sultans, and so sought to settle and register the tribes wherever its authority held sway. Having initially established itself in western Anatolia and Thrace, it began to turn its attention eastwards, where unruly Turkoman tribes gave increasing cause for concern.

By the beginning of the sixteenth century these tribes posed clear challenges to the Ottomans. They resented and resisted attempts to settle, control and tax them and their disorder encouraged many of the peasantry to abandon the land. Many of the Turkoman tribespeople in eastern Anatolia subscribed to an extreme and heterodox form of Shi'i Islam led by the Safavi order in Azarbaijan. Known as *qizilbash* (or 'Red Heads') after their red felt caps, they showed every sign of consolidating into a serious threat to Sunni Ottoman rule. Since the Turkomans, including *qizilbash* tribes, were still intermittently moving westwards, the borders of the Ottoman lands in central Anatolia were vulnerable to the resulting turbulence.

The Ottomans had already seen the emergence towards the end of the fourteenth century of two rival Turkoman dynasties in the region between Diyarbakir, Van and Azarbaijan – the Shi'i Qara Quyunlu or 'Black Sheep' and the Sunni Aq Quyunlu or 'White Sheep' (1378–1502) who superseded the former in 1469. In 1502, the Safavi leader, Ismail, overthrew the Aq Quyunlu and established the Safavid dynasty at Tabriz, proclaiming himself Shah. In 1505 Shah Ismail and his army, composed almost entirely of *qizilbash* troops, advanced westwards, capturing Kurdish areas as far as Marash, substantially west of

Diyarbakir, by 1507, and Mosul and Baghdad in 1508. Ismail also gave overt encouragement to *qizilbash* unrest inside Ottoman territories. By now the heterodox ideas had spread across much of eastern Anatolia, affecting certain Kurdish tribes or sections of them, and posing serious dangers to the Ottomans. In 1511 a major *qizilbash* uprising took place in central Anatolia.

The Ottoman sultan, Salim Yavuz, who had just seized power, immediately sought to destroy the *qizilbash* tribes. Forty thousand *qizilbash* adherents were said to have perished during his expedition of pacification. As soon as he was able, Salim moved against Ismail, bringing him to battle at Chaldiran (midway between Erzinjan and Tabriz) in 1514. Here he inflicted a sharp defeat on Shah Ismail, entering and plundering the Safavid capital of Tabriz.

With the onset of winter, Salim was compelled to withdraw into Anatolia to ensure his lines of communication. Nevertheless, the battle of Chaldiran effectively established a strategic point of balance between Ottoman Anatolia and Safavid Azarbaijan, and this in the longer term created the conditions for Kurdistan to enjoy a period of relative stability. Although both Ottoman and Safavid sought, and sometimes successfully, to shift the boundary in their respective favour, the border reverted to the approximate line marked by Sultan Salim's strategic withdrawal after Chaldiran. This line, formally established at the Treaty of Zuhab in 1639, persisted despite disputes, encroachments and invasions until 1914.

These events had a vital impact on Kurdistan, which now became the border march between the two empires. Each empire had to weigh up how far it could extend its control into the border marches, while Kurdish chiefs had the unenviable task of choosing which empire it was wisest to recognize, balancing a desire for maximal freedom from government interference against the local benefit of formal state endorsement of their authority.

The Safavids and the Kurds

Following his initial conquest of Kurdistan, the majority of chiefs recognized Shah Ismail, but probably with as little enthusiasm as they had accepted the Qara Quyunlu and Aq Quyunlu chiefs before him. For just as the Aq Quyunlu had deliberately exterminated those chiefly families which had supported the Qara Quyunlu, so also Shah Ismail dealt stringently with those chiefs who had supported his predecessors. It is therefore not surprising that even before Chaldiran some tribes had decided to help the Sunni Ottomans achieve their victory. Chaldiran led to further and widespread Kurdish defection from the Safavids.

Chaldiran apart, there were a number of reasons why many Kurdish chiefs renounced Safavid suzerainty. Primarily they were impressed by the demonstration of Ottoman military strength. There was also mutual religious suspicion between the mainly Sunni Kurdish tribes and the new rulers of Iran. For even though

Shah Ismail abandoned his *qizilbash* beliefs in favour of the more staid Ithna 'Ashari denomination of Shi'i Islam, he sought to extirpate all trace of Sunni Islam in his empire. Indeed, it was only among tribal groups on the fringes of Safavid Iran that Sunnism survived.

For the ruling Kurdish families there was a more practical consideration: Shah Ismail's intention was to govern through Turkoman or Persian administrators those areas of Kurdistan under his control, whereas the Ottomans relied on local chiefs. There was one major exception to Ismail's policy. Like their predecessors, the Safavids permitted the House of Ardalan to continue its rule over the central Zagros range and the fertile valleys lying to the west of it, most notably Shahrizur (roughly the valley area in which Sulaymaniya was later established). The *walis* (or governors) of Ardalan, as they were known, were hereditary rulers, whose capital was at Sinna (Sanandaj) on the eastern side of the Zagros. It is unclear why they were tolerated.[1]

Yet the policy of imposing Turkoman or Persian appointees proved difficult to enforce. The Safavids wanted to bring the tribes of Iran under their direct control as a matter of general policy. They were acutely aware that their predecessors had themselves been tribal, and that tribalism militated against the exercise of firm government. Some Kurdish tribes were almost certainly caught up in the Safavid struggle with recalcitrant *qizilbash* tribal regiments which perpetuated a state of unrest until almost the end of the century. Shah Abbas made strenuous efforts to replace tribal troops over which he had limited control with a standing army of slaves, but he had limited success, and tribes remained an important force in the social structure of Iran. Even where external governors were appointed by the state, their authority was often unenforceable. For example, the large Mukri confederation and those sections of the Bilbas and Harkis still within Safavid orbit remained only theoretically under government-appointed administrators. Many Kurdish tribes on the Safavid side of the border found that in practice they enjoyed considerable independence.

The Ottomans and the Kurds

The Ottomans, by contrast, were already highly centralized and perhaps could afford to make formalized exceptions for the tribes in the border marches. Following his withdrawal from Tabriz, Sultan Salim had insufficient manpower to ensure the submission of what had so recently been part of Safavid territory. He also faced two interconnected problems with regard to the newly acquired border marches: there was a danger of Safavid subversion or invasion, and the application of direct administration and taxation in the region would be extremely difficult and probably counterproductive.

As a result, Sultan Salim opted for pragmatism rather than the brutal ruthlessness for which he was better known. He did so on the advice of a Kurd, Idris Bitlisi, a man of considerable political judgement. Bitlisi was in the rare position of enjoying the confidence of both the sultan and the Kurdish rulers. As a former Aq Quyunlu official he had watched them destroy local loyalty with their heavy-handedness and saw Shah Ismail follow suit; as a high-born Kurd, he knew the region well and understood the ruling families and how to strike a bargain with them; as the son of a renowned religious mystic and teacher he would also have commanded wide respect.

Bitlisi persuaded Sultan Salim to give him a free hand to win over the Kurdish princes and chiefs. Equipped with blank *firmans*, or decrees,[2] Bitlisi reinstated rulers dismissed by Shah Ismail, and confirmed certain chiefs in semi- or virtual independence in return for their acknowledgement of nominal Ottoman suzerainty.

The majority of Kurdish leaders naturally welcomed reinstatement and willingly accepted an arrangement that gave them the benefit of Ottoman recognition and confirmation of their relatively independent status. In return, they undertook to produce armed and mounted men to serve the empire when called upon to do so. For a society in which the ruling class lived in the saddle, it must have been an attractive proposition. One should be cautious, however, about notions of reinstatement in terms of a revival of some kind of *status quo ante*. Ottoman formalization of Kurdish amirates must have changed fundamentally the configurations of Kurdish groups, in particular giving the amirs greater authority and security that they had ever before enjoyed.

Moreover, by this action the Ottomans created a formalized quasi-feudal system at a time when they were trying hard to eliminate such practices elsewhere in the empire. Altogether about 16 main *hukumats* (governments) or amirates were created over a period of years, in each case Bitlisi (or his successors) seems to have negotiated individual terms of local independence. The area of vassal states probably covered no more than 30 per cent of Kurdistan but it came to be seen, certainly by Kurds, as the ideal balance between localism and imperial government. These amirates were composed of sedentary Kurds.

Alongside the independent *hukumats* within the Ottoman administrative system, there were also *sanjaqs* (or counties) under hereditary Kurdish rulers, as well as directly administered *sanjaqs* under centrally appointed officials. Those well within the orbit of Ottoman control inevitably had to settle for greater state interference and control. Here the system of military fiefs prevailed, conditional on the provision of troops in time of war. But such fiefs were often heritable in practice, and a father might seek a fief certificate in the name of his son. The number and size of the Kurdish chiefdoms – be they amirates or hereditary *sanjaqs* – varied from one place to another, and from one time to another. In each case status reflected the balance between the ambitions, strengths and political skills of a Kurdish ruler, central government and local authorities.

The Ottomans also created nomadic tribal confederations, or peoples (*uluslar*), which seem not to have been subject to the amirate system. The largest in Diyarbakir province was the Boz Ulus (the Grey People), a remnant of the Aq

Quyunlu confederacy, consisting of Turkoman and Kurdish tribes, probably 75,000 or so souls, wintering in the Syrian desert and spending the summer in the Dersim/Tunceli region.[3] The other major group, almost entirely Kurdish, was the Kara Ulus (the Black People). Altogether there were probably over 400 tribal chiefs in the provinces of Diyarbakir, Van and Shahrizur, some wholly nomadic.

Approved Kurdish tribes were also authorized to move northwards to police the Armenian border region north of Van, while others seem to have moved westwards, possibly to dominate areas where there were still unpredictable Turkoman groups. The governing principle underlying all these arrangements was that where Kurdish tribes maintained good order, provided troops when necessary, defended the border regions and above all acknowledged Ottoman suzerainty, they would be allowed a measure of freedom enjoyed virtually nowhere else in the empire. Indeed, elsewhere the Ottomans were doing their best to eliminate the vassal system in favour of direct government.

At first Bitlisi's policy paid dividends. Substantial Kurdish forces under his command played a crucial role in the defence and relief of Diyarbakir in 1515 after a siege of 18 months, and in the capture of Mardin and other towns in northern Jazira. Other Kurdish forces purged the *qizilbash* from the regions around Mosul–Jazira bin Umar, Amadiya–Arbil and even Urumiya.[4] The *qizilbash* were decisively defeated at Qiziltepe, near Mardin in 1516. Bitlisi's system of appointments was in part a reward to those who fought for him.

Although the Safavids lost control of south-east Anatolia following Chaldiran, they gave up control of Iraq less easily. In 1530 Shah Tahmasp recaptured Baghdad, and the Safavids and Ottomans found themselves at war again.

Kurds in the Ottoman–Safavid Struggle

Throughout the period Kurdish forces played a vital part in these campaigns. Sultan Sulayman Qanuni (the Magnificent) led expeditions against Iran in 1533, 1534, 1548 and 1554, in which year the Ottomans wrested the Kurdish areas of Shahrizur and Bilkas from Iranian control with the help of the Kurdish amirs. In 1623 Mukri Kurds helped the Safavids recapture Baghdad. Forty thousand Kurds – from Mosul, Arbil, Kirkuk, Shahrizur, Suran and Amadiya – were vital to the Ottoman siege and recapture of Baghdad in 1638.

We have some picture of the importance of Kurdish troops within the Ottoman army. Kurds enrolled in the cavalry of the standing army alongside Turks. But it was in the provincial forces that the Kurds made a distinctive contribution, as light cavalry for scouting, raiding and skirmishing, usually in tribal formations. An Ottoman expedition into Iran in the mid-1630s used Hakkari and Mahmudi (Khushab) Kurds ahead of the main body, while the infantry of Bitlis formed the rearguard. However, when such expeditions withdrew, pro-Safavid Kurdish irregulars were equally adept in cutting off stragglers and capturing baggage trains.

Throughout the period the Kurdish region either side of today's Iran–Iraq border remained contested territory; its inhabitants played a major part in the continuing struggle. Some ruling families, despite the occasional conflict, were consistent in their support of the empire in whose orbit they fell. Others, however, were more openly opportunist, as were those tribes inhabiting the actual border areas.

Some deliberately placed tribal sections athwart the border to ensure their position against conflict with one of the two empires. The Jaf tribe, for example, largely abandoned Iranian territory at the end of the eighteenth century and were allowed to settle on Baban lands in Pizhdar and Halabja, but carefully left a section behind east of the border so that they could move either way over the border to escape government punishment. Once inside Ottoman territory Jaf chiefs still married across the border, notably into the Ardalan family. Northern Kurdistan, because military movement was impossible for almost half the year, was less susceptible to such vicissitudes and when inroads were made, as happened from time to time, both sides found it difficult to sustain their conquests.

The relationship between Istanbul and its Kurdish satraps was far from perfect. Because the system of semi-independent principalities lasted well into the nineteenth century, it is tempting to consider it a successful political arrangement. In practice neither side was satisfied. Both Istanbul and individual chiefs pushed for greater control whenever they thought they had the power to achieve it. In that sense the arrangements achieved by Bitlisi were understood to be a pragmatic recognition of the balance of forces at that time, a balance in which the chiefs benefited from official recognition.

However, it was a balance that could easily be upset by the excessive demands of either the sultan or local governors. Most Kurdish principalities and some hereditary *sanjaqs* were exempt from tax dues or other internal interference.[5] But at times local Ottoman officials did interfere in matters of succession and taxation, leading to such widespread dissatisfaction that Kurdish chiefs refused military service.[6] By 1633, according to the great traveller Evliya Chelebi, Kurdish rulers in the provinces of Diyarbakir, Van and Mosul were 'subject to oppression under the tyrannical hand of provincial governors' who 'through their avarice dismissed a part of them from office while executing others without reason'.[7] Certainly when Murad IV undertook the recapture of Baghdad in 1637–38, he levied food and fodder from the Kurdish amirates *en route*, despite their traditional exemption from tax. Some rulers were excused, but even where payment was required, rulers were significantly less punctilious than the *begs* of regular Ottoman *sanjaqs*.

In Diyarbakir, Murad IV's son-in-law, Malik Ahmad Pasha energetically sought to incorporate Kurdish territory into directly administered areas, possibly on account of the Kurds' reluctance to support the 1638 expedition.[8] But the process was less a steady government encroachment, and more an ebb and flow between the two sides, depending on their respective strengths and policies. Chelebi, visiting the region in the mid-1650s, found the Kurdish princes enjoying greater freedom than they had done for a generation. Ironically all this was to change, for Chelebi was travelling with the newly appointed Wali of Van, the old enemy of the amirs, Malik Ahmad Pasha, who soon showed he had lost little of his stringency.

If Kurdish rulers were sometimes ill-used, the sultan also had grounds for complaint. In the contest for territory between the two empires it would have been remarkable had Kurdish rulers not been openly opportunistic. Sharaf Khan, ruler of Bitlis, for instance, put the Ottoman position in the whole region in jeopardy when he suddenly defected to the Safavids in 1531; for Bitlis was one of the strongest principalities and its city commanded a strategic narrow pass connecting Azarbaijan with Diyarbakir and the Jazira.[9]

Others refused the military obligations implicit in their status. Amir Husayn Junbalat, for example, who ruled at Kilis (in the hill country north of Aleppo) at the beginning of the seventeenth century, refused to participate in an expedition into Iran when instructed to do so. He was killed for his contumacy. His brother Ali rebelled and, raising an army of 40,000 men, seized Tripoli and pillaged as far as Damascus.

Local conflicts were a significant element in the political uncertainties of the region. Rival amirates and tribes constantly had to watch their backs, and closer to home the heads of ruling families had to keep a sharp watch on ambitious relatives. Take, for example, the fortunes of the rulers of Bahdinan, in their dramatic hilltop capital of Amadiya during the sixteenth century. Hasan Bahdinan had shrewdly foreseen Ismail Safavi's ascendancy and had thrown off fealty to Ardalan in 1500, two years before Ismali destroyed the Aq Quyunlu. Fourteen years later, as the first news of Sultan Salim's great victory at Chaldiran reached his ears, he dropped Shah Ismail for Sultan Salim. He served his successor, Sulayman, zealously and was rewarded with *ayalet* (provincial) status, a reward which cut both ways since it drew Amadiya more closely into the Ottoman system. On his death, however, Hasan's two sons, Quhab and Bairam, quarrelled. Bairan fled to Shah Tahmasp who, he knew, would lend a willing ear. In the meantime, Quhab, who depended on his father's reputation in Istanbul but clearly lacked the necessary leadership qualities, found himself ousted by a powerful local tribe, the Mazuri, in favour of his cousin, Sulayman. Quhab fled to Istanbul and in due course returned to Duhuk, armed with a *firman* but without apparently taking any precautions for his own safety. By this time Bairam had installed himself at Zakhu and had reached an understanding with his cousin Sulayman. Having reach Duhuk, midway between Zakhu and Amadiya, Quhab let himself be captured by Sulayman, who then ceded Amadiya to Bairam, no doubt for some suitable reward. Quhab never regained Amadiya, but his son was installed with Istanbul's assistance in 1585.

The Houses of Ardalan and Baban

Two great rival Kurdish families, Ardalan and Baban, dominated the local scene on either side of the Iraqi–Iran border until the early nineteenth century. Ardalan was an ancient principality, which by the early fourteenth century had established itself over wide tracts of land on both sides of the Zagros range. It is an indication of its former extent that, unable to withstand Turkoman inroads in the early fourteenth century, it abandoned Arbil, Koi Sanjaq, Rawanduz, Harir and Amadiya. The Ardalans did not forget their claim on these territories and recaptured them in the last years of the fifteenth century. Local chiefs in these areas – for example, the Suran at Koi Sanjaq – gave their allegiance to Ardalan, as Ardalan gave it to Ismail Safavi.

The Ottoman triumph at Chaldiran, however, spelt the long-term dissolution of Ardalan holdings west of the Zagros. Straight after Chaldiran the Wali of Ardalan came to terms with Sultan Salim, but it was an accord that had no hope of lasting. The Ardalan rulers had to choose between Iran and Turkey and in the final analysis, since their heartlands lay along the eastern foothills of the Zagros range, that choice had to be for Iran and they consequently found themselves fighting a losing battle to hang onto lands west of the Zagros. In 1537 they were driven out of the fertile Shahrizur plain by Sultan Sulayman, only to hold it again on behalf of Iran from the turn of the century until 1630. The Treaty of Zuhab (1639) confirmed Shahrizur as under Turkish sovereignty.

While the Kurdish amirates were autonomous, imperial support could be a vital asset. Sultan Sulayman, for example, was thwarted in his attempt to cross the Zagros by Shah Tahmasp's vigorous support of Ardalan from 1538 onwards. One might have thought a non-Shi'i principality would have had a difficult relationship with a fervently Shi'i dynasty, but there was only one shortlived period of religious oppression at the outset of the eighteenth century when Shi'i governors were installed. Ardalan rulers generally worked assiduously to cultivate the imperial court in Isfahan (to which the Safavids moved in 1598), by keeping order among the tribes. Khan Ahmad Khan, the formidable Wali of Ardalan at the end of the sixteenth century,[10] became a close confidant of Shah Abbas, marrying his sister. He suppressed two great Kurdish tribes to the north, in the area between Rawanduz and Sawj Bulaq (just south of Lake Urumiya) – the Bilbas and Mukri – in the name of Shah Abbas, and thereby recovered almost all the ancient Ardalan dominions.

Proximity to the throne held its own dangers. As soon as Shah Abbas died in 1629, Khan Ahmad Khan's son, who had been brought up in Isfahan, was blinded, possibly to ensure the unchallenged succession of his cousin Shah Safi. There are limits to any person's loyalties and when an Ottoman army approached the western territories of Ardalan with the clear intention of laying them waste, Khan Ahmad Khan had no hesitation in offering the Ottomans his support. It was an act which automatically forfeited all Ardalan east of the Zagros. But his feud with Shalı Safi could not conceivably be repaired, and he was recompensed by the Ottomans with the government of Mosul and Kirkuk. Khan Ahmad Khan's successor in Ardalan, his cousin Sulayman Khan, repaid Shah Safi for his appointment, playing a critical role in repelling Sultan Murad's invasion of Iran in 1630. After his death in 1656 Sulayman's own son succeeded as *wali*, but the Shah carefully appointed other Ardalan family members to govern different parts of the Ardalan domain.

The Ardalans were probably more consistent in their loyalties than virtually any other border amırate, and only broke that loyalty under duress.[11] At times they were the most powerful of the shah's vassals. They epitomized the decentralized system of rule that characterized the later Safavids and the Qajars after them. Whether or not this reflected the trust of the rulers of Iran, it undoubtedly reflected the balance of power. For by the mid-seventeenth century the Safavids had lost the command they had held over the empire a century before. The regular army of Shalı Abbas more or less disintegrated into a motley array of ill-disciplined regiments (eventually displacing the Safavids), and in Kurdistan the Walis of Ardalan remained the dominant players. They were frequently made governors of all of Kurdistan lying within Iran's sphere, and were thus charged with ensuring the loyalty and orderly behaviour of the great confederations in the border areas: the Jaf, the Mukri, the Bilbas, the Hawrami and the Kalhur Kurds.

On the other side of the Zagros, the Baban dynasty was more typical of the opportunism which so often characterized the region. The Babans were relative newcomers, unable to claim the antiquity of Ardalan. Their eponymous founder, Baba Sulayman, hailed from the Pizhdar tribe which dominated the valleys around Raniya and Qala Dlza. He acquired sufficient local importance to displace the waning Suran clan[12] largely through his assiduous service to the Ottomans in their struggle against the Safavids during the 1670s.[13]

In the early eighteenth century the Babans achieved paramountcy in all the hill country east of the Kifri–Altun–Kupru road, between the Diyala and Lesser Zab rivers, and were strong enough to deal on equal terms with Ardalan. From this time on, the two houses took advantage of the other's weakness. When the Afghans invaded Iran (1721), plunging the country into chaos, the Babans seized Sinna on behalf of the Ottomans. They ruled Ardalan till 1730 when they withdrew on the approach of the Iranian army.

They had already discovered that loyalty to the Ottomans could be costly. When the Afghan army suborned other Kurds in the Ottoman forces outside Hamadan in 1726, the Babans remained loyal to their commander, sharing in his devastating defeat. Thereafter they became a good deal more calculating and less reliable for the Ottomans – with good reason. The Ottoman grip on Iraq was feeble for most of the eighteenth century. In Baghdad the governors recognized by the sultan were in practice virtually independent, and it was inevitable that unless they were strong, Ottoman weakness should affect local rulers like the Babans. Moreover, across the border the rise of Nadir Shah as the strong man of Iran, from the early 1730s until his death in 1747, persuaded some members of the Baban family that their best interests might lie there.

These factors provided the opportunity also for personal rivalries. From this time onwards leading pretenders to paramountcy of the Babans sought sponsorship from Iran. In 1743 Salim Baban obtained his investiture from Nadir Shah, displacing the Ottoman candidate, Sulayman. His incumbency did not last long, but he regained it in 1747 and raided Ottoman territories with impunity. In 1750, however, he was defeated by a joint Ottoman-Kurdish force north of Baghdad, and Sulayman was once again installed at Qara Cholan which, until the foundation of Sulaymaniya in 1785, was the Baban seat. In 1758 Salim was lured to Baghdad on false expectations and murdered.

Sulayman, as befitted a Kurdish paramount, exploited the weakness of his neighbours when he felt strong enough to do so, extending his rule south of the Diyala river, harrying the amirs of Rawanduz, and incorporating Koi. With Salim out of the way, Sulayman felt free to defy Baghdad and co-operate with Iran when it suited him.[14] In 1762 he raided Sinna with the approval of the then ruler of Iran, Karim Khan Zand, who had little love for the Wali, and the following year was confirmed by him as its ruler. When Sulayman was assassinated the following year (possibly by the rival Baban faction), Karim Khan Zand confirmed his brother as ruler at Qara Cholan (on the Ottoman side of the border), and his son as (shortlived) ruler in Sinna.[15]

When open war between the Ottomans and Iranians resumed in 1774, it was inevitable that this contest should be complicated with rival Babans seeking to co-opt one imperial army or the other. Control of the rich Shahrizur plain swung for the next 50 years between rival empires and the Baban surrogates.

It should not be thought that the Babans were merely tools in the hands of rival powers. Both empires recognized the Babans as both asset and danger to their authority. In 1810, for example, Abd al Rahman Baban was virtual kingmaker in Baghdad. 'It was he who had put to summary death suspected Aghas, he who appointed a new Kahya [major domo] and other officers and he who ... stamped out ... opposition.'[16] With the help of a rival Baban cousin the governor in Baghdad was strong enough to mount an expedition to bring Abd al Rahman into line in 1812.[17] Abd al Rahman was less duplicitous than many of his relatives. His objective, if we are to believe Claudius Julius Rich, the gifted East India Company Resident in Baghdad, was not to escape his status as a tributary of the Ottoman Porte but to remain independent of provincial officials.[18] As with so many Kurdish chiefs, it was local obedience which stuck in his craw.

His closest relatives, however, played off both Ottoman and Iranian without scruple. His son Mahmud told Rich, who visited him in 1820, of the difficulties with which he had to contend, sandwiched between two rival powers,

one of which [Iran] never ceased persecuting him for contributions, – the other, his natural sovereign, that is, the Turks, insisted he should neither serve nor pay Persia; and yet, Turkey was neither able nor willing to defend him, when the Shahzadeh of Kirmanshah carried out his exactions by force.[19]

Mahmud was being less than candid, for he had been in regular correspondence with Kirmanshah. When forces from Baghdad moved against him late in 1818, 10,000 Iranian troops crossed the border in his support, only to be pushed out the following year by Mahmud's uncle, Abd Allah. However, with inadequate troops on the ground, Baghdad accepted the Iranian demand that Mahmud be reinstated in Sulaymaniya.

Yet the story of Mahmud Baban and his uncle, Abd Allah, illustrates how fickle dynastic rivals could be towards their sponsors. Mahmud now sided with Baghdad, while Abd Allah turned to Iran. Rich, in Sulaymaniya at the time, tells us that Abd Allah was caught red-handed with correspondence from Kirmanshah, and was arrested as he prepared to escape. Rich was sure that Abd Allah had been shopped by Mahmud's dashing younger brother, Uthman, who was also corresponding with Kirmanshah. Despite their difficult relations, Mahmud seems to have decided not to hand Abd Allah over to the Ottoman authorities in Baghdad, possibly out of soft-heartedness because 'an exile in Baghdad is what the Koords most dread.'[20] If so, it was a foolish move. The following year, 1821, Abd Allah invaded Shahrizur at the head of 5,000 Iranian troops, seized Sulaymaniya and installed himself as paramount. Fearful that Baghdad itself might fall to the Iranians, the governor made terms including formal recognition of Abd Allah.

Alliances now criss-crossed at bewildering speed. Mahmud briefly and at great human cost ousted Abd Allah from Sulaymaniya. Iranian and Ardalani troops soon reinstated Abd Allah, who equally briefly enjoyed Ottoman as well as Iranian recognition. However, Mahmud abandoned Ottoman for Qajar allegiance when Ottoman authority looked particularly weak, and displaced Abd Allah. Baghdad's attempt to extend direct government to Sulaymaniya, however, sent Mahmud hot-foot to Iran, leading inevitably to Abd Allah accompanying Ottoman troops into the Baban state. All this was between 1821 and 1823, when a peace was theoretically established by the Treaty of Erzerum, with Mahmud back in Sulaymaniya, and Abd Allah consoled with Koi Sanjaq.

However, peace did not come to Baban. Mahmud found himself locked in a struggle with his brother Sulayman while Iran displaced Turkey as *de facto* suzerain, to the extent of putting a garrison in Sulaymaniya until 1834. Until their final suppression in 1850 the Babans remained a capricious and unpredictable presence in regional politics.

Yet despite the rivalries of the immediate ruling family, the Babans also enjoyed what Ardalan notably lacked, tribal solidarity. Ardalan was essentially a quasi-feudal polity, deriving its authority almost solely from imperial investiture. It was virtually the last surviving independent tributary from Safavid days.[21] The Wali of Ardalan once asked Abd al Rahman Baban why his own servants, though generously treated, would never follow him into exile nor show any personal loyalty, such as Baban retainers usually demonstrated.

> The answer of old Abdurrahman Pasha was very characteristic. 'You are not,' said the old chieftain, 'the lord of a tribe, nor are your men your tribesmen. You may clothe, feed them, and make them rich, but they are not your cousins; they are but your servants!'[22]

Yet Baban strength was also to do with the general weakness of Ottoman authority during the period and the physical distance between Kurdistan and Istanbul. On the Iranian side, whether the capital was at Tabriz, Qazvin, Isfahan or Tehran, imperial authority was more immediate, a few days rather than the better part of a month's ride away.

Locally, the existence of semi-independent rulers in both Baghdad and Mosul for much of the eighteenth century inevitably encouraged other local warlords and tribal chiefs, in both the mountains and the desert areas of Iraq, to treat imperial authority with truculence. In the nineteenth century all that was to change.

Sources

Secondary: J.A. Boyle (ed.), *The Cambridge History of Iran vol. 5: The Saljuq and Mongol Periods* (Cambridge, 1968); Martin van Bruinessen and Hendrik Boeschoten, *Diyarbakir in the Mid-seventeenth century. Evliya Celebi's Description of Diyarbakir* (Leiden, 1988); Claude Cahen, *Pre-Ottoman Turkey* (London, 1968); Robert Dankoff, *Evliya Celebi in Bitlis* (Leiden, 1990); *Encyclopaedia of Islam*, 2nd edition, 'Ahl-i Hakk', 'Ardalan', 'Bitlisi, Idris', 'Kurds, Kurdistan', 'Soran'; Kendal, 'The Kurds under the Ottoman Empire' in G. Chaliand (ed.), *A People without a Country* (London, 1993); Stanley Lane-Poole, *The Mohammedan Dynasties* (London, 1893, Beirut, 1966); S.H. Longrigg, *Four Centuries of Modern Iraq* (Oxford, 1925); Moosa, *Extremist Shiites*; Nikitine, 'La féodalité kurde'; Basil Nikitine, 'Les valis d'Ardalan' in *Revue du Monde Musulman*, no. 49, 1922; C.J. Rich, *Narrative of a Residence*; Steven Runciman, *A History of the Crusades* (Cambridge, 1954, London, 1965); S.J. Shaw and Kural Shaw, *History of the Ottoman Empire and Modern Turkey*, vol. i: *Empire of the Ghazis: the Rise and Decline of the Ottoman Empire, 1280–1808* (Cambridge, 1975); Guy Le Strange, *Lands of the Eastern Caliphate* (London, 1905, 1966); J. Wellhausen, *The Arab Kingdom and its Fall* (London, 1907, Beirut, 1963).

Notes

1. It may have been because of the strategic difficulty of holding land west of the Zagros, but it may also have been for religious reasons. The Ardalans may well still have been Ahl-i Haqq at this juncture. They certainly ruled over a large Ahl-i Haqq population, and this sect had been influential in the growth of *qizilbash* beliefs, holding the progenitor of the Safavi order, the thirteenth century mystic Shaykh Safi al Din, in particular reverence.

2. One must be a little cautious since the claims are based upon his own account, see van Bruinessen and Boeschoten, *Diyarbakir*, p. 14.

3. In 1540 the Boz Ulus had 7,500 households – perhaps 80,000 people in all – and two million sheep. While without military obligation, the Boz Ulus were liable to tax, van Bruinessen and Boeschoten, *Diyarbakir*, p. 27.

4. Bitlisi called on the rulers of the Mukri, Baradust and Suran Kurds to help him; see

van Bruinessen and Boeschoten, *Diyarbakir*, p. 15.

5. The first tax register for Diyarbakir province, made in 1518, does not mention any Kurdish chiefdoms except Chemishgezek (Dersim/Tunceli) as liable for tax, van Bruinessen and Boeschoten, *Diyarbakir*, p. 17.

6. For example in the 1630 campaign against Hamadan, the leader of the expedition had some Kurdish rulers executed for their disobedience, van Bruinessen and Boeschoten, *Diyarbakir*, p. 24.

7. Dankoff, *Celebi in Bitlis*, p. 13.

8. Several areas, the amirates of Amadiya, Bitlis and Sanjar, and the Mazuri tribe, suffered punitive expeditions.

9. Sultan Sulayman recaptured it four years later, giving it a Turkish governor, himself a deserter from Persian service. Almost 50 years later, in 1578, Sultan Murad III decided to restore Sharaf Khan's son, Sharaf al Din, who had grown up at the Safavid court. Sharaf al Din justified the trust put in him and five years later was also awarded the governorate of Mush. He had grown up and spent much of his life in the Iranian imperial service, but defected to the Ottomans in 1578 when he sensed his fortunes were waning, and was reinstated as ruler of Bitlis. His main claim to fame, however, is as a historian. He abdicated in 1596 in favour of his son in order to write a history of the Kurdish tribes. His *Sharafnameh* remains the most important source for mediaeval Kurdistan.

10. He it was who recaptured Rawanduz, Amadiya, Koi and Harir in the early 1600s, and had been rewarded with the governorship of all Iranian Kurdistan, Nikitine, 'Les Valis d'Ardalan', pp. 80–82.

11. There were moments when things went badly wrong, the most notable being the events following the death in 1629 of Shah Abbas already described; in 1721 Ali Khuli Khan sought Ottoman help when Iran disintegrated under the Ottoman onslaught; in 1742 Ahmad Khan, having loyally served Nadir Shah in India and Daghestan, was condemned to death for dispensing his grain reserve on famine relief; in 1751, Karim Khan Zand, Lur-Kurdish founder of the Zand dynasty (1759–94) sacked Sinna; and in 1859 court intrigues led the last *wali* to fear for his life (he sought assurances he would receive asylum in Ottoman territory if flight became necessary, but never had to put this to the test).

12. By tradition the Surans were said to be descended from an Arab shepherd who had sought refuge in Balikan, east of Rawanduz. Their capital was at Harir and they were said to be still powerful at the end of the sixteenth century, but succumbed to the attacks of their neighbours, presumably the Pizhdar, who were related to the Suran; *Elz* 'Soran'.

13. In 1694 Baba Sulayman invaded Ardalan and occupied several districts but was defeated the following year by a joint Iranian-Ardalan force, Longrigg, *Four Centuries*, p. 80.

14. His raids around Baghdad led to a punitive expedition which defeated him near Kifri in summer 1762.

15. The Ardalan wali was apparently restored in 1765, Nikitine, 'Les Valis d'Ardalan', p. 92.

16. Longrigg, *Four Centuries*, p. 227.

17. Abd al Rahman had built a line of fortifications along the Karadagh range, shielding Sulaymaniya, but his cousin, Muhammad bin Khalid, showed the Ottoman forces a little known and undefended pass through the hills, whereby Abd al Rahman was outflanked, Rich, *Narrative*, vol. i, pp. 55–59.

18. Rich, *Narrative*, vol. i, p. 96.

19. The Shahzadeh was Muhammad Ali Mirza, appointed in 1805, Rich, *Narrative*, vol. i, p. 71.

20. Rich, *Narrative*, vol. i, p. 87.

21. The others were Georgia, Hawayza (Khuzistan) and Luristan where the Wali of Pusht-i Kuh survived until the rise of Reza Shah.

22. Rich, *Narrative*, vol. i, p. 86.

CHAPTER 3

OTTOMAN KURDISTAN, 1800–1850

Introduction

By the end of the eighteenth century the Ottomans faced a severe crisis, that of a highly centralized empire that had lost control of its hinterland. The arrangements reached between tribe and state following Chaldiran had long since lost their value for Istanbul and finally foundered in the first half of the nineteenth century. As described in the preceding chapter, efforts to curtail the power of the amirs and chiefs of Kurdistan had been made intermittently by both state and regional authorities during the preceding three centuries. There had been phases of imperial progress, but the Kurds had usually managed to claw back their independence for a variety of reasons. By the end of the eighteenth century it was easy for the amirs and tribal chiefs to believe they had no need for an external sponsor. Their destruction during the next half century was a powerful reminder that leadership could not easily be maintained if the role of intermediary between state and subordinate tribal groupings ceased. External recognition remained an undervalued and undernoticed quality of chiefship, but its absence became potentially fatal when tribal groupings found themselves in conflict with each other.

The Roots of Ottoman Weakness

In reasserting control the Ottomans had to be careful. Given the underpopulation of eastern Anatolia, settlement and agricultural productivity were clearly in the interest of the state. Repressive measures by the state might impel a chief and his tribe to abandon their land in the prospect of finding fresh pastures elsewhere. On the other hand, the arrival of an irresolute local governor could quickly lead to the reassertion of old powers by the more ambitious chiefs. In other cases, corrupt officials might well strike bargains with local chiefs over the provision of troops, fodder or foodstuffs.

Overriding these factors, however, was the broader fact of declining imperial power. This decline may have been little more than relative to what was happening elsewhere, but it was manifest in the way the empire was beginning to crumble on the fringes. The second half of the eighteenth century saw the first serious inroads into the empire. Its swansong in eastern Europe, the unsuccessful attempt on Vienna in 1683, was followed four years later by the rout of its army at Mohacs in Hungary. Thereafter Europe's technological superiority, particularly in the military field, could no longer be denied. It was also clear that the Europeans, notably the Dutch, British and French, were building highly successful merchant enterprises in the Levant.

The greatest threat came from its increasingly ambitious northern neighbour, Russia, which inflicted a series of military and political humiliations during the second half of the eighteenth century.[1] After a temporary respite, thanks to Bonaparte's invasion of Russia, the empire experienced further humiliations. Its new fleet was completely destroyed by an Anglo-Franco-Russian fleet at Navarino in 1827, a prelude to the full independence of Greece, conceded in 1830. In 1828, Russia had renewed its assault on the Ottoman fringes, securing the principalities as far as the mouth of the Danube, and penetrating eastern Anatolia as far as Erzerum in 1829. Kars, Erzerum and Bayazid were all returned to Ottoman hands under the terms of the Treaty of Edirne, but the war had struck an entirely new note of danger. Not only had Ottoman Armenians assisted the Russian capture of Kars, but Muslim Kurdish tribes had also provided a regiment against the sultan. It was the first time the Russians had made use of the Kurds, having first come into contact with them during hostilities in 1804–5.

European inroads went well beyond the political and military sphere. In the late eighteenth century European merchants, already a longstanding presence, began to penetrate the empire as the potential for exporting the products of the growing European industrial revolution became clear. Furthermore, the empire faced the beginnings of an ideological assault. Its earliest manifestation was religious interest in the eastern churches under Islamic rule, to which the latter naturally began to respond as they recognized that Catholic and Protestant missionaries offered access to educational, commercial and political prospects. This ideological intrusion produced a crisis at the individual and community level even before it posed a threat to the empire. Each eastern church in turn was rent by schism, as one part abandoned its independence in favour of union with a powerful sponsor.[2] In the case of the new Chaldean, Armenian and Syrian Catholic Churches the impact was to be seen with the arrival of Catholic missionaries and teachers. The Protestants, not to be left out, soon set to work on the old Churches, hoping to bring the communities to a 'better' under-standing of the faith. Like the Catholics, one of the mission fields to which they turned was Kurdistan.

Besides Catholics and Protestants, the Orthodox Russians were hard at work with the Armenian community. Had Christians already been accepted on an equal footing as Muslims and had it not been feared (as it correctly was) that these activities implied European domination, all might have been well. But apart from the tribal Assyrians, who did live on a more-or-less equal footing with Kurdish tribesmen in the Hakkari mountains, the majority of Christians, certainly the majority of Armenians, were peasants and as such were inferior not only religiously but also socially. The consequences of European interest were destined to be explosive and tragic for Armenian and Assyrian alike.

The weakness of imperial authority was also evident in the landscape. Until the end of the nineteenth century, there were virtually no carriageable roads and no railways. In addition, in the summer an army could only cross large parts of the empire at the risk of epidemic disease in the heat, while in winter other parts remained impassable on account of snow. Season was even more important a factor in military campaigning in Turkey than it was in Europe.

In the Ottoman territories the eighteenth century had been characterized by nominally subject but effectively independent local rulers. Some of these arose when centrally appointed governors arrogated to themselves independent powers. The problem was not confined to the further flung areas of the empire. All over Anatolia, let alone in Kurdistan, local *derebeys* (or 'valley lords'), themselves theoretically holding military fiefs, turned their fiefdoms into hereditary holdings, failing to submit the requisite taxes to the capital.

When the Ottoman government finally resolved to bring the Kurdish chiefs to heel in the 1830s, the latter indignantly viewed their independence as of right. As a British consul reported of the Rawanduz chief, Mir Muhammad, in 1835:

> I inquired ... how he was so imprudent as to attempt to resist Reshid Mohammed Pasha, invested as he was with authority from his sovereign. The Haji replied that neither he nor his fathers were ever subjected to Pashas, or paid taxes to the Sultan, and he could not understand why he should be forced to do so; he had therefore resisted as long as he could.[3]

Inasmuch as Istanbul was able to extort taxes, the peasantry found themselves squeezed on both sides. In eastern Anatolia some peasants abandoned their villages and settled elsewhere in order to escape the intolerable burden. But whether the peasantry migrated, or the local notables successfully took their surplus, the growing fiscal crisis reduced the centre's capacity to deal with the problem.

By the beginning of the nineteenth century banditry had become a growing problem through much of Kurdistan. The main culprits were the Kurdish nomadic and semi-nomadic tribes on their seasonal migration. Government troops tried to retrieve what they could and would seize further livestock and goods as a penalty, but the jealousy between governors of neighouring provinces gave the tribes ample opportunity to make good their losses: 'the consequence is that on their winter migration back, the Kurds indemnify themselves by other robberies, repeating the same systematic plunder in the pashaliks of Angora and Koniyah alternately, each [provincial] government seeking an opportunity for reprisals within their own province, but neither pasha attacking the Kurds in the other's territories...."[4] If one wonders why there was not greater co-operation between one pashalik and another, the answer lies in the weakness of central government, its fear of the growth of provincial power and therefore its deliberate policy of discouraging inter-provincial co-operation on such matters.

All over the empire, central government was increasingly forced to recognize the power of tribal chiefs and provincial notables, and to confirm their status. In 1807 the Sultan was obliged to recognize formally that he shared his once-absolute power with local potentates, among them the Kurdish chiefs, who derived their power from local sources.

Something had to be done. In the first decade of the nineteenth century an attempt to overhaul the Ottoman army and to re-establish it on western lines precipitated a Janissary mutiny and the overthrow of Sultan Salim III. His successor, Mahmud II, recognized that to retrieve the empire from collapse he would have to restructure its institutions completely, not merely reform the army. This entailed the eradication not only of the Janissaries but the removal of all reactionary elements of government, for which the most careful planning and skilful execution would be required.

Mahmud began with the easier tasks in the provinces. By 1820 almost all the *derebeys* of Anatolia had been suppressed, and by 1830 those of the Balkans too. Where local notables were potentially dangerous they or their heirs were compensated with posts elsewhere. But everywhere newly confirmed government officials were installed, it being made clear that no holdings would be allowed to revert to hereditary inheritance.

Wherever strong enough Istanbul kept its new officials strictly answerable to the financial or military ministries in the capital. To follow up such measures, between 1831 and 1838 the government undertook a population census and a cadastral survey to establish the economic and human potential of the empire. For the time being, and until the Ottoman army was strong enough, Istanbul left Kurdistan well alone.

Reconstituting Ottoman military strength was more complex. In 1826 Sultan Mahmud had successfully overthrown and destroyed the Janissary regiments. But the first crucial tests of his new-style army hardly inspired confidence. In 1831–32 Ibrahim Pasha, the son of the Sultan's ambitious governor of Egypt, Muhammad Ali, seized Syria and proceeded to cross Anatolia, sweeping Ottoman resistance aside. He was only persuaded to withdraw to Syria by the European Powers.

Despite this humiliating setback, the Porte now set about bringing the tribal fringes of empire under its direct authority, something it had not attempted before. The destruction of the Kurdish amirates was a logical objective, part of the wholesale removal of local hereditary rulers necessary for the overhaul of empire. The most effective agents of this process were the amirs themselves. For having seen how easily the new Ottoman army had been worsted by the Egyptians, they one by one embarked upon reckless provocation against the capital, and upon short-sighted aggrandizement against each other.

Mir Muhammad of Rawanduz and the fall of the House of Suran

The first to founder was the ruthless and ambitious ruler of Rawanduz, Mir Muhammad. He displaced his father in 1814[5] and promptly eliminated opponents within the close circle of the Suran leadership. His father's old treasurer was the first to die, followed by both his uncles and their respective sons, after which no one in the principality dared oppose him.

Mir Muhammad was now free to turn his aggressive attention to his neighbours. He attacked and subdued one by one the tribes lying around his own principality – the Shirwan, Baradust, Surchi, Khushnaw and Mamash – killing those of their chiefs who seemed reluctant to submit. He also seized the nearby town of Harir, the old Suran capital which had been in Baban hands for at least half a century, thus re-opening a conflict which his father had put to rest some years earlier.

Mir Muhammad established control over a territory bounded by the two Zabs, the Tigris and the Iranian border. He seized another Baban town, Koi Sanjaq, in 1823 and widened his hold on the fringe of the Mesopotamian plain with the capture of Arbil and Altun Kupru. Raniya, centrally placed up in the mountains, fell the following year.

His next target was the Bahdinan amirate, where Mir Said of Amadiya was known to be weak. He used as a pretext Mir Said's failure to punish the Dasini (or Shaykhan) Yazidis for the murder of a dependent (Mazuri) chief in 1831. Mir Muhammad took it upon himself to ravage the villages of Shaykhan, east of Mosul. Thousands of men, women and children were killed and whole communities wiped out. A few escaped north to Tur Abdin, east of Mardin, or to Jabal Sinjar, west of Mosul. The destruction of so many Yazidis was easily justified on several grounds apart from the demands of vengeance. The Dasini were long-standing enemies of the Suran; they had defied their overlords, the mirs of Amadiya, on previous occasions. They, and their co-religionists in Jabal Sinjar, had routinely raided the villages of the Mosul plain, thereby provoking no less than eight Ottoman expeditions against them between 1767 and 1809. Since then the Yazidis had remained a formidable presence, and now again had proved their dangerous propensities. Above all, they were fair game because they were heretics.

Having demonstrated the failure of Mir Said in his duty as paramount to take vengeance on behalf of the Mazuri, Mir Muhammad seized the Bahdinan town of Aqra in 1833, expelled its ruler, and then moved on to take Amadiya after a brief siege. He threw out Mir Said, installing a Bahdinani puppet in his stead. He also acquired Zakhu and Duhuk, towns important not only for the trade which passed through them but because they lay strategically between Mosul and Jazira bin Umar.

The Ottoman authorities were aware of what was happening but had insufficient local forces to deal with Mir Muhammad. They had been preoccupied with Ibrahim Pasha's seizure of Syria and invasion of Anatolia and feared that Mir Muhammad was actually in touch with Egyptian forces. However, while Mir Muhammad was brutal and ruthless, it was undeniable that he had – once the ruins of his punitive work had ceased to smoulder – imposed on his territories a level of law and order unknown for generations. It was this, and apprehension concerning what he might do next, that persuaded the governor of Baghdad to obtain his investiture as a pasha. Had Mir Muhammad then acted as Ottoman agent imposing law and order in the region he controlled, as was expected of a Kurdish prince, he might have established a successful *modus vivendi* with Istanbul.

However, by now the alarm bells were sounding in Istanbul, and not a moment too soon. For Mir Muhammad marched up the Tigris against the amirate of Buhtan, seizing Jazira bin Umar, the seat of the amirs, the Badr Khans (Azizan), and filling the inhabitants of Husn Kayf, Nisibin and even Mardin with dread. However, following his attack on Buhtan, Mir Muhammad was compelled to return hot-foot to Amadiya, where Mir Said had regained control. He recaptured the town after a desperate struggle, put most of its leading inhabitants to the sword and formally annexed Bahdinan to Rawanduz, effectively eliminating the Bahdinani amirs.[6]

In 1834 Rashid Muhammad Pasha, formerly Grand Vizir and governor of Sivas at that time, appeared at the head of a substantial army with the specific task of suppressing the Kurdish princes. His first target, predictably, was Mir Muhammad, who had withdrawn to the almost inaccessible town of Rawanduz in the heart of Suran. As Rashid Muhammad entered Suran territory and approached the Rawanduz gorge, he was joined by forces from Mosul and Baghdad.

The circumstances of Mir Muhammad's submission cast valuable light on the local political scene. The conventional account[7] is that in order to avoid a bloody and possibly disastrous Ottoman progress through this easily defended gorge, Mir Muhammad was seduced by the offer from Rashid Muhammad Pasha of safe conduct to Istanbul with the prospect of being confirmed in his principality following submission. However, the correspondence of a British agent, Richard Wood, shows that the web of intrigue had a closer and more complex weave, directly involving Great Power rivalry, enmity between jealous Ottoman officials and Qajar intrigue. In 1835 Wood, as a young diplomat of promise, had been sent from Istanbul to Syria, to assess the chances in Egyptian-occupied Syria of a successful insurrection to restore Ottoman authority. He had then joined Rashid Muhammad Pasha (en route to suppress Mir Muhammad) to determine whether, as rumoured in Istanbul, Rashid Muhammad was in treacherous correspondence with the Egyptians. Wood rashly accused Rashid Muhammad publicly of treason and was compelled to slip away, escaping by night down the Tigris to Baghdad.

Wood was convinced that the Ottoman forces would suffer ignominious defeat if they tried to seize Rawanduz. In Baghdad he heard the East India Company Resident's belief that Russian influence in Tehran was prompting Qajar subversion in the border area. Both men were unhappy that Britain was training the Qajar army at a time when the shah was acting on behalf of Russia and against British interests on the eastern frontier of the Ottoman Empire.

Wood called on the governor of Baghdad, Ali Ridha Pasha, who knew Mir Muhammad personally. Wood had very little trouble persuading him of the danger of the destruction of the Ottoman army or of Mir Muhammad's Rawanduz forces. Either might create a vacuum into which the Qajars, whose forces had already recently invaded Sulaymaniya and Shahrizur, could move. Far better, Wood argued, to create a strong anti-Iranian bulwark out of a contrite Mir Muhammad and the Ottoman forces in Baghdad. Ali Ridha, who also wished to forestall Rashid Muhammad,[8] gave his blessing to Wood's proposal to make the dangerous journey to Rawanduz with the aim of persuading Mir Muhammad in person to submit to Istanbul.

Wood could hardly have been more successful. At Rawanduz he found not only Mir Muhammad but also a Qajar agent negotiating terms on which the Mir might flee to Iran, and on which the Qajars would support him against the Ottoman army.[9] Wood had the pleasure of discomfiting the Qajar agent by telling him how Iran was simultaneously offering to co-operate with the Turkish army in Mir Muhammad's defeat – an offer he was aware of since the British Embassy in Istanbul had conveyed it. He was also able to warn Mir Muhammad that Ali Ridha's forces were only four hours march away. Confronted with such news, but assured of safe conduct to Istanbul and seduced by Ali Ridha Pasha's promise to recommend his reinstatement in order to protect the border against Iran, Mir Muhammad abandoned his plan to flee and agreed to submit. However, he travelled to Istanbul in Rashid Muhammad's custody, not Ali Ridha's, and Rashid Muhammad had hoped to destroy Mir Muhammad on the battlefield. His journey to Istanbul was consequently one of open humiliation.

There are two postscripts worth noting to this story. First, the Qajar force that crossed the frontier to support Mir Muhammad included a Russian infantry battalion, 800 men strong[10] – more evidence of growing Great Power interest in the region. As for Mir Muhammad, he was received by the sultan with courtesy and honours, and may have been promised the governorate of all Kurdistan that he had hoped for. But this is doubtful. The reinstatement of a man like Mir Muhammad contradicted the core provincial policy of Ottoman reform: to replace the old hereditary rulers with men appointed and controlled by Istanbul. In any case the known facts fit this view better. For having set out on his return home Mir Muhammad simply disappeared, almost certainly killed on the sea journey from Istanbul to Trabzon.

Badr Khan Beg and the Fall of Buhtan

Badr Khan remains for many Kurds the most illustrious of an illustrious dynasty. He was brave, charming, pious and ambitious, but he was reckless, too. He was descended from the Azizan, mentioned in Sharaf al Din Bitlisi's *Sharafnameh*, which traced the family back to the thirteenth century. He is important partly because he was the last paramount chief to present a serious challenge to the Ottoman reformers. However, his real significance lies in the way local magnate, state and Great Power interests began to crystallize around the growing religious dimension of Kurdistan.

Badr Khan acceded to the principality of Buhtan in about 1820, when he was probably 18 years old. As in so many cases, his succession was resented by other family pretenders and it may be for this reason that he remained apparently quiet, consolidating power within his domain.[11] He certainly remained submissive to Ottoman authority, avoiding the widespread punitive actions of Rashid Pasha in the region, between 1834 and 1836. In 1839 he was given official rank in the Ottoman army in order to mobilize his tribal troops in the imminent battle with Ibrahim Pasha's Egyptian forces.

However, the battle at Nazib, close to his seat at Jazira bin Umar, ended in the rout of the Ottoman forces and, tempted by the patent power vacuum in the region, Badr Khan began to widen his sphere of influence. He was careful to avoid confronting Ottoman authority, but wholly underestimated the sensitivity of religion in the politics of the region. He had already shown his fervour by the duress he had applied to local Yazidis to convert to Islam and, incidentally, the character of his rule by the way in which he surrounded himself with these wholly dependent converts in preference to his old family retainers. He was, like a number of paramounts of whom Ardalan was the most notable, more of a monarch than a tribal chief.

Badr Khan's eye was attracted eastward, where the fall of Suran and Bahdinan and the weakness of the Hakkari amirate offered opportunity for aggrandizement without directly provoking the Porte. Hakkari was rent by schism between the Mir, Nur Allah Beg, and his kinsman, Sulayman, whom he had displaced.

The Mir of Hakkari's most important dependent was Mar Shimun, the spiritual and temporal paramount of the formidable (Nestorian) Assyrian Christian tribes inhabiting the Tiyari district of the Greater Zab valley and its precipitous tributaries. Indeed, despite his religion, Mar Shimun's importance within Hakkari placed him as second only to the Mir himself and, when the Mir might for some reason be absent from the principality, it was Mar Shimun, rather than a Kurdish chief, who acted as locum. However, the schism in the House of Hakkari had resulted in a permanent breech between the Mir and Mar Shimun, who supported Sulayman Beg, and the Mir now called upon his more powerful neighbour, Badr Khan, to punish the Assyrians.

The Assyrian tribes, too, were rent by schism as a result of missionary activity and this schism made attack on an otherwise formidable foe possible. In the 1830s they had repulsed both the Mir of Rawanduz and Badr Khan himself; but by 1843 serious differences had arisen between Mar Shimun and two influential clerics.[12] These now sided with the Mir of Hakkari and Badr Khan, who was already gathering his forces, on the understanding that their own village would be spared reprisals. In addition, one of the more formidable Tiyari tribes, the Tkhuma, promised to assist the Mir and Badr Khan against Mar Shimun.

The conflict between Mar Shimun and some of his flock throws light on the dangerous and destabilizing influence of foreign missionary endeavour. By 1835 American Protestants were hard at work in the area, establishing dispensaries and schools among the Armenian and Nestorian communities.[13] Mar Shimun feared this American endeavour because it undermined his own standing. Some church leaders welcomed the intrusion, since it reduced the authority of a patriarch for whom they had little liking. Among the missionaries, too, there was a polarization and while Anglicans supported Mar Shimun, their American competitors succoured his adversaries.

It was not difficult for Kurdish chiefs to find fault with the Assyrian community. In 1837 Mar Shimun had sent 3,000 men, with Nur Allah Beg's approval, to assist in the defence of Amadiya against Ottoman forces but had suddenly withdrawn them when cautioned by the governor of Mosul. Nur Allah Beg had every reason to welcome the discomfiture of a disobedient vassal, even at the hands of another chief.

At last, Christian missionary activity triggered alarm bells in the surrounding Muslim community. W.F. Ainsworth, travelling through Hakkari on behalf of the Church of England at the end of the 1830s had already noted the ominous implications for intercommunal relations.

> This sudden interest, so explicitly and so actively shown on the part of the Christian nations, towards a tribe of people [the Nestorian tribes], who have almost solely prolonged their independent existence on account of their remote seclusion and comparative insignificance, has called them forth into a new importance in the eyes of the Mohammedans, and will undoubtedly be the first step to their overthrow.[14]

Fears had certainly been awakened. As one Kurdish beg remarked to Ainsworth's Assyrian guide, 'You are the forerunners of those who come to take this country.'[15] In 1842 the Americans built a hill-top mission house above an Assyrian village. The rumour soon gained currency that it was a fortress against the Muslims, or a bazaar to draw business away from Jularmark.

Finally, it is likely that the Porte deliberately winked at Badr Khan. Certainly the governors of Mosul and Erzerum did nothing to discourage him from his well-publicized objectives. The Ottomans would have welcomed the reduction of the formidable and troublesome Nestorian tribes, and the persecution of Christians would inevitably lead to European demands that the culprits be punished and this would give the Ottoman authorities a convenient pretext to reduce another Kurdish amirate also.

Badr Khan does not seem to have foreseen this. The first round took place in July 1843 when he assembled a force of possibly 70,000 men which proceeded to move through the Nestorian region, massacring the inhabitants. Those who survived were sold as slaves. A second invasion occurred in 1846 when those Nestorian villages which had previous allied themselves with Badr Khan were also laid waste. Following stiff protests by Britain and France, the Porte decided to move against Badr Khan; but this was no simple matter, for Badr Khan had enlarged his confederation and also created a network of alliances with the chiefs of Hakkari, Van, Muks and Bitlis. He defeated the first expedition sent against him and declared himself independent of the Ottoman empire, minting his own coinage.

How he hoped to maintain a formally independent state is unclear. In any case he was unable to withstand a larger force and soon lost Jazira bin Umar. After an eight-month siege of his fortress at Urukh he surrendered in 1845, and he and his family were exiled to Crete.

Those who had helped Badr Khan were also suppressed. Yazidi tribesmen had some revenge for their earlier fate by assisting in the defeat of Khan Mahmud of Van,[16] who was tortured and killed. Nur Allah Beg of Hakkari was also captured but was spared death, to be exiled. Sharif Beg of Bitlis survived in rebellion until 1849, but was also exiled. A year later the Baban dynasty, which had limped on as ruling family in Sulaymaniya, was also dismissed from power. It was so enfeebled it accepted its lot without a struggle.

The Kurdish amirates were at an end, but it was not yet clear whether the Ottomans could substitute effectively for them. Just as the amirs had in the end been undone by undervaluing the importance of external recognition and support to their position, so also the Ottoman authorities were destined to underestimate the mediating role these princes had fulfilled with regard to the local population.

Sources

Secondary   W.F. Ainsworth, *Travels and Researches in Asia Minor, Mesopotamia, Chaldea and Armenia* (London, 1842); Bletch Chirguh, *La Question Kurde, ses Origines et ses Causes* (Cairo, 1930); A.B. Cunningham, *The Early Correspondence of Richard Wood, 1831–1841* (London, 1966); *Encyclopaedia of Islam*, 1st edition, 'Kurds'; J. Baillie Fraser, *Mesopotamia and Assyria* (London, 1842); Guest, *Survival Among the Kurds: A History of the Yezidis* (London and New York, 1993); Joseph, *The Nestorians and their Neighbours*; Austen Henry Layard, *Nineveh and its Remains* (London, 1850) and *Discoveries in the Ruins of Nineveh and Babylon; with Travels in Armenia, Kurdistan and the Desert* (London, 1853); Longrigg, *Four Centuries*; A.K.S. Lambton, *Qajar Persia* (London, 1987); F. Millingen, *Wild Life Among the Kurds* (London, 1870); Shaw and Shaw, *A History of the Ottoman Empire and Modern Turkey*.

Notes

1. In the winter of 1769 Russian forces pushed across the Danube, occupying Bucharest and destroying an Ottoman army at Kartal in 1770. The following year Russia destroyed the whole Ottoman fleet, leaving the entire eastern Mediterranean seaboard undefended. In 1774 it occupied Crimea, gaining access to the Black Sea. These humiliations were set out in the Treaty of Kutchuk Kainarji, 1774. Although Russia withdrew from the Danube provinces and both parties recognized the independence of the Khanate of Crimea, it was clear that these two regions now fell within Russia's orbit. Crimea was directly annexed in 1779.

2. The Chaldeans had walked out of the Nestorian Church as early as 1681 in order to enter into union with Rome. In Kurdistan a sharp and enduring conflict was unleashed between the old and new churches, with both playing hard for Ottoman approval. In 1716 the Orthodox (Melkite) church, in 1740 the Armenian Church, and in 1781 the Syrian Orthodox (Jacobite) Church were rent by similar schisms.

3. James Brant, 'Notes of a journey through part of Kurdistan in the summer of 1838', *Geographical Journal*, no. x, 1841, London, p. 356.

4. Ainsworth, *Travels and Researches*, p. 188.

5. His father, Mustafa, had only taken over Suran leadership in about 1810. He lived in retirement until his death in 1826.

6. Said's successor, Ismail, briefly returned to Amadiya after the defeat of Mir Muhammad, but was soon ousted by the governor of Mosul. He rebelled, was captured and exiled.

7. Compare variations, for example, Chaliand, *People without a Country*, p. 29; Jwaideh, *The Kurdish Nationalist Movement*, pp. 172–173, Longrigg, *Four Centuries*, p. 286; Zaki, *Khulasat*, pp. 232–233.

8. Ali Ridha Pasha had another motive. Rashid Muhammad and he disliked each other, and he welcomed the chance to forestall a victory for his rival.

9. These terms were complicated by the fact that for the past 20 years Mir Muhammad had waged war against Iranian-held territory, and had taken Koi Sanjaq from Iran only five years previously. Iran understandably wanted reparations.

10. These may have been deserters, but it is difficult to believe so large a body of men would be operating for the Qajars without Russian approval, Richard Wood to Lord Ponsonby, 19 September 1836, Cunningham, *The Early Correspondence*, p. 109.

11. Regarding his displacement of Saif al Din Shir and the subsequent betrayal of Badr Khan by Saif al Din's son Izz al Din, see Layard, *Discoveries*, p. 54 and Jwaideh, *The Kurdish Nationalist Movement*, p. 177.

12. These were Shamasha (deacon) Hinno, and Kasha (priest) Jinno of Ashita.

13. By 1835 there was an American missionary dispensary in Urumiya: by 1841 schools had been established in sixteen villages, more than doubling by 1845; one of the schools was for Muslim children, Lambton, *Qajar Persia*, pp. 204–6.

14. W.F. Ainsworth, *Travels and Researches*, vol. ii, p. 255.

15. Ainsworth, *Travels and Researches*, vol. ii, p. 242.

16. Khan Mahmud had made himself powerful in the region south of Van. His main stronghold Khush Ab, a dramatic mountain-top fortress, may still be seen.

CHAPTER 4

OTTOMAN KURDISTAN, 1850–1914

The suppression of the old amirates and other semi-independent satraps of Kurdistan led to less law and order in the countryside, not more. This may seem surprising, since if the Porte had the military power to suppress the amirs and chiefs it presumably could also suppress anyone else. However, while the Kurdish paramounts indubitably were responsible for major upheavals, conflicts and bloodshed in the region, they were also part of the regional balance of forces.

While eager to aggrandize themselves, they were also vital mediators between the tribes and tribal sections within their territory, and between these and the outside world. Without them, unrestrained inter-tribal conflicts arose all over Kurdistan, with both political and economic consequences.

While the Ottoman authorities were able to govern towns and their immediate environs, they were unable to exert control further afield except by reprisal. Such expeditions were an insufficient response to the challenge now posed. The absence of adequate restraint led to repeated fights between one tribe and another, to increased banditry and to a serious decline in the economic condition of the country. Hitherto, the peasantry had been protected from the worse excesses of pastoral tribes by the restraint of the paramount who expected to gain from peasant produce, and mediated between competing tribal claims on client villages.

The rapacity of the amirs and paramount chiefs had always been tempered by the knowledge that a peasant pushed too far would simply abandon the land. They valued Armenian peasants who were willing to colonize abandoned villages or entirely new sites. In their absence a free-for-all occurred, with tribes violating each other's pastures, and moving through agricultural areas in which they had no economic interest beyond exploiting them as much as they could before moving on. Kurdish tribes had always billeted themselves on peasant villages during the winter months. While this was extremely unpopular, particularly with Armenians, it was an accepted fact of life. In 1838 Ainsworth had already noted how many Armenians were migrating to the Russian-occupied parts of Armenia.

Now a new tendency arose of stripping villages on departure. Since this could now be done with impunity, it was not long before Kurdish chieftains and their men were also abducting Armenian girls and killing those who opposed them. The assistance given by Armenians to Russian invading forces could always be invoked as justification for such behaviour, and the Russians compounded this impression by busily rebuilding damaged or ruined Armenian churches and sending emissaries 'in the garb of travelling doctors'.[1] The tragic consequences of this process will be discussed later.

The Rise of the Shaykhs

Within Kurdish tribal society, however, the power vacuum led to a crisis in the settlement of disputes between one family or tribe and another, and even within each family or tribe. The old amirs and paramounts, because they were seldom blood relatives of the confederation, save for their own immediate family, had been able to act as mediators, with authority if not always impartiality. All that was now gone. In due course they were replaced in their role of mediators and unifying leaders by religious shaykhs.

For a number of centuries the shaykhs belonging to one of the Sufi or dervish orders, or *tariqas*, had been influential in Kurdish society, as they were in much of the region, particularly with the Turkoman and Kurdish tribes. These *tariqas* dated back to the rise of the Sufi brotherhoods in twelfth and thirteenth centuries to men like Shaykh Safi al Din, eponymous founder of the Safavids, and himself possibly a Kurd. His order had become the focus of the *qizilbash*. Another important one was the Naqshbandi order, which had emerged at the end of the fourteenth century and was particularly influential in Diyarbakir by the seventeenth century.

Such brotherhoods were viewed with some disquiet by the authorities, since they were independent of the formalized Muslim institutions of state, eccentric in their practices, if not beliefs, and thus prone to sedition. There was particular nervousness concerning the empire's eastern frontiers, where the *qizilbash* movement had represented a dangerous fusion of Sufism and Shi'ism. Many of the *qizilbash* belonged to or joined the Baktashi *tariqa*, which was prone to Shi'ite beliefs so extreme that they were barely recognizable as Muslim. The Baktashis had connections with the Naqshbandis – indeed the eponymous founder, Hajji Baktash, a thirteenth-century mystic from north-east Iran, was himself a member of the Naqshbandi order. In fact, despite this ambiguous connection, the Naqshbandiya was strictly orthodox, particularly in its emphasis on the *sharia* (Islamic law). Many of the *ulama* and other great men of learning in the seventeenth century, for example, belonged either to the Naqshbandiya or to another *tariqa*, the Khalwatiya, which had penetrated the Palace. In fact, the Naqshbandiya played (and still plays) a role of cardinal importance in the religious life of Turkey since the fifteenth century. Even so, however, like other orders, its activities were watched closely.[2]

However, the predominant *tariqa* in Kurdistan by the beginning of the nineteenth century was the Qadiriya, the brotherhood of the twelfth-century mystic and saint, Abd al Qadir Gailani. By 1800 there were only two Qadiri shaykhly dynasties in Kurdistan, the Barzinjis who hailed from the village of Barzinja near Sulaymaniya, and the Sayyids of Nihri (in Hakkari), who claimed descent from Abd al Qadir Gilani himself. Both families had *sayyid* status (descent from the Prophet), and both made sure that only family members, i.e. *sayyids*, should aspire to shaykhly status within the Qadiri order, thus maintaining hierarchical control over their followers.[3] A network based on these two families and their disciples, *murids*, was to be found through much of Kurdistan, but it was largely moribund.

A new and rival *tariqa*, however, was born out of the Mujaddidi ('revivalist') tradition within the Naqshbandi order which rapidly surpassed the Qadiris in Kurdistan. The instigator of this new Naqshbandi movement was Shaykh (or Mawlana) Khalid. Born into the Jaf tribe in Shahrizur in the late 1770s, Shaykh Khalid seems to have studied with both Qadiri *sayyid* dynasties,[4] before travelling to Damascus, making the *hajj* in 1805.

Shaykh Khalid went to India in 1810 to meet a particular Naqshbandi Mujaddidi shaykh. It was clearly a profound experience. He returned to Sulaymaniya the following year and swiftly acquired his own large following, thereby upsetting the Barzinji shaykhs and other Qadiris. His more sensational claims included knowledge of the future, an ability to preserve the living from harm and a facility to establish contact with the spirits of the dead. Such things eclipsed the powers claimed by the Barzinjis. At a more practical level, his influence on the Baban rulers must have directly threatened the Barzinjis. Such was the tension that Shaykh Khalid withdrew to Baghdad.

In 1820 Mahmud Baban invited Shaykh Khalid back to Sulaymaniya. It is possible that this was with deliberate Ottoman encouragement. Unlike some rival Sufi orders, the Naqshbandis enjoyed favour in Istanbul on account of their firm commitment to Sunni Islam.[5] It may have been hoped in Ottoman circles that bolstering Sunni feeling in Sulaymaniya would discourage the Babans from their inveterate flirtations with Shi'i Iran. Shaykh Khalid's sojourn in Sulaymaniya did not last long. He suddenly left, under a cloud it seems, and never returned. He spent the rest of his life (d. 1827) in Damascus, from where his influence spread throughout Syria and beyond.

Shaykh Khalid's new Naqshbandi *tariqa*, however, spread like wildfire in Kurdistan, rapidly outstripping the Qadiriya. The Qadiri system had been fine as long as there was no serious competition. Shaykh Khalid's followers, however, could become shaykhs and could train their own *khalifas* (deputies), who in turn could aspire to becoming shaykhs. For any ambitious cleric, the revivalist Naqshbandiya was clearly more attractive, since it offered the opportunity of establishing one's own network and sphere of influence. In fact many Qadiris converted to the new order including Shaykh Khalid's old teacher, Shaykh Abd Allah of Nihri.

We have early evidence, too, of the role the Naqshbandi shaykhs began to play as troubleshooters (and troublemakers) in the political sphere, and the high esteem in which they were held. In 1820 Shaykh Khalid himself acted as a referee between the leaders of the Babans with regard to Iranian intrigues, possibly with Ottoman encouragement. After Shaykh Khalid's departure for Damascus three shaykhly families became central players in the politics of Kurdistan, the Sayyids of Nihri, the Barzanis – both Naqshbandi, and the Qadiri Barzinjis who recovered their position in Sulaymaniya, inheriting the patrimony of the Babans.[6]

Martin van Bruinessen, the leading European expert on Kurdish society, has noted that shaykhly dynasties were most important in areas where tribes were most numerous and prone to feuds. Here they prospered on conflict resolution (and provocation) that made their own mediation skills indispensable. They were less influential in those areas either where there were still strong tribes, for example the Jaf, or where the area was basically non-tribal, for example the lands around Diyarbakir, and where consequently tribal conflicts requiring mediation either did not, or seldom, occurred.

These shaykhs not only encouraged tribal chiefs to resort to their mediation skills, but solicited the affections of rank-and-file tribal Kurds, particularly the low status non-tribal peasants who were subordinate to tribal chiefs. For example, the Barzani 'tribe' was, in the view of some, not strictly speaking a tribe at all, since apart from the shaykhly family itself, its adherents were mainly peasants who had defected from the Zibari and other neighbouring tribes. The ties were territorial and spiritual, not ones of kinship. The Barzani shaykhs conferred a protective structure and cohesion on this growing group of fugitives from tribal oppression.

The shaykhs wove themselves into the decaying power structure of the old chiefly families by marriage, thus authenticating their growing political authority. It was a formula which suited both shaykh and chief, since the latter's declining authority was in some measure protected by alliance to religious prestige.

Religious zeal was used as a political weapon. In 1843 we know that Shaykh Taha of Nihri, Shaykh Abd Allah's nephew and successor, played on local Muslim fears about the Christian threat and actively encouraged Badr Khan's attack on the Nestorians. The motivation was probably twofold: fear of European missionary encroachment and active dislike of Nestorian Christians who were both formidable fighters and in conflict with their Hakkari overlord.

Yet religious intolerance was not directed solely towards Christians. In 1848 Layard came across a shaykh 'notorious for his hatred of Yazidis ... one of those religious fanatics who are the curse of Kurdistan'.[7] Such behaviour was entirely consistent with Shaykh Khalid's exhortation to his disciples. For alongside strict adherence to the *sharia*, Shaykh Khalid had enjoined his followers to end their prayers with the supplication that God would 'annihilate the Jews, Christians, fireworshippers (*majus*) and the Persian Shi'ites'.[8]

Following the collapse of Buhtan in 1845, Shaykh Taha sought refuge with one of the last surviving independent tribal chiefs, Musa Beg of Shamdinan, whom he seems to have eclipsed in influence. Certainly by the time Shaykh Taha's son, Ubayd Allah, succeeded in the 1860s or 1870s, the Sayyids of Nihri ruled Shamdinan, exerting their influence as far as the erstwhile amirates of Buhtan, Bahdinan, Hakkari and even Ardalan.

Shaykh Ubayd Allah of Nihri

Shaykh Ubayd Allah remains for many the first great Kurdish nationalist, but the evidence is hardly conclusive. In 1880 he invaded Persia, claiming to be acting in the name of the Kurdish nation. He sent a message to William Abbott, the British Consul-General in Tabriz to explain his conduct:

> The Kurdish nation ... is a people apart. Their religion is different [from that of others], and their laws and customs are distinct ... the Chiefs and Rulers of Kurdistan, whether Turkish or Persian subjects, and the inhabitants of Kurdistan, one and all are united and agreed that matters cannot be carried on in this way with the two Governments [Ottoman and Qajar], and that necessarily something must be done, so that European Governments having understood the matter, shall inquire into our state. We also are a nation apart. We want our affairs to be in our own hands.[9]

British diplomats in Iran and Turkey took his words more or less at face value,[10] as the Qajars may also have done. Yet apart from such utterances, the revolt bore little evidence that it was anything other than the kind of tribal disturbance, but on a larger scale, that already bedevilled the region.

Yet it is important. For apart from the mayhem it caused in the area, it raises for the first time ambiguities implicit in the word 'nationalism' which surrounded subsequent risings.

The revolt was started in September 1880 by Shaykh Ubayd Allah's second son, Abd al Qadir, who was already inside Iran. Abd al Qadir was his father's representative in those border villages which acknowledged the Nihri Sayyids and, as a result of this status, also designated by governor of Urumiya as their intermediary responsible for the tranquillity of the local tribes. His act of rebellion seems to have been triggered by harsh treatment meted out to a number of tribal chiefs by the local authorities who had acted without consulting him.[11] This was a serious omission, for it undermined Abd al Qadir's role as intermediary on which his standing with the tribes was based. From his perspective he had little choice but to lead these disgruntled chiefs[12] in rebellion. This he proceeded to do by seizing Sawj Bulaq (Mahabad). He then called for the submission of tribes as far south as Bana and Saqqiz. Most obeyed although some, for example the Mamash, with very marked reluctance. He then advanced eastwards with up to 20,000 men, along the southern side of Lake Urumiya, and out of Kurdish territory. Before leaving Sawj Bulaq, he heard the senior Sunni cleric of the town declare *jihad* upon the Shi'is. When the inhabitants of the Shi'i town of Miandoab killed his envoys and refused to surrender, his forces put them to the sword slaughtering 2,000 men, women and children, before advancing towards Maragha.

In the meantime two other columns crossed into Iran from Hakkari, one under Shaykh Ubayd Allah's elder son, Muhammad Sadiq, on the west side of Lake Urumiya to protect Abd al Qadir's retreat, and another under the Shaykh's *khalifa*, Said, who had raised the Kurds of Hakkari and advanced further south. Among those cajoled into supporting the attack was the tribal Nestorian community of Tiyari.[13] Shaykh Ubayd Allah himself crossed the frontier in mid-October.

Shaykh Ubayd Allah seems to have been a master of disinformation. The Turkish authorities understood he had dissociated himself from his sons' uprising; yet he also called on Turkomans to join the fight against Iran and reportedly declared that once Iran was dealt with he would turn on Turkey. His *khalifa*, on the other hand, had been busy claiming that Turkey supported a Kurdish attack on Iran.

Ubayd Allah claimed he wanted an independent principality and undertook to repress brigandage on the part of the various tribes. All he wanted from the European powers, particularly Britain, was their moral support. In view of the advance eastwards beyond Kurdistan, particularly the carnage at Miandoab and the destruction of 'upwards of 2,000 villages', during which 10,000 had been rendered homeless, it was hardly a persuasive argument.

Before crossing the border, Ubayd Allah also unsuccessfully tried to draw in the Shah's half-Kurdish half-brother, Abbas Mirza, who had spent much of his life in exile in Turkey, a move that suggested a challenge to the Qajar throne itself. Meanwhile he told Abbott[14] that the Kurds could no longer bear the exactions of the Iranian government nor its inability to prevent the depredations of the two major Kurdish tribes of the region, the Shikak and Harki.

In other words, he claimed his revolt was against Iranian *incompetence* and local banditry. In both tribal cases Ubayd Allah was almost certainly demonstrating his intention to defend villages loyal to the Sayyids of Nihri from the depredations of formidable challengers. He had been quite happy to defend Harki banditry *elsewhere* against Ottoman interference the previous year. As for the Shikak, they had crossed into Turkey and had had a fruitful time marauding, in response to his call to *jihad* in 1877. But now Ubayd Allah must have been increasingly concerned by the way the rapidly expanding Shikak were beginning to encroach on his own area of patronage in Hakkari-Baradust, and that on either side of the border the government authorities were patently powerless. While his son may have risen in response to Iranian brutality to Nihri client chiefs and then run amok among the Shi'is, Ubayd Allah himself was probably as concerned by the Shikak threat. In both cases the Sayyids of Nihri had to demonstrate their worth as patrons. Only up to a point did this harmonize with 'nationalist' claims.

By the end of October Shaykh Abd al Qadir's force had shrunk from the 20,000 it had been two weeks earlier to 1,500 men, most of the tribesmen having gone home laden with booty. Shaykh Ubayd Allah and his son Muhammad Sadiq had invested Urumiya with probably no more than 6,000 men. Knowing that a relief column was on its way, Urumiya put up a stiff resistance and broke the spirit of the attackers. By now 12,000 Iranian troops were advancing, 5,000 of them down the west side of Lake Urumiya, and the remainder from the south-eastern edge of the lake. These perpetrated ruthless revenge on the non-Shi'a population, slaughtering with scant discrimination between the innocent and guilty. More Nestorians, for example, perished at the hands of the army than at those of the insurgents.

Shaykh Ubayd Allah's forces fled home, many being captured (and often killed) by government forces on either side of the frontier. Under European diplomatic pressure, the Shaykh was exiled, first to Istanbul, but after his escape in 1882, to the Hijaz where he died in 1883.

The devastation in the fertile Urumiya plain, renowned as the 'Garden of Persia', was felt for years to come and relief taxes were imposed elsewhere to restore the region. Indeed, it so surpassed the normal level of tribal disorder that an American missionary wrote, 'Until the World War, all events in Urumia dated from the "coming of the Sheikh".'[15]

If these facts hardly bear out the claim of a national revolt, what is to be made of Shaykh Ubayd Allah's utterances and actions? We get some clues from the despatches of the British consul-generals either side of the border. Visiting Urumiya from his post at Tabriz, William Abbott initially thought, 'His project is to place himself at the head of a Kurdish principality, and to annex the whole of Kurdistan, both in Turkey and Persia'.[16] Shaykh Ubayd Allah may have been after a wider domain than the mirs, as his spiritual authority suggested; but it is unlikely the Qadiri-inclined tribes would have welcomed him, still less the Shikak of whom he complained, let alone those tribes outside his area of influence.

Henry Trotter, consul-general at Erzerum, made a fine but crucial distinction in the question of loyalty to the Ottoman government which the mirs half a century earlier would readily have understood. 'I believe,' he reported to his ambassador, 'the Sheikh to be more or less personally loyal to the Sultan; and he would be ready to submit to his authority and pay him tribute as long as he could get rid of the Ottoman officials, and be looked *de lege* as well as *de facto* the ruling chief of Kurdistan.'[17] This was consonant with what Trotter had himself been told by his vice-consul in Van a year earlier: that the shaykh was quite willing to pay tribute to the sultan in lieu of taxes.[18] Shaykh Ubayd Allah had confirmed this orally when he had met Abbott outside Urumiya. Abbott had asked him whether it was

his object to form Kurdistan into a separate Principality, independent of the Porte or merely to weld together its rude components, reduce order out of chaos and become the responsible head of the Kurdish nation, answerable to the Sultan for their good conduct and the collection of taxes? To this the Sheikh replied that nobody ever doubted his loyalty to the Sultan, but that he had a very poor opinion of the Pashas [i.e. the provincial administration].[19]

It would seem that while using the vocabulary of contemporary European nationalism, he was more probably after the resurrection of an autonomous principality as these had existed before the extension of administration under the Ottoman tanzimat.

This alone does not explain why the government in Istanbul was apparently so relaxed about Shaykh Ubayd Allah or so reluctant to exile him afterwards.[20] It must be remembered that Shaykh Ubayd Allah inherited his uncle's mantle in a period of growing disorder and economic deprivation in eastern Anatolia. The Ottoman inability to achieve law and order beyond the immediate environs of each town, the increased and at times unreasonable tax burden, and the attempts to introduce conscription all undermined the wellbeing of a region already prone to lawlessness. Without the restraint of respected local leaders, each tribe extorted what it could from travellers and settled villagers. As innumerable foreign travellers through the region testify, brigandage had brought the economy at times almost to a standstill. Trade on the roads was liable to pillage. One tribe would fight with another, with the reverberations of their antagonism felt by villages in the surrounding countryside. Some local Ottoman officials found it lucrative to work hand-in-glove with bandit chiefs. More scrupulous officials knew that in a test of will with powerful local chiefs or shaykhs they would not necessarily enjoy firm backing from Istanbul. Disorder and deprivation merely increased the rapacity of the tribes when moving through peasant villages, be they Kurdish, Armenian or mixed. In other words the Shikak and Harki, while unbridled, were as much the Sultan's enemies as Ubayd Allah's.

Then there was the question of the growing hostility to the Christian communities. Armenians and Assyrians were both targets, Armenians because of their growing national feeling and consequent identification with the Russian threat, and the Nestorians because they were also suspect, for each year 5,000 or so in Urumiya (let alone Hakkari) visited Russia as migrant workers.

In this disordered scene, Shaykh Ubayd Allah had already shown himself willing to help the Sultan against the Christian threat. He had been appointed commander of Kurdish tribal forces in the Russo-Turkish war of 1877–78, giving him wider official powers than those enjoyed by any Kurd since the days of the amirs half a century earlier. He had proclaimed that war a *jihad*, one which the tribal chiefs took as a green light for attacking Armenian villagers.[21]

Shaykh Ubayd Allah's religious views of Christians may have been ambiguous but his political ones were less so. The Armenian community posed a serious threat to Kurdish interests. The war of 1877–78 had led to the Treaty of Berlin, whereby the European Powers had specifically called (Article 61) for protected status for the Armenian community a stepping stone, as Muslims saw it, towards the emergence of an independent Armenian state. In fact Britain was anxious for

Ottoman reform and proper protection of the Armenians in order to remove the justification Russia wanted (unrestrained Muslim persecution of the Armenians) to intervene.

Yet European pressure had its inevitable effect in the area. 'What is this I hear,' Shaykh Ubayd Allah expostulated to one Turkish official, 'that the Armenians are going to have an independent state in Van, and that the Nestorians are going to hoist the British flag and declare themselves British subjects?'[22] Here, surely, lies the clue to his own call to Britain to recognize the Kurds as 'a nation apart'. If, as feared, an Armenian or Nestorian protected entity was in prospect, it would be established partly in his area of influence. It was a clear case of 'them or us'. Shaykh Ubayd Allah therefore, it seems, made the case for Kurds in the secular nationalist vocabulary current in European chancelleries.

It may seem strange that the Sultan, having once suppressed the Kurdish amirates during the years of Ottoman tanzimat should have then vested Shaykh Ubayd Allah with so much power. Why not stem the Armenian and Russian threat by the reforms Britain wanted? The tanzimat period, 1826–76, had been one in which the Porte increasingly sought to re-organize the empire on European lines. But this could only be achieved at the price of growing discontent among the majority of Muslims in Anatolia who feared the implications of European-inspired reform.

In 1876 a new sultan, Abd al Hamid II, assumed office. He was not a reformer as this had come to be understood – with all its negative resonances (to Muslims) of allowing the European powers a greater influence in politics and trade, and the accordance of equal rights to non-Muslim Ottoman citizens. He was determined to defend his Islamic empire, not by a process of liberalization which had reached a short-lived climax in the Constitution of 1876, but by centralization in the person of the sultan himself and by an appeal to Muslim values and solidarity. Ottoman officials in the provinces, on the other hand, were part of the tanzimat, the Trojan horse of European reform, as well as the bane of community leaders like Shaykh Ubayd Allah.

Sultan Abd al Hamid felt safer with Muslim traditionalists. Shaykh Ubayd Allah, with his immense spiritual stature in eastern Anatolia, was too valuable a pillar in Islam's defence to ignore, in spite of his mercurial behaviour; once formally vested with so much temporal power he could not possibly relinquish it.

Istanbul had already had a little local difficulty with Shaykh Ubayd Allah in 1879. In September that year some of his protégé Harki tribesmen had been punished by the local district prefect, or qaim-maqam (of Gawar), for banditry. As with Abd al Qadir the following year, Ubayd Allah could not allow his own status to be undermined by local government; so he sent his sons to attack the local troops. But when his sons were worsted, Shaykh Ubayd Allah protested his innocence blaming all on his sons. Both sons now moved over the border to adherent villages just inside Iran, presumably till things quietened down. Istanbul discounted Shaykh Ubayd Allah's involvement, increased his state stipend and removed the offending *qaim-maqam* from his post. The sultan, who was rapidly taking control over many affairs in the empire, evidently felt happier working through the volatile shaykh than he did through his own reformist officials.

Surrounding this local disturbance there were also rumours concerning a 'Kurdish League', purportedly a nationalist group formed by Shaykh Ubayd Allah himself. The latter certainly wanted to expand his following, but its nationalist overtones should be treated with caution. We have little more than the accusations of the Armenian patriarchate to go on. The League, if it really existed, apparently never made any statement nor took any action in that name. But intriguingly the patriarchate claimed that the Porte itself was fostering the League in order to stifle the Armenian question. It is a perfectly credible explanation, a scheme cooked up in Istanbul which offered Shaykh Ubayd Allah undisclosed official sponsorship to form a movement that could act as a counterbalance to the Armenian threat.

A truly independent Kurdistan in such a troubled region, what the Shaykh seemed to be calling for in 1880, had little chance of survival. The Ottoman government must have realized this but the argument for Kurdistan, like the ephemeral League, was a useful counterweight to Armenian nationalist claims, especially if Shaykh Ubayd Allah managed to co-opt, as he tried to do, Armenians and Nestorians into his revolt. Had they co-operated it would have conveniently undermined the Armenian nationalist case for European-protected status. In the unlikely event of a Kurdish principality actually coming into existence, it was bound to remain dependent on the sultan.

There was also the question of improving the Ottoman position on its eastern bulwark. There was no doubt this would be qualitatively improved by incorporating Kurdish tribal territory overlooking the plains of West Azarbaijan. Shaykh Ubayd Allah had already demonstrated his influence over Iranian Kurdish tribes when some of the latter had rallied to his call for *jihad* against the infidel in 1877. The Porte, anxious about its position in the east, may have seen this foray in a strategic light. Twenty-five years later it was to take advantage again of Iranian weakness to encroach in the very same area.

The Ottoman government would not have wished to explain any of this publicly, since it had to deny any encouragement to Shaykh Ubayd Allah's adventurism. While the British Ambassador remained puzzled, it is now possible to guess what was going on:

> I again failed to ascertain to what extent the Porte believes in the intention of Sheikh Obeidullah to found an independent Kurdistan. My general impression was that Assim Pasha [the Ottoman foreign minister] himself did not believe in the serious existence of any such ambitious designs.[23]

Assim Pasha knew that Shaykh Ubayd Allah was a devout Naqshbandi. Mawlana Khalid had taught his followers to 'pray for the survival of the exalted Ottoman State upon which depends Islam, and for victory over the enemies of religion, the cursed Christians and the despicable Persians.'[24] Less apparent perhaps to European than to Ottoman observers, Shaykh Ubayd Allah to the very end had been true to his spiritual mentor.

The Hamidiya Cavalry and the Armenians

In 1891 Sultan Abd al Hamid authorized the establishment of an irregular mounted force in eastern Anatolia, designating it after himself, the Hamidiya Cavalry. The intention was to imitate the Russian Cossack regiments which had been used so effectively as scouts and skirmishers in the Caucasus.

Given the social context of the region, the Hamidiya was raised from selected Sunni Kurdish tribes,[25] preferably of proven loyalty, to form mounted regiments of approximately 600 men. In many cases these regiments were drawn solely from one tribe, and its commanding officer was the tribal chief. In cases where tribes were too small, each might provide a squadron for a composite regiment. In any case tribal solidarity was always maintained by keeping fellow tribesmen in one unit.

There were enormous advantages for both a chief invited to levy a regiment, and for his recruits. Chiefs and their officers were to be sent to a special military school in Istanbul. They were outfitted in dashing Cossack-styled uniforms to lend weight to their new status. Hamidiya tribes were exempted from one of the most unpopular measures of Ottoman centralization, the liability for conscription which was being introduced into the region for the very first time. Hamidiya chiefs were invited to send their sons to one of the tribal schools established in both Istanbul and Kurdistan, in order to absorb them into the Ottoman establishment. In some of the principal 'Hamidiya' villages the authorities also offered to establish schools for the population. Since Kurdistan was the most neglected, backward and impoverished corner of the empire, the offer held serious attraction.

The ostensible purpose of the Hamidiya Cavalry was to provide a bulwark against the Russian threat. It was important to stiffen the resolve of Kurds as part of the empire, especially as some tribes inside Ottoman territory had been willing to support czar versus sultan in previous wars. Besides, an increasing number of tribes had fallen inside Russia's orbit in the Caucasus. The formal deployment of the Hamidiya regiments was primarily along an axis from Erzerum to Van.

Yet the fact that the Hamidiya tribes were an irregular force only to be marshalled in units greater than regimental strength on the instructions of the *mushir*, or military commander, meant that in practice these regiments remained dispersed in their usual habitat except when called upon for duty. Furthermore it was generally suspected that most Hamidiya tribesmen would desert rather than move too far from their encampments and livestock.

It was not long before the creation of the Hamidiya led to trouble. For one thing, squabbles and fights broke out between various chiefs for senior rank within one tribe,[26] and for another, local commanders did not differentiate between enemies of their tribe *qua* tribe, and enemies of the Hamidiya Cavalry. Scores soon started to be settled between Hamidiya tribes, armed by the state, and local adversaries. The powerful Sunni Jibran tribe, which had fielded four Hamidiya regiments, soon started attacking the Alevi Khurmaks, confiscating their lands. As reviled Alevis, or Qizilbash, it was not surprising that the state authorities did nothing to obtain redress for them or for other Alevi tribes suffering similarly. But even Sunni tribes not similarly favoured with Hamidiya status were liable to land theft by force of arms. H.F.B. Lynch who was travelling in the region in 1894 wrote of recent pillaging bands around Erzerum:

> It is well known that these bands were led by officers in the Hamidiyeh regiments – *tenekelis*, or tin-plate men, as they are called by the populace, from the brass badges they wear in their caps. The frightened officials, obliged to report such occurrences, take refuge behind the amusing euphemism of such a phrase as "brigands, disguised as soldiers."[27]

When the government could not afford to pay Hamidiya officers, it offered them tax-collecting rights on local Armenian villages, causing further hardship for the latter. In several cases a Kurdish chief was not only commander of a Hamidiya regiment but also the local civil authority.

Such circumstances apart, those who sought recourse to government still found that the civil administration had no power to restrain the Hamidiya, who were answerable solely to the *mushir* of the Fourth Army in Erzerum. The *mushir*, Zakki Pasha, who happened to be the sultan's brother-in-law, was subject not to the wali but direct to Istanbul. He was clearly using the Hamidiya as the instrument of a policy that had little in common with the brief of the civil administration of the region. The civil administration had nothing but contempt for the Hamidiya, a view echoed by British military consuls:

> The Hamidiye troops, in fact, are under no control whatever, beyond that of their own native Chief, which does not appear to be exercised much in the interests of law and order. It is a curious sight to see Kurds walking about the streets of the town [Bashkale] in their native costume.... They have a habit of taking what they require out of the shops without payment.[28]

The lawless activities of the Hamidiya set an example which non-Hamidiya tribal Kurds were soon to imitate. In fact there were any number of young swells anxious to look the part. Local blacksmiths did a roaring trade with such dandies, forging Hamidiya badges for wear with lambskin busbies. As with the Hamidiya, the civil authorities found themselves powerless to curb them, while the army commanders ignored or indulged tribal excesses.

Although most affrays initially were inter-tribal ones, it was the client peasantry, Muslim and Christian, which suffered most. Soon it became clear both that the Armenians were the primary targets, and that the Hamidiya was egged on or even deliberately directed by the Ottoman military authorities.

The growth of the Armenian problem has already been discussed. By the early 1890s it had deteriorated considerably. Largely because after their experiences in the 1877–78 war some Armenians had finally begun to react to the provocations, depredations and persecution suffered at the hands of the Ottoman authorities, the Kurdish tribes and the Muslim citizens of mixed towns and cities. In 1882 'Protectors of the Fatherland', almost certainly a revolutionary group, was uncovered in Erzerum. In 1885 the Armenakan Party began to operate from Van, supported by groups in Russian Transcaucasia and Iran. After its formation in 1887 the internationalist Hunchak Party established armed cells in eastern Anatolia and Russian Transcaucasia. In 1889 an armed Armenakan group was caught crossing the frontier from Persia. Other militant groups appeared, giving rise to paranoia both in Istanbul and in the eastern provinces. In 1893 seditious placards appeared on the walls of several Anatolian towns. Agitators tried to arouse dissident Alevi tribes in Dersim and peasant Kurds around Sasun, reputedly descended from convert Armenians.

However, the event that paved the way for more widespread attacks on Armenians took place in Sasun district, south of Mush where a Hunchak group had intermittently ambushed and killed Kurds since 1892. In summer 1894 an affray between Armenian villagers and the local *qaim-maqam* concerning tax arrears gave the pretext for wholesale massacre in which local Hamidiya tribesmen played a prominent part. Over 1,000 villagers probably perished. By spring 1895 the representatives of Britain, France and Russia wanted reforms for the Armenian provinces: an amnesty for Armenian prisoners; 'approved' governors; reparations for victims of the outrages at Sasun and elsewhere; Kurdish nomadic movements to be allowed only under surveillance and for them generally to be encouraged to settle; and the Hamidiya to be disarmed. Abd al Hamid agreed to these demands but deliberately neglected to implement them. Continued level of insecurity had reduced agriculture to famine levels by 1897–98.[29]

For a year there was relative quiet, but on 30 September 1895 a violent incident took place between Armenian demonstrators and police in Istanbul, which marked the beginning of a more widespread attack on Armenians in the city, in which hundreds perished, some at the hands of the many Kurdish porters there. A week later over 1,100 Armenians were massacred in and around Trabzon. By the end of October there had been massacres in Erzinjan, Bitlis, Erzerum and elsewhere, in each of which hundreds were killed. In the first ten days of November about 1,000 Armenians perished in Diyarbakir, almost 3,000 each in Arabkir and Malatya. More massacres followed, in Kharput, Sivas, Kayseri and Urfa. The perpetrators were a mixture of Muslim citizenry, both Turks and Kurds, and Ottoman soldiers, including the Hamidiya.

Some Armenian villages stood up to this harassment and won the begrudging respect of the tribes. Some became Muslim, others invited Kurdish chiefs to settle in their villages at the cost of offering inducements, for 'policemen have to be paid'.[30] By 1897 even the urban Turkish population had begun to protest about the intolerably disruptive effect of the Hamidiya Kurds.

Why did Sultan Abd al Hamid allow such mayhem in his eastern provinces? Was the Hamidiya deliberately raised in order to destroy the Armenian population? Armenians were not alone in seeing sinister, indeed genocidal designs in the Hamidiya. They had been raised ostensibly in order to mobilize the Kurdish tribes as auxiliaries in the event of another war with Russia.

It was well known that some Kurds – both Sunni and Alevi tribes – had responded to intermittent Russian overtures since the war of 1827–29. The Russians had skilfully exploited tribal unhappiness with both the centralization that had led to suppression of the old amirates, and the reforms which seemed to favour the Christian peasantry. Similarly the Russians fomented the tribes, particularly the Alevi Kurds of Dersim, during the Crimean War in 1854, and 1877–78. Fear of Kurdish disaffection remained real. In fact, not long after the establishment of the Hamidiya, the Russians invited a disaffected Badr Khan to Tiflis to discuss the formation of a pro-Russian counterweight.

Enrolment of tribesmen, exemptions from taxation, the education of tribal officers, and particularly chiefs' sons, in Istanbul were all part of an attempt to draw the Kurds more closely into the fabric of the empire. In principle it was a good idea. The more the Kurdish tribes were integrated into the Ottoman regime, the more secure would be the eastern border and, hopefully, the tamer the Kurds. In practice integration never really happened. The tribes remained wild while some of the chiefs took town houses.

It was also a policy of weakness. Sultan Abd al Hamid could not afford to alienate the Kurds, neither militarily nor indeed with regard to tax collection. For the tribes, rapacious as they were, could facilitate or frustrate the collection of taxes in the countryside. So he permitted their depredations, and as Army Commander in Erzerum his brother-in-law, Zakki Pasha, indulged and protected them from local civil administrators. He could have crushed them, but only by virtual military occupation of the region, creating tension with Russia and alienating the Kurdish tribes.

It was also as much out of weakness as deliberate policy that Abd al Hamid allowed the Hamidiya to inflict such suffering on the Armenians. By 1895 neither the average Hamidiya tribesman nor Turkish soldier made any distinction between Armenian peasants and revolutionaries. The tanzimat had risked alienating the tribes already, better now to allow them free rein. So Abd al Hamid swallowed the European reforms thrust upon him in Istanbul but made sure, by putting the Hamidiya under Zakki Pasha rather than the civil authorities, that they could never be properly implemented. Law and order took second place to loyalty on this vulnerable border.

Nevertheless, the Hamidiya Cavalry was clearly a failure. On the whole, there was little sign of integration into a wider Ottoman context. On the contrary, through the licence allowed to the Hamidiya regiments, tribalism enjoyed a strong resurgence. Furthermore, as the local British consul reported, 'Zeki [Pasha] is a king among them; they recognize no authority but his. The opinion is that he means to make himself a Prince of an independent Kurdistan.'[31] It is unlikely Sultan Abd al Hamid distrusted Zakki Pasha for he was only removed from his post after his own overthrow in 1908.

Yet the revival of tribal power was a different matter. However much Abd al Hamid was opposed to reform, he could hardly have had in mind a reversion to the tribal principalities his forebear Mahmud II had abolished. By 1900, with fears of Russian attack abating and popular irritation with the Hamidiya mounting, Zakki Pasha began to curb their excesses and punish Hamidiya chiefs who only a year or two earlier could have counted on protection. Yet, even so, they remained a menace. As the empire slid towards revolution, it was not seditious Turks but the Hamidiya chiefs who still gave provincial governors the real cause for concern. Even on the battlefield the Hamidiya proved a disappointment, and several regiments were disbanded.

After the overthrow of Abd al Hamid's regime by the Committee of Union and Progress in 1908, a theme discussed more fully in the next chapter, the Hamidiya regiments were renamed as 'Tribal Regiments' (*ashirat alaylari*) but remained essentially the same. The triumph of the Young Turks, the threat which they posed to supporters of the ancien régime, and their reversion to authoritarian and explicitly Turkish rule after a brief spate of liberalism led to disorder in many parts of the empire: within Kurdistan itself, among the Bulgars of Macedonia, the Catholic tribes of northern Albania, in Yemen where a new Mahdi proclaimed himself, and among the formidable Druzes of the Syrian Hawran.

Tribal regiments were sent to some of these trouble spots alongside regular troops. Tribal contingents were despatched to Yemen in 1908 and to Albania in 1911 where they performed badly, sustaining heavy losses, and acquiring a reputation for savagery while restoring order. Indeed, it could be said that on the eve of the First World War, the Kurds were generally noted mainly for their disorderliness, banditry and harassment of the Armenians.

Thus the nineteenth century ended with a firmer Ottoman grip on the towns of the region, but a more volatile situation with simmering inter-communal conflict, lawless tribes and the now familiar pattern of periodic Russian land seizures – a mixture finally detonated in autumn 1914.

Sources

Great Britain, unpublished: Public Record Office: series FO 248/382 and 391; series FO 371 nos 346, 540, 953; WO 106/5964.

Great Britain, published: Parliamentary Papers, Turkey nos 16 (1877), 28 (1877), 54 (1878); 1 (1878), 10 (1879), 4 (1880), 5 (1881), 2 (1896), 3 (1896), 6 (1896), 3 (1897), 1 (1898); Captain F.R. Maunsell, RA, *Military Report on Eastern Turkey in Asia* (London, 1893).

Secondary sources: Butrus Abu Manneh, 'The Naqshbandiyya–Mujaddidiya in the Ottoman lands in the early 19th century', *Die Welt des Islams*, vol. xxii, 1982 (1984); Ainsworth, *Travels and Researches*; Hamid Algar, 'The Naqshbandi Order', *Studia Islamica*, vol. 44, 1976; W.E.D. Allen and P. Muratoff, *Caucasian Battlefields* (Cambridge, 1953); Julian Baldick, *Mystical Islam* (London, 1989); Brant, Notes, *The Geographic Journal*, vol. x, 1841; Martin van Bruinessen, *Agha, Shaikh and State*; Captain Fred Burnaby, *On Horseback Through Asia Minor* (London, 1887); Stephen Duguid, 'The politics of unity: Hamidian policy in eastern Anatolia', *Middle Eastern Studies*, no. 9, May 1973; *Encyclopaedia of Islam*, 1st edition, 'Kurds'; James Baillie Fraser, *Travels in Koordistan, Mesopotamia* (London, 1840); Ghilan, 'Les Kurdes persans et l'invasion ottomane', *Revue du Monde Musulman*, no. 5, May 1908; Geary Gratton, *Through Asiatic Turkey* (London, 1878); Albert Hourani, 'Shaikh Khalid and the Naqshbandi Order' in S.M. Stern, A.H. Hourani and H.V.B. Brown (eds), *Islamic Philosophy and the Classical Tradition* (Oxford, 1972); Richard Hovanissian, *Armenia on the Road to Independence* (Berkley and Los Angeles, 1967); Joseph, *The Nestorians and their Neighbours*; Dirk Kinnane, *The Kurds and Kurdistan* (London, 1964); Layard, *Discoveries*; H.F.B. Lynch, *Armenia: Travels and Studies* (2 vols, London, 1901); Serif Mardin, *Religion and Social Change in Modern Turkey* (New York, 1989); William Miller, *The Ottoman Empire, 1801–1913* (Cambridge, 1913); Moosa, *Extremist Shiites* (Syracuse, 1988); Basil Nikitine, 'Les Kurdes racontés par eux-mêmes', *L'Asie Française*, no. 231, Paris, May 1925, Annexe I; Olson, *The Emergence of Kurdish Nationalism and the Sheikh Said Rebellion, 1880–1925* (Austin, 1989); Earl Percy, *Highlands of Asiatic Turkey* (London, 1901); Rich, *Narrative of a Residence*; Mary Shedd, *The Measure of Man* (New York, 1922); Lt-Col J. Shiel, 'Notes on a Journey from Tabriz through Kurdistan, via Van, Bitlis, Se'ert and Erbil, to Suleimaniyah in July and August, 1836', *The Geographical Journal*, vol. viii, 1938; E.B. Soane, *To Mesopotamia and Kurdistan in Disguise* (London, 1912); Mark Sykes, 'The Kurdish tribes of the Ottoman Empire', *Journal of the Anthropological Institute*, no. 38, London, 1908, and *The Caliph's Last Heritage* (London, 1915); H.F. Tozer, *Turkish Armenia and Eastern Asia Minor* (London, 1881); C.J. Walker, *Armenia, Survival of a Nation* (London, 1980).

Unpublished research: Hakim Halkawt, 'Confrèrie des Naqshbandis au Kurdistan au XIXᵉ siècle' (doctoral diss., Sorbonne, 1983).

Notes

1. These may have been genuine doctors, but to Ainsworth, possibly as paranoid about Russian intentions as the Kurds, they were clearly 'emissaries', Ainsworth, *Travels and Researches*, vol. ii, p. 379.

2. It has already been noted how Sharaf al Din Bitlisi probably owed his influence partly to the saintly prestige of his father. Such was the potential danger of religious leaders that Sultan Murad IV had executed one charismatic Naqshbandi shaykh in the Kurdish region, Shaykh Mahmud of Urumiya, fearing the emergence of a mass and dissident movement, van Bruinessen & Boeschoten, *Diyarbakir*, p. 52.

3. Virtually the only exception to this rule was the Talabani shaykhly dynasty which made no sayyid claim.

4. One should be cautious regarding his sojourn with the Barzinjis since these and the Jafs were antagonistic. However, Shaykh Khalid was apparently authorized for initiation into the Qadiri order but never took up the invitation.

5. In fact in 1826 when the Baktashi order was suppressed its *takiyas*, or oratories, were handed to the Naqshbandiya.

6. Others, no less revered albeit with smaller constituencies, were the Qadiri shaykhs of Brifkan and the Naqshbandi shaykhs of Bamirni.

7. Layard, *Discoveries*, vol. i, p. 38.

8. Abu Manneh, 'The Naqshbandiyya-Mujaddidiyya', p. 15.

9. *Parliamentary Papers* (hereafter *PP*), Turkey No. 5 (1881) Correspondence Respecting the Kurdish invasion of Persia, Sheikh Obeidallah to Dr Cochran, 5 October 1880, Inclosure in Abbott to Thomson, Urumiya, 7 October 1880.

10. 'There seems to be no doubt ... that his design is to detach the entire Kurdish population from their allegiance to Turkey and Persia, and to establish under his own authority a separate autonomous Principality', *PP*, Turkey No. 5 (1881) Thomson to Granville, Tehran, 31 October 1880; see also Inclosure in No. 22, Trotter to Goschen, Therapia, 20 October 1880.

11. This included in one case inflicting 1,000 stripes on a chief and the execution of 50 tribesmen.

12. These included the Mukri, the Mangur, the Zaza and the Turkoman Shi'i Karapapakh.

13. The Nestorians deserted when they found out the true nature of the expedition.

14. Abbott met Ubayd Allah during the siege of Urumiya, when he had asked the shaykh for an escort out of rebel territory. This had been reported at the time, but it was only a year later that Abbott revealed what had been said; FO 248/382 Abbot to Granville, 1 October 1881.

15. Mary Shedd, *The Measure of Man* (New York, 1922), p. 45, quoted in Jwaideh, *The Kurdish Nationalist Movement*, p. 267.

16. *PP*, Turkey No. 5 (1881) Abbott to Thomson, Urumiya, 7 October 1880, Inclosure 1 in No 61.

17. *PP*, Turkey No. 5 (1881) Trotter to Goschen, Therapia, 20 October 1880, Inclosure in Goschen to Granville, Therapia, 24 October 1880.

18. His wish 'is to form an independent Principality of the country inhabited by the Kurds, undertaking to pay as tribute the amount now levied in taxes by the Turkish government', *PP*, Turkey No. 4, (1880) Clayton to Trotter, Van, 10 September 1879.

19. FO 248/382 Abbott to Granville, Tabriz, 1 October 1881.

20. By the beginning of 1881 Istanbul had still done nothing to discipline Ubayd Allah. Tehran was angry, since Shaykh Ubayd Allah was threatening a second campaign. He was only arrested and sent to Istanbul in June 1881. He escaped back to Nihri in September 1882.

21. In 1878 Ubayd Allah's influence saved many Christians from massacre in Bayazid and he enjoyed the confidence of the American missionaries in Urumiya. A decade earlier, however, he was known as a persistent instigator of attacks on Armenians and Nestorians.

22. *PP*, Turkey No. 5 (1881) Clayton to Trotter, Bashqala, 11 July 1880, Inclosure in No. 7.

23. *PP*, Turkey No. 5 (1881) Goschen to Granville, Constantinople, 29 November 1880.

24. Abu Manneh, 'The Naqshbandiyya-Mujaddidiyya', p. 15.

25. One or two Turkoman regiments were also raised.

26. For example, within the Haydaranli and Jalali, see Hampson to Fane, Erzerum, 27 February 1892, in *PP*, Turkey No. 3 (1896).

27. Lynch, *Armenia*, vol. ii, p. 219.

28. *PP*, Turkey No. 6 (1896) Hallward to Graves, Van, 10 September 1894. Inclosure in Graves to Currie, Erzerum, 18 September 1894.

29. Two leading culprits were the chief of the Haydaranli tribe, which had maintained a highly unsavoury reputation since the 1870s, and Shaykh Muhammad Sadiq, son of Ubayd Allah, who as a Hamidiya officer continued to harass Christian villages as his father had done before him.

30. *PP*, Turkey No. 1 (1898), Crow, Report on a Journey through Sasun and Guendj, Bitlis, July 1897.

31. *PP*, Turkey No. 1 (1898) C8716, Elliot to Currie, Van, 1 September 1897.

CHAPTER 5

THE QAJARS AND THE KURDS

Introduction

To the casual observer in 1914 it could easily seem that the Kurdish tribes posed as formidable a threat to the integrity and authority of the Qajar state as they had done a century earlier. Without a doubt they still appeared uncontrollable, playing fast and loose with provincial politics as well as with Russia and Turkey. The disorder was real enough, but the idea that it was still as insoluble as it had been a century earlier was illusory, explained partly by the unprecedented weakness of Tehran during the two decades up to 1914.

Yet various developments occurred during the second half of the nineteenth century which made the *possibility* of integrating Kurdistan into the state more likely by 1914 than ever before. In military terms there can be no doubt that breech-loading rifles, machine-guns and hydraulic-recoil field artillery, though as yet barely used against the Kurds, nevertheless spelt the death knoll for Kurdish tribal independence. Tribes – even armed with the latest rifles – were seldom able to achieve the discipline necessary for formal battle with such modern weapons, and their future lay with guerrilla warfare.

Socio-economic changes, however, were a good deal more important in the process of integration. In the first place, tribalism declined in the nineteenth century all over Iran, Kurdistan included. An increasing number of pastoralists adopted a sedentary life, and as they did so their chiefs were slowly transformed into landlords with a growing interest in tranquillity and in politics in the provincial capital. Finally, the constitutional revolution of 1906 marked a formal drawing of lines between urban and sedentary Kurds on the one hand and the pastoralist tribal Kurds on the other.

Qajar Weakness

Iran, like Ottoman Turkey, experienced acute weakness in the eighteenth century, leading to the final collapse of the enfeebled Safavid dynasty in 1735. After almost 60 years of political uncertainty and turmoil, the Qajar dynasty established itself in 1794. The Qajars were, by origin, a tribal group. They cherished the memory of their tribal origins, but sought to emulate the requirements of absolute monarchy.

They faced formidable problems. The decline of central authority from the latter part of the seventeenth century led to provincial insecurity in which tribal groups, including the Kurds, played a disorderly role. During the Afghan invasions from 1709 onwards Kurdish tribes, like Iran's external enemies, seized what territory and power they could. In 1719, for example, Kurdish tribes seized Hamadan and penetrated almost to Isfahan itself. When Nadir Shah fell in 1747, assassinated, incidentally, on an expedition to suppress a Kurdish rebellion, nomadic tribes from the Zagros – Kurds, Lurs and Bakhtiyaris – streamed into Fars to exploit the vacuum in authority.

Such disturbed conditions drove many unprotected sedentary folk to seek the security of their own tribal formations. By the end of the eighteenth century tribes formed a significantly more substantial proportion of the population than they had done a century earlier. Controlling these tribes constituted a major domestic preoccupation for the Qajars. The problem was not new, but the Qajars found it particularly acute, partly because they restored the idea of unity to Iran following the fragmentation of the state during the eighteenth century. Each Qajar ruler came into conflict with powerful tribal leaders in one part of the country or another.

Since central government (Isfahan, then Tehran) was comparatively close to the Zagros one might suppose it would try to take vigorous steps to suppress the Kurdish tribal chiefs. Many chiefs, however, had opted for Ottoman suzerainty, not only to be nominally subject to a Sunni suzerain, but also for the very practical reason that Istanbul was more distant and therefore less able to impose taxation or the provision of military service. Trying to enforce the submission of the remoter border Kurds, like those of Hakkari, was a particularly fruitless activity, since they were scattered in the most rugged country. Whenever necessary, semi-nomadic tribes would simply move across the perenially disputed 1639 border. Both sides – Turkey and Iran – gave happy refuge to the other's rebels.

Even where the Kurds fell well within Iran, central government was often too weak to enforce its authority. Subjection to the tenuous hold of provincial government frequently meant increased oppression rather than protection, for weak local government officials would strike profitable but corrupt deals with tribal chiefs rather than risk costly and indecisive confrontation. From the perspective of the peasantry, the dividing lines between provincial governor, tribal chief, military commander and landowner were often indistinguishable.

The Qajars were able to survive in spite of the relatively increased military strength of the tribes during the eighteenth century because of the latters' inability to combine against government. The Qajars were often obliged to acknowledge those chiefs able to command the unquestioned obedience of their tribes. Imperial recognition or authentication remained a valuable asset to most chiefs. While a shah might have no alternative but to accept a tribal chief or magnate as local governor, the latter also knew he was more likely to command unquestioned authority locally if he possessed imperial investiture, but there were always exceptions. In about 1810 the Crown Prince of Iran, Abbas Mirza, sought to restore a Hakkari chief deposed by insubordinate aghas, but without success. Formal Qajar recognition proved worthless in such inaccessible terrain.

With the larger and more accessible confederations, the Qajars tried to foster and manage feuds and rivalries, and thereby to rule through dependent chiefs rather than without them. This was even the case with the Walis of Ardalan who had been important loyal supporters of the Qajar bid for power in the 1790s and after. Despite the walis' proven loyalty, the Qajar shahs 'often exerted their influence and power to alter the direct line of succession and, by supporting the pretensions of younger branches, they have created feuds, which have rendered its rulers more dependent upon them'.[1] This had been the case with rivals for the position of Wali of Ardalan at the very end of the eighteenth century. Where possible the Qajars insisted on hostages from chiefly families in order to ensure loyal behaviour. Khusrou Khan Ardalan, whose mother was a member of the Qajar household, was brought up at court, an effective way to ensure the good behaviour of his father, the wali.

The Qajars also tried to absorb tribal leaders into the state system. Sometimes they married their daughters off to tribal chiefs or dynastic local rulers, enhancing the status of such chiefs but drawing them more closely into the orbit of imperial authority. Thus Khusrou Khan, who succeeded his father as wali, married one of Fath Ali Shah's numerous daughters. She proved 'of a very vigorous and determined character. She was the virtual ruler of Kurdistan, and administered the affairs of the province by virtually open *durbar* [formal audience]'.[2] And so she continued on behalf of her son, after Khusrou Khan's death. It was but a short step to the installation of a Qajar governor and the final extinction of Ardalan in 1865.

Elsewhere the process was slower, but by the end of the century Iranian governors, often members of the Qajar family, were replacing Kurdish chiefs as local governors. To the north of Ardalan, on the lands south and west of Lake Urumiya, lay the territory of the Mukri Kurds, a powerful confederation which provided the best cavalry the shah could call upon. While technically only required to field 200 cavalry, they could easily provide 4,000 and still have enough men to harvest their crops and protect their territory. But in order to use them, the shah – certainly in the 1830s – had to play their chiefs with care, taxing them very lightly, for 'the Persian crown had no hold whatever on their allegiance; and they are, at the same time, too powerful to be coerced into anything like tame submission.'[3] Indeed, there was great resentment in Sawj Bulaq later when the Qajars tried to replace the local Mukri chief with a princeling from Tehran, and they reverted to acceptance of the Mukri choice. A Mukri was still in place when war broke out in 1914. For, as was clear from the Shaykh Ubayd Allah episode, from the trouble the Shikak gave at the turn of the century, and from the turbulence that accompanied Turkish and Russian encroachments into Azarbaijan, those governors who enjoyed no local power base were destined to remain largely impotent, dependent on playing one local chief or magnate off against another.

Undoubtedly the Qajars were assisted by economic change. During the middle years of the nineteenth century the number of nomads began to decline, partly because of a devastating famine in 1869 (to which pastoralists were always more vulnerable than agriculturalists), and partly because of the introduction of crops, for example, tobacco, which made settled agriculture more profitable. By the end of the century the number of those still properly described as tribal had probably fallen from one third to one quarter of the Iranian population. The Mukri, for example were divided into two parts by 1900, one still pastoralist, the other not only sedentary but barely cognizant of its tribal origins. This, too, had its consequences for tribal leadership. Not only were chiefs acquiring title to the villages in which their tribesmen settled, but they also began casting around to acquire ownership of villages outside their tribal area. The possession of large landholdings, the need either to govern or to liaise with Qajar officials, and the seductive attraction of city life, persuaded many chiefs to settle in the provincial capital, thus weakening tribal ties.

The Qajars constantly faced daunting threats from their neighbours. In addition to the perennial efforts of the Ottomans, the Uzbegs and Turkomans to violate and occupy areas of Iran, the new pressure came from the European powers, primarily Russia and Britain, who competed for influence at the Qajar court until 1914. Russia and Turkey had already exploited the Afghan invasions to seize parts of northern and western Iran.[4] Kurdistan and Azarbaijan were always tempting morcels in the path of ambitious Ottoman and Russian armies, a fact not lost upon their freedom-loving tribes.

By the end of the eighteenth century Russia had acquired much Iranian territory north of the Araxes river, adding Georgia to the list in 1800. In order to counter Russian advances Iran sought European help to reform its army, and in 1812 tried to recover its losses while Russia was preoccupied with Bonaparte's invasion. In reaching a peace agreement in 1813 the Russian czar undertook on behalf of himself and his heirs to recognize whichever Iranian prince was nominated by the shah as heir apparent. While this may have contributed to stability, it also opened the state to foreign interference.

Britain, anxious about growing Russian influence and the possibility that this might eventually threaten its hold on India and anxious, too, about French efforts to secure Iranian co-operation against Russia, sent repeated military missions to the Qajar court to bolster Iranian defences against the Russians.

Russia's growing influence in Tehran, the Qajar capital, was expressed both in loss and gain of territory. For while Russia periodically took another bite out of Caucasia, it also encouraged Iran to compensate by invading Ottoman territory.[5] In 1827 the Russians took what remained north of the Araxes, the cities of

Erivan and Nakhchivan, and the area's Kurdish tribes. The permanency of the Araxes river boundary was established by the Treaty of Turkmanchai that year.

In their efforts to claw back central control, it was an understandable Qajar fear that any delegation of power or freedom would threaten their own position. Their own arbitrary exercise of power and the fact that delegation implied Qajar weakness, not strength, gave rise to a widespread and profound distrust of all government. Lacking developed state institutions and a trained standing army, Qajar sovereigns, like European kings of the Middle Ages, sought to remind their subjects of royal authority by making their royal progress with large retinues from one city or town to another. Thus the seat of government rested in the shah's saddle rather than in some chancellery in Tehran. This habit seriously disrupted the countryside through which the imperial retinue passed. In 1858 Nasr al Din Shah visited Sinna without warning, much to the embarrassment of the Wali of Ardalan. He happily accepted the gift of gold offered by the unfortunate wali in lieu of provender. The unannounced nature of the shah's arrival may have been deliberate, for gold was always highly acceptable since the shah's coffers were often empty.

The ability to raise revenue, the essential precondition for firm and efficient administration and a standing army, was compromised by dependence upon tax farming. The peasantry paid substantially more than the state required in order to give a sizeable cut to the landlord or fiefholder. This remained a problem throughout the century. In his report on trade and commerce for 1894/95 the British consul in Tabriz noted that the Farmer-General for Azarbaijan had paid taxes to the central government amounting to 180,000 tomans, retaining a balance of 370,000 tomans, of which a fraction was paid to his agents, and the rest was clear profit.[6] Of the revenues that actually reached Tehran, the Qajars treated what we should view as public funds as a private purse, sometimes for the pursuit of their own extravagances.

The Qajars took periodic steps towards reform but were thwarted by internal weakness, by distrust of European help and by a fear that reform would undermine autocracy as it threatened to do in Turkey. What efforts there were, were tempered by the fear of Russian encroachment on the northern borders and of Britain's potential appetite to swallow Iran as it had done India. By 1890 the few serious attempts at radical reform had been largely abandoned.

The Qajars never managed to create the standing army that would render reliance on tribal irregulars redundant. For much of the nineteenth century they could only command about 12,000 regular troops of indifferent fighting quality. Britain had sent a military mission to help beef up the army in 1835, but the attempt at reform had not been successful. This effort included the training of a regiment of Guran tribesmen at Kirmanshah by Henry Rawlinson. The Guran did not take kindly to European ideas of discipline and training, and the experiment was abandoned. From 1875 the army was largely conscripted but remained disorganized, underfunded and its troops irregularly and inadequately paid. Only a Cossack brigade raised in 1879 constituted a credible fighting force. Since it was commanded and largely officered by Russians it was questionable, however, where its loyalties lay.

The far greater part of the Qajar forces was composed of irregulars, provided regionally, or by tribe, on a quota system. The use of tribal irregulars as a key ingredient in the Iranian armed forces reflected the enduring importance of the tribes in Iranian society, unlike the Ottoman empire which had largely destroyed tribalism, certainly among the Turkic people. Nomadic tribes on the frontiers of Iran held land conditional on the provision of military service, cavalry or infantry and frontier outposts and guards as required, even after efforts to introduce conscription. In return they were exempt from land tax, only liable for herd and sometimes pasturage tax. At the northern end of western Azarbaijan, for example:

> He [the Khan of Maku] levies troops necessary for defence of the frontier.... The Persian Government has always considered the Khans of Maku as the valuable guardians of its frontiers. Thus, in the twentieth century, and in one of the Provinces most submissive to the royal administration, Azerbijan, we see this khanate enjoy all the prerogatives of feudalism.[7]

As late as 1910 it was possible for Walter Smart, recently arrived as British Consul-General in Tabriz to report:

> The administration of Kurdistan, such as it exists, is genuinely feudal. The Kurds are very lightly taxed, in fact scarcely at all, but the aghas, or chiefs, are expected to furnish armed contingents for active service when called upon by the Government or local governors. These contingents are generally maintained in the field by the chiefs at their own expense.[8]

One might quibble about the European term 'feudal' but Smart, acute observer that he was, recognized that essentially the same system operated as had done even before the Safavids had come to power. The system had its advantages. 'For instance,' Smart reported, 'in November last Imam Kuli Mirza collected some 2,000 Kurdish infantry and cavalry and marched against ... a rebellious chief. This little campaign did not cost the Persian authorities a penny, for the whole army was armed and maintained and fed by its chiefs.'[9] He also described how he saw 400 infantry and cavalry raised and assembled at Sawj Bulaq at 24 hours' notice.

Yet in practice the whole system of tribal levies was in ruins. Each of the larger tribes were required to field infantry or cavalry regiments as and when required. Although Iran had toyed with the idea of raising a force equivalent to the Hamidiya, this is the nearest they had got to it.[10] The nominal strength of tribal regiments seldom reflected reality. Sometimes such regiments were entirely fictitious,[11] while smaller tribes, unable to field a whole regiment, were nevertheless called upon also to provide armed men.

Tribal irregulars were of two-edged benefit, for they were generally as well or better armed than the small regular infantry, thus making them a threat to government authority. Discipline among the tribesmen was non-existent. They were also reluctant to stray too far from their own region and, when required to do so, the chief expected the state to finance his forces. In practice, therefore, they were used to putting down rebellious rival tribes.

Throughout the Qajar period the army remained breathtakingly inefficient by European standards, its troops unpaid and denied the essential equipment and munitions for training. In 1871 the newly appointed minister of war discovered that no stocktaking had taken place for 20 years. The army was also corrupt at the highest level. In the 1890s one of the shah's own sons, as commander-in-chief, was selling rifles to Kurds and Lurs, 'thus in the position of arming the very groups it was his task to prevent from becoming a threat to the government'.[12] By 1900 breech-loading rifles were common among the tribes, and by 1910 they were universal. In the jaundiced view of one of its own officers, the army in 1914 was:

> quite incapable of fighting against the numerous and much better armed tribes, and when some of these became unruly the matter had to be settled by negotiation, or by mobilising against them the forces of rival tribes which were induced to take the field by a prospect of loot or in order to settle their private feuds.[13]

This, given recent developments in military technology – particularly the development of the machine-gun and hydraulic-recoil systems for field artillery – and the clear superiority of regular troops in open country, was an overly pessimistic assessment. But it was true that the army's ability to control the more distant parts of the empire was still limited by the lack of infrastructure. By 1890 Iran had only two carriageable roads of any extent: Qazvin to Tabriz and Tehran to Qum.

Independence for the tribal chiefs meant not only freedom from government control and taxes, but in practice the freedom to extort without restraint provender and service from the peasantry within the tribal sphere of influence. One result of the Qajar failure to mediate between tribe and peasantry, was that agriculture, the single most important component of the state economy, failed to raise adequate revenue for the state. It was small comfort that a situation which was deteriorating under the Qajars had existed since the Saljuq period.

Another result was acute poverty for most of the Kurdish peasantry as vividly described by one traveller in the mid-1830s:

> At length we emerged into a Koordish village, in which we could scarcely obtain the hospitality of *water*, for these people are but little removed above the flocks and herds they live amongst, and one feels degraded to see human beings reduced to anything so low in the scale of creation: they merely vegetate on the soil which feeds them, their dens sometimes disturbed by the cattle, and they lie down together amidst the mutual dung and rubbish.[14]

The only sanction enjoyed by the peasantry, as in Ottoman territory, was to abandon the land. Overly oppressive chiefs risked losing their peasantry to the more lenient who, with a surplus of land and room for an expansion of labour, might welcome refugees. Almost half a century later relations were much the same. A report in 1879 describes how the fertility of Kurdistan was wasted by the rapacity of landlords and by poverty and disorder, the only relief for the peasantry being to migrate.

The same year the government began to transfer crown estates to individuals, a belated recognition that many fiefs were already, practically speaking, in private hands. In Kurdistan a substantial number of landlords were also tribal chiefs, for example the Sanjabi and Kalhur chiefs in the south who owned villages well outside their tribal areas. It was an indication of how such men exercised a multiplicity of functions as tribal chiefs, as political and economic intermediaries between town and country, and as landlords.

Kurdish Azarbaijan

Apart from its relations with the wider Iranian world, Iranian Kurdistan had its own specific and internal characteristics, and these differed between the northern and southern parts. Tribal chiefs within the province of Azarbaijan, especially the districts around Urumiya and Maku, were closely involved in cross-border matters of a political, economic or social nature.

Sometimes the tribes created tension and disorder by raiding across the border into Turkey. At other times they acted in cahoots with the Ottomans to create mayhem among the *rayyat* of Azarbaijan. Certain tribes became notorious. Outside Sawj Bulaq the Mamash and Mangur were locked in longstanding feud. It was the Mangur who were in the greater disfavour with Tehran, ever since Hamza, the paramount, had thrown in his lot with Shaykh Ubayd Allah. Hamza had been executed but his brother, Qadir Agha, maintained the Mangur reputation for banditry and recalcitrance. Muhammad Agha, chief of the Mamash, on the other hand, had been rewarded for his loyalty in 1880 with the title *amir al asha'ir* (commander of the tribes) although locally it was common knowledge he had only refused to join the rebels because he could not bear taking orders from Hamza Mangur. The Mamash, now locally supreme, were always willing to march with imperial authority against their old enemy. The tribes enjoyed considerable latitude under Qajar rule, but they were responsive to the wider Sunni community of Ottoman Kurdistan and were susceptible to the spread of the *tariqas*. Hence they helped Shaykh Ubayd Allah to widen his constituency into Iran, driving the Christian peasantry from villages he wished to control, for example, in the Margavar valley. Disturbances in Margavar and Targavar continued to be frequent, partly because of the unsettling proximity of the Turkish border and the slow expansion of Shaykh Muhammad Sadiq eastwards, but more particularly because of the absence of any acknowledged paramount who could mediate or impose order between fractious tribes there, notably the Targavar and Begzada Dasht Kurds.

Yet further north lay the Shikak, which from the 1870s had constituted a significant confederation. Although by no means the largest of the Kurdish tribes, they had established a reputation for predatory activities, attacking both Kurdish and Christian *rayyat*, refusing to pay taxes or fines, and behaving in a generally lawless manner.

Where possible, government officials sometimes used Kurdish predatory instincts to their advantage, but this was often of questionable value. In 1896 the Shikak had ambushed 800 Armenian revolutionaries on their retreat from Van. Two years later Jafar Agha of the Shikak was hunting down Armenian revolutionaries at the behest of Tehran. Yet men like Jafar Agha were too rebellious to be an asset to government. Through his banditry and refusal to pay taxes he created more trouble than he was worth, and it was decided to get rid of him. In July 1905 he was invited on safe conduct to Tabriz, where he was murdered and his corpse dragged through the city's streets.

Such behaviour might seem shortsighted, but treachery was part of the world Kurds inhabited. Like government officers, Kurdish chiefs themselves practised betrayal between themselves and in their dealings with outsiders. Particularly savage cases included the execution of Said Sultan, chief of the Hawrami, by the governor of Jawanrud after being guaranteed safe conduct in 1871. In 1886 Qazi Fattah, a leading *alim* (religious leader) of Sawj Bulaq 'disappeared' after his safe conduct was torn up in Tabriz. A succession crisis in the Sharafbayni in 1907 led to fratricide and blood feud with the Walad Begi, since the murdered man's mother was from that tribe. In 1909 the Walad Begi convened a conciliation meeting where they duly massacred the unsuspecting Sharafbayni chiefs. In 1910 Daud Khan Kalhur (see below) had destroyed Shir Khan Sanjabi's forts, having sworn on a sealed Quran not to do so. In 1913 the Hawrami put to the sword a village with which they had just concluded a peace settlement brokered by the local mullas and sworn on sealed Qurans. Given the frequency of betrayal, it is remarkable that safe conducts or sealed Qurans were trusted at all.

Like Ottoman Kurds, Azarbaijani Kurds keenly felt the Christian threat and routinely harassed Armenian and Nestorian villages on the lowlands between Urumiya and the Kurdish mountains. There had always been perennial dangers for Christian communities. This was on account of their status: peasants subordinate to the dominant nomad culture. A favourite way to expand tribal control was to demonstrate to *rayyat* villages that they were inadequately protected by their current tribal patron. The obvious means of doing this was by raiding, thereby challenging the patron to defend his village. If raids went unrevenged, the village in question might abandon its patron and seek the protection of the raider. Such challenges usually led to counter-raids. In these contests people tended not to be killed, but thousands of livestock might be driven off, often across the border. Two major examples occurred in 1890, in July, between the Iranian Jalali and Turkish Haydaranli, and during the autumn between the Turkish

Harki and the Iranian Targavar Kurds. The economic cost of these epidemics of sheep rustling frequently led to the abandonment of villages.

Christians were also apt to be drawn into local rivalries, often as unsuspecting victims, since their death seldom led to blood feud. In 1896 Shaykh Muhammad Sadiq arranged the ambush and murder of a Nestorian bishop and his party who were passing from his territory into Iran, and then tried to intimidate Nestorian villagers into signing statements denouncing a rival Kurdish chief for this murder and other criminal acts. In 1907 one Kurdish faction murdered a German missionary in Sawj Bulaq for no other reason than to secure the removal of the Mukri chief whose appointment as district governor was bitterly resented. It worked; the Iranian authorities were sufficiently embarrassed to remove him. In 1914 a British member of the frontier demarcation commission was shot by one Shikak chief to embarrass a rival, Ismail Simqu, who had been vested with responsibility for that section of the frontier by the Russians.

Yet it is important to note that the relationship was not merely one of exploitation. Christian shepherds and their flocks spent the summers in the high pastures with the tribal livestock. When undisturbed by external forces, there could be a strong element of symbiosis between tribe and peasantry.

We know such details about the Christian population because the American and Anglican missionaries were so assiduous in reporting them to the British consuls-general in Tabriz. We know less about the Kurdish *rayyat* (peasantry), partly because they were of less interest to Europeans, but also because in Iran the term 'Kurd' normally meant 'tribal', and that carried its own censorious resonances. In fact, with the decline in nomadism, the more observable difference between tribesman and peasant was lessening daily. Even so, we know that the relatively young confederation of the Shikak, for example, frequently plundered the Kurdish *rayyat* – hence Shaykh Ubayd Allah's wrath in 1880 – and one must assume other tribes acted similarly. Certainly by 1913, on the Turkish side of the border, and one must assume on the Iranian side also, it was possible for the British vice-consul in Bitlis to conclude that:

> The material condition of the Kurds is worse than that of the Armenians in these provinces. They live in almost feudal conditions under the rule of their chiefs, work for their benefit and have no opportunity of improving their position.... It would appear that the only real remedy is to emancipate the Kurds by breaking the power of the chiefs and giving land to the tribesmen.[15]

Another 50 years were to pass before land reform finally destroyed the grip of landowning chiefs in Iran.

To the east, the northern Kurds felt the chill winds of enmity with the Shi'i majority, mainly on the eastern side of Lake Urumiya. This found its most bitter expression in the sack of Miandoab and the army reprisals following it, in the autumn of 1880. The event remained firmly in the local memory and the animosity persisted. After the Constitutional Revolution of 1906 it intensified, with growing nationalist distaste for non-Persian minorities, especially those that were also non-Shi'i.

The Constitutional Revolution

Although the Constitutional Revolution of 1906 affected Kurdistan only tangentially, it merits a brief description as a background to events in Kirmanshah province. The causes of the revolution lay primarily with foreign political and economic penetration, the failure of the Qajars to protect Iran from its baleful effects, and possibly with significant local resentment at Qajar attempts to raise revenue in the provinces. In part this last was an attempt to share in the increased wealth derived from the gradual shift to cash crops, and also to displace tribes in the raising of tolls on caravan routes. Growing popular frustration against Qajar rule succeeded in creating an opposition coalition of *ulama*, intellectuals, and merchants in Tehran and several provincial capitals, most notably Tabriz. These local coalitions were in some cases supported by landlords and tribal chiefs, including certain Bakhtiyaris, who had begun to feel the chill winds of Qajar taxation.

Fear of Russian intervention inhibited the opposition from acting, but in 1905–6, following Russia's defeat by Japan and its own revolution, the opposition took control of Tehran and forced the shah to accept the establishment of a consultative assembly (*majlis*) and the drafting of a constitution. Broadly speaking the merchants and artisan classes strongly supported the newly established Majlis. In major cities like Tabriz and Kirmanshah, in smaller towns like Urumiya and Sawj Bulaq and even in some villages, popular committees (or *anjumans*) were formed in deliberate opposition to the local governor.

The Kurdish tribal chiefs generally identified with the monarchy and the hierarchical system of which they were part, and were hostile to the constitutional movement. Legitimation resided in a man, not an institution founded on fancy foreign notions. But the chiefs also resented growing Qajar intrusion into provincial affairs, and their response was therefore mixed. They favoured local autonomy from the centre, but resented political activity by townspeople. However, the chiefs hardly acted as a class. Each pursued his own narrow interests.

The urban Kurdish populations in Sawj Bulaq, Urumiya, Saqqiz, Sinna and Kirmanshah tended to identify with the constitutional movement, and more specifically with the desire to escape arbitrary and corrupt government by landlords, chiefs and governors. So also perhaps did many villagers, hence *anjumans* were to be found even in certain small towns and villages. When some of these *anjumans* tried to force down the price of meat and grain, the chiefs saw it as a direct threat to their own position. Thus divisions of loyalty lay across ethnic lines in Kurdistan, and tended to follow socio-economic ones.

The efforts of the new shah, Muhammad Ali, to overthrow the constitution following his accession in 1907 finally led to his abdication and exile in July

1909. He was defeated primarily by an axis of Tabrizi revolutionaries and the Bakhtiyari confederation. However, having successfully removed the obstacle to constitutional progress, the Majlis in Tehran found itself broadly divided between radicals, who wanted social reform, and conservatives, who wished to safeguard a constitutional monarchy and also the position of religion. The failure of the two tendencies to reconcile their differences and the resulting power vacuum in the countryside gave rise to widespread disorder. A number of tribal confederations sought to reduce the power of the Bakhtiyaris, but were defeated by their own rivalries. Tribes around Kirmanshah used the national struggle as a pretext for competition locally.

The Kirmanshah Kurds

Little has been published hitherto concerning the Kurds of Kirmanshah. Here the Kurds were either Ithna 'Ashari Shi'is like the Iranian majority or belonged to the Ahl-i Haqq. Unlike the confessional conflicts further north, there is little evidence of tension between the Shi'a and the Ahl-i Haqq in southern Kurdistan. Conversion to Shi'ism by the latter seems to have been an act of convenience. The House of Ardalan, for example, was possibly once Ahl-i Haqq, but by the 1820s the wali and chief members of the family were professing the Shi'i faith. This facilitated a wider range of marriage alliances and strengthened Ardalan credentials for local government.

Kirmanshah itself was a city of about 50,000 inhabitants at the turn of the century. It was important as the last centre of any size on the Mesopotamian caravan route. While imports to Iran from the Gulf came mainly through Bushire, a substantial amount still came up the Tigris to Baghdad, thence via Khaniqin and Qasr-i Shirin, the respective border towns between Mesopotamia and Iran. But there was a more sensitive traffic that gave Kirmanshah particular importance. Each year 120,000 live Shi'is and 8,000 dead ones passed along this road bound for Najaf and Karbala. Generally, tribes along the caravan routes levied dues on passing traffic, opposing government attempts to replace them with gendarmerie. By banditry they also tried to disrupt alternative caravan routes that were controlled by rival tribes or government in order to divert traffic onto their own routes. Travel in Luristan and Kurdistan was notorious for its insecurity.

The two largest southern tribes were the Kalhur (mainly Shi'i) and the Guran (Ahl-i Haqq), both reckoned to have roughly 5,000 tents (or families) in the 1890s. The Kalhur were still Ahl-i Haqq in the 1830s but by the early 1900s the majority outwardly professed Shi'ism.[16] They became major players in Kirmanshah at the turn of the century, and it is likely that their chiefs, like the Ardalans before them, decided that a Shi'i identity was politically prudent, and that one by one the Kalhur sections followed suit.

The Guran, on the other hand, were solidly Ahl-i Haqq. They were divided between eight rival sections and their reluctance to allow the emergence of an undisputed paramountcy offset their numerical superiority. This allowed the spiritual leadership provided by the Haydari *sayyids* to grow in political importance. Following the demise of the temporal chiefs in the 1920s the Haydaris rapidly began to fill the political vacuum.[17]

Apart from the Mangur (near Sawj Bulaq), the Kalhur and Guran were significantly larger than any other Kurdish confederation in Iran. But the Guran's internal divisions gave smaller but relatively sizeable tribes, for example the Sanjabi, Kerindi and Zangana,[18] the chance to play a major role in the politics of southern Kurdistan. In between the larger Kurdish tribes of Azarbaijan and Kirmanshah lay a plethora of smaller, mainly Sunni, tribes in erstwhile Ardalan, now renamed the province of Kurdistan.

The most powerful chief in the region was the Luri Wali of Pusht-i Kuh, south-west of Kirmanshah. On the whole he avoided conflict with the central government. Ensconced on the west-facing side of the Zagros, he enjoyed virtual independence. Unlike Ardalan, the walis of Pusht-i Kuh still had their title at the beginning of this century, uncompromised by the judicious marriages the family had concluded with the Qajars and neighbouring tribes. These marriages reflected the important balance to be maintained with the centre and with neighbours. The wali in 1907 was, for example, father-in-law to Salar al Dawla, the younger brother of Muhammad Ali Shah and also son-in-law to Daud Khan, Ilkhan (paramount) of the neighbouring Kalhur.

Daud Khan, a man of humble origin[19] but limitless ambition, successfully usurped the leadership of the Kalhur in about 1900. He did so with ruthless determination, killing those who got in his way, including his own father, in order to ascend the tribal hierarchy. Uncharacteristically, he spared the old Ilkhan, who was packed off to Kirmanshah as a pensioner. By his acts Daud Khan was hated by many and feared by all the Kalhur.

Once Ilkhan, Daud Khan cast his eye further afield. To consolidate his position he needed to forge alliances with other tribes and make himself indispensible to the governor of Kirmanshah for control of the countryside. He married outside the tribe with relentless determination. By 1906 he had 12 wives and his son Jawan had five – numbers which do not suggest that they were particularly assiduous in either the spirit or letter of Muslim law. Such marriages had a serious political purpose. The previous year Jawan had become infatuated with the daughter of Muhammad Ali Khan, the chief his father had ousted. Since it touched upon his own legitimacy, Daud Khan predictably ruled out any such alliance. Jawan was willing to fight to fulfil his passion and his father equally determined to prevent it. In a pitched battle in May 1905, Jawan's 800 warriors slew a brother and another son of Daud Khan. Jawan then marched on Kirmanshah to demand of the governor that the old Ilkhan be reinstated and his own father displaced.

For the governor such events required steady nerves. He might take pleasure in a powerful tribe led by a dangerous family tearing itself apart, but if one party brought his warriors to town, mayhem was in prospect. In the Kalhur case, one branch (the Hajizada) were already strongly represented in Kirmanshah. *In extremis* a rival tribe could always be mobilized, but this virtually guaranteed further disorders and depredations in the town and neighbouring countryside, for the tribes would strip the landscape bare. So Jawan's arrival at the gates of Kirmanshah was the kind of situation which brought governor, citizenry and local village landlords rapidly together.

It was in everyone's interest to send the Kalhur peacefully home, none more so than the governor himself who, since his appointment, had been quietly buying up villages obtainable at very low prices on account of the very disturbances he had been sent to deal with. The last thing he wanted was for his new acquisitions to be sacked. Fortunately for him, the city's mullas achieved a reconciliation between father and son. Daud Khan saved his position as Ilkhan, but was probably compelled to accede to the marriage.[20]

It was not long before Daud Khan sought to assert his ascendancy over neighbouring tribes. One target was the Ahl-i Haqq Sanjabi tribe. The Sanjabi were traditionally loyal to the government. Hence their chief was entrusted with the governorship of Qasr-i Shirin and the profitable task of protecting traffic passing through the hill tracts. The provincial governor could hardly have garrisoned Qasr-i Shirin himself since, while his troops might hold the town itself, he simply did not have the resources to guarantee the road through the hills as well. The Sanjabi chief at this juncture was Shir Khan (Samsam al Mamalik), who had usurped his uncle, Ali Akbar Khan, with the help of the then provincial governor, in about 1900. Shir Khan Sanjabi and Daud Khan Kalhur were bitter rivals.

Any governor had to weigh up very carefully the balance of forces at play. It was all very well entrusting Qasr-i Shirin to the Sanjabis, but could they or could he hold the ring against the Kalhur and their allies? Each governor had to decide whom to befriend, whom to betray. In 1908 Zahir al Mulk Zangana, himself a local tribal chief and landlord, was appointed governor of Kirmanshah. Daud Khan successfully concluded an understanding with him that year, sealed by the marriage of Jawan to Zahir al Mulk's daughter. Daud Khan was appointed *rais al asha'ir*, the acknowledged senior among the tribal chiefs of the province and the most important player in the governor's pledge of 10,000 tribesman to support the shah against the constitutionalists that year.

None of this can have pleased Shir Khan Sanjabi, who realized that Daud Khan was now much stronger than he had been a few years earlier, and that Zahir al Mulk's support for Daud could prove fatal for himself. Shir Khan's fears were well founded. Daud Khan was indeed waiting for a pretext to move against him.

The struggle between constitutionalists and monarchists had led to conflict in a number of cities across Iran. Kirmanshah was no exception. The city had expelled the monarchists and elected a mayor. Outside the city walls the lapse in authority had two effects on neighbouring tribal chiefs. First, they felt free to commit depredations and secondly they were tempted to throw in their lot with whichever party might give them the best personal advantage. By October 1908 the struggle for Kirmanshah had led to serious fighting between the Kalhurs and a smaller force of Sanjabis in the city. Having driven the Sanjabis out of the city, Daud Khan moved his Kalhur troops towards Qasr-i Shirin, joined now by Guran tribes who had grievances against the Sanjabi. One of the Guran chiefs hoped to receive the lucrative governorship of Qasr-i Shirin as reward for his support, but Daud Khan had his own plans. He produced Shir Khan's cousin and heir to the Sanjabi leadership, Habib Allah Khan and, in the contemptuous words of the British consul, the Sanjabi warriors 'seeing superior force did the Persian thing and went over to the Pretender' (Habib Allah Khan).[21]

Daud Khan was a wholly untrustworthy patron. By April 1909 he was arranging Shir Khan's reinstatement at Qasr-i Shirin, sending the disconsolate Habib Allah back into retirement. He simply appointed and dismissed at will, dictating who would be chief of the Sanjabis without reference to the provincial governor. In fact, from that year Daud Khan also saw no need to pay any taxes. Humiliating though this situation clearly was, Zahir al Mulk needed Daud Khan's support against his enemies in the city itself. In June, at Zahir al Mulk's request, Daud Khan brought 1,000 footsoldiers into Kirmanshah, to intimidate the rival party in the city. As usual, wherever they went the Kalhur stripped the neighbourhood bare.

At the end of the year a new and able governor, Nizam al Saltana, replaced Zahir al Mulk in response to mounting complaints about the latter's governorship, not least his reckless use of the Kalhur. The new governor immediately demanded payment of tax arrears by Daud Khan and provision of the fictitious Kalhur regiment for government service. Daud Khan, as rais al asha'ir, made the other chiefs promise to back him against the new governor. Within the Kalhur, Daud Khan tried to raise the money but encountered resistance from those who hoped the new governor would reduce his power. When he was refused extra dues by the chief of the largest section of the Kalhur, Daud Khan promptly had him shot, an unprecedented act which caused huge dissension. He withdrew into the border marches where he continued his vendetta against the Sanjabi. Now the cost of tribal warfare on the local non-tribal economy was seen for what it was, with 180 villages sacked during the conflict.

The new governor was simply not strong enough to deal with Daud Khan. Even with the use of Sanjabi tribesmen, he could only raise 2,700 troops locally against Daud Khan's 4,000, and lacked the money to raise more. So he resorted, unsuccessfully, to stratagems, including a promise to Daud Khan's son-in-law, the Wali of Pusht-i Kuh, that he would be appointed minister of war if only he would arrest Daud Khan. The wali shrewdly did not respond. In July 1910 Daud Khan made a formal submission empty of substance, buying the governor off with renewed promises of tax arrears and the provision of his promised regiment.

As he knew, the governor needed his help in the wider politics of the region: to confront the growing power of the Bakhtiyari confederacy to the east and the prevailing lawlessness in Luristan to the south-west.

All this, of course, affected the Kalhur contest with the Sanjabi. Shir Khan, who had provided 500 cavalry and lost many of them in fights with the rebel Kalhur over the previous nine months, learnt in November that the constitutional government in Tehran had rescinded reimbursement of his costs, a blow to his prestige as well as his pocket. On the Kirmanshah–Khaniqin road it was the Kalhur and their Bajilan allies[22] who extorted money from passers-by. Shir Khan Sanjabi, albeit the government's appointee, was unable to reach Qasr-i Shirin, let alone govern it. In March 1911 Daud Khan appointed the Bajilan chief, Karim Khan, as his deputy in Qasr-i Shirin, earnest of the marriage of his daughter to Karim Khan's son. In April he bribed the governor to appoint him officially as governor of the frontier district, including Qasr-i Shirin, and to appoint a pliable Sanjabi as the town's new chief.

Yet Daud Khan's triumph carried the seeds of its own destruction. Rewarding Karim Khan Bajilan with the revenues of Qasr-i Shirin provoked jealousy on the part of Karim Khan's brother, and disappointment among sections of the Guran, who began mending their fences with the Sanjabis. Previously disaffected Sanjabis also rallied again around Shir Khan, insulted by Daud Khan's appointment of placemen over their tribe.

As southern Kurdistan and the border region slipped further into lawlessness and conflict, fresh alliances began to fall into place, characterized by rival sections of different tribes taking either the Kalhur or Sanjabi side.[23] By the end of April the anti-Daud Khan faction (for loathing of Daud Khan was what held these forces together) began to outnumber the Kalhur. In June Daud Khan suffered defeat, but not before he had destroyed Sanjabi villages in an area of approximately 200 square miles, and looted others.

These inter- and intra-tribal contests were interrupted by an event of national importance. Salar al Dawla, the ambitious younger brother of Muhammad Ali Shah, who had been deposed and exiled in 1909, raised the flag of revolt near Saqqiz and entered Sinna in July 1911 at the very moment that Muhammad Ali Shah himself separately returned from exile to make a final (and unsuccessful) bid for the throne. Salar al Dawla was accompanied by the highly revered Naqshbandi Shaykh of Tawila,[24] armed with letters to the Sunni *ulama* of Kurdish towns indicating that opposition to Salar al Dawla would constitute opposition to himself and to the *shaykh al islam* in Istanbul who, it was claimed, supported the venture.

It was no accident that Salar al Dawla had chosen this part of Iran as his springboard. He had close connections with the Kurdish and Lur chiefs. He had been governor of Luristan in 1906, had married a daughter of the Wali of Pusht-i Kuh with a view to achieving semi-independence from his brother, and in 1907 had attempted to arm the tribes for this purpose. Now he offered to lead them against the constitutional government in Tehran and achieve the restoration of the shah. As he knew, the tribes were generally hostile to the constitutional movement. So, among others he persuaded the Kalhur and Sanjabi tribes to a temporary reconciliation.[25]

It cannot have been easy for Daud Khan, Shir Khan or other leading tribesmen to judge how to respond to the new situation in which a widespread but fragile coalition of tribes seemed to be challenging Bakhtiyari ascendancy in Tehran. There was potentially much at stake, and they all wanted to assess the balance of forces. Daud Khan momentarily hesitated, sending simultaneous promises of support to Salar al Dawla and to Tehran until, that is, Salar al Dawla asked him to govern Kirmanshah. Very soon Daud Khan had intimidated the majority of tribal leaders into supporting Salar al Dawla, and the leading merchants of Kirmanshah into financing him, by the simple expedient of having one or two of them beaten.

Salar al Dawla now had a force of 10,000 Kurds, but they were troops of dubious value. The Kalhur were only there for the loot and the others for fear of Daud Khan, and many deserted once they had taken as much as they could carry. In September 1911 Salar al Dawla was defeated by the constitutionalists near Sultanabad, barely 80 miles from Tehran, and retreated to Kirmanshah, thence into Kalhur country. Daud Khan now found his authority no longer acknowledged by the important Qalkhani section of the Guran.

In the spring of 1912 Daud Khan found himself in a contradictory position. His fortunes with Salar al Dawla had somewhat improved when the latter retook Kirmanshah and gave it over to his Kurdish tribesmen to plunder. But on the tribal arena things were going badly. The Guran and Sanjabi had renewed their anti-Daud compact, and many of the smaller tribes, tired of Kalhur overbearing, were joining them. At the beginning of May the Kalhur badly upset the powerful Kerindi. Only the agreement of the tribes to stay their hand until Salar al Dawla's rebellion was resolved one way or the other, saved Daud Khan from serious defeat.

Daud Khan never faced the humiliation he so richly deserved at the hands of the combined tribes. He accompanied Salar al Dawla in a desperate march on Tehran. He and his eldest surviving son perished on the battlefield at Sahna, mown down by government maxim machine-guns. Many of the Kalhur perished with him. As for Salar al Dawla, he fled to Luristan. His revolt, which at one point had come close to success, petered out in October.[26]

With Daud Khan dead, the Kalhurs made their peace with their numerous adversaries. Leadership of the tribe fell to a couple of youths, Daud Khan's surviving son, Sulayman Khan and his grandson Abbas Khan. Inevitably, they competed for sole leadership, and the Kalhur chiefdom suffered temporary eclipse.

Meanwhile Shir Khan Sanjabi enjoyed undisputed ascendancy over the tribes, making a profitable business out of protecting the road on the eastern side of

Kirmanshah as far as Kangavar. But neither he nor the Kalhur chiefs could control their people. Kirmanshah remained in disorder well into 1913, as new tribal configurations began to form in the aftermath of Daud Khan's demise and as the ageing Shir Khan lost his vigour.

Turkey, Russia and Iran's Kurds

Tehran was extremely sensitive concerning Turkish and Russian interest in this part of the country. First there had been Shaykh Ubayd Allah's incursion in 1880, which Tehran justifiably believed enjoyed tacit Ottoman approval. Six years later 6,000 Ottoman troops massed at Van and Bashqala, creating alarm in Iran. Then, in the late 1890s the Russians began to show greater interest, with the despatch of seemingly innocent religious missions to convert the Nestorians to Russian orthodoxy.

Istanbul shared Tehran's apprehensions concerning Russian designs. Like Tehran, it feared that Russia was likely to occupy Iranian Azarbaijan. In that case the Porte wanted to ensure it had secured sites of tactical importance along the ill-defined border. But any pre-emptive action had always been inhibited by the fear that it would precipitate Russian intervention. By 1906, however, Turkey felt able to act while Russia was distracted by its humiliating defeat at the hands of Japan and its internal political turmoil. It made a series of minor incursions, laying claim to and then seizing one customs post after another. In May 1906 its troops occupied Margavar and Dasht. In June and October it seized Sardasht and Ushnaviya respectively. Its actions seemed justified first by Russian moves in 1906 to protect its interests in northern Azarbaijan, and then by the Anglo-Russian agreement of 1907 whereby the two Powers delineated Iran into spheres of influence. All Iranian Kurdistan fell within Russia's orbit.[27]

Kurdish tribesmen predictably exploited the power vacuum, frequently acting as stalking horse for the Turks. For example, in February and April 1906, Shaykh Muhammad Sadiq introduced Turkish troops into the Targavar, Margavar and Dasht valleys, chasing out the customs staff. When they learnt that Iranian forces were to march against them in the spring of 1907, local tribal Kurds appealed as Sunnis to the sultan for protection and the pretext was used for Turkish troops to seize high ground west of Urumiya, occupying that town in August. By the end of the year the Turkish consul in Urumiya was openly inviting the population (including the Shi'i Karapapakh) to apply for Ottoman nationality. In January 1908, 1,500 Turkish troops with a large body of Kurds occupied Sawj Bulaq. Kurdish chiefs in the surrounding countryside were summoned before the Turkish commander and reminded that they owed their allegiance to sultan rather than shah.

In many cases of incursion Turkish troops did not stay for long, but they left behind them a vacuum in which the tribes were allowed free reign to jostle for position, inevitably damaging the local economy. Troops and tribes colluded in a protection racket for caravans passing through the area. Local Turkish commanders continued to warn their Iranian counterparts that they would intervene if Iran tried to discipline its Kurds. Tribal activities reached a climax in June 1909 with the sack of Urumiya, and the subsequent defeat of Russian troops by Turks and Kurds near the town two months later. By the end of 1909 it was clear that Turkey could not be prevailed upon to withdraw from Iran until Russia demonstrated its willingness to follow suit.

It was only in December 1911 that Britain and Russia agreed on joint action to protect their commercial interests. A protocol on the Turco-Iranian frontier was signed that month. Russia asked Turkey to withdraw its troops to their positions of 1905. When this was not responded to, it assembled a force in Khoi. By October 1912 Turkey had backed down.

Russia replaced Turkey as occupying power, deploying troops at Salmas, Urumiya and even Sawj Bulaq. During 1913 Russia ran Azarbaijan as a protectorate, purposely weakening the ties between Tabriz and Tehran, but also giving the province greater order than it had known for years. It maintained a garrison of 10,000 troops, over half of whom were stationed in the country between Khoi and Sawj Bulaq. Since such numbers were inadequate either to maintain order or defend the region, the Russians co-opted certain tribes just as the Turks had done.

Here was another opportunity for ambitious chiefs to improve their position locally, offering service in return for support against local enemies. This, for example, is precisely what Ismail Simqu did to strengthen himself against rivals within the Shikak confederation. Thus the Russians were drawn into local feuds, either sponsoring one tribe against another, or themselves coming under attack.

Meanwhile the Mixed Boundary Commission worked hard to resolve delineation disputes between Iran and Turkey, with the mediation of Russian and British officials. However, it was not to be. Resolution of the Turco-Iranian frontier question was thwarted for the fourth time in sixty years by the outbreak of a European war which spread to the region in October 1914.[28]

Sources

Great Britain, unpublished: Public Record Office: series FO 60 nos 464, 483, 516, 580, 598, 612; series FO 248 nos 246, 289, 330, 391, 505, 547, 654, 675, 847, 851, 938, 944, 968, 999, 1031, 1053, 1059; FO 371 nos 304, 306, 313, 346, 498, 540, 953, 956, 2079; FO 416/111; WO 106/5964; India Office Library L/P&S/10/345, 11/36.

Great Britain, published: Parliamentary Papers, Turkey No. 3 (1896); Indian Army, Intelligence Branch of Quartermaster-General's Department, *Gazetteer of Persia* (Simla, 1905).

Secondary sources: Ervand Abrahamian, *Iran Between Two Revolutions* (Princeton, 1982); Hassan Arfa, *Under Five Shahs* (London, 1964); Peter Avery, Gavin Hambly and Charles Melville, *The Cambridge History of Iran*, vol. vii (Cambridge, 1991); Shaul Bakhash, *Iran: Monarchy, Bureaucracy and Reform under the Qajars, 1858–1896* (London 1978); Lois Beck, 'Tribes and states in nineteenth and twentieth century Iran' in Khoury and Kostiner, *Tribes and State Formation*; Isabella Bird Bishop, *Journeys in Persia and Kurdistan* (London 1891, reprinted London 1988); Martin van Bruinessen, 'Kurdish tribes and Simko's Revolt' in Richard Tapper (ed.), *The Conflict of Tribes and State: Iran and Afghanistan* (London, 1983); G.N. Curzon, *Persia and the Persian Question* (London, 1892); C.J. Edmonds, *Kurds, Turks and Arabs* (London, 1957); *Encyclopaedia of Islam*, 1st edition, 'Sawdj Bulak'; George Fowler, *Three Years in Persia with Travelling Adventures in Koordistan* (London, 1841); Ghilan, 'Les Kurdes persans et l'invasion ottomane', *Revue du Monde Musulman*, no. 5, May 1908; P.M. Holt, Ann K.S. Lambton and Bernard Lewis, *The Cambridge History of Islam: The Central Islamic Lands* (Cambridge, 1970); Nikki Keddie, *The Roots of Revolution* (New Haven, 1981); Nikki Keddie, 'The Iranian Power Structure and Social Change', *International Journal of Middle East Studies*, vol. ii, 1971; A.K.S. Lambton, *Landlord and Peasant in Persia* (London, 1953); A.K.S. Lambton, *Qajar Persia*; Robert McDaniel, *The Shuster Mission and the Persian Constitutional Revolution* (Minneapolis, 1974); Sir John Malcolm, *A History of Persia* (London, 1829); Vanessa Martin, *Islam and Modernism: The Iranian Revolution of 1906* (London and Syracuse, 1989); F.R. Maunsell, *Military Report on Eastern Turkey in Asia* (London, 1893); Ziba Mir-Hosseini, 'Inner truth and outer history: the two worlds of the Ahl-i Haqq of Kurdistan', *International Journal of Middle East Studies*, vol. 26, 1994; J. de Morgan, *Mission Scientifique en Perse*, vol. ii (Paris, 1895) and 'Feudalism in Persia', *Smithsonian Institution Annual Review* (Washington, 1913); Morgan Philips Price, 'A Journey through Azerbaijan and Persian Kurdistan', Lecture to the Persian Society (London, 1913); H.C. Rawlinson, 'Notes on a march from Zohab at the foot of the Zagros along the mountains to Khuzistan (Susiana) and from there through the provinces of Luristan to Kirmanshah in the year 1839', *Journal of the Royal Asiatic Society*, no. 9, 1839 and 'Notes on a Journey from Tabriz through Persian Kurdistan', *The Geographical Journal*, no. x, 1841; Ra'iss Tousi, 'The Persian Army, 1880–1907', *Middle East Studies*, no. 24, 1988; H.J. Whigham, *The Persian Problem* (London, 1903); A.T. Wilson, *South West Persia: A Political Officer's Diary, 1907–1914* (London, 1941); S.G. Wilson, *Persian Life and Customs* (New York, 1900); A.C. Wratislaw, *A Consul in the East* (Edinburgh, 1924); Denis Wright, *The English Among the Persians during the Qajar Period, 1787–1921* (London, 1977).

Notes

1. Malcolm, *A History of Persia*, vol. ii, p. 134.
2. Indian Army, *Gazetteer of Persia*, p. 393.
3. Rawlinson, 'Notes on a Journey', p. 34
4. In 1722/23 Russia seized Caucasian territory including Derbent and Baku, and temporarily penetrated as far as Rasht on the Caspian.
5. Hence Iran's strong support of the Babans in 1818–20, its occupation of Sulaymaniya, and its shortlived capture of Bayazid and Bitlis in 1821.
6. FO 60/613 Wood to Durand, Tabriz, 1 June 1899.
7. J. de Morgan, 'Feudalism in Persia', p. 592.
8. FO 371/953 Barclay to Gray, Tehran, 23 January 1910, Inclosure No. 1, Smart to Barclay, Tabriz, 3 January 1910.
9. FO 371/953 Smart to Barclay, Tabriz, 3 January 1910.
10. Unlike the Hamidiya, they were hardly an auxiliary force but an essential part of the Iranian army. Moreover, unlike the Hamidiya, they do not seem to have been assigned regular officers and NCOs to oversee training.
11. There was a glaring discrepancy between theory and reality. The nominal strength of the irregular cavalry in 1899, for example, was 37,600, the actual strength 13,660, Reza Ra'iss Tousi, 'The Persian Army, 1880–1907', p. 217.

12. Bakhash, *Iran*, p. 277.

13. Hasan Arfa, *Under Five Shahs*, pp. 50–51.

14. George Fowler, *Three Years in Persia with Travelling Adventures in Koordistan*, vol. i, p. 110.

15. L/P&S/10/345 Smith to Mallet, Bitlis, 16 April 1913.

16. Written sources are contradictory, see Rawlinson, 'Notes on a March from Zohab', p. 36, Curzon, *Persia and the Persian Question*, vol. i, p. 557, Bishop, *Journeys in Persia and Kurdistan*, vol. i, p. 84, Moosa, *Extremist Shiites*, p. 191, Maunsell, *Military Report on Eastern Turkey in Asia*, p. 484, Soane, *To Mesopotamia and Kurdistan in Disguise*, p. 387. Edmonds, *Kurds, Turks and Arabs*, p. 193, indicates it was still widely believed in the 1920s that a large number of the Kalhur were Kakai, as the Ahl al Haqq are known in Iraq. The only branch of the Kalhur who remain Ahl al Haqq today are the Minishi, also known as the Kufravar (lit. bringers of *kufr*, or unbelief). See also the forthcoming important work by Ziba Mir-Hosseini on the Ahl al Haqq.

17. See Ziba Mir-Hosseini, 'Inner truth and outer history' which shows the difference played by the Ahl-i Haqq leadership in the tribal and non-tribal Kurdish areas near Kirmanshah.

18. The Sanjabi: 1,500 tents, mainly Ahl-i Haqq; the Kerindi, 2,000 tents, also Ahl-i Haqq; the Zangana, 1,500 tents, Shi'a.

19. Daud Khan is variously described as originally a menial of the ruling family or a *khadkhuda*, see L/P&S/11/36 E.B. Soane's Reports on the southern Kurds, 1913; FO 248/938 Kirmanshah Consulate Diary, 11 May 1908.

20. In 1908 ex-Ilkhan Muhammad Ali was invited by disaffected tribal sections to seize power. Yet despite Daud Khan's unpopularity, Muhammad never had a chance and fled beyond Kalhur reach, taking sanctuary with the Wali of Pusht-i Kuh.

21. FO 248/938 Kirmanshah Diary, 17 November 1908.

22. The Bajilan inhabited the Turkish side of the border and were also of Ahl al Haqq origin but had become Sunni.

23. For example Husayn Khan and his section of the Guran joined the Shir Khan, bringing with him previously disaffected Sanjabis. The Muradi Jaf too soon joined, for they were in feud against two of Daud Khan's allies, Fatah Beg Jaf and Karim Khan Bajilan. In April 1911 Fatah Beg Jaf had killed the chief of Sharafbayni (a smaller tribe in the border region) allied to the Muradi Jaf.

24. This was Shaykh Ala al Din, son of Shaykh Umar Tawila.

25. Daud Khan even conceded the governorate of Qasr-i Shirin to Shir Khan. He was willing to do this since he had fallen out with Karim Khan Bajilan (who had broken the terms of marriage to Daud Khan's young daughter which stipulated the marriage was not to be consumated for three years on account of her extreme youth).

26. It says much for the low esteem in which Tehran's authority was held that the government commander at Sultanabad defected to command Salar al Dawla's forces in a final assault on Kirmanshah in October, and that the Sanjabis and other Kurdish tribesmen offered support to whomsoever seemed in the ascendant at any particular time. Salar al Dawla was still trying to rekindle revolt in Kurdistan in 1913.

27. Russia's sphere ran from the Ottoman border at Khaniqin to Yazd and thence to the Russo-Afghan border in the east. The British sphere, the south-east of the country, included Bandar Abbas, Kirman and Birjand near the Afghan border.

28. The previous wars were in 1857 (Crimean), 1876 (Serbian) and 1877 (Russo-Turkish).

CHAPTER 6

REVOLUTION, NATIONALISM
AND WAR, 1908–1918

It will be clear from the preceding chapter that by the end of the nineteenth century profound conflicts and tensions existed within the body politic of Ottoman Turkey. The desire to modernize was qualified by a fear of losing control, the wish to establish effective provincial administration matched by an obsession to maintain central authority, the desire to import European technical efficiency tempered by the imperative of protecting the Muslim heart of empire.

Similar tensions and characteristics are evident when comparing the region in 1900 and today: the use of a widespread network of informers and spies; the physical abuse of detainees, extrajudicial (as well as judicial) killings, and internal exile for both individuals and groups of people who present a risk to state security; attempts openly to publish criticisms or proposals for reform; the arrest and exile of those who speak openly; the formation of clandestine groups dedicated to change the system or even overthrow it by extra-legal means; the resort to open warfare and finally, as happened increasingly in the last half of the nineteenth century, self-imposed exile in order to escape the authorities and yet continue to be active politically.

Not everyone, either then or now, fitted neatly into such crude categories. Furthermore the tensions between reaction and reform, authority and liberty persisted not only on the central stage of Istanbul (or later in Ankara and Baghdad), but also at the local level among the many communities of empire.

Among Kurds, primarily in Istanbul but subsequently in the neglected provinces of Kurdistan, a profound dilemma of identity arose in response to the crisis of empire, one that persists to this day. Some sought a political solution in which their identity was something wider than purely Kurdish and for whom participation within a greater and more sophisticated political culture seemed natural. One should not be surprised that Kurds born, or at least educated, in Istanbul should have been comfortable with this kind of solution. To be a 'Kurd' just as to be a 'Turk' was, until the closing years of the nineteenth century, to be a rural unsophisticate. Those with any ambition aspired to cast off that description and to become Ottoman subjects in the fullest sense of the word, educated and civilized city dwellers. To this day, there are Kurds for whom, on account of their political or economic activities, ethno-national identity is a good deal less important to them than their modern state identity.

There is a second category which for quite different reasons sought membership of the wider Ottoman community. Those in Kurdistan who felt threatened by the political changes now affecting the whole empire, clung to the old verities of caliph and sultan which offered certainty and security in a now rapidly changing world. The 'Kurdishness' of their existence was defined essentially by the pursuit of traditional, usually tribal, identity which the ancien régime seemed willing to foster.

For others the question of ethnicity posed problems of loyalty and identity, as it had already begun to do for Turks, the people of the Balkans, the Armenians and the Arabs. Among this category two distinct tendencies developed during the first two decades of this century. One did not wish entirely to sever its wider socio-economic relationships, and so sought autonomy within the broader embrace of a generally Muslim though ethnically varied community. The other wanted to achieve complete political separation, and so opted for ethnic independence.

These divisions have not disappeared and remain important. The first category, which claims membership of a wider whole, may still be found in state capitals and in the countryside – 'traitors' or 'collaborators', as they are frequently described among those who insist that ethnic difference demands political autonomy or independence. In riposte, some of those willing to deny their ethnicity or at least to subordinate it to the dictates of state, frequently anathematize nationalist Kurds as separatists, rebels or terrorists. Among those who favour outright independence the greatest animosity is frequently reserved for the 'heretics' of their church, those who both for ideological and pragmatic reasons, favour autonomy over independence. The bitter quarrels which took place early in this century undoubtedly seriously weakened the impact of the Kurdish cause then, just as similar conflicts continue to impede the thrust of nationalism today.

The First Kurdish Reformists

The very first Kurds to challenge the nature of the regime did so in response to the despotism of Sultan Abd al Hamid and essentially as Ottoman citizens rather than as Kurds. Ethnic emphasis was to come later. Kurds featured prominently in the very first organized opposition to the sultan, in 1889. Four medical students at the Military Medical School, an Albanian, a Circassian and two Kurds, formed the nucleus of an initially 12-member secret society, the Committee for Union and Progress as it later became known. The committee was modelled upon the Carbonari, forerunners of Il Risorgimento in Italy.

It is not surprising that the imperative for reform should have taken root among young cadets at one of the few modern schools in Istanbul (the university was not founded until 1900). They were more exposed by their education, location and youth than others in the empire. Perhaps, too, as scions of the provinces rather than the Istanbul establishment, all four were particularly prone to radicalism.

Abdallah Jawdat and Ishaq Sukuti, the two Kurds in question, illustrate the early travails of Kurdish intellectuals, less nationalists than Ottomans committed to reforming the empire as a whole. Yet they represent an important link in the intellectual progress made by educated Kurds from thoughts of reforming empire to those of redemption for the Kurdish people. Jawdat came from Arabkir, whence he had progressed through secondary education at Elazig (Mamurat al Aziz), to Istanbul at the age of 15 in 1884. Sukuti came from Diyarbakir, a larger town but still a provincial backwater. In 1892 several of the conspirators, by now spread through the colleges and training establishments of Istanbul, were picked up by the secret police. Jawdat and Sukuti seem to have been let off with a warning. Both resumed not only their studies but also their subversive extramural pursuits. But in 1895 they were rounded up again and this time exiled to Tripoli, north Africa. Both escaped to Europe via the French protectorate of Tunisia in 1897. Jawdat wrote for Kurdistan (see below), supporting Armenian demands and pleading that Armenians and Kurds 'should walk hand-in-hand'.[1]

However, Jawdat and Sukuti soon revealed their own irresolution. In 1899 they negotiated the suspension of Osmanli, a Young Turk publication established in Geneva two years earlier with the assistance of, among others, another Kurdish exile, Abd al Rahman, son of the great Badr Khan. They persuaded their Young Turk colleagues to agree this price in return for the release of political prisoners (internal exiles) from the notorious fortress of Tripoli. It was a humane act but it contradicted the determination of the Young Turk movement. Their next move the following year was less easy to defend. Both accepted non-political posts in Ottoman embassies, Jawdat in Vienna, and Sukuti in Rome. Neither was forgiven by their erstwhile colleagues. Sukuti died in France in 1902. Abd al Rahman Badr Khan gave him a generous epitaph in Kurdistan,[2] emphasizing Sukuti's devotion to the land of Kurdistan, but his end was a disappointment for other critics of the system.

Jawdat remained an exile, his honour compromised. He had joined the Young Turk Decentralization Party after its formation in 1902, but any political ambitions had already been destroyed by his perceived defection in 1900. He returned to Istanbul in 1911. Although he joined the Kurdish Club at the end of the war he seems to have remained an Ottoman Decentralist.

The Beginnings of Ethnic Awareness

Meanwhile other Kurds had become involved in the political fate of the empire. Two Kurdish dynasties feature prominently in the story, one religious, the other secular: the Sayyids of Nihri (or Shamdinan) and the Badr Khans. Although it only became apparent later, one could describe them as the founders of the two broad strands of Kurdish nationalism, the autonomists and the secessionists. At first both sought solutions within the Ottoman context but when forced to decide they chose different routes. As great families from adjacent parts of central Kurdistan, their rivalry was also symbolic of the factionalism that has been a persistent feature of Kurdish nationalism.

Both families had grounds for discontent. The most active member of the Nihri dynasty was Ubayd Allah's second son, Shaykh Abd al Qadir. After his father's death Abd al Qadir was allowed back to Istanbul, but apparently not to Kurdistan where his elder brother Shaykh Muhammad Sadiq, who seems either to have escaped exile or to have been amnestied sooner, took over the shaykhly leadership;[3] Abd al Qadir resented his brother's spiritual ascendancy and had grounds for hoping that he himself would inherit his father's mantle.[4]

Shaykh Abd al Qadir, on his return to Istanbul, found a channel for his ambitions in political activity. Like Jawdat and Sukuti, he became embroiled in the Committee for Union and Progress. In August 1896 he was among those rounded up when a new conspiracy to overthrow Abd al Hamid was uncovered. Once again, he and his family were exiled. His dissidence, essentially his decision to identify with modernizing reformers, contrasts with the behaviour and beliefs of his father. It would seem that away from Kurdistan where loyalty to the *padishah*, especially one so indulgent as Sultan Abd al Hamid, made sense, Shaykh Abd al Qadir found that the only channel for his ambition lay with the reformists. He was not allowed back to Istanbul until the revolution in 1908.

The Badr Khans had an equally stormy and unreliable record. They had never fully accepted the defeat of Badr Khan himself in 1847. In 1879 two of his many sons, Uthman and Husayn, mounted a short-lived rebellion in Buhtan.[5] In 1880 another son, Badri, played a double game between Istanbul and Shaykh Ubayd Allah. In 1889 two more sons, Amin Ali and Midhat, attempted to rally the tribes, but word got out and they were captured before they had assembled their forces. It is unclear when they were released from custody; but by the late 1890s Midhat was in Cairo where, in April 1898, he commenced publication of a bilingual journal (Kurmanji–Turkish) entitled *Kurdistan*, which both supported 'Union and Progress' and stirred up feelings in support of the Kurdish people, led by its notables and shaykhs. Subsequently *Kurdistan* was published in Geneva, and then London and Folkestone, possibly because the politically active Badr Khans wanted to be in closer touch with Ottoman exiles in Europe. Midhat's brother, Abd al Rahman, an enthusiastic supporter of the Committee for Union and Progress, took over editorship. Together with Hikmat Baban, another Ottoman Kurdish notable, he attended the Young Turk Liberal Congress in Paris in 1902.

The congress proved a landmark in the Young Turk movement, with a decisive split between Ottoman liberals and Turkish nationalists. The former supported Armenian delegates believing that the empire must fulfil its international treaty obligations implicitly regarding protection of the Armenian community. The latter insisted that no outside powers should have any say in the internal affairs of the empire. Abd al Rahman clearly numbered himself among the Ottoman liberals and joined the new Ottoman Decentralization Party which stood for a federal and decentralized Ottoman state. But it failed to attract the Christian *millets*, while with so many external threats most Turks found the call of the nationalist Young Turks, to 'Union and Progress', more attractive.

Because of the development of such currents of thought, it became progressively harder to think in terms of Ottoman citizenship. From 1876 Sultan Abd al Hamid had tapped powerfully into the Muslim sense of embattlement, mobilizing a dimension of Ottoman life which not only permeated society but was the vital link between Sultanate and people, between the political institution and society. That dimension, of course, was embodied in the range of Muslim institutions that existed, from the *shaykh al Islam* in Istanbul to the more pervasive *tariqas* of small towns and countryside. The further one travelled from Istanbul the more the Islamic idea was espoused, particularly in eastern Anatolia, given the Christian threat there. The Sayyids of Nihri, of course, were an integral part of that Muslim network, Shaykh Muhammad Sadiq having extended his father's constituency.

In Istanbul Abd al Hamid's Islamic policy had always had many opponents and sceptics, particularly among the bureaucracy and intelligentsia that had so welcomed the Constitution of 1876. They wanted modernization, as conceived in European terms. Sukuti and Jawdat were clearly among the modernizers. To the end of his life Jawdat remained committed to political, social, intellectual and religious liberty, as he spelt out in a couple of articles entitled 'A Very Wakeful Sleep' in his own journal, *Ijtihad*, in 1912. His own voluminous translations of European (English, German, French and Italian) literature into Turkish (not Kurdish) was in its way a testimony to the consistency of his modernizing belief that 'Civilization means European civilization',[6] an idea later embraced by Ataturk.

Since religion permeated virtually every aspect of everyday life, it was viewed by thinkers like Jawdat, especially those in the bureaucracy, as the most fearful brake on what they sought to do. It was also an instrument for mobilization and manipulation and the Young Turks did not hesitate to use it as such, but it was too a vehicle for the ignorance, prejudice and fanaticism which prevented modernization. The Young Turks therefore had to be careful. Islam was the cement that held together the Ottoman city culture and the folk culture of the countryside, expressed in 'village Islam' and particularly in the *tariqas*. The shaykhly families had to be treated with circumspection.

Yet by 1908, secularism was already a firmly established idea among the Young Turks, even if this could not yet be acknowledged publicly. In 1912 Abdallah Jawdat called for the closure of the religious schools (*madrasas*) and the oratories (*takiyas*) of the sufi *tariqas*, an emerging opinion 'brought to its logical end by the Founding Fathers of the Turkish Republic'[7] when they established a laicist regime in 1923.

Alongside this growing frustration with the empire's Muslim institutions, Young Turks had watched as Greeks, Serbs and Armenians had moved from *millet* to ethnic national identity. Muslims, on the other hand, remained part of one *umma*, regardless of whether they were Sunni or Shi'i, Turk, Arab or Kurd. It was inevitable that this traditional identity should come under scrutiny, since it contradicted the modern ideas that had invaded the empire, and since the *millets* had themselves rejected the system. A specifically Turkish awareness was the first to become apparent, stimulated by the flow of Turkish refugees from Russian rule. By the end of the century Turanic and pan-Turanic ideas were attracting interest among Istanbul's intellectuals.

The Turkish reassessment of the *millet* system and their own assertion of ethnic identity made it inevitable that other members of the Muslim *umma* should do likewise. The opportunity of the latter group to do so openly came with the Young Turk Revolution of July 1908. The Committee of Union and Progress (CUP) which took power immediately proclaimed the revival of the 1876 Constitution and the equality of all Ottoman citizens, Muslim and non-Muslim, and announced elections. *'Dastur'* (constitution), *'mashrutiyat'* (constitutional government) and *'hurriya'* (freedom) became the ill-understood slogans of revolution all over the empire.

Among the educated these developments were received with euphoria and rejoicing. There seemed to be an emphasis on *Ottoman* brotherhood, yet by now ethnic identity was already an issue, even among the Kurds.[8] Not every Kurd felt the appeal of Kurdish identity. Then, as now, some identified wholeheartedly with the official ideology and embraced the growing Turkic identity of the new ruling elite. There were some striking examples. Ismail Hakki Baban, arguably not really Kurdish, was influential in the CUP's inner circles. He was elected deputy for Baghdad in the new parliament, was closely associated with *Tanin*, the principal organ of the CUP, and became minister of education in the new government, intent on promoting Turkism.

Two other Kurds also stood out as pioneers of Turkism. One was Sulayman Nazif, a politician, administrator and noted journalist. He served as Wali of Mosul in 1914, where he took vigorous action against the Barzani Kurds, and from 1915 as Acting Wali of Baghdad. The other was Ziya Gokalp, who played a major role laying the ideogical basis of Turkish nationalism.

Gokalp, or Muhammad Ziya to give him his original name, was born in Diyarbakir in 1876. His father was a minor administrator in the city and Gokalp, though Kurdish, grew up with the outlook of an urban Ottoman and with a natural disdain for the Kurdish culture of the countryside. As a young man he was gripped by the writings of Abdallah Jawdat. He rose to national prominence at the CUP Conference of 1909, where he represented Diyarbakir. He was elected a member of the party's executive council, and such was his ideological contribution to Turkish national identity (see chapter 9) that beyond his death in 1924 his 'ideas created an intellectual movement that provided the inspiration needed for a change in popular mentality from empire to nation, from religious to secular, from East to West.'[9]

However, other urban notables wished to qualify their support of the Ittihadist movement with their own ethnic identity. A handful of Istanbul's educated Kurdish elite formed a number of Kurdish societies about which we know little. The first was The Society for the Rise and Progress of Kurdistan (Kurdistan Ta'ali wa Taraqi Jamiyati).[10] Among the founders were Amin Ali Badr Khan, Shaykh Abd al Qadir of Nihri and General Muhammad Sharif Pasha, a Baban from Sulaymaniya, a Decentralist and hostile to the Young Turks. Similar Kurdish groups were also formed in Diyarbakir, Bitlis, Mosul and Baghdad. A cultural affiliate in Istanbul, the Society for the Propagation of Kurdish Education, was also established, opening a school (under the direction of Abd al Rahman Badr Khan) to serve some of the children of the 30,000 or so Kurds in the city. Among those associated with the school was Sayyid Nursi of Bitlis.

Sayyid Nursi deserves mention because he inhabited that ambiguous terrain where religious and ethnic identities overlap. He had already made a reputation for himself in Istanbul as a proponent of Kurdish identity. In 1896 he had given Sultan Abd al Hamid cause for suspicion when his proposals for Islamic reform gave special emphasis to the Kurdish population. Far from being separatist in intent, however, Sayyid Nursi probably hoped to foster a sense of Muslim identity that would transcend kinship networks in Kurdish society. He petitioned the Sultan a decade later, probably only weeks before the revolution, arguing for Kurdish-speaking teachers to be sent to Kurdistan to extend Ottoman secular education. It was, he asserted, essential to produce an educated Kurdish-speaking cadre to turn the Kurdish tribesmen into good Ottoman citizens. He wanted to upgrade the *madrasas* (religious schools) to provide a mixture of religious and secular studies, and establish an eastern university along the lines of al Azhar to provide higher education:

> I have seen the miserable state of the tribes in the Eastern provinces.... Everyone knows that in those provinces the fate of the semi-nomadic citizens is in the hands of the *ulama*. And it is this which led me to come to the capital.[11]

Sayyid Nursi never became a Kurdish separatist. Two years after the revolution, he advocated regional autonomy for Diyarbakir. This, of course, could have been no more welcome to the CUP than his association with the Muslim Union, implicated in the abortive Hamidian counter-coup of April 1909. But it suggests that, like Shaykh Abd al Qadir, Sayyid Nursi remained committed to the integrity of the Ottoman sultanate. He simply wanted his own woefully backward people to achieve full stature within it.

A number of journals began to appear. A Turkish language journal, *Kurt Teavun we Teraki Gazetesi* (Kurdish Mutual aid and Progress Gazette) was produced by the society of that name, the first legally circulated Kurdish journal. *Kurdistan* moved from exile to Istanbul and came under the editorship of Suraya Badr Khan, Amin Ali's son.

Competitive tensions between the Badr Khans and Shaykh Abd al Qadir arose almost immediately. The latter, not to be outdone by Kurdistan, started his own journal, *Hitavi Kurd* (Kurdish Sun). He may also have formed a breakaway group from the original party. Despite his previous absence in exile, Shaykh Abd al Qadir almost certainly enjoyed a bigger following in Istanbul, with considerable influence over its artisan guilds. Indicative of this, he became a member of the Ottoman Senate and President of the Council of State. The Badr Khans enjoyed no such power base, either in Istanbul or in Kurdistan itself. However, these rivalries were rapidly overtaken by political developments.

The liberalism of the Young Turks proved shortlived. The CUP members' chauvinist inclinations were exacerbated by Austria's immediate seizure of Bosnia and Herzegovina and by Bulgaria's declaration of independence. After the abortive countercoup of April 1909 in which, incidentally, the insurgents had been mobilized with the cry 'the *sharia* (Muslim law) is imperilled', the CUP cracked down. Abd al Hamid was deposed, the liberals banished to the sidelines, and in August a 'Law of Associations' prohibited the formation of political associations based on or bearing the name of ethnic or national groups. Although the primary targets were Greek and Bulgarian groups, the Kurdish Society was also closed down and apparently went underground. Amin Ali Badr Khan and General Sharif Pasha were both condemned to death for contumacy and had to flee the country. Given General Sharif's known loyalty to the deposed sultan, it is likely that he and Amin Ali were associated with the abortive counter-coup.[12]

In Istanbul the CUP continued on its authoritarian and chauvinist path. Turkish ethno-nationalism spread rapidly. As far away as Muhammara (Khoramshahr) Arnold Wilson, a British political officer, listened to the Turkish consul, who three years earlier had been filled with a euphoric sense of Ottoman brother-hood, now including 'Arabs and Armenians, Christian Syrians and Jews, Kurds and Assyrians within the ambit of his comprehensive curses. Turks and Turks alone, can govern them, and only with rods of iron and whips of scorpions.'[13]

The CUP was quite correct in sensing the rapid spread of ethno-nationalism among other groups. In 1910 Shaykh Abd al Qadir apparently issued a notice in the Istanbul press to the effect that the Kurds wanted autonomy. Its probable intention was to allay CUP suspicions, but it must have increased them for it produced schism within Istanbul's Kurdish ranks.[14] As a result, a group of young Kurds organized a new group, Hivi-ya Kurd Jamiyati (Kurdish Hope Society), which began to distribute a weekly paper, *Ruji Kurd*. Hivi enjoyed a wider mem-bership, with many more fresh and younger faces, sons of urban notables and of Hamidiya chiefs who had been sent from Kurdistan to receive a formal Ottoman education.[15] Yet, as with subsequent schisms in 1919, the members of Hivi never fully separated. On the whole individual members represented tendencies, not clear-cut factions.

How far were these groups nationalist, and what does nationalism in the Ottoman context mean? No one can doubt that they were an expression of Kurdish identity, but they did not yet express a desire to secede. That is clear from the composition of the groups: young notables, most of whom welcomed the revolution of 1908, and one or two, like General Muhammad Sharif Pasha, who regretted the overthrow of Abd al Hamid.

There is another important facet to this expression of Kurdish distinctiveness. The centralizing measures of the CUP, once it was firmly in the saddle, were perceived by many provincial notables as a danger to their own position. Where the influence of provincial notables can be traced at that time, in Ottoman political parties and as deputies in parliament, it is clear that they were made very uneasy by the authoritarian implications of the CUP on their own status locally. This may in part explain why Hivi-ya Kurd Jamiyati included deputies from the provinces and the sons of notables and chiefs whose importance lay in Kurdistan, while the Kurdistan Taali wa Taraqi Jamiyati, established in the first liberal flush of 1908, was solely composed of Istanbul notables.

Kurdistan and the Young Turk Revolution

There was good reason for the air of rejoicing in the towns and villages of Kurdistan when freedom and the revival of the constitution were proclaimed. Whatever else it might turn out to mean, people understood that it heralded orderly rule and an end to the Hamidiya regiments, which were duly disbanded. The whole notion of *mashrutiyat*, however, also unleashed wild speculation. In 1909 a new journal, *Payman*, appeared in Diyarbakir. One contributor wrote enthusiastically that *mashrutiyat* meant 'the agha system is about taking from the poor.... There is not an agha system anymore. We are all Ottoman citizens.'[16]

How threatening all this was to the agha class is demonstrated by the vivid description of their influence, written by Ziya Gokalp the very same year:

> Once the village agha has got a member of the administration in his hands through his capacity in the art of surreptitiously gaining the ear of the powerful, he immediately tries to save the men of conscription age in his village from the army, the criminals from the courts, those who owe taxes and labour commutation dues from the tax collector. He lives like an independent prince in the confines of his villages through these services. He collects dues from crimes, marriages, 'marriage by capture' and receives various other benefits. The villagers, who in their opinion are now under obligation, pay the sums for animal taxes in the exact amount to the agha, and in order not to permit any other tax farmer in the villager except the agha, become secretive, commit false accusations, give false evidence, and do all else that is necessary.[17]

It might, incidentally, be thought that the growing number of migrants to Istanbul had escaped the clutches of their old aghas, but even there some migrants learnt to expect a visit from tribal retainers collecting the agha's dues.

No wonder those associated with the old regime saw the revolution as a direct threat. There was another specific reason why certain aghas and shaykhs felt threatened. They had seized Armenian lands following the massacres of 1895 and, in the first liberal flush of revolution, the CUP indicated a desire to restore these lands to their rightful owners. One of the Sultan's protégés whose depredations had been indulged for years, was Ibrahim Pasha, chief of the Milli, a large confederation which included Arab tributaries in northern Jazira.[18] It was his harassment of Diyarbakir that had led to popular protests in that city *against the sultan*. Ziya Gokalp had been among the demonstrators.

Four weeks after the declaration of the constitution in Istanbul, Ibrahim Pasha rose in revolt. He may have hoped to incite all Syria but his men were rapidly surrounded by a large Ottoman force at his seat, Viranshahir. He died in a Shammar ambush in the nearby hills and the Milli, deliberated crushed by the authorities, disappeared as a formidable unit.

Ibrahim Pasha's rapid demise delighted the citizens of Diyarbakir but sent a shock wave through the old classes of chiefs, notables and shaykhs who had done well under Sultan Abd al Hamid. In the autumn of 1909 a group of these, mainly old Hamidiya officers led by Husayn Pasha Haydaranli, slipped over the border where the Khan of Maku, who fancied independence from Tehran, made them welcome. Their dislike of the new constitution was increased by the new government's determination to extract tax arrears for their freebooting years pre-1908.

Meanwhile, a number of religious shaykhs began stirring up local feeling against the new regime. Ever since the beginning of the *tanzimat* the shaykhs had disliked the new vocabulary of the Ottoman reformers that included terms like 'nation' and 'society' in place of '*umma*', appealing to abstract and secular concepts rather than loyalty to the sultan and caliph. Sultan Abd al Hamid had offered a respite for thirty years; now the alarm bells were ringing again and nowhere more than in eastern Anatolia. 'This is the end of Islam,' exclaimed the Kurdish Mufti of Kharput, on hearing of the revolution.[19]

In the wake of the failed counter-coup of April 1909, other conspiracies were made. There was talk of simultaneous risings in Istanbul and Syria, and groups of conspirators met in northern Kurdistan/Armenia under the leadership of Hamidiya chiefs and religious shaykhs.[20] These, according to Arshak Safrastian, the British vice-consul in Bitlis, had

> taken oath upon the Koran and their religion to be faithful to their vow and to the cause of the Sheriat ... to carry on a relentless campaign against everything undertaken by the Young Turks.... The Young Turks are represented as entirely irreligious and violators of Mahommadan traditions, as laughing at prayers, *namaz*, and all such religious duties.[21]

A rumour began to circulate that a certain 'Ibrahim Pasha' was touring the region raising recruits and spreading sedition. Even dead, Ibrahim Pasha's name was clearly potent as a rallying call for dissident shaykhs and chiefs interested in general uprising. A year later Safrastian reported from Bitlis that 'common talk says there's a secret organization among the chiefs to rise against the constitutional government.'[22]

Further south there was trouble too. Shaykh Said Barzinji, leader of the Qadiri order in Sulaymaniya, instigated a revolt against the new regime as soon as word of the new constitution reached him. Fear of loss of power and status seem to have been the reason for revolt. The Barzinji shaykhs had exploited the power vacuum following the demise of the Babans to extend their control over trade in Sulaymaniya itself, a prosperous town on the Baghdad–Tehran trade route, and over villages in the surrounding countryside. The Barzinjis enjoyed an aura of sanctity among the faithful, but among the ordinary traders of Sulaymaniya and the peasants of the neighbourhood they were known for their rapacity. Shaykh Said had been a favoured son of the ancien régime having scored a success in Istanbul by healing Sultan Abd al Hamid's favourite son. Thereafter it was said that he enjoyed carte blanche with local officials enriching himself at the expense of Sulaymaniya's citizenry. By intermarriage with the Hamawand, he had bought himself into the lucrative business of looting caravans between Sulaymaniya and Kirkuk.[23]

Threatened with the new Ittihadist broom, Shaikh Said encouraged the Hamawand, who had already been raiding unchecked for the preceding two years, to revolt against the irreligious *dastur*. With insufficient troops to defeat them, the authorities had persuaded the shaykh in March 1909 to come to Mosul to parley. While there he was killed during a public affray. Whether or not the authorities were behind his murder, the event plunged the Sulaymaniya region into renewed disorder. His son, Shaykh Mahmud, instructed the Hamawand to renew their insurrection. They were still in revolt at the outbreak of the First World War.

It should have been a source of encouragement that, in spite of such local difficulties, the Ittihadists substantially improved the economy and general level of order in the region after 1908. The Armenian and Kurdish peasantry were more secure and prosperous than they had been in living memory. Yet this was precisely the source of anxiety: with many chiefs skulking over the border, the growing signs of harmony between Kurds and Armenians posed a threat to the eastern ramparts of empire.

This was no idle fear, there being specific grounds for government apprehension. In the autumn of 1909 Shaykh Abd al Qadir, albeit President of the Ottoman Council of State, travelled to Shamdinan where he organized a Kurdo-Armenian congress. His words, loyal to the CUP's official rhetoric, were nevertheless disturbing to his increasingly authoritarian and Turkicist rulers, 'We must live like brothers with the Armenians. We must restore those lands which they claim and which have not yet been restored. We will work to strengthen understanding and concord among Ottoman compatriots.'[24] Abd al Qadir was also rumoured to have conferred with local chiefs, possibly with those sulking over the border. Whatever his game, he was detained on his return to Istanbul.[25]

It was not the first time such fears had surfaced. Following three visits to the region in the 1890s, Lord Percy had written: 'While the government is not afraid of either the Kurds or the Christians singly, they view with considerable apprehension the possibility of an understanding between the two races for the purposes of common defence'.[26] Percy said he knew cases where Kurdish chiefs had made overtures to Armenian village headmen. Eighteen months before the 1908 revolution the governor of Erzerum had intercepted a letter from Armenian revolutionaries to certain Hamidiya chiefs encouraging them to join them.

There was something particularly disturbing about religious dignitaries befriending the Armenians. In the autumn of 1910 Sayyid Nursi himself passed through Diyarbakir and, while careful to claim loyalty to the CUP, he urged Kurds to unite and sink their differences. 'Kurdistan belonged to the Kurds and Armenians, not to the Turks,' he told his audience, repeating an appeal to ethnicity which had previously disturbed Abd al Hamid.[27] While he may not yet have advocated political union, the implications of his feelings of brotherhood towards the Armenians were unmistakable: 'Union is the great task of our time. Love is the innate nature of that union, that non-Muslims may be convinced that our unity is an offensive against three ills – ignorance, poverty and discord.'[28]

If Sayyid Nursi was a mere flash in the pan, the government might have been less concerned; but other shaykhs, too, had tilted towards regional autonomy in Kurdistan. North-east of Mosul, Shaykhs Abd al Salam of Barzan and Nur Muhammad of Dohuk organized a petition for the five qadhas (administrative districts) of Bahdinan, demanding the adoption of Kurdish for official and educational purposes; the appointment of Kurdish-speaking officials; the adoption of the Shafi'i school of law and the administration of law and justice according to the *sharia*; and finally taxation only in accordance with *sharia*, or in exemption from the *corvée*, the revenue being applied to public works within the five qadhas. Copies of the petition were sent to the three perceived leaders of Kurdish sentiment in Istanbul, Shaykh Abd al Qadir, Amin Ali Badr Khan and General Sharif Pasha, suggesting that awareness of the ethnic dimension was really taking hold even in the remoter parts of Kurdistan.

Meanwhile, Shaykh Abd al Qadir's rivals, the Badr Khans, had themselves been in contact with discontented shaykhs and chiefs ranging from Buhtan to the Iranian border. By the end of 1911 those Badr Khans resident in Buhtan were co-ordinating the groundswell of opposition to the CUP among aghas and shaykhs in the region, as far afield as the notorious Shaykh of Khizan, near Bitlis. 'There is no apparent propaganda,' reported the British vice-consul in Diyarbakir, 'but a very secret understanding, which has not yet been ripened.'[29] However, rumours of the Badr Khans' ability to raise 50,000 men had the CUP worried. During 1912 Badr Khan activity increased.

There was another alarming dimension to the rumours that flurried around Kurdistan, that of Russian intrigue. Russia's occupation of Khoi and Urumiya in 1909, ostensibly to evict the Ottomans from their seizure of Iranian territory in 1905, had already created apprehensions in Istanbul.[30] In August 1910 Abd al Razzaq Badr Khan had come out of his Parisian exile to travel to Tabriz and disseminate tracts on the idea of Kurdish autonomy under Russian protection.[31]

In December 1911 he crossed the border and began whipping up fears of Armenian rule in Anatolia, informing his listeners that Russia could give the Kurds protectorate status. In Iran he was also negotiating with Simqu of the Shikak, himself on close terms with the Russians, another warning to Istanbul that Russia might be serious about creating a dependent Kurdish enclave.

There was growing disquiet in Istanbul at the number of Kurds who had responded to Russian overtures. Apart from Abd al Razzaq the most prominent of these was Shaykh Taha, the new head of the Sayyids of Nihri. Shaykh Taha had taken over on his father's death in 1911. The authorities had always been suspicious of Muhammad Sadiq but had never been able to pin anything on him. Shaykh Taha, however, lacked his father's discretion and word of his Russian correspondence was soon out.

By the spring of 1913 the potential line-up of nationalist Kurds was beginning to look formidable. The charismatic head of the Badr Khans in Buhtan, Husayn, and his cousin Abd al Razzaq were both independently campaigning to advance the idea of autonomy and whip up resistance to the CUP. Now they were trying to involve important local leaders, for example Shaykh Abd al Salam of Barzan, Shaykh Taha of Nihri, Mar Shimun and even Yazidi leaders. With Shaykh Taha's rumoured ability to raise 30,000 men, such a coalition might field an irregular force of 100,000 easily enough with Russian support to pose a major threat to Ottoman sovereignty over Kurdistan.

Faced with such mounting dangers, Kurdish dissidence, Armenian and Russian intrigue, and the same social conditions that Abd al Hamid had faced, the government had to admit that the agha system had proved too strong and it resorted to the Hamidian habits which it had disavowed in the first flush of revolution. In July 1910 the governor of Van had sent Shaykh Muhammad Sadiq to Iran to entice the old Hamidiya chiefs back from Iran. Having abolished the Hamidiya it now reconstituted it under a new name, the Tribal Light Cavalry Regiments, and the whole policy of breaking the power and lawlessness of the Kurdish chiefs on the eastern marches began to be reversed. Some aghas even enrolled in branch committees of the CUP, though it was anyone's guess whether this represented a success for the CUP or for the aghas.

These new broom secularists of the CUP even revived the Hamidian pan-Islamic policy to keep the Kurds away from the Armenians and wary of the Russians. From autumn 1910 several delegations were sent from Istanbul to ginger up the Kurdish chiefs against the infidel. This helped stem Kurdo-Armenian co-operation. At the end of the year three CUP inspectors, all belonging to a pan-Islamic society, toured among the tribes telling the chiefs to prepare for war against Russia. The ex-minister of finance made a similar tour in summer 1911, leaving 'a strongly pan-Islamic impression in Bitlis'.[32]

Bitlis was a well-known troublespot, not least because of the notoriously unruly shaykhs of Khizan. When Abd al Razzaq made them his first port of call during his visit in December 1911, the government immediately rushed substantial quantities of ammunition to Bitlis. With regard to Shaykh Taha in Shamdinan, the government adopted a policy of divide and rule. Late in 1912 they reluctantly pardoned Shaykh Abd al Qadir, untrustworthy though he seemed, since he would waste no time in trying to undermine his nephew.[33] That left the Badr Khans as their chief concern.

It was at this juncture that the government enjoyed a stroke of good fortune. Husayn Badr Khan, the dynamo behind the conspiracy, was killed in May 1913. His brother Hasan soldiered on, informing the British vice-consul visiting Jazira that he was ready to revolt but would be satisfied if the government granted the Kurds what it had promised to the Arabs, namely the appointment of officials who spoke the vernacular, and the expenditure locally of tax revenue.[34] But the whole enterprise had quickly run out of steam with Husayn's death.

Possibly because of these developments the co-ordinated rising so feared in Istanbul never materialized. Instead, two quite separate and spontaneous risings occurred, both with religious overtones.

The Barzan and Bitlis Risings

On the Greater Zab in the Mosul vilayet, the shaykhs of Barzan had been an uncomfortable presence for about 50 years. Their establishment at Barzan had caused conflict with the powerful Zibari chiefs on the left bank, by attracting non-tribal Zibari peasantry to switch fealty. To the north their relations had remained consistently bad with the Sayyids of Nihri, to whom the Barzanis had originally been disciples. By the end of the nineteenth century the Barzanis had become one of the five most powerful religious families of Kurdistan. This caused plenty of tension with the governor of Mosul who tended to exert authority through the Barzanis' enemies, the Zibari chiefs.

Relations seriously deteriorated, however, following the 1908 revolution. On the one hand Shaykh Abd al Salam Barzani viewed the new 'atheistic' regime with horror; on the other, the new government was determined to compel men like him to pay their tax dues regularly, yield conscripts and integrate within the ambit of government administration. The next few years were characterized by repeated armed clashes in which the government suffered heavy casualties. Shaykh Abd al Salam's petition (see p. 98 above) indicated his ambitions were more than those of a mere mountain chief and implied association with ethnic nationalists in Istanbul. Thereafter he was a marked man. The two reassuring facts for the Ottomans were his repudiation of Russian overtures and hostility to Shaykh Taha of Nihri.

Early in 1914 word reached Mosul that the shaykh had buried his differences and formed an alliance with Shaykh Taha, Abd al Razzaq Badr Khan and, by implication, the Russians. In March Ottoman troops moved against him. Defeated in battle Shaykh Abd al Salam fled to Urumiya and briefly to Tiflis. On his way to meet Simqu in the border area of Somai-Baradust he was waylaid by Shikak tribesmen, possibly on Simqu's orders, and handed over to the Ottomans. He was hanged at the end of the year.

At a pinch, Shaykh Abd al Salam's rising could be dismissed as a local difficulty that had occurred in an isolated region, and his appeal to religious and ethnic identity ignored. It was less easy to be sanguine over the revolt that erupted in Bitlis. Here it was well known that a certain Mulla Salim had been deliberately stirring up local shaykhs in Khizan district to rise against the government. Khizan was the hub of a *tariqa* network with long tentacles, one that was in liaison with the Badr Khans in Buhtan and with opponents of the CUP in Istanbul. This network was also relatively close to the Russians now deployed on the Iranian side of the border. There was reason to think that this agitation was fermenting into a general uprising. The authorities sought to nip it in the bud. In March they tried to arrest Mulla Salim, and the Khizan shaykhs decided to act. One of them called on the Bitlis governor to restore the *sharia* and to withdraw all 'atheist' officials. In the absence of a response the Kurdish rebels occupied part of Bitlis. The townspeople, however, wanted nothing to do with the rebellion. Thirty years of lawlessness had not made town-dwellers remotely sympathetic to people they saw as rural riff-raff. Without wider support Mulla Salim dismissed his men and sought asylum in the Russian consulate. Thus the Bitlis rising ended as a damp squib.

The problem for would-be Kurdish rebels was one of co-ordination. As the British vice-consul in Bitlis reported, 'Could the Kurds combine against the Government even in one province, the Turkish troops in their eastern part of Asia Minor would find it difficult to crush the revolt.'[35] Lack of co-ordination remained the Kurds' Achilles heel.

Istanbul remained apprehensive of Kurdish intentions and did what it could to stamp out any hint of sedition. When it learnt that certain Kurds had secretly met the Russians in Khoi in July 1914, it sent its agents to assassinate those involved. When war with Russia was declared three months later, it was rumoured in Van that all the Kurdish tribes had gone over to the enemy. No wonder Istanbul was nervous.

Iran

In contrast with events in the Ottoman world, there was barely a whisper of Kurdish national sentiment in Iran at this stage. We have only one hint of early inclinations towards autonomy, other than the natural desire of the chiefs to throw off external interference. In 1886 there was apparently a brief autonomy movement in Sawj Bulaq led by the Mukri governor. After his accidental death it petered out. Then, in about 1900 Shaykh Qazi Fattah, chief mulla of the town, led a fresh movement supported by a few dissident chiefs. Most prominent of these, predictably, were the Mangur aghas who must have been partly guided by their feud with the Mamash, who equally predictably offered to assist the

authorities suppress this dissidence. Shaykh Qazi Fattah was guaranteed safe
conduct to Tabriz to present his two demands: a freeze on tax increases and an
assurance that the governorship of Sawj Bulaq would normally be held by a local
man. It was the second demand, of course, which was unacceptable. Qazi Fattah
was seized and taken to Tehran.

Following the 1906 revolution tension between Sunni and Shi'i in Azarbaijan
grew rapidly, fuelled by growing Shi'i consciousness, but also because Kurdish
tribes were creating so much disorder and deliberately, or so it seemed, trying to
undermine the constitutional movement.

In fact, religious tensions masked an essentially class, rather than ethnic,
conflict. All over the Kurdish region, in towns such as Khoi, Salmas, Urumiya,
Sawj Bulaq, Saqqiz, Sanandaj, Kirmanshah and in certain villages *anjumans* were
formed as elsewhere in Iran in support of the constitution. In the case of Sawj
Bulaq, Shaykh Qazi Fattah, released in the wake of the revolution, assumed
leadership of the town *anjuman*.

The impulse for these committees was not some kind of ethno-nationalism
but the desire to run affairs locally on a representational basis. Townsfolk wished
to be rid of corrupt and manipulative governors imposed upon them from
outside, and village peasantry wished to mobilize themselves against their landlords, many of whom were tribal chiefs. Townspeople and villagers shared a
common aim: that of reducing landlords' profits, either from their villages or
from highly priced food stuffs.

It was inevitable, therefore, that Kurdish aghas were hostile to the *anjumans*
and some were willing to act. Ismail Simqu, leader of the Abdui branch of the
Shikak, for example, gave the Khan of Maku his unsolicited support in the
suppression of the *anjuman*s, and was rewarded with the governorship of Qutur.[36]

World War

The Turks need not have been so anxious about Kurdish loyalties. In the end
only a handful of Kurds were attracted to the Russian cause, and Kurdo-Armenian
solidarity never materialized. The Jaf, Hamavand and Dizai all toyed with Russian
offers of help. Only three Kurds of any note actually defected: Shaykh Taha of
Shamdinan, who ended up distrusted by everyone;[37] Abd al Razzaq, already in
Tiflis, who continued to hope Russia would fulfil his hopes for Kurdish independence; and his uncle, Kamil, who went to Tiflis to persuade the Russian
commander, the Grand Duke Nicholas, of the Kurdish national cause.[38]

For all their flirtatious behaviour, the Russians never evolved a coherent policy
towards the Kurds, largely because Kurdish aspirations were bound to clash with
Armenian ones. It suited Russia in its policy with both Kurds and Armenians to
encourage dissidence in order to weaken the Ottoman hold on the region, but
not in order to permit either Armenian or Kurdish independence. Russia wanted
eastern Anatolia for itself.

World war plunged Kurdistan into greater disorder than at any time since Chaldiran. During the next four years armies marched and counter-marched across the land, laying waste life, property and landscape. Turkey pre-empted the formal declaration of war on 30 October with a raid by 400 tribal cavalry intended to disrupt Russian positions around Urumiya at the beginning of the month. It was anxious to prevent a thrust from the direction of Khoi or Urumiya, since the Russians had built a railhead to Julfa. The Russian response was to expel not only the raiding party, but also all Kurds and other Sunnis from around Urumiya. Turkey responded in kind, expelling Armenians from the border zone.[39]

Ethnic cleansing now became an essential ingredient of the conflict, as some had forseen.[40] When Russian forces briefly penetrated beyond Bayazid (Dogu-bayazit) to Alashkirt in December 1914, they garrisoned the area with Armenian troops, many of whom were ex-Ottoman citizens. By the time they left, only one tenth of the largely Kurdish population of the area, it was claimed, had survived.[41] While the Turkish Third Army destroyed itself in the snows around Sarikamish in January 1915,[42] a subsidiary force moved through further south to capture Urumiya and Tabriz at the beginning of January, while the Russian forces occupying Iranian Azarbaijan retired northwards. Most Armenians and Assyrians fled in panic northwards in the wake of the Russian army. Many died of exposure. Those who remained flocked into Urumiya. Here and in the surrounding villages, the Christian population was subjected to all manner of atrocity at the hands of Turkish troops and Kurdish auxiliaries.

Iran had, in fact, declared its neutrality almost as soon as war had erupted. It repeatedly asked Russia to withdraw its forces from Azarbaijan; but with Russia using the compliant governor-general of the province against Turkish forces, Turkey was able to argue that Iran was far from neutral. It sent letters to the tribal chiefs in Iran, telling them that a refusal to help the Turkish *jihad* to get rid of the Russians was tantamount to disloyalty to the shah. Further south similar calls to *jihad* were made by Shaykh Abd al Qadir of Nihri and by the Tawila shaykhs. Those tribes that had failed to benefit from the Russian troops' presence since 1909 now had an opportunity to fight the Russians and undermine those tribes patronized by them, while those that had enjoyed Russian patronage also reassessed where the balance of advantage lay. Tribesmen of the Shikak, Mamash, Mangur, Zarza, Herki and Begzadeh tribes all now played an active part in the reign of terror. Relief came to the Christians of Urumiya when Russian forces reoccupied Azarbaijan in May, but it was shortlived, since they were compelled to withdraw in July.

Inside Ottoman borders the Turks had been preparing themselves for the Russian onslaught in spring 1915. Essential to that preparation was the removal of all those potentially friendly-to-the-enemy forces, in short the Armenian and other major Christian communities of the region. On 27 May the Council of Ministers in Istanbul approved the deportation of populations 'suspected of being guilty of treason or espionage'.[43]

In fact the deportations and massacres had already begun. By the last week of April 1915 soldiers and Kurdish tribesmen were

> sweeping the countryside, massacring men, women, and children and burning their homes. Babies were shot in their mothers' arms, small children were horribly mutilated, women were stripped and beaten.[44]

These were not isolated incidents but a state of general mayhem in Erzerum, Bitlis, Mush, Sasun, Zaytun, and a number of other locations including most of Cilicia. The Armenians of Van came under seige by the Kurds after those in surrounding villages had been massacred. On 30 May Muslims, which in practice broadly meant Turks and Kurds in the towns and Kurds in the countryside, were formally allowed to take over 'abandoned' Armenian property. Over the next twelve months or so, about one million Armenians perished.

The Turks and Kurds also moved against the warlike Tiyari Assyrians of Hakkari. They were probably motivated by the fear of a Russian advance into the area and the known desire of the Assyrians for Russian protection. The Tiyari Assyrians knew of the fate of their brethren on the Urumiya plain and, when faced with the Ottoman attack in the summer of 1915, decided to respond to indications of Russian material support by declaring war on Turkey. Mar Shimun had already made his way to Urumiya with a small fighting force to make contact with Russian forces. His hope had been for a Russian advance into Hakkari. When he learnt this was not possible he returned to evacuate his whole flock, which was already under repeated assaults by neighbouring Kurdish tribes. About 15,000 reached Urumiya.

In some cases Kurds spared their Christian victims because they were neighbours with whom they had enjoyed cordial relations or because they had been subject *rayyat* who merited protection. But these occasions were probably the exception rather than the rule, for friendly Kurds were threatened with punishment by the authorities if they did not obey orders to evict or kill. Some of the Alevi (*qizilbash*) Kurds, possibly on account of fellow feeling with another persecuted minority or because some of them were themselves recent converts, gave refuge to Christians.[45]

Why did the Kurds co-operate in government orders so willingly? It is tempting to accept the argument that the struggle was purely an ethnic one. That certainly may have been true for the Young Turk ideologues who had little time for the old ideas of Sultan and *millet* and had a nasty surprise in store for the Kurds themselves; but it is no explanation at all for Kurdish behaviour. This could be seen as revenge for reported atrocities at Bayazid and Alashkirt. Yet the massacres would probably have happened in any case, for they were also a climax to the tribal lawlessness that had developed since the latter part of the nineteenth century, and to the rising tension between a Muslim empire and its enemies. Muslim identity certainly counted for much. The Kurds were constantly reminded of their own potential weakness and vulnerability by the connections their Christian neighbours enjoyed with the hostile European powers. It is no accident that atrocities were worse the further east one went, where the Russian danger was greatest, and those areas where tribes gave protection to Armenians were well away from the battlegrounds. In short, most Kurds involved in the massacres probably felt it was a question of 'them or us'.

When the Russians advanced into Anatolia in July 1915 they expelled the few Kurdish villagers they found and relieved Van. On the whole they acted with restraint, and did not permit Armenians to colonize abandoned Kurdish settlements. Some Armenians revenged themselves on those Kurds who fell into their hands, giving excuse for future atrocities on the Christian population. When the Russians were compelled to withdraw at the end of the month, 200,000 Christians abandoned their homes and followed the army, ambushed repeatedly by roving Kurdish bands.

Besides their involvement in the Armenian genocide, the Kurds also provided substantial manpower for the Ottoman army. Thousands of Kurdish conscripts perished with the Third Army at Sarikamish, and on other fronts. Naturally, there was an almost universal reluctance to serve in the regular army, but even so, many were enrolled and the greater part of the Ottoman forces in the region were Kurdish.[46] Service with the tribal regiments was preferred since at least privation and death were endured *en famille*, so to speak. Some tribes refused conscription point-blank, among them certain Alevi tribes of Dersim.

After the first couple of years the authorities changed their tack and raised territorial regiments, locally based and commanded by Kurds, the rank and file made up of army deserters and refugees – hardly the stuff of glory, but in practice it kept marauding bands on the Ottoman side. Tribal troops were offered food but no pay, but were allowed to take turns with other family members.

It is a grim irony that the Kurds participated in the destruction of the Armenian people unaware of Young Turk plans for themselves. An imperial decree authorized the deportation of Kurds for resettlement in west Anatolia, in locations where they were not to exceed 5 per cent of the population. Notables and chiefs were to be settled in towns and cities and all connection with their tribes or followers forbidden. It was intended that no tribesmen were to return to the ancestral habitat at the end of hostilities. It is unclear when this programme was first evolved. Sultan Abd al Hamid had spoken of the need to assimilate the Kurdish element into the Ottoman state but that was an ambiguous statement. However, in 1913 the CUP had introduced an administrative order to regulate tribal locations, and in 1917 this was amended making it crystal clear that the specific intention was to eliminate Kurdish identity by dispersing Kurds in small groups. It was a case of genocide for the irredeemable Armenians and forcible assimilation for the quarrelsome but Muslim Kurds.

The CUP never advertised its plan but did partially implement it. It could do so under cover of its scorched earth policy, removing the civilian population and destroying everything as it retreated In order to deny the Russians any kind of succour. Probably as many as 700,000 civilians were forcibly removed by the Turkish authorities, apparently to deny the enemy shelter or revictualling. It was unlikely that much pressure was needed: thousands of civilians instinctively fled from advancing Russian or Armenian forces in the provinces of Van, Bitlis and Erzerum. Half of those displaced may have perished, but some thousands were also resettled in the west – as the assimilation plan had intended.

A significantly different situation developed in the southern part of Iranian Kurdistan. Here, too, the conflict had a strong religious dimension. To be sure, Russia was profoundly unwelcome but so also were the Sunni Turks. Only the Kalhur toyed with helping the Turks and then only as mercenaries.[47] The Sanjabi worked closely at first with the authorities in Kirmanshah to uphold Iranian sovereignty, but they received scant help from the state they were attempting to defend. By June 1915 there were 10,000 Turks on the border whom the Sanjabi and the Guran managed to defeat at Karind at the end of the month.

The Turkish slaughter of some Ahl-i Haqq Sayyids, followed by the desecration of Baba Yadgar, a shrine sacred to many nearby Shi'is as well as Ahl-i Haqq, gave the war a strong religious flavour. Shaykh Rustam, the senior Haydari shaykh, had little trouble in rallying the faithful against the Turk. In May 1916 a new Russian thrust was made towards Rawanduz, in order to relieve pressure on British forces in lower Mesopotamia. Although this was abandoned after four weeks, it created a new dilemma for Iran's southern Kurds. On balance they considered the Turks the lesser evil, and so did not oppose the subsequent Turkish counter-attack which led to the capture of Kirmanshah in July. They had already responded favourably to German agents, partly because Britain had failed to woo them, partly because Germany was supportive of the Iranian government, but mainly because its agents were busy buying tribal support. These agents soon found themselves in a labyrinth of tribal venality, as chiefs competed to maximize on this new source of wealth, by reminding their paymasters they might get a better price from Britain or Russia. 'What we get for this extraordinarily high expenditure is practically very little,' protested one German general. 'Only for their own selfish ends are the tribal warriors wont to fight well.'[48]

In the February of 1917 a new Russian offensive made serious inroads on Ottoman-held territory. Erzerum and Hamadan fell in February, Kirmanshah and Qasr-i Shirin in March, Van in early summer and Erzinjan by July. During the Russian advances Turkey forcibly evacuated inhabitants from Diyarbakir, Bitlis and Mush. Most of these evacuees were marched to Mosul, Aleppo and Adana, many dying on the way or in the streets of these cities.

Russia, however, was already subject to the first tremors of revolution. The czar had abdicated in March. On the direction of the liberal government in Moscow, the Armenians took charge of the provinces of Van, Erzerum, Bitlis and Trabzon, but they were operating on shifting sands. A rapid collapse in morale and discipline soon undermined the Russian forces, which were then pushed out of Mush and Bitlis by the Second Army under Mustafa Kemal and

Kiazim Karabekir, both of whom were destined to play a crucial role in the area in 1919–20.

The Bolshevik revolution in October paralysed Russian military activity and thereby undermined the Armenians. A truce concluded at Erzinjan in December 1917 between the Transcaucasian Commissariat (responsible for territory inhabited by Georgians, Armenians and Azeris south of the Caucasus) and Turkey soon collapsed as the Turks and Kurds sensed the chance to recapture lost possessions. Four thousand Armenian troops strung out on a forty-mile front around Erzinjan were constantly harassed by Kurdish cavalry and unable to hold the line. When Turkish forces recaptured this city in February 1918, another disorderly multitude of Christians fled eastwards, as they had done from Van in 1915. This time they trudged through snow, attacked by Kurdish bands. Half of them died before reaching safety. On 12 March Erzerum was back in Turkish hands, Kurdish bands operating north and south of the city. What restraint there had been on the Christian side seems at this stage to have been finally extinguished and, as the Russian and Armenian forces retreated, they slew any Muslims that fell into their hands.

Turkish objectives seem to have progressed from the restitution of the 1914 borders to the recapture of territories lost in 1878, and finally to the capture of Caucasia if possible. The first two of these objectives fell into Turkey's lap with the Treaty of Brest–Litovsk, March 1918, which cut the remaining ground from under Armenian feet. Russia, in its anxiety to extricate itself from war, agreed to cede Kars, Ardahan and Batum, all of which had been acquired from Turkey in 1878. In April Turkish forces occupied Batum and Alexandropol amid Transcaucasian requests that at least marauding Kurdish bands should be curbed by the Turkish army. In late May, following inconclusive talks in Batum, the Turks pushed forward again but were repulsed at Sardarabad. A treaty was concluded at Batum in June, leaving Turkey in control of the Kars–Julfa railway, and Alexandropol.[49]

Further south British forces were unable to occupy Khaniqin until December 1917. In spring 1918 they advanced northwards, occupying Kifri, Tuz and Kirkuk, and negotiating with its notables the recognition of British authority in Sulaymaniya. When its eastern flank was threatened, however, British forces withdrew from Kirkuk and Sulaymaniya which were promptly reoccupied by Turkish forces. Kirkuk was only finally taken by British forces on 25 October, five days before an armistice was agreed at Mudros.

Meanwhile, the Russian collapse had persuaded Britain to adopt a more active policy to 'preserve' Iran's neutrality, in reality to deny Iran to the enemy. In December 1917 it decided to occupy Qasr-i Shirin, and then secure the road northwards to Enzeli. Military operations commenced in March.

The Sanjabi, who believed they would suffer a curse if they opposed the state, had already made it clear they would oppose any violation of Iranian neutrality, and decided to oppose the British advance. They had been decisively alienated by Russian behaviour and so had co-operated with German policy, helping to thwart the conjunction of Russian and British forces in 1917. Seeing their chance, the Kalhur and Guran formed an anti-Sanjabi coalition and now had little difficulty in obtaining British material support to ambush the Sanjabi on their summer migration. The Sanjabi lost 250 men and the victorious tribes made off with 100,000 Sanjabi sheep, thereby dealing a formidable economic as well as political blow to the Sanjabi.

It was time to count the cost. Much of Kurdistan, from Bayazid in the north to Khaniqin in the south, as far west as Erzinjan and Mush, was also laid waste by opposing forces and raiding bands. Famine, death by exposure, typhus, typhoid or some other disease all took their toll. The hardship was considerably aggravated by the failed harvest of 1917 and by Russian troops who, given the collapse of discipline during the summer, now acted without restraint, stripping the country-side of flocks and herds, cutting or destroying all standing crops. They even razed Sawj Bulaq. All but the richest were left destitute.[50] The tribes of Kifri, for example, which had successfully concealed their food stocks from the Turks were now driven by hunger to reveal them. British troops advancing northwards were appalled by what they found:

> In no part of Mesopotamia had we encountered anything comparable to the misery which greeted us at Khaniqin. The country harvested by the Russians had been sedulously gleaned by the Turks who, when they retired, left it in the joint possession of starvation and disease.... The destruction of the Persian road exceeded, if possible, that of Khaniqin. The villages had been gutted by passing armies, Russian and Turkish, the roof beams and all wooden fittings torn out and used as fuel, and the rain and snow of winter had completed the destruction of unprotected mud walls. The fields lay untilled, and if any of the husbandmen remained, it was because they were too greatly extenuated by hunger to flee.[51]

As usual in such situations, the poor had suffered worst of all, and the survivors tended to be aghas, village headmen and their relations. But there was hoarding too. Outside the zone of direct British control landlords near Sanandaj were deliberately withholding grain from the market in the autumn of 1918, waiting while people starved, until the roads were closed by winter snows and floods, so as to force prices upwards.[52]

By the end of 1917 people were dying of hunger in many parts of Kurdistan, for example around Sawj Bulaq and Sulaymaniya. By November 1918 the latter city had dropped from it pre-war population of 20,000 to 2,500, and 'Dead bodies were collected in the bazaar every morning, and in some cases people were eating their dead babies.'[53] In Nihri of Shamdinan, only ten houses out of 250 were left standing, in Rawanduz only 60 out of 2,000. In the same area only three of the one hundred or so villages of the Balik tribe had not been razed. Of approximately 1,000 families of the Baradust tribe at the outset of war, only 157 had survived; of the thirty-odd villages of its Rawanduz section, 'neither man, woman or child remained.'[54]

British forces undertook an extensive relief operation, providing food for the relief of hunger and seed for the restitution of agriculture. Hardly surprisingly, the Kurds generally welcomed British forces as saviours, and one may forgive the self-congratulatory tone of the official record:

> Forgetting their fears they [the Kurds] came down from their retreats in the hills and made friends with this surprising army, which distributed its surplus rations and paid in cash for what it took.[55]

The war, as far as the Kurds were concerned, was over.

How many perished in all? There had probably been approximately 3 million people living east of Sivas in 1914.[56] Kurds probably slightly outnumbered Armenians, but both were around the one million mark, with a largely Turkish urban population of about 600,000. The total Armenian death toll, which included those living in Cilicia and central Anatolia, was probably in the order of one million. Very few survived in eastern Anatolia. Probably over 500,000 Kurdish civilians also perished, together with combatants probably totalling very approximately 800,000.[57]

Once the initial euphoria had dissipated, Britain's dealings with the Kurds soon revealed that the complexities and conflicts between government and the tribes were far from resolved. But first Britain had to decide how to deal with the vanquished Turks and what new borders it wanted. It had wanted possession of Mosul for political and economic as well as strategic reasons, and therefore invoked the armistice terms authorizing British forces to occupy 'strategic points'. The Turkish commander, Ali Ihsan Pasha, was ordered to evacuate; the city was occupied on 8 November and the rest of the vilayet on 10 November, ten days after Mudros. It was to become a bone of contention between Britain and Turkey, in which both sides courted the loyalty of its Kurds.

Sources

Great Britain, unpublished: Public Record Office: series FO 248 nos. 698, 722, 851, 1112, 1188, 1204, 1205; series FO 371 nos. 346, 540, 559, 956, 1009, 1011, 1112, 1244, 1245, 1249, 1250, 1261, 1263, 1509, 1783, 2080, 2146, 4192, 7824, 7844; WO 106/63 and 64; India Office Library L/P&S/10/345, 652, 781; L/P&S/11/3, 8, 18, 36, 74, 84, 115.

Great Britain, published: Parliamentary Papers: *Turkey No 1, Correspondence Respecting the Constitutional Movement in Turkey 1908*, Cmd 4529 (London 1909); *Miscellaneous No 31: The Treatment of Armenians in the Ottoman Empire, 1915–16* (London, 1916); Other official publications: E. Noel, *Note on the Kurdish situation* (Baghdad, 1919); E.J.R., *Precis of Affairs in Southern Kurdistan during the Great War* (Baghdad, 1919); G. Bell, *Review of the Civil Administration from 1914 to the summer of 1920*, Cmd 1061 (London, 1920); E.B. Soane, *Adminstrative Report of Sulaymaniya for the Year 1919* (Baghdad, 1920).

Secondary sources: Kamal Madhar Ahmad, *Kurdistan During the First World War* (London, 1994); Emir Sureya Bedr Khan, *The Case of Kurdistan against Turkey* (Philadelphia, 1927); Gertrude Bell, *Amurath to Amurath* (London, 1924); Hamid Bozarslan, 'Entre la umma et le nationalisme' (Amsterdam, 1991); Chirguh, *La Question Kurde: ses origines et ses causes* (Cairo

1930); F.N. Heazell and Margoliouth, *Kurds and Christians* (London, 1913); Hovanissian, *Armenia on the Road to Independence*; Imperial War Museum, *Operations in Persia, 1914–1919* (London, 1987); Joseph, *The Nestorians and their Neighbours*; Kendal, 'Kurds under the Ottoman empire'; Naci Kutlay, *Ittihat Terakki ve Kurtler* (Istanbul, 1991); Bernard Lewis *The Emergence of Modern Turkey* (London, 1968); S.H. Longrigg, *Iraq, 1900–1950: A Political, Social and Economic History* (London, 1953); Serif Mardin, 'Ideology and religion in the Turkish Revolution', *The International Journal of Middle East Studies* 2 (1971), 'Centre–periphery relations: a key to Turkish politics', *Daedalus* (winter 1973), and *Religion and Social Change in Modern Turkey: The Case of Bediuzzaman Said Nursi* (New York, 1989); Kenneth Mason, 'Central Kurdistan', *The Geographical Journal*, vol. liv, no. 6 (1919); Nikitine, 'Les Kurdes racontés par eux-mêmes'; Olson, *The Emergence of Kurdish Nationalism*; Earl Percy, *The Highlands of Asiatic Turkey* (London, 1901); Peresh, *Barzan wa harakat al Wa'i al Qawmi al Kurdi, 1826–1914* (n.p., 1980); E.E. Ramsaur, *The Young Turks: Prelude to the Revolution of 1908* (Princeton, 1957); Abd al Sitar Tahir Sharif, *Al Jami'at wa'l manzimat wa'l ahzab al Kurdiya fi nisf qarn 1908–1958* (Baghdad, 1989); Shaw and Shaw, *History of the Ottoman Empire and Modern Turkey*; E.B. Soane, *To Mesopotamia and Kurdistan in Disguise* (London, 1912); C. Sykes, *The Caliph's Last Heritage* (London, 1915); Walker, *Armenia*; W.A. and E.T.A. Wigram, *The Cradle of Mankind* (London, 1914); Wigram, *The Assyrians and their Neighbours* (London, 1929); Arnold Wilson, *S.W. Persia: A Political Officer's Diary, 1907–1914* (London, 1941); Nur Yalman, 'On land disputes in Turkey' in G.L. Tikku (ed.), *Islam and its Cultural Divergence* (Ann Arbor, 1977).

Notes

1. It was republished in 1899 in the Armenian journal *Troshak*, Kutlay, *Ittihat Terakki*, p. 17.
2. Issue No 30 of 14 March 1902, see Sharif, *Al jami'at*, p. 17.
3. Muhammad Sadiq, in spite of an unsavoury reputation, had taken only a minor part in his father's rebellion. He was a good deal more shrewd than his father, concentrating on tobacco smuggling but ensuring that the Ottoman Tobacco Regie officials received their cut of the profits, thus amassing enough wealth to invest in London banks.
4. There was no fixed line of primogeniture, see Nikitine 'Les Kurdes racontés par eux-mêmes', p. 149.
5. Centred on Jazira bin Umar it quickly spread to Zakhu, Julamirk, Amadiya, Mardin and Nusaybin. Uthman's name was even announced in the Friday prayer as the legitimate *amir*. Sultan Abd al Hamid persuaded them to make their submission.
6. Quoted by Lewis, *The Emergence of Modern Turkey*, p. 267.
7. Mardin, 'Ideology and religion', p. 208.
8. Even as far afield at south-west Iran, Arnold Wilson, then a political officer, already considered 'the [Ottoman] Kurds are at heart set upon autonomy.' Wilson, *S.W. Persia*, p. 85.
9. Shaw and Shaw, *History*, ii, p. 302.
10. Also known as the Kurd Taraqi wa Ta'awun Jamiyati, the Kurdish Society for Progress and Mutual Aid.
11. Quoted in Sherif Mardin, *Religion and Social Change*, p. 80. See also pp. 19, 35, 79, 86.
12. Amin Ali's son Suraya was also compelled to flee. He, it seems, had spurned an invitation by one of its leaders, Taalat Pasha, to join the CUP.
13. Wilson, *S.W. Persia*, p. 175.
14. FO 371/10089 High Commissioner Iraq to Amery, 4 December 1924.
15. These included Khalil Khayali of the Mutki tribe, Umar and Qadri sons of Jamil Pasha Zada, a Diyarbakir notable, and Fuad Timu Beg a tribal scion from Van. Hivi also allegedly included Shaykh Abd al Qadir, Amin ali Badr Khan (possibly back from exile), Murad Muhammad Ali, Khalil Rami, Kamuran Badr Khan, Fuad and Hikmat Baban (and

at least four other Babans), Husayn and Muhammad Awni (deputies respectively of Kharput and Malatiya, and many others. Some of these had attended the tribal schools which had been closed down in 1907.

16. Kutlay, *Ittihat Terakki*, p. 54.

17. Quoted by Yalman, 'On land disputes in Turkey', p. 215.

18. Ibrahim Pasha was a brigadier-general in the Hamidiya and the only local chief capable of seeing off the Shammar bedouin. He had rebuilt the confederation after his forebears' exploits had brought down the wrath of the tanzimat reformers.

19. *Parliamentary Papers*, Turkey No 1, Lowther to Grey, Therapia, 26 August 1908.

20. Ibrahim Beg of the Jibranli, Kuli Khan of Khinis, the Hasananli chiefs of Malangird, the Shaykhs of Till (Mush), and Shaykh Sulayman of Abri (Bulanik) and Musa Beg of Khavnir on the Mush Plain. Musa Beg owed the CUP a debt of gratitude, for it had released him after twenty years of exile, a punishment for outrages against Armenian villages. On Musa Beg's original crimes and trial, see *Parliamentary Papers*, Turkey No 1 (Cmd 5912, London, 1890).

21. FO 371/1009 Safrastian to McGregor, Bitlis, 22 April 1910.

22. FO371/1249 Safrastian to McGregor, Bitlis, 12 June 1911.

23. He was also said to run a network of secret informers. In 1881 there had been a major popular protest at his rapacity, but he survived unscathed. For an account of Shaykh Said and the Hamawand tribe, see Soane, *To Mesopotamia*, pp. 173–190.

24. France, Ministère des Affaires Étrangères NS, vol. xiii, Van, 8 November 1909, quoted in Bozarslan, 'Entre la umma et le nationalisme', p. 19.

25. It was variously speculated that he was stirring up the Kurds against the government, or that he had ambitions to become Wali of Van, FO 371/1009 Morgan to Lowther, 3 and 25 April 1910.

26. Percy, *The Highlands*, p. 222.

27. FO 371/1244 Matthews to Lowther, Diyarbakir, 31 December 1910. As early as 1896 Sultan Abd al Hamid had expressed unease at Sayyid Nursi's mixture of religious revivalism and ethnic advocacy, Mardin, *Religion and Social Change*, p.19.

28. Bozarslan, 'Entre la umma et le nationalisme', p. 19.

29. L/P&S/11/8 Lowther to Grey, Istanbul, 11 February 1912, Enclosure 1 Mugerditchian to McGregor, Diyarbakr, 31 December 1911.

30. It will be recalled that Russia's occupation of Tabriz in 1909, Urumiya and Khoi in 1910 and the border area west of Khoi as far south as Sawj Bulaq (Mahabad) following the Ottoman withdrawal in 1911, gave it road access to Van via Khoi from its own railhead at Julfa.

31. Abd al Razzaq, incidentally, had been exiled having killed the governor of Istanbul in a personal quarrel. He had been to Moscow in 1909 where, no doubt, he received sufficient encouragement to proceed.

32. See for example the article in *Tanin*, quoted in FO 371/1013 in Lowther to Grey, Therapia, 30 August 1910.

33. Abd al Qadir had fought Taha for the succession to Muhammad Sadiq in 1911, and had shed blood in the process. He reluctantly accepted a financial settlement in 1911.

34. L/P&S/10/345 Molyneux Seel to Marline, Van, 22 July 1913 and Hurst to Mallet, Diyarbakir, 14 May 1914.

35. L/P&S/10/345 Smith to Mallet, Bitlis, 16 April 1914.

36. Simqu seems to have been instrumental in the suppression of the *anjumans* of Khoi and Salmas. In the case of Salmas, the *anjuman* took what revenge it could by prompting the rival branch of the Shikak to raid villages occupied by Simqu's men.

37. He tried to interest the Russians in Kurdish independence, but tried also to maintain relations with Turkey, was caught doing so and imprisoned by the Russians. He fled following

the October Revolution.

38. When the Russians briefly occupied eastern Anatolia in the summer of 1917, they appointed Kamil and Abd al Razzaq Walis of Erzerum and Bitlis respectively.

39. *PP, The Treatment of Armenians*, p. 100.

40. See for example, FO 371/2080 Buchanan to Grey, Petrograd, 6 October 1914; Townley to Grey, Tehran, 11, 14 and 16 October 1914.

41. Ahmed Emin, *Turkey in World War*, pp 218–219, quoted by Jwaideh, *The Kurdish Nationalist Movement*, p. 363. It is extremely difficult to know how reliable this account is. Given Kurdish treatment of Armenians it is perfectly credible. On the other hand the Turks had the strongest possible motive for alleging that the Armenians began the atrocities.

42. This was a major offensive with the aim of recapturing Kars, lost in 1878. Given the climatic conditions, it was an act of lunacy. Out of 95,000 men who set out, approximately 80,000 had perished by February, mainly from exposure, Hovanissian, *Armenia on the Road to Independence*, pp. 41, 45, 46; Walker, *Armenia*, p. 199.

43. Hovanissian, *Armenia on the Road*, p. 46.

44. *The Treatment of Armenians*, pp. 36, 60, narrative of Miss G.H. Knapp of the American Mission at Van.

45. Armenian revolutionaries had established relations with the Dersim Kurds twenty years earlier.

46. The Eleventh and Twelfth Armies at Elazig and Mosul respectively were entirely Kurdish, while the Ninth and Tenth Armies at Erzerum and Sivas were largely Kurdish. Kurds also provided 135 cavalry squadrons, gendarmerie forces and border guards.

47. Sulayman, Daud Khan's son was promptly imprisoned for treating with a potential enemy, presumably under British pressure. In June 1915 the Kalhur agreed to uphold Iranian neutrality, on condition Sulayman was released.

48. In fact German involvement with Iranian forces was abandoned during the summer of 1916, in disagreement over Turkey's insistence on launching an offensive towards Kirmanshah; Field Marshal von der Goltz, 'The Situation in Persia', 16 February 1916, reprinted in Imperial War Museum, *Operations in Persia*, pp. 175, 472.

49. It did not hold. In September Turkish forces captured the Black Sea port of Baku, massacring 20,000 of its Armenian inhabitants.

50. When Russian troops withdrew into Iran in June 1917, Turkish forces rapidly reoccupied the area as far as Khaniqin, ravaging whatever was left, and punishing those who had co-operated with the Russians or been in communication with British by demolishing their homes and by execution. A year later, when Britain was forced temporarily to withdraw, those who had aided the invaders were again punished and their homes plundered and demolished.

51. *Review of Administration from 1914*, pp. 46, 47.

52. The most notorious of these was Farjallah Asaf of Sinna, who was credited with the death of some 2,000 during famine in 1916.

53. Capt Charles Beale, an eyewitness, quoted in Mason, 'Central Kurdistan', p. 345.

54. Overall, 52 out of 81 Baradusti villages were razed. The smaller Kawaruk tribe, 150 families in 1914, was reduced to seven families by 1919, the final trial being the great influenza epidemic of that year, Mason, 'Central Kurdistan', pp. 339, 345.

55. *Review of Administration from 1914*, p. 47.

56. See FO 371/4192 Noel, Note on the Kurdish situation, 18 July 1919, and Robert Olson's discussion of the conflicting figures in *The Emergence of Kurdish Nationalism*, pp 19–21, comparing the figures in Justin McCarthy, *Muslims and Minorities: The Population of Ottoman Anatolia and the End of Empire* (New York, 1983) and Hovanissian, *Armenia on the Road to Independence*.

57. Zaki, *Khulasat*, p. 259, footnote; Olson, *The Emergence of Kurdish Nationalism*, p. 21.

BOOK II

INCORPORATING THE KURDS

CHAPTER 7

REDRAWING THE MAP: THE PARTITION OF OTTOMAN KURDISTAN

Introduction

With the defeat of Turkish forces in Syria and Mesopotamia during the course of 1918, it was inevitable that the map of the Middle East would be redrawn. The first intimations of fresh borders had been made before the end of the war, with the Husayn–McMahon correspondence regarding the future of Ottoman Arab lands.

Then, in November 1917, the Bolsheviks revealed details of the Sykes–Picot Agreement (May 1916) which proposed to strip most of Anatolia from Turkish control. Imperial Russia was to have been rewarded for its co-operation with Istanbul, the Straits and the eastern provinces, Italy with south-west Anatolia and Greece with the region around Izmir. The Bolsheviks wanted nothing of such imperialist schemes, except to expose them to the light of day. Embarrassed Anglo-French planners now hurriedly filled the vacuum created by Russia's withdrawal, awarding 'the Cossack territories, the territory of the Caucasus, Armenia, Georgia, Kurdistan' to Britain as 'zones of influence'.[1]

Anxious to take the peace settlement onto higher moral ground, President Woodrow Wilson hastened to publish his Fourteen Points for World Peace in January. The twelfth point affirmed:

> The Turkish portions of the present Ottoman Empire should be assured a secure sovereignty, but other nationalities which are now under Turkish rule should be assured an undoubted security of life and an absolutely unmolested opportunity of autonomous development.

Such an assurance hardly allayed the fears of the Turks, since those who secured Turkish lands by force were unlikely to relinquish them willingly, regardless of the Fourteen Points.

It was clear that the Allies had far-reaching territorial ambitions but unclear now what their plans might really be. With Russia ineligible for the fruits of victory but the United States now in, the situation had changed. New Allied

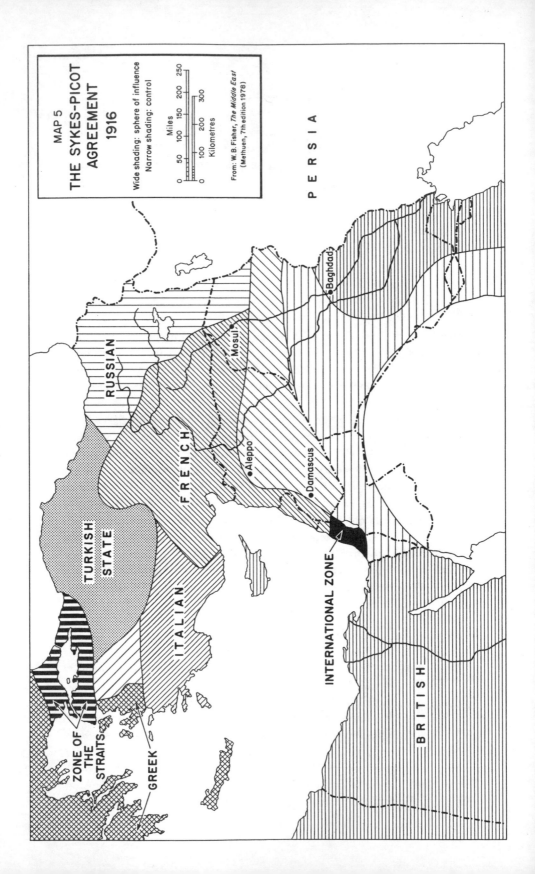

MAP 5
THE SYKES-PICOT
AGREEMENT
1916

Wide shading: sphere of influence
Narrow shading: control

Miles
0   50   100 150 200 250
Kilometres
0   100   200   300

From: W. B. Fisher, *The Middle East*
(Methuen, 7th edition 1978)

PERSIA

RUSSIAN

TURKISH
STATE

FRENCH

ITALIAN

GREEK

ZONE OF
THE STRAITS

INTERNATIONAL ZONE

BRITISH

●Baghdad

Mosul●

Aleppo●

●Damascus

talks were necessary, particularly in view of the United States' avowed interest in Armenia.

For the Turks, the key issue was to minimize the territory they might lose. The general consensus among Ottoman statesmen was that only co-operation with the Allied victors would salvage something from the wreckage. The possible loss of the eastern provinces weighed heavily on Ottoman minds. Toleration of Kurdish claims seemed prudent to deter them from making common cause with the Armenians.

The Armenians, too, were left wondering where they stood. In spite of Allied sympathy, an Armenian state was unlikely to come into being except by their own efforts. They were worried by the implications of Sykes–Picot that their ancestral lands in Anatolia were to be divided between Russian and French spheres of influence. There was no suggestion yet that France would yield her claim to Cilicia (Lesser Armenia), so a re-created Armenia was likely to be a divided one.

The few Kurds who were aware of Sykes–Picot would also have been alarmed by its intention to divide them between several different spheres: one of British influence, another of French influence, a third area of direct French rule and a swathe of land of now undetermined status hitherto awarded to Russia. This area extended along the Iranian border from Raniya and Rawanduz northwards through Bitlis and Van and up to the Black Sea, and westwards as far as Erzinjan. Thus the Kurds found themselves uncertain about the future and some of them apprehensive of Allied retribution for their part in the Armenian genocide.

Turks, Kurds and Armenians were far from alone in facing great uncertainty. At climactic moments of victory it is easy for great powers to assume they will dispose of the peace as convincingly as they have done with the war. The aftermath of the war faced victors as well as vanquished with considerable problems, not least in resolving the future of Kurdish areas.

For Britain the question of Kurdistan was bound to remain secondary to a political settlement for the main territories of interest, greater Syria and Mesopotamia. Indeed, as the Sykes–Picot map had shown, Britain was not primarily interested in Kurdistan at all. But it was drawn inexorably into consideration of Kurdistan's fate by its strategic position in Mesopotamia.

British Strategic Concerns

In October 1918, British officers in Baghdad recognized that Mesopotamia's political and economic future would be greatly enhanced by the inclusion of the vilayet of Mosul. From a military viewpoint it would give Britain control of the foothills edging the plain. The economic (and social) argument was the close commercial integration between Mosul, Baghdad and Basra. Furthermore, the Turkoman towns on the edge of the Mesopotamian plain, most notably Arbil and Kirkuk, along with the peasant economies around them, fell naturally within this view of Mesopotamia since here were some of the richest wheat districts of the region. Thus the decision was made to secure Mosul while the state of war still made this possible.[2] It followed that Britain no longer had any wish to see Mosul under French control, for which Sykes–Picot had provided.

In Baghdad it was also immediately recognized that the peace and prosperity of northern Mesopotamia would depend directly on what happened north of the border and furthermore, that the fate of a putative Armenian state in eastern Anatolia – an Allied brainchild – would be contingent on peace in Kurdistan.

The question was how to achieve all of this. At face value Britain was more powerfully placed than the US, France or Turkey to determine the future of Kurdistan. Its forces occupied Syria, Mesopotamia and southern Kurdistan, the Straits Zone around Istanbul, and there were British officers in western Iran. It was easy in London to feel bold when it came to redrawing the maps.

Before the guns had even fallen silent, Arnold Toynbee at the Foreign Office was proposing to Sir Mark Sykes:

> If there is to be an individual Mesopotamia under Arab government with British administrative assistance, the natural corollary would be an autonomous Kurdistan, likewise assisted by H.M.G. and performing the same function towards Mesopotamia as the NW Frontier province performs towards India. This was proposed recently by Cherif Pasha [see below]. Such a Kurdistan would include not merely the country south of the Lesser Zab, but Rowanduz, Hakkiari, and Bohtan districts up to the line, wherever that may be drawn, of the Armenian frontier....[3]

Toynbee, anxious to reinstate the Assyrians of Tiyari and Urumiya, even suggested the transfer of Turkish Kurdistan to Iranian sovereignty on condition it was an autonomous province with foreign, presumably British, assistance. However, his proposal was dismissed by a sceptical Sykes. The latter preferred the idea of a Cilician Armenia under French tutelage, a Kurdo-Armenia from the Black Sea down to Siirt and Urfa[4] and finally an autonomous Southern Kurdistan excluding Kirkuk, Altun Kupru and Arbil where the largest urban communities were Turkoman, but including territory up to Siirt and across to Urumiya and including Sawj Bulaq (Mahabad).

The Creation of a Strategic Border in Kurdistan

It was easy to wield coloured crayons on a map. In southern Kurdistan Britain had already established relations with certain chiefs well before the Turks had been decisively driven back. Shortly after General Maude's capture of Baghdad in March 1917, representations were received from tribal chiefs controlling Khaniqin, Kifri and Halabja, in spite of Turkish attempts to frighten the Kurds into believing Britain planned to put them under Arab rule.[5] Early in May 1917 British political officers established relations with chiefs in Tuz Khirmatu, Kirkuk and Sulaymaniya. At the latter a meeting of notables decided to create a provisional Kurdish government, with Shaykh Mahmud Barzinji at its head, that would 'adopt a policy of complete friendliness to the British'.[6]

British authorities in Baghdad soon received word from Shaykh Mahmud Barzinji, claiming to represent all Kurds not only in Sulaymaniya district but as far as Sinna, in Iran, 'offering either to hand over the reins of Government to us or to carry on as our representative under our protection'.[7] These contacts had to be abandoned when British troops were compelled to withdraw from the area during the summer of 1917, but when an advance could be made again at the end of the year, friendly contacts were resumed.

No sooner had an armistice been declared than Britain sought to regularize its relations with the Kurdish tribes on the fringes of Mesopotamia. A Major Noel, who already had four years' experience of Iranian Kurdistan, was despatched to Sulaymaniya and other towns lying between the Lesser Zab and the Diyala to negotiate local arrangements and to make clear that Britain would not support a united Kurdistan embracing parts of Iran. Britain would reach agreements with those chiefs lying within its zone of occupation but so far had not identified any one single leader for all the Kurds, although Shaykh Mahmud was the nearest thing to one. It also understood that some of the chiefs preferred protection to rule.

Other things were less clear. The undertaking to local Kurdish chiefs clearly echoed the wording of the Anglo-French Declaration made three weeks before in Syria and Mesopotamia, which sought 'the setting up of national governments and administrations that shall derive their authority from the free exercise of the initiative and choice of the indigenous populations....'[8] The decision to attach South Kurdistan to Mesopotamia suggested Mesopotamian rather than Kurdish self-determination. It was equally unclear whether the tribes were free to disown Britain's 'assistance and protection' if they later so chose.

Nevertheless, arrangements south of the Lesser Zab were the very essence of simplicity compared with the difficulties north of it. Until it was substantively replaced, the Sykes–Picot agreement marked some of this as a French area of interest, while the area abutting the Iranian border had no provision after the Russian withdrawal. Anyone with even a rudimentary understanding of economic geography could see the lunacy of the Sykes–Picot partition lines since they ran smack across trade routes and grain-producing hinterlands.

Yet until a more practical arrangement had been agreed with France, nothing could be done to suggest that Britain had decided the fate of the area unilaterally. Although Britain was now loathe to hand the vilayet of Mosul over to France, its whole approach to the problems north of Mosul was contingent on reaching a substantive arrangement with France. That was only achieved in spring 1920 when a provisional understanding, made between Lloyd George and Clemenceau in early 1919, was formalized.

Another complication was the existence of a substantial Christian population in the vilayet. The proximity of Turkey and the presence of Turkish agents conspired to make the Kurds nervous about the future. General Sharif Pasha, now in exile in Paris, warned Britain as early as October 1918 that the Turks intended to foment hatred between Kurds and Armenians, 'with the object of destroying the Armenians and, later, of depriving the Kurds of any chance of real autonomy'.[9] It was all very well for someone like Sharif Pasha to talk of Kurdo-Armenian amity from the comfort of his Paris salon, as he had now begun to do (in contrast to the fears of Armenian intentions he had expressed when meeting Percy Cox the previous June). It was a wholly different matter in the region where massacre and counter-massacre had taken place. Turkish agents lost no time in reminding the Kurdish population of the dangers of European tutelage, including retribution for the Armenian massacres. Kurds also feared that if France, with its special interest in the Catholics (Chaldeans and Syrian Catholics), took over the vilayet as provided for under Sykes–Picot, it would place Christians in office over them.

Finally, there was the problem (which meshed with the other ones) of delineating the border with whatever political entity should exist north of the British occupied zone and what that political entity should be. If, as the Allies had in mind, there should be an Armenian entity in the north-eastern part of Anatolia, Britain had no desire at all for the area between Armenia and the British zone to be either unstable or, worse, a springboard for subversion or attack on the British zone.

The obvious thing would be to create an intermediate area of British influence. In theory some kind of Kurdish confederation was envisaged. In practice, however, there were real problems in defining a secure boundary for Mesopotamia, a buffer zone north of this to keep the Turks away, and finally a satisfactory northern border of that buffer zone with the putative Armenian state.

A variety of options concerning the northern boundary of Mesopotamia were aired. One proposal was to demarcate one along the watershed between Lake Van and the Tigris. Major Noel, the political officer in Sulaymaniya, however, had more elaborate ideas. He was a leading exponent and champion of Kurdish aspirations and argued strongly for three Kurdish polities: southern Kurdistan based on Sulaymaniya and embracing Nihri, Rawanduz, Arbil, Kirkuk, Kifri and Khaniqin; Central Kurdistan, centred on Mosul, and Western Kurdistan centred on Diyarbakir and stretching as far north as a Kurdish majority persisted, all implicitly enjoying British protection and advice.[10]

Both the Foreign Office in London and General Headquarters in Cairo proposed with the simple clarity of distance, a total withdrawal from all Kurdistan, keeping only the Mesopotamian plain. Wilson, Acting Civil Commissioner in Baghdad, hoped he had scotched this idea, stating

> The whole basis of our action as regards Kurds should be in my opinion the assurance of a satisfactory boundary to Mesopotamia. Such a boundary cannot possibly be secured,

I imagine, in the plains, but must be found in the Kurdish mountains ... [and that] entails a tribal policy.[11]

The whole strategic argument was based upon Britain's financial crisis at the end of the war. Mesopotamia had to be defended with insufficient troops. Defending the Kurdish hills required half the troops necessary for holding the plain. Wilson had first made the case in April 1919, but it was the end of the year before London accepted the view that clean ethnographic borders were strategic and economic nonsense, a fact immediately realized by Kurds living within the economic orbit of Mosul and Baghdad. Yet Wilson had no wish to extend his borders either, incurring greater liabilities without more troops. Wilson's view was dictated by defensible borders and he made it clear that Diyarbakir, Urfa, and Nusaybin must be excluded from British Mesopotamia. He wanted a fringe of autonomous states along the edge of Mesopotamia, centred on Sulaymaniya, Rawanduz, Amadiya, and possibly Jazira bin Umar. That was quite enough. Further penetration into Kurdistan might bring security problems similar to those on the North West Frontier of India. Even Turkey back in Diyarbakir was preferable to that.

Britain and Turkey Compete for the Kurds

All this still left the problem of what should happen north of the vilayet of Mosul. The obvious thing was to find suitable Kurdish leaders with whom it would be possible to work out a solution. This was easier said than done.

The oldest and most persistent contact had been with General Muhammad Sharif Pasha, erstwhile member of the Kurdish party of 1908. Sharif Pasha had little in common with the rough-hewn chiefs of Kurdistan. He was an educated notable accustomed to life in Europe. Ever since his exile in 1909 he had been seeking opportunities to remain active in Ottoman affairs. He felt loyal to the sultanate, but had liberal, decentralist inclinations.[12] He had settled into a comfortable exile in Paris, where he became active in Ottoman liberal opposition activities,[13] but with a reputation among other Turkish exiles as a 'phenomenally stupid' dandy whose sole asset was his money.[14] With the outbreak of war Sharif renewed his interest in the Kurdish issue, and made more approaches to the Allies.[15]

In May 1919 Sharif Pasha informed the British embassy in Paris that he was willing to shoulder the 'burden' of becoming Amir of an independent Kurdistan, presiding over a federal council of chiefs. With no constituency in Kurdistan, it was difficult to take the ageing Sharif Pasha seriously. As one official tartly commented, 'I understand that he is quite unsuited for the position he covets, his qualifications being those of a Parisian pamphleteer.'[16]

Besides, Shaykh Mahmud Barzinji, son of the murdered Shaykh Said, was cock of the walk in Sharif's native city and was already co-operating with British forces. In any case it was hard to see how Sharif Pasha as a southern Kurd could speak authoritatively on behalf of those Kurds further north who had traded atrocities with the Armenians. It was also unclear what Sharif Pasha was up to, since he had also openly and actively pursued ideas of Ottoman decentralization,[17] which were hardly consonant with his avowed objective of either autonomy or independence under British tutelage.

In Cairo a 'Committee for Kurdish Independence' had also appealed for British assistance in establishing a Kurdish state in January 1919.[18] This, it turned out, was little more than a group of emigrés, led by the exiled Suraya Badr Khan. It was hardly representative of the people of Kurdistan, and was never taken seriously although an intermittent dialogue took place throughout 1919.

In Kurdistan itself there were a number of unsatisfactory candidates, of whom Shaykh Mahmud Barzinji was the most obvious, and of whom more will be said later. From Sulaymaniya he had claimed his leadership of all Kurdistan, yet even neighbouring towns like Kifri and Khaniqin disowned him, let alone important nearby tribes like the Jaf. There was little possibility of places further afield, where he was barely known, accepting him. He was the leading Qadiri, but the more numerous Naqshbandi Kurds were likely to turn to their own shaykhs.

Then there was Shaykh Taha of Nikri, a man noted for his intellectual powers. It will be recalled that he had spent most of the war in Russian custody. After the war his own power base was so eroded that he had made common cause with a relative by marriage, Ismail Agha Simqu, the ruthless young chief of the Shikak who had established *de facto* independence in Iran, west of Urumiya. Taha approached the authorities in Baghdad in April 1919, anxious to make a visit. He, too, hoped he might become leader of the Kurds. When he reached Baghdad in May 1919 he urged the idea of a united Kurdistan, including the portion lying in Iran. Taha had personal reasons for such a suggestion, since the Sayyids of Nihri had always held sway across the border. Moreover, Shamdinan was economically dependent on trade with Urumiya. Finally, it was a policy which neatly tied up with Taha's newfound ally, Simqu.[19]

Such ideas had been mooted before. In July 1918, at a time when some of Iran's Kurdish chiefs were discussing the idea of an independent Kurdistan under British auspices, a Mukri chief from Sawj Bulaq had approached the British consul for Kirmanshah with the idea that a free Armenia in the northern provinces of Turkey would be acceptable to the Kurds, provided an independent Kurdistan was established between an Armenian and an Arab state. That idea had already been squashed once, when Arnold Wilson visited Sulaymaniya at the beginning of December. Since then the Jaf and the Rawanduz chiefs had been propagating the idea of a united Kurdistan. They, after all, possessed grazing or villages either side of the border. A few weeks before Taha's visit, Iran's Kurds had demonstrated their discontent by attacking the governorate-general in Sinna (Sanandaj), while Simqu had seized Urumiya itself.

However, Baghdad and London had no intention of infringing Iran's border,

even if British troops at war had recently marched across Iranian territory with
such disregard. So the British made a counter-suggestion, that Taha become
hukumdar (governor) of a northern Kurdish entity that he should establish under
British tutelage, from Rawanduz to Shamdinan – but they refused to give him
the rifles necessary to achieve it, and so he declined the proposal. He was well
aware that without the Iranian component, Simqu *et al.*, his credibility as a
leader was much diminished. He might still be revered by many tribesmen even
beyond Hakkari and Van, but his absence since 1914 had left him without a
strong retinue of his own. Without rifles he had no means of assembling a
credible force. In any case, like many other Kurdish leaders, he was hedging
his bets. When he learnt the same month that his unloved uncle, Shaykh Abd
al Qadir, might be coming to Kurdistan under British auspices, he turned to
the Turks.

The most powerful chief in Buhtan was Ibrahim Pasha's son, Mahmud, head
of the Milli. He had professed strong nationalist feeling when a British officer
visited Viranshahir in May 1919. He could not claim the prestige of the Badr
Khans, hereditary amirs of Buhtan, but he commanded sufficient respect to rally
thousands of warriors from miles around. It was unlikely any of the emigré Badr
Khans could marshall anything like that number. But, again, it was difficult to
gauge Mahmud's loyalties. Was he really more concerned with his neighbour and
longstanding tribal enemy, Abd al Rahman of the Karagich in nearby Shirnakh,
who was so openly pro-Turk and anti-British? There were grounds for thinking
so. Whatever the case, when Mahmud opted to support Mustafa Kemal's nascent
Turkish nationalist movement in Sivas a few months later, Abd al Rahman
suddenly became ardently pro-British.

Finally there were the Kurds of Istanbul. These, too, had to be taken seriously
since they were on hand to negotiate with the Ottoman government and to
proposition the British High Commissioner. With the government prostrate and
the city surrounded by Allied troops, Istanbul's Kurds had no difficulty in
resurrecting their nationalist groups. Before the end of 1918 Shaykh Abd al
Qadir and the leading Badr Khans, Amir Amin Ali and his two sons Kamuran
and Jaladat Ali, had reconstituted the Kurdish Club, with its modified pre-war
title of The Society for the Rise of Kurdistan (Kurdistan Ta'ali Jamiyati). Ten
years since their first activities in 1908 such groups may still have been led by
the old notable class, but there was much greater provincial and tribal involvement. Affiliate branches soon opened in Diyarbakir, Siirt, Elazig and other towns.

But from the outset the British saw difficulties with the Kurdish Clubs. Shaykh
Abd al Qadir had been absent from Kurdistan for so long and had such a bad
relationship with his nephew, Taha, that his claim to leadership outside Istanbul
could only be viewed with scepticism. It was also unclear what precisely the
Kurdish Club in Istanbul, and its affiliates in the provinces, represented. It
included integrationists like the pro-CUP liberal Abdallah Jawdat, whose pro-
European ideas were influential on Mustafa Kemal, and the fervent CUP

supporter Sulayman Nazif, the ex-governor of Mosul who had hanged Shaykh Abd al Salam Barzani.

It was no easier for Kurds in Istanbul than it was for those in the provinces. There was everything to play for at the awaited Peace Conference but what should the Kurdish position be? Herein lay the difficulty. Britain was clearly considering the viability of a Kurdish state with some diffidence. It did not wish to offend France which had already indicated its lack of enthusiasm for a Kurdish state, and seemed undecided whether or not to maintain a separate administration for southern Kurdistan as an adjunct to Mesopotamia, in which case Kurdistan would effectively be partitioned. Yet a partitioned Kurdistan might be tolerable if Britain were to act as protector and adviser to both parts.

Kurdish nationalists were probably aware by spring 1919 that the Allies were thinking of partitioning eastern Anatolia between an Armenian state in the vilayets of Erzerum and Trabzon under American auspices, and a Kurdish state in the remaining four vilayets of Bitlis, Van, Diyarbakir and Elazig, presumably under British auspices.

Yet since the Allies had made no move to occupy the region, was it not rash for the Kurds to burn their boats with the Ottoman government? Abd al Qadir at certainly thought so and, possibly loyal to his Naqshbandi upbringing, did not really wish to sever all ties with the Ottoman sultanate. He was not alone. Speaking over fifty years later about the Kurdish Club, Kamuran Badr Khan remarked 'The majority had one foot in the Kurdish camp and the other in the Ottoman-Islamic establishment ... they wanted to become ministers....'[20] Personal ambitions apart, Abd al Qadir knew that the Ottoman establishment feared the loss of the eastern vilayets and might therefore offer the Kurds what they wanted in order to keep them within the empire.

The Turks were understandably anxious to keep the Kurds on board. It was easy to penetrate the Kurdish clubs. In December 1918 the General Staff had been instrumental in forming an Association for the Defence of the Eastern Vilayets. Alongside his membership of the Kurdish Club, Sulayman Nazif took a lead in the association. He castigated those in Istanbul who favoured conciliating the Allies, offering to travel to Europe to lobby the case for Turco-Kurdish independence on behalf of the CUP. He was sure to be well received since he had at personal risk denounced the Armenian massacres and refused to implement executions while governor in Baghdad.

Indeed, CUP Turks were sufficiently desperate for Kurdish loyalty 'to pretend to support a policy ... of decentralized local government by the subject races'.[21] At the beginning of 1919 a network of CUP activists established local groups under the title of 'Committees for Turco-Kurdish Independence' in Kharput, Urfa, Mardin, Diyarbakir and Jazira bin Umar. Thanks to the centralized system of the CUP these were highly co-ordinated, making declarations against foreign (i.e. Allied) interference, arming civilians and recruiting for the gendarmerie. The CUP network of informers ensured that civil servants or notables stepping out of line were quickly reported to the local committee. Some CUP activists were actually inveigling Kurds into newly formed Turkish parties, even into explicitly neo-Turanian ones like the Turkish Nationalist (literally 'Hearth') Party (Turk Ojaghy).

At such a perilous moment in the east it was worth co opting a leading Kurd into government. Shaykh Abd al Qadir was the obvious target. He was a widely acknowledged Ottoman notable, still President of the Council of State and also commanded a large Kurdish following, including the 15,000 or so members of Kurdish artisan guilds in Istanbul. In March 1919 he was invited into the new cabinet of Damad Farid Pasha. He insisted that Kurds must be given the chance to take greater control of their affairs and obtained a promise, an empty one as it turned out, that Kurds would be appointed as governors in Kurdistan. However, he also risked Ottoman suspicion by suggesting that the British oversee such an arrangement.

The government also prevailed on some members of the Kurdish National Committee (as the Kurdish Club also called itself) to travel from Istanbul as far afield as Sulaymaniya with letters to tribal chiefs urging them to throw off the British yoke. In response the British were tempted to lean on the Ottoman government to remove Turkish troops from Kurdish towns and to appoint members of Shaykh Abd al Qadir's entourage as governors in Van, Bitlis, and other Kurdish towns.[22]

Kurdish Hopes Dashed

By the spring of 1919 there were three strands of political thinking among the Kurds: pro-Turkish, pro-Allies and finally, among the Dersim Kurds, a desire for complete independence from all outside interference. The trouble was that these strands were not distinct. Many Kurds, perplexed by the uncertainties involved, did not wish to commit themselves irretrievably to one course of action.

Two developments in May 1919 destroyed Kurdish hopes of achieving either autonomy or independence in eastern Anatolia. The first of these was the Greek landing at Smyrna, encouraged by the Allies in the hope of achieving its share of the Sykes–Picot spoils by force. Further south Italy landed forces at Antalya. The psychological effect of these landings was dramatic for the Muslim population of Anatolia. It was already known how sensitive the Kurds were to the Christian threat. Admiral Calthorpe in Istanbul had telegraphed the Foreign Office only a fortnight before the Greek landings: 'The most important factor in situation is fear that the [eastern] section of Turkey will be placed under Armenian rule. There is otherwise a strong tendency for Kurds and Turks to drift apart but this fear drives them into Union.'[23]

The Kurdish reaction was inevitable. For thousands living in eastern Anatolia will-o'-the-wisp ideas of nationalism were instantly eclipsed by the heightened

Christian threat. The Ottoman government had no difficulty mobilizing pan-Islamic solidarity:

> News was spread of a massacre of Mohammedans by the Greeks. The Kurds were invited to apply the analogy of Smyrna to Diarbekir; the English would come first and occupy the town, which would be but a prelude to the arrival of Armenian troops. All these measures had their natural effect.[24]

However, if it was a Turkish aim to whip up Kurdish apprehension against the Christian threat, it was equally the aim to use the danger of *Kurdish* fanaticism and anti-Christian violence as grounds for closing the Kurdish clubs. In view of their part in the Armenian massacres of 1915, this was an easily justifiable move. On 4 June the Diyarbakir club was closed and its leaders arrested.

In the meantime, the Kurds had begun to run into serious difficulties in Istanbul. With Greeks and Italians seizing parts of Anatolia and the Allies discussing the reconstitution of Anatolian Armenia, talk of Kurdish autonomy within the cabinet itself was more than even Damad Farid Pasha could stomach and, in the first week of June, Shaykh Abd al Qadir was dismissed.

Abd al Qadir's dismissal caused understandable anger in Istanbuli Kurdish circles. In early July a meeting between certain cabinet members and Kurdish Club leaders was arranged by a cabinet member, Ibrahim al Haydari who was a former *shaykh al islam* and scion of an Arbili Kurdish family. Its purpose seems to have been to repair some of the damage between the two parties, but it got off to a shaky start. The Turks accused the Kurds of 'working with organizations tending towards independence and refusing to recognize our government', a charge that was vehemently denied. Ibrahim al Haydari warned 'England ... is trying to form a big Kurdistan and annexe to it the eastern vilayet [sic].' Abd al Qadir, or his representative, countered that Farid Pasha's statements to the Peace Conference suggested he was willing to sacrifice Kurdistan in favour of the Armenians. Al Haydari conceded Farid Pasha's mistakes in Paris and Abd al Qadir pressed home his advantage by complaining that having chosen two Kurds to be Walis of Diyarbakir and Elazig respectively, the cabinet then failed to appoint them. It was promised that a Kurdish wali and a proportionate number of Kurds would be appointed to Kurdistan. But the meeting ended badly when Rifat Mawlana Zada, a journalist from Diyarbakir, argued on behalf of Abd al Qadir in favour of British protection and asked 'how it could be possible for the Turkish Government to grant any form of autonomy to the Kurds seeing that the Turks themselves were not sure of their own position.'[25]

The Turks were furious, but their policy had already crystallized decisively, after the Greek landings at Smyrna, to take a tough line with any hint of Kurdish distinctiveness. Noel's views were relayed from Istanbul in early July:

> Idea of Kurdish autonomy under Turkish sovereignty seems dead. Turks are working on exclusively Pan-Islamic lines. Word Kurdish is rigorously suppressed and Moslem used instead.[26]

Furthermore, as the same despatch noted, Kurdish leaders now had wind of a proposed revival of the war-time Kurdish resettlement programme, to distribute Kurdish refugees

> so that they can never form a block of more than 5 per cent of the Turkish population presumably with a view to their speedier Turkification whilst every effort is being made to prevent their return to Kurdistan.

It also noted that the Turks had started propagating 'Pan-Islamic and Chauvinistic propaganda which makes use of Armenian bogey' to win over tribes ignorant of the broader political picture.

It was now that a second disaster for Kurdish nationalism began to be felt. Mustafa Kemal, the founder of modern Turkey, arrived in Samsun in May 1919 as newly appointed inspector-general of the Ninth Army. His orders were to collect in arms and ammunition and ensure obedience to Istanbul, as the Allies insisted. Contrary to such instructions he urged local commanders to organize popular resistance to all foreign intrusions, the Greeks in the west, the Armenians in the east, the French in Adana, the Italians in Antalya and Konya, and the British in Urfa, Marash and Ayntab (Gaziantep).

When Britain demanded his recall four weeks later, Kemal resigned his commission, thus becoming a rebel. In late June his colleagues and he signed a protocol in Amasya that renounced Istanbul's authority and called for a National Congress in Sivas to organize the defence of the Fatherland. Even before the Sivas Congress was called, the Society for the Defence of the Rights of Eastern Anatolia had arranged for a congress in Erzerum, which took place from 23 July to 7 August. Its ten-point resolution declared *inter alia* the six eastern vilayets an integral and inseparable part of Ottoman territory; vested the national forces with authority to preserve the integrity of the empire and the protection of the sultanate and caliphate; and rejected any privileges to Christians in a manner to alter political control or social balance. Although written in Turkish, it was careful to speak in terms of Muslim citizens:

> We are calling for a decision based on right and justice, one that respects our historic, cultural and religious rights, and that rejects totally the theory of dividing lands and separating peoples who are within the boundaries established by the armistice signed by the Allies on October 30, 1918 and in eastern Anatolia, as well as in other regions, inhabited by a majority of Muslims and dominated by Muslims culturally and economically.[27]

How could any Kurd reject the preservation of eastern Anatolia's integrity against the Christian threat or, for that matter, the preservation of the sultanate and caliphate, those elements that bound together Muslims of different ethnic origin?

In August it was rumoured that the French were about to march on Sivas, and also that all the political parties in Istanbul had assured the Americans that Turks in the eastern provinces would agree to surrender territory to an Armenian state.[28] As the carve-up of Anatolia seemed imminent, Kemal did not hesitate to write personally to those Kurdish chiefs he knew in Diyarbakir, Bitlis, Van and Bayazid for their active support.

The Noel Mission

It was perhaps partly on account of the activities of Mustafa Kemal that the Ottoman government now gave its blessing to a visit to Turkish Kurdistan by Major Noel and Amin Ali's two sons, Jaladat and Kamuran Ali. The idea had been cooked up in Baghdad by Noel and Wilson. Noel arrived in Istanbul in July exuding pro-Kurdish enthusiasm, 'a nice fellow' as the British political adviser, J.B. Hohler, remarked, 'but he is another fanatic.... I am afraid Noel may turn out a Kurdish Col. Lawrence.'[29] Hohler's instincts did not mislead him, and he took every care to impress upon Abd al Qadir and his colleagues that their sole task was to encourage the chiefs north of the Mosul vilayet to remain quiet at this difficult time:

> I made it as clear as words five times repeated can make things clear that we were *not* out for intrigues against the Turks, and that I could promise *nothing whatsoever* as regards the future of Kurdistan.[30]

Hohler probably knew he was wasting his time. What use was it to impress such things on the mission when every Kurd and Turk they met on the way could only logically believe that Britain had designs on south-east Anatolia? Moreover they were correct to believe such things. Noel had been less than candid in discussing the mission in Istanbul, for he intended 'counteracting the Pan-Islamic propaganda of the Turks and their efforts to turn the Kurds against us'.[31] He hoped to strengthen British influence, preferably by the installation of Amin Ali Badr Khan as Wali of Diyarbakir and commensurately to weaken Turkey's hold on the region.

It is unlikely Istanbul believed the Noel mission to be half as innocent as officially pretended. As could have been forseen Noel's mission, as he himself reported by telegraph, 'led to [the] thought that [the] formation of [a] Kurdish state would be seriously discussed at [the] Peace Conference'.[32]

Meanwhile Noel had set out from Istanbul, amidst misgivings at the High Commission. He met the brothers Kamuran and Jaladat Badr Khan in Aleppo, travelling with them to Ayntab and to Malatya, where unlike in Mardin and Diyarbakir the population was allegedly more nationalist. That, as Noel himself later admitted, was partly owing to his own incitement. But in Ayntab and Malatya the Kurds were predominantly Alevi and so did not share feelings of Muslim unity or loyalty to the sultanate, and were hostile to Kemal's national movement. Furthermore, unlike Mardin and Diyarbakir, there was no Armenian threat. It will be recalled that Alevi Kurds had been notable for protecting Armenians from extermination in 1915. Ayntab and Malatya were unrepresentative of the general state of apprehension in Ottoman Kurdistan.

Mustafa Kemal had been aware at the beginning of July of the impending visit and purpose of the Badr Khans. Once they were known to have left Istanbul, Kemal had instructed a local force 'to proceeed in such a manner as to destroy the possibility of a separatist movement by the Kurds.'[33] Kemal's Sivas Congress was in full swing when Noel reached Malatya on 3 September and made contact with the Mutasarrif, Khalil Badr Khan, an uncle of Kamuran and Jaladat who had been entrusted by Farid Pasha with rallying anti-Kemalist forces in the region.

Kemal learnt on 9 September that Noel and the Badr Khans were in Malatya. He had also learnt that Farid Pasha had given instructions to the Mutasarrif of Kharput nearby to rally some Kurdish cavalry, presumably old tribal regiments, in order to surprise the Sivas Congress in session and arrest the delegates. His darkest suspicions about Noel were confirmed: 'We understood that their real object was to rouse the Kurds and incite them to attack us, promising them a constitution for an independent Kurdistan.'[34] Noel and his colleagues were compelled to withdraw hastily into Syria.

Kemal and his colleagues had little difficulty in using the Noel mission for propaganda purposes. Kurds in the east were already apprehensive after Armenian operations in the Caucasus during July had sent thousands of Muslims fleeing to the Ottoman frontier. Fighting had been taking place between Kurds and Armenians on the north-eastern slopes of Ararat since the spring, and in September Armenian forces had razed Kurdish villages between Ararat and Bayazid. The Noel mission suggested collusion on the part of the British and Farid Pasha's government in Istanbul against those trying to defend Anatolia. Even the Americans were persuaded of 'deep British designs in Kurdistan'.[35]

Kurdistan and the Turkish National Movement

In September Kemal informed the Great Powers that the government in Istanbul was an illegal tyranny and that its delegation to Paris did not represent the nation. One month later Farid Pasha resigned from office, embarrassed by his inability to halt Kemal's progress. He was succeeded by Ali Riza, a more resolute nationalist. That autumn Kurds began to feel the heat. A new 'Kurdish Democratic Party' was refused registration. Newspaper articles began to warn that to speak of Kurdish independence was to help Armenian nationalism. Certain Kurds were rounded up and condemned to death for treasonous statements.

In Istanbul some Kurdish nationalists still clung to Britain. In the light of the abortive Noel mission and the successes of the Kemalists, members of Kurdistan Ta'ali Jamiyati held an extraordinary meeting on 8 October to reiterate their confidence in the Peace Conference, and to affirm 'They have no common cause whatever with the Anatolian movement.... England is our only friend, and the Kurds have resolved to have no other protector than England.'[36]

Yet in Kurdistan the tide of events was clearly flowing against both British and Kurdish nationalist interests. Not only the Kemalists but also the Kurds in the region, in the words of the British High Commissioner, 'see us abandoning the Caucasus, and leaving behind between Ararat and the Caspian, a fruitful field for Pan-Islamic and Pan-Turkish propaganda. To the south east, they see us slowly drawing in our horns in south eastern Kurdistan.'[37]

By the autumn Kemal's propaganda was rapidly turning many tribes in his favour. Turkish nationalists believed, possibly correctly, that Britain was financing the Kurdish clubs in places like Diyarbakir and that these in turn were sending supplies to the rebellious tribes in Dersim.[38] At any rate they seem to have had little difficulty in mobilizing Kurds still loyal to the Ottoman state to move against such groups. By the end of the year at least 70 Kurdish tribes, apart from a number of influential urban notables, had declared for Kemal. These lived mostly where the threat seemed greatest, on the southern and eastern marches of Anatolia, and of these the most important were the Milli in the south and the Jalali and Haydaranli tribes in the east.

Meanwhile, Mustafa Kemal had been strengthening his position elsewhere. His demand for the election of a genuine national assembly was accepted by Sultan Mehmet VI. In January 1920 its large Turkish nationalist majority affirmed a National Pact, based upon the declaration made at Sivas. This formally confirmed the Kemalist position on Turkey's complete independence and its claim to all non-Arab Ottoman territories, including Kurdistan *beyond* the armistice line.

The rise of the Kemalists in Anatolia had increased British anxiety for a buffer zone between Mesopotamia and the Turks. By autumn 1919 there were fresh grounds for apprehension when the Kemalists received support from the Bolsheviks. Mustafa Kemal had secretly conferred with Soviet representatives at the end of May, obtaining an assurance of support against Allied attempts to carve a separate Armenia or Kurdistan out of Anatolia. Britain had already run into difficulties with Bolshevism in the Caucasus, on the Caspian shore in 1918, and in Batum. It began to worry that Kurdistan, even the southern part, might prove susceptible to the joint efforts of Turkish nationalists and Bolsheviks. Indeed, the term Bolshevism, wholly misunderstood, was nevertheless gaining currency among the tribes. In February word came from French-occupied Nusaybin 'we will have no foreign power over us, we are Bolsheviks and will rule ourselves.'[39]

Britain was still working on the hope that an Armenian state would be created. Its enthusiasm was predicated on the American interest in acting as mandatory. In the United States, Woodrow Wilson had told the National Democratic Committee in February, 'I am not without hope that the people of the United States would find it acceptable to go in and be trustee of the interests of the Armenian people and see to it that the unspeakable Turk and the almost equally difficult Kurd had their necks sat on long enough to teach them manners.'[40] By June President Wilson was all for telling Istanbul which territories in the east it could no longer have, but at the same time he was unable to confirm that the United States would assume the mandate. By the autumn it was clear that the United States would not take it.

The Road to Sèvres

America's withdrawal put the fate of all eastern Anatolia into flux and made a reconciliation between the Kurds and the Armenians all the more desirable, despite Kurdo-Armenian fighting on the ground. Thus, the fate of Kurdistan became strategically more important to Britain at precisely the moment when the prospects for its materialization were significantly lessened. In Paris, British officials persuaded the Armenian representative, Boghos Nubar, of the desirability of a Kurdo-Armenian declaration of solidarity against the return of Turkish rule. Believing the Armenian case to be in jeopardy Nubar immediately negotiated an agreement with Sharif Pasha. On 20 November they issued a joint declaration

> We are in complete agreement in jointly seeking from the [Peace] Conference the constitution, in accordance with the principals of nationalities of a united and independent Armenia and an independent Kurdistan, with the assistance of a Great Power.... We confirm moreover our complete agreement to respect the legitimate rights of the minorities in the two states.[41]

The declaration accepted the verdict of the Peace Conference regarding the delimitation of borders between the two states. At first, reactions in both camps were positive. Shaykh Abd al Qadir and several of the Badr Khans expressed their satisfaction, largely because it was the first occasion on which Armenians had formally recognized Kurdish rights. A sense of euphoria prevailed in both camps that Kurdo-Armenian animosity might be a thing of the past, and the actual text of the declaration was eagerly awaited in Istanbul and Yerevan.

America's withdrawal also left the east Anatolian question essentially to Britain and France. Until now it had been possible to assume that, with a political settlement to the north of it, somehow Kurdistan would 'fall into place' with a fringe of autonomous states providing a buffer for Mesopotamia. This was now no longer realistic. Britain and France would have to act.

France shared British unease about a vacuum north of Syria and Iraq which the Kemalists seemed bound to fill. In late December M. Berthelot, Chief Political Secretary at the Quai d'Orsay, reminded Lord Curzon that the only extant agreement for the area was Sykes–Picot, and now proposed a federal arrangement between a northern (French) and southern (British) Kurdistan.[42]

Curzon was unenthusiastic. He told Berthelot he wanted to avoid repetition of the problems Britain had on the North West Frontier, and that it would be better to let the Kurds decide whether they preferred one state or loosely knit autonomous fiefdoms. He was so determined to avoid further troop deployments that, still deaf to the strategic argument of Baghdad, he confirmed that Britain did not intend to remain in southern Kurdistan. But he certainly did not want France on the northern approaches to Mesopotamia.

Thus, as Kurdistan continued to assume greater strategic importance, Britain was also abandoning hope of effective co-operation with Kurdish leaders. 'I think it should be left principally to the Kurds themselves,' Hohler had written in November from Istanbul, ' to work out their own salvation and to disentangle themselves from the Turks.... [The Kurds] are like a rainbow of every shade of colour.'[43] By March the British High Commissioner sceptically summed up his view of the realities:

> there exists much doubt whether independence or autonomy of Kurdistan is a propo-
> sition at all and in any case no such thing as 'Kurdish opinion' in the sense of coherent
> public opinion can be said to exist ... few [Kurds] looking higher than tribal aghas or
> religious Sheikhs amongst whom there is little common ground ... [the] few educated
> Kurds outside Kurdistan holding Separatist ideas are very apt to exaggerate their own
> influence and importance.[44]

In Istanbul Damad Farid Pasha, now out of government, believed he could replace the new administration if only he could come up with a credible plan for defeating Mustafa Kemal. He sought to enveigle Shaykh Abd al Qadir into a bargain similar to the one he had failed to keep twelve months earlier. He promised the Kurds virtually complete autonomy in return for a Kurdish assault on the Kemalists in the east. But Abd al Qadir was reluctant to compromise his prospects without cast-iron guarantees from Farid Pasha and an assurance of British protection for Kurdistan, guarantees that simply could not be provided.

Meanwhile, rumours of partition between the two Allies pushed the Kurds back into Ottoman arms. In January 1920 a group of Young Kurds travelled to Switzerland to see Sharif Pasha, armed with an Ottoman offer of autonomy subject to the Sultan and to a Turkish parliament in which they would be represented. Despite their mistrust, the Young Kurds preferred such an arrange-ment to partition. A Kurdish delegation also called on the British High Commis-sion to protest at the separation of southern Kurdistan. It insisted 'that Kurdistan is treated as an integral ethnic and geographical whole' but also 'admitted that loyalty to the Caliphate was a real force in Kurdistan',[45] a view that contrasted with previous talk of separation. Sure enough, before the end of March chiefs and notables in Elazig were petitioning that their country should not be sepa-rated from the caliphate.

Abd al Qadir also wanted Kurdistan to remain united preferably under British protection, but said he was not against Turkish sovereignty. He emphasized another growing Kurdish anxiety: that Armenian rule was unacceptable. The Badr Khans were reluctant to take a position until the Allies made a formal announcement.

From Paris Sharif Pasha also started to campaign against the rumoured Anglo-French partition, arguing that autonomy under Turkish sovereignty was prefer-able. This did not prevent him from formally presenting the Peace Conference with maximalist claims for an independent Kurdistan, and repudiating Armenia's territorial claims as egregious. Invoking the right to self-determination and the right to free development of different peoples following their national aspiration, he affirmed

> Kurdistan forms an indivisible whole, which, if it is to be detached from the Ottoman empire, may only be assigned to one single mandatory for its economic development.[46]

It was his most glorious moment, but it was shortlived.

When the verbatim text of the Sharif–Nubar accord became known in Armenia and Kurdistan it provoked outrage and embarrassment. Boghos Nubar was accused of demolishing the Armenian case for the six eastern vilayets submitted to the Peace Conference in February 1919. Among Kurds it provoked equal distress, for it brought out into the open the ambiguity that had existed between the true separatists and those for whom a guaranteed autonomy was enough. In Kurdistan dozens of Kurdish chiefs and notables, some of them engaged in bitter conflict with Armenian troops, denounced the accord. For it spoke of 'emancipation from the cruel domination of the Turkish governments ... deliverance from the yoke of the CUP...' at the very moment when a growing number of Kurds wished to mend their fences with the Turkish government.[47]

There were mixed Kurdish reactions in Istanbul. The Babans dissociated themselves from the accord. Abd Allah Jawdat interpreted his decentralist views in support of a Kurdo-Armenian union.[48] A group led by Amin Ali Badr Khan wrote to Lloyd George 'we solicit the kind assistance of the British Government for the development of our country within her national limits.'[49] Shaykh Abd al Qadir was not one of the signatories.

He had already outraged a number of his Kurdish Club colleagues when he gave an interview to the Istanbuli journal *Ikhdam* at the end of February in which he had minimized the significance of the accord, disclaimed any Kurdish hostility towards Turks, and spoke of autonomy of the Kurdish vilayets as his aspiration, within 'the one fold of Ottomanism'.[50] It was this last phrase which had stung his colleagues most. They accused him of going back on a commitment to independence. But Abd al Qadir had always been 'actuated a great deal by veneration for the Caliphate'.[51] In this he was true to his Naqshbandi roots. In mid-April he was declared deposed as president of the Kurdish Club and expelled. He retorted by pronouncing the club committee dissolved and calling for new elections. He knew he could win because the Kurdish guilds of Istanbul supported him.

New elections soon demonstrated his popularity among the ordinary Kurds of Istanbul. The Badr Khans and 'intellectuals' withdrew from the Kurdish Club and formed their own Kurdish Social League,[52] motivated as much by personal rivalries as issues of principle. The Badr Khans were already longstanding rivals of Abd al Qadir, no doubt jealous of his popular following among the Kurdish masses, in Istanbul and Kurdistan. Some members of the new league, for example

Jawdat, were a good deal more pro-Turkish than Abd al Qadir himself. In reality so similar were the positions of the rivals that a few months later the Kurdish Social League and Abd al Qadir's 'League of Kurds and Kurdistan' made almost identical objections to the delimitation of Kurdistan as proposed for the Peace Treaty.

As for Sharif Pasha, disowned by both factions in Istanbul, his brief nationalist career ended in ignominy. His dalliance with both the Turkish government and the Armenian delegate left everyone distrustful of his position. When he announced his resignation as Kurdish representative to the British Ambassador in Paris, his self-justification contradicted most of what he had been telling British representatives since 1914: 'My principal objective had been to establish cordial and straight relations between England and the Ottoman Empire.'[53]

Thus, on the eve of the peace treaty to be forged by the Allies, the Kurds found themselves without a representative in Paris, deeply divided by personal rivalry and factionalism in Istanbul, and divided by the harsh choices that had to be made in the face of Kemalist and Armenian forces in Anatolian Kurdistan.

Yet, some of the fears that gave rise to such destructive tensions proved ill-founded. Britain never welcomed the idea of extending the French sphere as far as Diyarbakir, Siirt and Bitlis, which in any case ceased to be feasible when Kemalist forces drove the French from Marash in February 1920.

It was not difficult for Britain to persuade France now to accept the idea of an autonomous Kurdistan. This should be free from Turkey as Britain wanted, on account of its pan-Turan and Bolshevik fears, but not a single protectorate, which Britain could not contemplate for itself because it was unready to commit the necessary troops and which it could not assign to the French because of the mutual suspicions between the two Allies.

Yet the idea that Britain had evolved a clear-cut policy towards Kurdistan is misleading. The possibilities that seemed clear in November 1918 were painfully narrowed by April 1920 when decisions at last had to be made. Only Arnold Wilson had maintained a reasonably consistent and realistic policy throughout, liking the idea of a Kurdish confederation but reconciled to the probability of eventual Turkish rule.

The failure of the Kurds to produce a credible leadership was undoubtedly a blow to British hopes, but the greater failure was that of the Allies. They failed to offer a credible alternative to Sykes–Picot in 1918 and so failed to give the people of eastern Anatolia clear indications for their future. More damaging, they allowed time to slip by. The length of interval between Mudros and Sèvres proved a hostage to fortune: the Greek and Armenian attempts on Anatolia, the rise of the Kemalists and quibbling between the Allies. No wonder most Kurds of eastern Anatolia responded to the Muslim call of Mustafa Kemal in the autumn of 1919, for it was the only credible proposition to hand.

Nothing illustrates Britain's disarray on Kurdistan more than the crucial inter-departmental meeting at the Foreign Office on 13 April 1920. Curzon, who took the chair, knew that within the week he would be in San Remo explaining the terms of peace Britain believed the Allies should offer Turkey. He reminded those present that during their previous three or four meetings to discuss the Kurdish question they had arrived at contrary conclusions resulting from the changing situation: first, to form a fringe of autonomous Kurdish states around the borders of the Mosul vilayet; then to divide Kurdistan into French and British spheres of influence; at the last meeting they had decided to cut Britain free from all of Kurdistan but found themselves 'in a position where we desired to cut Kurdistan off from Turkey, but were unable to find anyone to set up an autonomous State in that country'.[54] Now they found themselves modifying this position to retain southern Kurdistan *pro tem*, and with the proviso made by Edwin Montagu, the India Secretary, that 'hope might be held out to it that it should join Northern Kurdistan at some future date'.

Curzon finally bowed to the hard fought argument from Arnold Wilson in Baghdad, that it made more sense to defend Mesopotamia by retaining southern Kurdistan than to allow Turks or Bolsheviks the chance to encircle northern Mesopotamia from the east. In the long run it would require fewer troops. Britain had already had a taste of Turkey fomenting unrest around Rawanduz in February. Besides, by this time certain Arab Nationalists were suggesting that the southern Kurds would accept the suzerainty of the Hashimite Amir Abd Allah if the latter were installed at the head of an Arab government in Baghdad.[55] If Southern Kurdistan later joined Northern Kurdistan to form a single political entity, well and good, just so long as the Turks and Bolsheviks could be kept well away from the approaches to Mesopotamia.

There was now a new economic consideration. In early December Arnold Wilson had toured Sulaymaniya and Arbil by air, and confirmed that 'geological reports indicated greater oil potential than previously thought.'[56] Indeed, Britain had harboured rather low expectations of the Kirkuk oilfield, its preliminary geological survey in February 1919 opining that the field should be tackled by a company 'rich enough to face indifferent success or failure'.[57] By March 1920 this new economic factor crystallized into policy, with the cabinet concluding that 'the oil bearing regions of Mosul are essential to the revenues on which the future of the whole country will depend.'[58] But on 13 April, those cabinet ministers deciding the fate of Kurdistan failed to mention oil; not one of them seems to have apprehended the importance of the Kirkuk oilfields. Even those representing the Treasury and the Admiralty, which has most to gain from oil, remained silent throughout the meeting. They did not even challenge Montagu's hope that Southern Kurdistan would in due course be separated from Iraq. The oil consideration never arose.

For Curzon the prevailing force of argument to hang onto southern Kurdistan was embarrassing since he had already assured Berthelot of British intentions to withdraw. However, he would now have to go to San Remo with a volte-face, one that was bound to strengthen the French belief in British duplicity.

Yet he could conveniently but truthfully claim that the exclusion of southern Kurdistan from British-administered territory would go against the wishes of the majority of Kurdish inhabitants. Rumours that Britain might be about to abandon Sulaymaniya had already led to a general panic. The Civil Commissioner had smugly reported only the week before that the governor in the Iranian border town of Mariwan had made a special trip to plead for the British to stay, otherwise his own position would be untenable. Local chiefs and notables had also sent deputations in similar vein. He proudly pointed out the prosperity Britain had brought to a region wracked by years of despoliation: the acreage of cereals had doubled, 100,000 trees had been planted, the tobacco harvest trebled, and Sulaymaniya sufficiently recovered to the degree that it had a 50 per cent higher population density than the rest of Iraq. Withdrawal, he concluded, would be regarded by 'our Kurdish friends' as 'perfidy', and the British would be lucky to withdraw without loss of life.[59]

And so at San Remo the following week, Lord Curzon obtained acceptance from the Allies of the terms he wanted for a peace treaty with Turkey. It would provide for the appointment of a Commission of the three Great Powers to draft within six months of the coming into force of the treaty a scheme of local autonomy for the predominantly Kurdish areas, with the right of appeal within one year to the League of Nations for complete independence. The scheme also incorporated Montagu's wish that 'provision should be made for the two parts of Kurdistan eventually to come together if they desired it.'

Until they knew the terms on offer some Kurds understandably began to bridle. Shaykh Abd al Qadir cabled Paris that since the Kurdish Committee was not represented at the Peace Conference it reserved the right to protest any decision made 'contrary to the principles of nationality'.[60]

Once the proposals were formally known Shaykh Abd al Qadir and the rival Badr Khans protested the exclusion from the Kurdish autonomous area of the Kurdish parts of Jazira, Urfa and Mardin in French Syria, and certain lands, notably Malatya and Kochgiri [Dersim] west of the Euphrates. The Kurdish Social League rashly expressed its delight to President Wilson that he had been designated arbiter of the border delineation between Armenia and Kurdistan. Meanwhile the Turks were trying to get Sharif Pasha's support for a counter-proposal for an autonomous Ottoman Kurdish state, one presumably for which independence would never be an option.

Yet by now the situation was radically altered. Alarmed by the French defeat at Marash, Britain occupied Istanbul militarily in mid-March and installed Farid Pasha as virtual puppet vizir. Britain's action justified Mustafa Kemal's establishment of a separate government of the Grand National Assembly in Ankara in late April. For most Turks it was the only credible government, for it was careful to declare the Sultan in Istanbul 'a prisoner of the Allies'.[61] In May, Kemal defeated the French in Cilicia.

Despite the growing power and authority of the Grand National Assembly in

Ankara, however, the Allies pressed on with negotiating the peace treaty with the government in Istanbul. Farid Pasha himself protested the terms of the treaty but he and his government were prisoners of the British forces. On 10 August his representatives were compelled to sign at Sèvres a surrenderist treaty of which they strongly disapproved.

For the Kurds, Sèvres (articles 62 and 64, see appendix) promised the formation of an autonomous region which would have the right to elect for complete independence one year after the formation of the autonomous area, if the League of Nations were persuaded of their capacity for such independence. It also allowed for the adhesion of southern Kurdistan to such a future Kurdish state. But the terms were flawed by the exclusion of Kurdish territories in Syria, Dersim lying west of the Euphrates and, above all, by the failure to demarcate Kurdistan's boundary with Armenia. This was foreseeably bound to outrage either the Kurds or the Armenians, as President Wilson's pro-Armenian proposed boundary accompanying the treaty clearly showed.

However, such flaws were as nothing compared with the fundamental fact that the treaty had been forced upon an unwilling and token government that lacked a constituency even in Istanbul. On the same day the Allies concluded a tripartite treaty to partition much of Anatolia in favour of Italy and France, leaving only a fraction for the Turks. Already the Greeks had launched a new offensive in western Anatolia. For any self-respecting Turk there was only one government now, the government that was willing to fight to the end, be it on the eastern, western or southern fronts, the government of Mustafa Kemal. Sèvres, as far as the Turks were concerned, was void before the ink was dry.

From Sèvres to Lausanne

The Treaty of Sèvres had been signed in disregard of the facts. Turkey was now fighting for its life, facing civil war within and invasion from without. Rebel Turkish and Kurdish bands roamed the countryside. In the summer of 1920 the Alevi Kurds of Dersim and Kharput, whose independence had only been reduced in the 1870s, rebelled against Ankara's attempted imposition of authority. One year later they were still defying Kemalist forces (see chapter 9). Moreover, through Mush, Bitlis and Siirt government authority was negligible. In Diyarbakir, Nusaybin and Mardin there had been short-lived risings by tribes resentful of Ankara's attempts to impose control. These disorders constituted nuisance value. The real danger was that they would distract and divert Ankara's forces from the more serious external threat.

In May Armenian bands had begun to raid the eastern borders. Only after the Greek invasion had been contained were troops deployed to counter them. In October, Turkish forces captured Kars and moved on to recapture territories lost in the 1877 war with Russia. The Armenians sued for peace, repudiating all claims on Turkish territory. A new frontier was established. Unless Turkey collapsed on its western front, the idea of an Armenian state and consequently a Kurdish one, no longer seemed feasible. It became increasingly important to bring Ankara into a political settlement.

Attempts to convene a conference in London in March 1921 to persuade the Kemalists to accept Sèvres in tandem with Ottoman representatives ended in failure. As soon as they had wind of the London conference both factions of Istanbuli Kurds called on Britain's High Commissioner to emphasize that the Ankara delegation could in no way represent the wishes of the Kurdish people. But they also sensed a weakening of Allied resolve, and asked that there should be no dilution of the autonomy principle adumbrated in Article 64, renewing their claim to areas of Kurdish population density excluded from the autonomous region and allocated to French Syria and British Mesopotamia.

The Kurdish nationalists were right to be suspicious. Britain was already willing to drop all reference to a future independent Kurdistan in a revised treaty, though it still hoped to retain autonomy clauses, and accordingly informed the Turkish delegate on 12 March:

> In regard to Kurdistan the Allies would be prepared to consider a modification of the Treaty in a sense in conformity with the existing facts of the situation, on condition of facilities for local autonomies and the adequate protection of Kurdish and Assyro-Chaldean interests.[62]

What Britain badly wanted was an assurance from Ankara that it would cease fomenting unrest on the Iraqi border.

Meanwhile the Bolsheviks and Kemalists, both friendless so far, needed to confront the Western Allies and so concluded a Treaty of Friendship in March 1921. It was the first formal foreign recognition of the new Ankara government. It was just the kind of fillip it needed, for Greece launched a second major offensive the same month.

The Greeks were well aware of the diversionary advantages of a Kurdish uprising in the Kemalist heartlands. Discussions had taken place with the Badr Khans and other nationalists in Istanbul. Throughout the summer scraps of information surfaced concerning Greek material and financial support for a Kurdish rising. This had included the Greek release of Kurdish soldiers captured with Kemalist forces. In August the Greek prime minister urged that Europe assist the Kurds form an independent state.

British officials debated whether to give discreet help. The idea of fomenting an anti-Kemalist rebellion had been discussed intermittently since the autumn of 1920 when Ankara had so vehemently rejected Sèvres. The British had already turned down Shaykh Taha, who had visited Arbil in September 1920, seeking arms and equipment for an independent Kurdistan. Then they had thought of a joint strategy with the Ottoman government. But such a venture was contingent on re-occupying Jazira bin Umar, supplying the Kurds with arms, and assuring them that they would not fall under French rule. All three were ruled out as not being feasible.[63]

At the time it seemed desirable to deal not only with the Kemalists but also with the growing Bolshevik threat, since the Kemalists and Bolsheviks were increasingly friendly.[64] Now, with the Greeks themselves attempting to make common cause with the Kurds, the idea was raised again.

The plan was to work through the Shirnakh tribes with leadership provided by Major Noel and the Badr Khans. But fears that, once unleashed, a Kurdish movement could not possibly be controlled, brought such schemes to nought. Only *in extremis* would Britain follow such a policy.

Nevertheless, British interest in fomenting revolt was revived by the arrival in Rawanduz in June 1921 of a platoon of Kemalist soldiers, intent on goading the Surchi and other local tribes into revolt, and another 300 troops in early August. Although a Turkish advance on Raniya was repulsed at the end of the month, it was clear that Ankara was intent on wresting the Kurdish areas from British control and was doing all it could to stir up the tribes, using pan-Islamic and anti-Arab propaganda to attract the Kurds. By the end of the year the Turks were still firmly ensconced in Rawanduz in spite of RAF bombing, and were likely to remain there until the snows melted.

There was a natural desire to repay Ankara in the same coin. Abd al Rahman of Shirnakh now offered the British and the newly acclaimed king of Iraq, Faysal, the prospect of a small buffer state on the northern border of Iraq, one that might abut the growing fiefdom of the ambitious Simqu, who had thrown off Tehran's authority the previous April. It was a tempting prospect. In October Khalil Badr Khan (ex *mutasarrif* of Malatya) and other members of the Istanbul Kurdish club arrived in Baghdad. He offered the prospect of simultaneous risings in Dersim, Diyarbakir, Bitlis and Van which would achieve unity under Badr Khan leadership. What he needed, Khalil Beg argued, was a few officers like Major Noel, a couple of mountain guns, several heavy machine-guns and 5,000 rifles and ammunition. The Greeks had already promised a shipload of weapons conditional on Britain permitting transit of such material through Iraq. The High Commissioner was tempted, for the simple reason that if the Kemalists prevailed, they might try to retake all Kurdish and Turkoman land as far as Kifri. But in London Churchill deprecated any such adventure; the diplomatic and military dangers of such a commitment were too great.[65]

If Britain felt threatened on the northern Iraqi border, this was as nothing compared with the dangers the Kemalists faced in Anatolia. By July Ankara itself seemed likely to fall to the Greeks and most of Anatolia with it. Taking personal command of the Turkish forces, Mustafa Kemal fought a desperate but finally victorious battle against the invaders on the Sakarya river, August–September 1921. The tide had turned.

Now that Ankara seemed likely to prevail, France broke ranks with its Allies. It had already faced major disorder in northern Syria exacerbated by Kemalist armed bands and now wanted to bring hostilities in Cilicia to an end, where the price in manpower was proving too high. In October it concluded a treaty (of

Ankara), based on the National Pact rather than Sèvres, and ceding Cilicia and other claims. It only retained Alexandretta. It was a great triumph for the Ankara government, for besides French recognition it had now struck a separate peace behind Britain's back. Curzon was incandescent. By ceding Nusaybin and Jazira bin Umar to Turkey, France had provided the Kemalists with an ideal assembly area for an assault on Iraq.

Inevitably the British thought again about orchestrating a Kurdish rising to the north but, in spite of the heightened danger to Mosul, they preferred to strike a deal with the Kemalists if they could, rather than risk unforeseen difficulties in a tribal revolt. As for the Kurds, they found that the new borders that divided them had been arbitrarily revised yet again. Abd al Rahman Badr Khan bitterly complained 'France promised us protection but then handed us to the Turks.' He hoped Jazira, Buhtan's old capital, would be incorporated into Iraq.

In March 1922 Turkish and Allied officials met in London, Ankara's purpose being to negotiate a treaty based upon the National Pact, the Allies' being to remodel Sèvres in more a concessionary mould. Thus they affirmed their 'desire for the protection and security of the various minorities, whether Muslim or Christian, or of other races and creeds, who, whether in Europe or Asia, find themselves placed in the midst of larger political or ethnic aggregations'.[66] The Allies still wanted an Armenian state, but Ankara would have none of it.

Despite its victory against the Armenians eighteen months earlier, Ankara's authority in eastern Anatolia remained tenuous. In October 1921 the level of unrest among the Kurdish tribes was sufficient for the Grand National Assembly to send a mission of conciliation to the east. Some deputies had urged the use of immediate 'strong methods', but some of the Kurds in the Assembly reminded their colleagues that a substantial force would be required to bring an estimated 40,000 rebel horsemen to submission, and insufficient troops were available.

Just as Kemalist penetration of northern Iraq had provoked acute anxiety in Baghdad, so the danger of British subversion of the tribes in Anatolia provoked a similar state of mind in Ankara. By March things had not improved. There was an understandable conviction in Ankara that the disorder was supported by King Faysal and the British. Certainly some continued to advocate subversion. Colonel Rawlinson, a liaison officer in Anatolia reported, 'The Kurdish chiefs are entirely dissatisfied ... and extremely anatagonistic towards the Turks, and would require very small inducement (arms or money) to carry out raids,' and proposed the delivery of weapons, principally machine guns, to three Kurdish tribes he thought capable of seizing Erzerum, Bayazid and Erzinjan.[67] In London the temptation was resisted.

In the late summer of 1922 Turkish forces swept the Greeks out of Anatolia and invaded the Straits Zone. The commander of British forces in the Straits Zone, faced with the imminent likelihood of fighting the Kemalists in the streets of Istanbul, agreed to armistice talks in late September and a formal armistice of Mudanya on 3 October.

In the meantime, Ankara's own efforts among the tribes of Kurdistan seemed to be bearing fruit. In the early spring of 1922, at the very moment when Rawlinson was urging a British-sponsored adventure in Anatolia, a Kemalist *qaim-maqam* installed himself in Rawanduz.[68] In June he was succeeded by a Colonel Ali Shafiq, more popularly known as Oz Demir, who made clear that his mission was the reconquest of the Mosul vilayet. Since troops had also concentrated in Jazira, the claim was credible.

It was not long before Oz Demir had the support of important sections of major tribes: the Surchi, Khushnaw, Zangana, Hamavand and Pizhdar, affecting a swathe of country through the administrative divisions of Arbil, Kirkuk and Sulaymaniya. During the summer months more tribal sections threw off British authority, so that in early September Turkish troops occupied Raniya unopposed, and threatened Aqra. A British relief column to Raniya was badly mauled without reaching its objective. Oz Demir proceeded to occupy Koi-Sanjaq also.

It had long been recognized in Baghdad that the unsteady behaviour of the Kurds was in large measure due to uncertainty concerning the future in general and British intentions in particular. The preceding decade or so had seen unprecedented changes in the regional order, beginning with the 1908 revolution and culminating, after the horrors of war in 1915–18, in an entirely new form of foreign (and Christian) administration.

Moreover, it seemed as if the full outcome had not yet been reached. In the north Mustafa Kemal fought against the odds in the name of the Muslim fatherland, and from 1920 was inciting certain chiefs in southern Kurdistan to revolt against Britain. In the east the Kurdish leader Simqu repudiated Iranian authority in 1920 to establish an independent region which inevitably excited Kurdish feeling on the Iraqi side of the border. Like the Kemalists, Simqu was apparently benefiting from the Bolsheviks.

By the summer of 1921 Simqu's successes had offered Britain the enticing prospect of an independent Kurdish entity, carved out of both Iran and Turkey. Although it suspected Iran of facilitating the passage of Turkish troops into Iraq through its own territory, Britain resisted such adventures, this time because of the dangers of dismantling the Turco-Iranian border.

Kurdish chiefs had to consider their position, particularly if the Kemalists won. For a moment this seemed a likely outcome. The Kemalists had successfully repulsed one threat after another, the Armenians, the Greeks, and then the French. Would they now forego the recapture of the Mosul vilayet already publicly claimed in the National Pact? During autumn 1922 intense speculation regarding the rendition of the vilayet to the Kemalists gripped its inhabitants.

In Baghdad it was hoped that with the prospect of peace talks, and the de facto autonomy allowed to its own Kurds, the Turkish danger in southern Kurdistan would recede. Indeed, as Oz Demir soon reported to Mustafa Kemal,

the establishment of an independent Kurdish administration had severely embarrassed the Turkish and pan-Islamic position.

When the Allies formally invited both the Ankara government and the residual
one in Istanbul to Lausanne to discuss peace terms on 27 October, the Grand
National Assembly in Ankara responded by announcing the abolition of the
sultanate, on 1 November. This destroyed the legal foundation for the Istanbul
government and three days later it ceased to exist. At Lausanne this left the
Ankara government as the undisputed government of Turkey. But in Kurdistan
the measure caused dismay among devout Sunnis and, alongside the armistice on
3 October, reduced local support for the Turkish presence in southern Kurdistan.

Although peace talks were scheduled to begin in Lausanne in November,
Britain remained nervous concerning the continued Turkish military presence at
Rawanduz. Anxious not to antagonize the Turks as negotiations began, the
colonial office told the high commissioner to refrain from attacks on Turkish
positions even on the *Iraqi* side of the border, an instruction the High Commissioner was pleased to report had arrived too late.

Curzon, still foreign secretary, was even more fearful. He telegraphed from
Lausanne suggesting that Britain should offer to surrender Kurdish areas to the
Turks in order to secure a peace agreement. This view got short shrift in London.
The air ministry and war office considered these areas strategically vital to the
rest of Mesopotamia, while the Admiralty was anxious to retain the oilfields.
Besides, it meant going back on pledges given to King Faysal concerning the
extent of his domain.

Once commenced, the peace talks in Lausanne rapidly became an attritional
struggle. The treaty, signed on 24 July 1923, achieved what Turkey demanded,
with the exception of the vilayet of Mosul. Here Britain and Turkey had been
unable to agree or to compromise, and it was decided to submit the dispute to
League of Nations arbitration if bilateral compromise proved impossible (as it
did) over the following nine months (Article 3 (2)). This left the vilayet in
continuing uncertainty. Pro-Turkish groups sprang up in many towns, in which
the notable families ensured the attendance of one or more of its junior members.

At Lausanne Curzon had told Ismet Inonu, the Turkish representative, unequivocally that 'The whole of our information shows that the Kurds, with their
own independent history, customs, manners and character, ought to be an
autonomous race,'[69] but to no avail. Any provision for an Armenian or Kurdish
state was abandoned in the new treaty. So also were any safeguards for the
Muslim minorities, notably the Kurds, Circassians and Arabs. The best they got
was an undertaking that:

> No restrictions shall be imposed on the free use by any Turkish national of any lan-
> guage in private intercourse, in commerce, religion, in the press, or in publications of
> any kind or at public meetings. Notwithstanding the existence of the official language,
> adequate facilites shall be given to Turkish nationals of non-Turkish speech for the oral
> use of their own language before the courts (Article 39).

Curzon, no lover of the Turks, recorded his own unease, 'I do not feel very confident but I hope for the best.'[70] As it turned out, Turkey exceeded his worst forebodings. From that day onwards it sought to hammer the Kurdish people on a Turanic anvil, sweeping aside its own modest treaty undertakings.

The Mosul Vilayet

The question of Mosul remained deadlocked. The Kemalists were unwilling to compromise the National Pact which claimed all non-Arab parts of Ottoman Turkey. They feared that Kurdish national feeling in the vilayet would undermine their own 'Turcification' endeavours just north of the border.[71]

Yet the British were unwilling to yield. Oil was becoming an increasingly important issue as the extent of the reserves became better understood. Yet it was still not the overriding consideration. Britain had been willing to give away half the Anglo-Persian Oil Company's 70 per cent holding in Mosul to Standard Oil to get US support for Britain retaining Mosul in 1923. Curzon had even been willing to surrender Mosul in order to clinch Lausanne, but he was shouted down by those who had a stake in the defence of Mesopotamia, namely the colonial office, the India office, the air ministry and the war office. Both Britain and Turkey tried to bribe the other into ceding its claim with a generous share of the oil. Neither side was interested, and the first Kirkuk oil gusher was not struck till 1927.

Mesopotamia, or Iraq as it was now called, was not viable politically, militarily or economically without southern Kurdistan. This was the crux. When Britain and Iraq ratified their treaty of alliance in 1924, it included an important rider that the treaty would become void if Britain failed to safeguard the rights of Iraq in the whole of the Mosul vilayet

At Lausanne Turkey had demanded a plebiscite, but this had been discounted by Britain.[72] Britain favoured arbitration by the League of Nations, an option Turkey disliked since it considered the league to be in the pocket of the Great Powers. Turkey remained committed to plebiscite, willing to accept an indefinite passage of time in the belief that this might provide fresh opportunities for the seizure of Mosul.

This left the population of the region in a quandary. One reason for their difficulties and for increased danger was the absence of any defined northern border of the vilayet. This was not simply a cartographical omission. The Ottomans purposely drew boundaries to divide up some unruly Kurdish confederations, and then changed them as local political circumstances required. Of all the vilayet boundaries, that between Mosul and Van had always been the most vague. In fact, no official map existed.[73]

It was not surprising therefore that minor clashes occurred. In August these reached a climax when Assyrian villagers in the border area captured the local Turkish governor. In response a Turkish force marched through Iraqi-held territory to attack these Assyrian villages in September, expelling their 8,000 inhabitants with considerable brutality.

Meanwhile, on 6 August 1924, Britain had formally referred the question to the league. Despite British protests on 29 September and 5 October, Turkey refused to withdraw from territory claimed by Britain. War was only avoided by the league on 29 October when it delineated the 'Brussels Line', a temporary border that would not prejudice the final outcome, pending a league commission of inquiry.

This commission reached Mosul in January 1925, after visits to London, Ankara and Baghdad. Its task was not an easy one. The majority of the vilayet's population was undeniably Kurdish. Yet the city of Mosul itself was primarily Arab, while the towns and villages along the high road running to Baghdad were mainly Turkish speaking, being Turkoman. But, as the commission noted, the Kurd 'is taking possession of the arable land and is "Kurdizing" certain towns', especially the Turkoman ones of the high road.[74] Trying to draw a line between Arab and Kurdish areas, the only possible ethnic line to attempt, made a nonsense of the economic interdependence of Mosul and its Kurdish hinterland. On the other hand, as the commission reasoned,

> if the ethnic argument alone had to be taken into account, the necessary conclusion would be that an independent Kurdish State should be created, since the Kurds form five eighths of the population.[75]

This figure excluded Yazidi Kurds. If these were included the proportion was nearer three quarters. Yet the council believed that the Kurds were not yet motivated as a whole by national solidarity:

> Among the Kurds we find a growing national consciousness, which is definitely Kurdish and not for Iraq; it is more strongly developed in the south and decreases as one goes northward to die entirely in the plain of Mosul and the mountains of Aqra.

Another broad division existed

> Of the Kurds who inhabit the disputed territory, those who live north of the Greater Zab are, as regards language, ethnic affinities, and personal and economic relations, more closely connected with the Kurds of the vilayets of Hakkiyari and Mardin in Turkey, while those who dwell south of the Lesser Zab have more in common with the Kurds of Persia. It would be difficult to draw a boundary in the territory between these two rivers.[76]

Furthermore, in each zone there were the divides between nomad and peasant, between neighbouring tribes, or between factions within tribes. Kurdish national feeling, the commission believed, expressed itself only in opposition to external political interference, or in the activities of persons of Kurdish origin in places like Istanbul, who had largely lost touch with their kinsmen. There was only one exception to this general view, the Sulaymaniya Division, where we found a Kurdish national feeling which, though yet young, was reasonable enough; for, though the people stated that their supreme desire was for complete independence, they recognized the advantages of an enlightened and intelligent trusteeship.

But overall

Opinion among the Kurds is divided, the group in Sulaymaniya and the neighbouring districts which asks for autonomy within the Iraq State includes almost half the total Kurdish population.

That left just over half less convinced. There were other arguments against attempting an ethnic Kurdish state in the vilayet:

neither the political frontiers of the disputed territory with Persia and Syria, nor the existing boundaries, nor the frontiers claimed by Turkey and by Iraq, are racial frontiers.[77]

Furthermore, the commission argued, the Kurds of the vilayet were a 'negligible' (in fact about 20 per cent) proportion of the entire Kurdish people.

Thus the League of Nations commission abandoned ethnic considerations in favour of economic and strategic ones and, above all, the preferences of the population. Here, of course, the commission found both reticence to speak for fear of reprisals, and conflicting outlooks:

The absence of any Iraqi national feeling explains the large number of conditional preferences. The most strongly nationalist Arabs say that they would prefer Turkey to an Iraq under foreign control. On the other hand, a large number of Christian chiefs say that they would feel less suspicious of a Turkish Government than of an Iraq Government without European control [i.e. better the devil they knew]. The same views are to be found among the Yazidi. The Kurds of Sulaymaniya ask for a wide measure of local autonomy with the assistance of British advisers. Taken as a whole, the opinions expressed in favour of Iraq were in most cases based on considerations of private or community interest rather than on common patriotism.[78]

The commission found the Turkish claim that the population desired a return to Turkish rule to be incorrect.

By now, however, two events in Turkey had seriously undermined the dwindling pro-Turkish camp in the vilayet. In March 1924 Ankara had abolished the caliphate, repudiating the last crucial link between erstwhile Muslim Ottoman citizens and Turkey, and nowhere more so than in Kurdistan where Naqshbandis had always stressed the importance of the *khilafa*. Now there was a more telling demonstration of its new secularist and Turkicist culture. At the very moment the commission was making its inquiry, a revolt led by a Kurdish Naqshabandi, Shaykh Said, was being brutally suppressed, with whole villages being forcibly deported (see chapter 9).

In its conclusion, the League of Nations commission awarded the territory south of the Brussels Line to Iraq, subject to two important conditions:

(1) The territory must remain under the effective mandate of the League of Nations for a period which may be put at twenty-five years; (2) Regard must be paid to the desires

expressed by the Kurds that officials of Kurdish race should be appointed for the administration of their country, the dispensation of justice, and teaching in the schools, and that Kurdish should be the official language of all these services.[79]

This did not amount to autonomy. The commission indicated that were its two conditions not adhered to, the population would have preferred Turkish to Arab sovereignty. In its final deliberations the league was willing to waive its first condition if Iraq itself acquired League of Nations membership within 25 years. However, when Iraq acquired its independence in 1931, no provision was made to guarantee Kurdish political or cultural rights.

Turkey challenged the decision, insisting on the reinstatement of *de facto* Turkish sovereignty. It had made one final attempt in March 1925 to persuade Britain to cede the vilayet in return for exclusive oil exploitation rights, but Britain was not interested. Strategic interests far outweighed oil ones. When pressed upon the commission's requirement regarding Kurdish desires, its spokesman stated that: 'All Kurds possess in Turkey, without any restriction, all the rights possessed by the Turks.'[80] This remained Turkey's position during the succeeding decades of denial and repression of those Kurds who fell within its borders.

While the League of Nations sought the opinion of the Permanent Court of International Justice, fresh complaints were made by both parties concerning infringements of the Brussels Line. Another 3,000 Assyrian Christians fled or were expelled from Turkish areas, and others killed.[81] In November 1925 the court finally gave its opinion that the league's decision was binding on both parties and 'will constitute a definitive determination of the frontier between Turkey and Iraq'.[82] In December 1925 the league confirmed that the commission's recommendations were binding. Turkey and Britain indicated their acceptance of the League of Nation's decision in a bilateral treaty on 5 June 1926.

Sources

League of Nations: Report submitted to the Council by the Commission instituted by the Council Resolution of September 30th, 1924, Document C.400, M.147, vii (Geneva, 1925).

Great Britain, unpublished: Public Record Office: series FO 248 nos 1246; series FO 371 nos 1010, 3384, 3407, 4141, 4149, 4157, 4162, 4192, 4193, 5067, 5068, 5069, 6346, 6347, 6348, 6360, 6369, 6467, 6526, 7772, 7781, 7782, 7858, 9005, 9006; India Office Library L/P&S/10 nos 745, 781, 782, 815, 818.

Great Britain, Printed, Command, Parliamentary and other papers: Kurdistan and the Kurds by G.R. Driver (Carmel, 1919); *Review of the Civil Administration of Mesopotamia from 1914 to the Summer of 1920* by G.L. Bell, Cmd 1061 (London, 1920); *Precis of Affairs in Southern Kurdistan During the Great War* by E.J.R. (Baghdad, 1919); *Mesopotamian Geological Reports, 1919* (Baghdad, 1920); *Diary of Major E.M. Noel on special duty in Kurdistan from 14 June to 21 September, 1919* (Basra, 1919); *Correspondence Respecting the Conditions of the Population of Asia Minor,* Turkey No 10, C 2432 (London, 1879); *Correspondence between H.M.G. and the French Government respecting the*

Angora Agreement of October 20th, 1921, Turkey No. 1 (London, 1922); *Pronouncement by the Three Allied Ministers for Foreign Affairs Respecting the Near East Situation*, Miscellaneous No. 3, Cmd 1641 (Paris, 27 March 1922); *Lausanne Conference on Near Eastern Affairs, 1922–23, Record of Proceedings and Draft Terms of Peace*, Turkey, No. 1, Cmd 1814, (London, 1923).

Secondary sources: George Antonius, *The Arab Awakening* (London, 1938); *Ataturk, A Speech Delivered by Ghazi Mustapha Kemal, October 1927* (Leizig, 1929); Peter Beck, 'A tedious and perilous controversy: Britain and the settlement of the Mosul dispute, 1918–1926', *Middle Eastern Studies*, no. 17, 1981; Briton Cooper Busch, *Mudros to Lausanne: Britain's Frontier in West Asia, 1918–1923* (New York, 1976); Stuart Cohen, *British Policy in Mesopotamia, 1900–1914* (London, 1976); Roderic Davison, 'Turkish diplomacy from Mudros to Lausanne' in Gordon Craig and Felix Gilbert, *The Diplomats, 1919–1939* (Princeton, 1953); C.J. Edmonds, *Kurds, Turks and Arabs* (London, 1957); W.R. Hay, *Two Years in Kurdistan: Experiences of a Political Officer, 1918–1920* (London, 1921); Richard Hovanissian, *The Republic of Armenia*, vol. i, *The First Year, 1918–1919* (Berkley, 1971) and vol. ii *From Versailles to London*; Chris Kutschera, *Le Mouvement National Kurde* (Paris, 1979); Shaw and Shaw, *History of the Ottoman Empire and Modern Turkey*, vol ii; Peter Sluglett, *Britain in Iraq, 1914–1932* (Oxford, 1976); Arnold Toynbee, *Survey of International Affairs, 1925: The Islamic World since the Peace Settlement* (London, 1927); Walker, *Armenia*; Wilson, *Loyalties: Mesopotamia 1914–1917* (London, 1930) and *Mesopotamia, 1917–1920: A Clash of Loyalties* (London, 1931).

Notes

1. Agreement of 23 December 1917, Ronald Grigor Suny, *The Baku Commune, 1917–1918* (Princeton, 1972), p. 275, cited in Walker, *Armenia*, p. 259.
2. L/P&S/10/781 P4635 Political to IO, Baghdad, 16 October 1918.
3. FO 371/3407 Toynbee to Sykes, memorandum 22 October 1918.
4. Defined by a line along the Black Sea coast from Trabzon across to Kars, Bayazid, down the Iranian frontier, across to Siirt, Urfa, north to Divrigi, thence to the Black Sea.
5. Turkish agents were using General Maude's declaration to the inhabitants of Baghdad as evidence of British intentions to put Kurds under Arab rule, Wilson, *Loyalties*, p. 266.
6. E.J.R., *Precis of Affairs*, p. 6.
7. Ibid.
8. For the full text, see George Antonius, *The Arab Awakening* (London 1938), Appendix E.
9. FO 371/3384 Secretary of State for India to Civil Commissioner, Baghdad, 28 October 1918; Wilson, *Mesopotamia*, p. 130; *Precis of Affairs*, pp. 7–8.
10. FO 371/4149 Memorandum: Future Constitution of Mesopotamia dated 6 April 1919, Enclosure 8 note by P.O. Sulaymaniya.
11. FO 371/4192 C-in-C Egypt to War Office, 12 September 1919 and Wilson's response.
12. It was because of his decentralist inclinations that Abd al Hamid had posted him as envoy to Stockholm, allegedly 'to keep him out of the way'. After the 1908 coup he had been disappointed that the CUP passed him over for the post of ambassador to Paris. This may explain how he became compromised in the counter-coup of 1909.
13. He started *Mashrutiyat*, the journal of the Ottoman Radical Party. It opposed the centralist, nationalist policy of the CUP, advocating a constitutional sultanate, two elected legislative chambers and complete religious toleration with Islam as the official state religion. He was enough of a nuisance for the CUP to try to assassinate him.
14. IO L/P&S/10/745 Note on General Cherif Pasha, 19 April 1920.

15. In December 1914 he had offered help in the conquest of Mesopotamia: 'if assured ... that his country [Kurdistan] would at the end of the war be made into an autonomous state', he would 'place 2,000,000 armed men at once in the field against Turkey, and would not ask for a penny'. His offer was declined. In June 1918 he urged Britain to make a declaration that would rally Kurds to the Allied cause, arguing that the establishment of autonomous states in Kurdistan and Mesopotamia would present any Peace Conference with a *fait accompli*. Over the next year he made proposals to both Britain and France for liberating Kurdistan, see L/P&S/10/745 P3432 Note on Cherif Pasha, 19 April 1920, and P5006/14 Shuckburgh Note, 14 June 1918, FO 371/1010 files 44/26783 and 44/27510, FO 371/4192; *Precis of Affairs*, p. 8, Wilson, *Mesopotamia*, p. 130.

16. IO L/P & S/10/745 P 2614 Secretary of State for India to Civil Commissioner Baghdad, 6 June 1919, and enclosed memorandum from Sharif Pasha to Sir Louis Mallet, 20 May 1919.

17. In January 1919 Sharif Pasha convened a congress of Ottoman liberals in Geneva, the purpose of which was to examine ways in which the Ottoman rights and integrity could be protected through the principles of decentralization and local autonomy. One of the delegates proposed the election of Sharif Pasha as Delegate for the 'Turks of Geneva' to Paris, charged with the defence of Ottoman interests in general.

18. FO 371/4192 Inter-departmental Conference on Middle Eastern Affairs, Secretary's Note on the Situation in Kurdistan, September 1919.

19. Kamil Badr Khan in Tiflis had had a similar idea as early as February 1918, proposing to the British that he should create a united Kurdistan in alliance with Simqu.

20. Interview with Chris Kutschera, Paris, July 1975, in Kutschera, *Le Mouvement National Kurde*, p. 26.

21. FO 371/4157 Intelligence Summary, GHQ Cairo, 4 March 1919.

22. FO 371/4141 G.H.Q. Egypt to DMI War Office, Cairo, 6 March 1919; GHQ, GSI No. 2838 Salonika on the CUP, in High Commission to Foreign Office, Istanbul, 8 March 1919.

23. L/P&S/10/781 Calthorpe to FO, Istanbul, 2 May 1919.

24. *Review of the Civil Administration*, p. 67.

25. FO 371/4192 Report of a Conversation between members of the Kurdish Committee and the Turkish Government, 10 July 1919, and Hohler to Tilley, British High Commission, 21 July 1919.

26. FO 371/4192 Calthorpe to Foreign Office, 10 July 1919.

27. Article 6, as translated in Shaw and Shaw, *History*, vol. ii, p. 345.

28. These rumours also said that the eastern Turks did not want their position to be made public 'because they have made common cause with the Kurds who are by no means favourable to the idea of abandoning any territory to the Armenians...' Ataturk, A *Speech*, pp. 71, 87.

29. FO 371/4192 Hohler to Tilley, Istanbul, 21 July 1919.

30. FO 371/4192 Hohler to Tilley, 21 July 1919.

31. FO 371/5068 Diary of Major E.M. Noel on special duty in Kurdistan from 14 June to 21 September 1919 (Basra 1919), p.1.

32. FO 371/4192 Civil Commissioner to India Office, Baghdad, 20 September 1919, quoting Noel's cable of 19 September 1919.

33. Ataturk, *A Speech*, pp. 102, 109.

34. Ataturk, *A Speech*, p. 100.

35. FO 371/4193 44/153094 Minute on Relations between Kurds and the Nationalists, 19 November 1919.

36. FO 371/4193 GSI, Army of the Black Sea, Istanbul, 13 October 1919, Note on the Kurds and the Nationalist Movement.

37. Quoted in Hovanissian, *The Republic of Armenia*, vol. ii, p. 427.

38. Diyarbakir was a case for anxiety. In the words of one Kemalist officer 'under the mask of Kurdish nationalist the Diyarbakiris were working for a British protectorate. Judging by the propaganda which the Young Kurds were conducting and the steps they were taking ... they were working in Great Britain's interest.... The refusal of the Diyarbakiris to participate in the Erzerum Congress, in spite of our advice to them to do so ... showed clearly where the truth lay.' FO 371/5068 *Diary of Major Noel*, p. 19.

39. FO 371/5067 Civil Commissioner to India Office, Baghdad, 22 February 1920, but see also FO 371/4193 Internal Memorandum by H.W. Young, 10 January 1920, and FO 371/5069 Secretary of State for India to Baghdad, London, 27 October 1920.

40. Hovanissian, *The Republic of Armenia*, vol. i, p. 316.

41. FO 371/4193 File 44/156272 of 28 November 1919.

42. IO L/P&S/10/782 Note on Kurdistan by M. Berthelot, London, 23 December 1919.

43. FO 371/4193 Hohler to Curzon, 12 November 1919.

44. FO 371/5068 de Robeck to Curzon, Istanbul, 29 March 1920.

45. FO 371/5067 Kurdish Club to High Commission, Istanbul, 28 January 1920; de Robeck to Curzon, Istanbul, 3 February 1920.

46. FO 371/5067 Mémoire présenté par le Général Cherif Pacha, Président de la Délégation Kurde a M. Le Président du Conseil Suprême de la Conférence de la Paix, 1 March 1920.

47. FO 371/5068 de Robeck to Curzon, 15 March 1920; Hovanissian, *The Republic of Armenia*, vol. ii, p. 444.

48. *Ikhdam*, 27 February 1920, quoted in FO 371/5068 Webb to Curzon, Istanbul, 3 May 1920. Jawdat was an autonomist and it is unlikely he had abandoned his old decentralist position in favour of outright independence, for it would have contradicted his recent willingness to serve in Farid Pasha's government, and also his subsequent career.

49. FO 371/5068 Letter of Amin Ali Badr Khan, vice-president of Society for the Elevation of Kurdistan, and representatives of Hiva, The Kurdish Democratic Party *et al.*, to Lloyd George, 24 March 1920.

50. FO 371/5068 Webb to Curzon, Istanbul, 16 April and 3 May 1920; and Kutschera, *Le Mouvement National Kurde*, p. 31.

51. FO 371/5068 Webb to Curzon, Istanbul, 3 May 1920.

52. For membership see FO 371/5069 de Robeck to Curzon, Istanbul, 20 May 1920.

53. FO 371/5068 Sharif Pasha to the British Ambassador, Paris, 27 April 1920.

54. FO 371/5068 Minutes of Inter-Departmental Conference on Middle Eastern Affairs, Foreign Office, 13 April 1920.

55. FO 371/5068 Inter-Departmental Conference on Middle Eastern Affairs, 13 April 1920; Wilson, *Mesopotamia, 1917–1920*, p. 257.

56. FO 371/4193 Second Additional Note on the Situation in Kurdistan and L/P&S/10/815 *Mesopotamian Geological Reports 1919* (Baghdad, 1920).

57. L/P&S/10/815 *Mesopotamia and Kurdistan Geological Reports.*

58. L/P&S/10/4722/1918/1920/3/2463 quoted in Sluglett, *Britain in Iraq*, p. 137, n. 47.

59. FO 371/5068 Civil Commissioner to India Office, Baghdad, 5 April 1920.

60. FO 371/5068 Vansittart to Curzon, Paris, 19 May 1920.

61. Davison, 'Turkish Diplomacy to Lausanne', p. 182.

62. FO 371/6467 E 3357.

63. Jazira bin Umar was in the putative French zone of influence. To occupy it or offer the Kurds guarantees concerning the French risked major ructions in Paris. Given the intermittent troubles on the border, arming the Kurds seemed like giving a hostage to

fortune, FO 371/6346 High Commissioner Mesopotamia to Secretary of State to the Colonies, 21 June 1921.

64. See for example, FO 371/6346 Rumbold to Curzon, 29 December 1920 (enclosing Mr Ryan's memorandum of 23 December) and 1 January 1921.

65. FO 371/6346 and FO 371/6347 High Commissioner Iraq to Colonial Office, 4 August, 28 October, 21 November 1921 and the Colonial Office reply of 11 November 1921.

66. *Parliamentary Papers*, Miscellaneous No. 3, Pronouncement by the Three Allied Ministers for Foreign Affairs respecting the Near East Situation, Paris, 27 March 1922 (Cmd 1641).

67. FO 371/7858 Rawlinson, Memorandum on the Position of Angora Government, 4 March 1922.

68. For a personal account of events, see C.J. Edmonds, *Kurds, Turks and Arabs*, chapters 17, 20, 21 and 22.

69. *Lausanne Conference*, p. 357.

70. *Lausanne Conference*, p. 296.

71. See Toynbee, *Survey of International*, p. 494, no. 1.

72. Britain's objections were: the difficulty of carrying out a census and registration in a remote and pastoralist area; the difficulty of framing the choice for such a referendum; the fact that the border of the vilayet of Mosul remained undefined; the fact that one of the contestants (Britain) remained in physical control of the area, hardly a premise on which an impartial referendum could be conducted, *Proceedings of the Lausanne Conference*, pp. 399–400.

73. FO 371/9006 Notes on the Mosul Frontier by Col. F.R. Maunsell, 22 September 1923.

74. *Commission Report*, p. 39.

75. *Commission Report*, p. 57.

76. *Commission Report*, pp. 57–58.

77. *Commission Report*, p. 87.

78. *Commission Report*, p. 78.

79. *Commission Report*, pp. 88–89.

80. Toynbee, *Survey of International Affairs*, p. 513.

81. Yet again, as with the Armenians in 1915, the Turkish troops committed widespread atrocities, Toynbee, *International Survey*, pp. 517–18.

82. Toynbee, *Survey of International Affairs*, p. 518.

CHAPTER 8

THE KURDS, BRITAIN AND IRAQ

Introduction

Trying to master Kurdistan and its inhabitants has never been easy for outsiders. Britain, with its experience on the North West Frontier of India, had a better idea of what was required than most and started out with relatively honourable intentions. Yet the promise of the first few weeks was not fulfilled. The exigencies of Mesopotamian policy drove Britain step by step to betray its own promises to the Kurds, and it is doubtful that its successor Arab administration ever intended to fulfil its own obligations.

The Kurds were politically inept in their response to the post-war situation. Poor communications, diffusion of society and the adversarial nature of intra-tribal relations made the presentation of a united political position virtually impossible. On the whole most aghas and shaykhs were happy to fall in with British plans, since these included administration through the traditional patronage system; but subordination to Arab rule stuck in their craw. Direct Arab rule was imposed just as a new class of Kurds began to emerge: the non-tribal educated professionals of the towns of Kurdistan. It was their misfortune that by the time they were ready to mobilize the Kurds as a people rather than as tribes, Britain had long since betrayed its offer of self-determination. In the meantime both Britain and the Arabs in Baghdad confirmed the agha class as an intermediary through which to ensure Kurdish compliance with their policies.

Introducing Order

Political uncertainty before the settlement of the Mosul question had been increased by a number of factors. Turkish efforts to destabilize the vilayet had begun early in 1919. Yet Britain had only itself to blame for much of the atmosphere of indecision. As noted, Britain only definitively opted for the inclusion of the vilayet within Mesopotamia in April 1920 when it could delay its decision no longer, and even then it was not certain until the end of 1925 that it would remain within the British sphere. Furthermore, it had assured the Kurds that the idea of self-determination would guide its approach yet gave no idea of how this principle was to be implemented.

The first essential had been to return order and prosperity to a devastated region. With this in mind Major Noel had visited the area between the Lesser Zab and the Diyala in November 1918, his instructions being to avoid a definitive arrangement:

> It should be your object to arrange with local chiefs for the restoration and main-
> tenance of order in areas outside the limits of our military occupation.... [It] should be
> made clear to the chiefs, that any arrangements you may make are of necessity provi-
> sional and subject to reconsideration at any time. You are authorized to appoint Shaikh
> Mahmoud as our representative in Sulaimaniyah should you consider this expedient and
> to make other appointments of this nature at Chamchamal, Halebja, etc., at your dis-
> cretion. It should be explained to the tribal chiefs with whom you enter into relations
> that there is no intention of imposing upon them an administration foreign to their
> habits and desires. Tribal leaders will be encouraged to form a confederation for the
> settlement of their public affairs under the guidance of British Political Officers.[1]

Major Noel set to work with a will, energetically making arrangements with Shaykh Mahmud of Sulaymaniya and others. Shaykh Mahmud had already appealed to Britain not to exclude Kurdistan from the list of liberated peoples.[2] On 1 December Arnold Wilson, as Acting Civil Commissioner, visited Sulaymaniya and met the shaykh and about 60 chiefs of Southern Kurdistan, including major ones from across the Iranian border. He was able to explain some of the constraints of the situation and learn the wishes of these chiefs. There seemed to be virtual unanimity that the Turks should not return and a general recognition of the need for British protection. But several chiefs were less sure of the wisdom of allowing Britain to administer Kurdistan. Others insisted Kurdistan must be separated from Iraq and directly administered from London rather than Baghdad, clearly hoping to return to the freedom they had enjoyed when ruled from Istanbul. Wilson also discovered that Shaykh Mahmud, whom the British were minded to appoint as paramount in the region, was by no means universally respected. The chiefs of Kifri and Kirkuk stated that they and the townspeople were unwilling to fall under his authority, and were allowed to make separate arrangements.

Wilson signed an agreement with the chiefs to the effect that:

> H.B.M.'s Government having announced that their intention in the war was the libera-
> tion of the Eastern peoples from Turkish oppression and the grant of assistance to
> them in the establishment of their independence, the chiefs, as the representatives of
> the people of Kurdistan, have asked H.B.M.'s Government to accept them also under
> British protection and to attach them to Iraq so that they might not be deprived of the
> benefits of that association, and they requested the Civil Commissioner of Mesopota-
> mia to send them a representative with the necessary assistance to enable the Kurdish
> people under British auspices to progress peacefully on civilised lines. If H.B.M.'s

Government extended its assistance and protection to them they undertook to accept H.B.M.'s orders and advice.[3]

This hardly indicated the form of government Britain had in mind. On the contrary, its preamble might easily have suggested in Kurdish minds a return to the independence of the old amirates, with friendly help from an acknowledged suzerain in London. If so, they did not baulk at the ominous final phrase of the agreement.

By this time it was clear to British administrators that a single Southern Kurdistan was not immediately feasible 'owing to the underdeveloped state of the country, the lack of communications, and the dissension of the tribes'.[4] It was also recognised that Southern Kurdistan was both economically and strategically interdependent with the Mesopotamian plain. British thinking moved towards creating a network of states or administrative areas reflecting the tribal fragmentation and economic catchment areas, pending consolidation into a single Kurdish entity at a later date.

Kurdish confidence in the durability of these initial arrangements was shaken by the tenuous hold Britain seemed to have on the region. Britain had already demonstrated its unreliability. Some chiefs had co-operated with advancing British forces in May 1918 only to be left facing reprisals when these forces suddenly withdrew. As Arnold Wilson subsequently wrote,

> The Kurds, who were by no means ill-disposed to us, became once more prey to doubts and suspicions. It seemed clear to them that the assurances of support, freely given by some irresponsible officers ... were not to be relied on ... we had induced them to show their hand to their enemies the Turks, and we had left them in the lurch. The Hamawand leaders, in particular, never forgave us, and remained hostile to us for many years after.[5]

Then, having conquered Mespotamia, Britain sent its troops home. By March 1919

> Merchants and others returning from Basra and Baghdad to Sulaimani told of soldiers leaving daily by ship and train; and in the minds of many the belief that we would once more evacuate Kurdistan and leave the inhabitants to their own devices, or to the machinations of rival claimants to power, hardened into certainty.[6]

A quite different tension existed in the presence of Assyrian refugees, from Hakkari and Urumiya. These had been ejected from Amadiya area by local and Baradusti Kurds during the war. In spring 1919 two battalions of Assyrian levies were used to 'clear certain areas' with a view to refugee resettlement. Kurdish fears were raised by the Allies' apparent enthusiasm to award Christians self-determination and by talk of retribution for those guilty of war crimes. Only at the end of May 1919, once it was already facing serious revolt, did Britain make clear it would not prosecute guilty Kurds. That did not remove old animosities. When the Assyrians unsuccessfully attempted to return to their homes in October 1920, they razed Barzan village.

Such frictions were additional to more longstanding ones. The most obvious of these was the volatile disposition of many tribal chiefs towards both government and their rivals, and their unwillingness to accept a single leader. And, as was soon discovered, many Kurdish landholders, particularly up in the mountains, did not want awkward questions about land ownership, as many held no title to their lands, keeping them by forcible possession. As a result it was decided it would be more tactful to leave the land registers in Sulaymaniya than bring them to Baghdad for scrutiny. There was also the newly apprehended fact that whatever the British might have in mind when they began talking of overall direction from Baghdad, the Kurds had no intention of being ruled by Arabs, whom they held in disdain.

It might seem that the British were blundering through the political under-growth of Kurdish society, but those directly involved had previously worked in Iranian Kurdistan before or during the war and their approach was based on experience there and in India.[7] In Baluchistan, British success had been largely due to two factors: the acknowledged authority of certain chiefs and initial military domination of the whole countryside – thus indicating that those who wielded authority did so on behalf of a proven suzerain. But where chiefs did not enjoy absolute authority and where British troops had not first subjugated the tribes, this policy had been a failure, most notably among the Mahsuds of the North West Frontier Province. Powerful religious figures and cross-frontier agitation from Afghanistan brought the system to a point of collapse. In these respects, similar conditions prevailed among the Kurds as among the Mahsuds. The Kurds had not witnessed a British military occupation of Southern Kurdistan and, like the Mahsuds, each tribal section in Kurdistan was often inclined to behave independently of the rest of the tribe, let alone neighbouring tribal groups. Like the Mahsuds, too, many Kurdish tribesmen were susceptible to the call of religious leaders, like Shaykh Mahmud in Sulaymaniya.

Britain tried to control the Kurdish tribes with a light but efficient hand, using only a network of political officers to maintain relations with the chiefs, to arbitrate disputes, to ensure the collection of revenue and to recruit men for the gendarmerie and levies with which Britain hoped to manage the region. These were all delicate matters, which had occasioned conflict between different chiefs and the Ottoman authorities in the past.

It would have been miraculous had the novel circumstances of the situation not led to outbursts of violence, and such affrays were not long in coming. In April 1919 Abd al Rahman of Shirnakh, himself encouraged by Turkish Islamic propaganda, goaded the Goyan Kurds into attacks on Assyrians in the border area, culminating in the murder of the British Political Officer from Zakhu who had set out to parley with them. Reprisals by ground forces were discounte-nanced, since they would violate the ceasefire line. Enlisting Turkish help was also discounted, partly because Turkey was believed to be the instigator, but also because of the loss of prestige involved. So Britain resorted to aerial bombard-ment, a technique it began to use as a standard tactic to economise on troop deployment. It had the advantage of instant effect and economy of cost. Quite apart from the inevitability of civilian casualties, it had the disadvantage of creating a gulf between government and the governed.

Then there was trouble at Amadiya in June when an Assistant Political Officer and his colleagues were murdered. Both the notables of Amadiya and also several local aghas, primarily the Barwari, were implicated. A variety of factors had come into play: the recent withdrawal of a nearby troop detachment, suggesting that local warlords might be free to do as they pleased; fears over the repatriation of Assyrians; efficient and energetic tax collection; and measures which undermined the power and authority of local chiefs and notables. The latter included the raising of a gendarmerie, which implied the removal of such men from tribal authority, and the direct provision of cash and seed for agricultural revival, undermining the commercial patronage wielded by chiefs. It was only during August–September that a sufficiently strong punitive force reimposed British control.

Then a third serious outbreak of disorder occurred on the Greater Zab, in the Barzan–Zibar region, and spread into Aqra district. The region was notoriously unruly, largely on account of the almost endemic feud between the shaykhs of Barzan and the Zibari chiefs. The conflict was partly territorial, since the Barzani shaykhs had established themselves on the right bank of the river in the mid-nineteenth century, almost opposite Zibar. But the spiritual leaders of Barzan also threatened the Zibaris more directly since they attracted many peasant cultivators away from the Zibaris and other neighbouring tribes, thereby becoming a new and formidable political power in the region.

Both Barzan and Zibar fell within the admininstrative remit of Aqra. In order to hold the ring between Barzan and Zibar, Faris Agha of Zibar was forbidden to cross the Zab into Barzan territory. Shaykh Ahmad of Barzan, on the other hand, had wanted Barzan to be transferred administratively to Rawanduz, away from Zibari-dominated Aqra.

Following the imposition of a fine by the local political officer, two Zibari chiefs unexpectedly appealed to Shaykh Ahmad of Barzan for support in November 1919. Together they ambushed and killed the political officer and most of his retinue. Then they moved on to loot Aqra, joined by the Surchi. The whole affair seemed to have been an outburst of anger rather than a preconceived rising. A British-led force of Kurdish levies proceeded through the area burning the homes of the Zibari and Barzani chiefs, who fled into the mountains. Local chiefs now offered to assist in dealing with the rebels, a commentary less on their loyalty than on the endemic and treacherous nature of inter-tribal politics.

Shaykh Mahmud of Sulaymaniya

Nevertheless, the most serious trouble occurred in Sulaymaniya. Everywhere else Britain administered the occupied territories directly through a network of political officers. Sulaymaniya was the one area which enjoyed special status.

On 1 December 1918 Wilson had confirmed Shaykh Mahmud as *hukumdar* (governor) of Sulaymaniya division, a large tract of land between the greater Zab and the Diyala. Other Kurdish officials had been assigned to the administration of various sub-divisions under the guidance of British political officers. In return, the British understood Shaykh Mahmud to have undertaken to obey British orders. Indeed, they assumed he derived his authority from the British administration.

Shaykh Mahmud was the single most influential leader in Sulaymaniya. As far afield as Rawanduz, Koi-Sanjaq and Raniya there was a willingness among impoverished communities anxious for aid to accept him as Britain's appointed Kurdish paramount:

> Thus tribe after tribe which hitherto had been barely cognisant of Shaikh Mahmud, or at best had known him as an unworthy descendant of a good man, signed the sterotyped memorial praying for inclusion in the new State under Shaikh Mahmud, a condition which they imagined the British Government to have made essential, for reasons of its own.[8]

So wrote a sceptical Major Soane, who knew the area well from before the war.

Soane was by no means alone in his dislike of Shaykh Mahmud. All around Sulaymaniya, the Shaykh had his opponents, among the Jaf and Bajalan tribes and notably among the shaykhs – the Talabani shaykhs of Kirkuk, who were his Qadiri rivals, and the Nashqshbandi shaykhs of Biyari and Tawila. Indeed, on account of such opposition the townspeople and tribesmen of Kirkuk and Kifri were specifically excluded from Shaykh Mahmud's area of authority, a measure to which he had consented.

Shaykh Mahmud had a completely different understanding of the political arrangement. He did not envisage his authority to be circumscribed geographically by the Greater Zab and the Diyala, nor did he consider his authority to derive from the British. On the contrary, as he saw it, he had been recognized on account of his moral authority over the Kurds and within this definition he generously included all the Kurds of the vilayet, an understandable vanity, since the sixty chiefs who had met Wilson had claimed to represent all the Kurds of the vilayet.

It was not long before such fundamental misunderstandings became clear. Shaykh Mahmud used the British subsidy, provided for salaries and to assist recovery from the ravages of war, in order to consolidate his power base, buying the loyalty of chieftains and seeking, in Soane's hostile estimation,

> to fill every post with his own relations regardless of their character of capability, and to exclude all whom he did not consider personal adherents.... Every important post from that of outside petty governor to that of judge of the Sulaimaniyah Religious Court was held by his relatives and sycophants.[9]

Civil administrators and even the Kurdish levies, under British training, were required to swear allegiance to him.

It is important to remember that regardless of Shaykh Mahmud's shortcomings (and these soon became apparent), trouble might well have arisen with another Kurd in his place. For behind the clash of personality, lay conflicting systems and expectations. There was a fundamental conflict between institutionalized government on the one hand, in which officials were appointed on merit and owed their loyalty to an abstract idea – the state, the administration, the Crown or whatever – and, on the other hand, the highly personalized form of government based on patronage still existing in the religious and tribal strata of Kurdish society. From his own perspective, Shaykh Mahmud could only be secure through the building of his personal power base, attracting men by patronage, and removing those who seemed either hostile or to have minds of their own.

Things were going awry before the year was out, but it was only in March 1919 that steps were taken to curb Shaykh Mahmud's activities. Noel, who had initiated the tribal policy and appointed Shaykh Mahmud, was replaced by Soane. His appointment was a clear warning: as well as Kirkuk and Kifri, Koi Sanjaq, Rawanduz, Halabja and the Jaf lands were now specifically excluded from Shaykh Mahmud's orbit.

However, by their enthusiasm for 'tribalism', British political officers had already encouraged the very culture that in their more sober moments they deplored. Soane, an open dissenter from this policy, explained his view:

> Revival of the tribal system was ... a retrograde movement. Already South Kurdistan had become largely detribalised and a measure of prosperity, in consequence, had been its lot in pre-war times. Now, the Political Officer [Noel], accepting the views of Shaikh Mahmud, devoted his energies to re-tribalising. Every man who could be labelled a tribesman was placed under a tribal leader. The idea was to divide South Kurdistan into tribal areas under tribal leaders. Petty village headmen were unearthed and discovered as leaders of long dead tribes.... Law was to be administered by this chief, who must only recognise Shaikh Mahmud as Hukmdar.... Ideal for the clansman but fatal for trade, civilization and tranquillity.[10]

Wilson, aware of the deteriorating situation, had planned to visit Sulaymaniya towards the end of May 'to meet Shaikh Mahmud in person and to endeavour to reach a solution which would make it possible to retain the framework of Kurdish autonomy [sic].'[11] Before that visit could be made, however, Shaykh Mahmud had raised three hundred tribal followers on the Iranian side of the border, and on 23 May imprisoned all British personnel and ejected the garrison of levies. Shaykh Mahmud's supporters from neighbouring districts now rallied to him. Flushed with this auspicious start he now proclaimed himself Ruler of all Kurdistan, appointing his own retainers throughout the Division. His prestige rose further with the successful ambush of a light British column that strayed beyond Chamchamal. On both sides of the border tribes now proclaimed themselves for Shaykh Mahmud. The authorities in Baghdad now moved swiftly to reassert their shaken authority. They assembled two brigades which rapidly defeated Shaykh Mahmud's 500-strong force in the Bazyan Pass in mid-June.

Shaykh Mahmud himself was captured, reprieved from execution, and sent into exile. His short-lived rebellion subsequently became a symbol of Kurdish nationalism.

The scheme for a 'free united Kurdistan' suggests that Shaykh Mahmud was a nationalist, as indeed he was. Not only did he believe in a Kurdish political entity under his own authority but he also justifiably believed that Kurdish self-determination was effectively what the Allies had promised. 'Strapped like a talisman to his arm' was a Quran on the flyleaves of which was written in Kurdish the texts of Woodrow Wilson's twelfth point and the Anglo-French Declaration of 8 November.[12]

It is tempting retrospectively to clothe Shaykh Mahmud in the garb of modern nationalist ideas. But it is clear he had little in common with today's Kurdish leaders. Both the vocabulary and style are quite different. It is significant that Shaykh Mahmud did not waste his time appealing to nationalist sentiment. He was a sayyid, and the language his constituency understood was the language of Islam. In 1919 he appealed for a *jihad*, not a national liberation struggle. Further-more, his style was to use kin and tribal allies and his aim was the establishment of a personal fiefdom.

Shaykh Mahmud offered Kurds liberation from British rule, but not from himself. The notorious rapacity of the Barzinja *shaykhan* was a distinct disincentive for many Kurds of the Sulaymaniya Division. So it was tribal allies from Iran, the Hawrami (Hawraman) under Khan Mahmud Dizli and the Marivi (Mariwan) under Mahmud Khan of Kanisanan who triggered the revolt.

Yet Shaykh Mahmud's revolt took place in the most nationalist of locations in Kurdistan, where the inhabitants had made it perfectly plain that they had no wish for Arab rule. Had he really represented national aspirations, one might have expected greater support in Sulaymaniya town itself, yet here he was unable to command a spontaneous rising. Apart from personal adherents, local forces were largely Barzinja tenantry and tribesmen, the Hamavand under Karim Fattah Beg, and disaffected sections of the Jaf, Jabbari, Shaykh Bizayni and Shuan tribes, all in Sulaymaniya's hinterland. The majority of the Jaf and the Pizhdar, the two most powerful confederations, offered to help suppress the revolt – hardly suggestive of Kurdish unity.

After Shaykh Mahmud's defeat, Soane returned to administer Sulaymaniya with a rod of iron. He acted like a local paramount inspiring both fear and loyalty and, according to his obituarist, achieved greater prosperity for Sulaymaniya than it had known before.[13] He was an enthusiast for public works funded out of local revenue, and encouraged the adoption of written Kurdish and its use in schools. Before the end of the year he had launched Sulaymaniya's first Kurdish newspaper *Pishkutin* (Progress), which, owing to the novelty of written Kurdish, was initially ridiculed by literate Kurds, but in due course became established and popular.

If Soane was a colonialist, he was undoubtedly a maverick one, for he believed passionately in Kurdish self-determination, helping 'to secure a degree of local autonomy which was not enjoyed by any other part of the occupied territories and which caused much discontent among certain departmental chiefs in Baghdad'.[14] Soane was dismissed in March, his autonomist views in conflict with Britain's growing integrationist policy.

Shaykh Mahmud's Second Revolt

Britain recalled and pardoned Shaykh Mahmud in September 1922 in order to deal with the growing Turkish threat. It was essentially a cynical act, driven by its wish to co-opt the growing sense of Kurdish nationalism as a bulwark against Turkish propaganda. It needed Shaykh Mahmud because it had virtually no troops to deploy in Kurdistan, thanks to the stringent budgetary policy decided in London.

The growing sense of Kurdish particularism had two bases. One was a growing national awareness of non-tribal Kurds in the towns and on the edge of the Mesopotamian plain. But this had barely expressed itself beyond the consultations which Britain had so far undertaken. More obvious and dramatic were the periodic outbreaks of tribal violence, directed largely against government and essentially to do with resentment of interference rather than a positive ideology for the future of Kurdistan.

In August 1920 Arbil division had fallen into disorder. Shaykh Mahmud had already shown others that it was possible to defy British interference. In July 1920 insurrection had spread across southern Iraq and this instigated 'the spirit of unrest which spread upwards from the south'.[15] In Kurdistan the Surchi confederation became openly rebellious. In April sections lying in the Mosul division had ambushed a military convoy and then attacked Aqra. Then their relatives in the Arbil division made common cause with dissident Rawanduzi Kurds and drove out the political officers in Rawanduz and Koi-Sanjaq. Now most of the Khushnaw, previously well-disposed to the British, and other tribal groups joined the rebels. In September Arbil itself was threatened by the Surchi and only saved by the Dizai tribe on behalf of the government. Things petered out with the unexpected defeat of the Surchi when they attacked an Assyrian refugee camp. By the end of the year most had submitted, but they had shown how volatile the tribes could be and how weak the government appeared.

Ever since the capture of the vilayet there had been intermittent efforts at subverting British rule. Six weeks before they crossed the Greater Zab, the Surchi had been busy spreading Turkish propaganda in Koi and Shaqlawa. North of the Zab, the Surchi were led by shaykhs, of whom Ubayd Allah was the most important. He made no secret of his pro-Muslim Turkish leanings (though these were fast becoming anachronistic) and his distaste for infidel rule.

In the winter of 1921–22 fresh disturbances began. In mid-December a major clash took place in the north, at Batas, between police and the Surchi. Then, in the south, Mahmud Khan Dizli, Shaykh Mahmud's old ally, began cross-border raids in the Halabja region, egged on by the Turks. In late spring Sayyid Muhammad, chief of the Jabbari, rebelled again, and was soon joined by Karim Fattah Beg of the Hamavand, who had arranged for the killing of the local British political officer and commander of levies. When levies pursued the Hamavand into the Pizhdar mountains they found that the more powerful section of the Pizhdar was sympathetic to the rebels, and could only re-establish the authority of the pro-British Pizhdar chief, Babakr Agha, temporarily. As soon as British authority looked shaky, the Pizhdar went over to the rebels.

In the meantime, Karim Fattah had made his way to Rawanduz where the Turkish presence had given coherence to tribal dissidence in the region, and had mobilized the most influential tribal groups in the region. These were the Surchi (under Shaykh Ubayd Allah), the Zibari (under Faris Agha), the Barzanis (under Shaykh Ahmad), the Khushnaw, and from Kifri in the south, the Zangana, a tribe of Turkoman origin. By August these dissident Kurdish forces had been augmented by men defecting from Simqu after his defeat in Iran (see chapter 10).

Britain's strategy for Iraq was now in crisis. On 1 October 1922 ground forces handed overall responsiblity to the RAF:

> Had the air control scheme not offered a cheap but effective alternative to military occupation, it is likely that the British presence would have been curbed or ended, the Arab Kingdom would have been stillborn and the reviving power of Turkey would have engulfed the Mosul and possibly the Baghdad and Basra vilayets.[16]

It was in this sense of crisis, too, that Baghdad decided to appeal to Kurdish national sentiment against the Turks. Attempts had already been made to get the Jaf Begzadas, who held sway in the lands around Halabja 'to take a lead in a process of "home rule" which, it is generally agreed, cannot be long delayed'.[17] But the Jaf Begzadas were timorous, fearful of backing the wrong horse.

The ideal solution was still to find someone all the Kurds could unite behind. In August it was decided to invite Shaykh Taha, who had now lost his position in Shamdinan,[18] to consider the post of *hukumdar* of Rawanduz and Raniya once the Turks were evicted. He was enticed with the prospect of becoming Governor of Sulaymaniya and thus effectively the ruler of an autonomous Kurdistan subject to Iraqi sovereignty. At the time, however, Taha was preoccupied with the last gasp of Simqu's revolt against Tehran. In October he offered to evict the Turks from Rawanduz and Raniya by rallying the tribes. Thirteen weeks of relentless rainfall and his own inability to raise even the Harki, traditional supporters of his family, left the plan stillborn.

Baghdad had not been able to await Shaykh Taha's moves. At the end of August its force sent to recover Raniya had been routed by Oz Demir's forces. So dangerous had the situation become that in the first week of September

British and other non-Kurdish government personnel were evacuated from Sulaymaniya by air (the first such air evacuation) and administration of the division entrusted to the elective council.

If Britain could persuade the Kurdish population that its own best interests were better served in association with Britain than with Turkey, the danger posed by Oz Demir would recede. But the rout outside Raniya and the precipitate withdrawal from Sulaymaniya both argued strongly in favour of Turkey. Britain urgently needed a credible Kurdish leader to pull its chestnuts out of the fire. Shaykh Taha was otherwise engaged and, besides, his standing did not really extend to Sulaymaniya. Only one man had the credentials to restore confidence despite his proven unreliability.

At the beginning of September Shaykh Qadir, Shaykh Mahmud's brother, was appointed president of the Sulaymaniya Council. This fillip to Kurdish national feeling persuaded the council to close Sulaymaniya's doors to the Turks. However Shaykh Mahmud himself seemed a logical and desirable choice for leader, a view probably held by Shaykh Qadir himself, and in mid-September he was recalled from his enforced detention in Kuwait and reappointed as president of the council, on his undertaking to prevent the Turks entering the city and to expel them from the division.

Once reinstated, Shaykh Mahmud was understandably more concerned to establish a Kurdish kingdom. He began persuading local tribal leaders – even some Kirkukli chiefs beyond Sulaymaniya's jurisdiction – to recognize him as head of an independent Kurdistan. He demanded the incorporation of areas outside the Sulaymaniya division and by November was designating himself 'King of Kurdistan'. He also began to remove those who crossed him, if necessary by assassination.[19]

In the hinterland of Sulaymaniya, sections of the Jaf at Halabja and the Pizhdar at Qala Diza, his antagonists in the past, now seemed willing to co-operate with him. More ominously, Shaykh Mahmud entered into correspondence with Oz Demir at Rawanduz, from whom he wanted assurances concerning Kurdish autonomy under Turkey, and began marshalling supporters and allies, including Simqu, on the Iranian side of the border.

Shaykh Mahmud's conduct seems to have created unease both among the townspeople who disliked his attempt to put the town under tribal control and among the more canny of his relatives and supporters. The most influential of these, perhaps, was his cousin, Shaykh Abd al Karim of Qadir Karam, an important taqiya south-west of Sulaymaniya in Talabani country, who shared Shaykh Mahmud's ambition for a Kurdish state under Barzinja rule but was apprehensive of his cousin's poor political judgement. When the Talabani shaykhs felt compelled by the course of events to swallow their pride and make a formal submission to their sworn enemy Shaykh Mahmud, Shaykh Abd al Karim suggested they make their submission conditional on Mahmud's promise to remain loyal to British policy. Talabani adhesion was vital to Kurdish solidarity, so Shaykh

Mahmud accepted these terms. This, of course, gave Shaykh Mahmud's uneasy allies grounds for withdrawing support.

The situation was still too volatile for the British to risk direct action against Shaykh Mahmud. In November they summoned him under safe conduct in order to clarify his terms of reference. Fearing duplicity, Mahmud sent his brother, Shaykh Qadir.

From 1 October onwards air action drove the Turks from Koi and Qala Diza, and the rebels from Raniya; but while air action could disrupt the Turks it could not secure the region. The very fact that Turkey would not abandon its claim to the vilayet of Mosul inevitably caused continuing uncertainty.

Consequently British political officers were authorized to tell local notables informally that Britain intended to allow the Kurds to run their own affairs. This was followed up by a formal statement of intent regarding the Kurds published in Baghdad on 20 December 1922. It promised that the Kurds could establish a Kurdish government (over an unspecified area) if they so wished. This declaration had some effect. On 13 January a petition signed by notables of Sulaymaniya sought independence under British protection but, less welcome, with Shaykh Mahmud as king.

Meanwhile, Shaykh Mahmud had received a visit from Turkish officers in late January and from Oz Demir himself in March to discuss the projected capture of Kirkuk and Koi, in association with the Pizhdar and Dizli tribes. Aware of these meetings, the British summoned him again under safe conduct and, following his refusal, declared his administration suspended on 24 February and ordered him to leave town by 1 March. After dropping warning leaflets, the RAF bombed government buildings on 3 March. Shaykh Mahmud fled the following day.

The tide had turned in Britain's favour. In April Surchi, Zibari and Harki leaders and even Simqu had gone to Oz Demir's headquarters in Rawanduz, but elsewhere tribes previously in correspondence with Oz Demir melted away. Koi was re-occupied in early April, Rawanduz two weeks later, and Sulaymaniya in mid-May. The official proclamation of Kurdish autonomy had served its immediate political purpose, as a growing number of aghas began to mend their fences with Baghdad.

Once Sulaymaniya was re-occupied, an attempt was made to incorporate the division into the Iraqi state under a regime of local self-government, resting on the faction hostile to Shaykh Mahmud. But these opponents dared not govern without a British garrison. When this was withdrawn a month later, Sulaymaniya's new government immediately resigned and fled to British lines. Shaykh Mahmud triumphantly re-entered Sulaymaniya on 11 July. In an attempt to avoid further conflict, Baghdad informed Shaykh Mahmud that no further action would be taken if he accepted a reduced territorial mandate, and desisted from all acts of hostility.

Shaykh Mahmud refused to accept the new restrictions, and his quarters were bombed again, in August and then in December 1923. Finally his quarters were destroyed from the air in May 1924. By this stage many of Sulaymaniya's traders, fed up with the conflict, had moved to other towns like Kirkuk in order to continue their commerce. Once more Shaykh Mahmud fled to the mountains, and an Iraqi force entered the town in July, followed by 7,000 residents who had temporarily abandoned the city.

A loose administration was set up by the Iraqi government, temporarily administered by the high commissioner. Until early 1927, Shaykh Mahmud continued to worry the government with raids on settled areas, the interception of tax revenues from mountain tribes, and the waylaying of tribes like the Jaf on their annual migration across the border to and from Iran. His chief allies in this were tribes who still owed him loyalty, notably the Hawrami and Hamavand, whose fortunes had been so closely tied to those of Barzinja since the beginning of the century.

Promises Betrayed

Behind these events, however, lay a dismal trail of abandoned assurances which Britain had given the Kurds, retreats that can be explained but for which no real excuse can be made. On 7 November 1918, it will be recalled, Britain and France had jointly declared that their goal was

> the complete and final liberation of the peoples who have for so long been oppressed by the Turks, and the setting up of national governments and administrations that shall derive their authority from the free exercise of the initiative and choice of the in-digenous populations.[20]

It was to this declaration that Wilson referred in his agreement with the Kurdish chiefs on 1 December 1918. At that stage 'attachment to Iraq' quite clearly meant British rather than Arab administration, a fact well understood by Wilson and his colleagues.

Yet there was a dissonance between Britain's policy-makers, committed, however reluctantly, to the principles of self-determination, and the practitioners led by Wilson. For policy-makers the prime attraction of self-determination was the possibility of running a quasi-colony without the expense. Wilson, schooled in India, believed in running Iraq efficiently, according to the 'best principles' evolved in British colonial experience. Fancy notions like self-determination were all very well for vague statements of intent, but the administration of Iraq must remain in the hands of the best-qualified personnel available, the Indian Expeditionary Force's team of political officers.

Nothing illustrated better the cast of mind of such officers than the comments of Major Hay, P.O. Arbil, on his charges:

> The Kurd has the mind of a schoolboy, but not without a schoolboy's innate cruelty. He requires a beating one day and a sugar plum the next. Too much severity or too

much spoiling renders him unmanageable. Like a schoolboy he will always lie to save himself....[21]

As Hay informed his principals, Kurdish chiefs, like native chiefs elsewhere, fell into straightforward categories:

> The Kurds may be divided into good Aghas, bad Aghas and the people. Every area has its bad Agha.... These are the people that cause all the trouble and whom it is necessary for us to suppress by every means possible. They are actuated purely by greed and selfish ambition.... It is the bad Aghas and they alone who have anything to say against the Government and by suppressing them we protect ourselves, and do a service to Kurdistan generally. Fortunately the good Aghas, who wish to live in peace, and see their tenants prosper are not rare and where they are to be found, I consider we should use every endeavour to associate them with *our* [author's emphasis] rule.

Just as this simplistic state of mind ignored the implications of self-determination, so it also conveniently ignored longstanding conflicts between rival neighbouring tribes, and between rival aghas within the same tribe. By co-opting one agha, political officers often predetermined his rival to adopt an anti-government attitude, as Ottoman officials had also done in their time. Hay himself, in over-throwing the choice of paramount among the Khushnaw aghas in favour of his own, unleashed resentment to government and within the Miran family still felt by its descendants today.

It is not surprising, therefore, that while policy was clear that its executors 'were charged with the foundation of an independent South Kurdistan under British auspices',[22] events on the ground demonstrated a practical determination to bring the Kurds under the 'benefits' of British order, whether they liked it or not, hence the outbursts of fury in Amadiya, the Barzan–Zibari area and indeed, Shaykh Mahmud's first rising in 1919.

When it had come to actually ascertaining what the Kurds of southern Kurdistan wanted, the British administration found itself floundering. In early 1919 it had gone through a public consultation later ludicrously described as a plebiscite. In fact only the views of leading notables, shaykhs and aghas were sought and these were neither individual nor secret. Since the British were physically in control and also providing urgently needed post-war relief, no one was going to oppose their presence. The material benefits of belonging to a 'unitary' state under British tutelage clearly outweighed the uncertainties, famine and deprivation of those beyond British lines. Implicit in these arrangements were the economic benefits of not being separated from the outlets and markets of Iraq. However, it did not mean the Kurds had no wish to govern themselves and the British knew it.

Even before the Armistice, British administrators realized that if they were to press ahead with the idea of an independent Southern Kurdistan, greater unity than the tribe would be needed since, as Noel noted, Kurdish solidarity was still 'clannish' rather than 'nationalist'.[23] Yet this was almost impossible to achieve, for no sooner was it rumoured that Shaykh Mahmud might be made wali of Southern Kurdistan than others made known their opposition. The notables of Kirkuk, for example, apparently

> felt that the path of progress lies in the direction of Baghdad, not in that of Sulaymaniya. Moreover there is no trace of Kurdish national feeling in Kirkuk. British control is strongly desired as well as the absence of any administrative frontier between Kurds and Arabs.[24]

But by the same token, Kirkuk adamantly sought British protection, *not* Arab government.[25]

And so, by May 1919, in their first retreat from a single Southern Kurdish state, the focus began to shift to the idea of an Arab province of Mosul fringed by autonomous Kurdish states under Kurdish chiefs with British advisers. As yet there was no intention to renege on the idea of political separation between Kurd and Arab. Indeed, with an altruism that ran in tandem with the conviction 'nanny knows best', it was acknowledged in Baghdad that 'we have not yet freed them [the Kurdish peasantry] from the tyranny of Mosul landowners who constitute the pro-Arab party and the only class in favour of Arab government.'[26]

Then came the risings of 1919. These persuaded the British in Iraq of the need for a closer grip on local affairs but the policy-makers in London of the need to abandon a mountainous region that was costly to control. While the former won the day, talk of an independent Kurdistan, even of autonomous states, underwent modification. Wilson cabled his principals in London in the aftermath of Shaykh Mahmud's rising:

> Recent events have in no way altered my view as regards necessity of giving effect to policy approved by HM's Government on May 9th for autonomous Kurdish States, but degree of supervision must depend on need of country and on strategic considerations.[27]

That meant a free hand, unfettered by fresh promises. Wilson now favoured a mandate from the League of Nations in which 'no special regime [is] to be stipulated for non-Arab areas.'[28] In the meantime it seemed wise to play along with Kurdish sensibilities in a non-committal way,[29] tolerating the jealousies between one region and another, or between one tribe and another.

It was at this stage that Southern Kurdistan began to fall victim to the exigences of Arab nationalism. Arab national frustration with Wilson's style of rule came to a head during early summer, bursting into full scale rebellion in July 1920. Wilson had resisted for too long growing nationalist sentiment in Iraq and growing impatience in London with the failure to implement indirect control through a pliable local ruler.

Sir Percy Cox replaced Wilson in October and within a fortnight had persuaded the elderly Naqib of Baghdad to head a Council of State, thereby signalling his intention of establishing Arab government in Iraq. This in turn begged the question of who should be head of state and what precisely the borders of that state should be. When the electoral law was revised in December 1920 it contained no recognition of the safeguards to which Iraq's Kurds were entitled under the Treaty of Sèvres, signed only four months before. It is difficult to avoid the conclusion that Britain no longer had any real intention of safeguarding Kurdish interests. These were to be wholly subservient to British (and Iraqi) strategic concerns.

At the end of the year responsibility for Iraq passed from the India Office to the Colonial Office under its new Secretary of State Winston Churchill. He immediately convened a conference in Cairo in March 1921, the fundamental purpose of which was 'to maintain firm British control as cheaply as possible'.[30]

In Cairo the idea of allowing the emergence of a separate southern Kurdistan was finally discarded in favour of retaining it as a part of Iraq. The overwhelming argument was a strategic one, but Churchill and Cox both recognized the need for a distinct 'Anglo-Kurdish' administration that was sensitive to Kurdish feeling, and believed 'the best policy being to consider the Kurds as a minority in Iraq but give them a chance after three years to reconsider their [sic] decision.'[31] So the cosmetic of possible and discretionary local autonomy was slipped into the draft Mandate.

In Sulaymaniya Soane was as hostile to the incorporation of the division into Arab Iraq as Shaykh Mahmud had been. He had seen the writing on the wall with Cox's establishemnt of an Arab Council of State. At the end of the year he had made clear that in his view the subordination of Sulaymaniya to an Arab government could only be temporary, pending the creation of a state of South Kurdistan. So he was summarily dismissed after the Cairo Conference. Like his colleagues, Soane may have worked from the paternalistic conviction that he knew what was best for the natives, but no one could doubt his commitment to the wellbeing of Sulaymaniya.[32]

Baghdad was still willing to recognize Kurdish identity, albeit within Iraq, but Cox had decided it was necessary to 'consult' Kurdish opinion formally, and issued a statement on 6 May 'to obtain an indication of the real wishes of the Kurdish communities [sic]. Should they prefer to remain under Iraq Government...'[33] Cox offered to form a sub-province for the Kurdish parts of the Mosul division (Zakhu, Aqra, Dohuk and Amadiya), and similar arrangements for the Arbil division (Arbil, Koi-Sanjaq and Rawanduz).

In both cases British officials were to be replaced by Kurds or Kurdish-speaking Arabs as soon as candidates were available. Everything would be done with consultation and after due consideration of the wishes of the people. Sulaymaniya, however, was offered the status of *mutasarriflik*, governed by a Mutasarrif-in-council. At first the Mutasarrif would be a British officer.

If the Kurds wanted an autonomous entity, now was the crucial moment to fight for it. But although later described as a plebiscite, Cox's consultation was no more than a public sounding taken of notables, elected local councillors and recognised aghas. Most notables knew exactly which way the wind of British policy was blowing and few felt ready to challenge it. Even if a quorum of notables had wished to form a united front (extremely unlikely in the circumstances), they hardly had the chance to mobilize themselves.

So they gave localist responses. Dohuk and Aqra seemed perfectly content with local arrangements, not even wanting semi-separation from Arab Mosul, and while Zakhu and Amadiya both harboured ambitions of becoming the centre of a new Kurdish *mutasarriflik*, both also recognised that separation from Mosul was economically suicidal. Quite apart from the question of markets for Kurdish produce, all roads led down off the mountains onto the Mesopotamian plain. There was no direct route worthy of the name from Amadiya to Sulaymaniya. Arbil insisted on being administratively separate from Kirkuk. As for Sulaymaniya, it resolutely rejected any form of inclusion under an Iraqi government, but it was alone in this stance.

Cox had now lured most Kurdish areas into co-operating with British policy. The new regime in Iraq was extended to Kirkuk, Arbil and Mosul divisions while Sulaymaniya 'remained at its express wish under direct British control' and 'every effort' was made 'to develop native administration along normal lines'.[34] Cox still had to deal with London's residual sense of obligation to the Kurds. Churchill had argued that Arab rule should be limited to purely Arab areas, but Cox could now point out that most Kurds had been consulted and had opted for a non-separatist policy. One could hardly ignore their wishes. Besides, Arab nationalists now counted on an Iraq that included all of the Mosul vilayet. To disappoint them now might risk another explosion like that in 1920. That was the view from Baghdad. While Churchill reminded Cox that inclusion of Kurdish districts in the new National Assembly must respect the principle that 'Kurds are not to be put under Arabs if they do not wish to be',[35] the exigencies of creating the Iraqi state outweighed special claims for the Kurds.

For by now the question of how to establish a compliant form of self-government for Iraq overshadowed all others in British minds. The question of a ruler seemed to be resolved in the form of the Amir Faysal. He was religiously tolerant, thus acceptable to the Shi'a of southern Iraq, and a proven Arab nationalist. Yet it was necessary that he should appear to be chosen by the people of Iraq rather than foisted on them as a puppet ruler by the British. Elections were therefore carried out in late July giving a barely credible 96 per cent vote in favour of Faysal ascending the throne. In reality, of course, everyone perceived Faysal to be Britain's choice.

In Kurdistan the result was equivocal. Kirkuk demanded a Kurdish government but one separate from Sulaymaniya, just as Arbil had insisted on administrative separation from Kirkuk only a couple of months before. Sulaymaniya itself refused to participate in the election at all. Faysal was now assured of the Iraqi throne and Kurdistan, usefully disunited, could be definitively dealt with later.

For Faysal, however, the question of Kurdistan was not confined to strategic or oil concerns. In September 1921, only four weeks after formally ascending the brand-new throne of Iraq, he had made clear he wanted no chance of Kurdish districts seceding from his kingdom, as allowed for in the Treaty of Sèvres. For all his tolerance, he had no wish to see the Shi'i population of Mesopotamia emerge as the dominant force in Iraqi politics. The Kurds were essential to the balance of Sunnis against a Shi'i preponderance, an entirely novel factor to British policy-makers.

Faysal also feared that a separate Kurdish entity might make common cause with the Kurds of Iran and Turkey, thus posing a permanent threat to Iraq. Caught between assurances that the Kurds would not be coerced unwillingly into an Arab state and the political imperatives of creating a viable state, Cox assured Faysal that the Kurds would remain within the economic and political union of the Iraqi Crown, even if they enjoyed different administrative status. He also indicated that he would work for their participation in the Iraq National Assembly. Thus the Kurds had become essential confessional ballast for the new kingdom.

It was a year later, in October 1922, that Faysal issued a decree to convene a Constituent Assembly. It was decided to include all Kurdish areas, even Kirkuk which had demurred to swear allegiance to Faysal, in the process of electoral registration. Only Sulaymaniya was excepted, where what Baghdad had in mind was perfectly understood. Major Noel reported:

> I am up against the universal suspicion, in some cases almost amounting to a certainty, that we are determined to get the Kurds into Iraq by hook or by crook and that the election business [for the Constituent Assembly] is all eyewash.... I would point out that to the Kurdish mind the assurances that no Kurds will be forced into Iraq cannot be squared with the principle of Kirkuk *liwa* [division] as an electoral college.[36]

It will be recalled that at this juncture a Turkish fomented insurrection was rapidly spreading southwards from Rawanduz and that Shaykh Mahmud had been recalled to save the day. Certain nationalists in Sulaymaniya seemed determined to maximize their opportunities. On 2 November a delegation met the high commissioner in Baghdad, demanding recognition of the independence of southern Kurdistan; the transfer of all predominantly Kurdish areas to the government of southern Kurdistan; the establishment of a commission to delineate the boundary between Southern Kurdistan and Iraq; recognition of Shaykh Mahmud as *hukumdar* of Southern Kurdistan and finally that secondary electors (emerging from the electoral process already taking place elsewhere) should form the nucleus of a Kurdish National Assembly.

The high commissioner demurred, asking them to moderate their demands, but he knew that the fate of Sulaymaniya and the whole Kurdish mountain range now hung in the balance and if Turkey regained it, the rest of Mesopotamia might prove untenable. The Kurds would have to be bought off. Thus, as the danger increased in Sulaymaniya, a joint Anglo-Iraqi statement of intent regarding the Kurds was agreed in London and issued on 20 December 1922:

His Britannic Majesty's Government and the Government of Iraq recognize the right of the Kurds living within the boundaries of Iraq to set up a Kurdish Government within those boundaries and hope that the different Kurdish elements will, as soon as possible, arrive at an agreement between themselves as to the form which they wish that that Government should take and the boundaries within which they wish it to extend and will send responsible delegates to Baghdad to discuss their economic and political relations with His Britannic Majesty's Government and the Government of Iraq.[37]

It contradicted what Cox had previously given Faysal to understand, but this was unimportant. He privately assured Faysal that this declaration 'in no way implied separation politically or economically of Kurdistan from Iraq'.[38] Iraq would not brook the political or economic separation of any part of Kurdistan. Those who drafted it knew the Kurds were too divided to 'arrive at an agreement between themselves'.[39] Meanwhile, Shaykh Mahmud was demonstrating his unsuitability for the diplomatic task now required. If through Shaykh Mahmud the Kurds appeared as politically inept, then through Cox the British were now seen to be perfidious.

No sooner had British forces re-occupied Sulaymaniya at the end of May, than the Iraqi prime minister was sent to discuss with Kurdish leaders the idea of a form of autonomous Kurdistan 'in loose subordination' to Iraq. It would be officered by Kurds, of whom only the senior ones would be subject to approval by the king and the high commissioner. Its deputies would not be required to take an oath of allegiance, but would sit in the Baghdad Assembly. Faysal, fearing another nationalist revolt in Sulaymaniya and the danger that the League of Nations might yet allocate the region to Turkey, was even willing to proclaim the immediate autonomy of Sulaymaniya on condition it remained in permanent association with Iraq. But the collapse of the anti-Shaykh Mahmud faction in July following the British troop withdrawal rescued Faysal from such hostages to fortune.

Notwithstanding, Faysal still faced the reluctance of the Kurds in Kirkuk and Arbil to participate in the elections for the Constituent Assembly. Their participation was essential to bring them fully into the Iraqi state and to isolate the obstinacy of Sulaymaniya. On 11 July 1923, the very day on which Shaykh Mahmud re-entered Sulaymaniya, the Iraq Council of Ministers formally resolved that (i) the government would not appoint any Arab officials to Kurdish districts, except technical officials; (ii) that it would not force the inhabitants of these districts to use Arabic in official correspondence; (iii) that the [unspecified] rights of the inhabitants and religious and civil communities in these districts would be properly safeguarded.[40]

By October 1923 the crisis had passed, and Britain and Iraq edged the Kurdish question back within their policy confines. The British reckoned the idea of Kurdish independence had abated everywhere, except for the immediate area around Sulaymaniya, and that Kurdish areas could be incorporated into Iraq on the basis of minimal interference. Apart from Sulaymaniya, the Kurds now participated in the Constituent Assembly elections. In fact, many Sulaymaniya residents went to vote in neighbouring districts, and as a result five deputies were returned for Sulaymaniya, including Shaykh Qadir. Meanwhile, Sulaymaniya's leading citizens seem to have made no move to obtain Baghdad's substantive commitment to its offer in May.

Even now the Council of Ministers kept a declaration of Kurdish cultural rights up its sleeve, to be used in case of difficulties in Kurdistan during the elections. London reminded Baghdad that the previous year Churchill had promised the Commons that the Kurds would indeed be given a real opportunity to decide their position for themselves.[41] Sulaymaniya remained subject to the high commissioner rather than the Iraqi government for the time being.

By 1925 when the League of Nations' Boundary Commission came to the region it seemed as if, Shaykh Mahmud apart, the Kurdish question was in abeyance. Kurdish urban and tribal notables represented the region in parliament. True, a few clouds lurked on the horizon. Sulaymaniya remained a centre of nationalist feeling and Kirkuk still harboured strong nationalist sentiments. But at the representative level such nationalists were easily outnumbered by those who now saw their best interests served by allegiance to the Crown. After the League's Mosul ruling, British promises concerning the use of Kurdish officials and the Kurdish language in Kurdish areas seemed to be generally accepted. Britain felt it had got off lightly, having dreaded a requirement for some form of formal autonomy.

By now the Kurds had proved how essential they were to British policy for Iraq. As Sir Henry Dobbs, Cox's successor, stated, quite apart from the strategic and confessional considerations, they had proved themselves

> the sheet anchor of British influence in Iraq.... It was only through the pro-British Kurdish 'bloc' in the Constituent Assembly that the 1922 Anglo-Iraqi Treaty was finally accepted in June 1924. And since then they have consistently supported British policy by their votes and influence.[42]

Now the dreaded word 'autonomy' could be finally abandoned, even from the emollient vocabulary that Baghdad had used for so long with the Kurds. The new treaty with Faysal in January 1926, that took account of the League's ruling, contained no guarantees for the Kurds. Only an annexure referred to League requirements.

The final nail in the autonomy coffin was the question of Iraq's relations with Turkey. As early as January 1922 it had been noted that negotiations with Turkey would be eased if it could be seen that arrangements for Kurds inside Iraq ignored the provision made at Sèvres, since this eliminated the danger of a cross-boundary autonomy movement. Once the Lausanne negotiations were under way, Iraq and Britain agreed a protocol on 23 April 1923, which 'involved the abandonment of the former policy whereby the administration of Sulaimani *liwa* was to remain the direct responsibility of the high commissioner [and] the establishment of an administration which ... should definitely unite the *liwa* with the Iraqi State'.[43] Thus, within four months of the December 1922 Declaration, the promise of Kurdish government had been quietly junked.

Britain did not hesitate to satisfy Turkish as well as its own interests by abandoning once and for all the question of Kurdish autonomy. Of all Britain's undertakings, the most incriminating had been that given in December 1922. It could now be dismissed from mind and conscience:

> ...both His Majesty's Government and the Government of Iraq are fully absolved from any obligation to allow the setting up of a Kurdish Government by a complete failure of the Kurdish elements even to attempt, at the time this proclamation was made, to arrive at any agreement among themselves or put forward any definite proposals....'[44]

Thus, by 1926 the promises and policy declared in 1918 had been massaged down to the residual rights as promised to the League of Nations. Kurdish leaders may have been guilty of political incompetence, but Britain had been guilty of a betrayal.

Into the Hands of the Arabs

Had Britain ensured that these residual rights – pledged to the League of Nations on behalf of the fledgling Iraqi government as well as itself – were actually fulfilled it might have relinquished its responsiblities for Southern Kurdistan with a little of its honour intact. Instead, it wittingly abandoned the Kurds to an Arab government intent upon evading these pledges.

During the latter 1920s it seemed as if the Kurds were relatively content with their lot. In January 1926 Britain's fresh treaty with Iraq on the League's instruction ensured its responsibility as mandatory for 25 years unless Iraq were admitted as a member of the League. It had laid before the League Council 'the administrative measures which will be taken with a view to securing for the Kurdish populations mentioned in the Commission of Enquiry the guarantees regarding local administration recommended by the Commission.... '[45] A few days later, on 21 January, the Iraqi prime minister, Abd al Muhsin al Saadun, had warned the Chamber of Deputies

> This nation cannot live unless it gives all Iraqi elements their rights.... The fate of Turkey should be a lesson to us and we should not revert to the policy formerly pursued by the Ottoman Government. We should give the Kurds their rights. Their officials should be from among them: their tongue should be their official language and their children should learn their own tongue in the schools. It is incumbent upon us to treat all elements, whether Muslim or non-Muslim, with fairness and justice, and give them their rights.[46]

There was the odd murmur of disgruntlement. For example in February 1926 there had been a fruitless attempt to mobilize Kurdish deputies in Kirkuk to make demands regarding the use of Kurdish and regarding the proposed Kurdish administration. On the whole it seemed as if the area had been integrated happily into the Iraqi state, with Britain still in a reassuringly supervisory role. All Kurdish areas took part in the general election of May 1928, and there were no disturbances nor any shortage of willing candidates. Indeed, there was nothing to suggest anything substantial was wrong. When Khoybun, a new pan-Kurdish movement in Syria (see chapter 9) tried to foster a following in Iraq, it was notably unsuccessful.

Britain, as mandatory, could therefore report a generally satisfactory state of affairs to the League Council. The impression that the government of Iraq was already acting responsibly, particularly in areas of specific League concern, was vital if Britain was successfully to recommend a termination of the mandate and Iraq's membership of the League as an independent state. Britain was motivated mainly by the prospect of retaining its influence by treaty, while being absolved of the more costly aspects of responsibility as mandatory power.

During the course of 1930 Britain negotiated a treaty with Baghdad whereby Iraq might become independent at the beginning of 1932. Britain was assured of the rent-free air bases and strategic communications it wanted, privileges which the Iraqi public realized qualified the kind of independence Britain had in mind. Not a word was mentioned about the special position of the Kurds, as stipulated by the League of Nations in 1926.

Had Iraq implemented the League's requirements of 1926, the Kurds might well have accepted this omission, relying on the proven good faith of Baghdad. But this was not the case. True, there were insufficient qualified Kurdish officials or teachers, and nothing in the way of textbooks for use in schools. Kurdish, too, was problematic. From the plethora of local dialects, a form or forms of Kurdish had to be used that were both workable and met the League's requirement.

Yet no steps had been taken since 1926 to rectify the situation. The promised Local Language Law intended to guarantee the use of Kurdish had not even been drafted, let alone introduced. Barely three weeks after his altruistic declaration to the Chamber of Deputies, Saadun received a British recommendation to establish a Kurdish Translation Bureau, to provide official translations of all laws and regulations applicable to Kurdish areas, and to produce school books in Kurdish, a measure which would 'do much to satisfy the Kurds that their interests are receiving the full attention of the Government'.[47] But nothing had happened. The high commission sent the government the occasional reminder from 1927 onwards but recognized, in the words of one British adviser, government reluctance to act:

> Nobody denies that the practical application of the solution to the Kurdish problem bristles with difficulties, but all efforts are concentrated on not overcoming them.[48]

There was a tendency to blame inertia, but it was well known that Baghdad feared Kurdish separatism and wondered whether the British might use the Kurds as a political lever, or even detach them completely.

Kurdish anxiety began to gather pace as soon as Britain announced in September 1929 its support for Iraq's entry into the League of Nations. The high commission was faced with embarrassing requests for elucidation on the safeguards Britain would provide for the Kurds, and growing disaffection in Kirkuk and Arbil. On learning the terms of the proposed treaty of independence in March, Kurdish opinion was outraged. One petition after another arrived either at the League in Geneva, or on the high commissioner's desk in Baghdad. These petitions were signed by many leading urban and tribal notables of the region, including representatives of the Jaf, Hawraman, Pizhdar, Dauda, Talabani and Dizai tribes. Almost without exception they sought local autonomy, or even independence under British auspices. But they also drew attention to the failure to implement the League's pledges, particularly on education and the use of Kurdish.

It was embarrassing, for these petitions drew attention to previous ones addressed to the high commissioner in the spring of 1929, which appeared to have been ignored. These petitions had been been passed to the Iraqi government for reaction, but the petitioners had gone unanswered. All this became public in the new spate of petitions. What did not become public was Britain's own position on the April 1929 petition. King Faysal and his British adviser, Kinahan Cornwallis, had both agreed that any hint of separatism should be checked at once. So, while the high commissioner reminded Iraq's prime minister of the need to fulfil its pledge to the League, he went on to say 'I have no reason to think that the Government is failing to study the interests of the Kurds.... I should deprecate the adoption of any measure which tended towards separation rather than unity ... it is the wish of His Britannic Majesty's Government to see the eventual unification of all the elements which go to make up the population of Iraq into a stable and homogeneous state.'[49] How could Baghdad possibly create the homogeneous state Britain thought so desirable while pandering to Kurdish particularism?

Britain found itself in a bind of its own making. Publicly, as Baghdad knew perfectly well, it could hardly now admit that it had misled the League all these years, that nothing had been done and that the Kurds were, contrary to everything Britain had previously indicated, profoundly unhappy. At the end of such an honest road lay inevitable rejection of Iraqi independence by the League. Britain would be exposed as incompetent as well as dishonest. So Britain found itself publicly reassuring the outside world that there was no difference between the Iraqi government and itself on this issue and that Baghdad merely needed time in which to rectify its oversights.

Privately though, it deplored Baghdad's failure to implement any of the pledges given to the League, and started chivvying Baghdad to put its house in order. It pressed for the appointment of a Kurdish assistant director-general to the Ministry of the Interior with responsibility for Kurdish areas; the adoption of Kurdish officially in such areas; the creation of a Kurdish educational inspectorate; steps to insure that all officials and the police in Kurdish areas could speak the language; and creation of the long awaited translation bureau.

British officials in Iraq could hardly claim Kurdish outrage came as a total surprise. The petition of April 1929 had been warning enough. Besides, they had known ever since 1918 that the Kurds did not welcome Arab rule. It was known that the Kurds had to be gently discouraged from thinking themselves back to the heady days of 1918–20. When the high commissioner had visited Sulaymaniya in May 1927, for example, he had made a point of reminding them how much better off they were than their cousins in Turkey and in Iran, and that 'they must put aside all ideas of Kurdish independence.'[50]

There were now indications that Kurdish nationalism was no longer confined to conservative shaykhs or aghas and their adherents as it had tended to be in the early 1920s. Then it had been relatively easy to play off one notable against another. By the mid-1920s, however, a small but growing professional class in the Kurdish towns were beginning to show interest in Kurdish national identity.

Ever since the early 1920s there had been a tiny handful of educated nationalists in Sulaymaniya and other main centres. A handful of townspeople had formed Komala-i Sarbakhoi Kurdistan (The Association for the Independence of Kurdistan) in July 1922. Their basic tenet was that Kurds should not be ruled by Arabs, but they were equally hostile to Shaykh Mahmud's tribal style of rule. After 13 issues (from August 1922) Shaykh Mahmud closed down their weekly paper, *Bang-i Kurdistan*, and dismissed its editor, the eminent retired Ottoman general and moderate nationalist, Muhammad Pasha Kurdi. He replaced it with a more openly nationalist organ, *Rozh-i Kurdistan*, the mouthpiece of Shaykh Mahmud himself. In the very first article in November 1922, Arif Saib articulated the position he sought for Kurdistan within Iraq, a position not so very far from the early ideas of British administrators:

> We never expected our great and friendly neighbour [Iraq] to trample under foot all our thousand year old rights and the good relations of these two governments [Iraq and Kurdistan] and peoples, or … to violate our frontiers…. The formation of a government of Kurdistan offers a hundred thousand benefits for Iraq…. History and geography bear ample witness that the Kurdish people have always had an individuality in the world…. The law and principle of self-determination are strongly impressed on the mind and soul of every individual of the nation. In the blessings of rights and frontiers, which have been justly allotted by the League of Nations we, too, have our share. To preserve this share we shall make all necesary sacrifices with our moral and material being…[51]

When the Mosul question had come up at Lausanne the editor, Muhammad Nuri, had written in emphatically nationalist terms:

> As the population of Mosul is generally Kurdish, why should the recovery or retention of this vilayet be demanded by outside peoples. The Turks, Arabs, and Assyrians base their claims on the presence of a small number of their people…. The demand we make

of the Lausanne Conference is not the protection of a minority; it is the vindication of the right to live of a great independent people with a country of its own.[52]

At the time it is doubtful how many Kurds shared this view. As already noted, localist identities predominated and were fatally divisive in the crucial early phase of British policy. But they were views that began to have wider appeal as power was drained away from local notables and chiefs towards Arab Baghdad. The fear of such a spread had been a key factor in bringing Sulaymaniya's special status to an end in 1923.

So, by 1926, it was hardly surprising that there was irritation among educated Kurds that 'only the most colourless Kurds' were allowed to become members of parliament, and that the Kurdish press was censored. Kirkuk might still not want too much to do with Sulaymaniya, for example, but it was a good deal more ready for contact than it had been in 1921. Meanwhile national sentiment was spreading to towns like Kifri and even Altun Kupru, where Turkomans felt they were better off with the Kurds than with the Arabs.

An example of how Kurdish feeling was beginning to spread was the Zanisti-i-Kurdan or Literary Society of Sulaymaniya established in 1926. It was not long before it was being used as a springboard for a wider Kurdish movement. When Shaykh Taha and Ismail Beg Rawanduzi (the previous qaim-maqam) sought permission to form a cultural club in Rawanduz, the government in Baghdad refused it despite their insistence that it would be strictly non-political. In Sulaymaniya itself, Zanisti-i-Kurdan became a cockpit for local political rivalry in which Kurdish nationalist credentials were exploited.

Now that Kurdish sensitivities had been allowed to boil over, there was a need to allay them before they shipwrecked Iraq's projected independence. In April 1930 the Iraqi cabinet announced legislation for Kurdish to be the official language in Kurdish localities and promising that all the pledges would be honoured. It was showered with telegrams of thanks, indicating how easily it could allay Kurdish fears if it wanted to. But it did nothing, and Kurdish anxieties were reawakened.

On the surface things momentarily seemed better, but the tensions soon began to show. In London Nuri Pasha bitterly complained that the RAF Special Service Officers (who had replaced political officers) were deliberately encouraging Kurdish demands. From Baghdad the high commission sent impatient despatches on the inadequate steps of the Iraqis.

Now a new problem loomed. In Sulaymaniya there was a move to boycott the forthcoming elections to be held in September. It was important that Kurds participate and that they did not begin to believe Iraq and Britain were at loggerheads. Consequently the acting high commissioner and acting prime minister arranged a joint tour of Arbil, Kirkuk and Sulaymaniya, to demonstrate Anglo-Iraqi unity and reassure the Kurds regarding Iraqi policy. In Arbil and Kirkuk they persuaded Kurdish representatives momentarily to renounce any separatist ambitions [53]

But in Sulaymaniya army and police pickets and rooftop machine-gun emplacements deployed to protect the tour created exactly the opposite impression to the reassuring one that had been intended. The assembled crowds were un impressed by honeyed words concerning the fulfilment of long overdue promises, and demonstrated in favour of British protection and the removal of Arab rule. A group of city notables led by Shaykh Qadir and by Azmi Baban presented a petition seeking independence under Britain. The acting prime minister, Jaafar Pasha, was only dissuaded from arresting them when reminded that to do so would jeopardize the image necessary if the bid for independence were to gain League approval. A few days later the government removed Sulaymaniya's popular Kurdish *mutasarrif*, Tawfiq Wahbi, who was known to sympathize with moderate nationalist demands.

It was hardly surprising, therefore, that the 6 September election in Sulaymaniya disintegrated into mass demonstrations and stonethrowing. Troops were brought in to restore order. By the evening fourteen civilians had been killed. It was an event that produced international speculation, British embarrassment, and a new round of Kurdish petitions unequivocally demanding administrative separation from Baghdad for a united Kurdish region. Leading notables, including Shaykh Qadir and Azmi Baban and other petitioners, were rounded up. From just over the border in Iran Shaykh Mahmud sent a petition accusing Baghdad of atrocities and demanding a united Kurdistan under British mandate, stretching from Zakhu to Khaniqin. In late October Shaykh Mahmud crossed the border from his exile in Iran and began to raise the tribes.

Now the situation hung in the balance. Without immediate political and military steps the whole of Kurdistan might rise. It was vital to Britain and Iraq that Shaykh Mahmud should be neutralized before his rising gathered any pace. RAF and ground troops operations thwarted his movements and began to contain him, although he was not defeated until well into the new year. Denied asylum in Iran, Shaykh Mahmud made his submission at Panjwin in May 1931, accepting enforced residence in south Iraq. At the political level it was now essential to get Iraq to implement the promises it had made in April and to allay fears when the League of Nations' Permanent Mandates Committee met at the beginning of November. At face value, the government seemed finally to be acting. On 24 August a Kurd was appointed as assistant director-general at the Ministry of the Interior with special responsiblity for Kurdish affairs. A month later a Kurd was appointed inspector of Kurdish schools. But nothing had been done about the Local Languages Law, and it quickly became apparent that the assistant director-general had been left twiddling his thumbs, while Arab *qaim-maqams* were still being appointed to Kurdish areas. Britain now tried to distract attention. Its memorandum to the Permanent Mandates Committee shied away from the inadequacies of its protégé and its own neglect by stressing how wrong-headed the Kurdish petitions were in assuming the League had promised them any form of separatism.

When the committee deliberated, It rejected the Kurdish petitions, much to the relief of Baghdad. But it recommended that Britain be requested to ensure that all administrative and legislative measures necessary to fulfil the Kurdish pledges be promptly and properly enforced, and recommended that Britain ensure the position of the Kurds following Iraq's independence.

Meanwhile, the government of Iraq, resentful of its bossy nanny, had seen the strength of its position, for Britain had more to lose than itself. In December it prepared a memorandum which deliberately quoted from British annual reports for 1925 and 1926 to confirm that Britain had indeed been perfectly satisfied that its policies had not caused dissatisfaction among the Kurds, and that 'Everywhere in the Kurdish areas, officials, with very few exceptions, were Kurds.... The policy enunciated by the Prime Minister on 21 January 1926 has been loyally carried out...'[54] Iraq was, in effect, warning Britain that it ran the risk of exposure of its falsifications. Rather than run this risk British policy-makers chose to continue the deception.

A unity of view, or rather its semblance, was now all the more important for Iraq and Britain lest the Council turn down Iraqi independence. 'Do your best,' the colonial secretary instructed his high commissioner, 'without sacrificing any principle, to secure their [Iraqi] joint concurrence' with the British memorandum to the Council on the Kurdish question.[55] But while London wanted a bullish posture in Geneva, the high commissioner in Baghdad pleaded for silence on the Kurdish question 'until His Majesty's Government can honestly say that the policy is being implemented'.[56]

By late February it was feared that Iraq might succumb to Turkish enticement and openly renege on its League pledges. A stiff warning was given of the dire consequences of open rejection of the League requirements. Meanwhile Nuri Pasha was reminded of the urgency of the Local Languages Law. This was finally ratified on 19 May, the text betraying Iraq's determination to erode the substance: Kurdish speakers rather than actual Kurds were required for administrative and teaching posts; even this requirement was waived for technical posts. In July, as if to thumb its nose at British counsels for restraint, the government arrested respected Kurdish nationalists like Tawfiq Wahbi on charges of high treason.

Despite this provocative incident and the manifest reluctance of Baghdad to grant the Kurds even modest safeguards, the League of Nations formally admitted Iraq as a member at its independence at the beginning of 1932.

Thus Britain found itself a compromised accomplice in Iraq's determination to integrate Kurdistan bereft of any special status. It was a shabby end to the high-flown promises with which British political officers had entered Kurdistan in 1918, and a betrayal of the assurances given by Arab Iraqi ministers during the formation of the Iraqi state.

As for the Kurds, their failure was in unity of leadership and of purpose. Had Zakhu, Dohuk, Arbil, Kirkuk, Sulaymaniya, Kifri and Khaniqin produced a common front before 1923, both Britain and Iraq would have had great difficulty in denying them the formation of an autonomous province. In part they were inhibited by the fear that Turkey would recover the vilayet of Mosul. Yet the underlying reason was their insufficient maturity to recognize the dangers and the strategies necessary to confront Anglo-Iraqi schemes during the brief post-war period when they could have determined the course of events.

Shaykh Ahmad Barzani

Few Kurds welcomed government by Arabs. Indeed, it acted as a spur to Kurdish national feeling. However, the first outbreak of trouble in Kurdistan after inde-pendence had less to do with national feeling as such, than with traditional tribal resentment of government interference in its own territory. Shaykh Ahmad of Barzan already had a stormy relationship with Baghdad. However, he had been left, like many chiefs, in unmolested control of his villages. In practice it was an informal state of local autonomy. But in June 1927 the district began to be brought under administrative control with the construction of blockhouses, a fact distinctly unwelcome to Shaykh Ahmad himself. By October he was preparing to fight the government, demanding an end to the provocative presence of Assyrian levies and the restoration of his right to collect revenue within his tribal area. By February 1928 he was in touch not only with his formidable neighbours, the Zibaris and the Surchis, but was also rumoured to be in touch with Shaykh Mahmud and the Iranian Kurdish chief Simqu. The British also reckoned he was receiving arms and ammunition from the Turks. Fearful of revolt again in Kurdistan, the British opted for compromise. In April an agreement was reached whereby the *qaim-maqam* of Zibar 'delegated' tax collecting responsibilities of Barzan district to Shaykh Ahmad. But by August Shaykh Ahmad was handing in excuses rather than taxes.

British officials were apprehensive about taking Shaykh Ahmad on. They probably feared that open conflict would inflame Kurdish national feeling, some-thing Britain wanted to avoid at all costs, particularly in the run-up to the Anglo-Iraqi treaty. By 1931 Assyrian levies and Iraqi army units were still patrolling through Barzan district. Government troops implied government control, some-thing Shaykh Ahmad still wanted to avoid. Apparently he appealed unsuccessfully to King Faysal. There seems to be no evidence that Shaykh Ahmad was remotely interested in the wider Kurdish picture. He had declined Shaykh Mahmud's invitation to join a co-ordinated demand for autonomy among the chiefs in 1930. He was engaged, like his forebears, in the defence of his tribal patch. He had a retinue of formidable warriors, and instilled respect in the chiefs of Barush and Mazuri Bala, the districts north of Barzan.

Shaykh Ahmad also used his spiritual status to ensure obedience. It is not altogether clear whether he had religious delusions or deliberately used novel ideas to reinforce his authority. He was, however, central to a religious cult that had nothing to do with Naqshbandi beliefs. In 1927, at the very time that Barzan was brought under administrative control, one of his mullas, Mulla Abd al Rahman, was going about proclaiming Shaykh Ahmad to be 'God', and himself 'the Prophet' – strong meat even in a region given to extreme religious eccentricity. The credulous were invited to abandon the Mecca *qibla*. Mulla Abd al Rahman did not last long, killed by Shaykh Ahmad's brother, Muhammad Sadiq, for attempting to substitute Shaykh Ahmad's name and his own in the call to prayer. Yet such ideas lingered on. About ten weeks later the small Balik tribe announced its attachment to Shaykh Ahmad, recognizing no other master than the 'Divine Shaykh'.

Four years later, in 1931, Shaykh Ahmad's religious eccentricity led to war with an old Naqshbandi rival, Shaykh Rashid of Lolan, leader of the Baradust Kurds. Shaykh Ahmad apparently told his followers to eat pork, symbolic of the synthesis of Christian beliefs with Naqshbandi Islam, and encouraged destruction of copies of the Quran. In July Shaykh Rashid called on his own people to deal with this unbelief by attacking Barzani villages. One cannot help wondering whether Shaykh Ahmad was really religiously deranged or whether he had deliberately intended to provoke Shaykh Rashid. Whatever the reason, the ensuing cycle of raid and counter-raid reached a crescendo in November when Shaykh Ahmad's retinue stormed its way through Baradust, burning villages and driving Shaykh Rashid into Iran.

Baghdad had for some time intended to march against Shaykh Ahmad to enforce his submission to its demands and end his provocative religious eccentricities. His despoliation of Baradust now spurred Baghdad to action. But Shaykh Barzan's behaviour was not a significantly greater challenge to government authority than the behaviour of other tribal leaders. He had sailed close to the wind in 1927–28, but backed away from confrontation.

Why the Iraqi government chose to make an example of Shaykh Barzan remains unclear. Like the Ottomans, it seems to have found the Barzanis a particular provocation. Perhaps as a newly independent and unconfident regime it felt it could brook no trouble from Kurdish tribesmen. If so, it made a great mistake. An Iraqi strike force despatched in December was soundly beaten near Barzan and only extricated with British air support. In spring 1932 another force occupied Margasur, east of Barzan, with a view once again of marching on Barzan itself. Again, it was defeated with heavy loss. In June Iraqi forces supported by British air support finally occupied Barzan. For the next year Shaykh Ahmad was pursued through the mountains. Delayed action bombs killed or maimed unsuspecting villagers and deterred Shaykh Ahmad's men from obtaining supplies from abandoned villages. In late June 1932 Shaykh Ahmad surrendered to Turkish troops on the frontier, rather than to Iraqi forces.

But it is doubtful whether Shaykh Ahmad had enjoyed wide support in his villages. There were plenty of people, for example in Mazuri, who strongly opposed his religious views. Furthermore, it seems that he was ruthless in seizing his villagers' grain in order to support his war and that many fled his oppressive rule. When those who had fled returned, they were supplied with grain to replace their lost crops.

Shaykh Ahmad's surrender to the Turks did not mark the end of the rebellion. His two brothers, Muhammad Sadiq and Mulla Mustafa continued to fight from the border area and the recesses of Mazuri Bala for another year. But they surrendered with their small force when the RAF dropped amnesty leaflets in June 1933 and Shaykh Ahmad, now in Turkish detention in Eskishehir, advised them to accept Iraqi terms. After months in the mountains they were half-starved and in rags. Remarkably, rebels were allowed home with their weapons, once they had taken an oath of allegiance to King Faysal. As a further douceur to the tribe, a small grant was made to assist 'loyal' Barzani cultivators retrieve their agriculture, and for the opening of dispensaries. It was paltry recompense for the destructive manner in which the Barzanis had been brought to heel. RAF bombing had destroyed 1,365 out of 2,382 dwellings in 79 villages. In addition, the use of delayed action bombs, in violation of the 1907 Hague Convention and of the British *Manual of Military Law* (1914), caused widespread civilian casualties.

The Kurds were among the first to learn that aerial war was indiscriminate in its victims, something which fuelled Kurdish indignation with Baghdad. As Arthur ('Bomber') Harris had written in 1924:

> They [Arabs and Kurds] now know what real bombing means, in casualties and damage; they now know that within 45 minutes a full sized village can be practically wiped out and a third of its inhabitants killed or injured...[57]

Presumably on guarantees for his life, Shaykh Ahmad returned to Iraq and was exiled with his brothers. At first he stayed in Mosul, until he was caught corresponding with the Mazuri chief, Khalil Khushawi, who remained in rebellion. So they were moved to Nasiriyya in southern Iraq, then to Sulaymaniya.

Shaykh Ahmad's war was a conflict between tribe and government, and as such it proved damaging to Iraqi prestige. For after Shaykh Ahmad's defiance, the continued rebellion of Khalil Khushawi until 1936 demonstrated that the Iraqi army was not yet strong enough to deal with determined tribal resistance. Baghdad's difficulty in dealing with Khushawi led it to enrol tribesmen as an irregular local force, a step in the direction of restoring and incorporating agha authority into the government system for Kurdistan, a 'confession that they can only control Kurdistan with the armed assistance of the Aghas'.[58]

Sources

League of Nations. Decision Relating to the Turco-Irak Frontier Adopted by the Council of the League of Nations, Geneva, December 16, 1925 Cmd 2562 (London, 1925)

Great Britain.   Public Record Office: series FO 371 nos 3385, 3404, 4147, 4149, 4192, 4193, 5067, 5068, 5069, 6346, 6347, 6348, 7772, 7782, 9004, 9005, 9007, 9009, 9014, 10097, 10098, 10833, 10835, 10868, 11458, 11459, 11460, 11464, 11468, 11478, 12255, 12265, 13027, 13032,

13759, 14521, 14523, 15310, 15311, 16038, 16917, 17874, 18948, 18949; series CO 730 nos. 13, 14, 16, 19, 22, 23, 133/6, 150/6, 157/5, 157/6, 157/7, 157/8, 161/1, 161/2, 161/4.

Great Britain, Command Papers, Internal Prints etc. *Precis of Affairs in Southern Kurdistan; Review of Civil Administration in Mesopotamia, 1914–1920; Administration Report for Sulaimaniyah Division for 1919;* Major W.R. Hay, *Note on Rowanduz* (Baghdad, 1920); Major E.W. Noel, *Note on the Kurdish Situation* (Baghdad, 1919); *Report on Iraq Administration for the Period October 1920 – March 1922* (London, 1923); *Report on Iraq Administration for the Period April 1922 – March 1923* (London, 1924).

Secondary sources: Anon., 'Major Soane in Sulaimaniyah', *Journal of the Royal Central Asia Society* (hereafter JRCAS), vol. x, 1923; Antonius, *The Arab Awakening;* Joyce Blau, *Le Problème Kurde: Essai Sociologique et Historique* (Brussels, 1963); Edmonds, *Kurds, Turks and Arabs;* C.J. Edmonds, 'A Kurdish Newspaper: "Rozh-i Kurdistan"', *JRCAS,* vol. xii, 1925; A.M. Hamilton, *Road through Kurdistan* (London, 1937); W.R. Hay, *Two Years in Kurdistan;* G.M. Lees, 'Two years in South Kurdistan', *JRCAS,* vol. xv, 1928; Longrigg, *Iraq 1900–1950;* Philip Mumford, 'Kurds, Assyrians and Iraq', *JRCAS,* vol. xx, 1933; Nikitine, 'Les Kurdes racontés par eux-mêmes', *L'Asie Française,* May 1925; David Omissi, *Air Power and Colonial Control: The RAF 1919–1939* (Manchester, 1991); Piresh, *Barzan wa Harakat al Wa'i al Qawmi al Kurdi* (n.p., 1980); Sluglett, *Britain in Iraq;* Soane, *To Mesopotamia and Kurdistan in Disguise; The Times;* Arnold Toynbee, *A Survey of International Affairs;* Wilson, *Loyalties;* Wilson, *Mesopotamia;* A.T. Wilson, 'The early days of the Arab government in Iraq', *JRCAS,* vol. ix, 1922; W.C.F. Wilson, 'Northern Iraq and its peoples', *JRCAS,* vol. xxiv, 1937.

Unpublished: Siyamand Othman, 'Contribution historique a l'étude du Parti Dimokrati-i Kurdistan-i Iraq, 1946–1970' (Dissertation, Paris, 1985).

Notes

1. FO 371/4192 *Precis of Affairs,* p. 9.
2. FO 371/3407 Political, Baghdad to India Office, telegram, 1 November 1918.
3. FO 371/4192 *Precis of Affairs,* p. 10.
4. Wilson, *Mesopotamia,* p. 133.
5. Wilson, *Loyalties,* p. 88.
6. Wilson, *Loyalties,* p. 135.
7. For the following analysis I am indebted to Jwaideh, 'The Kurdish nationalist movement', pp. 474–480.
8. *Review of Civil Administration 1914–1920,* p. 61. It will be recalled that Soane had spent time in Sulaymaniya in 1909, and considered Shaykh Mahmud and his father as rogues. See *To Mesopotamia and Kurdistan in Disguise,* pp. 187–195.
9. FO 371/5069 Major E.B. Soane, *Administration Report of Sulaimaniyah Division for the Year 1919,* pp. 1–2.
10. *Administration Report of Sulaimaniyah Division for 1919,* p. 3. Soane had been unable to prevent this situation since he had been on sick leave during winter and spring 1918–19. The conflict between Noel and Soane regarding Shaykh Mahmud may be followed in CO 730/13.
11. Wilson, *Loyalties,* p. 136.
12. Wilson, *Loyalties,* p. 139.
13. Anon., 'Major Soane in Sulaimaniyah', *Journal of the Royal Central Asia Society,* vol. x, 1923, p. 146.
14. Anon., 'Major Soane in Sulaimaniyah', *JRCAS,* vol. x, 1923, p. 146.

15. Hay, *Two Years in Kurdistan*, p. 349.

16. David Omissi, *Air Power and Colonial Control: The RAF 1919–1939* (Manchester 1991), p. 37; see also Edmonds, *Kurds, Turks and Arabs*, p. 297 and p. 244f.

17. FO 371/7772 Iraq Intelligence Report no. 17, 1 September 1922.

18. As a result both of his adventures with Simqu and because the Kemalists had found his younger brother, Shaykh Muslih, with whom he had strained relations, ready to support them; FO 371/9009 Iraq Intelligence Report No. 10, 15 May 1923.

19. For example, Jamal Beg Urfan, a Kurdish officer seconded from the Iraqi army to assist the Sulaymaniya administration and who dared criticise Shaykh Mahmud's methods openly; and Arif Sa'ib, appointed by Shaykh Mahmud as his personal secretary in December 1922 and editor of *Rozh-i Kurdistan*. He was executed in the presence of his master some months later; Edmonds, *Kurds, Turks and Arabs*, p. 304, and 'A Kurdish newspaper: "Rozh-i Kurdistan"', *JRCAS*, vol. xii, 1925, pp 86, 88.

20. Antonius, *The Arab Awakening*, (London, 1938), Appendix E.

21. FO 371/5068 W.R. Hay, *Note on Rawanduz*, 26 December 1919.

22. *Precis of Events*, p. 12.

23. FO 371/4149 Memorandum on Mesopotamia's future constitution, 6 April 1919, Enclosure No. 8.

24. FO 371/4149 Monthly Administration Report for the Period 15 December 1918 to 15 January 1919.

25. FO 371/4149 Memorandum on Self-Determination in Iraq, 9 July 1919.

26. FO 371/4147 Political to India Office, Baghdad, 26 December 1918.

27. Wilson, *Mesopotamia*, p. 143.

28. FO 371/5067 Civil Commissioner to India Office, Baghdad, 4 February 1920.

29. For example, see FO 371/5069 S.H. Longrigg, Administrative Report for Kirkuk Division 1 January 1919 – 31 December 1920.

30. Sluglett, *Britain in Iraq*, p. 49.

31. FO 371/6346 High Commissioner Mesopotamia to Secretary of State for the Colonies, 12 June 1921.

32. Two colleagues went with him, see Lees, 'Two Years in Kurdistan', *JRCAS*, vol. xv, 1928, p. 269 and 'Soane in Sulaimaniyah', *JRCAS*, vol. x, 1923 pp. 146–147.

33. Iraq, *Report on Iraq Administration, October 1920–March 1922*, p. 126.

34. *Iraq Report 1922–23* and Toynbee, *Survey of International Affairs*, p. 487.

35. FO 371/6347 Secretary of State for the Colonies to High Commissioner Baghdad, 3 October 1921.

36. BHCF, *Events in Kurdistan*, 13/14/vol. II Noel to Bourdillon, Sulaymaniya, 10 October 1922, quoted in Sluglett, *Britain in Iraq*, p. 120.

37. This was issued as an official communiqué in Kurdish by Baghdad, and communicated orally by a Political Officer, C.J. Edmonds to Shaykh Abd al Karim of Qadir Karam, Edmonds, *Kurds, Turks and Arabs*, p. 312.

38. FO 371/9009 Iraq Intelligence Report No. 1, 1 January 1923.

39. FO 371/9004 Edmonds, Note on the Kurdish situation, 4 January 1923.

40. FO 371/15311 Humphrys to Passfield, Baghdad, 27 February 1931, included in the draft section on Kurds for the Ten Year Report to be submitted to the League of Nations.

41. The promise was made in the Commons on 11 July 1922.

42. FO 371/11460 Dobbs to Shuckburgh, Lismore, Ireland, 16 March 1926.

43. FO 371/15311 Humphreys to Passfield, draft section on Kurds for inclusion in Ten Year Report to the League, 27 February 1931, quoting from *Report on Iraq Administration for the Period April 1922 – March 1923*, p. 37.

44. FO 371/11460 Bourdillan to Amery, Baghdad, 10 February 1926.

45. League of Nations, *Decision relating to the Turco-Irak Frontier Adopted by the Council of the*

League of Nations, Geneva, December 16, 1925 (London, 1925), Cmd 2562, p. 4.

46. *Proceedings of the Chamber of Deputies*, 21 January 1926, quoted in Sluglett, *Britain in Iraq*, p. 182.

47. FO 371/11478 Bourdillon to Saadun, Baghdad, 12 February 1926.

48. Delhi, BHCF, File 13/14 vol. vi, *Events in Kurdistan*, Edmonds to Holt, 9 May 1928, in Sluglett, *Britain in Iraq*, p. 186.

49. FO 371/13759 Clayton to Abd al Muhsin Saadun, Baghdad, 20 April 1929.

50. FO 371/11464 Iraq Intelligence Report No. 11, 24 May 1927.

51. *Rozh-i Kurdistan*, no. i, 15 November 1922, in Edmonds, 'A Kurdish newspaper', p. 86.

52. *Rozh-i Kurdistan*, no. vi, 12 December 1922, in Edmonds, 'A Kurdish newspaper', p. 87.

53. But after their departure Kirkuk notables and the Dauda tribe demanded separation from Arab rule, and identified with Sulaymaniya's nationalist stance.

54. CO 730/157/8 High Commissioner Iraq to Secretary of State for the Colonies, 19 December 1930, and quotes from *Iraq Report 1925*, pp. 22–23 and *Iraq Report 1926*, p. 14, in Sluglett, *Britain in Iraq*, p. 193.

55. FO 371/15310 Colonial Secretary to High Commissioner, London, 19 January 1931.

56. FO 371/15310 High Commissioner Iraq to Secretary of State for the Colonies, 10 February 1931.

57. Omissi, *Air Power*, p. 154.

58. FO 371/18949 Air HQ, Iraqi Review of Events 1934, Hinaidi, January 1935.

CHAPTER 9

INCORPORATING TURKEY'S KURDS

Introduction

Nothing that Iraq's Kurds could complain of remotely compared with the oppression meted out to Turkey's Kurds. Yet at first this was neither apparent nor necessarily planned by the Kemalists. Kurds helped the Kemalists prevent the infidel, Greek, Armenian, French or British overrun the homeland. It is unclear whether Mustafa Kemal premeditated his ruthless suppression of Kurdish identity, or whether his thinking underwent a radical change in 1923.

Either way, the Kurds proved quite unable to create any effective opposition. They were too dispersed geographically, and too fragmented by religious and tribal affiliation, by socio-economic activity and by language. Furthermore, few Kurds had yet evolved any coherent idea of Kurdish identity, let alone the political consequences of such ideas. But while the state was therefore able to repress one rising after another and impose its new racial and centralizing ideologies, it seriously underestimated the durability of the primordial ties that bound groups of Kurds together. Yet these ties, which gave an unsuccessful structure for resistance in the 1920s and 1930s, showed every sign of outlasting Kemalist ideology by the 1990s.

The Kuchgiri Rebellion[1]

Kurdish nationalists, particularly those who explored the chances for a Kurdo-Armenian alliance, could only mobilize national feeling among those who felt least threatened by Armenian ambitions. Of these the clearest group was Alevi, which did not share the fear felt by many Sunni Kurds further east.

On the whole relations between Sunni and Alevi Kurds had been fractious, going back to the Sunni–Shi'i struggle in Anatolia in the sixteenth century. It will be recalled that the Hamidiya aghas used their authority and power to reduce local Alevi rivals. Conflict between the two groups was widespread. The most notable example had been the feud between the Alevi Khurmak and the Sunni

Jibrans. The former were a leading Alevi landowning family, while the latter were one of the strongest tribes of Kurdistan. The Jibrans had slain the Khurmak chief, Ibrahim 'Ialu, in 1894, and his son 12 years later. At the tribal level there was little love lost between Alevi and Sunni Kurd.

Nevertheless, when Kurdistan Ta'ali Jamiyati was formed in Istanbul at the end of the Great War, one or two Alevis were among them, for example Mustafa Pasha, chief of the Kuchgiri in western Dersim, his son Alishan Beg, and Nuri Dersimi, an agha's son, who was anxious to forge Sunni–Alevi solidarity and who, in October 1920, opened party branches among the Alevi Kuchgiri tribal group. The establishment of these branches was the prelude to a major rising in November, led by Alishan Beg against the Kemalists.

This was not the first occasion on which the Alevis had crossed swords with the Kemalists, for they had tried to foil the Sivas Congress in September 1919 by blocking the Pass of Erzinjan. They were hostile to the recovery of the Turkish state, because this suggested growing control of Dersim, which had been temporarily subdued for the first time only in 1878. The 1919 incident had coincided with the Noel mission arousing Kemalist fears of a co-ordinated rising to establish a Kurdish state.

The timing and location were significant. West Dersim, lying west of the Euphrates, had been excluded from the area formally designated at Sèvres in August as part of an autonomous Kurdish state. During July and August Kurdish bands had attacked police posts and ammunition convoys. The Kemalists had appointed Alishan and his brother Haydar as *qaim-maqams* of two towns (Rafahiya and Umraniya) on the Sivas–Erzinjan road on the optimistic but, on this occasion, misguided principle of poacher turned gamekeeper.

In September 1920 the position of the Kemalists had begun to look more fragile as the Armenians launched a major offensive in the east. A month later the Greeks mounted their offensive in the west. On 20 October the Kurds seized a large shipment of arms and, rather than returning it to the Kemalists, Alishan Beg used this windfall to rally the Dersim tribes in rebellion.

Having cut the road between Sivas and Erzinjan, the rebel leaders presented Ankara with their demands in mid-November. The influence of the Kurdistan Ta'ali Jamiyati can be discerned in the nature of the demands, which were far from sectarian: (i) acceptance by Ankara of Kurdish autonomy as already agreed by Istanbul; (ii) the release of all Kurdish prisoners in Elaziz, Malatya, Sivas and Erzinjan jails; (iii) the withdrawal of all Turkish officials from areas with a Kurdish majority; (iv) the withdrawal of all Turkish forces from the Kuchgiri region. A response was required within ten days.

The Ankara government was in a critical position. It had no wish to concede but could not risk its supply route while fighting off external enemies. It decided to play for time and sent a commission to Dersim to parley; this was driven away. Then it received a statement on 25 November that if an independent Kurdistan were not established as stipulated at Sèvres, the Dersim chiefs would continue their rebellion. Ankara may have sensed uncertainty in this abrupt change of terms, and refrained from rejecting the demand. Rather, it continued to make overtures to the rebels, while quietly strengthening its garrison at Sivas. Mustafa Kemal even met Alishan Beg who accepted candidacy to the Ankara Assembly, a curious position for a rebel chief to take.

The beginning of winter rendered movement difficult. While garrisons could be strengthened at Erzerum, Erzinjan, Sivas and Elaziz to prevent the rebellion spreading, conditions made it difficult for the rebels to recruit further afield. No one in their right minds would take to the hills until winter was over.

If the Alevi Kurds had hoped by their demands to broaden the appeal of their rising to include Sunni Kurds, they were disappointed. Few Sunnis joined them. On 11 March they made a fresh demand for a vilayet administered by Kurds wherever they formed a majority. But it was already too late. When the snow began to melt in March and April Dersim was encircled by Turkish forces which began to advance on rebel positions. Word of atrocities committed by both sides almost certainly proved a strong disincentive to Kurdish tribes further afield. Kurdish deputies in Ankara sat on their hands. Further south, around Malatya, the Alevi Kurdish tribes which Noel had visited in 1919 likewise remained passive. By the end of April the rising was over. Haydar Beg had been imprisoned, but his brother Alishan was still at large.

It is doubtful whether Sunni tribes would have rallied to the cause even had it not been winter. Many had already committed themselves to the Kemalists who, at this juncture, had not yet even hinted at the Turanic and secularist ideology they would subsequently impose. They suspected the Alevis not merely *per se* but for their links with the Armenians.

When Mustafa Kemal had first rallied support in the east in the summer of 1919 he had made a point of bringing in the Kurds. He had written to a number of chiefs whom he had known while stationed in Diyarbakir in 1916, and, following the Congress of Erzerum in July 1919, he deliberately tried to co-opt three key constituent groups of Kurdistan: the urban notables, chiefs and shaykhs.[2] By the end of the year he had rallied a substantial proportion of the Kurdish tribes to his support.

To the Kemalists the first Kuchgiri revolt was like previous revolts, essentially a matter of troublesome aghas. It attracted only particular tribes for particular reasons. Some Alevi tribes had supported the government, so it was not even as if Alevis *qua* Alevis stood shoulder to shoulder. The nationalist rhetoric employed by Kuchgiri leaders had evinced no perceptible response from the Kurdish masses. It had only been dangerous because of Ankara's critical communications while committed on two fronts.

Six months later, however, fresh disturbances occurred in Dersim. By now the area had become the centre of Kurdish nationalist activity. Those who meant business had fled Istanbul and gone to Kurdistan. Consequently there was a much stronger nationalist flavour, and it seemed as if many parts of Kurdistan might also join the rebellion. Meanwhile Turkish troops were heavily committed containing the Greek threat.

On 9 October the Kurdish deputy for Dersim addressed a secret session of the Turkish Grand National Assembly, to explain how the Kurdish Social League, the separatist wing of the nationalist movement led by the Badr Khans and by Alishan Bey, had established itself in Dersim and elsewhere, exploiting the general discontent arising from heavy tax levies. A heated debate ensued with several deputies urging the use of 'strong methods'. But much of Kurdistan, apart from Dersim, was already plunged into disorder. With rebels rumoured to have 40,000 horsemen, there was no question of raising a credible punitive expedition. The moderates, essentially the Kurdish deputies, won the day and the Grand National Assembly sent a conciliation commission to examine the whole question of how to administer Kurdistan. But there was considerable apprehension concerning Kurdish demands, particularly that these might include autonomy behind frontiers defined by an Allied commission (as provided for at Sèvres), and the complete withdrawal of all Turkish state personnel from this region. If so, Ankara had no intention of yielding.

'A Mixture of One Muslim Element'

It is important to bear in mind that until the foundation of the republic and the crystallization of ideology in 1923, the Kemalists envisaged, or pretended to, a Muslim state, composed of the Turkish and Kurdish remnants of the empire. This was implicit in the National Pact, and explicit in Kemalist action and utterance.

Mustafa Kemal was perfectly aware of Kurdish separatist tendencies, of the Kurdish clubs in Istanbul and of the dangerous implications of the Noel mission. There was a Kurdish question undoubtedly, but at this stage its threat was as a Trojan horse for the British or the Armenians to wrest eastern Anatolia from Ottoman control. Whether in sincerity or in deceit, Mustafa Kemal pragmatically stressed the unity of Turks and Kurds, condemning foreign (essentially British) plots to wean the Kurds away. This was consonant with the resistance movement already operating when Mustafa Kemal arrived in Anatolia. For the Society for the Defence of Rights of Eastern Anatolia was already issuing rallying calls that appealed to Kurdo-Turkish unity. Such calls appealed to ethnic identity, but unity centred on the controlling religious idea of empire. In the words of Mustafa Kemal in September 1919,

> As long as there are fine people with honour and respect, Turks and Kurds will continue to live together as brothers around the institution of the *khilafa*, and an unshakeable iron tower will be raised against internal and external enemies.[3]

Islam was to be the linch-pin of the Kemalist struggle against the Christian invader. Mustafa Kemal was explicit on the existence of different ethnic groups within the Muslim *watan* (homeland).

...there are Turks and Kurds. We do not separate them. But while we are busy to defend and protect, of course, the nation is not one element. There are various bonded Muslim elements. Every Muslim element which makes this entity are citizens. They respect each other, they have every kind of right, racial, social and geographical. We repeated this over and over again. We admit this honestly. However, our interests are together. The unity we are trying to create is not only Turkish or Circassian. It is a mixture of one Muslim element.[4]

The idea of the Kurds *qua* Kurds as an essential component of Turkey remained part of his expressed thinking in this phase. For example, in 1921 he wrote to certain Kurdish chiefs 'the loyalty of the Kurdish people has been known to us for a long time. The Kurds have always been a valuable help to the Turks. One can say that the two peoples form one.'[5]

Yet he was a good deal more vague on the future relationship between the two groups. That, he claimed, could be decided later once the external threat had been repelled. 'Do not imagine,' he told the Grand National Assembly,

there is only one kind of nation within these borders. There are Turks, Circassians and various Muslim elements within these borders. It is the national border of brother nations whose interests and aims are entirely united ... the article that determines this border is our one great principle: around each Islamic element living within this home-land's borders there is a recognition and mutual acceptance in all honesty to their race, tradition and environment. Naturally there are no details and explanations belonging to this tradition because it is not the time to answer details and explanations. God willing, after saving our existence this will be solved among brothers and will be dealt with.[6]

Thus, on 10 February 1922 the Assembly undertook to establish 'an autonomous administration for the Kurdish nation in harmony with their national customs'.[7] However, what it proposed robbed the word autonomy of any meaning: a Kurdish National Assembly was to be elected by universal suffrage, but the Grand National Assembly reserved the right to approve or otherwise the governor-general chosen by the population of the Kurdish region. The Assembly also reserved the right to command the gendarmerie in Kurdistan and insisted on Turkish being the language of the Kurdish National Assembly. But the real message regarding autonomy and the powers of an elected Kurdish National Assembly lay in Article 16: 'The primary duty of the Kurdish National Assembly shall be to found a university with a law and medical faculty.'[8]

Little wonder therefore that the commissioners, none of whom seem to have been Kurds, and the Kurdish deputies vigorously opposed the proposal on their return to Ankara a few days later. The Erzerum deputy, Khoja Salih Effendi, spoke for them when he blamed the Kurdish problem on government tyranny. Tax levies made for military purposes, in particular the seizure of livestock, and corruption surrounding the issue of receipts for such seizures had already created widespread resentment. He also drew attention to Ankara's attitude to the caliphate, evidence that eight months before the abolition of the sultanate and almost exactly two years before the demise of the caliphate, Kemalist hostility towards this institution was already causing disquiet in Sunni Kurdish circles.

Were the Kemalists already bent upon the eventual abolition of the caliphate in March 1922? It is difficult to be sure when this point was reached or when the inner circle of Kemalists decided on a specifically Turkish state in which other ethnic groups must be denied. The Turkish language restriction was a harbinger of repressive measures. Yet, while the proposed Kurdish National Assembly was to use only Turkish, Article 15 permitted the governor-general to encourage the use of Kurdish, provided it was not made the basis for the future recognition of Kurdish as the official language of government.

Although approved in draft form, this autonomy plan never saw the light of day. Eastern Anatolia remained plunged in chaos during the spring and summer of 1922, while the Kemalists dealt with the Greek threat, and there was no credible Kurdish national leadership with which Ankara could negotiate even if it were so inclined. As Colonel Rawlinson, emerging from long months of incarceration at Erzerum reported,

> the Kurds are left enormously in the majority in the eastern districts of Anatolia and all Turkish posts there being very weakly held are at the mercy of the local Kurds, being particularly vulnerable should Kurdish raids be carried out approximately simultaneously, say within the same month. The principal Kurdish chiefs are entirely dissatisfied.[9]

But herein lay the fatal fact, that although they might be dissatisfied, the chiefs were incapable of the concerted action necessary to eject the Turks. Ankara had only to wait until the Greeks were defeated before dealing with Kurdistan.

The steps eventually taken by the Kemalists completed a process begun when the Young Turks had questioned the basis of empire at the end of the nineteenth century. Kemalist interest in strong central government, with its firm grip felt in every part of Turkey, the emphasis on a kind of 'Turkishness' that must be embraced by all citizens of the republic, and their secularism are all easily traceable to the early mentors of modern Turkey. Significantly, Ziya Gokalp had published his seminal *The Principles of Turkism* in 1920. His writings gave the Kemalists the line of argument for dragooning minorities into a Turkish identity:

> ...since race has no relationship to social traits, neither can it have any with nationality, which is the sum total of social characteristics ... social solidarity rests on cultural unity, which is transmitted by means of education and therefore has no relationship with consanguinity ... a nation is not a racial or ethnic or geographic or political or volitional group but one composed of individuals who share a common language, religion, morality or aesthetics, that is to say, who have received the same education.[10]

Gokalp was writing before Kurdistan had been incorporated into the new republic. He did not live to see the Kurds rebel against Kemalist policy and he viewed Kurds as a distinct national and cultural movement: 'Among the Kurds and Arabs, too, nationalism started as a cultural movement. Political and economic forms of nationalism followed as second and third stages.'[11] Kurds, he knew, were of Iranian rather than Turanic origin. He did not include himself among Kurds because he considered his culture to be Turkish: 'I would not hesitate to believe that I am a Turk even if I had discovered that my grand-fathers came from the Kurdish or Arab areas because I learned through my sociological studies that nationality is based solely on upbringing.'[12]

During the first two months of 1923 Gokalp's ideas on Turkish identity, essentially that the nation is the outward expression of a specific culture, became accepted to mean that all those within the bounds of the new (but as yet un-declared) republic belonged to this Turkish identity.

In January, when the negotiations at Lausanne were well under way, Turkey's new leaders still found no embarrassment in speaking of the Kurds as a distinct group within Turkey. But now there was a new tone. In Lausanne Ismet Inonu shamelessly told Curzon that the Kurds were of Turanian origin, the *Encyclopaedia Britannica* told him so and that 'as regards manners, usage and customs, the Kurds do not differ in any respect from the Turks.'[13] To drive his point home he informed Curzon that

> The Government of the Grand National Assembly of Turkey is the Government of the Kurds just as much as the Government of the Turks, for the real and legitimate representatives of the Kurds sit in the Assembly and take part in the government and administration of the country to the same degree as the representatives of the Turks.[14]

Technically this was true but it was already contingent on the subordination of Kurdish particularism to the evolving Kemalist idea, and the Kurdish deputies found it progressively harder to defend their corner.

Yet it was also a moment of hesitation. Some provision for the Kurds was still conceivable as long as it was not imposed by foreign powers and as long as Ankara's authority still held sway. Mustafa Kemal himself was still thinking in terms of special status for the Kurdish region, but less emphatically than before. This was expressed most clearly on a visit to Izmit in mid-January 1923:

> Those in our national borders are only a Kurdish majority in limited places. Over time by losing their population concentration, they have settled with Turkish elements in such a way that if we try to draw a border on behalf of the Kurds we have to finish with Turkishness and Turkey, for example in the regions of Erzerum, Erzinjan, Sivas and Kharput, – and do not forget the Kurdish tribes on the Konya desert. This is why instead of considering Kurdishness in isolation, some local autonomies will be established in accordance with our constitution. Therefore, whichever provinces are predominantly Kurd will administer themselves autonomously. But apart from that, we have to describe the people of Turkey together. If we do not describe them thus, we can expect prob-lems particular to themselves.... it cannot be correct to try to draw another border [between Kurds and Turks]. We must make a new programme.[15]

Thus, while it was not proposed to draw a boundary between the two, Mustafa Kemal still seemed inclined to allow some form of Kurdish identity, albeit one stripped of political power.

A fundamental policy change took place during the next four weeks. When Kemal's speech to the Izmir Economic Congress (17 February 1923) was published, all reference to the Kurds had been excised.[16] We may speculate on what changed his mind. First, it was only after the Armistice in October when Turkey's external enemies were finally defeated that he had been free to consider state-building and its necessary ideological foundations. It is possible that only now had he had time to read Gokalp's writings. To someone bent upon rebuilding the country on European lines, the social and political traditions of Kurdistan presented a profound obstacle. Only now was he free to give the implications of this obstacle real thought. Secondly, the 1922 disruptions in Kurdistan and the estrangement of Kurdish chiefs who had co-operated in 1921 must have caused a major re-assessment in Ankara. The very fact that Kemal was asked about the Kurdish *problem* on his visit to Izmit, indicates the change in perception that had taken place. In the summer of 1922 the minister for the interior had spoken of bringing the Kurds to a higher level of civilization through the building of schools, roads and (more ominously) gendarmerie posts and military service. This theme was to be elaborated later. Implicit now but explicit within only a few months was the idea of turning Kurds into good Turks.

Finally, negotiations at Lausanne had produced a major stumbling block: the vilayet of Mosul. Turkey found Britain's apparent willingness to offer the Kurds of southern Kurdistan a measure of local autonomy threatening, because it would excite secessionist tendencies north of the border. Inonu may have been alarmed by Curzon's attempt to persuade Turkey to recognize the Kurds among its minorities. Turkey had not fought off Sèvres to concede an undertaking now to grant the Kurds special status imposed by international treaty. If events in southern Kurdistan could not be prevented, then it might be possible, or even necessary, to extinguish Kurdish identity inside Turkey's borders.

The Kurds under Mustafa Kemal

The chill breeze from Ankara was soon felt. During the elections for the new Grand National Assembly in summer 1923, deputies were denied the chance to return to their constituencies. The new candidates fielded and returned for Kurdish areas had, in the Kurdish view, been nominated by the government rather than elected by the people. Kurdish dissent, therefore, was exiled from the *soi-disant* democratic forum of the new republic. As the months passed, other straws indicated which way the wind was blowing. For example, all the senior administrative appointments, and half the more junior ones in Kurdistan were soon filled by Turks. Kurds still officiating as *qaim-maqams* only hung on if cleared of all nationalist taint. All reference to Kurdistan was excised from official materials, and Turkish place names began to replace Kurdish ones. Meanwhile, at the common level Kurds serving in the army complained of ill-treatment and abuse, and of being picked upon for unpleasant duties.

In March 1924 these measures reached a climax. The insistence on the sole use of Turkish in the law courts, and the prohibition of Kurdish officially, including its use in schools, indicated a radical change in Kemalist thinking, for the draft autonomy law two years before had allowed for 'encouragement of the Kurdish language'. Turkey had banished Kurdish to the periphery, abandoning its undertaking (Article 39) at Lausanne a year earlier. It was now clearly embarked upon a racist policy which proposed to expunge all non-Turkish expression. The language decision effectively excluded Kurdistan from the benefit of education. By 1925 only 215 of the 4875 schools in Turkey were located in Kurdistan, providing education for 8,400 pupils out of Turkey's total of 382,000 enrolled. Without Kurdish-medium schools the number of Kurds who could benefit was strictly limited. The levy of an education tax in Kurdistan in such circumstances predictably caused great resentment, as did the progressive colonization by discharged Turkish soldiers of Armenian and Kurdish lands made empty by death or deportation during the war years.

On 4 March Mustafa Kemal abolished the caliphate. This was the real body blow. He deterred opposition by establishing 'Tribunals of Independence' with full powers of life and death and extending the Law of Treason to include all discussion of the caliphate or any appeal to religion in political life. This cut the last ideological tie Kurds felt with Turks. The closure of the religious schools, the *madrasas* and *kuttabs*, removed the last remaining source of education for most Kurds. By stripping Turkey of its religious institutions, Mustafa Kemal now made enemies of the very Kurds who had helped Turkey survive the years of trial, 1919–22. These were the religiously-minded, the shaykhs and the old Hamidiya aghas who had genuinely believed in the defence of the caliphate.

Azadi

It was among such people, who on the whole had repudiated any previous connection with them, that the Kurdish nationalists now built their resistance. Indeed, the nationalist removal from Istanbul to Dersim in 1921, and the subsequent establishment of a new organization, Azadi (Freedom) marked the real arrival of Kurdish nationalism in Turkish Kurdistan. Until then nationalist sentiment had been confined to the educated notable class in Istanbul, to the larger towns of Kurdistan and a handful of aghas. Now the new movement, probably formally established in Erzerum in 1923, spread like wildfire through the oratories, or *takiyas*, of the Sufi orders, from the encampment of one ex-Hamidiya agha to another, and finally through the commissioned and other ranks of Kurdish battalions in the army.

The leadership of Azadi reveals this broadening and essentially provincial dimension: Yusuf Zia Beg, scion of the old princely house of Bitlis and one of the Kurdish deputies who lost his seat in the Grand National Assembly in 1923; Khalid Beg Jibran, probably a founding member, who in his time had commanded the two Hamidiya regiments raised from among his tribesmen; his kinsman by marriage, Shaykh Said of Palu, whose reputation as a leading Naqshbandi shaykh made his *takiya* a place of pilgrimage for the devout; finally, Captain Ihsan Nuri and Yusuf Zia's brother Riza, fellow officers in the Seventh Army Corps quartered at Diyarbakir where, no doubt, they were entertained and encouraged by the local branch head, Akram Beg Jamilzada.

A meeting of Azadi's leadership in 1924 resolved upon preparing for a rising in May 1925 to establish an independent Kurdistan. When precisely this meeting took place is unclear, but by May 1924 groups in Erzerum and Van were reportedly receiving subsidies from the Bolsheviks. But, as had been seen in the past and was to be repeated more painfully in the future, the difficulties of communication, co-ordination, secrecy and command proved too great for Azadi's organizational abilities.

In August certain battalions of 18 Regiment of the Seventh Army Corps were moved to Bayt al Shabab in Hakkari, to deal with the troublesome Assyrians in the border area. It may also have been believed that Turkey intended invading the vilayet of Mosul. At the end of August, company commanders Ihsan Nuri and Riza received a cypher telegram from Yusuf Zia in Istanbul where he had found considerable dismay at the abolition of the caliphate and at Mustafa Kemal's increasingly dictatorial methods. Believing the telegram indicated the readiness of Azadi and also possibly Turkish dissidents to rise against Mustafa Kemal, Ihsan Nuri and Riza planned a mutiny on the night of 3/4 September in Bayt al Shabab. However, they were unable to raise any local tribes, and the 500 officers and men who mutinied fled to Iraq.

Thus Azadi's first attempt ended in fiasco. It revealed an absence of the discipline, co-ordination and secrecy necessary for success. At Bayt al Shabab the garrison commander got wind of the mutiny and began to arrest suspects before it took place. In fact the authorities in Ankara were keenly aware of Kurdish discontent. With the forthcoming League of Nations arbitration in Mosul in mind, they had arranged a meeting in Diyarbakir with Kurdish leaders on 1 August in order to defuse Kurdish resentment. They had promised to consider a special regime where Kurds formed a majority, the provision of finance for the recovery of the region, suspension of conscription for five years, restoration of *sharia* courts, the removal of unpopular Turkish commanders and an amnesty of Kurds in prison. In return the Kurds were to support Turkey's claim to Mosul. The Ankara government was well aware of the depth of Kurdish resentment. It knew about the committees, for it had already offered Turkish officers 'to train them'. It therefore must have realized the danger of an uprising.

It did not take long for Ankara to discover some of Azadi's ringleaders. By the end of the year waves of arrests had taken place, including Yusuf Zia Bey and two Hamidiya chiefs, Khalid Beg Jibran and Hajji Musa Beg Mutki of Bitlis. Another official meeting with Kurdish nationalists took place in Diyarbakir on 4 November, but it seems to have achieved nothing. Three weeks later the town governor was assassinated.

The Shaykh Said Revolt [17]

The round-up of suspects was a major setback, for it seems that virtually all officers sympathetic to Azadi were purged. Despite this and the many desertions from Azadi that followed, some surviving members still hoped for a widespread rising in spring 1925. Now Azadi was stripped down to those who acted out of conviction, among whom the religiously motivated were bound to predominate. Many shaykhs and their followers were quite willing to risk martyrdom in order to restore the *khilafa*.

Pre-eminent among these was Shaykh Said of Palu. Towards the end of 1924 he left his abode at Khinis partly to avoid arrest but also to tour the Zaza-speaking heartlands of his support: Palu–Lijja–Hani–Chabaqchur area. As their spiritual leader he had little difficulty in rallying his *murids*. It proved harder to persuade the tribes beyond the Zaza-speaking areas either to set aside long-standing quarrels, or to commit themselves unequivocally to an uprising. In particular he failed to attract the Alevi Khurmak and Lawlan to the cause. There were two simple reasons for their refusal. First, a Naqshbandi shaykh had no standing for them and, if anything, Shaykh Said's religious identity was likely to have negative rather than positive impact on Alevis. Secondly, the Jibran seemed resolved to support Shaykh Said. The Khurmak had neither forgotten nor forgiven Jibran oppression in the pre-war years. The last thing they wanted was a victorious Jibran tribe lording it over them again.

It was intended to rise in the second half of March. Tribes led by their own chiefs would seize control of their own areas, driving out or arresting Turkish officials. They would then join one of five fronts planned to expand the extent of the rising. Almost all the senior commanders were to be shaykhs.

Once again, however, things went awry. On 8 February a clash occurred at Piran between Shaykh Said's retainers and Turkish gendarmes seeking the surrender of a group of outlaws who had sought the shaykh's protection. This may have been a Turkish ploy to flush out the conspirators, for Ankara claimed it knew Kurdish intentions and was expecting a rising at the end of March.

Despite Shaykh Said's efforts to hold back, disorders spread quickly and he was compelled to raise the flag of revolt. Lijja and Hani fell within the week, and Chabaqchur soon after. Troops sent to confront the rebels either defected or fled. In order to rally support, Shaykh Said issued a manifesto in favour of a Kurdish government and the restoration of the caliphate, and this was followed by the proclamation of one of the late Sultan Abd al Hamid's sons as King of Kurdistan.

The insurgents, by now several thousand strong, marched southwards towards Diyarbakir, which was invested by up to 5,000 rebels at the end of the month. On the night of 7–8 March a small party penetrated the Zaza quarter via recently dug drainage ditches but were driven out again. Shaykh Said appealed to the Milli paramount, Mahmud bin Ibrahim, in the belief that he was an Azadi member, to help take Diyarbakir, but no reply came.

While Diyarbakir absorbed and withstood the main thrust of the revolt, advances were made elsewhere. Madin and Arghani fell in the first week of March. In the north-east the Hasanan and Jibran took Malazgirt and Bulanik respectively but ran into fierce opposition from the Khurmak and Lawlan. On 11 March Varto fell to the Jibran. Many of the gendarmes there, Kurdish and some Naqshbandi, went over to the rebels. But after five days it was abandoned on account of Turkish and Alevi forces in the area. Indeed, it was largely the Khurmak and Lawlan who inhibited the planned advances on Erzerum and Erzinjan.

Meanwhile, rebel parties advancing across the plain of Mush towards Bitlis, found local tribes unwilling to support them. To the west, an advance was made to Elazig which was captured and sacked on 24 March. For several days a rabble looted the town without restraint, while the main body of rebels moved on. Finally the Kurdish citizens of Elazig themselves ejected their unwelcome guests. By the end of March rebel impetus had petered out.

Ankara took its time responding to revolt. It was only after a fortnight, as rumours reached the street, that the government finally admitted it had serious trouble in the south-east, and proclaimed martial law in virtually all of Turkish Kurdistan. Government forces in the area were inadequate to deal with the disorder, partly because they were insufficient in number but also because some of the troops, particularly in the Seventh and Eighth Army Corps, headquartered at Diyarbakir and Erzerum respectively, were not wholly trustworthy. The former had many Kurds in its ranks, and the latter had until recently been commanded by Kemal's leading political opponent, Kazim Karabekir. In late February eight infantry divisions, approximately 35,000 men, were mobilized. On 1 March France consented to the use of the railway running through its territory to move some of these forces to the scene of revolt, and by the end of April Turkish forces in the region numbered about 52,000, or just under half the army's new peace-time strength.

On 4 March the newly appointed prime minister, Ismet Inonu, announced draconian measures. Two 'Tribunals of Independence' were to be established, one in the east and the other in Ankara. The eastern tribunal was empowered to apply capital punishment without reference to Ankara. This was justified under a Law for the Restoration of Order:

> The Government is directly authorized, with the approval of the President, to stifle all reaction and rebellion, as also all instigation or encouragement thereof, or the publication of anything susceptible of troubling the order, tranquillity or social harmony of the country. The authors of such movements will be brought before the Tribunals of Independence.[18]

The British ambassador found it 'difficult to imagine how the net for repression could have been thrown out more widely, for it gives the Government a free hand to do what it will'.[19] This law lasted for two years

On the ground massive troop concentrations quickly brought the revolt to a halt and then retreat. By 26 March rebel groups were encircled. Villages in the affected area were warned of military severity unless the inhabitants declared before the nearest civil or military authority that they had no sympathy with the revolt and offered proof by surrendering any rebel leaders in their midst. As the ring closed, some rebel bands managed to escape, but large numbers were killed or taken prisoner in the fights that ensued. The last stand was made between Ganj and Palu. Shaykh Said and his entourage slipped through the ring, but were caught crossing the Murad river north of Mush on about 14 April, apparently betrayed by a Jibran chief.

Suppressing Kurdistan

Reprisals in the area were brutal. By mid-April 30 rebel leaders had been executed. Multiple executions took place as the Independence Tribunal moved from one town to another. On 4 September Shaykh Said himself and 46 others were hanged in Diyarbakir. Before their abrogation, the Independence Tribunals arrested 7,500 suspects of whom they executed 660.

A meeting in Diyarbakir in June decided on the extirpation of 'the remnants of feudalism'.[20] Consequently, other shaykhs, aghas and their families not directly implicated in the revolt were now deported to western Anatolia. The army acted ruthlessly as it moved across the countryside. 'Whole villages were burnt or razed to the ground, and men, women and children killed.'[21] Around Diyarbakir, for example, Zazas were rounded up and massacred. Thousands of sheep were seized and auctioned, for example no less than 30,000 in Lijja and Diyarbakir, effectively removing the food resources of the tribal population.

The revolt also gave an excuse to take secularization all the way, by closing down remaining institutions. Every *takiya* was proscribed. Even the pro-government Alevis found their religious institutions suppressed. As Mustafa Kemal asked, 'Could a civilised nation [*sic*] tolerate a mass of people who let themselves be led by the nose by a herd of shaykhs, dedes, sayyids, chelebis, babas and amirs?'[22] It was believed that with their closure the *tariqas* would wither away.

Ankara used the rebellion as a pretext for dealing with many of its enemies. Yusuf Zia Beg and Khalid Beg Jibran, already in prison, were executed in April. In Diyarbakir and other Kurdish towns known nationalists were arrested and some subsequently executed. In Istanbul Shaykh Abd al Qadir was framed and charged with dealing with the British. Many others were rounded up, for example Khoja Salih Effendi, the former deputy for Erzerum who had spoken up for the Kurds in the Assembly in 1922.

The net was thrown yet wider. In early April Kazim Karabekir and a colleague, both vociferous critics of Mustafa Kemal's autocracy, were denounced by two *khojas*, as supporting the insurgents in their attempt to restore the caliphate. Despite the absurdity of the accusation, it served notice of the government's

intention to crush him and his associates. Karabekir was accused of writing to
Khalid Beg Jibran two years earlier complaining 'They [the Kemalists] are attacking
the very principles which perpetuate the existence of the Muhammadan world',
while his Progressive Republican Party was accused of sending delegates to stir
up religious fervour in the Eastern vilayets. That the Progressives roundly condemned the revolt did not protect them. In the second week of April the party
headquarters suffered a night raid by the police and all its papers were confiscated. The party was suppressed. Likewise the government began to harry journalists who wrote unwelcome commentaries on political events.

Thus ended Shaykh Said's revolt. On the Kurdish side it demonstrated yet
again the difficulty of uniting the different geographical, linguistic, socio-economic
and religious elements among the Kurds. Only the Zaza Sunni tribes rose *en
masse*. Of all the Kurmanji-speaking majority, only the Jibran and the Hasanan
rose, and possibly only sections of them. The non-tribal peasantry around
Diyarbakir did not lift a finger and were almost certainly not invited to do so,
peasants being considered unfit for combat. Inside Diyarbakir, Zaza tribals who
had migrated to town helped the rebels penetrate the walls but did not themselves fight. As for the town's nationalist notables like the Jamilzadas, they sat on
their hands either frightened or disdainful of these rustic rebels.

The religious dimension deserves notice, for it is in exactly the same part of
modern Turkey that the Naqshbandi order still exerts its greatest influence. Shaykh
Said's fatwa had announced that the *'jihad* is an obligation for all Muslims without
distinction of confession or *tariqa*',[23] but it failed to stir other *tariqa* networks, let
alone the Alevis. Had Azadi been able to recruit leading Kurmanji-speaking
shaykhs like those of Khizan near Bitlis and Nursin near Mush, the revolt might
have spread throughout their constituencies, making it substantially more threatening to Ankara. Had Azadi attracted Alevis, then the Khurmak and Lawlan might
not have inhibited the spread of the revolt to the north-east.

Yet even had the revolt been widespread, it is unlikely that it could have
succeeded. Ankara only had to bide its time while marshalling its forces. Disorder
might be temporarily inevitable, but there was little prospect of the insurgents
wresting sovereignty. For Ankara had three supreme assets: a battle-experienced
standing army, the resources necessary to revictual large concentrations of troops
and, finally, the ability, through its communications network, to concentrate its
forces more rapidly than the rebels could ever do at any place it chose. It was
therefore only a question of time before the revolt would be suppressed, a point
painfully borne out in later uprisings.

What did the insurgents want? In simple terms it is clear they wished to be
free of Ankara's rule and once more subject to the caliphate. These were sound
Naqshbandi objectives. Yet the announcement of a non-Kurd as king of Kurdistan
raises an interesting question concerning the nature of Shaykh Said's nationalism.
His willingness to nominate a caliphal rather than Kurdish candidate to his proposed throne of Kurdistan suggests his idea of 'Kurdishness' was based less on

ethnicity *per se* than on Kurdish *religious* particularism. At its most obvious, this was expressed in Kurdish devotion to the Shafi law school, which, unlike the Hanafi school, made a distinction between devotion to the person of the caliph and acknowledgement of the pre-eminence of the state. This, of course, had been exploited by Sultan Abd al Hamid thirty years earlier in his efforts to thwart the reforms of his own administration. Had the caliphate not been important, Shaykh Said might well have chosen Shaykh Abd al Qadir or one of the Badr Khans as ruler-in-waiting. But devotion to the caliphate pointed up the difference between Kurdish 'folk Islam', rooted in the *tariqa* networks, compared with mainstream institutionalized Islam. It was the last time the caliphate was invoked to rally the Kurds, but by no means the end of Kurdish religious particularism.

Shaykh Said's revolt marked the beginning of 'implacable Kemalism'. Systematic deportation and razing of villages, brutality and killing of innocents, martial law or special regimes in Kurdistan now became the commonplace experience of Kurds whenever they defied the state. The army, deployed in strength for the first time since Lausanne, now found control of Kurdistan to be its prime function and *raison d'être*. Only one out of 18 Turkish military engagements during the years 1924–38 occurred outside Kurdistan. After 1945, apart from the Korean war, 1949–52 and the invasion of Cyprus, 1974, the only Turkish army operations continued to be against the Kurds.

The revolt also marked the beginning of an authoritarian one-party state which persisted until partial political liberalization in 1946. Journalists discovered they worked on sufferance, liable to censure or arrest. After 1925, it proved impossible to function effectively without infringing the array of restrictive regulations concerning what might or might not be discussed in the public domain. Later it was the turn of associations, trade unions and other movements concerned with citizens' rights. Thus, Shaykh Said's revolt was a catalyst for more than Kurdish nationalism or religious obscurantism. It became a symbol of state inflexibility not yet abandoned.

Kurdish resistance outlived the suppression of Shaykh Said's followers, and was partly a response to the policy of repression. The rest of the year – and much of 1926 – was characterized by such disorder in the eastern provinces that the French in Syria believed the situation had become more rather than less critical for Ankara by late summer 1925.

Not only did resistance continue among tribes in the affected area, but elsewhere one tribe after another took up arms rather than undergo the humiliations inflicted by the security forces. In April the Goyan had asked the League of Nations Commission if they could be included in the British sphere. By June they found themselves fighting the Turks and the following month both they and the neighbouring Shirnakh tribes were seeking refuge in Iraq. Insurgents around Midyat and Mardin fled to Syria. In August Shaykh Abd al Qadir's son, Abd Allah, was ambushing Turkish forces around Shamdinan, before finally seeking asylum for his and his supporters' families in Iraq.

In Tabriz, Ali Riza, Shaykh Said's son, begged the British consul for consent to visit to London to canvass support for an independent Kurdish state. When the latter waxed sympathetic, his ambassador sharply reminded him: 'You are no doubt aware that it forms no part of the policy of His Majesty's Government to encourage or accept any responsibility for the formation of any autonomous or independent Kurdish state.'[24] Barely five years had elapsed since Sèvres. In November no fewer than 500 families, at least 5,000 men, women and children, were seeking asylum around Salmas in west Azarbaijan. In January another 5,000 Goyan and Artushi sought asylum in Iraq.

In the spring of 1926 the troubles started again. In the vilayet of Van, which had escaped involvement in the revolt, Turkish troops re-establishing government authority committed, so it was rumoured, widespread massacres. Dersim was up in arms and remained defiant, despite exemplary executions. Without doubt much of the reluctance concerned the deportations. As the British consul in Trabzon noted, 'Travellers report having seen great numbers of Kurds with their families and cattle being driven along the Erzerum–Erzinjan road presumably bound for Angora and Western Anatolia. Whole villages are deserted, and trade is at a standstill over a large area.'[25] At Batman a whole regiment was routed by local Kurds, with the loss of well over 100 men. At the same time the Havarki around Nusaybin rose under their illustrious leader Haju, before fleeing across the Syrian border. By June 1926 the Jalali and Haydaranli Kurds of Bayazid were also up in arms, deeply resentful of a deportation policy inflicted even though they had not rebelled. In December 1927 part of Bitlis town rose briefly in revolt. In response to continued Kurdish recalcitrance, Ankara introduced a new law in June 1927 whereby, as Sir George Clerk the British ambassador reported, the government was empowered

> to transport from the Eastern Vilayets an indefinite number of Kurds or other elements ... the Government has already begun to apply to the Kurdish elements ... the policy which so successfully disposed of the Armenian Minority in 1915. It is a curious trick of fate that the Kurds, who were the principal agent employed for the deportation of Armenians, should be in danger of suffering the same fate as the Armenians only twelve years later.[26]

Technically there was a right of appeal on transfer against the liquidation of property. In practice it was worthless because victims never had enough notice of deportation. Furthermore, as Clerk reported, 'No indication is given of the districts to which they are to be sent, and in the case of the poorer ones [deportees] at all events, it may be excusable to wonder how many will reach their allotted destinations.'[27] With the region shut off and complete press silence, it was difficult to be sure how many were being moved, but in August Clerk reckoned the figure to be not less than 20,000, 'on a scale,' he said, 'which to some extent recalls the mass deportations of Armenians in 1915.'[28] The agha and shaykhly class was singled out. According to The Times at least 150 such notable families, which implies perhaps five or six thousand men, women and children, were deported to western Anatolia. 'Many died on the way and some of the better-looking women are said to have disappeared.'[29] No wonder observers thought of the Armenians.

In fact, the events of 1925–26 had produced an almost genocidal state of mind in Ankara. In May 1925 the journal *Vakit* had announced 'There is no Kurdish problem where a Turkish bayonet appears.'[30] In October Sir Ronald Lindsay, Britain's new ambassador, had already noted how Turkey 'would welcome with open arms any and every Turkish speaking peasant in the world. Aliens are not wanted; but Kurds are a necessary evil.'[31] But did that imply acceptance of a Kurdish presence? It was not long before Turkey's foreign minister, Tawfiq Rushdi [Saracoglu], expressed the frank views circulating in the cabinet:

> in their [Kurdish] case, their cultural level is so low, their mentality so backward, that they cannot be simply in the general Turkish body politic ... they will die out, economically unfitted for the struggle for life in competition with the more advanced and cultured Turks ... as many as can will emigrate into Persia and Iraq, while the rest will simply undergo the elimination of the unfit.[32]

Unrest continued throughout 1927, particularly in Diyarbakir, Mush, Khinis, Bitlis and Bulanik. Towards the end of that year there was an expectation of repression involving 'Kurds being hanged wholesale, massacred, and practically crushed beyond recovery'.[33] Such forebodings were borne out by leaks of information from the east, of razed villages and killings.

Some such reports may have been exaggerated. Two important Kurdish propaganda documents were published in 1928 and 1930. These claimed that, in the winter of 1926–27, 200 villages with a population of 13,000 were razed, while in the whole period 1925–28 almost 10,000 dwellings had been razed, over 15,000 people massacred, and more than half a million deported of whom some 200,000 were estimated to have perished.[34] It was easy, perhaps, for British diplomats to dismiss such material as 'clumsy propaganda', full of 'grossly exaggerated details'.[35] It was far harder to dismiss Turkish officers who 'recounted how they were repelled by such proceedings and yet felt obliged to do their duty'.[36] In December 1927 the British Embassy reported

> A gendarmerie major on short leave from Diarbekir told a friend that he was disgusted with the work he had had to do and that he wanted to be transferred. He had been in the eastern provinces all through the period of tranquillisation [*sic*] and was tired of slaughtering men, women and children.[37]

Yet now there seems to have been a spell of relative moderation in Turkish policy, inspired perhaps by momentary concern for the young republic's international reputation. The large number of refugees in Iraq, Syria and Iran bearing tales of atrocities hardly helped the republic's external relations. At the beginning of 1928 Ankara appointed one Ibrahim Tali as governor-general of the eastern provinces. Tali sought to repair the damage of the previous years. Regeneration could only take place with the active engagement of local people. No sooner was he in the saddle than he arranged for a partial amnesty. In April many commoners deported to the west were allowed to return to the east, although those aghas and shaykhs who had not already been killed were excluded. In May the Grand National Assembly introduced a Law of Amnesty including rebel leaders and covering virtually all of Turkish-controlled Kurdistan. Among those who returned were two of Shaykh Said's brothers, and two of his sons.

Ibrahim Tali also attempted to create an infrastructure for growth. While it proved difficult to recruit the doctors, teachers and other officials necessary to develop the region, he did manage to initiate a road-building programme, and proposed the redistribution of the large estates of Kurdish magnates. A law in June 1929 allowed for the break-up of big agha estates to the peasantry, but progress on implementing the law was very patchy. Some peasants were trained in the use of the steel plough.

However, there were darker aspects to the reconstruction programme. Kurds were excluded from even modest positions of economic or political authority. Take, for example, staff changes in the Ottoman Bank: all non-Turkish staff were removed from the one or two branches in the eastern provinces. Steps were taken to ensure strategic control, for Tali's extensive road-building programme had an essentially military rather than economic purpose. Furthermore, Tali's clemency did not extend to Kurds incarcerated in Diyarbakir prison, some of whom were summarily shot.

A serious effort was made to erase Kurdish identity through the Turkish Hearth Organization. The *ocaks*, or 'hearths', were first established in 1912, committed to the defeat of Islamist and Ottomanist ideas and the proposition of Turkish nationalism, objectives developed by Diyarbakir's most famous son, Zia Gokalp. They had been condemned by the men of religion, suspected by the CUP, and feared by the Palace because ethnic nationalism might incite non-Turkish elements to rebel.

With the triumph of the Kemalists, these *ocaks* had been revived in 1924 as a vehicle for the spread of Turkish nationalism in the provinces. Special cadres were now sent to Kurdistan to persuade the population to be good Turks. They found an enthusiastic response from the garrisons and officials of the area, who flocked to the tea dances, mixed tennis parties and the other necessary appurtances of modernity.

Yet even among the native Kurdish population, Turkish language classes soon began to have an impact. Education meant 'turkification'. Every young urban Kurd knew his future depended on functional competence in the language of his masters. In Diyarbakir, for example, the library and reading room were heavily used. The town boasted the only primary-level teacher-training institute east of the Euphrates, the other nineteen such institutes being located outside

Kurdish areas. In the meantime, young Kurdish conscripts were automatically posted to western Anatolia where they could be turned into dutiful Turks.

In parts of Kurdistan the success of 'turkification' was already apparent by 1930. In both Gaziantep (Ayntab) and Urfa, for example, where Kurds were, in any case, barely 50 per cent of the population they, like the substantial Arab minority, were quite ready to pass as Turks. But no uniform pattern existed. Local experience affected popular responses. In Marash, for example, noted then as now for its strong religious sentiments, the Sunni population sulked, held down by a strong garrison. Alevis, by contrast, welcomed Kemalist secularism for they no longer felt oppressed by Sunni clerics.

At last there were the faintest signs of recovery from the rigours of war with Russia, the destruction of the Christian population, the loss of trade with Iraq and Syria and the suppression of Kurdish rebellion. Yet Kurdistan had no prospect of developing an economy in parallel with the rest of Turkey. Trade was still a shadow of what it had been in 1914. In 1930 the countryside was still littered with ruined Christian villages. In Bitlis the famous gorge was lined for a mile with gutted Christian homes, and its pre-war population of 40,000 reduced to 5,000. In Mush, the population was still one tenth of its pre-war level of 30,000 souls.

While the destruction of the Christian communities may have seemed necessary for Turkish survival from 1915 onwards, it also wiped out the greater part of Turkey's wealth-creating middle class and set back economic recovery by at least half a century. The loss left Kurdistan permanently impoverished. No one ever really replaced this entrepreneurial class. As a result of the disorders, the balance of personnel in Kurdish towns in 1927 reflected the disastrous imbalance between the productive and non-productive sectors: 46,925 soldiers (discounting those troops mobilized to deal with specific risings) and 1,254 magistrates as against 29,241 artisans and workers, 29,677 merchants and 23,591 others in a variety of professions.[38] The roads fell again into a hopeless state of disrepair but if it were any comfort, compared with the rest of Turkey there were virtually no motorized vehicles to use them.[39]

The almost universal absence of banks meant that loans were virtually impossible and those Kurds with any resources to invest were likely to migrate westwards. Besides, any commodities that were not locally produced might cost up to ten times as much in Kurdistan as in the west, on account of transit costs. The question of Kurdistan, therefore, was destined to remain economic as well as political.

Kurdish Resistance: Khoybun, Agri Dagh and Dersim

With the ruthless suppression of Kurdistan, 1925–27, followed by the mix of relative clemency and 'turkification', it seemed that Kurdish dissidence was at an end. But beyond Turkey's borders in Paris, Cairo, Tabriz, Aleppo, Beirut and

Damascus, many of the old Istanbul nationalists who had fled the city on the approach of Kemalist troops in 1922, continued to believe in a Kurdish national movement. Virtually none of them had played any part either in Azadi or in the 1925 rising. They had watched while Britain, in which so many had placed so much hope, did nothing, while Turkey stamped out one insurrection after another. They found it difficult to understand, since Britain had, judging by its previous statements, so much to gain from denying eastern Anatolia to the Turks.

Some of these exiles met in Bhamdoun, Lebanon, in October 1927 to form a new party 'Khoybun' (Independence). They hoped to avoid the mistakes of the past, particularly the schisms that had dogged their efforts. They therefore formally subsumed the old parties within the identity of Khoybun, under the presidence of Jaladat Badr Khan. They also believed that after the disasters of 1924 and 1925, they could only hope to succeed with a military enterprise if it were properly conceived, planned and organized. This implied a move away from risings led by tribal leaders, and the constitution of a trained, non-tribal fighting force. They decided to establish a permanent headquarters in Aleppo to put together a viable liberation movement. This movement would send a revolutionary army to establish itself in the mountains of northern Kurdistan, proclaim a government and unify the local tribes under its leadership. Ihsan Nuri, who had taken a leading part in the abortive Bayt al Shabab (Beytussebap) mutiny was chosen as operational commander.

All this required funding, and Khoybun sought it by appealing to expatriates and to those who might favour such an enterprise, like the Caliphal Monarchist Party with which presumably most tribesmen would have felt comfortable. Despairing of Britain and France which it had approached at the outset, the party now sought friends elsewhere. While distrusting the Bolsheviks, Khoybun's leaders were happy to accept funds from the International Minority Movement, headquartered in Odessa. They were also happy to forge an alliance with the Armenian Dashnak Party, which promised to provide practical assistance to a venture in eastern Anatolia. Indeed, a leading Dashnak had been instrumental in the establishment of Khoybun, travelling through the region in the summer of 1927 to urge the Kurds to act together against Turkey, and to obtain Greek and Italian help. Khoybun sought Italian and American experts (presumably mercenaries) to assist with military training.

Some Kurds, especially those who feared their position in Syria might be compromised, watched Khoybun with disdain or hostility. Assurances were given to Britain and France that Khoybun would encourage Kurds living within the borders of Iraq and Syria to obey the law. Even so, France prohibited Khoybun's activities in Aleppo in the summer of 1928, following strong protests from Ankara.

However, this did not prevent Ihsan Nuri from raising the flag of revolt in the chosen region for the revolution, Ararat (Agri Dagh) the same year. Ararat had been chosen because the local tribes were already in revolt there, because of its proximity to the international border which ran across Ararat's north-eastern foothills and because its rocky slopes afforded substantial shelter against military action and against the elements. Nuri assembled a small group of men trained with modern weapons and versed in modern infantry tactics, and moved them to Ararat to join up with the various tribes already there. He worked in partnership with the Jalali chief, Ibrahim 'Bro' Haski Talu. Talu was already highly experienced in the tactical use of Ararat, since he had resisted all Russian attempts to capture it during the war. Indeed Jalali men, women and children were able to subsist with their flocks during this period, and were even re-victualled by the Russians in return for undertaking not to attack the Russian lines of communication.

Talu's career illustrated the alienation of many aghas who had so far been loyal to the Kemalist regime. In 1925 he had assisted the government to crush Shaykh Said's revolt by closing the frontiers, but this did not protect him from the wholesale deportation policy directed at the agha class. Warned of his intended fate, he fled to Ararat in the winter of 1925, where several other chiefs had joined him by the summer of 1927.

By the time Nuri reached Ararat in 1928, Turkish forces were already grappling with Talu's men. In September 1927 the Turks suffered a sharp reverse on the Zilan plain and lost substantial material. In December they were repulsed again. In January Kurdish forces seized the Mutki–Bitlis road. In March another major battle took place near Bayazid. These developments attracted more support for the rebels, in spite of a general amnesty in May 1928.

Then the authorities tried conciliation in an effort to persuade the insurgents to lay down their arms, offering a cessation to all deportations in addition to the amnesty. But they failed to convince the Kurdish leaders of their sincerity, partly because they were unwilling to concede the use of Kurdish as a sop to nationalist sentiment. Nuri demanded Turkish evacuation of Kurdistan, so there was no prospect of a settlement.

Meanwhile Khoybun sought to develop two fronts, the massif of Ararat where their main forces were concentrated, and among the heterogeneous mass of Kurdish and Armenian refugees in north-eastern Syria. In September another battle took place, in which the Wali of Bayazid was captured and executed.

Although some tribes supported the government forces, the nationalists were heartened by attacks on Turkish troops in different parts of Kurdistan, for example in Sasun, Botan (Buhtan) and Bitlis in late 1927, and that of Haju Agha of the Havirki on the Syrian border in 1928.[40] In February 1929 Kurdish forces, estimated at up to 5,000 strong, destroyed a Turkish battalion. On the north side of Ararat some Alevi tribes joined the revolt. To the south Kur Husayn Pasha, who had assisted in the suppression of Shaykh Said's revolt, crossed the Syrian border to rally the powerful Haydaranli. Although he was ambushed and killed by pro-government Mutki tribesmen near Sasun, his sons brought the tribe to the nationalist cause. Government forces were busy enough dealing with minor outbreaks elsewhere.

By the autumn of 1929 the Kurdish forces dominated an area from Ararat as far south as Khushab, south of Van. Turkish forces were frustrated by the fact that the north and eastern slopes of Ararat abutted the international border, making it impossible for Turkish troops to surround and isolate the rebels. It was common knowledge that the insurgents were being resupplied by Jalali kinsmen in Iran.

The authorities bided their time until spring 1930 when they began to concentrate their forces around Ararat. While the 5,000 or so rebels wished to absorb the area lying between their two principal areas of control, Ararat and land just north of Arjish (on the northern shore of Lake Van), Turkish forces were deployed in two groups, one to drive eastwards from Erzerum, the other from the north-west side of Lake Van towards Arjish and Bayazid.

Both protagonists enjoyed external assistance. The Kurds were resupplied by Kurds and Armenians from Iran, while Turkish forces were helped by a Soviet promise to seal the Araxes border and allow the use of Soviet rail facilities. On 12 June a major battle took place involving 15,000 troops, artillery and several aircraft, with heavy casualties on both sides. The Turkish effort was frustrated by the international border on the east side of Ararat. A month later another costly but indecisive action took place. In early July Turkey warned Tehran that it would assume 'liberty of action' if Iran did not prevent the rebels using Iranian territory. There was now a real danger of conflict between Turkish and Iranian forces.

In early July the Kurdish forces launched a major counter-offensive, with tribesmen crossing from Iran in order to cut off Turkish forces around Ararat before marching on Diyarbakir. It was hoped villagers would rally *en route*. Rosita Forbes, the English writer, crossed the border into Ararat district at this very moment and reported 'The Kurds, whose women seemed all to carry babies on their backs and rifles in their hands, appeared to regard the fighting more as an amusement than anything else.'[41] But the mood cannot have lasted long, for they were driven back after a series of sharp encounters on the Zilan Plain. Of the few villagers who answered the call to arms, most were motivated by religious rather than nationalist propaganda.[42]

Turkish forces pursued the Kurds into Iran, forcing the authorities in Tabriz to instruct all Kurdish insurgents (both Turkish and Iranian), either to return immediately to Turkey to fight or to lay down their arms. By the end of August 3,000 Kurds were surrounded on Ararat, dispersed in about 60 small camps. The Turks, by now over 50,000 strong, had two objectives: to clear Ararat and to drive the insurgents into Iran. They were able to take their time in the knowledge that winter would drive the Kurds off the mountain. In September they captured the saddle between Lesser and Greater Ararat, killing many and driving the remainder south-eastwards

Turkish forces now began to take their revenge for the reported mutilation and killing of those captured by the Kurds. Instructions had been issued long before the offensive began to exterminate Kurds who fell into their hands. The authorities had already made widespread arrests of suspected sympathizers in Erzerum and elsewhere, many of whom were hanged. Now Turkish forces shot the 1,500 Kurds they captured. By the end of August they had destroyed over 3,000 non-combatants, men, women and children, during their *nettoyage* operations around Arjish and the Zilan plain, razing villages wherever they went. Then they moved on to other local outbreaks, Julamark (Hakkari), Siirt, Lijja, Diyarbakir, almost to the Iraqi border, to which over 1,500 families had fled by the end of January.

A law (No. 1850) was passed in order to ensure that no one engaged in suppressing the Kurds could be prosecuted for any excess. By the beginning of 1932 the vilayet of Van, the scene of the greatest unrest, had been completely subdued. Now it was divided into four zones, each under the watchful eye of a co-opted local chief authorized to arm his own tribe in order to keep order. Yet, even by the end of 1932 the government had still not finished with either executions or deportations:

> One hundred Kurds, mostly women and children, arrived here [Mersin] by road from the interior.... They were very scantily clad and many went barefoot. Four carts containing their ill and dying, and their few personal belongings, completed the procession. They are the remnant of the Ararat Kurds...[43]

With Turkey's violation of its territory and the subsequent flight of so many Kurds, Iran changed its attitude to Turkey's Kurdish question. It reluctantly agreed to the border amendation Turkey so wanted, ceding the north-eastern slopes of Ararat, and receiving in return small strips of land near Qutur and Bazirgan.

The Iranian authorities began deporting Kurdish communities from around Khoi and the border region, communities already bereft of men of arms-bearing age. One traveller came across a column of deportees, mainly women and children, six kilometres long. From May Iranian troops around Qara Ayni found themselves repeatedly attacked by groups of Kurds, mainly Jalali and Haydaranli tribesmen. By the end of July the army was in full control. It was a cruel irony that the severity of the Iranian army operations drove 405 families of the Iranian Jalali to seek asylum in Turkey, to be resettled in western Anatolia.

Afterwards there was plenty of time to assess the causes of Kurdish failure. It is doubtful whether, even in the most advantageous circumstances, the Kurds could have ejected Turkey from Kurdistan. As with the Shaykh Said rebellion, Turkey had the advantages of superior communications and logistics, and were thus able to concentrate forces significantly larger and faster than the Kurds. It also had the benefit of superior weaponry, including aeroplanes. The Kurds' ability to sustain a credible force in the field remained contingent on the willingness of Iran to turn a blind eye. Once Turkish troops had entered Iran in July, the rebels were finished.

Yet beyond such factors lay the fundamental weaknesses of Kurdish tribalism. The lack of homogeneity of the Kurdish forces and the lack of co-ordinated action seriously weakened the Kurds' fighting capacity. Moreover, while a substantial number were willing to rise against their Turkish oppressors, tribes could always be found to do the state's bidding, as had been true in the nineteenth century.

The Road to Dersim

In June 1934 a draconian new law was enacted, granting the state wide-ranging powers over the population. Law No. 2510 divided Turkey into three zones: (i) localities to be reserved for the habitation in compact form of persons possessing Turkish culture; (ii) regions to which populations of non-Turkish culture for assimilation into Turkish language and culture were to be moved; (iii) regions to be completely evacuated.

The state was vested with full powers of compulsory transfer for those categories requiring assimilation. Furthermore, this law abrogated all previous recognition of tribes, their aghas, chiefs and shaykhs, with the automatic sequestration of all immoveable property pertaining either to tribes or to their leaders. Such leaders and their families were to be transferred for assimilation into Turkish culture. All villages or urban quarters where Turkish was not the mother tongue were to be dissolved, and their inhabitants distributed in predominantly mother-tongue-Turkish-speaking areas. Any kind of association or grouping in which the majority were non-Turkish-speaking was forbidden. It was intended to disperse the Kurdish population, to areas where it would constitute no more than 5 per cent of the population, thus extinguishing Kurdish identity. It was even proposed that village children should be sent to boarding establishments where they would be obliged to speak only in Turkish and to lose their Kurdish identity entirely.

Although the word 'Kurdish' was studiously avoided, no one could mistake the intention to destroy Kurdish identity in its entirety. Today such legislation seems wholly repugnant, yet one must remember that Turkey was practising the crude ideas of social engineering which had currency not only in Nazi Germany but among many European intellectuals. Only the impracticability of transferring and assimilating up to three million people prevented the law from being implemented except in a localized and piecemeal fashion. Even so, complaints made by Kurdish refugees from Van, Bitlis, Mus (Mush) and Siirt suggested that massacres, deportations and forced assimilation were proceeding apace.

Even before this bill had had its first reading in the Grand National Assembly in May 1932, Dersim had attracted government attention. Dersim was notoriously defiant. No fewer than eleven military expeditions had tried to quell its inhabitants since 1876. It had given trouble in 1925–26 and in 1927 4,000 troops had been sent to subdue the Kutch-Ushagh tribe. From 1930 onwards, the government began a policy of deportation, diasarmament and forced settlement of nomadic tribes 'in a manner which resembles the operations against Armenians in 1915'[44] in order to achieve greater control of Dersim. At first it was piecemeal, but it was clear that the suppression of all Dersim was only a matter of time.

At the end of 1935 the government announced its intention to tackle Dersim in earnest, promising a plan which combined administrative reorganization with military repression. Dersim was redesignated as a vilayet, to be known by the Turkish name of Tunceli. When making the announcement the interior minister innocently described the region as 'comprising a purely Turkish population'.[45] A state of siege was declared for Tunceli in 1936, and a new military governor, General Abd Allah Alp Dogan, appointed. He spent the rest of the year marshalling troops for what promised to be an arduous task, and building military roads across the region.

It was not until spring 1937, however, that military operations commenced in earnest. By then approximately 25,000 troops had been assembled around Dersim. At least 1,500 Dersim Kurds were determined to resist their progress. The Dersim leaders sent emissaries to Elazig, with a letter to General Alp Dogan pleading to be allowed to administer themselves. In reply, Alp Dogan had the emissaries executed. In early May the Kurds took their revenge, laying an ambush that left ten officers and fifty troops dead. Torturing, execution and mutilation of the bodies excited considerable indignation.

In June the government reassured the Grand National Assembly that its losses had been slight and that authority was re-established in Tunceli, claims that seemed more credible with the surrender of 600 guerrillas a month later. In August government forces compelled the Kurds to abandon their villages which were immediately razed, and to move to the less accessible summer high pastures. But the cost had been high. Turkish troops suffered significant casualties from snipers.

In July the septuagenarian leader of the rebel tribes, the Alevi cleric Sayyid Riza had appealed to Anthony Eden, Britain's Foreign Secretary. He set out the reasons for his compatriots' resistance. The government had tried to assimilate the Kurdish people for years, oppressing them, banning publications in Kurdish, persecuting those who spoke Kurdish, forcibly deporting people from fertile parts of Kurdistan for uncultivated areas of Anatolia where many had perished. The prisons were full of non-combatants, intellectuals were shot, hanged or exiled to remote places. 'Three million Kurds,' he concluded, 'demand to live in freedom and peace in their own country.'[46] But no one could or would come to his aid. He and many of his fellow leaders were unable to endure the rigours of winter and surrendered. Seven, including Sayyid Riza himself, were executed immediately.

Others decided to hold out in the more remote areas. During the spring of 1938 the aerial bombing, gas and artillery barrages were resumed. With the rebel refusal to surrender, more villages were razed. By August, three army corps, with a total strength of over 50,000 men, had been concentrated around Dersim, in 'a military parade of irresistible strength'. Forty airplanes were deployed for reconnaissance and bombing. Although described as the army's Grand Annual Manoeuvres, foreign military attachés were not invited to witness the advance across Dersim, for it was undesirable for foreign eyes to see Turkish forces in action. These traversed the whole of Dersim from one end to another, rounding up rebels, burning villages and declaring as 'uninhabitable zones' all those areas, for example with caves, which favoured guerrilla warfare. Ugly rumours began to filter out:

> It is understood from various sources that in clearing the area occupied by the Kurds, the military authorities have used methods similar to those used against the Armenians during the Great War: thousands of Kurds including women and children were slain; others, mostly children, were thrown into the Euphrates; while thousands of others in less hostile areas, who had first been deprived of their cattle and other belongings, were deported to vilayets in Central Anatolia.[47]

It was estimated, possibly with exaggeration, that some 40,000 Kurds perished.[48] Three thousand notables and others were deported. The remainder of the surviving population was put under the supervision of local garrisons. Once the area had been completely subdued, a special Mountain Brigade was formed to remain permanently stationed in Tunceli.

The diplomatic missions in Turkey knew enough of what was going on but even they found it difficult to believe Turkish excesses. The rest of the outside world had little idea. *The Times* merely parrotted the first mendacious announcement by Prime Minister Ismet Inonu, namely that there was hostility in Tunceli to the introduction of compulsory education.[49] Nothing was further from the government's mind, as a Turkish journalist visiting Dersim in 1948 (after the lifting of the emergency regime) discovered:

> I went to Tunc Eli, the old Dersim. The place was desolate. Tax collectors and policemen are still the only state officials the people have ever seen.... There are no schools, no doctors. The people do not even know what the word 'medicine' means. If you speak to them of government, they translate it immediately as tax collectors and policemen. We give the people of Dersim nothing; we only take. We have no right to carry on treating them like this.[50]

Dersim marked the end of the 'tribal' revolts against the Kemalist state. Only at the end of 1946 was it decided to lift the special emergency regime for Tunceli, and allow deported families to return home.

Meanwhile the deportations and settlement of Turks in order to 'turkicize' the rest of Kurdistan continued. In 1942 Khoybun circulated a report by the Inspector General of the First Inspectorate (covering the vilayets of Bitlis, Diyarbakir, Van, Hakkari, Mus, Mardin, Urfa and Siirt) which indicated that another 3,000 aghas and shaykhs had been identified for deportation to the west.

This report went on to express concern over the demographic balance. In the 1927 census the First Inspectorate General covering eastern Anatolia had a population of 870,000 of whom 543,000 were Kurds. By 1935 the population had risen to almost one million of whom 765,000 were mother-tongue-Kurdish-speakers, compared with only 228,000 Turks. Thus the Kurds had increased from 62 to 70 per cent of the population. Only assiduous settlement would solve the problem and the report recommended the construction of three Turkish villages annually, each of 100 households, hardly the basis on which the demographic balance could be changed. The report went on to urge Turkish-language boarding schools for Kurdish children, where all trace of Kurdish culture could be expunged. Yet such recommendations echoed objectives that had been set out in the Grand National Assembly almost a decade earlier. Turkey had unmistakably intended genocide of the Kurdish people. In practice its intentions were defeated by the sheer size of the task.

However, few could dispute that Kurdistan seemed thoroughly cowed. The Kurds had, it seemed, accepted their lot. It still remained to turn these subdued people into good Turks, or rather 'Mountain Turks', as Kurds began to be described from 1938, and it was hoped that the passage of time would succeed where forcible population exchange had failed. In 1965 it seemed safe enough to allow foreigners to travel east of the Euphrates for the first time since the 1930s.

The Survival of Kurdish Folk Islam

Meanwhile, the attempt to destroy the Sufi brotherhoods by exile of their leaders was falling short of its intention. Wherever they found themselves sent, many of the shaykhs re-established their networks – now over long distances by letter or by oral messages carried by trusted disciples. Furthermore, they provided a focus for local religiously observant Turks. For example, some Naqshbandi shaykhs exiled to Menemen formed an anti-Kemalist movement. When it was uncovered in 1931 the authorities were sufficiently fearful to hang them wholesale.

No one demonstrated the power of the religious impulse more clearly than Said Nursi,[51] who was living in Van at the time of the Shaykh Said rebellion. Nursi, it will be recalled, had been involved in the early expressions of Kurdish cultural identity. Now he was unwisely put in Isparta, a westerly equivalent of Bitlis, with its *madrasas* and conservative atmosphere. It was not long before he acquired a following and the crowds he attracted persuaded the governor to move him to a village outside. Here he defied the decree of 1932 forbidding the call to prayer in Arabic and was sent back to Isparta in disgrace. By this time his following was expanding, his followers circulating his tracts. He was again arrested and given an eleven-month jail sentence for pamphleteering. In his defence Said Nursi insisted his concern was not with founding a new *tariqa* but with strengthening faith, the sole path to paradise. Moreover, he averred his unshakeable belief that to be a Muslim was infinitely more important than to be

Turkish, Kurdish or any other nationality. On his release in 1936, Nursi was sent to Kastamonu. Thereby he maintained his old connections in Isparta and elsewhere and also forged new ones. In 1943 he was re-arrested, acquitted and sent to Afyon. Once more, in 1948 he was accused of establishing a secret religious society. To the end of his life, in 1960, the authorities obstructed his freedom of movement. Yet his followers of Nur (Light), the 'Nurculuk', relentlessly grew in number, and remain significant to this day.

Said Nursi was the most famous of these shaykhs but he was not alone. The notables of Bitlis and Erzincan (Erzinjan), for example, had close ties with the Naqshbandi shaykhs of these provinces and those of Erzerum more particularly with Qadiri shaykhs. Such ties survived exile. The traditional following in villages may have been weakened but the essential ties survived, to resurface once allowed to do so.

As yet unrecognized, the paths of Kurdish nationalism and of Kurdish folk Islam were destined to part company. When both resurfaced, after the first faltering gestures of democratic pluralism in the 1950s, the shaykhs generally encouraged their disciples to support conservative clerical or right-wing parties in national politics; Kurdish nationalists, on the other hand, sought strength from the political left. Each, in the fullness of time, was destined to become a *bête noir* for the other.

Sources

Great Britain, unpublished: Public Record Office: series FO 371 nos 6347, 6369, 7781, 7858, 10078, 10089, 10121, 10833, 10835, 10867, 11473, 11528, 11557, 12255, 12321, 13032, 13037, 13089, 13792, 13827, 14579, 14580, 15369, 16035, 16074, 16981, 16983, 20087, 20092, 20864, 21925, 130176; FO 424/261; CO 730/133/6 and 730/157/7; CO 732/21/2.

Great Britain, command papers etc: Lausanne Conference

Secondary sources: Ataturk, *A Speech Delivered;* Suraya Bedr Khan, *The Case of Kurdistan against Turkey* (Philadelphia, 1929); Martin van Bruinessen, *Agha, Shaikh and State;* Bletch Chirguh, *La Question Kurde: ses origines et ses causes* (Cairo, 1930); Ziya Gokalp, *The Principles of Turkism* (Ankara, 1920 and ed. Robert Devereux, Leiden, 1968) and *Turkish Nationalism and Western Civilisation: Selected Essays of Ziya Gokalp* (ed. Niyaz Berkes, London, 1959); Kendal, 'Kurdistan in Turkey'; Ihasan Nouri, *La Revolte de l'Agridagh* (Geneva, 1986); Olson, *The Emergence;* Sharif, *Al Jamiyat wa'l; Manzimat wa'l Ahzab al Kurdiya.*

Periodicals: *Ikibine Dogru* (Istanbul); *The Times* (London).

Unpublished: Hamit Bozarslan, 'Le problème national kurde en Turquie kemaliste' (Mémoire de diplôme de l'EHESS, Paris, 1986)

Notes

1. I have relied primarily on the account in Olson, *The Emergence,* pp 26–41.
2. Ataturk, *A Speech,* p. 57.
3. *Sacak* no. 39, April 1987 quoting from the recorded speeches, instructions and secret meeting records of the Grand National Assembly.

4. Statement made on 1 May 1920, Grand National Assembly records, quoted in *Sacak*, no. 39, April 1987.

5. *Hakimiyet-i-Milliye*, 6 May 1921, in *Bulletin Périodique*, 12 April – 25 May 1921, quoted in Bozarslan, 'Le problème national kurde en Turquie kemaliste', p. 40.

6. Statement, 24 April 1920, Grand National Assembly records, *Sacak*, no. 39, April 1987.

7. Olson, *The Emergence of Kurdish Nationalism*, p. 40.

8. FO 371/7781 Rumbold to Curzon, Istanbul, 29 March 1922; and Olson, *The Emergence of Kurdish Nationalism*, pp. 39–40.

9. FO 371/7858 Rawlinson, Memorandum on the Position of the Angora Government, 4 March 1922.

10. Ziya Gokalp, *The Principles of Turkism* (Ankara, 1920, trs. Robert Devereux, Leiden, 1968) pp. 12–15.

11. 'Historical materialism and sociological idealism', Ankara, 8 March 1923, quoted in Berkes, *Turkish Nationalism and Western Civilisation*, p. 65.

12. 'My nationality', Kucuk Mecmua, no. 28, Diyarbakir, 1923, quoted in Berkes, *Turkish Nationalism and Western Civilisation*, p. 44.

13. Great Britain, *Lausanne Conference*, p. 342.

14. Great Britain, *Lausanne Conference*, p. 345.

15. This statement was in reply to a journalist, Emin, in Izmit. It received press coverage in the Izmit papers on 16 and 17 January 1923, see *Turk Tarih Turumu* – Ataturk ve Turk Devrimi Arastirma merkezi, no. 1089, p. 15 cited in *Ikibine Dogru*, 6 November 1988, vo. ii, no. 46.

16. *Ikibine Dogru*, vol. ii, no. 46, 6 November 1988.

17. Except where noted otherwise, this account draws almost exclusively on van Bruinessen, *Agha, Shaikh and State*, pp. 281–305, and Olson, *The Emergence*, pp 91–127.

18. Law for the Reinforcement of Order (*taqrir-i-sukun*), *The Times*, 6 March 1925.

19. FO 371/10867 Lindsay to Chamberlain, Istanbul, 10 March 1925.

20. FO 371/10867 Hoare to Chamberlain, Istanbul, 3 August 1925.

21. FO 371/14579 W.S. Edmonds, Notes on a tour of Diabekir, Bitlis and Mush, May 1930.

22. Ataturk, *A Speech*, p. 722.

23. Bozarslan, 'Entre la umma et le nationalisme', p. 13.

24. FO 371/10835 Loraine to Gilliat-Smith, Tehran, 7 October 1925.

25. FO 371/11528 Knight to Lindsay, Trebizon, 16 June 1926.

26. FO 371/12255 Clerk to Chamberlain, Istanbul, 22 June 1927.

27. FO 371/12255 Clerk to Chamberlain, Istanbul, 22 June 1927.

28. FO 371/12255 Clerk to Chamberlain, Istanbul, 9 August 1927.

29. *The Times*, 7 April 1928.

30. *Vakit*, 7 May 1925, in Ghassemlou, *Kurdistan*, p. 52.

31. FO 371/10867 Lindsay to Chamberlain, Istanbul, 16 October 1925.

32. FO 371/12255 Clerk to Chamberlain, Ankara, 4 January 1927. For an almost identical conversation, see also FO 371/11557 Clerk to Oliphant, Istanbul, 20 December 1926 enclosing a shocked report by Dobbs, following his meeting with Tawfiq Rushdi in Ankara on 23 November 1926.

33. Fo 371/12255 Hough to Chamberlain, Aleppo, 15 November 1927.

34. Sureya Bedr Khan, *The Case of Kurdistan against Turkey* (Philadelphia, 1929), p. 63; Bletch Chirguh, *La Question Kurde* (Cairo, 1930), p. 33.

35. FO 371/13827 minuting on the enclosed copy of *The Case of Kurdistan Against Turkey*.

36. FO 371/14579 Edmonds, Notes on a Tour to Diabekir, Bitlis and Mush, May 1930.

37. FO 371/12255 Hoare to Chamberlain, Istanbul, 14 December 1927.

38. *Annuaire Statistique 1932/33*, cited in Bozarslan, 'Le Problème national kurde', p. 23.

39. Of 4,400 km of roads in Kurdistan only 989 km were in useable condition in 1930. In 1932 only 233 out of 4,606 cars, 372 out of 2,637 lorries, and 30 out of 432 buses were to be found in Kurdistan, *Annuaire Statistique 1932–33*, cited in Bozarslan, 'Le problème national kurde', p. 12.

40. For the story of Haju, see van Bruinessen, *Agha, Shaikh and State*, pp. 101–105.

41. FO 371/14580 Clerk to Henderson, Istanbul, 16 July 1930, Inclosure, see also *The Times*, 17 July 1930.

42. FO 371/14580 O'Leary to Clerk, Istanbul, 16 July 1930.

43. FO 371/16981 Matthews to Morgan, Mersin, 20 December 1932. Most families were settled in Thrace or Chanak, FO 371/16983. Annual report for Turkey 1932, refers to 300 arrested since the end of the Ararat rebellion, 30 of them receiving death sentences.

44. FO 371/14580 Matthews to Clerk, Trebizond, 15 November 1930; FO 371/16074 Tabriz Consulate Diary, 5 January and September 1932.

45. FO 371/20087 Loraine to Eden, Ankara, 3 January 1936.

46. FO 371/20864 Sayyid Riza to the British Foreign Secretary, Dersim, 30 July 1937.

47. FO 371/21925 Pro-Consul to Loraine, Trebizond, 'Memorandum on Military Operations in Dersim', 27 September 1938. Sir Percy Loraine reserved judgement. He could not believe the government would allow such excesses.

48. L. Rambout, *Les Kurdes et le Droit* (Paris, 1947), p. 39, quoted by Jwaideh, *The Kurdish Nationalist Movement*, p 39.

49. 'Kurds who Object to Education', *The Times*, 16 June 1937.

50. Osman Mete, *Son Posta*, April 1948, quoted by Kendal 'Kurdistan in Turkey', p. 72.

51. The following is taken almost exclusively from Serif Mardin's *Religion and Social Change in Modern Turkey*.

CHAPTER 10

THE KURDS UNDER REZA SHAH

Introduction

During the 1920s and 1930s the situation in Kurdistan was radically affected by the establishment of a government strong enough to impose centralizing measures on a hitherto highly decentralized state and the ruthless suppression of tribal independence, including the severe curtailment of transhumant movement.

Military technology was a key reason for the ability of the centre to impose its will on the periphery. The Kurds' first serious whiff of the new technology was probably at the battle of Sahna, when Daud Khan Kalhur was killed. Machine-guns and rifled weapons (not least field artillery equipped with hydraulic-recoil systems) favoured regular troops rather than tribesmen, even when these obtained modern weaponry. The new generation of field artillery and machine guns required proper training and direction to be really effective, and only regular forces could ensure this. The essential ingredient missing in Iran before the 1920s was a leader capable of imposing order, discipline and co-ordination on the country as a whole. From 1921 Reza Khan fulfilled that role. Although he did not succeed in destroying the tribes, he transformed the context in which they operated. By the time of his abdication in 1941, the status and power of tribal chiefs was largely dependent on their landholdings and on their standing in Tehran, or the provincial capital, and tribal power was in its twilight, only to enjoy a brief revival in the years 1941–46.

The Story of Simqu

By the end of the First World War Iran was in administrative and financial chaos. Tribal fighting, anarchy and famine plagued many areas; Gilan was in revolt; both Soviet and British forces were still on Iranian soil; in Tehran the government had fallen as a result of its universally unpopular acquiescence to the 1919 agreement with Britain which implied protectorate status. By the end of the year Iran's dismal circumstances included the imminent threat that rebel groups in the

Caspian region would march on Tehran, backed by the Red Army. Iran seemed weaker than at any time in the nineteenth century.

In early 1921 General Reza Khan, the first Iranian to command the Cossack Division, marched on Tehran and formed a new government, designating himself as Minister of War and Commander-in-Chief. Reza Khan was driven by fierce patriotism, and a determination both to rid Iran once and for all of any foreign presence and to modernize the country. His first self-appointed tasks, however, were to achieve the cohesion and control of the army and restore government authority in the provinces. The fulfilment of these objectives marked the beginning of Iran as a modern centralized nation state.

In Kurdistan the implications of Reza Khan's coup were not immediately apparent. The region was still struggling with the rigours of war. Regarding the settled population, for example, many of the 300 villages of the Urumiya plain had been destroyed, while the population of Urumiya had been reduced from 25,000 to only 5,000. The area was in anarchy, with tribes seeking to control or seize what they could. Of these the most active were the Abdui Shikak, led by Simqu, who were both looting and taking possession of villages between Khoi and Salmas.

Had such tribes been capable of uniting they might well have been strong enough to frustrate any government attempt to regain control. There had been one or two attempts to mobilize a pan-tribal movement for independence, or at any rate for freedom from Iranian misrule. In July 1918 certain Kurdish chiefs had apparently met to consider Kurdish independence under British auspices, and this had been suggested by a Mukri chief to a British representative in Saqqiz. At the beginning of December a group of chiefs representing the dominant tribes of Sinna, Saqqiz and Hawraman had visited Sulaymaniya to supplicate for inclusion in the British administered zone. In February 1919 another meeting of chiefs reportedly took place to consider a revolt against Iranian authority, but it came to nothing.

Such developments were the aspirations of certain individuals; in reality, however, many of the larger tribes were fraught with internal rivalries, let alone quarrels between one tribe and another. In the northern reaches of Kurdistan the main tribal groups, the Shikak, the Zarza, Mamash and Mangur were all riven. Most contestants sought external sponsors, one brother seeking help from the Turks, another from the Russians, and the occasional one from the Iranian government or its local officials.[1] The Shikak, the most important group during this period, was divided into three rival main sections: the Abdui led by Simqu, the Mamadi and the Kardar. All three had experienced a high turnover of leaders as a result of the violence that accompanies the life of a chief.[2] Even within the Abdui, Simqu was threatened by several challengers, of whom the most formidable was Amr Khan.[3]

Simqu, it will be recalled, had exploited the instability of the frontier region to get support from Iran and Russia before the war. From 1914 he had intermittently acted on behalf of Iran. While never in actual rebellion it had been clear that in practice he had acted independently, enjoying official blessing, in so far as he provided a measure of authority locally and helped to resist the Turkish or Russian threats.

From 1918, with the political possibilities wide open, Simqu began to strengthen his ties with Shaykh Taha of Shamdinan. He had already married one of the Shaykh's sisters before the war. He needed an external ally, both to deal with his challengers within the Shikak, and to exploit the power vacuum in the region. Together Simqu and Shaykh Taha formed a formidable cross-border (Iran–Turkey) bloc, one that in the absence of any credible alternative, could realistically dream of independence. By January 1919 it was reported that a crossborder 'pan-Islamic' alliance had been forged under Simqu's leadership among Kurds near Bashqala, and that this was based upon a determination to prevent the return of Assyrians and Armenians to the region.[4]

It is inconceivable that the Iranian government trusted Simqu. He was a notorious adventurer. Everyone knew of his dalliance with the Russians before the war, and of his co-operation with the Turks primarily against the Assyrians, who in the last year of the war threatened to create a new power base on the Urumiya plain. It was also well understood that in treacherously killing Mar Shimun in March 1918, he had done the governor of Tabriz's bidding as well as serving his own interests, namely the removal of any Assyrian threat to his control over the Urumiya plain. Now he evidently intended to exercise his independence, just as the Azaris and Armenians also intended to do. This was certainly the British impression as early as January 1919.

For some time the Iranian government had hoped to mount an expedition against Simqu, but it was bankrupt. In April 1919 it unsuccessfully sought a British loan for the project. Now it tried stealth. In mid-May Simqu was sent a parcel bomb, disguised as a box of sweets, which failed to slay its intended victim but killed a brother. The following day the Iranian garrison attacked Kurdish and Christian civilians in Urumiya, following an affray with a body of Simqu's supporters. Simqu promptly lay seige to the town, cutting off its water supply and creating mayhem in the nearby Azari settlements.[5]

In June Britain, anxious to restore calm, seems to have favoured the appointment of Simqu as Governor of Urumiya, a move that in the government view would have made West Azarbaijan an independent province. Under pressure from Britain, the authorities agreed in July to a settlement that recognized Simqu as warden of certain highways in the locality and of the frontier districts of Dilman and Lahijan, contingent on his loyalty.

Loyalty could hardly have been further from Simqu's thoughts, for he was already intent on seizing the moment for independence. As he told a British officer, 'The Turks were dead and now we [British] were merely asking the Kurds to tie themselves up to another dead nation misruled by a dead king.'[6] In fact Simqu fancied striking a deal with Britain, since it seemingly wanted to help create a Kurdish entity in Turkey 'Do by us, the Kurds on the Persian side of the frontier,' he told his British interlocutor, 'as you are doing by Sayyid Taha's Kurds on the other side of the frontier.' (As we have seen, Shaykh Taha had already learnt the limits of British encouragement.) When Simqu was refused the weapons necessary to acheive independence he turned to the Turkish nationalists for help, presumably invoking the potential Armenian and British threats and the help he could offer in preventing Christian repatriation. He was already busy buying rifles and ammunition and recruiting deserters from Turkey, whom he enticed with the prospect of loot and even of wives – Christian and Muslim women whom he had been abducting from Salmas and other settled areas.

In early September Simqu tried to convene a meeting of West Azarbaijan's Kurdish chiefs. It was not a success. Too many of those who attended were engaged in their own petty rivalries, and several important Harki and Begzada Dasht chiefs did not attend, being allied to Bahri Beg, one of Simqu's rivals in the Shikak. Meanwhile, his other rival, Amr Khan, had already offered to assist the governor of Urumiya against him.

As more recruits joined him that autumn, Simqu consolidated his position north of Lake Urumiya, warning the population around Salmas and Qutur to consider themselves under his jurisdiction. He demonstrated his wider importance by giving sanctuary to 40 of Shaykh Mahmud Barzinji's relatives, despite his hostility to the shaykh's rising.[7]

The Iranian authorities were sufficiently concerned by the deteriorating situation to begin assembling a strike force to deal with him. After an initial setback, this force defeated Simqu in February 1920 and he fled, first to his mountain stronghold of Shahriq in Sumay, and thence up into the snowbound passes. Many of his 3,000 followers melted away and he sued for a settlement, which the Iranian authorities unwisely agreed to. Simqu undertook to restore loot stolen from the Qaraqishlaq; to provide 50 horsemen under his brother Ahmad as a contribution to the Cossack Brigade; and not to interfere in Urumiya and Salmas districts.

Simqu took clemency as a symptom of weakness. By April he was re-arming with machine-guns and field artillery, thoughtfully provided by the Turks in Van. In August he re-occupied the Salmas plain, then the Urumiya plain including the town itself, which he occupied in December. By now he was also receiving support from the Bolsheviks, who wanted to undermine the integrity of Iran. So it was not surprising that he was able to assemble local chiefs at Dilman in order to consolidate his support, nor that he now tried to interest the chiefs of Sawj Bulaq and Lahijan in joining him. In January 1921 the two great Mukri tribes, the Dihbukri and Mamash, met Simqu's representatives at Ushnaviya and indicated their willingness to seize Sawj Bulaq. In February Shaykh Taha's men seized Haydarabad, on the southern shore of Lake Urumiya, and threatened all of Solduz. In Hawraman further south, Jafar Sultan, the Hawrami chief at Nawsud, now wanted Simqu to join him in an assault on Sulaymaniya.

Yet it would be wrong to think Simqu enjoyed universal Kurdish support. We know he had many opponents. One of them, the Khan of Maku, knowing the Turkish nationalists badly needed grain supplies for their own military contest with the Greeks, unsuccessfully offered substantial supplies at low cost, if only they would stop supporting Simqu. Others, one must assume, bent with the prevailing breeze.

Simqu at this stage had 1,000 cavalry, 500 infantry, and possibly some regular Turkish troops. In March, fighting under a Turkish flag, he inflicted a sharp defeat on a 600-strong Cossack force at Qizilja, at the northern end of Lake Urumiya. It is difficult to understand why the authorities risked a fight with so small a force. Out of 600 only 250 returned.[8] Tribal sections began once again to rally to Simqu's cause. By midsummer 1921 he had a following of 4,000 men.

Simqu's success must largely be ascribed to the general uncertainty prevailing in the region. It will be recalled that Reza Khan seized Tehran in February 1921. There were rumours of Soviet ambitions to break up Iran into petty states and it was easy for Simqu, since he was receiving Soviet assistance, to boast of 'assistance of [a] most powerful character from a foreign power'.[9] Some took this to be British rather than Soviet intrigue, and this was certainly the impression deliberately given by Shaykh Taha in Solduz.

Certainly Simqu recognized the value of an external sponsor to validate his undertaking. He sought British backing, probably at the behest of Shaykh Taha. Strategically Britain was much better placed than the Soviet Union, since his fiefdom abutted British-occupied Kurdistan, and he knew it would tempt the British in Baghdad. In July 1921 he made an indirect and disarmingly candid approach. 'I am aware,' he wrote, 'that my reputation is one of treachery and deceit in dealing with governments.'[10]

Would Britain support him? It was an interesting proposition promising the possibility of a barrier against Turkish adventures in the Baradust region and along the British eastern flank. It was also thought that Tehran might accept the loss of territory, over which it had only ever had nominal control, in return for much needed stability and order. Set against this were several negative considerations. Simqu was already letting Turkish troops move through his fiefdom to infiltrate the area around Rawanduz, and since he was routinely receiving ammunition supplies from Van, it was unlikely he would break with the Turks except for substantial war material from Britain. Then there was the explosive question of repatriating the Assyrians of Hakkari and Urumiya, so many of whom had already been slain by Simqu's men in 1918. It was inconceivable, even if he allowed them back, that the Assyrians would not be persecuted. Then there was the question of frontier stability. Britain had already committed itself to the integrity of Iran within its agreed international borders, and that suggested no adventures beyond the frontier. Finally there was the question of Kurdish nationalism. On the one hand Britain did not wish to identify with repression of Kurdish national aspiration and so offend Iraqi Kurds; on the other it did not wish to give Tehran further grounds to accuse it of interference in Iranian affairs. Tehran was already accusing it of encouraging unrest in Kurdistan. So Britain sat on its hands.

By now, however, Simqu controlled virtually the whole area from the outskirts of Khoi as far south as Bana. Only Sawj Bulaq was still in government hands, but not for long. In early October the garrison commander had treacherously arrested two chiefs he had invited to parley. Without hesitation Simqu marched on the town, sacking it and killing the gendarmerie that fell prisoner into his hands. He appointed a local Mamash chief as governor, then raced his troops back along the west bank of the lake to confront and rout a large irregular force of Qaradaghi tribesmen just north of Salmas. In early December he inflicted another sharp defeat on government forces at Qara Tappa, on the northern approachs to Salmas. Simqu's prestige surged again. By the end of the year he could field at least 5,000 men.

However, whatever the expectations, Simqu's revolt remained fatally handicapped by the nature of tribal politics. For all his success Simqu remained, like Daud Khan Kalhur, feared and disliked as well as admired. He still had his opponents within the Shikak, albeit now silenced. To the north, Kurds around Maku, who were anxious for paid employment, went on the rampage insisting the government form a local contingent against Simqu. To the south, the Mangur, in their habitual hostility to government, were ready to join Simqu, but both main tribes of the Mukri, the Dihbukri and the Mamash, were divided into pro- and anti-Simqu factions. The majority probably did give Simqu qualified support, and they may well have been influenced in his favour by the capture of Sinna by local tribesmen in mid-March. At any rate, these tribes in theory added another 3,000 warriors to Simqu's force of 5,000.

The alliance of Mukri chiefs with Simqu did not last long. By March 1922 they and he were at loggerheads. It is doubtful he had ever enjoyed their enthusiastic support. When he advanced on Sawj Bulaq in October 1921 – 'I sent for all the chiefs [to support me] but they would not come'[11] – he allowed his tribesmen to pillage their town houses. Those who subsequently sided with Simqu did so because he was the prevailing force of the moment. It is unlikely they were remotely inspired by loyalty either to Simqu or to a nationalist ideal.

In Kurdistan province the Dizli decided to support Simqu, as did Sardar Rashid of Rawansar, who was already alienated from the government. He offered to seize Sinna if Simqu took Saqqiz. But the Mariwan chief, Mahmud Khan Kanisanan spurned Simqu's invitation to join the revolt, even when this was spiced with the offer of the governorate of Sinna should he seize it. Mahmud Khan must have found this offer insulting, since he was the strongest chief in the area and could take Sinna at any time he wanted.[12]

Further south there was little interest in the revolt. The British consul in Kirmanshah thought the independence movement was 'greatly exaggerated.... The attitude of the majority of people in southern Kurdistan is that they are willing to support a movement provided it is financed by the British, but will not act unless they are paid',[13] a view that echoed German experience in the war. The Sanjabi and Qalkhani were united in their disdain for Simqu, even at the height of his power. And it is unlikely that other non-Sunni tribes would have rallied to his cause, except possibly rivals of these two tribes.

Despite the lack of interest further south, it is easy to see why Simqu felt increasingly sure of his position. Each expedition against him was easily defeated, while Reza Khan was preoccupied elsewhere. In September 1921 the revolutionary movement in Gilan had finally been defeated, and in early February 1922 a shortlived rising led by gendarmerie officers had taken place in Tabriz. By midsummer, in addition to Simqu's rising, Reza Khan still faced raids by the Lurs on Burujird, Turkoman raids around Gurgan and Shahsevan raids near Ardebil. Such disorders justified fears that Iran might disintegrate.

Even without open rebellion, the government had to face Soviet and Turkish subversive activities. A widespread underground Bolshevik-supported network, 'Milyun', was active in Kurdistan as far south as Kirmanshah, and there were signs of fruitful Bolshevik propaganda among the mullas around Khaniqin. Meanwhile the Kemalists were still supporting Simqu. A Kemalist faction even existed in Tehran, containing a disproportionate number of Kurds. These Kurds were probably motivated more by dislike of Reza Khan than affection either for Mustafa Kemal or Simqu.

In May Shaykh Taha, who had based himself at Sawj Bulaq, took his men out looting Dihbukri country around Bukan, a rich agricultural area 30 miles to the south-east. In his absence a pro-government force of Kurdish irregulars[14] from Miandoab, realizing Sawj Bulaq was undefended, quickly repossessed it. When Shaykh Taha learnt of this he swiftly retook it, killing 200 defenders and moving on to occupy Miandoab. This caused widespread panic among the Shi'i population, and even the people of Maragha took flight. In June Simqu extended his territories further by the seizure of Sayn Qala, east of Bukan.

The Iranian government was biding its time, marshalling sufficient forces to be sure of success. At the beginning of August 8,000 men moved southwards from their assembly point north of Lake Urumiya. On 9 August a major battle took place north of Salmas in which Simqu's men were soundly beaten. The following day the government retook Dilman. Simqu's force now disintegrated, with different tribal groups quietly making their way home. His stronghold of Shahriq was captured on 14 August, and Urumiya reoccupied on the 16th, by which time Simqu and other leading rebel chiefs had fled to Turkey.

Simqu's last years were spent trying to regain his former glory. He moved to Iraq where he hoped to obtain support from Shaykh Taha and also Shaykh Mahmud Barzinji, but the former had abandoned his ambitions in Iran while Shaykh Mahmud reciprocated Simqu's disdain for his own 1919 revolt. In 1923 Simqu returned to Turkey, but no longer found support there either. In 1924 Reza Khan pardoned him, presumably on the assumption that it would be safer having him inside than just beyond the frontier.

Simqu returned in spring 1925. His first task was to displace his rival Amr Khan, who had taken over the tribe since his submission in 1922.[15] By January 1926 Simqu was again cock-of-the-walk and bent upon re-creating the freedom he had previously enjoyed. The government was naturally nervous and resumed support for Amr Khan. By October 1926 Simqu's raiding that had been going on since the previous autumn slipped into open rebellion. He allied with the Begzada Dasht of Margavar and Targavar and with a Harki chief invaded Salmas plain. However, he was easily defeated when half his troops defected to Amr Khan outside Dilman. Simqu fled to Iraq this time, leaving Amr Khan to resume leadership of the Abdui Shikak.

Simqu still looked for opportunities to relaunch his career. In exile in Iraq he was soon in correspondence with like-minded spirits and with Turkey, which may have wanted Simqu's assistance in the suppression of its own Kurds in eastern Anatolia. In 1928 he left Iraq for Turkey lured by the promise of a regiment of tribal cavalry and the award of an estate on the Iranian frontier. Tehran must have viewed Turkey's use of Simqu as a threat to its own control of the border area, and this time decided to kill him. In 1929 it amnestied him, inviting him to be governor of Ushnaviya. Shortly after his return, government troops ambushed and killed him.

Was Simqu a nationalist? He spoke of independence and successfully united a number of tribes around himself, and by his alliance with Shaykh Taha in Turkish Kurdistan for a short span made it a cross-border affair. Yet he also found it hard to recognize anyone else as a national leader. Neither he nor Shaykh Taha saw Shaykh Mahmud as anything but a potential rival. It was only after his own defeat that Simqu changed his attitude towards Shaykh Mahmud. No manifesto or political programme seems to have survived that records Simqu's national vision, leaving it questionable whether he ever produced one. Although a Sawj Bulaq man produced a shortlived journal, *Ruji Kurdistan*,[16] on his behalf, its nationalist line is not clear. Simqu does not seem to have attempted a unified administration or tax regime over the territories he controlled. In Urumiya and Sawj Bulaq (and possibly elsewhere), he installed tribal chieftains as governors. This, of course, was not significantly different from previous Iranian practice, but it hardly suggested the vision of a nascent Kurdish national state. It is clear that Simqu had disdain for urban and settled non-tribal folk, except as *rayyat* for the benefit of the tribes. His treatment of the *anjumans* in the constitutional period and his sack of the Kurdish 'capital', Sawj Bulaq, suggest that his nationalism was defined more by socio economic status (tribal pastoralist *versus* settler) than by ethnicity.

Simqu remained a tribal chief *par excellence*, exploiting the advantages of a tribal culture to mobilize supporters and suppress rivals. The Shikak had come together as a significant tribal confederation in the second half of the nineteenth century. It was itself a conglomerate of unrelated septs, welded together by a determined family. It could be argued that Simqu was carrying this process further in his drive to become paramount of the Kurdish tribes of West Azarbaijan. Yet he was also fatally weakened by tribal culture, of which he himself was so much a part. This was demonstrated most clearly in the rapid dissolution of his forces following his defeat, and the quarrels and jealousies inherent in tribalism.

Kirmanshah

A contemporary illustration of the difficulties inherent in forging unity among tribes already gripped by their own networks of feuds and alliances may be found in Kirmanshah. The Sanjabi tribe, it will be recalled, suffered a severe reverse at the hands of hostile neighbours and the British in May 1918. By 1920 it had recovered its position relative to the other great tribes in the region.[17] The Guran confederation was breaking up, while the Kalhur were weakened by uncertain leadership.[18]

In early autumn 1921 Qasim Khan (Sardar Nasir) Sanjabi, the new British-sponsored paramount, formed a confederation with Rashid al Sultana Qalkhani and Sardar Rashid Ardalani (or Kurdestani) against the Waladbegi tribe, with whom the Sanjabi were in feud. This feud had been going since the time of Shir Khan Sanjabi, and was exacerbated by Waladbegi treachery towards Shir Khan's son, Ali Akbar. It had came to the boil with the Waladbegi's persistent theft of Sanjabi livestock that summer. Sardar Rashid had his own grudge against one particular chief involved in this looting, since the latter had deliberately fomented trouble between himself and the governor of Sinna. Rashid al Sultana Qalkhani had contributed men out of a longstanding friendship with the Sanjabi. There had been no difficulty in looting the Waladbegi, but the Sanjabi and Qalkhani had put themselves in a dangerous position, since their winter quarters lay between the Waladbegi and the Kalhur. They would be outnumbered if the Kalhur and Waladbegi allied, a real danger, given the longstanding competition between the Kalhur and Sanjabi confederations. Furthermore the Sanjabi knew that the governor at Qasr-i Shirin was hostile to them. Qasim Khan Sanjabi feared the governor might persuade the Kalhur to attack Rashid al Sultana Qalkhani, in which case he would be honour-bound to assist the Qalkhani, almost certainly prompting the Waladbegi to attack the Sanjabi from the rear.

Sure enough, the Waladbegi chiefs took refuge with the Kalhur, an act which implied a duty of revenge, and the Kalhur chief was then ordered by Tehran to punish the Sanjabi-led confederation. Tribal war was only averted by the timely arrival of a new governor in Kirmanshah, who foresaw the economic damage and disorder that might result and persuaded the Kalhur and Sanjabi chiefs to submit to his arbitration.[19]

Subjugating the Tribes

Like Mustafa Kemal in Turkey, Reza Khan was determined to exert central authority throughout the state with a similar policy of integrating a pluralistic society into a homogeneous one. This included attempting to bring tribes under direct government control for the very first time, to impose a single language, Persian, on a country of linguistic diversity (primarily a variety of Turkish and Kurdish dialects, Arabic, Luri and Baluchi), and to impose elements of uniform dress on urban, agrarian and pastoral peoples.

Simqu's rebellion had been crushed because it was a direct threat to the state, but Reza Khan now intended to remove the latent threat to his aims posed by tribal society in general. At first he was preoccupied dealing with immediate problems, for example the defiance of the Turkoman and Lur tribes, and building up a regular military force. So he resorted to the old strategems: the use of one tribe against another, the keeping of hostages and, within certain powerful tribes, the playing off of a pretender against the incumbent chief.

Like the Qajars before him, Reza Khan still needed tribal irregulars to assist in the maintenance of order. When quelling disorders among the Lurs in 1923, for example, he accepted help from the Kalhur once he realized the difficulties for regular troops of operating against a wily enemy in the mountains. In 1924 tribal auxiliaries were raised among the leading Kurdish tribes in anticipation of trouble on Simqu's return that year. Altogether, 4,000 armed retainers were reckoned available for service, some of which were used later the same year against the Wali of Pusht-i Kuh.

A real difficulty, however, was the proximity of the border, which offered Tehran both disadvantages and opportunities. On the one hand dissident tribes could slip over the border to safety at the first sign of trouble. On the other, when Kurds came over from Iraq seeking refuge from the British, they offered Tehran the chance to punish Britain for its interference in Iran. The Iranian government had plenty of grudges against Britain, dating back at least to the Anglo-Russian agreement of 1907. It was particularly suspicious of British policy with the tribes. It resented the way Britain gave asylum to Simqu in 1922, and to Sardar Rashid the following year. It was outraged when the British started paying the turbulent Jafar Sultan a subsidy in 1924 to discourage him from helping Shaykh Mahmud. This amounted to bribing a chief in a neighbouring country. Little wonder Tehran found it tempting to offer sanctuary to men like Shaykh Mahmud and allow them the freedom to operate across the border to repay Britain, as Tehran saw it, in its own coin.

On the other hand, it was unsettling for Tehran to see that Shaykh Mahmud's nationalist fervour was so contagious, appealing to influential chiefs like Mahmud Khan Dizli and Mahmud Khan Kanisanan of Mariwan. If these chiefs were troublesome for Iraq, they were hardly less so for Iran. By 1927 Tehran had had quite enough of Shaykh Mahmud's troublesome presence. The danger implicit in increasing talk of 'the ideal of Kurdish autonomy' easily outweighed the nuisance value the shaykh had been to the British.

The other major border problem arose from the migratory habits of frontier tribes. The summer migrations were always moments of potential friction with the people through whose lands the tribes moved. But additionally, with state centralization came awkward questions about land ownership, military service and taxation. Disagreement could easily lead to explosion. The most notable example involved the Pizhdar, who traditionally came over the mountains from Qala Diza each summer to graze their flocks in the Sardasht area.

Throughout the 1920s the Pizhdar remained in conflict with the government. During the years of Qajar impotence, the Pizhdar had acquired proprietorial rights over a number of villages around Sardasht, probably because no one was strong enough to challenge their encroachments. In 1923 government troops occupied Sardasht and dealt stringently with tribal leaders. On the pretext of tax arrears, Pizhdar flocks were seized and tribal representatives ousted from the villages and properties they occupied. Some chiefs were temporarily detained. In 1924 the government tried to extract annual poll tax, taxes retrospective to 1914, and to disarm the tribe. While the Pizhdar accepted poll tax as legitimate, they absolutely refused to pay back tax, still less to disarm. They soon found themselves fleeing from Cossack cavalry, but were not so easily broken of their customary practice. Each summer they were antagonized by government interference on their lands during their winter absence. In summer 1926 they drove government forces from Bana and Sardasht, and burnt down 38 villages before retreating into Iraq. In 1927 the peace was kept, but in 1928 they again felt provoked by government treatment and became bellicose as they prepared for the 1929 migration.

Two factors prevented trouble. First, they received a stiff warning from the government in Baghdad against any 'misbehaviour'. Second they found themselves courted by Tehran which needed their co-operation against a revolt by the Mangur, old allies of the Pizhdar. With the Mangur already occupying Sardasht, Tehran was willing to accommodate certain Pizhdar grievances.

Reza Khan's primary objective was the disarmament of all the tribes. The Kurdish tribes may have been less important than large confederations like the Bakhtiyari and the Qashqai but nevertheless presented a direct threat to the stability of the western fringe of the state. Yet disarmament was contingent on relative strength and an air of general stability. Setbacks occurred when revolt broke out among the turbulent spirits of the region, men like Mahmud Khan Dizli, Jafar Sultan of the Hawrami, and Sardar Rashid Ardalani of Rawansar, all of whom were a priority for disarming. In 1925, for example, Salar al Dawla made yet another attempt to raise the tribes and it was to precisely these leaders that he appealed.

Tehran still needed the active co-operation of other tribes or the ability to placate them so as to avoid a more general conflagration. During 1925–26, for example, when Turkey was creating tension in the frontier region, the Soviets were making approaches to the Maku chiefs and further south the Pizhdar and Hawramis were giving the army a hard time, it seemed wiser to have strong but neutral tribes in the border areas than risk alienating them. Tehran was also dogged by the private enterprise of individual soldiers, who readily sold rifles and ammunition to insurgents to supplement their own meagre earnings.

Towards the end of the 1920s the government began the hardest part, disarming the tribes on the frontier itself. This required substantial manpower and tactical surprise, since it had already been discovered that tribesmen would hand over the weapons to the Jaf or some other tribe inside Iraq, rather than surrender them to the government. Between 1927 and 1934 there were repeated clashes between government forces and the tribes of Hawraman and Mariwan, and with them instances of growing brutality on the part of the government.[20] In 1926 troops fighting the Pizhdar, Mariwi and Hawrami executed all prisoners they took. It may have been incidents like these that prompted 37 chiefs to seek British suzerainty over their territory that year. By 1931 it appeared to British consular staff that a 'policy of open cruelty was deliberately adopted', with troops executing those tribal captives unable to march.[21] Such reports echoed those emerging from Turkish Kurdistan.

Ruthlessness was already the order of the day with recalcitrant chiefs. Simqu had perished in 1929, while his nephew, Umar Khan (Jafar Agha's son), died in suspicious circumstances in prison five years later. This was standard fare.[22] The chief of the Mukri died mysteriously in Sawj Bulaq prison in 1931. Not even Shaykh Taha was spared, though apart from his earlier alliance with Simqu, he had hardly offended Reza Shah. He had been relieved of his post as *qaim-maqam* of Rawanduz in 1928 at Iran's request. He went to Tehran to negotiate over the lands to which he laid claim in the border marches of Margavar, apparently at the invitation of Reza Shah, but was imprisoned and subsequently poisoned in 1932.

Disarming the tribes was made considerably more difficult by the added provocations of Reza Shah's drive toward national uniformity. In 1928 all traditional honorific titles, for example Ilkhan, beg, amir, or agha were banned. New dress requirements, too, in particular the obligatory Pahlavi hat (a specially designed kepi), which came into force in March 1929 caused widespread anger. Both the Mamash and Mangur, for example, attacked Sardasht and drove the garrison out.

The tribes were also fiercely antagonistic towards plans to conscript their young men and this caused repeated trouble. In 1937, for example, twelve soldiers were shot dead in a village when they tried to compile a conscription list. Two years later the Sardasht tribes rebelled rather than submit to conscription, disarmament and the adoption of European clothes. Another cause for widespread discontent was the linguistic policy, with the prohibition of Kurdish dialects first in schools in 1934, then on any public notices the following year.

Finally, throughout Iran Reza Shah deliberately settled the tribes and tried to destroy their organization. Had he not been forced to abdicate in 1941 he might have succeeded. During the 1930s he inflicted severe damage on the Kurds. Some were forcibly transferred from Kurdistan, for example the Jalali from the north, largely on account of their attacks on Iranian army contingents deployed to frustrate the Agri Dagh rebels, and the Kalbaghi were moved from Kirmanshah to Isfahan, Hamadan and Yazd, their place taken by Turkic-speaking groups. But such measures inevitably persuaded some young men to take to the hills. Many greater chiefs were detained permanently in Tehran. Others had their lands sequestrated, sometimes being compensated with 'equivalent' estates far from their tribal habitat, where they were required to reside. Certain lesser chiefs who gave trouble were also rounded up, but as late as 1936 chiefs were still success-fully bribing local officials to leave them free. In many cases military officers took over the responsibilities of chiefship, many becoming notorious for their corrupt and cruel dealings.

Where his authority was unopposed, Reza Shah left tribal organization at lower levels intact as a bulwark against Bolshevik ideas among settled peasantry concerning their land or water rights. Through the Land Registration Department he encouraged local aghas to register communal property under their own name. Forcible transfer, confiscation of herds, the prohibition on tribal migration all had a damaging effect on tribal solidarity and life. Furthermore they had severe economic consequences, not only for the tribes themselves which became im-poverished, but also for food supplies locally. Many towns on the edge of Kurdistan depended on the tribes for their meat.

By the late 1930s the Kurds had been beaten into resentful submission. On a visit to Kurdistan in 1936 Reza Shah had hectored the assembled aghas to avoid politics, leaving them, in the words of the British consul, with the feeling that 'the future which Iran offers to a race of free and proud mountaineers is unbearably hum-drum'.[23] No sooner, however, had Reza Shah abdicated in 1941 than the chiefs returned to their ancestral lands, tried to rebuild their retinues and reverted to their traditional activities. But that belongs to another chapter.

In the meantime, Iraq, Iran and Turkey agreed that their respective use of discontented Kurds in order to foment trouble for each other was less valuable than co-operation in order to stifle Kurdish dissent. In July 1937 a pact was signed at Reza Shah's palace of Saadabad, in which the signatory parties recog-nized the existing borders and undertook to observe the canons of good neigh-bourliness. It marked a discouraging development for the Kurds in inter-state co-operation against their aspirations.

Sources

Official Great Britain, unpublished: Public Record Office:s series FO 248 nos 1224, 1225, 1226, 1246, 1278, 1331, 1400; series FO 371 nos 3858, 4147, 4192, 4930, 5067, 6347, 6348, 6434, 6442, 7781, 7802, 7803, 7805, 7806, 7807, 7808, 7826, 7827, 7835, 7844, 9009, 9010, 9018, 10097, 10098, 10124, 10158, 10833, 10841, 10842, 11484, 11491, 12264, 12265, 12288, 12291, 13027, 13760, 13781, 16063, 16076, 17912, 17915, 18987, 20037, 23261; FO 416/112; CO 732/21/2.

Official Great Britain, published: Driver, *Kurdistan and the Kurds.*

Secondary: Ervand Abrahamian, 'Kasravi: the integrative nationalist of Iran', *Middle Eastern Studies*, vol. 9, no. 3, October 1973 and *Iran Between Two Revolutions* (Princeton, 1982); Arfa, *Under Five Shahs*; Beck, 'Tribes and state in nineteenth and twentieth century Iran'; van Bruinessen, 'Kurdish tribes and the State of Iran: the case of Simko's revolt' in Richard Tapper (ed.) *The conflict of Tribe and State*; Hassanpour, *Nationalism and Language*; Hoshang Sabahi, *British Policy in Persia, 1918–1925* (London, 1990).

Notes

1. FO 371/5067 Gracey to Wardrop, 'Kurds in Urumiya District', Erivan, 23 January 1920 lists contestants by name and affiliation. See also FO 248/1225 Packard to Bristow, Urumiya, 7 May 1919, on Shikak rivalries.
2. We have already noted the murder of Simqu's brother Jafar in 1904 or 1905. Umar Agha, leader of the Mamadi, was killed by Iranian officials in 1902. Mustafa Agha, leader of the Kardar, had been killed by his Abdui rivals in 1906.
3. Threats to Simqu came from his brother Ahmad, 'a dashing warrior', the sons of Taymur, one of whom, Bahri Beg had had a major quarrel with Simqu, and Amr Khan, son of Muhammad Sharif Pasha. The latter is variously described as Simqu's brother, uncle or cousin.
4. This alliance received support from Tabriz, but we do not know from whom precisely.
5. He seized Dilman, looted Khoi, and massacred the Azari Qaraqishlaq population of Lakistan (north-west of Dilman).
6. FO 248/1225 Brig. Gen. Beech, Report on Unrest in Urumiya District, Tiflis, 14 July 1919.
7. Both Simqu and Shaykh Taha expressed hostility towards Shaykh Mahmud and his rebellion. In fact, after his own defeat Simqu visited Shaykh Mahmud in Sulaymaniya.
8. 120 were killed on the battlefield, another 230 went missing or were taken prisoner.
9. FO 371/6347 High Commissioner Iraq to Secretary of State for the Colonies, 26 August 1921.
10. FO 371/6347 APO Raniya to PO Sulaymaniya, 20 July 1921. See also High Commissioner Iraq to SS Colonies, 21 October 1921 and inclosures.
11. See letter of Kurd Mustafa Pasha, which also cites Simqu's justification for killing prisoners at Sawj Bulaq: that they had been captured and released before (i.e. during the World War) on the promise of not fighting the Kurds again; FO 371/7781 Kurd Mustafa Pasha to his son Abd al Aziz, Sulaymaniya, 12 December 1921.
12. Sardar Rashid must have been outraged at Simqu's offer to Mahmud Khan, given his claim to the governorship of Sinna ever since the Russians had offered it to him in 1917. He was already on bad terms with Mahmud Khan. Perhaps it was the latter's refusal to rebel that induced he himself to do so.
13. FO 371/6347 Cowan to High Commissioner, Iraq, Kirmanshah, 25 September 1921.
14. This Kurdish force was originally with the nationalist guerrillas of Kuchik Khan in Gilan in April 1921. It surrendered and enrolled in Reza Khan's forces following Kuchik Khan's defeat in October 1921. Its leader, Khalu Qurban, was a chief from Kirmanshah area. He was killed, and his force disbanded following its mauling at Sawj Bulaq.
15. Both had friends in government. Amr Khan was favoured locally, but Simqu enjoyed the patronage of the war minister, who had accepted his submission. In 1925 Amr Khan was summoned to Tabriz, but refused to go. It is possible the summons was the result of intrigue between Simqu and his friend in Tehran. At any rate it was Simqu who took government troops to arrest him.
16. Its title page is reproduced in Hassanpour, *Nationalism and Language*, p. 260. According

to van Bruinessen there was a journal called *Kurd dar sal-i 1340*, 'Kurdish tribes', p. 399, no. 36.

17. In 1918 Ali Akbar Khan (Sardar Muqtadar) had fled to Turkish territory. The British took Qasim Khan (Sardar Nasir) as a hostage to Baghdad. They knew the Sanjabi had been provoked by Russian excesses into opposing the Allies, and understanding the danger now of a vacuum, sent Qasim Khan back as paramount. Ali Akbar and the third brother, Husayn Khan (Salar Zafar) were detained in Tehran, but were released by Reza Khan in 1922 on the promise of good behaviour.

18. Although Sulayman Khan was formal chief, he remained nervous of nephew Abbas Khan who lived in Kirmanshah and schemed against him, sometimes with government help.

19. When this governor resigned a month later, the British consul persuaded the Kalhur chief to stay out of it. His motive was to maintain tranquillity on the Iraqi frontier and prevent disorder on the trade route from Khaniqin to Kirmanshah.

20. Such brutality was not new. In 1924, for example, about 20 Lur chiefs, some rebel, others already supporting the government, had been enticed to parley under the guarantee of a sealed Quran sent by the army commander, only to be promptly executed and their severed heads sent for display to Hamdan.

21. Fo 371/16076 Kirmanshah consulate Diary, March 1932.

22. Umar Khan, son of Jafar Agha, fell victim to a rival, Sartip Khan, who reported Umar Khan for intended disobedience. For other extra-judicial killings by the state, see Abrahamian, *Iran between Two Revolutions*, pp. 150–151.

23. FO 371/20037 Urquhart to HM Minister, Tabriz, 18 November 1936.

BOOK III

ETHNO-NATIONALISM IN IRAN

CHAPTER 11

TRIBE OR ETHNICITY?
THE MAHABAD REPUBLIC

Introduction

The impulse of ethnic nationalism first found full expression in Iran where, ironically, the Kurds were weaker than in either Iraq or Turkey. It was the power vacuum during the Second World War that provided the conditions in which this idea could take powerful root. Ostensibly the Mahabad republic was crushed by the Iranian state. In reality the success of Mahabad as an expression of ethnic nationalism was frustrated by the tribal culture which continued to dominate Kurdish affairs.

The Road to Mahabad

The Second World War, like the first, marked a watershed in Kurdish history in Iran. This was partly on account of the war itself. Britain and the Soviet Union occupied western Iran in August 1941, compelling the apparently pro-German Reza Shah to abdicate and leave the country the following month allowing his son, Muhammad Reza, to succeed to the throne. The British sphere, intended to protect Iraq's eastern flank, was centred on Kirmanshah. The Russians occupied most of northern and western Azarbaijan as far south as a line across from Ushnaviya to Miandoab. The occupying powers allowed a vacuum to occur in the intervening Kurdish lands from Mahabad to Saqqiz, within the Russian sphere of influence but outside its direct control, and the country running south from Sanandaj, in the British sphere but outside the effective control of the Iranian forces operating there on British sufferance. This vacuum was contested by local forces as well as by the much weakened Iranian government and allowed for the first autonomous Kurdish government.

The Allies had differing concerns. The Soviet Union, wishing to safeguard its flank position in western Azarbaijan, wanted the Kurds to be more favourably inclined to themselves than to Tehran. But the desire to win Kurdish goodwill for so modest a purpose was liable to misinterpretation and this soon happened.

Britain took a different approach. It was aware of the difficulties inherent in controlling the tribes. It had plenty of experience from Mesopotamia, let alone its longer experience in India on the North West Frontier. The last thing it wanted was for the Kurdish tribes to throw off fealty to Tehran and declare some form of independence or autonomy. 'If the Kurds in Persia succeed in getting local autonomy supported by us,' the British military attaché in Tehran argued, 'the Arabs of Khuzistan will want it and Heaven knows who else.'[1] Worse yet, it would give a disastrous example to the Iraqi tribes and the nationalist agitators in Kirkuk and Sulaymaniya. Finally Britain was acutely aware that Turkey, already sympathetic to Germany, was extremely apprehensive about Allied encouragement of the Iranian Kurds and the destabilization this might provoke in its own Kurdish territory.

So Britain wanted to uphold Iranian authority and the system as it was, but without the steamroller tactics of Reza Shah. It told Tehran to settle legitimate Kurdish grievances, to reinstate tribal leaders where they had good title to lands confiscated by Reza Shah; to assist those tribesmen who wanted to settle; to permit unfettered annual tribal migration so long as this did not breach the peace; and to prosecute those officers who had abused their position in Kurdistan during the previous decade.

Being kind to Kurds sounded all very well, but inevitably rang alarm bells in Tehran. As Allied rhetoric proclaimed its struggle for democracy against dictatorship, for the weak against the strong and other similarly subversive ideas, it was easy for those in Tehran to imagine that Iran would slide back into a state of decentralized weakness similar to that which had existed a generation earlier. Indeed, disorders broke out within a week of Reza Shah's abdication. But now, when there was disorder in western Azarbaijan, Iranian forces were denied access by the Soviets. On those occasions when the Soviet Union did allow its forces access, it seemed in retrospect to have been a deliberate ploy to allow Iranian forces to incur the odium from unpopular but necessary measures.

Things were easier further south, but the British presence was highly inhibiting. Tehran could welcome British support for its authority in Kirmanshah, but felt it was expected, unreasonably, to use kid gloves on incorrigible tribes. Furthermore, regardless of their fair words, the very presence of the British and the visible fact that they, rather than Tehran, held the political whiphand did nothing for government authority. Finally, there was the irritating but persistent belief among the Kurds that somehow the British might help them realize their national aspirations. Several tribal and other leaders, including the volatile chief of Bana, Hama (Muhammad) Rashid, and the more calculating leader in Mahabad, Qazi Muhammad, soon approached British officials with a view to obtaining British protection.

So desperate were they in Tehran to prevent the secession of Kurdistan that a government commission went there in November 1941. At Mahabad it convened the local chiefs, promising them the freedom to bear arms and wear

Kurdish costume, if they would only accept the return of Iranian administration. This was no more than the tribes had already enjoyed since Reza Shah's fall, so the offer was rejected. The chiefs wanted assurances concerning the restoration of confiscated lands and, more significantly, the employment of chiefs or their delegated representatives in government in Tehran. Eight months later, in June 1942, a Tribal Commission was established to investigate Kurdish land complaints and to appoint local *bakhshdars* (or community heads) in place of army officers. In the meantime the tribes, glad to be shot of Reza Shah's stringent regime, were determined to retrieve the *status quo ante*, before the Allies had time to impose a new order. Before Soviet troops entered Urumiya, tribesmen had already looted and burnt its bazaar. They had also picked up large quantities of arms abandoned by the fleeing Iranian soldiery and made off into the hills. In the south tribesmen around Sanandaj and Kirmanshah soon had the countryside in disorder, looting indiscriminately or raiding enemy villages. By the end of the year Kurdish tribesmen were swaggering even in Tabriz, clothed in their proscribed traditional costume and armed to the teeth.

In Urumiya relations between Azaris, Kurds and Christians became explosive. In January 1942 a group of Kurds, Armenians and Assyrians formed a party entitled 'Liberation', which began to pillage nearby Azari villages. In April there was renewed tribal disorder provoked by the government's arming of the Shi'i peasantry. Over 2,000 peasants fled their homes. The tribes were only mollified once the government agreed to remove gendarmerie forces from lands between Khoi and Mahabad.

In central Kurdistan Hama Rashid seized Bana, where he had been governor during the First World War, and set up his own administration. By December 1941 he was threatening to seize Sanandaj and was only dissuaded by a warning that to do so would precipitate conflict with British forces. In February his men seized Saqqiz and were only driven out in April. By then they had even removed doors, windows and electrical wiring.

In early autumn 1942, having initially spurned Tehran's overtures, Hama Rashid agreed to enter government service as a local official but as the British consul Urquhart reported, 'Neither side would hesitate to abandon this relationship if it could find something more attractive.'[2] Two years later, in 1944, that moment came. When Hama Rashid attacked the Mariwan territories of his neighbour, Mahmud Khan Kanisanan, who had been appointed (governor) in October 1941, Iranian forces came to Mahmud Khan's rescue and helped drive Hama Rashid into Iraq, but not before he had burnt almost all Bana's 1,000 houses to the ground. Once they had dealt with Hama Rashid, government troops turned on Mahmud Khan and drove him into Iraq too.

By June 1942 Tehran had released virtually all Kurdistan's tribal leaders and it was inevitable that those who had suffered under Reza Shah should now seek restitution, be it the lands that were taken from them, or their tribal position. The story of Abbas Qabudian, Daud Khan Kalhur's grandson, illustrates how landlords adapted to the circumstances created by Reza Shah. On Daud Khan's death in 1912 there had been a succession struggle between his son Sulayman, and his grandson Abbas (Sulayman's nephew). Both were young and relatively inexperienced but Sulayman had more powerful backers and became paramount. But his fear of his nephew weakened his standing among the Kalhur.

Abbas, like previous pretenders, lived in Kirmanshah from where he tried to undermine his uncle. When Sulayman was murdered in a family quarrel in 1922, Abbas protested his innocence; but he was the chief beneficiary, for he became Ilkhan and one of the greatest landlords of the region. His paramountcy did not last long. Like so many chiefs, in 1926 Abbas was detained in Tehran where he remained until autumn 1941 when he was able to return to Kirmanshah. During his absence a military officer had administered the Kalhur, alongside Ali Agha Azami, a Kalhur appointed by Reza Shah to nominal chiefship.

Abbas effected his release from Tehran to Kirmanshah by offering to help restore government authority, tribal loyalty and collect in firearms. In return he hoped he would be reinstated formally as Kalhur paramount. In practice he had to lower his sights since he needed the co-operation of the rival Daudi branch (Sulayman's descendants). When Ali Agha Azami was murdered the following year, Abbas again protested his innocence. Although Ali Agha's son became *bakhshdar* of Gilan, Abbas was appointed *farmandar* (governor) of the more important Shahabad, and soon sought to place relatives in other suitable positions.

In 1943 Abbas, with British help[3], was elected one of Kirmanshah's four deputies to the Majlis, the national assembly. This gave him a vantage point from which to join the Majlis Tribal Commission, established to reinstate confiscated tribal lands.[4] One may be sure he felt no reticence in giving his own claims priority, since he was single-minded in recovering the land and power he had enjoyed before 1926. It also gave him the wherewithal to displace Kalhur rivals.

Abbas was not alone. During this period many chiefs worked assiduously to incorporate themselves into the institutional structure of the centralizing state, helping to place relatives in key local positions in order to achieve, if possible, a monopoly of local power. When, in 1945, a new prime minister[5] found himself short of assured support in the Majlis, Abbas offered his loyalty in return for the appointment of his brother, Khusrou, as governor of Shahabad, a post he himself had had to give up on becoming a Majlis deputy. This effectively gave him total control over the Kalhur and undisputed ascendancy over the upstart Azamis. Khusrou took advantage of the governor-general's first absence from Kirmanshah to take government troops into Azami villages 'to disarm the Kalhur'. By October Abbas was planning the appointment of his uncle Karim Khan Daudian (Sulayman's brother) as governor of Qasr-i Shirin, a coup which would have made effectively over half Kirmanshah province Abbas's fiefdom.

Tehran, however, began to take fright. With a new government in office, Khusrou was removed from Shahabad. When Mahabad (see below) declared itself an autonomous republic, Abbas organized a 'Union of the Western Tribes' ostensibly to help the government bring Mahabad to heel. But Tehran was impressed more by the power this gave Abbas, and ordered the union's immediate disbandment. Abbas was summmoned to Tehran and warned to curb his ambitions.

Similar things were happening further north. The three deputies elected for Sanandaj were all major landlords, ambitious for power and control.[6] In the land between Mahabad and Bukan, Ali Agha (Amir Asad), the unpopular leader of the Dihbukri, also sought to ingratiate himself with the authorities. He, like Abbas Qabudian, offered to raise a mounted force to maintain tranquillity in the area, and to act as envoy for Tehran's peace parleys with Hama Rashid. He returned as governor of Mahabad, with authority to raise 300 levies. But he lacked the skill or the allies to exploit his position. Hama Rashid angrily threatened to singe his whiskers.[7] Meanwhile Ali Agha's failure to share Tehran's subvention equitably caused jealousy with his estranged brothers and with leaders of the Mamash and Mangur, who soon combined to eject him from Mahabad.

It comes as no surprise that alongside their jealous rivalry and their bitterness towards Tehran, the chiefs exploited and oppressed their own tribes almost as much as government had done. Returning chiefs had to extort the appurtenances of power either from their own tribesmen or plunder it from neighbouring ones. Only village headmen, the *kadkhudas*, were – in the view of one British political officer – worth retaining, for the simple reason that, unlike the chiefs with their armed retinues, the *kadkhudas* were directly answerable to their villagers. In a perfect world, he thought, what the villagers and tribesmen needed were local government officials well versed in the fields of agriculture, hygiene, revenue and education.[8] It was, of course, dreaming the impossible. The chiefs were still a fact of life, with their own political agenda to be played within the tribe, within the wider context of town and countryside and between the external powers, Tehran, the Soviet Union and the British.

It was inevitable that in the Soviet zone, or more particularly on its fringes, Kurdish leaders weighed up carefully the balance of benefit between the Soviet administration and Tehran. When Ali Agha Dihbukri, for example, affirmed his loyalty to Tehran, his estranged brothers sought the patronage of the Soviets. Others deliberately sought recognition with both. While Qazi Muhammad, the acknowledged principal in Mahabad, sought Soviet support for his nationalist purpose, his brother Sadr Qazi stood for and was elected as deputy for Mahabad in the Iranian Majlis. The Qazi brothers were no strangers to political poker. Their father, Qazi Ali, had had to negotiate with Simqu.

Like some tribal chiefs, Qazi Muhammad had seen the Allied intervention in Iran as a chance to achieve a measure of autonomy for Kurdistan. Like them he had at first approached the British in September 1941, hoping for protectorate status for a united Kurdistan. It was in the belief that the British were planning another meeting with Kurdish leaders, that Soviet officials suddenly invited and sent thirty leading chiefs, including Qazi Muhammad, to Baku that November.[9]

The Soviets wanted the Kurds, particularly those just beyond the Soviet occupied zone, to look to the Soviets, not the British.

On their return, the excited delegates formed a Kurdish High Committee of Health and Safety as the nucleus for some kind of autonomous or independent entity. In Urumiya, the organization 'Liberation' may well also have derived the belief that it had been given *carte blanche* by the Soviet Union.

Two notables stand out for their efforts to build upon the Baku trip, Qazi Muhammad and Shaykh Abd Allah Gilani. Qazi Muhammad was the highly respected leading notable (and cleric) of Mahabad, the great nephew of Qazi Fattah who at the turn of the century had also attempted self-government for Mahabad. Abd Allah Gilani was a son of Shaykh Abd al Qadir and had come from Iraq to Margawar in 1941 after the Allied occupation. His influence spread far and wide because of his standing as the most saintly Naqshbandi shaykh in the region.

Together they sought to persuade the chiefs in the Mahabad–Urumiya region to set aside their old feuds, to control their unruly followers and to unite in 'spiritual harmony'.[10] But it was frustrating work, for some chiefs refused to set aside longstanding enmities. Qazi Muhammad found himself relying on two friends, Haji Qara Ayni of the Mamash, and Abdallah Bayazidi of the Mangur, both of whom had to deal with opponent sections within their respective tribes.

Worse yet, the Soviet Union seemed to blow cold on Kurdish ambitions. A second trip to Baku was arranged in May 1942, when Kurdish delegates were told that the Soviet Union supported self-determination for minorities, but that the time was not yet ripe for Kurdish independence. In September a meeting of Mahabad and Urumiya chiefs was held in Ushnaviya with the aim of forging their unity and electing a leader. Shaykh Abdallah and Qazi Muhammad wanted that leader to be Haji Qara Ayni Mamash, ostensibly because of his acknowledged seniority as *amir al asha'ir*, but more practically because he was close to Mahabad and a committed ally of Qazi Muhammad's. However, Soviet officials present at the meeting engineered the election of Amr Khan of the Kardar Shikak as their leader. They also repeated the view that it was premature to think of autonomy.

Qazi Muhammad and Shaykh Abd Allah were clearly frustrated that their own nominee was passed over and accused Soviet officials of convening the meeting only to render it ineffective. In fact Qazi Muhammad probably convened the meeting himself, inviting Soviet attendance to endorse nationalist decisions. The Soviet Union, realizing it was likely to lose control of the Kurdish movement, decided to spike the meeting, forcing those present to accept a leader, Amr Khan Shikak, who was pliable and who lived within the Russian-occupied sector.

Komala and the New Nationalists

It was easy to construe events as reflecting the endemic and characteristic disorders of Kurdistan. But there was something new in the wind, itself a commentary on the fact that Kurdish society, like neighbouring societies, was in a phase of accelerating transition at the time of the Second World War. An increasing number of tribesmen were settling down to a sedentary existence, partly because of Reza Shah's repression but also because economic changes since the late nineteenth century were leading to a rapid decline in nomadism.

Tribal chiefs had become an increasingly important component in urban politics not merely by the traditional means, the threat of tribal mayhem and the exercise of landlord interests and power, but also because they recognized that with centralization their own interests could only be satisfactorily protected by incorporation into the provincial state system and economy. Abbas Qabudian of the Kalhur exemplified that changing function. Along with the process of in-corporation, the chiefs were also acquiring a taste for city life. Indeed, the towns of Kurdistan were becoming cockpits of competition between the aghas. In Kirmanshah, for example, the British political adviser described the presence of so many tribal chiefs as 'too many and too large fish for so small a pond'.[11]

Towns themselves were growing and with them a newly educated urban class. This was distinct from the older educated notable class which had led the movement in Istanbul a generation earlier. Take, for example, a man destined to play a leading role in the nationalist movement in Mahabad, Abd al Rahman Zabihi. He came from a family of petty traders inhabiting a one-room dwelling. He had dropped out of secondary school at the age of 15 or so, and earned a modest living tutoring the sons of local landlord or agha families.

Zabihi was one of 15 townspeople who met in a private home in Mahabad in September 1942 to organize a political party that would realize their dream of an independent Kurdish state. Their professional composition reflected the changes taking place, for example a junior civil servant, a primary school teacher, a trader, and a policeman.[12] Not one belonged to the notable class, and they seem to have been motivated solely by ethnic nationalism. They founded Komala-i Jiyanawi Kurdistan (The Committee for the Revival of Kurdistan) popularly known as JK Society, and Zabihi was appointed party secretary. Present also at this inaugural meeting was an Iraqi army officer, Captain Mir Hajj, representing Hiwa (Hope) one of several shadowy Iraqi Kurdish nationalist groups based on Sulaymaniya and Kirkuk (see p. 289) From the outset these new urban nationalists in Mahabad and in places like Kirkuk and Sulaymaniya welcomed cross-border links. Zabihi was one of the liaison officers between Irani and Iraqi Kurds.

Komala was organized in cells. Within six months it had 100 members. In April 1943 its first central committee was elected and began to send emissaries as far as the Soviet border in the north and almost to Sanandaj in the south, the extremity of Mahabad's orbit of influence. In 1944 they were making contact with the Kurdish movement in Turkey as well as Iraq. In August 1944 delegates of the three countries met on Mount Dalanpur, where the three borders intersect, to pledge mutual support and a sharing of resources. By this time the movement was attracting interest among young men even among the tribes.

Did Komala seek Kurdish independence? It is difficult to be sure. A Komala memorandum dated November 1944 sought language rights (in education and administration) but was willing to leave the issue of political status for a post-war peace conference.[13] Perhaps the more significant feature of Komala was its social outlook. Two publications by Komala (or 'JK Society', as it called itself) throw valuable light on a debate scarcely noticed outside educated nationalist circles. In July 1943 the first number of its magazine *Nishtman* (Fatherland), printed in Tabriz, attacked the agha class head on:

> You, the aghas and leaders of Kurdish tribes, think for yourselves and judge why the enemy gives you so much money ... they give it because they know it will become capital to delay the liberation of the Kurds and hope that in a few years this capital will create intrigues detrimental to the Kurds.[14]

Nishtman urged their reform. Zabihi may well have been the author of this piece.[15] As tutor to children of the notable class, he had had the opportunity to see the socially divisive implications of tribal politics at first hand. In any case, tribal disorder must have been freshly in his mind. In April that year two damaging inter-tribal conflicts had taken place which undermined efforts for the unity of Mahabad tribes.[16]

Then there was the equally vexed question of the tariqa shaykhs and mullas, arguably an even greater obstacle to progress. Mulla Muhammad, a progressive reformer of Koi-Sanjaq,[17] had recently bitterly attacked them:

> The mullas are traitors, they praise the shaykhs but do not tell people the truth about God and their religion.... As long as shaykhs and mullas remain in Kurdistan, there is no hope of a new life. All of them are Sufis with beards and beads, thick necks and big bellies.... How can they, with their begging bowls and poverty, be expected to push forward the Kurdish cause or serve in a Kurdish state?[18]

Komala soft-pedalled its response in its '*JK Society*' booklet which appeared at the same time:

> It is a great mistake and falsehood to say that [all] the shaykhs and mullas have hindered the Kurds from progressing ... the shaykhs and mullas criticized by Mulla Muhammad of Koi are quacks who claim to perform miracles and believe in superstitions.... These people along with tribal chiefs bear the full responsibility for backwardness, differences and strife among the Kurds.[19]

Komala was probably anxious not to alienate Qazi Muhammad, the unquestioned leader in Mahabad, and his associate, the Naqshbandi Shaykh Abd Allah Gilani.[20]

Finally both publications had emblazoned on their covers 'Long live the President, the Kurds, Kurdistan and Hope', a toast to the efforts of Hiwa and its president, Rafiq Hilmi, in Iraq. There was something for the Soviets too. The editor had added a footnote, possibly either suggested by Soviet officials in Tabriz or included to flatter them, which drew attention to the Red Flag under which 'the [Soviet] people rose and expelled their khans and beys and thus achieved unity, peace and strength.'[21]

By early 1945 most aghas around Mahabad were attracted to Komala in spite of its class rhetoric, presumably because it symbolized independence from central government.[22] This did not imply solid support. The chiefs were notorious for their mercurial politics.[23] Some were motivated by the fact that Mahabad was about the most orderly part of western Azarbaijan, thanks to the local militia force organized by Qazi Muhammad. Others feared the economic penalties that would come with government control. They had had their fill of corrupt and lazy officials and with the food shortages this incompetence led to. They had already faced acute wheat shortages in 1942. Rather than sell grain to a government procurement agency that might never pay, it was preferable to sell to local or Iraqi merchants or smuggle produce into Turkey. But could they manage as an independent entity? Few of the aghas, apparently, thought so.[24]

However, Qazi Muhammad's membership of Komala had not been spontaneous. He had offered support some time in 1944. He knew its programme and of its contact with Hiwa. He was also candid with foreign diplomats. Not every Kurd desired independence but they all wanted better health and education services, better communications, a degree of autonomy and guarantees against a return to the brutality of the Reza Shah period. But it was only in April 1945 that Qazi Muhammad became formally admitted as Komala's new president. At the time of his first approach, Komala had demurred, uneasy at so powerful and authoritative a member. If he joined he would have to be leader, and Komala would rapidly find its internal ideological base shifting from a middle-class democracy to rule by notables, something it greatly feared. Yet his membership, as a respected public figure, was the inevitable outcome of Komala's progressive success.

Qazi Muhammad's admission to Komala also indicated Soviet manipulation. Until 1944 the Soviet Union had permitted the Kurds considerable leeway outside the control of Tehran in order to keep their good will, but had discouraged separatism. But as the end of the war came into sight in 1944, the Soviets began to encourage Azarbaijan, where the Iranian communist Tudeh party was particularly strong, and northern Kurdistan, with its well-known autonomist tendencies, to demand formal separation from Iran, as a prelude to seeking incorporation in the Soviet Union. The Kurds required little encouragement. As Ann Lambton wrote of her visit to Kurdistan in 1944 'the few Kurds I talked to ... all spoke of Kurdish independence with enthusiasm'.[25]

The Soviet Union had an ulterior motive in which both Azarbaijan and Kurdistan appear to have been bargaining chips. In 1944 it had put pressure on Iran for an oil concession. When Tehran resisted, the Soviets began to encourage the two separatist movements. This was easy to do since, although the Tudeh had not taken root in Kurdistan, Komala, as its publications indicated, looked to Soviet ideology for guidance. If Tehran refused to concede oil exploitation rights, northern Kurdistan would be a useful strategic adjunct to the more important province of Azarbaijan since it would secure the latter's south-western flank. It would also, of course, flank both Turkey and Iraq's eastern frontiers

The Soviet Union was able to expoit Komala's success. As it expanded, so its cell structure collapsed with its existence increasingly becoming public knowledge. What it needed was a party centre and this was provided by the Soviets in the form of the Kurdistan–Soviet Cultural Relations Society. In April 1945 Komala formally 'came out' at a public event at the new centre, where it staged a drama, *Daik-i Nishtiman* (Motherland), in which a woman (the Kurdish motherland) was violated by three ruffians (Iraq, Iran and Turkey) until a hand bearing a Hammer and Sickle came from behind a screen and unlocked her chains. 'Her veil fell and revealed on her bosom was a Red Flag bearing the words "Long Live Stalin, the Liberator of Small Nations."' In the words of Archie Roosevelt, who followed these events from the US Embassy in Tehran, 'The audience, unused to dramatic representations, was deeply moved, and blood feuds generations old were composed as life-long enemies fell weeping on each other's shoulders and swore to avenge Kurdistan.'[26]

However, the Soviet Union was anxious to gain some control over the independently-minded Komala and they succeeded in doing this by acclaiming Qazi Muhammad as president.[27] The Soviets moved quickly to strengthen Qazi Muhammad's position, leaning on the government in Tehran to appoint his cousin Sayf Qazi as the commander of the gendarmerie. They also began to arm the Kurds.

As the Kurdish administration acquired an increasing semblance of practical autonomy from Tehran, the Soviet Union strengthened its hold. In September 1945, Qazi Muhammad, Sayf Qazi and the leading chiefs were summoned to Tabriz to meet the Soviet consul who sent them straight to Baku, where they were received by the president of Soviet Azarbaijan. He explained how the Tudeh Party had been ineffective in Iranian Azarbaijan and was being replaced by the Democratic Party, and how in order to achieve their freedom the Kurds should do the same. Komala, he told them, was the creation and instrument of British imperialism. They were exhorted to form their own democratic party.

The Mahabad Republic

On his return Qazi Muhammad convened a meeting of notables to announce the formation of the Kurdish Democratic Party (KDPI).[28] This resulted in the dissolution of Komala and absorption of its membership into the new party. A manifesto signed by many leading Kurds demanded:

> why do they [the Iranian government] not let Kurdistan become an independent province administered by a Provincial Council, for which provision was made in the consitutional law.... We must fight for our rights.... It is for this sacred aim that the Kurdish Democratic Party has been established in Mahabad.... It is the party which will be able to secure its national independence within the borders of Persia.[29]

They listed among their aims: (i) autonomy for the Iranian Kurds within the Iranian state; (ii) the use of Kurdish as the medium of education and administration; (iii) the election of a provincial council for Kurdistan to supervise state and social matters; (iv) all state officials to be of local origin; (v) unity and fraternity with the Azarbaijani people; (vi) the establishment of a single law for both peasants and notables.

It is the last objective which is the most interesting, for it was clearly reformist in character and indicated that regardless of what the law actually said, the legal status of peasants and notables was significantly different. The KDPI intended to change that. The chiefs presumably dissociated themselves from such a distasteful objective but in any case were adept at protecting their interests. The KDPI failed to take any measures to reform land tenure.

Indeed, it is possible that, but for the fortuitous arrival of Mulla Mustafa and Shaykh Ahmad Barzani with about 1,000 fighters and their families, the aims of the KDPI would have been quickly thwarted. These two leaders entered Iran near Ushnaviya in October 1945 as fugitives from the Iraqi army, following the failure of their rebellion (see p. 290). Soon after his arrival the Soviet Union instructed Mulla Mustafa to place himself under Qazi Muhammad. It is unlikely that he was fully aware of the local political situation but, as a fugitive, he was dependent upon Soviet goodwill and local Kurdish hospitality. Local Kurds were ordered to feed and house his destitute forces.

Towards the end of the year Tehran lost control of Azarbaijan as armed members of the Azarbaijan Democrat Party drove Iranian forces into the safety of their barracks. On 10 December the garrison of Tabriz surrendered to the Democrat forces, and the 'Azarbaijan People's Government' assumed authority in all eastern Azarbaijan. Now Qazi Muhammad decided to declare the independence of western Azarbaijan. On 15 December a small ceremony in Mahabad marked the foundation of the Kurdish People's Government. A national parliament of only 13 members was formed and on 22 January 1946 Qazi Muhammad proclaimed the establishment of the Kurdish republic, a miniscule territory which incorporated the market towns of Mahabad, Bukan, Naqada and Ushnaviya. Beyond it were certain lands whose chiefs, even the Jalalis in the far north, acknowledged the Republic. Qazi Muhammad himself formally became President of the Mahabad Republic. His cousin Sayf Qazi was appointed Minister of War, something of a promotion from his rank of local gendarmerie commander, while the Prime Minister was Haji Baba Shaykh, one of the Sayyids of Zanbil, near Bukan, a popular choice. Virtually all the founder members of Komala were included in the administration, but the weight of power had now shifted decisively in favour of the established families of Kurdistan.

Besides Mulla Mustafa, three local chiefs were appointed marshalls of the Mahabad forces, Sayf Qazi (ex officio), Amr Khan Sharafi Shikak, for whom discretion had always been the better part of valour, and Hama Rashid, recently returned from Iraq and as volatile as ever. Ziro Beg Harki, with a similarly notorious reputation, was appointed colonel. Mulla Mustafa was sent off to earn his keep by attacking the garrisons of Saqqiz, Bana and Sardasht, each of which was already isolated by heavy winter snow.

In Mahabad itself schools began to teach in Kurdish, translating Persian textbooks into the mother tongue. Thanks to the Soviet provision of a printing press, a daily newspaper and a monthly journal, both entitled *Kurdistan*, and certain literary magazines, for example, *Hiwa-i Nishtiman*, *Giru Gali* and *Mindilan-i Kurd*, appeared.

Yet from the outset, the Mahabad Republic was flawed by the absence of cohesion. The Barzanis were by no means universally welcomed. The very fact that they provided the Republic with its most credible fighting force disturbed the world of tribal politics. Within the Kurdish leadership, too, there were serious tensions. For example, Shaykh Abd Allah, Qazi Muhammad's only potential challenger, was denounced by Ziro Beg Harki at the inaugural republican festivities in Mahabad, not only for his half-hearted attitude but also for his pro-British sympathies.[30]

Although the majority of tribal chiefs had attended the festivities in Mahabad, many of them harboured misgivings about the venture, some because they saw the Republic as a puppet state of the Soviet Union, others because they did not wish to burn their boats with Tehran. Indeed, some of the Dihbukri chiefs who found it difficult to swallow Qazi Muhammad's leadership were shortly in touch with General Humayuni commanding Iranian forces on the southern flank of the republic. By April Hama Rashid, albeit a marshall of the Mahabad Republic, was offering to defect if Tehran would kindly reinstate him as *bakhshdar* of Bana.

It was not long, either, before tensions developed with the Democratic Party of Azarbaijan which did not like the idea of Mahabad being independent of its authority. There had already been trouble over the Tudeh Party's recruitment of peasants and Kurdish tribals in Urumiya district. No sooner had the Kurdish republic been declared, than Qazi Muhammad was summoned to Tabriz to be told he could only form a local government under Democrat guidance. It was only the Soviet support he enjoyed which persuaded the Azarbaijanis to tolerate a Kurdish administration independent of Tabriz. Then there was the question of control of Urumiya and Miandoab districts, largely on account of their mixed populations; in Urumiya, the Shikak and other Kurdish tribes in the hills had scant regard for the Azarbaijani administration in town.

In April 1946 Qazi Muhammad returned to Tabriz at the behest of the Soviets to resolve the differences between Kurds and Azaris so as to present a united front against Tehran. These talks culminated in a treaty on 23 April. In order to meet the frictions in Urumiya and Miandoab districts, this allowed for the appointment of Kurdish or Azari officials and full cultural encouragement in those parts of the respective administrations where these communities formed a minority. But the treaty also smacked of complete independence from Tehran, allowing for the exchange of representatives between the administrations; the formation of a joint economic commission; mutual military assistance; and negotiations with Tehran to be in 'the joint interest' of the two administrations. In a fit of amnesia regarding long years of mutual dislike, both signatory nations undertook to punish any individual or group seeking to destroy the 'historic friendship and democratic brotherhood of the Azarbaijanis and the Kurds'.[31]

Standing together had now become much more important. Those chiefs who had harboured suspicions of Soviet motives had seemed well justified. By the Anglo-Soviet-Iranian Treaty Alliance of January 1942 the two occupying powers had undertaken to withdraw from Iran six months after the end of hostilities between the Axis and Allied powers. In theory this meant a Soviet evacuation by 2 March 1946, in practice they looked likely to stay. On 4 and 9 March respectively Britain and the United States expressed grave concern. On 26 March Andrei Gromyko promised all Soviet troops would be out of Iran within six weeks and this timetable was adhered to, but only after Tehran had agreed to form a joint Soviet-Iranian oil company, subject to ratification by the Majlis. The agreement went on to recognize that 'since it is an internal affair, peaceful arrangements will be made between the Government and the people of Azarbaijan.'[32]

While this allayed Iranian and Western concern of permanent Soviet occupation, it precipitated fears in Tabriz and Mahabad that they would no longer enjoy protection against a vengeful government in Tehran. They were well aware of the furore caused by their apparent secession. Mahabad, in particular, had cause for concern because it was only recognized as part of Azarbaijan.

By the end of April the government in Tabriz decided an agreement with Tehran was imperative, and finally reached one in mid-June. By its terms all Azarbaijan, including the Kurdish areas, formally reverted to Iranian sovereignty, and its government ministers were re-appointed as administrators of the revived province of Azarbaijan. Thus the Azarbaijanis legalized their position and avoided Iranian reprisals, but left Mahabad isolated as a rebel enclave *within* the province of Azarbaijan, in disregard of their agreement with the Kurdish Republic.

In the meantime Iranian and Mulla Mustafa's forces eyed each other warily on the edge of Saqqiz. Soviet officials bribed Amr Khan to take the Shikak and the Harki south to support Barzani's forces. In Mahabad it was hoped that with the build-up of tribal forces (with a putative strength of 13,000 troops), it might launch an offensive against Saqqiz and even Sanandaj, since government forces were only 5,000 strong and insufficient to take the offensive.

At the end of May a series of skirmishes took place in which Barzani's men distinguished themselves for their steadiness under fire and Amr Khan's men for their timidity. Kurdish prisoners captured by Barzani's men were pressed into Mahabad's forces. But with the news of the Tabriz–Tehran agreement, the Soviet Union warned Mahabad to abandon its offensive on Sanandaj and to open negotiations with Tehran. As tribesmen withdrew northwards, so Mahabad's army dwindled.

In Mahabad itself the uneasy alliance between townspeople and tribesmen quickly crumbled, with the Soviet Union clearly favouring the latter. The social divide between tribesman and urban dweller may not have been as great as that between Kurd and Azari, with all its religious, linguistic, as well as ethnic resonances, but it was still a fundamental fact of life.

Qazi Muhammad himself went to Tehran in August to negotiate for a new autonomous Kurdish province stretching from the Soviet border to a point midway between Sanandaj and Kirmanshah, in short the whole of Sunni Kurdistan, including those parts in the province of Azarbaijan or under direct government control. He had grounds for optimism. Prime Minister Qavam was a moderate who had sought to steer a middle path between the authoritarian establishment (the Shah, the army and the tribes) and the democratic movement. By August Qavam had begun to align himself with the Left, arresting those personalities most symbolic of reaction, including Abbas Qabudian. It seems that he agreed to the creation of a semi-autonomous Kurdish province, possibly of the size Qazi Muhammad demanded but under a governor-general appointed by Tehran. He envisaged an electoral alliance for the 15th Majlis not only with the Tudeh but also with the Azarbaijan and Kurdistan Democratic Parties. From his point of view it was important to keep the Left together. So he apparently insisted that his proposal must be acceptable to the governor of Azarbaijan, which predictably it was not. In October, however, Qavam's administration came under intense pressure as a result of widespread anti-Leftist tribal disorders and army unrest instigated by the shah. In an attempt to save his administration Qavam rapidly dissociated himself from the democratic parties. With the dramatic change of mood in Tehran, Qazi Muhammad and his colleagues trimmed their sails, abandoning such nomenclature as 'president' and 'minister' in favour 'party leader', or 'chief of finance', and so forth. It was a conciliatory gesture, but an inadequate one.

In the meantime, tribal support for Qazi Muhammad was dwindling. The tribes had supported him only because he held the key to economic as well as military assistance. It was inevitable that the tribes should begin to abandon Mahabad from the moment the Tabriz–Tehran deal was broadcast. They had their situation to consider. The mainstay crop produced in tribal areas was tobacco, but without access to their market elsewhere in Iran they began to experience serious hardship, in spite of Soviet arrangements to exchange the tobacco and wheat crops for sugar and cotton.

Acrimony increased. There was growing resentment among the tribes that they had to share their dwindling resources with the powerful (but destitute) Barzanis. As for the Barzanis, it was rumoured that Mulla Mustafa harboured ambitions of ousting Qazi Muhammad, since only his forces had fought credibly for the Republic. Disputes broke out between certain chiefs of the Mamash and Mangur and Qazi Muhammad. To support the latter the Soviet Union despatched Mulla Mustafa to chase the former into Iraq.

Qazi Muhammad still had trouble with the Dihbukri and having failed by diplomacy, marched the Shikak and Harki under Amr Khan towards Bukan to compel Dihbukri acquiescence. It was Amr Khan's last duty to Mahabad. By the end of September, representing not only the Kardar Shakak but also a clutch of other tribes, Amr Khan asked the US Consulate in Tabriz to inform Tehran of his allegiance, asking merely for an assurance of fair treatment. Only the Gawrik of Mahabad, the Fayzallah Begi and a section of the Zarza remained loyal to Qazi Muhammad.

The chiefs were aware of the broader picture in Iran. During October most of them had sympathized with the tribal unrest against Qavam's administration. They, too, felt distrustful of the Tudeh and the Left. They knew, as they had done in 1906, that their interests generally lay with the authoritarian Right. When Qavam reluctantly authorized the military re-occupation of Azarbaijan and Kurdistan on 10 December most chiefs were already clear in their own minds whose side they were on.

Five days earlier, Qazi Muhammad's now isolated war council had pledged armed resistance against the Iranian army. Why it did so remains a mystery. It is possible that it still believed the Soviet Union might intervene to protect them. But within the week the Shikak and Harki were taking part in the government's recapture of the countryside around Urumiya and Tabriz. On 13 December Iranian troops re-entered Tabriz. The following day the first group of tribal chiefs and notables drove north to Miandoab to make their submission. Among them was Sadr Qazi who, as a deputy in the Tehran Majlis, had acted before as go between for his brother. Now he told General Humayuni that Mahabad was ready to receive government forces peacefully. Humayuni sent forward tribal allies, the very men of the Dihbukri, Mamash and Mangur who had opposed Qazi Muhammad previously. However, fearing that they might loot the town, and at Qazi Muhammad's request, he also sent regular troops to secure Mahabad on 15 December.

The Republic of Mahabad had lasted not quite a year. Government forces were quick to close down the Kurdish printing press, ban the teaching of Kurdish and burn all the books they could find in Kurdish.

On 31 March Qazi Muhammad, his brother and his cousin were hanged in the town square. It was a vindictive act, particularly on Sadr Qazi who had spent the year in Tehran, except when sent by the government as an envoy to his brother. Furthermore, their act of rebellion had been an orderly and largely non-violent one. But for a few skirmishes in the summer and his ill-judged declaration of armed resistance on 5 December, Qazi Muhammad had made it perfectly clear that he wanted a negotiated settlement and was willing to visit Tehran in order to achieve this. Nothing he had done compared with the criminality of, say, Hama Rashid.

However, Tehran recognized that the very orderliness of the Mahabad Republic and the new Kurdish nationalism were infinitely more dangerous to its authority

than tribal rebellion. The Qazi trio perished because they personified the nationalist ideal. Other members of the Republic's administration were executed a
week later in April. Apart from executions among the Gawrik and Fayzallah
Begi, most of the tribal chiefs got off scot free, for in early February Muhammad
Reza Shah had issued a general amnesty.[33]

Tehran offered Mulla Mustafa the choice between returning to Iraq, or being
disarmed and resettled near Varamin. Shaykh Ahmad returned to Iraq with the
Barzani families and some of the fighting men. But neither option was acceptable to Mulla Mustafa or his followers and he decided to fight his way out. He
demonstrated his superlative tactical skills and captured the imagination of Kurds
everywhere by his epic march through the border marches of Iran, Iraq and
Turkey. At the climax of this epic, his men covered 220 miles of highland in
fifteen days, hotly pursued by regular forces. Barzani dodged their attempted
encirclement, and finally crossed the Araxes river to the safety of the Soviet
Union on 15 June.[34] He had created the legend on which one day he would
make his come-back.

The idea that the Republic of Mahabad was the critical moment at which the
Kurds realized their freedom is arguably a rosy version of reality. Mahabad was
beset with overwhelming political, social and economic problems. It never had
a hope without serious Soviet support and the Republic's leaders knew in their
hearts that such support was not dependable. Furthermore, the ambiguity always
present in the Republic's posture between autonomy and independence[35] made
it virtually inevitable that Tehran would, if it could, reassert its control militarily.
In that respect the Azarbaijanis played their hand with greater prescience.

From the moment that Komala was dissolved, nationalist cohesion fell victim
to the politics of the notables and tribal chiefs and to the social divisions, between
one tribal section and another, between tribal and urban Kurds, and between
urban notables and the lower middle class. Finally, the Republic was established
in conditions of economic bankruptcy and remained that way to the very end.
The economic future of Mahabad, or of a wider sweep of Kurdistan, could only
be assured in harmony with the Iranian hinterland. Inspirational though the
Republic was to Kurdish nationalists everywhere, its foundations were cruelly
flawed.

Sources

Official Great Britain, unpublished: Public Record Office: series FO 195/2589, FO 248 nos
1405, 1410; series FO 371 nos 7824, 17915, 27080, 27244, 27245, 31388, 31390, 31391,
31402, 34940, 35092, 35093, 40173, 40177, 40178, 45488, 45503, 52698, 52702, 61986; WO
106/5961

Secondary sources: Abrahamian, *Iran Between Two Revolutions*; Henri Binder, *Au Kurdistan, en
Mésopotamie et Perse* (Paris, 1887); W. Eagleton, *The Kurdish Republic of 1946* (London, 1963);
Fred Halliday, *Iran: Dictatorship and Development* (Harmondsworth, 1979); M.R. Ghods, *Iran*

in the Twentieth Century (Boulder and London, 1989); F. Koohi-Kemali Dehkordi, 'The Republic of Kurdistan: Its rise and fall' (M.Litt. diss., Oxford, 1986); Archie Roosevelt, 'The Kurdish Republic of Mahabad', *The Middle East Journal*, vol. i, no. 3 (July 1947), reprinted in Chaliand, *People without a Country*; Sharifi, *Al Jamiyat wa'l Manzimat.*

Notes

1. FO 248/1405 Military Attaché, memorandum, Tehran, 3 December 1941.

2. FO 248/1410 Urquhart to Bullard, Tabriz, 22 October 1942. Hama Rashid apparently lost more of his men quarrelling over government rifles than in battle against the army.

3. To assure his election the British arrested Karim Sanjabi, the Iran Party candidate in southern Kurdistan. Born in 1904 Karim Sanjabi had been exiled in 1918 to Tehran from the arena of tribal politics in Kirmanshah. From there he had been educated in Paris, where he had imbibed leftist ideas and returned to Tehran as a radical law professor. The Iran Party, led by Musaddiq, was nationalist and deeply hostile to British interference. Another Iran Party candidate, Dr Abdul Hamid Zangana, obtained a seat mainly because his father was the Zangana chief.

4. In June 1942 the Majlis had passed an act to restore Reza Shah's land expropriations to their previous owners.

5. This was octogenarian Muhsin Sadr, whose premiership lasted only a few months in the summer and autumn 1945.

6. Farjallah Asaf came from a notorious landed merchant family in Sanandaj. He had been responsible for grain hoarding while the people of Sanandaj starved in 1916. After the war Asaf had schemed through his supporters and through those in debt to him, to place his henchmen at the top of the local security forces, judiciary and religious establishment. The other two deputies, Salar Said Sanandaji and Nasir Quli Ardalan, were both scions of notable families.

7. The removal of beard or moustache is a ritual humiliation of manhood that can easily precipitate a blood feud.

8. FO 371/40177 Fletcher, 'Note on Tribal Policy in Kurdistan and Kirmanshah', December 1943.

9. Those who went to Baku included Haji Baba Shaykh, Majid Khan (Miandoab), Ali Agha Dehbokri and his son Umar Aliar (Bukan), four Harki chiefs including the volatile chief Ziro, two Shikak chiefs but not the paramount Amr Khan who pleaded he was 'unwell', Zarza, Piran, Gawrik, Mangur and Mamash chiefs, and also Shaykh Taha's son, Muhammad Sadiq (popularly known as Shaykh Pusho).

10. FO 248/1410 Cook to Bullard, Tabriz, 8 April 1942.

11. FO 371/35092 Kirmanshah Consulate Diary, December 1943.

12. Kutschera, *Le Mouvement National Kurde*, p. 164.

13. FO 371/40178 Tabriz Consulate Diary, no. 20, 30 November 1944.

14. FO 371/34940 Combined Intelligence Centre for Iraq and Persia, Report No. 138, 4 October 1943.

15. We know he was a principal contributor, and helped with the publication of *Nishtman*, FO 371/40177 Tabriz Consulate Diary, 15 June 1944.

16. These were between the Piran and the Mangur, in which the rival sections of the Mamash had taken opposite sides, and another conflict between Majid Khan of Miandoab and Ali Agha, Amir Asad, Dihbukri.

17. Mulla Muhammad was well known for his radical views. He had sent his daughter to the secular school in Koi as soon as it had been established. She later married Umar Mustafa, a KDP activist.

18. FO 371/34940 Combined Intelligence Centre for Iraq and Persia [CICIP], No. 138, 4 October 1943.

19. FO 371/34940 CICIP No. 138, 4 October 1943.

20. In 1942 the Soviet Union had favoured Shaykh Abd Allah as leader of the Kurds on account of his popularity but had then been misinformed that he was a British agent. Abd Allah Gilani was aware of and apparently favoured Komala but he seems to have eschewed prominence.

21. FO 371/34940 CICIP, No. 138, 4 October 1943.

22. For early adherents, see Eagleton, *The Kurdish Republic*, p. 35. But one should be cautious. Some chiefs complained in Tabriz that their men were being weaned to the nationalist cause, FO 371/45503 Wall to Bullard, Tabriz, 7 May 1945.

23. For example, the Ilkhanzada Dihbukri aghas had been among the first to support Komala, but abandoned it once Qazi Muhammad became its leader.

24. FO 371/40178 Tabriz Consulate Diary, no. 20, 30 November 1944.

25. FO 371/40173 A.K.S. Lambton, 'Kurdish–Russian Relations', Tehran, 13 September 1944.

26. Roosevelt, 'The Kurdish Republic', p. 139.

27. The Soviet first choice had not been Qazi Muhammad but the three leading chiefs of the region, Ali Agha (Amir Asad) Dihbokri, recently invested in Tehran as local chief of gendarmerie, Amr Khan Sharafi of the Shikak, and Qara Ayni Agha Mamash, none of whom fancied the political dangers of leading the nationalist movement, Roosevelt, 'The Kurdish Republic', p. 139.

28. The acronym KDPI (Iran) is used to distinguish it from the subsequent KDP in Iraq.

29. FO 371/45436 file 73400, Declaration of 8 November 1945.

30. His son, Abd al Aziz, who had joined the Republic from Iraq was promptly despatched to the Soviet Union 'for further training', in reality as a hostage for Shaykh Abd Allah's good behaviour.

31. Roosevelt, 'The Kurdish Republic', p. 143.

32. *New York Times*, 6 April 1946, quoted in Eagleton, *The Kurdish Republic*, p. 73.

33. The KDPI claimed up to 15,000 were killed, but this figure should be treated with caution, Halliday, *Iran*, p. 221.

34. For an account of Barzani's stirring exploits, see Eagleton, *The Kurdish Republic*, pp. 116–126, or trace in FO 371/61986.

35. In September 1946 the British Consul in Tabriz reported that Qazi Muhammad had virtually admitted that the claim to autonomy was a blind, and it was independence he was really after; FO 371/52702 Wall to Le Rougetel, Tabriz, 11 September 1946.

CHAPTER 12

IRAN: CREATING
A NATIONAL MOVEMENT

Introduction

Following state suppression of the movement in 1947 Kurdish nationalists led a twilight existence, unable to offer any serious threat to the state. The KDPI posed no serious threat except as the physical expression of an ethnic ideal that a growing number of Kurds seriously began to cherish only a full 20 years after the collapse of Mahabad. They did so less in response to political ideas propagated by the KDPI than because of changed circumstances of life. It was socioeconomic change in the 1960s and 1970s, agrarian reform, improved communications, worker migration and population growth which not only destroyed the tribal system but created the conditions in which ethnicity became the central cohesive identity for Iran's Kurds. However, this only found open expression with the demise of the Pahlavis in 1979.

The Locust Years, 1947–78

Following the collapse of the Mahabad Republic the KDPI in Iran effectively ceased to exist. A handful of Kurds who had some connection with the short-lived republic continued to meet and dream. Significantly these were intellectuals and members of the petty bourgeoisie, men who were civil servants, merchants, teachers and the like, notably Aziz Yusufi, Ghani Bulurian and Abd al Rahman Sultanian, the last two close relatives of senior members of the Mahabad administration.[1] The notables who had dominated the Republic all went to ground.

This KDPI rump was ideologically close to the Marxist Tudeh Party but remained distinct from it. This may partly have been because until March 1947 the KDPI had been run by notables while the Tudeh, founded in September 1941, was overwhelmingly dominated by young urban intellectuals. However, the Tudeh's influence was undeniable. It had inherited a modest following created by the Communist Party (before its suppression) in the mid-1920s, and its special regard for minorities.[2] One or two members of the KDPI belonged to a short lived Tudeh affiliate, the Kurdish Communist Committee. The Tudeh had a strong and active following among the Assyrian population of Urumiya region, townspeople with whom, unlike the notable class, young Kurdish intellectuals were happy to associate. It gave moral and ideological succour when the survivors of the Republic most needed it. Those Kurds interested in socialism, however, tended to stay with the KDPI. When Tudeh members were arrested in their hundreds in the early 1950s, barely 3 per cent were Kurdish.

There was little the KDPI rump could at first do. As yet it had neither a belief in, nor the means for, armed struggle. Instead it began to distribute a few clandestine publications around Mahabad in 1948, but not for long. Aziz Yusifi was arrested that year and only released in 1952.

At this time the political atmosphere in Iran was beginning to change. At the end of 1947 the pro-monarchist National Unionists, holding the balance of power in the Majlis, had brought about the resignation of Prime Minister Qavam. From now on Muhammad Reza Shah began to intervene in public affairs, something he could more easily do with the National Unionists holding the balance of power in the Majlis and with a rapidly growing army loyal to him. In February 1949 an abortive assassination attempt gave him the pretext to move against the democratic development of the country. He declared martial law, closed down hostile newspapers, outlawed the Tudeh and convened a Constituent Assembly which agreed to the creation of a Senate, half of whose members would be the Shah's appointees, and to new powers for the Shah allowing him to dissolve the Majlis at will. In a further profoundly unpopular move in the countryside, the extensive estates acquired by Reza Shah and made over to the state in 1941 were now surrendered to Muhammad Reza.

Inevitably Muhammad Reza's encroaching dictatorship invited opposition. In 1950 General Razmara, a man of leftist sympathies, was appointed prime minister.[3] It is possible he might have satisfied Kurdish aspirations in part, for he intended to introduce administrative decentralization. However he was assassinated by a Muslim *fida'i* in early 1951.

Razmara was replaced in May by Dr Muhammad Musaddiq, specifically on the issue of carrying through the proposed oil nationalization law. Musaddiq was a populist radical who appealed to the public when he encountered resistance in the Majlis or the court. He surrounded himself with educated radicals, some of whom, like Karim Sanjabi and Abd al Hamid Zangana,[4] were from the highest echelons of society. Like Razmara, Musaddiq wanted a liberal democracy but he was also a confirmed centralist. Thus, while he created the atmosphere in which democratic groups, most notably the Tudeh, could flourish, he would probably have ridden roughshod over Kurdish or other appeals for decentralization. His administration was a tumultuous one, which reached a climax in summer 1953 when it looked as if he would succeed in definitively reducing the Shah to no more than a constitutional monarch and perhaps even remove him in favour of a republic. In August, however, an American-inspired *coup d'état* was carried out by the army and the Shah reinstated with wide powers.

During this period the KDPI could breathe more freely. In 1951 it recruited members to create a popular following. In Mahabad it enjoyed widespread sympathy because of the bitterness felt among ordinary townsfolk over what had happened in 1947, particularly the execution of Qazi Muhammad, who had acquired the aura of a martyred saint. The Shah was widely loathed, not least because he had vindictively decided not to appoint another senior Sunni cleric to replace Qazi Muhammad in Mahabad. So in the January 1952 elections for the Seventeenth Majlis, Mahabad ignored police intimidation and overwhelmingly voted for a candidate of known KDPI membership. As a result the poll was declared invalid, and a Tehrani cleric appointed representative of a constituency he had never seen. It was not surprising therefore that Mahabad remained passionately hostile to the Shah and everything he stood for. On 13 August 1953, less than a week before his own downfall, Musaddiq had held a national referendum to limit the powers of the Shah. In Mahabad only two voters out of 5,000 supported the monarchy.

Once back in power, the Shah began to expunge all traces of the democratic movement. Between 1953 and 1958 3,000 Tudeh members were rounded up. The KDPI went to ground, operating as two separate committees in Mahabad and in Sanandaj.[5] During 1954 these two committees fused at a party conference at a secret location outside Mahabad. Here the KDPI forged its priorities: the overthrow of the monarchy, the creation of a Kurdish entity with its own elected government, the liberation of *all* Kurdistan and the enfranchisement of women. It also recorded its dissatisfaction concerning the current regime in Kurdistan, specifically that all education was in Persian, that all senior officials were appointed from Tehran and that Kurdistan was effectively run under martial law.

In May that year Ghani Bulurian plucked up courage to publish the first edition of *Kurdistan* since the collapse of the Mahabad Republic, distributing it in Mahabad, Saqqiz and Sanandaj. This paper reflected an essentially socialist line while treating Kurdistan as a separate entity. It was this separatism which so upset the Tudeh Party and other Iranian leftists and was destined to keep KDPI in constant tension with its natural Iranian allies. *Kurdistan* did not last long. Police found the secret printing press in Tabriz shortly after the fifth (September) number was issued. This had advocated an independent Kurdistan 'freed from the oppression of Iran, Turkey and Iran',[6] a sentiment less often heard from Iranian Kurds. About 150 were arrested, of whom 50 stood trial.

The regime was fearful that Kurdistan was a vulnerable gap in Iran's Cold War armour. It feared Soviet influence, in particular its Kurdish language radio broadcasts which had started in 1947, some of which hinted at a coming signal for revolt. It was sufficiently worried from the beginning of 1951 to arrange for its own broadcasts to counter Soviet ones. But it also feared other Soviet interventions in the border region. It was therefore an embarrassment for the Tehran government that in the harsh winter of 1949/50 Soviet relief reached starving peasants in Maku before it could itself react. It was disturbing, too, to learn that Soviet-trained religious clerics, some belonging to the tariqas, were being used for propaganda work in Kurdistan.

To his friends, the Shah's fears seemed valid. In the British view, the Jalali Kurds in the north would support any Soviet invasion of Azarbaijan. By mid-1954 the British reckoned that the Shikak and many of the tribesmen (but significantly not their chiefs) around Mahabad and Saqqiz were also under Soviet influence.

In the light of the regime's increasing ability to deal with them, it is easy retrospectively to be dismissive of troublesome tribes. But they were still a real worry to Tehran. The Dihbukri still had 3,000 fighting men, and an estimated 7,000 spare rifles. The Mamash and Mangur could still field 1,500 fighters each and they too, like all self-respecting tribes, had at least one spare rifle per fighting man.[7] Mahabad, where so many tribes converged and where the Kurdish national idea had been born, was naturally viewed in Tehran with suspicion and apprehension. The Iranian army still had a healthy respect for the damage an angry tribe could inflict, and it chose its targets cautiously.

It was with this in mind that in 1948 it began a running battle with the Jawanrudi, a formidable but small tribe, which had returned to its traditional independence of action since 1941. In September 1950 it overran the Jawanrudi stronghold with the assistance of the Jawanrudi's many local tribal enemies. Yet it was only in 1956 that a major offensive dealt with this tribe once and for all. It was easy for Kurdish nationalists to portray such an assault as one against the Kurdish people as a whole. It is more likely, however, that the government had identified the Jawanrudi as an easy target, something the formidable tribal confederations of the Bakhtiari and Qashqai clearly were not.

In 1958 the regime had cause again to be fearful of developments in Kurdistan. It was well aware of Kurdish recalcitrance and of the rebellious effect Cairo's Kurdish language anti-Hashimite broadcasts might have in Iranian Kurdistan also. By early July it was extremely apprehensive, and this seemed justified a week later when Qasim overthrew the Hashimite monarchy in Iraq and openly wooed the Kurdish people. The army was immediately deployed in Iranian Kurdistan to prevent demonstrations or, worse, a Soviet-orchestrated rising.

After his return as a hero to Iraqi Kurdistan in October 1958 Mulla Mustafa Barzani proposed the unification of the Kurdistan Democratic Party and Kurdistan Democratic Party of Iran under a single secretary-general, implicitly himself. But before any decision could be taken SAVAK, the Shah's newly created secret police, arrested 250 suspected KDPI activists, among them Aziz Yusifi and Ghani Bulurian, both central committee members.[8] Once again, the KDPI almost ceased to exist but for a handful of exiles in Iraq.

It was inevitable that KDPI survivors came directly under Mulla Mustafa's powerful influence. When Mulla Mustafa rebelled against Baghdad in 1961, the skeleton KDPI in Iran provided food, clothing and ammunition to assist his revolt. At an ideological level the KDPI also moved rapidly away from its leftist position under the direction of its new leader, Abd Allah Ishaqi (*alias* Ahmad Tawfiq). Ishaqi had been a founder member of the Mahabad committee and was now very close to Mulla Mustafa. As in Iraq, major tension grew between leftists and traditionalists. When Ishaqi convened the party's second congress near Qala Diza (just inside Iraq) in 1964, Mulla Mustafa helped prevent the attendance of undesirable delegates, just as he chased off his own troublesome leftists. The congress condemned Qazi Muhammad of treason and the progressives of 1954 of 'deviationism.'

The Barzani–Ishaqi alliance did not last. Mulla Mustafa agreed to restrain the KDPI's political activities as the price for the Shah's aid against Baghdad. He demanded that the KDPI suspend all activities hostile to Tehran, thus subordinating the struggle in Iran to that in Iraq. He also warned that KDPI militants would not be tolerated in Iraqi Kurdistan.

Most of the KDPI and its supporters were outraged by Mulla Mustafa's decision, particularly in view of the material support given to Barzani since 1961. A new Revolutionary Committee, formed to continue the struggle against Tehran, rapidly marginalized Ishaqi, who was denounced as a 'collaborator',[9] and expressed defiance of Mulla Mustafa. Some members were new blood, ex-members of the Tudeh, like Abd al Rahman Qasimlu, the future party leader. Others had impeccable nationalist antecedents, for example Abd Allah and Sulayman Muini, sons of a Mahabad veteran. The Revolutionary Committee hoped to support peasants in the Mahabad–Urumiya region already in conflict with the police.

It launched its campaign in March 1967. Two months later those still in Iraqi Kurdistan were evicted by Mulla Mustafa. In the summer of 1968, 5 of the 11 who formed the Revolutionary Committee leadership had been killed, including Abd Allah Muini. In addition to this disaster on the battlefield, Sulayman Muini had been captured by Barzani fighters that spring, trying to slip over the border into Iran from Iraqi Kurdistan. He was executed and his body handed over to the Iranians who displayed it in Mahabad, one of over 40 killed or turned over to the Shah's men by Mulla Mustafa. Within 18 months it was all over.

Many Iranian Kurds were bitter against Mulla Mustafa's 'stab in the back'. Even Ishaqi, who had blamed the Revolutionaries for their headstrong lack of caution, condemned Barzani's behaviour as 'filthy'.[10] But it would be wrong to assume that Barzani was responsible for the KDPI's defeat. Even with a safe base in Iraq, the KDPI at this juncture lacked the skills or resources to survive. It lacked modern or adequate weaponry,[11] secure bases, or a real grasp of guerrilla warfare. By confining its struggle to the Mahabad–Bana–Sardasht area it allowed the army to concentrate its forces, thus failing in the guerrilla imperative to dissipate and exhaust an army's efforts by operating over a large area and in an unpredictable fashion.[12]

The surviving elements of the KDPI soldiered on, with bitterness against Mulla Mustafa and determination to continue the struggle. A second KDPI conference in 1969 expelled the disgraced Ishaqi from the party and espoused a clearly leftist policy, in line with the Revolutionary Committee. From March 1970 a new 'Provisional Central Committee' began to prepare a new party programme which was approved at a third conference in Baghdad in June 1971, and a new party secretary-general elected, Abd al Rahman Qasimlu. Qasimlu had gone to Paris to study in the late 1940s, had come into contact with the Tudeh and moved to Prague. After living clandestinely in Mahabad, where he tried to help KDPI organize itself, he fled to Europe, and while the Revolutionary Committee was destroyed on the battlefield he worked in Europe to build up KDPI's intellectual following among expatriate students. Under his guidance, the Third Congress in September 1973 adopted the slogan, 'Democracy for Iran, autonomy for Kurdistan', and committed itself formally to armed struggle.

Over the next few years the KDPI found itself side by side with the other Iranians fighting the regime, who tended to belong to either Islamic or Marxist groups. Of those with whom KDPI at this time co-operated, the Marxist Fida'in-i Khalq and Mujahidin-i Islami were the most important groups.

To argue that the KDPI during the 1970s had little significance since it did not give the Shah much cause for concern, ignores the important psychological impact of the KDPI struggle during this decade. Ordinary Kurds were aware, however unpromising the prospects, that a tiny band had refused to abandon the nationalist dream and were prepared to risk their lives for its eventual realization. As the Shah's regime suddenly lost conviction and authority in 1978, this psychological transformation rapidly bore fruit as a large swathe of Kurdistan demonstrated its desire for autonomy.

Socio-economic Change

Before considering the Kurdish part in the revolution that swept Iran in 1978, it is important to note the social and economic changes that had occurred since 1918. With the collapse of government authority during the First World War, local leaders, tribal chiefs and landlords had asserted virtual independence, arrogating to themselves the privileges of the old land assignment holders of the Qajar period. In many cases dating back to before 1914, villages had invited a *sayyid* or tribal chief, often a citizen of Tabriz, Sanandaj or Kirmanshah to provide protection from the excesses of Qajar tax farmers. Villagers rewarded the patron in produce, and in time he naturally began to think of the village as his possession.

The temptation for patrons to assume proprietorial powers, where these did not legally exist, was increased by the absence of an independent class of peasantry able to subsist without the landlord class. The peasantry was illiterate and largely unable to handle any matters outside the village context. It was not difficult therefore for protective patrons to become also the providers of sowing loans, marketing facilities and other essentials beyond the village. The inability to control such functions robbed the peasantry of experience of the outside world and increased its psychological and financial dependence. It was a short step in many cases for peasant status to be transformed from smallholder to share-cropper. Landlords and patrons held all the instruments of economic and social power.

Reza Shah may have reduced the great tribal chiefs, killing some, and impris-oning or detaining others, but he left the lesser chiefs and the landlord class virtually untouched. He had no argument with landlords who concentrated on wealth acquisition or who used their wealth to establish their influence in the provincial towns to which they moved in increasing numbers during the 1920s.

The disappearance of a chief to town and his consequent abandonment of the social, political and economic role he had traditionally played, inevitably attenuated tribal ties. This process was already happening with the decline in nomadism from the nineteenth century, but was accelerated by Reza Shah's programme of coerced settlement. Settlement may have occurred unevenly, with the north-west (Urumiya–Mahabad–Bukan) more advanced than the more moun-tainous south, but everywhere its eventual effects were much the same. Land-lordism weakened tribal ties and fostered a sense of common peasant identity among all tillers of the land, be they tribal or non-tribal. The chief, who once protected their interests from the predatory inclinations of government and of neighbouring tribes, as landlord himself became predator. Those who tried to defy their landlord were liable to find themselves facing the army. Neither land-lord nor government would brook evidence of peasant power.

On account of their poverty and weakness the peasants did not revolt, but there were indications of the dissatisfaction that existed. They were quick to note that landlords and patrons no longer fulfilled the same functions they had once done. With Reza Shah's creation of certain state monopolies, for sugar, dried fruit and wheat, for example, peasant produce was purchased by govern-ment agents at fixed prices. In 1935 the application of a new direct agricultural tax rendered the protective function of village patrons obsolete. Peasants refused to pay protection and rushed to register their holdings. In some cases shrewd tenants misrepresented real landowners as patron protectors so as to escape dues in produce and service.

During the wartime occupation, the Soviet authorities deliberately fomented unrest among the Kurdish peasantry in order to weaken Tehran's hold there. Their intention had been to persuade the peasantry to look to the Soviet Union rather than Tehran for direction, and their task was not difficult in view of the oppressive and rapacious behaviour of many landlords, particularly following Reza Shah's downfall.

The Tudeh, which had signally failed to make inroads into a conservative and frightened peasantry before the war, now began to make progress, first with those living in the more open and settled areas of West Azarbaijan where it expanded its efforts through peasants' unions. In 1945 the Tudeh office in Urumiya enrolled thousands of Hurki and Shikak peasants into the party.[13] In

Bukan it recruited over 1,000 villagers and thereby forced landlords to increase the peasants' share of the sugar beet harvest.

It was the notables class that had held the social implications of the democratic movement in Kurdistan at bay. While the Azarbaijan Democratic Party advocated land reform, the Mahabad Republic eschewed it. In 1952 there was trouble for the landlords in Bukan. No doubt the general atmosphere was encouraged by the Musaddiq administration, but this time it was the KDPI which fomented it.

Elsewhere, the Musaddiq period marked a dramatic shift against the landlord class which had acquired so much power in Kurdistan. Back in the early 1920s the great magnates had tended to place their agents in the new Majlis, but had then begun to enter the Majlis themselves. Only 8 per cent of the First Majlis were landlords, but this proportion increased to 12 per cent in the Fourth, and to 26 per cent in the Twelfth.[14] Such landlord-deputies spread their mantle of patronage to represent as well the interests of lesser landlords. In Sanandaj, for example, Farjallah Asaf and Wakil al Sultan[15] were able to represent tribal chiefs who had no other spokesman in Tehran. It followed naturally therefore that such tribes, for example the Zand between Sanandaj and Mariwan and the Galbaghi between Sanandaj and Saqqiz, became clients of those who represented them.

With the rise of Musaddiq the natural rivalry between two neighbouring magnates was complicated by the growing challenge from the peasantry which forced them to act together against this class threat. When Musaddiq fought his 1952 election campaign, he had hoped to widen the franchise. His intention was to weaken the royalist and pro-British conservatives, by implication the landlord class. In Kurdistan province the battle lines were drawn between Hizb-i Saada-i Melli (National Prosperity Party), representing peasant and lower middle class interests, and Hizb-i Wahdat (Unity Party), the party of the landed magnates. As Hizb-i Saada became more of a threat, the Asafs and other landlords financed Hizb-i Wahdat to feast the people of Sanandaj for three days, each man who attended being paid five tomans. It was a sign of the times that such barefaced bribery no longer worked. Hizb-i Saada easily took Sanandaj for the seventeenth Majlis. It was one of the few rural areas in the country where the conservatives were defeated.

Agriculture, however, remained acutely neglected. Travelling through Kurdistan in 1956, Ann Lambton commented 'The most striking feature ... is its apparent under-development.'[16] She found agriculture primitive, the use of wooden ploughs and harvesting by sickle widespread, and deforestation uncontrolled. Kurdistan and Azarbaijan were notorious for their large estates. Less than half the villages in these two provinces were in multiple ownership. In fact about 64 per cent of Kurdish cultivable land was in the hands of 0.3 per cent of the population. In Sanandaj the Asafs and Sanandajis were bitter rivals to rule the roost, each owning several villages in their entirety. In Bukan and Mahabad land had been parcelled out through the Dihbukri and other magnate families. It was reckoned that in Iran as a whole possibly 100,000 families owned whole villages or substantial parts of them. Tenants still handed over 20 per cent of their cereal crop to the owner and dues to the *kadkhuda* and mulla. They were even liable for corvée. Technically such things were abolished by Musaddiq's decree increasing the share-cropper's portion in October 1952, but his decree was never really implemented. Besides, where the peasant consented, dues in kind and corveeé were still acceptable, and most landlords and headmen knew how to ensure consent.[17] It is not surprising that in many places – Lambton picked out Mahabad and Mariwan for special mention – landlord–peasant relations were acutely antagonistic. Without the charismatic leadership of a Barzani, the agha class was associated almost universally with the regime, and no longer had any place in nationalist thinking. In such circumstances, despite government suppression of the Tudeh, socialist or egalitarian ideas found fertile ground, regardless of their origin.

In 1962, goaded by the United States, the Shah finally initiated a programme of land reform, the price of US assistance in resolving the deep economic crisis. The Shah embarked on such a land reform unwillingly, since half the Majlis was composed of the landed class. Yet, as one US specialist had forecast four years earlier, 'it is certain that no land distribution law would put the upper limit of area low enough to interfere with the property of a large number of petty landlords.'[18]

In fact all landlords were required to sell agricultural land in excess of one village (or six *dangs*, or village portions), receiving compensation in lieu. Land bought by the state was to be promptly sold to the share-croppers who worked it. Overall, something like 5,000 families in Iran managed to find loopholes in the law and to hang onto 100 or more hectares, while another 45,000 families or so managed to keep 50 or more hectares, thereby retaining control of 20 per cent of the country's cultivable land. A fair share of this was in Kurdistan. Around Urumiya a number of Azari magnates hung onto more than one village. Likewise, further south, the Begzada Jafs held onto substantial estates. Such examples were not innocent oversights but favours to those useful to the state. Salar Jaf, for example, was a tribal member of the Majlis, while his brother, Sardar, was a high-level official at the Shah's palace.[19]

The government tried to create a class of independent farmers instead. Small landlords in Kurdistan, owning up to 20 hectares each, nearly doubled in number, but they only comprised 2.5 per cent of the rural population. But the proportion of peasants with 3 to 5 hectares rose from 3 per cent in 1960 to over 30 per cent by 1970. The landless Kurdish peasants and workers were less favoured. Their proportion was reduced by the land reform from 80 per cent to only about 50 per cent.

Unfortunately, virtually no beneficiaries of the land reform received the generally acknowledged minimum for economic viability: 7 hectares. In order to solve this problem the state encouraged the formation of state-run farm corporations and co-operatives. By the mid-1970s many smallholders found their land had become effectively state property. The introduction of mechanization further accelerated the loss of both small landholding and employment, leading to the rapid transition from an agrarian society to a rural proletariat. While some smallholders were losing their land, others were still trying to obtain their due from the 1960s reforms. As late as September 1978, no fewer than 1,400 farmers were still trying to get 750 hectares from the Khan of Mariwan promised nine years earlier by the state. As far as they were concerned the state and the old 'feudal' landlord class still worked hand-in-hand.

Despite such exceptions and despite the fact that the reform took a decade to implement, the land reform struck the death knell of the landed magnate class and tribalism as political forces in Kurdistan. Other factors conspired in this process. The spread of the radio and of carriageable roads, and the beginnings of peasant literacy put once wholly isolated communities in touch with the outside world and its ideas. Population growth forced mobility and migration. In the century, 1850–1950, the population of Kurdistan had increased rapidly, well over tenfold. From the 1950s onwards the rate increased, as elsewhere in Iran, to the point of doubling roughly every 20 years. Villages and hamlets proliferated, but even so, increasing numbers of people were squeezed off the land. Some of these drifted to live in Kurdish towns, while others commuted daily in search of work. In such situations Kurdish migrants were exposed to a whole new range of ideas.

Land reform, improved communications, literacy and migration had different effects in different parts of Iran. While in central Iran it tended to accelerate the transition of localist identities towards that of the state, on the periphery people abandoned village or tribal identity in favour of an ethnic one. Thus during the years 1960–79 a mass Kurdish identity in Iran – regardless of the struggles and failures of the KDPI – was forged.

This new Kurdish self-conciousness was made more acute by the recognition of migrant Kurds of the comparative backwardness of Kurdistan. Pahlavi economic effort was focussed on building an industrial base, and this was located in central and northern Iran. Kurdistan – like Baluchistan, the other Sunni region – dropped further behind in relative terms during the 1960s and 1970s, years of economic centralization and industrialization.

Kurdistan was exiled to the edge of economic progress. The loss of cross-frontier trade undermined the Kurdish pastoralist economy, while the introduction of a state tobacco monopoly and other centralizing measures drew the region into the state system – but very much as a peripheral participant. Investment in the centre and in the oil industry led to polarization, with the periphery receiving proportionately least money. It was natural to expect some disparity between the centre and periphery, but its degree by the mid-1970s was considerable. By 1977 the ratio of industrial worker to agricultural labourer in East Azarbaijan was 1:2.6; in Kurdistan it was 1:20;[20] 80 per cent of central Iran's population was urban compared with only 25 per cent in Kurdistan; 80 per cent of central Iran's households were electrified, compared with less than 20 per cent in Kurdistan; 75 per cent of central Iran's households had piped water compared with only 12 per cent in Kurdistan; over 66 per cent of central Iran was literate, compared with only 36 per cent in Kurdistan (males 43.8 per cent, females 20 per cent).[21]

Such changes both within Kurdistan and in its relationship with the rest of Iran inevitably instigated changes with clear political consequences. An ever growing body of young men drifted off to find work elsewhere, driven by Kurdish population growth and drawn to richer parts of Iran. They became politicized by the evident disparities and by exposure to the mainstreams of clandestine political opposition. Those who remained became more integrated into the Kurdish region and thereby became more conscious of their ethnic identity. It only required a lapse of central power for the Kurds to try to establish their ethnic identity as the basis for local government. That chance came with the 1979 Revolution.

Sources

Official Great Britain: Public Record Office: series FO 195/2589, FO 248/1400, FO 371 nos 18987, 45503, 68472, 82000, 82307, 91449, 91450, 109994, 114809, 114810, 120749, 127143, 133005, 133007, 140789, 140856.

Secondary works published: Abrahamian, *Iran Between Two Revolutions;* Akbar Aghajian, 'Ethnic inequality in Iran: an overview', *International Journal of Middle East Studies,* no. 15, 1983; Nader Entessar, 'The Kurds in post-revolutionary Iran and Iraq', *Third World Quarterly,* 9 (4) October 1984 and *Kurdish Ethno-nationalism* (Boulder and London, 1992); Abd al Rahman Ghassemlou, 'Kurdistan in Iran' in Chaliand, *People without a Country;* Halliday, *Iran: Dictatorship and Development;* Margaret Kahn, *Children of the Jinn* (New York, 1980); A.K.S. Lambton, *Landlord and Peasant in Persia* (London, 1953), *The Persian Land Reform, 1962–1966* (London, 1969) and 'Land Reform and Rural Co-operative Societies in Persia', *JRCAS,* vol. lvi, June 1969.

Unpublished: Wilson Howell, Jr, 'The Soviet Union and the Kurds: a study of a national minority' (PhD. diss., Univ. Virginia, 1965).

Interviews: Khalil Rashidian (London, June 1993), Hassan Ghazi (by cassette, autumn 1993).

Notes

1. Wahhab Bulurian, Ghani's brother, had been one of the official representatives to the Azarbaijan Republic, and Abd al Rahim Sultanian's father, Mustafa, had also been a senior official.

2. At its second congress in Urumiya in 1927 the Communist Party had called for the formation of a federal republic to protect the many nationalities of Iran.

3. Despite his distaste for him, Muhammad Reza appointed Razmara as the only man capable of saving Iran from political instability and financial bankruptcy, Abrahamian, *Iran Between Two Revolutions,* p. 263.

4. On Sanjabi's background, see chapter 11, note 3. He had assisted Qavam negotiate with the Kurds in Azarbaijan and Mahabad in 1946, and like Qavam had deeply dis-

approved of the executions that followed Mahabad's collapse. Dr Abd al Hamid Zangana had been elected as a deputy for Kirmanshah in 1943 because he was the son of the Zangana chief. In fact, like Sanjabi, he was a radical. Both belonged to Musaddiq's cabinet, 1952–53, and the subsequent National Resistance Movement after Musaddiq's fall.

5. In Mahabad led by Yusifi, Bulurian and Sultanian, and in Sanandaj by Shari Atti, Kutschera, *Le Mouvement National Kurde*, p. 187.

6. FO 371/114809 Fearnley to Stewart, Tehran, 18 January 1955.

7. FO 371/82000 Dundas to Tehran, Tabriz, 18 October 1950.

8. Aziz Yusifi was released in 1977 with broken health, and died in June 1978. His funeral in Mahabad occasioned mass demonstrations.

9. Either to control or to protect him, Mulla Mustafa detained Ishaqi at Kanimasi, in the inner fastness of Bahdinan. After his election as secretary-general, Qasimlu sought to welcome Ishaqi back into the fold, but the latter refused Qasimlu's invitation. He was arrested by the Iraqi authorities and disappeared in 1972.

10. Ishaqi (Ahmad Tawfiq) to Mulla Rasul, 7 January 1969, information from Hassan Ghazi.

11. Apparently they initiated their struggle with a total of four Kalashnikov rifles, two machine-guns and 85 old rifles, Kutschera, *Le Mouvement National Kurde*, p. 346.

12. The KDPI recognized its own shortcomings in these respects at its Third Congress in 1973.

13. Ziro Beg thwarted this process among his Harki by collecting in all the membership cards and insisting on a refund.

14. Abrahamian, *Iran Between Two Revolutions*, p. 149.

15. Both owned about 50 villages apiece, Asaf in the direction of Hamadan, Sultan towards Kirmanshah. They were rivals politically, but naturally allied on class matters.

16. FO 371/120749 A.K.S. Lambton, Note on Persian Kurdistan, September 1956.

17. The regime finally banned tribute in kind as corvée unconditionally in October 1958. Even so corvée was still in existence in Urumiya villages in the 1970s.

18. FO 371/140856 Wordsworth to Kellas, Beirut, 31 December 1958.

19. Entessar, 'The Kurds in post-revolutionary Iran', p. 923, where the two Jafs are wrongly interchanged, according to a Jaf informant.

20. Abrahamian, *Iran Between Two Revolutions*, p. 449.

21. Akbar Aghajian, 'Ethnic inequality in Iran: an overview', *International Journal of Middle East Studies*, no. 15, 1983, pp 215–21.

CHAPTER 13

SUBJECTS OF THE SHI'I REPUBLIC

Introduction

Like the rest of Iran, Kurdistan welcomed and exploited the Pahlavi regime's collapse. The turbulence of autumn 1978 contrasted strongly with Prime Minister Hoveida's denial only a year earlier that there was no problem and that the Kurdish community 'feels a great loyalty towards the country'.[1] Kurdish repugnance for the Shah, already considerable, had greatly increased with the 1975 Algiers agreement whereby he had abandoned Iraq's Kurds. As army garrisons in Kurdish areas lost confidence during the autumn of 1978, the Kurds seized as much weaponry as they were able and became the effective power on the ground by the close of the year. Although they initially welcomed Khomeini's arrival in Tehran, they had acted to throw out the hated old regime, not to usher in an Islamic republic. It was less clear what they now hoped to see in its place, although the majority probably would have given joyful assent to the KDPI slogan of 'democracy for Iran, and autonomy for Kurdistan'.

Within three weeks of Khomeini's triumphal return from exile, a major battle took place close to Bana, between local Kurds and forces loyal to the newly declared Islamic Republic, and over 100 were killed. This conflict was initially sparked by the clash of fervour between local Shi'i and Kurdish forces. Yet behind events on the ground, the fundamental conflict between the new regime and the Kurds was one of incompatible expectations. For the new Islamic regime the political aspiration for Iran was necessarily inclusive of all Muslims within the republic. Opting out cast doubt on fidelity to the faith. At the same time the new regime, unsure of itself and of the constituency which had installed it, was terrified of national disintegration. It could brook no fragmentation at the edges, and this is precisely what it feared of the Kurds.

On the other hand, the Kurdish expectation after 35 years of progressive centralization was that it would be possible to regularize the decentralization that had resulted from the power vacuum. The overwhelming majority of Kurds conceived of local administration as being along secular and democratic lines,

That was the cast of mind of the leftist KDPI, one that was bound to conflict with the Islamic view in Tehran. During the next year or so, Kurdistan was rocked by repeated clashes and pitched battles between Kurdish fighters and the newly formed volunteer Revolutionary Guards, or Pasdaran, a formation which aggressively asserted the Shi'i values of the new regime.

Broadly speaking, most of the countryside remained in Kurdish hands until 1982–83 while most towns, though subject to periodic rebellions, remained in the tenuous grasp of the regime. Mahabad repeatedly fell into rebel hands, sometimes for months at a time. Bukan remained a Kurdish stronghold for a period of over two years. The border town of Sardasht, once recovered by the government, could only be retained by air supply since road access remained in rebel hands until late 1982.

Much bitterness was added to the conflict by the regime's use of the Pasdaran rather than the regular army, and by the brutality of pacification in which an estimated 10,000 Kurds died in the first two years, some in battle, and some in the summary and mass executions carried out by Ayatollah Sadiq Khalkhali, the 'hanging judge' sent to terrorize the population into submission.[2]

Yet on both sides there were efforts to bring the fighting to an end and to reach a *modus vivendi*. On the Kurdish part this was motivated by the desire for autonomy and for an end to the widespread suffering that had resulted from the conflict. On the regime's side, the overriding motivation was to reduce the number of challenges it faced both internally and externally, if necessary by making concessions which would not endanger the territorial integrity of the country.

During the first year three rounds of parley were attempted. In early March 1979 the Kurds presented their first set of eight demands which, while acknowledging the Islamic Republic, demanded autonomy for all Kurdistan as one administative unit within a federated Iran.[3] Their claim went far beyond the province of Kurdistan to include West Azarbaijan, where there was in fact an Azari majority, and Kirmanshah and Ilam, where the majority were Shi'i, and in the case of Ilam arguably Lur rather than Kurd. It is unlikely any agreement would have been possible. The regime rejected so wide a definition of Kurdistan and countered with an offer of full cultural and language rights, with senior Kurdish officials to run the local administration, and specific minority guarantees in the new constitution. The Kurds reiterated their vision:

> Our people have fought for two major goals; the overthrow of the dictatorship and its replacement by a humane regime which would respect political freedoms and rights throughout Iran, and the realization of national rights for all nations in the form of autonomy or a federation in free Iran.[4]

In Qum Khomeini had already vetoed the government's offer. In Kurdistan scant attention was paid to such exchanges, as fighting raged first around Sanandaj, then further north at Naqada.

In early August another ceasefire was attempted at the behest of a Kurdish religious leader, Shaykh Izz al Din Husayni, after hundreds had died and thousands had been displaced in a summer of fighting all over central and northern Kurdistan. The lull lasted barely a fortnight before major fighting broke out at Pawa, prompting Ayatollah Khomeini to anathematize both Qasimlu and Shaykh Izz al Din. The furthest he was prepared to go was to offer an amnesty for all who surrendered, and a day's oil revenue ($75 million) for immediate development purposes. Qasimlu pleaded for a ceasefire to be based upon the government's agreement: (i) to cease sending troop reinforcements to the region; (ii) to release all political prisoners; (iii) to free all Kurdish hostages; and (iv) to cease the execution of captured Kurds; but his plea fell on deaf ears.

During the autumn of 1979 the regime's position deteriorated as it became clear that the rebels were intercepting Pasdaran communications to launch effective ambushes against its troop movements. In October the Pasdaran lost control of Mahabad, central symbol of the Kurdish national movement.

At the end of the month the government obtained Khomeini's reluctant agreement to negotiate again with the rebels. It offered the Kurds control over the economic, political, social and cultural affairs of the province. On 2 December the Kurds responded with another eight-point plan, with the same wide geographical remit as previously, but this time with Kurdistan's autonomy to be written into the draft constitution.[5]

A few days later, however, Kurds boycotted the referendum on the new constitution when it was learnt that the revised text omitted any mention of the Kurds, even as one of Iran's peoples. The Kurds were not alone in their opposition to the proposed constitution, for 80 per cent of Azarbaijan voters also boycotted the referendum. In the middle of the month the government offered the Kurds a plan for local administration through two provincial councils, based on Mahabad and Sanandaj, and cultural autonomy.[6] In January Khomeini enlarged the government proposal with an offer to amend the Islamic Constitution to guarantee Sunni religious practices in areas of Sunni majority; but this offer, inadequate though it was, did not materialize.

Fighting broke out afresh between local Kurds and Pasdaran early in the new year, first in Sanandaj and then proliferating to Pawa, Nawsud, Jawanrud, Piranshahr and Ushnaviya in March and April. This provoked another major military assault on Kurdistan. Although most towns were recaptured, the countryside remained in the hands of the Kurds. With the onset of the Iran–Iraq war in September 1980, relations broke down irretrievably.

Why a Negotiated Settlement Failed to Materialize

The reasons for failure: divisions in the Islamic Republic

At face value failure had resulted from a gap between the minimum requirements of each party. Had this been the only reason, it is just possible that a tolerable compromise might have been found, one that fell short of full autonomy but allowed the Kurds a significant degree of decentralized government. However, there were other major impediments to successful negotiations. Neither side possessed a united leadership in control of the constituency it claimed to represent. On the contrary, both sides were hydra-headed. In practice there were two regimes in Iran: the government in Tehran, which had full responsibility but severely circumscribed power, and the religious regime in Qum personified in Ayatollah Khomeini. Even such a description is simplistic, for the senior mullas were highly factionalized. However, the administrations in Tehran led first by Prime Minister Mahdi Bazargan, then by President Abu'l Hasan Bani Sadr, were repeatedly undermined by the dictates emanating from Qum, or by the schemes of individuals in the clerical camp, and subject to factional struggles among the religious hierarchy. In late August 1979, for example, after a particularly bad bout of fighting, the veteran nationalist, Rahim Sayf Qazi,[7] went to Tehran to forge a ceasefire agreement with the highly regarded cleric Ayatollah Taliqani. Twenty-four hours later Khomeini vetoed it. A couple of days later Prime Minister Bazargan was sharply criticized by the clerical hierarchy for his 'liberal' handling of the situation in Kurdistan. President Bani Sadr fared no better. At his back were clerical hard-liners who made sure he made no substantive concessions to the Kurds.

The civil and religious authorities of the republic sought to exert their authority through rival forces, the regular army and the Pasdaran. The former was a shadow of its former self. Large-scale desertions had amounted to about 60 per cent of the 171,000 strong imperial army. Purges, dismissals and executions accounted for the loss of another 12,000 or so. Almost half the army's middle rank officers (company and battalion commanders) were removed, devastating its combat effectiveness. Their loyalty was still doubted, for several military coups were attempted up to July 1980, one of the more serious being in the Kurdish border town of Piranshah in June 1980.[8] Understandably there was great reluctance to deploy the army in Kurdistan. Even after it became necessary to do so in response to growing insurgency in April 1980, the government found itself using an army that had to be warned against 'indiscipline', in reality the refusal by some to bomb or attack Kurdish villages. Lacking the certainties of faith, the army had a natural distaste for civil war.

It was natural therefore to turn to the Pasdaran, the ideologically motivated volunteers raised for internal security. But the Pasdaran, certainly at the outset, were barely under central authority. They were answerable to the *imam komiteh*s (Committees of the Imam), Shi'i committees established across the country to provide provisional local government, and to themselves. Both forces were characterized more by their Shi'i triumphalism than by either civic or military skills, let alone discipline. It is hard to imagine bodies more calculated to cause friction both in Sunni Kurdistan and with the regular army. Much of the fighting stemmed from the heavy-handed Pasdar presence. Tehran found itself neither in control of the Pasdaran nor of the *imam komiteh*s. Yet it was unwilling to accept demands for their removal.

The reasons for failure: divisions among the Kurds

Yet the Kurds also suffered the frailties of disunity. The largest party, the KDPI, claimed to represent the Kurdish people but had no mass base at the time of the revolution. Qasimlu, who had returned to the country in November 1978, hurriedly began to make contact with trusted lieutenants in Tehran and Mahabad, and with other returning exiles. Some of those already in Iran had tried to keep KDPI networks alive. But it was quite another matter to mobilize a mass movement in order to claim autonomy from the new regime now taking shape.

The KDPI had to establish its authority in the maelstrom of revolutionary events and it tried to do this through the establishment of village councils. Yet it was powerless to control or contain the outbursts of popular anger against the Pasdaran. As one hapless merchant remarked after the first major bout of fighting in Sanandaj, which had left about 100 dead, 'When all this is over, it will be our own lack of leadership that beats us. Look around. We have no leaders; even worse, every man thinks he is a leader.'[9] The Kurdish struggle during the crucial 18 months was dogged by disunity.

If indiscipline was one problem, acknowledgement of KDPI leadership was another. The KDPI could count on unanimous if undisciplined support in its traditional heartlands around Mahabad and Urumiya, but less so further north or south.[10] In the north it faced competition from the Iraqi KDP, led by the Barzani brothers, which now sought to rally the Kurmanji-speaking tribes in support of the republic and against Kurdish autonomy. To the south the KDPI was challenged by Komala (The Organization of Revolutionary Toilers of Iranian Kurdistan) which took issue on ideological grounds and, like the Fida'in-i Khalq which was also operating in Kurdistan, resented the KDPI's presumption as representative of the Kurdish people.

Komala, so its members claimed, had been founded by a group of students in Tehran in 1969 dismayed by the easy defeat of the KDPI's Revolutionary Committee and by its subsequent apparent passivity. In reality it only declared itself publicly at the end of 1978. Komala was inspired by the Chinese revolution and hoped to emulate it through the creation of cadres who would return to the industrial and agricultural centres of Kurdistan to educate the masses and evangelize them.

Although they derided KDPI leaders as 'bourgeois nationalists', many of Komala's founders were themselves scions of the notable families of Bukan, Saqqiz and Sanandaj,[11] for the simple reason that none of the lower classes had the same opportunity for university education.

Komala aimed at the mobilization of the masses, to be achieved through education, service, and through the rural health clinics which it subsequently established. It vehemently condemned the 'Soviet revisionism' of the Tudeh, and it dismissed Kurdish nationalism as parochial in ambition. It wanted power to be returned to all the communities of Iran, and the defeat of central government.

Decentralization rather than nationalism was its guiding aim. The Kurds were just one community in that process and could only hope for success in concert with others.

Nowhere was Komala stronger than in the Sanandaj-Mariwan region. Historically this was partly because of the large number of senior Komala members from the region, and possibly also because Sanandaj had eschewed previous Kurdish movements whose power base had been further north, for example the Simqu rebellion and the Mahabad Republic. So there was an element of regional loyalty.

However Sanandaj had always been more closely integrated into the affairs of the neighbouring province of Fars, and had consequently been more exposed to the class ideologies which had played an important part in opposition groups in central Iran. It also had a history of class solidarity. In 1917–18, for example, a group of lower class traders, influenced by Democrats elsewhere in Iran, had formed Hizb-i Sosial Dimuqrat (Social Democratic Party). As the famine in Kurdistan reached its climax, they seized control of the town and distributed hoarded grain from the warehouses of local magnates, notably Farjallah Asaf. They were quickly ousted by local aghas and mullas acting on behalf of Tehran.

However, the seed had been sown. In the early 1920s the Socialist Party organized a branch in Sanandaj until the party was forced to dissolve in 1926. Its advocacy of an egalitarian society in practice implied renewed struggle against aghas and landlords. Subsequently, the Tudeh had been more closely involved in Sanandaj than in other parts of Kurdistan. Thus, when the KDPI failed to support those fighting the Pasdaran in Sanandaj and Mariwan in the spring of 1979, Komala and the Fida'in were quick to denounce it, and Komala established itself locally as the dominant party.

Finally, Komala was attractive to many people in the area because it seemed more democratic. Its central committee co-ordinated semi-autonomous cells, but allowed much local decision-making. Not everyone felt the same way about the KDPI, despite its own local networks.[12] In Sanandaj the KDPI had a thin but active base, but it reinforced an impression of lofty detachment by sending a Mahabad man as its agent in Sanandaj rather than choosing a local man.[13]

Komala was less willing than the KDPI to brook compromise with Tehran and more determined than the KDPI to continue fighting. This inevitably weakened the Kurdish negotiating position. In November 1979 when the KDPI agreed a ceasefire with the government as a prelude to negotiation, it found its endeavours undermined by Komala's repeated attacks on government forces. Komala remained sceptical, and it took a month to persuade it reluctantly to relent. When talks broke down in December it returned to the battlefield. It refused to participate in the next ceasefire attempt in June 1980, and gained further support among a sceptical populace at KDPI's expense.

Then there was the 'conservative' constituency, composed of certain aghas, shaykhs and landlords, which still commanded a modest though disparate following. One or two aghas, most notably Simqu's son Tahir Khan, had tried to exploit the chaos in Kurdistan at the end of 1978 to make a come-back. Others added to the chaos when they tried to claw back land lost in the 1960s reforms. Some who regretted the passing of the *ancien régime* hoped to join the Kurdish General Palizban, ex-governor-general of Kirmanshah, who threatened to march back into Iran from Iraq.

The new regime sought help among those Kurds who had co-operated with the Shah on the assumption that these depended on the centre, regardless of the regime. As in Iraq there were certain tribal sections which, possibly for reasons of local rivalry, were initially willing to side with the government, for example the followers of Haji Jawhar in the Margavar valley. Yet it was not always easy to predict an agha's policy. Tahir Khan in the north, for example, had initially fought the local army and gendarmerie hoping to re-establish himself, but by July 1979 was reluctantly compelled to call upon the KDPI for help, something that hardly enhanced his leadership with the tribal rank-and-file. Then he allied with the Barzanis, the most formidable pro-tribal force in the northern part of Iranian Kurdistan and one with which his family was historically associated,[14] and thus found himself in the government camp against the KDPI. Several of his Abdui Shikak relatives, however, fought against Tehran.

Then there were one or two who supported the KDPI out of conviction. Sinar, leader of the Mamadi Shikak, for example, had a long record of nationalism. He was no friend of the Barzanis, for Mulla Mustafa had caught and delivered him to the Shah in 1967 while fighting for the KDPI's Revolutionary Committee. He was lucky only to have been imprisoned. After the Shah's overthrow he rejoined the movement and was elected to the KDPI central committee in February 1980. That summer he defied many of his own family, destroying Iran's sole rail link with Turkey and Europe where it ran though his fiefdom in the Qutur valley.

One of the more notable of those wooed by Tehran was the senior Sunni cleric of Sanandaj, Ahmad Muftizada. Muftizada had established Quranic schools in the town during the 1970s, and was a proponent of Kurdish cultural rights. He was approached during the first serious bout of fighting in Sanandaj in March 1979, almost certainly to undermine the popular Mahabad mulla (commonly called 'Shaykh') Izz al Din Husayni, who had become a focus for Kurdish resistance. Although Muftizada had associated with Kurdish activists, he was widely seen as a reactionary.[15] This stood him in poor stead with townspeople fired with revolutionary fervour. Shaykh Izz al Din echoed popular sentiment when he described him as 'for autonomy, but with no idea of its meaning'.[16] In due course Muftizada had to flee Sanandaj for his own safety.[17]

The religious class, as exemplified in Ahmad Muftizada, tended towards the conservative. But there were always exceptions. Shaykh Izz al Din was the most celebrated leftist cleric, but several others took a liberal or leftist line on social and nationalist issues. One or two had anticipated the land reform of the 1960s to make their villages over to the inhabitants, or encouraged women's education at government schools.[18] Thus, the liberal stance of some clerics helped Komala's strident Marxism seem less shocking to ordinary people than it might otherwise have seemed.

Other clerics sought their fortune elsewhere. Shaykh Izz al Din's brother Shaykh Jalal took weaponry from Saddam Husayn to mobilize a strongly conservative Sunni militia, 'Khabat' ('Struggle'), at odds both with Tehran and with Komala and the KDPI.[19]

For many of the old landlord class, the collapse of the imperial regime was an opportunity to regain lands distributed to the peasantry following the White Revolution, or at least to obtain tenant dues for what could not be repossessed. Elsewhere peasants took the law into their own hands to possess lands of which they believed they had been cheated. Nowhere was this more stark than in Mariwan, where landlord–peasant relations were so notoriously bad. Komala supported, indeed, led the peasantry in their struggle against the landlord class. When angry peasants marched on the *imam komiteh* in Mariwan in July 1979 demanding 'the expulsion of feudal elements', it was not difficult for the landlords to persuade the *komiteh* and the Pasdaran that their feudalism was distinctly preferable to Komala's communism.

So, even in a context where in many parts of Iran local agencies of the government supported the peasants, here it was different, a local class dispute over land becoming a nationalist one that seriously damaged relations with Tehran at an early stage. Only later did the regime act with greater understanding of the land issue – after it had mishandled it all over Iran.

Komala adopted a stridently pro-peasant position on land tenure, especially around Mariwan and Sanandaj. It was a good deal more reticent around Bukan where Dihbukri relatives of Komala's leadership lived. The KDPI also favoured socialist socio-economic reform. When aghas around Urumiya and Mahabad tried to levy customary dues, the KDPI forced them to withdraw. Yet it also wished to avoid the kind of confrontation that Komala sought. It wanted to win tribes over to its viewpoint, not crush them because of it. Nevertheless, there was a natural process of polarization, aghas seeking help from the state authorities, the peasantry turning to Komala or the KDPI.

Finally, the regime co-opted the Barzani forces in the Kurmanji-speaking northern reaches of Kurdistan to clear the KDPI from positions close to the border, and to woo Kurmanji aghas away from the Surani-dominated KDPI on the basis of linguistic solidarity.[20] The Barzanis co-operated as willingly with the Islamic Republic as they had done with the Pahlavis. However, most of these aghas tried to remain outside the conflict, willing to acknowledge Tehran's authority and thereby remain more or less independent, but not actually to be drawn into the Kurdish war.

The Republic's Attitude Towards the Kurds

The new regime viewed Kurdish national expression apprehensively. Altogether, Iran's non-Persian minorities constituted approximately half the population. In the early days when the regime was still unsure of itself, it was feared that concessions made to the Kurds would then be demanded or seized by other groups. These minorities straddled Iran's borders, Kurds and Arabs on the Iraqi border, Azaris and Turkomans on the Turkish and Soviet borders, and Baluchis on the Afghan and Pakistani borders. In three cases (Kurds, Turkoman, Baluchis) the sense of cross-border affinity was heightened by being a Sunni minority within Iran.

Rather than soothe state paranoia, it was tempting for Kurds to use the external danger as a goad to concessions. In March 1979 Ghani Bulurian (who had been released in December after 25 years in prison) rashly observed 'If the revolutionary government agree to give national rights to the Kurdish people, it will be very easy to defend Iranian frontiers from any aggression abroad. But if it does not, some forces from abroad can abuse the feelings of the Kurdish people.'[21] The threat was unmistakable. In any case, the Kurdish question had already struck a sensitive nerve in Tehran, because it was redolent with memories of Simqu, Mahabad and the way in which Iraq had allowed its territory to be used as a springboard for Kurdish dissidents.

So, 'autonomy' as uttered by the Kurds sounded like 'secession' in Tehran. For instance, when fighting began in Mariwan and Sanandaj over the land tenure dispute in July and August 1979, Prime Minister Bazargan concluded 'They [the Kurds] didn't simply want autonomy, they wanted to be separate from Iran', even though the Kurdish leadership had been careful to explain that its demand for autonomy held no such implication. Indeed, in Qasimlu's view 'it was reactionaries who shouted about secession. The Kurdish left wanted a constructive autonomy.'[22] But Tehran's view of the Kurds was immovable: separatists they were and separatists they remained.

The Kurds faced another impediment, one with both practical and ideological aspects. This was the religious divide that marked most Kurds as a Sunni minority in a Shi'i land. At the practical level, Sunni Kurdish relations with their non-Kurdish Shi'i neighbours were traditionally poor, with periodic explosions of violence.[23] Now the regime sent Shi'i enthusiasts to control Kurdistan in the form of the *imam komiteh*s and Pasdaran, with the predictable succession of gun battles in almost every Kurdish town: Mariwan, Sanandaj, Saqqiz, Bana, Pawa, and so on. After the first round of fighting in Sanandaj, Tehran exasperated local feeling further by appointing a Shi'i dignitary, Ayatollah Hojjat al Islam Saftdari, to command the Pasdaran garrison.

The most serious conflict, however, took place in Naqada, a town with a mixed population. In late April 1979 the KDPI organized a major rally in a football stadium located in the Azari part of town. The Azari local committee asked the KDPI to hold its rally elsewhere to avoid provocation. The KDPI not only refused this request but some KDPI groups arrived armed. The Azaris were ready for them. As the rally commenced shots were fired which rapidly led to heavy fighting. As Azari bands moved on to loot Kurdish villages, at least 200 died and some 12,000 Kurds were made homeless.[24]

Shi'i Kurds south of Sanandaj felt differently from their Sunni brethren concerning the Islamic revolution. Those of Kirmanshah province indicated they had no interest in autonomy. They wanted, initially at any rate, to remain part of a Shi'i republic and the regime had little difficulty in recruiting 'Muslim peshmergas' among them to fight the nationalists and leftists further north. In 1979 Sunni and Shi'i Kurds actually came to blows in mixed villages of Kurdistan province.

Yet it was at the ideological level that Kurdish prospects for a measure of self-government were seriously dimmed. Before his accession to power, Khomeini had never expressed his view about ethnic minorities, in spite of his extensive writings on social, theological, economic and political issues. He probably had not thought about it. However the problems of revolutionary Iran gave him plenty of opportunity to do so. Khomeini's initial concern was strategic. This is clear from Shaykh Izz al Din's first meeting with him in April 1979: 'When I was leaving, he [Khomeini] took me by the hem of my cloak and said to me: "What I am asking you for is the security of Kurdistan." So I took him by his hem and said, "What I am asking you for is autonomy for Kurdistan."'[25] In the first months he was willing to allow the government to negotiate with the Kurds over their autonomy demands. As Prime Minister Bazargan said (even though his own idea of autonomy was severely circumscribed):

> We wanted to reach an agreement with the Kurds, even though we were dealing with radicals who were a little too extremist. We said, 'Let them choose what they want.' And when they started talking of autonomy, we accepted even that.[26]

The draft Islamic constitution published in June 1979, while not offering autonomy, promised that 'Persians, Turks, Kurds, Arabs, Baluchis, Turkomans, and others will enjoy equal rights.'[27] It did not even propose the doctrine later adopted, of goverment by a supreme spiritual leader (vilayat-i faqih). Khomeini had been willing to allow the draft to go directly to popular referendum. Catastrophically, it was Bazargan and Bani Sadr who insisted the draft should first be submitted to, and refined by, an elected constitutional assembly. They entirely failed to foresee it would open the floodgates to clerical radicals. On the contrary, it was Ayatollah Ali Akbar Rafsanjani who warned them, 'Who do you think will be elected to a constituent assembly? A fistful of ignorant and fanatic fundamentalists who will do such damage you will regret ever having convened them.'[28] And so it proved to be. A 73-member Council of Experts was elected and convened in August; 55 of them were clerics.

It was not difficult for these fundamentalists to help Khomeini change his mind about the draft. In November he explained why all mention of ethnic minorities had been dropped:

> Sometimes the word minorities is used to refer to people such as Kurds, Lurs, Turks, Persians, Baluchis, and such. These people should not be called minorities, because this term assumes there is a difference between these brothers. In Islam, such a difference has no place at all. There is no difference between Muslims who speak different languages, for instance, the Arabs or the Persians. It is very probable that such problems have been created by those who do not wish the Muslim countries to be united.... They create the issues of nationalism, of pan-Iranism, pan-Turkism, and such-isms which are contrary to Islamic doctrines. Their plan is to destroy Islam and Islamic philosophy.[29]

Thus, even to talk about ethnic minorities in the Islamic domain was an offence against true religion.

If the Kurds could not be distinguished as an ethnic minority, perhaps the majority of them could invoke minority status as Sunnis. There was no doubting their different and inferior position in the Shi'i state, a mirror image to that of Shi'is in Saudi Arabia and other Arab countries. They were common people, *amma*, compared with Shi'is who were a special people, *khassa*. Yet here again, where the original draft constitution recognized by name the four Sunni law schools, the final draft omitted them while it emphasized the Shi'i nature of the state by requiring that the senior officers of the state, the president and prime minister, must be Shi'i.

If they had no identity either as Kurds or as Sunnis, then there was no point in voting on the Constitution. So the Kurds abstained almost unanimously, burning ballot boxes where they could. Only the Shi'i Kurds of Kirmanshah participated.[30] In January 1980 Khomeini softened sufficiently to promise an amendment to the constitution to guarantee Sunni religious practices in areas of Sunni predominance. Yet no such amendment was forthcoming, and Kurds interpreted it as a ploy to get them to participate in the presidential election.[31]

From the outset Shaykh Izz al Din Husayni gave Kurdish nationalists a religious justification for opposing the obscurantism of the new regime. As a religious liberal and as a leftist more comfortable with Komala than the KDPI, he made an unusual Sunni cleric. Yet however controversial his views, his exemplary personal standards guaranteed him wide respect.[32] Thus, given his personal, spiritual and nationalist standing, he was a natural candidate to fill the leadership vacuum in Mahabad once the Pahlavi regime collapsed.

Shaykh Izz al Din dismissed the doctrine of the *vilayat-i faqih*, thus, in practice, Khomeini himself and the Council of Guardians, in the following words:

> What we have is not religious government, but a dictatorship under the name of Islam.... The role of the clergy is to be *murshid* [guide] in knowing God. You will also find some Shi'i clergy who reject Khomeini's concept of *faqih*. It is not an Islamic regime.... Any religious government will end in dictatorship, and religion will become a means of beating, executing and killing in the name of God.'[33]

It was unlikely that Khomeini could forgive or forget such criticism. Yet Shaykh Izz al Din went further:

> I believe in the separation of state and religion. Whenever religious government is established it is dogmatic and against democracy. Government must allow democracy and political disagreement within society.[34]

Such ideas seemed to belong to European rather than Islamic political thought and certainly had no place in Shi'i Iran. It was therefore not surprising that the shaykh was viewed as anathema in Qum.

How far Shaykh Izz al Din's *religious* views were shared by pious Kurds is difficult to say, but his arguments in favour of national autonomy and the integrity of his own lifestyle created a groundswell of support. He sidestepped universalist claims of Islam advanced in Qum to deny ethnic autonomy with the argument:

> Islam does not require that all Muslims should be governed by a single group of people. It recognizes that people are divided into different groups, nations and tribes. There is no reason within Islam why these groups should not order their own affairs.[35]

Such views, however, served to confirm Khomeini's view of the Kurdish world. He held Shaykh Izz al Din and Qasimlu directly responsible for the original land tenure conflicts of July–August 1979, although they were patently swept along by the tide of events. Shaykh Izz al Din (Glory of Religion) began to be referred to by the regime's propagandists as Zed al Din (Anti-Religion). Qasimlu was debarred from the 73-seat Council of Experts to which he had been elected. Both of them were viewed as 'seditious' and the KDPI was outlawed as 'the party of Satan', 'corrupt and [the] agent of foreigners'.[36]

It was only later, under the stress of war with Iraq, that the regime took a more tolerant view of Sunnis and made serious efforts to woo Sunni Kurdish clerics to support the government.

Discord Without and Within

By the end of the first tumultuous year, such circumstances had understandably led to a loss of patience on the part of the regime and a loss of hope on the part of the Kurds.

The disorders of March–April 1980 provoked the government in Tehran into a major assault on Kurdistan. It was determined to achieve mastery of the whole country, and feared that a liberated Kurdistan would be a dangerous example elsewhere in Iran. Bani Sadr, acutely aware of his clerical enemies in Qum, could not afford to appear weak. Such, however, was the unpopularity of the war in Kurdistan that he had to warn the army of the consequences of disobedience. By the end of April the government was in control of most of Kurdistan, but at the cost of almost 1,000 killed in battle.

When it came to seeking a negotiated solution, Bani Sadr's efforts were swept away by hardline clerics like Ayatollah Muhammad Bihishti who wanted the whole region 'purged'.[37] Ghani Bulurian, who had refused to take his seat in the Majlis as representative for Mahabad, found himself defending his colleagues to the press against the criminal excesses of Ayatollah Khalkhali. It was his last service to the party.

There had always been a tension in the KDPI between two seemingly incompatible desires: to seize the moment to achieve autonomy and to welcome, accommodate and support the revolution. It was a gap that was increasingly impossible to bridge. Quite apart from the difficulties in dealing with Tehran, attempts at fresh dialogue tended to be undermined by Komala's determination to continue the fight.

Furthermore, Kurdistan had become the battlefield for many radical opponents of the regime and this diminished Kurdish political control of the struggle. Throughout the summer, the KDPI, Komala, Fida'in-i Khalq and the Mujahidin maintained a formidable guerrilla campaign, ambushing Pasdaran convoys. For three months the government made no attempt to retake Mahabad, Bukan or Sardasht.

Intermittent attempts by the KDPI to negotiate with the regime achieved nothing, except to encourage some Kurds to defect to Komala. At its Fourth Congress in February, the KDPI had favoured continuing its attempts to find a negotiated solution. But given the disappointments over negotiations and the constitution at the end of 1979, it was inexorably driven towards war. It ordered its membership to retire to the mountains. Some felt increasingly uneasy with the way the party seemed to abandon the decisions of the Fourth Congress, and how it diverged from the efforts of the Tudeh to negotiate from within the system.

In late May Ghani Bulurian and six others of the party's central committee renounced their party membership in protest at Qasimlu's leadership and his alleged departure from Congress resolutions.[38] They also condemned Qasimlu for receiving aid from Baghdad at a time of growing danger for Iran and argued that the autonomy of Kurdistan must come *after* Iran's anti-imperialist revolution had been safeguarded. They accused the KDPI armed struggle of playing into the hands of imperialism. The argument was in line with the Tudeh's policy of supporting the Islamic regime. Subsequently Bulurian published some of Qasimlu's correspondence with the Iraqis but failed to provide documentary proof of the charge against him.[39] In fact the KDPI never co-operated with Iraqi forces against Iran.

The revolt sent shock waves through the party. Bulurian, after all, had proved his patriotism with a 25-year jail sentence. But the balance of loyalty was in Qasimlu's favour and the rebels were soon labelled 'the Gang of Seven Jash',[40] thus relegating them to the same category as the regime's Kurdish mercenaries. A similar split occurred at this time in the Fida'in-i Khalq but it was the majority which decided to adopt a similar policy to the Tudeh. Only a minority remained committed to the armed struggle.

Iran had been busy with its own provocations. It had antagonized Iraq by its Shi'i propaganda and denuciations of Saddam Husayn. It already assisted the KDP, albeit mainly to defeat the KDPI inside Iran, and now held discussions with the Iraqi Kurdish Patriotic Union of Kurdistan (PUK). By midsummer 1980 open war was likely, but Iran was ill-equipped to face it. Its army had been decimated by desertions and purges. Three of its remaining 11 army divisions were already deployed to hold down Kurdistan. When Iraq attacked in late September 1980, Iran was expected to capitulate quickly.

Iraq's invasion seemed a golden opportunity for the Kurds to throw off government control completely, or to dictate the autonomy terms they wanted. One option could have been the KDPI's unconditional support for Iran's territorial integrity in the hope that Tehran would reward such a gesture. But Qasimlu, who had little expectation of a reciprocal spirit in Tehran, felt strong enough to insist that Tehran admit the principle of Kurdish autonomy and withdraw its forces from Kurdistan *before* the KDPI turned its weapons on the Iraqi invader. Given the mind-set in Tehran, such an ultimatum could only be treated as treason.

Defeat and More Discord

Kurdish hopes proved shortlived, for the Iranian army defied expectation by their resolute defence of Khuzistan in October. For the next few months the army was concerned with absorbing the Iraqi assault, and left the Kurds largely to themselves. On the ground the KDPI and Komala were able to establish schools and elected village and municipal councils in the population centres they held.

Yet in political terms both were marking time, awaiting the Iranian attempt to recapture the region. In August 1981 Masud Rajavi, the Mujahidin leader, and the now fugitive ex-President Bani Sadr announced the formation of a National Resistance Council. *Inter alia*, the NRC's charter promised civil liberties, the consolidation of farm lands as collectives, respect for property, equality for women and elected and consultative councils, all things calculated to appeal particularly to the lower middle classes, from which the resistance drew most of its strength. At its Fifth Congress in December, the KDPI decided to join the NRC, but some felt the decision precipitate and ill-considered, and the KDPI remained an uneasy member.

In summer 1982 the long-awaited Iranian assault was launched. At first government forces were unable to push through southwards to meet the army deployed along the southern front. It was only in November that they recaptured the tactically important Sardasht–Piranshahr road along which the KDPI had been able to move troops and supplies. The loss of this road forced the KDPI onto a purely guerrilla footing, mounted from the high ground around Sardasht. In September it temporarily recaptured Bukan, demonstrating that it was not yet a spent force. By the end of 1983 virtually all Kurdish rebel-held territory had been recaptured by Iranian forces.

In July 1984 Iranian forces finally cleared the KDPI out of its border fastnesses in Hawraman, using helicopters to seize mountain peaks and dominate the surrounding country. Where necessary, just like Iraq, Iran expelled villagers in the border area in order to create a *cordon sanitaire* and deny the guerrillas local assistance. The KDPI was driven into Iraq where it received armed assistance from the PUK against Iranian forces.

From the summer offensive of 1982 it was increasingly clear that the KDPI and Komala could ill-afford to ignore each other. Despite disagreement over the KDPI's membership of the National Resistance Council, Komala agreed in November 1982 to co-ordinate its military activities under a joint headquarters. During two years or so the two parties, KDPI and Komala, carried out some successful joint operations. However, in November 1984 a quarrel over land ownership and the killing of a KDPI commander by Komala set off a savage internecine war that dragged on for four years or so, and during phases of which neither side took prisoners.[41] A ceasefire was only agreed because of the pressure both groups faced from Iranian forces.

Behind this clash lay the deep ideological divergence between the two groups. In July a KDPI delegation had explored the chances for a resolution of its quarrel with Tehran. This contributed to its quarrel with Komala but also led to its resignation from the NRC. The decision to leave the NRC was made by Qasimlu himself, and upset many leftists inside the KDPI. The KDPI was now rent between those who shared NRC's or Komala's commitment to the overthrow of the regime and those who still hoped for a compromise.

There had been other signs of stress within the KDPI over the leadership question. Following the party's Sixth Congress in January 1984 it had purged the doubters from its ranks, of whom the most notable was Karim Husami, a senior veteran of the party who had been a marked man since 1980 because he had sympathized with the views, but not the resignation, of the Band of Seven four years earlier.[42]

Komala also entered a period of setbacks. Ideologically, it had always repudiated the 'bourgeois' idea of struggling purely for the Kurdish nation. This was a viewpoint, however, which appealed more to its strong representation of intellectuals than its comparatively small body of workers and peasants. In 1982 it joined two smaller Iranian leftist groups (Sahand and some members of Paykar, itself a splinter from the Mujahidin)[43] to form the Communist Party of Iran (Hizb-i Kumunist-i Iran) under the leadership of one of Komala's founders, Abd Allah Muhtadi.

Formally Komala ceased to exist although it remained known by this name in Kurdistan. In denouncing not only the contemporary KDPI but also its moment of glory at Mahabad in 1946, it wholly miscalculated Kurdish feeling. During the next six years many of its fighters and supporters drifted away from the Communist Party of Iran, since despite its disproportionately strong Kurdish component, it had now lost its specifically Kurdish flavour.

When it finally resumed its Kurdish identity in 1991, Komala was weaker numerically than those smaller groups with which it had united in 1982. The decision to revert to a Kurdish identity now triggered another schism, with a new group, the Proletarian Communist Party of Iran, denouncing Muhtadi and his followers for clinging to the vestiges of nationalism.

The end of the Iran–Iraq war in 1988 brought scant comfort to Iran's Kurds. Qasimlu's boast that Kurdish forces still tied down a quarter of a million troops was a vain one. His position was weak and he was now convinced he had to talk with the regime.

In spite of the controversy which the suggestion of negotiations with the regime triggered in KDPI ranks, Qasimlu had already made this central to the party's Eighth Congress, held in January 1988. He had rested his case on three factors: there was no military solution; when the Iran–Iraq war was over Tehran would feel able to reassess its attitude to the Kurds; finally, with Khomeini rapidly losing his vigour, there was a real chance for a fresh beginning for Kurdish relations with the republic.

However, such arguments and Qasimlu's efforts to push them through triggered a serious revolt within the KDPI. There had always been a strongly socialist faction within the party, one that was arguably as doctrinaire as Komala. Members of this group now accused Qasimlu of turning the KDPI from socialism to social democracy and, in so doing, risking the party's mass base. Fifteen executive committee members protested that after an estimated 50,000 Kurds had perished as a result of the regime's repression, parley was unthinkable. Behind such specific matters, however, lay the deep dissatisfaction with Qasimlu's auto-cratic style which had been growing since the Sixth Congress.

Under their leader, Jalil Ghadani, these rebels walked out of the Congress, to form a Kurdistan Democratic Party of Iran – Revolutionary Leadership. They attracted a substantial following of KDPI leftists and others who resented what they considered Qasimlu's undemocratic methods. This schism was quite as bitter as that of 1980, for like Bulurian, Ghadani was one of the oldest activists, almost synonymous with the KDPI itself.[44]

The Revolutionary Leadership rapidly made its peace with Komala, something the KDPI found difficult to do. Yet the weight of the party remained with Qasimlu, and during the next two years the collapse of the Soviet empire and of the credibility of pro-Soviet Marxism left the KDPI–RL weakened. Although it sought a compromise with the KDPI, the leadership of the latter did not feel inclined to make concessions and deeply resented the 'deviationists', as they called them, using their name.

In the meantime, Qasimlu was informed by his friend, Jalal Talabani, that Tehran was interested in talking. This was good news, and a series of secret meetings were arranged in Vienna in December 1988–January 1989. Qasimlu was greatly encouraged to find that Tehran's emissaries did not reject out of hand either the demand for autonomy or the plea that the Kurdish region should be united administratively, although neither did they accept them. In March Qasimlu learnt with disappointment that Iran wished to discontinue this dialogue.

In June, shortly after Khomeini's death, Qasimlu heard that Tehran wished to resume talks. He was excited by the prospect, even though the agenda merely concerned an amnesty programme for his peshmergas, not a political settlement. After Khomeini there was the chance for a new beginning. Qasimlu was already waiting with his aide and a trusted intermediary at a Viennese apartment when the Iranian delegation arrived. All three were shot dead.[45] It was the fortieth day of mourning for the late ayatollah.

The assassination of Qasimlu was a profound blow to Kurdish hopes. Many who knew him personally considered him the most skilful politician in the whole of Kurdistan. Dr Sadiq Sharafkindi, a close colleague, took over party leadership. The KDPI-RL could not resist crowing over Qasimlu's fate:

> Dr Qasimlu became a tragic victim of his own political mistakes and compromising stance toward the reactionary terrorists who govern the Islamic Republic.... We hope that Dr Qasimlu's death would teach a lesson to those who sanctioned the policy of compromise over armed struggle at the VIIIth Congress.[46]

Six weeks later a senior Komala member was assassinated in Larnaca.[47] Sharafkindi did not last long either. He was shot dead along with three colleagues in Berlin in September 1992, shortly after attending the Socialist International. He was succeeded by a little-known party member, Mustafa Hijri.

A Continuous Struggle

By 1993 both the KDPI and Komala had suffered brutal reverses: defeat on the battlefield, internal disarray and assassination. A garrison of 200,000 troops held Kurdish areas under control – except for attacks after dark.

The regime had felt sufficiently secure long enough to allow a degree of cultural freedom, including the propagation of Kurdish cultural events and publications.[48] Yet it remained unrelenting in its hostility to Kurdish political groups, partly because the number of Pasdaran being ambushed and killed was beginning to grow.

There was no question of talks now. Instead, the government embarked upon a series of artillery and air attacks on KDPI and Komala bases inside Iraqi Kurdistan, causing few casualties but forcing many Iraqi Kurds to flee border hamlets. In part Tehran may have reacted against the threat of the Iraqi Kurdish example of relative national freedom from 1991 onwards, but in the autumn it formed a Rapid Reaction Force to seal the border following the refusal of Talabani and Barzani to evict from Iraq Iranian Kurdish rebels – as they had done the previous year with Turkey's rebels.

Yet Tehran's policy made little sense. It had no realistic prospect of expunging either the KDPI or Komala, since by now both parties were synonymous with the national sentiments felt by most Kurds. The disintegration of either party seemed more probable from internal dissension than external attack.

The KDPI repeatedly and explicitly stated that it harboured no belief or expectation that it could win a guerrilla war, and that there was no alternative to a negotiated solution.[49] Yet within its ranks some spoke with a new stridency of secession if the Islamic regime proved obdurate to the demand for autonomy. As in Turkey, an adamant refusal to brook the idea of autonomy was beginning to show signs of generating genuine separatism.

Tehran's response to the insurgency ignored two crucial facets of the Kurdish challenge. The first of these was that most guerrilla action was nowhere near the Iraqi border, operating out of the homes of sympathizers the length and breadth of Kurdistan. As one KDPI politburo member remarked, 'They [Tehran] are much better equipped; they have all the advantages of a state. But they have no political base. Their only base is a fort on the top of each hilltop.'[50] The militarization of Kurdistan provided more potential targets for the guerrillas and deepened nationalist sentiment among the civil population.

Guerrilla freedom to live among the Kurdish population was a key indication of the progress of the national movement since the revolution. Another indicator was demonstrated in the presidential election of June 1993. Kurdistan distinguished itself as the only province where a majority of the electorate favoured an opposition candidate rather than the incumbent, Ali Akbar Rafsanjani. Finally, nationalist sentiment had seeped southwards into the predominantly Shi'i area, partly because of disgust with government savagery against Kurds further north and partly because of the unpopularity and human cost of supporting an ideological regime in its war against Iraq in the 1980s.

Ironically, Tehran's most reliable allies in Kurdistan by 1993 were among the extreme Shi'i Ahl-i Haqq tribes of the Guran and Sanjabi. There had been a remarkable growth in the authority of the Haydari *sayyids* since the suppression of the tribal chiefs by Reza Shah. Shaykh Nasr al Din emerged as the powerful leader of the Guran, a belated parallel to the rise of Sunni shaykhs in the latter part of the nineteenth century in Ottoman Kurdistan. Conscious of their vulnerable position as a heterodox minority, the Ahl-i Haqq had supported the Pahlavis; the imperative for such a policy grew, rather than decreas, with the establishment of an assertively Shi'i republic in Tehran. Shaykh Nasr al Din personally led Ahl-i Haqq forces in defence of the border during the Iran–Iraq war, and these acquired a reputation for greater steadfastness under fire than the Basij units either side of them. In addition, tribes like the Sanjabi which had suffered under the Pahlavis, even though they had supported them, found the Islamic regime much readier to foster tribal life again, partly as an intrinsically important cultural component of Iran and partly because of the value of stockbreeding in a country suffering severe meat shortages. But these were interesting exceptions to a process of alienation already well under way.

The other factor that posed a long-term challenge to the regime was an economic one, in which impoverished Kurdistan represented an acute facet of a wider problem. With a population that doubled every twenty years or so, it was doubtful whether the country still had the ability to meet the demand for food production, education and employment. In 1992 unemployment among those aged under 25 ran at 70 per cent, and real inflation at 100 per cent. Survival rather than development seemed the order of the day.

In Kurdistan these economic changes were evident in employment and migration. In the mid-1970s the towns of Kurdistan had expanded to absorb the growing labour force. By 1990 probably over 60 per cent of Kurds were town-dwellers; but now a growing number of them were travelling to Khuzistan in search of work in the oil industry or in the ports, or to Tehran. Far from creating a new and homogeneous national identity, as so fervently hoped by centralizing regimes in the region, the drift to the great industrial centres tended to emphasize the sense of difference, alienation and localist identity. It was in the burgeoning slum quarters of such cities, where government failed to provide even the basic services, that the Kurdish movement seemed most likely to grow and forge ties with other political movements wishing to achieve a measure of decentralization. Komala was particularly assiduous in exploiting this growing social phenomenon, but there was a long way to go. In the words of Komala's leader, Abd Allah Muhtadi, 'In order to mobilize the people, the government must be visibly destabilized.'[51]

Kurdish hopes of liberalization were raised by the election of the Islamic reformer, President Mohammad Khatami in 1997. Indeed, 76 per cent of the electors in Kurdistan province supported his candidacy. His vision of social and political pluralism offered an escape from the stifling conservative local authorities imposed on the region. Khatami appointed a Western-educated ethnologist, Abd Allah Ramazanzadeh, as governor to oversee the rehabilitation and reconciliation of Sunni Kurdistan. Ramazanzadeh was the first Kurd to hold this post since the Revolution. He got off to a good start, allocating substantial funds from Tehran for infrastructural development of this much-neglected province. He also sought to empower local communities, holding town meetings with local residents and actively promoting Kurds within his administration.

It was not surprising, therefore, that in the local elections in February 1999 reformist candidates were swept into office all over the province. Later that month this political impulse was more overtly expressed as news broke of Ocalan's capture in Nairobi. Major demonstrations took place in all the major towns and cities of the region.[52]

It was now that the limitations of Khatami's reforming process suddenly became apparent. Neither he nor his Kurdish governor would brook disorder. Both supported the harsh crackdown in which at least 30 were shot dead, hundreds wounded and possible 2,000 arrested.

Though government treatment of the February demonstrations proved a profound disappointment for Iran's Kurds, they have no better option currently than Khatami. He has already demonstrated his encouragement of civil society and, despite set-backs, working even with snail-pace liberalisation may yet be preferable to armed opposition from across international borders.

Sources

Secondary Sources: Nozar Alaolmolki, 'The new Iranian Left', *Middle East Journal*, vol. 41, no. 2 (Spring 1987); Shaul Bakhash, *The Reign of the Ayatollahs* (London, 1985); Abol Hassan Bani Sadr, *My Turn to Speak* (Washington, 1991); Ali Banuazizi and Myron Weiner, *The State, Religion and Ethnic Politics* (Syracuse 1986); van Bruinessen, 'Kurdish tribes and the state of Iran: the case of Simko's revolt'; van Bruinessen, 'The Kurds between Iraq and Iran', *Middle East Report*, no. 141 (July–August 1986); Shahram Chubin and Charles Tripp, *Iran and Iraq at War* (London, 1988); Nader Entessar, 'The Kurds in post-revolutionary Iran and Iraq', *Third World Quarterly*, vol. vi, no. 4 (October 1984) and *Kurdish Ethnonationalism*, Kahn, *Children of the Jinn*; Charles MacDonald, 'The Kurdish question in the 1980s' and David Menashri, 'Khomeini's policy towards ethnic and religious minorities' in Milton Esman and Itamar Rabinovich, *Ethnicity, Pluralism and the State in the Middle East* (Ithaca and London, 1988); Christiane More, *Les Kurdes Aujourd'hui* (Paris, 1984); Bo Utas, Carina Jahani, Ferhad Shakely, Muhamad Mohtadi, 'Present situation of the Kurds in Iran' (mimeograph paper, Stockholm, March 1991); Sapehr Zabih, *The Iranian Military in Revolution and War* (London and New York, 1988).

Newspapers, etc. BBC, *Summary of World Broadcasts, The Daily Telegraph, The Financial Times, The Guardian, Hawkar, Al Hayat, The Independent, International Herald Tribune, Liberation, Le Monde, Middle East International, New York Times, The Observer, The Times.*

Interviews: Hama Ali (London, 26 July 1993); Kemal Davoudi (Stockholm, 17 March 1991); Hassan Ghazi (by cassette, autumn 1993); Mustafa Hijri (London, 18 June 1993); Shaykh Izz al Din Husayni (Stockholm, 16 March 1991); Abd Allah Muhtadi (Stockholm, 16 March 1991); Khalil and Haydar Rashidian (London, 9 June 1993); Kawa and Bayan Rezannezhad (London, 30 June 1993); Abbas Vali (Swansea, 17 October 1993).

Notes

1. *The Egyptian Gazette*, 9 February 1977.
2. By February 1981 the death toll among Iranian Kurds was reckoned at 10,000, *Daily Telegraph*, 11 February 1981.
3. It was drafted by the Kurdish Revolutionary Council, a rapidly convened body representing major Kurdish groups out of an elected assembly of 500 'elders'.
4. Franjo Butorac, 'Iran's revolution and the Kurds', *Review of International Affairs* (Belgrade), 20 April 1980, p. 17, quoted by Charles MacDonald, 'The Kurdish question in the 1980s' in Milton Esman and ItamarRabinovich (eds.) *Ethnicity, Pluralism and the State in the Middle East* (Ithaca and London, 1988), p. 242.

5. These demands were: (i) Kurdish autonomy should be formally recognised and mentioned in the constitution; (ii) The Kurdish region should extend from Ilam to West Azerbaijan; (iii) The National Assembly of Kurdistan should be freely elected by secret ballot; (iv) Kurdish should be the primary language in school and in official correspondence; (v) Part of the [Iranian] national budget should be allocated to Kurdistan, to remedy its backwardness; (vi) Kurdish representatives should be appointed to central government; (vii) Foreign policy, national defence and economic planning should be a responsibility of central government; (viii) All Iran should enjoy the basic democratic freedoms of assembly, speech and religious practice. (*The Times*, 4 December 1979.)

6. The actual terms of the proposal for local administration were: (i) A provincial council would administer the local population, except regarding: national defence, foreign affairs, the monetary system and long-term planning, large industrial enterprises, telecommunications, rail and major roads. (ii) Senior appointments, for example city governors, local police and gendarmerie commanders, would be made by central government on the recommendation of the provincial council. (iii) A judicial system would be operated autonomously but subject to the Supreme Council of the Islamic Republic. (iv) Local responsibility for the maintenance of order. (v) The Provincial Council's legislative powers would be confined to traditional personal, family and religious law. (vi) The religion of the majority would be considered 'official'. (vii) The budget would be supplemented in two ways by government: by subsidy from central government and by local taxes and duties. (viii) Extra finance would be made available for backward areas. (ix) Freedom of expression and organization for all political, religious and cultural activity. (x) Freedom to teach in Kurdish, Baluchi, Azari, Armenian, Assyrian, Hebrew, Arabic or Turkish. The principal languages to be taught alongside Persian at school. (xi) The local language may be used for administrative purposes but not in dealing with central government. (xii) Each province to have its own university, radio and television services. (xiii) The provincial council to fix the size of the army and gendarmerie in proportion to the population (*Le Monde*, 18 December 1979.)

7. The younger brother of Sayf Qazi, Rahim had been in Soviet Azerbaijan undergoing military training at the time of the collapse of the Mahabad Republic. He was sentenced to death *in absentia*, was invited back after the collapse of the Pahlavi dynasty, and was elected to the KDPI Central Committee at the Fourth Congress in Mahabad, February 1980. He later defected with the Gang of Seven (see page 273). He died in Baku in May 1991.

8. Altogether, 62 officers and men were executed and 115 condemned to life imprisonment; 200 men were rescued by the KDPI; Zabih, *The Iranian Military*, p. 124.

9. *New York Times*, 12 March 1979.

10. In March 1980 the election for the Iran National Assembly had revealed the strength of the KDPI's hold in north-western Kurdistan. In Mahabad it obtained 80 per cent of the vote, and 96 per cent in Naqada-Ushnaviya. It was weaker to the south: only 57 per cent in Bukan and Saqqiz respectively, and further south the results were declared void. No election was attempted in Sanandaj; *Le Monde*, 22 April 1980.

11. For example, Abd Allah Muhtadi and Umar Ilkhanzada were both from the Dihbukri of Bukan.

12. Alaolmolki, 'The new Iranian Left', p. 231.

13. A man with the unfortunate family name 'Baghdadi'.

14. It will be recalled that Mulla Mustafa made his legendary march through Shikak territory in spring 1947.

15. Muftizada may possibly have suffered from association with his uncle, Muhammad Sadiq Muftizada, who had been editor of the Pahlavi propaganda journal, *Kurdistan*. There was also an unsubstantiated rumour of his links with Idris Barzani, associated in some minds with support for the old agha class against the peasantry; *Le Monde*, 23 March 1979.

16. *Le Monde*, 30 March 1979.

17. Muftizada was subsequently imprisoned by the regime and after his release died in 1992.

18. For example, Sayyid Abd Allah Hazrati Malakshan, who sold his lands to the people who worked it. Mulla Abd al Rahim Mudarrisi was the first cleric in Sanandaj to send his daughter to government school. His son joined Komala.

19. Shaykh Jalal severed his connection with Baghdad following the chemical attack on Halabja.

20. Martin van Bruinessen, 'The Kurds between Iraq and Iran', *Middle East Report*, no. 141, July–August 1986, pp. 14, 17.

21. *Egyptian Mail,* 3 March 1979.

22. *Le Monde*, 6 March 1979.

23. Kurds resented the appointment of Shi'is to govern them during the Pahlavi period. This sensitivity led to violence when Shi'i Azari peasants around Urumiya were armed by Tehran in April 1942 to keep order, implicitly against lawless Kurds. An American living in Urumiya in 1975 noted 'One of the reasons Kurds give for hating the Turks is their very Shi'iness', Kahn, *Children of the Jinn*, p. 119.

24. The best account of the Naqada affair is to be found in Karim Husami's memoirs, published in Stockholm in 1990.

25. *Middle East Report*, no. 113, March–April, 1983, p. 9.

26. *New York Times Magazine*, 28 October 1979.

27. Article 5 of the draft appeared in *Iran Voice*, 2 July 1979, see Hamid Algar, 'Documents: draft constitution of the Islamic Republic of Iran', *Ripeh* 3 (Fall 1979), pp. 20–51, quoted in Charles MacDonald, 'The Kurdish challenge in revolutionary Iran', *Journal of South East Asian and Middle Eastern Studies*, vol. xiii, nos 1&2, (Fall/Winter 1980), p. 61.

28. Bakhash, *The Reign of the Ayatollahs*, p. 75, quoting from Bani Sadr's own account.

29. Radio Tehran, 17 December 1979, in BBC/SWB 19 December 1979, quoted in Menashri, 'Khomeini policy', p. 217.

30. In Kurdistan province ballot boxes in 36 locations were removed by Kurds, and in the 37th it was burnt. But in Kirmanshah the vote was overwhelmingly in favour; in Qasr-i Shirin there were 9,460 votes in favour and only 21 against.

31. Kurds and Turkomans might have participated had the pro-autonomy candidate, Masud Rajavi, not been disqualified on account of his opposition to the recently introduced constitution. Bani Sadr offered 'Islamic autonomy' in July 1980, but it was insubstantial.

32. Unlike many religious figures, he lived modestly, supporting his wife and seven children by dint of Arabic classes to theological students, owning no land and taking no money gifts from his admirers.

33. *Middle East Report*, no. 113, March–April 1983, pp. 9–10.

34. Interview with the author, Stockholm, 16 March 1991.

35. Interview with Shaykh Izz al Din Husayni, Stockholm, 16 March 1991.

36. *Financial Times*, 20 and 21 August; *New York Times*, 19 August 1980; Menashri, 'Khomeini's Policy', p. 218.

37. *Financial Times*, 24 May 1980.

38. The signatories were Fawziya Qazi, Nafidh Muini, Rahimi Sayfi Qazi, Fatuq Kaykhusri, Ahmad Azizi and Muhammad Amin Sarraji (in consultative status to the Central Committee), information from Hassan Ghazi.

39. Karim Hussami's memoirs dismiss Bulurian's evidence as insubstantial. One of the letters related to Qasimlu's secret meeting with the Iraqi Vice-President Taha Yasin Ramadan at Hajj Umran.

40. 'Jash', literally small donkey, but popularly used to mean collaborator.

41. The catalyst for conflict was a quarrel over tree felling. Komala insisted on the people's right to fuel, while KDPI protested that the trees in question were private property, Hassan

Ghazi, personal information; *The Times*, 24 January; *Le Monde*, 9 February; *The Guardian*, 4 March 1985.

42. Karim Husami defended his position with his own version of events in his memoirs, published in Stockholm, 1993. Having deplored the Gang of Seven's departure he did not hesitate to criticize Qasimlu and his advisers for branding them as 'jash'; information from Hassan Ghazi.

43. For further information on Paykar, see Alaolmolki, 'The new Iranian Left.'

44. Ghadani had spent 10 years in prison after his arrest with 250 others in 1959. He was re-arrested when attending the funeral of Sulayman Muini in 1968. As an active organizer in Tehran, he gave Qasimlu the base from which to work in 1978. That year he had been one of three main orators (along with Shaykh Izz al Din Husayni and Umar Qazi) at Aziz Yusifi's funeral, calling for Kurdish autonomy.

45. The best account available is in *Liberation*, 7 August 1989.

46. *Aghazi No*, special bulletin, 18 July 1989, quoted in Entessar, *Kurdish Ethnonationalism*, p. 42.

47. This was Bahman Javadi (*nom de guerre* Ghulam Kisharvaz).

48. A Kurdish culture and literature congress was held in Mahabad in September 1986. A Kurdish cultural magazine, *Sirwa*, was commenced in Spring 1985. Work began on Kurdish primary level school texts, Utas, Jahani, Shakely and Mohtadi, 'Present Situation of the Kurds in Iran', p. 19.

49. Kemal Davoudi, KDPI spokesman, Stockholm, 17 March 1991; interview with Mustafa Hijri, London, 18 June 1993.

50. Salam Azizi in The Independent, 23 June 1993.

51. Interview with Abd Allah Muhtadi, Stockholm, 16 March 1991.

52. Urumiya, Mahabad, Bukan, Piranshahr, Sardasht, Saqqiz. Sanandaj, Bana and Pava.

BOOK IV

ETHNO-NATIONALISM IN IRAQ

CHAPTER 14

THE BIRTH OF A NATIONAL MOVEMENT UNDER HASHIMITE RULE

Introduction

In Iraqi Kurdistan, as in Iran in the early 1940s, a new educated class of people took up the cause of ethnic nationalism. This class was destined to challenge the aghas as national leaders. It challenged them because they were incorporating themselves into the Hashimite system of control and were increasing their economic hold on Kurdistan. As a result the nationalist movement found itself closely associated with a leftist struggle to liberate the peasantry from landlord exploitation. But it failed to overcome the culture of patronage in which Kurdish society remained steeped.

The Early Political Activists

After the bloodshed in Sulaymaniya in 1930, the Kurds seemed to accept their lot and the incident faded in the official memory – an unfortunate occurrence to be quietly forgotten. Most aghas were willing to leave community grievances in abeyance because their own position seemed assured under King Faysal's moderating influence, and this was an effective palliative to Arab rule.

Following Faysal's death in September 1933, however, the state was thrown into disarray as one cabinet after another found itself unable to govern on account of factionalism, Sunni–Shi'i tensions or the undermining of government by politicians temporarily out of office. It was this loss of authority at the centre which emboldened about 40 Kurdish chiefs in spring 1935 to challenge government on its continuing failure regarding the undertakings of the League of Nations.[1] They thought they held the balance of Sunni power *vis-à-vis* the Shi'is, and could therefore force Baghdad's hand. They demanded official use of Kurdish as required by the League of Nations in 1926. They did not want administrative autonomy but sought representation in the National Assembly by genuine natives of their constituencies, and they called for a fair share of national resources and genuine development of Kurdish agriculture and industry. The furthest they

287

went on the nationalist path was to ask for the detachment of the predominantly Kurdish *qadhas* from the Arab administration in Mosul, and the formation of a Kurdish *liwa* based on Dohuk; this request was largely because of friction with the people of Mosul who manifested Arab nationalist leanings. However, Baghdad refused to make any firm undertaking.

It was easy for politicians in Baghdad to assume that they had fobbed the Kurds off yet again. Apart from the periodic disgruntlement of chiefs and land-lords, there was little overt sign of any communal cohesion or organization. On the contrary, the politicians could congratulate themselves on the apparent ab-sence of the tiresome paraphernalia of growing communal solidarity. By 1936 Kurdish civil activity was still notable by its absence. Of 150 officially registered associations only five were located in Kurdistan, two of which were Islamic rather than Kurdish in identity.[2] Even the Christian minorities had more offi-cially registered 'self-improvement' associations.

Yet, unnoticed at the time, September 1930 had been a watershed for it marked the awakening of national consciousness among the first generation of secular educated and urban Kurds. In the words of Ibrahim Ahmad, then six-teen, 'from that day I thought it my duty to work as a Kurd.'[3]

Like a handful of other middle-class Kurds of Sulaymaniya, Ahmad went to Baghdad to receive a professional education. Baghdad was where the brightest young Kurds gathered and where they could watch the political process at close quarters. Some students had already formed an informal Komala-i Liwan (Young Men's Club) in 1930, ostensibly concerned with cultural and literary affairs, but with an unstated political programme. Ahmad soon joined it.[4] There were only about 100 Kurdish students in Baghdad at the time and only a few joined the club. It was a modest beginning but it was inevitable that in seeking to foster Kurdish language and literature, the issues central to Kurdish identity were dis-cussed, including the question of Kurdish political rights.

In the absence of any overt Kurdish party, however, some joined the Iraqi Communist Party (ICP), which had been founded in 1934 and which in 1935 briefly advocated the complete independence of the Kurds. During the next few years it built local branches in Arbil, Kirkuk and elsewhere. Even after its retreat from Kurdish independence, its advocacy of minority rights gave it appeal for many in the newly educated classes. Others opted for Al Ahali, a liberal reform-ist group which rejected both conservatism and authoritarian socialism, but sought social reform to advance conditions for urban and rural workers. In October 1936 the Ahali group was implicated in a *coup d'état* by the army commander, Bakr Sidqi.

Although Bakr Sidqi was of Kurdish origin he was hardly a Kurdish nationalist. Nevertheless, his coup provoked anti-Kurdish feeling among Arab nationalists. Pan-Arabists viewed the Kurds as an impediment to their political dreams. With the 1935 foundation of the Muthanna Club, with its express purpose of advancing their ideas, tension with the Kurds was bound to increase. Now the pan-Arabists accused Bakr Sidqi of pandering to the Kurds, an accusation based less on Bakr Sidqi's own Kurdish origins than on his failure to espouse pan-Arabism.

The provocations of pan-Arabists in turn excited Kurdish national feeling. When the Arab press accused the Kurds of Alexandretta of supporting Turkey's claims to this part of Syria in 1937, Ibrahim Ahmad wrote an impassioned response. In *Al Akrad wa'l Arab* (The Kurds and the Arabs) Ahmad claimed that the cause of conflict between the Kurds and Arabs was not inter-communal tension but government oppression which fell on all communities regardless. He warned against blind nationalism that disregarded others, avoided nationalist claims for the Kurds *per se*, and advanced the idea of democracy and brotherhood in equality for the nations of the region. But he also unmistakably asserted the right of each people to real control over its own affairs.

Suddenly it became clear that a new class of young professional Kurds which hoped for a degree of independence was coming into existence. Other groups began to form clandestinely. One of these, Komala Brayati (Brotherhood Society), was led by Shaykh Mahmud's son, Shaykh Latif. Its membership was largely confined to urban notables and one or two religious dignitaries. Younger and more radical nationalists in Sulaymaniya formed another group, Darkar (Wood-cutters), a clear reference to the Carbonari of the Italian Risorgimento. Darkar had close links with the Iraqi Communist Party (ICP), and particularly with its Kurdish wing known by its journal *Azadi*. As a component of the ICP, Azadi proposed the freedom of both Kurds and Arabs. Darkar could afford to be more clearly nationalist in its ideology, and it soon established chapters in Kurdish towns, and in Mosul and Baghdad.

It is hardly surprising that Baghdad was unaware of such developments. Brayati and Darkar had little significance in themselves. Each had only a handful of members, and were really small coteries rather than organizations. In 1938 the government proscribed unlawfully constituted political associations but everyone took this to mean the Communist Party and its fellow travellers, not Kurdish groups *per se*. As late as 1940 C.J. Edmonds, by then Adviser to the Ministry of the Interior, who had a more intimate knowledge of Kurdish society than most, could write 'In recent years there has been virtually no manifestation of political Kurdish nationalism in Iraq', and he put rumours of pro-Bolshevik Kurdish committees down to 'the normal working of the bazaar mind'.[5] However, as yet unseen, the seeds of Kurdish nationalism were germinating.

It was at this time that Darkar formed the nucleus of a new party, Hiwa (Hope), intended to bring together the different groups which had come into being. As in the case of Darkar, Hiwa's initial centres, Arbil, Kirkuk, Kifri, Kalar and Khaniqin as well as colleges in Baghdad, indicated the geographical and social shift taking place, away from the stereotyped mountain and tribal context of Kurdish identity.

Hiwa soon had 1,500 members, young trainee professionals in Baghdad's new colleges, officers and NCOs in the fledgling Iraqi army and a few landlords, shaykhs and tribal aghas. Yet there were virtually no peasants. Whether this was because recruitment was blocked by the landlord class, as Hiwa activists themselves claimed, or because the average peasant simply could not relate Hiwa nationalist rhetoric to his/her own highly circumscribed world is a moot point, but it undoubtedly weakened the party. When the government security services at last began rounding up activists, those landlords who had shown interest quickly dissociated themselves, and intellectuals on the run found nowhere outside their own middle class quarters to hide.

Indeed Hiwa, like Darkar, had better connections with the activists of Mahabad than it did with the traditional leadership in Iraq. It had barely formed when it sent two army officers, Mir Hajj Ahmad and Mustafa Khushnaw, as delegates to the founding meeting of Komala JK Society in Mahabad in September 1942. From then until the collapse of Mahabad, activists made the journey to and fro, hoping to build pan-Kurd solidarity.

Mulla Mustafa Barzani's Revolt 1943–45

The failure of the new intellectual leadership to attract the old agha class was clearly illustrated in the revolt of Mulla Mustafa Barzani in 1943. Although sometimes described as a nationalist rebellion, the evidence indicates that it was not.

Mulla Mustafa, like Shaykh Ahmad, was kept in detention after the previous rebellion, first in Nasiriya in southern Iraq and then in Sulaymaniya, where apparently he had contact with Brayati, if not with more overtly nationalist groups. The links he forged were probably with local notables like Shaykh Latif rather than with nationalists *per se*. Certainly there is no indication that Mulla Mustafa's escape and rebellion was motivated by anything other than the acute hardship the government foolishly inflicted on his brother and himself.

When Mulla Mustafa reached Barzan in July 1943 he petitioned the government merely for his brother and himself to live peacefully there. For two months the government did nothing and, almost inevitably, an armed clash took place between Barzani men and a police post, transforming Mulla Mustafa from fugitive to rebel. Britain warned Baghdad that continued victimization of the Barzanis would only drive them further into a corner, and was bad in principle for Arab–Kurdish relations.

Britain feared that Barzani might set all Iraqi Kurdistan ablaze. It was sensitive to continuing Kurdish grievance over Baghdad's betrayal of the League of Nations requirements of 1926 and its general neglect of Kurdistan. More immediately, Baghdad had done nothing to alleviate the Kurdish famine of 1943 – because of failed harvests people had been starving since the beginning of the year. Ever since 1922 Britain had cajoled the aghas into compliance with the new order; now it feared a combustion between general Kurdish discontent and Mulla Mustafa's private quarrel with government. It watched Arab distaste for the Kurds translated into a vindictive and short-sighted policy. In the last resort only the fear of military action might hold the Kurds in check. But was the army up to it? Britain did not think so and warned Baghdad of the dangers of open conflict. Baghdad was reluctant to listen and Barzani soon made a laughing stock of the armed forces with his skilfully laid ambushes.

As a result of British pressure, Mulla Mustafa was offered a pardon in November, with an indication that his case would be sympathetically considered after his submission. Having been kept on a starvation allowance for years, Mulla Mustafa was now treated like a miscreant; there was little doubt as to his victimization. As one highly placed Iraqi official remarked 'If Mulla Mustafa had been an Arab sheikh from Diwaniya, it is more than likely he would have been a Senator by now instead of being hounded by the government as if he were a mad dog.'[6]

In fact Mulla Mustafa no longer trusted (if he ever had) Baghdad's good faith, and began to correspond with the British embassy. In view of the Rashid Ali coup of 1941, he probably hoped Britain would welcome a Kurdish counter-weight to the uncertain loyalty of Baghdad: 'Whatever your orders,' he wrote to the ambassador, Sir Kinahan Cornwallis, 'I shall obey them as a child would the orders of a compassionate father ... our friendship for the merciful British government knows no bounds.'[7] These were hardly the words of a Kurdish nationalist. Cornwallis crisply told him to accept Baghdad's terms.

In January Baghdad sent a Kurdish minister, Majid Mustafa, to sort things out peacefully with Mulla Mustafa. He was chosen because he knew Barzani and was held in esteem in Kurdish circles. Many politicians in Baghdad viewed him with suspicion but probably did not realize that he was closely associated with Hiwa. They simply disliked the idea of being soft on the Kurds.

Majid Mustafa persuaded both parties to accept a formula that saved the government's face but gave Mulla Mustafa what at this point he demanded. Mulla Mustafa agreed to come to Baghdad to make his submission, an event he turned into a personal triumph, much to the irritation of Arab nationalists. But Majid Mustafa's proposals[8] were frustrated by Arab nationalist opposition and by a change of government.

Majid Mustafa had also uncovered an Augean stable in the north. The *mutasarrif*s of Arbil and Mosul had never once toured Barzan district and so it was hardly surprising that their subordinates had not done so either. Grain supplies for relief work had not been distributed, much had been misappropriated.

Government negligence had fostered widespread sympathy for the Barzanis. By the middle of the year Majid Mustafa found himself caught between rising hostility to his efforts in Baghdad, and increasing scepticism and suspicion in the north at the failure to implement the agreement.

As time passed without implementation of the brokered settlement, Mulla Mustafa began to raise the stakes, tempted by the support he enjoyed among discontented tribes across a swathe of country northwards to the border from a line drawn from Aqra through Amadiya to Rawanduz. By July 1944 it seems he no longer had any intention of obeying the government. Even his old adversaries, the Zibari chiefs, seemed willing to collaborate with him. Unlike the Baradustis and Surchis, the Zibaris had given no assistance to the army at all. Mulla Mustafa now allied himself with them by marriage to Mahmud Agha's daughter. With acute shortages of food and clothing throughout the north, the prospect of death by starvation or exposure with the advent of cold weather and widespread disgust with the government's failure to remedy the situation, the growing danger was unmistakable.

Baghdad had allowed Majid Mustafa the use of Kurdish army officers for his liaison work with Barzani. Two of these officers, Mir Hajj Ahmad and Mustafa Khushnaw, now used their freedom of movement to stimulate Kurdish nationalist activity. In Sulaymaniya they convened a meeting of tribal leaders to discuss their grievances. Then they went to Barzan and thence to Mahabad, where they discussed nationalist aspirations with Komala leaders and met the Soviet consul. It was clear they had overstepped the mark as far as Baghdad was concerned. As Mustafa Khushnaw naively confessed to the British:

> Our sole aim in contacting our Kurdish brothers in Iran was to establish the conception of a general union to include all Kurds living in the areas under British control whether in Iraq or Iran. For we believe we are all in a single house and a single type of country and disregard the boundaries laid down by the dictator Shah of Iran.[9]

From about this time onwards, fewer Kurdish officers were admitted to Staff College as Baghdad concluded that Kurds were too dangerous to be allowed positions of power in the forces.

A stalemate continued through the winter. In December 1944 Mulla Mustafa demanded fulfilment of previous undertakings, in particular to detach the Kurdish *qadhas* from the Arab administration in Mosul, something Prime Minister Nuri Said had offered to do the previous spring. He also wanted the release of Kurdish political prisoners, the appointment of a Kurdish commissioner in Baghdad with veto powers over any government order affecting Kurdistan, and a gift of £144,000 for his personal discretionary use as agricultural loans.

Strong enough to hold his own, Mulla Mustafa gave the government a fortnight in which to reply. It was difficult to see how Baghdad could concede the last two demands, for the one would effectively surrender its sovereignty over Kurdistan, while the other would give Mulla Mustafa new powers of regional patronage.

If Mulla Mustafa was, in the words of Cornwallis, 'vain, predatory amd dictatorial',[10] then the government for its part remained corrupt, untrustworthy and vindictive. Under British pressure, it had been constrained to remain patient alongside its failure to improve conditions in Kurdistan. Britain feared more than ever that government inflexibility would consolidate the Kurds behind Mulla Mustafa and that this would lead to conflict that would destabilize Iraq further.

By summer Britain felt unable to continue its counsel of restraint since Mulla

Mustafa remained evasive and provocative.[11] In April the government had made yet another offer of amnesty, and was unlikely to do so again. In the wings stood the army, determined to restore its shattered prestige by military action against Barzani. In August it was authorized to march against Mulla Mustafa and his allies. At first it took heavy casualties, but its use of friendly tribes, notably Shaykh Rashid's Baradustis, soon forced Mulla Mustafa onto the defensive. In September the Zibaris deserted to the government side, receiving a full pardon in return for help against their erstwhile allies. Mulla Mustafa never forgave them. In mid-October Mulla Mustafa and Shaykh Ahmad fled to Mahabad (chapter 11). From exile Mulla Mustafa vowed revenge on those he accused of betraying the Kurdish cause: Shaykh Rashid of Lawlan, Mahmud and Ahmad Agha Zibari, and Raghib Agha of the Surchi.

There is little solid evidence that Mulla Mustafa had espoused the Kurdish cause during the course of his revolt. Only his demands for a Kurdish commissioner in Baghdad and for the reorganization of the Kurdish *qadhas* of Mosul suggest a political agenda. He must have known that no government in its right mind could possibly allow a Kurdish commissioner the power of veto. Why did he not demand a negotiation along the lines of self-administration, something that carried a greater chance of acceptability? One must conclude that either Mulla Mustafa lacked political realism or that he made his proposal knowing it was completely unacceptable. His second demand (the detachment of the Kurdish *qadhas* from Mosul) had a better chance since it had been conceded in principle in spring 1944. But was this a nationalist demand or Mulla Mustafa trying to enlarge his own sphere of influence? If one looks at his actions rather than his statements, for example his removal of police posts and other appurtenances of government authority, and his attempt to act as both mediator and focus among the tribes in the area (the traditional shaykhly role), it is plausible that he not only wanted the kind of autonomy which both the Pizhdar and the Arab Shammar had been allowed, but that, like any good tribal leader, he was constantly seeking to widen his regional authority.

It also seems that, rather than Mulla Mustafa choosing nationalism, the nationalists chose him. They did this because of his proven tactical skills, and his successful embarrassment of the government. This choice was later vindicated when he achieved legendary renown in Iran transforming his standing among all Kurds. He had become the obvious charismatic leader for the Kurdish national movement.

Hiwa and its Successors

Hiwa had unsuccessfully tried to exploit the Barzani rebellion. At first it had been rebuffed, presumably because Mulla Mustafa distrusted it. Majid Mustafa's appointed liaison officers, almost entirely Hiwa members, were another matter, presumably because they were part of the deal Mulla Mustafa had forged and because he trusted Majid Mustafa. Nevertheless, they failed to transform the rebellion into a nationalist one. The revolt remained intrinsically tribal, its outcome settled more by tribesmen than by regular troops, let alone by nationalist volunteers.

The Barzani rebellion also worked as a catalyst on the tensions already existing within Hiwa, between the conservatives who clung to the hope of help from Britain and the radicals who believed the Soviets offered both practical and ideological rescue from British and Arab colonialism. Some had contempt for the pro-British line upheld by Hiwa's leader, Rafiq Hilmi. More conservatively minded members were outraged to learn that Shaykh Latif, now a fugitive in Sardasht, was in parley with the Soviets. When it was thought that Barzani was receiving Soviet assistance, others withdrew their financial support. By mid-1944 many were voting with their feet. Hiwa disintegrated and had ceased to function as a party by the end of the year.

Once again a plethora of small groupings formed, some within the ICP. Of these, a Kurdish Communist group known by the name of its journal, *Shurish* (Revolution), was the most important. It took a principal role in the foundation of a new party, Rizgari Kurd (Kurdish Liberation) in 1945, intended to be a popular front. Like its predecessors, Rizgari proved short-lived, but it was more successful in attracting supporters, possibly as many as 6,000. It rapidly established itself in the colleges of Baghdad and among students in Kurdish towns, and made contact with the Barzanis in Mahabad. Unlike Hiwa, which never produced a formal party programme, Rizgari Kurd unequivocally sought the freedom and unification of Kurdistan. Its interim objectives included administrative independence inside Iraq and the establishment of co-ordinated co-operation with Kurdish parties outside Iraq.[12] In January 1946 it appealed formally to the UN for Kurdish self-determination and sovereignty.[13]

There could be little doubt that potentially the Kurdish nationalists' best ally in Iraq was the ICP. A disproportionate number of ICP members, possibly 35 per cent, were Kurds who came mainly from Sulaymaniya. But there was also an uncomfortable tension. Many Kurds had faced a difficult choice between giving primacy to national identity or to social justice as expressed in Marxist theory. As its organ, *al Qa'ida*, made clear, the ICP believed in 'the right of self-determination for every community and nationality',[14] but there was an uncomfortable conflict between the geographical limits set by the ICP and the Kurdish national movement. The Kurds felt part of the Kurdish nation. While willing to work within Iraq pro tem, they refused to lose sight of the wider Kurdish context or the inspiration of Mahabad. The ICP viewed the Kurds as an Iraqi minority, and thus wished to harness Kurdish nationalism for its objectives *within* Iraq; so it criticized those Kurds who insisted on the need for a separate Kurdish Communist party.

This tension was also felt by those in Shurish and Rizgari. Shurish angrily reminded the ICP that it had authorized the Kurdish Communists to create their own national front, and that was precisely what it had done. Kurds had the right to struggle for self-determination and unity and this in no way invalidated their struggle against colonialism and imperialism, nor their willingness to co-operate with Arabs in that process.

The Birth of the KDP in Iraq

Rizgari Kurd undoubtedly raised the profile of Kurdish nationalism, and came to public notice during the (21 March) 1946 Nawruz (Kurdish New Year) celebrations in Arbil. The authorities now began to cast aside the insouciance that had prevailed only a year before when the prime minister had dismissed the nationalists as 'Only a few students and they will grow out of it.'[15] In view of the growing number of educated Kurds this had been an extraordinary remark to make. Within a couple of years Sulaymaniya was the explosive scene of left-wing and nationalist unrest.

So serious had the movement suddenly become that the British apparently tried to influence the shaykhs and other religious leaders in Kurdistan to issue *fatwas* against Rizgari;[16] but it is difficult to believe they did so with any conviction.

The position of the shaykhs had been radically weakened since 1918. They had lost their power base primarily because the arbitration of disputes was now handled by government officers, or government-approved *aghas*. Most had become redundant and the flow of gifts and pilgrims had largely dried up. Only those with economic power and the 'odour of sanctity', like the shaykhs of Biyara, still enjoyed local standing. Others, like the Tawila cousins of the Biyari shaykhs, were by 1949 reduced to penury, and Tawila itself had been repossessed by the voracious Jaf. Without their traditional function, shaykhs had to find new ways of living. One, as a British report in 1949 cynically noted, had 'renounced his religious duties in favour of smuggling'.[17]

Besides, the shaykhs were too closely identified with the traditional order, in a context in which young Kurds increasingly looked to radical left-wing ideologies for inspiration and guidance. Islam was universalist, nationalism particularist. Without Sultan or Caliph as a focus for both, it was inevitable that the nationalist drive should be increasingly secular.

Be that as it may, Rizgari came under increasing pressure, dozens were arrested and an attempt was made to stifle Kurdish publications. Even *Gilawizh*, Ibrahim Ahmad's literary journal was suspended.[18] By August 1946 both Rizgari and Shurish had decided to dissolve themselves, less the result of governmental pressure than a new dilemma created by Mulla Mustafa in Iran.

As a result of the privations his forces faced living on the charity of the people of the Mahabad Republic, Mulla Mustafa had sought to create financial (and presumably political) independence from Qazi Muhammad. It was well known in nationalist circles that relations between the two men were not easy.

In February 1946 Mulla Mustafa and Hamza Abd Allah, a Shurish envoy, had tried to create a special committee for the Barzanis in Iran. Qazi Muhammad had warned them 'There is to be only one party, and you must not operate separately from it.'[19]

Shortly thereafter, Mulla Mustafa sent Hamza Abd Allah to Iraq with two letters, one asking Shaykh Baba Ali (Shaykh Mahmud's son) to intercede with Baghdad for his return, the other proposing the formation of an Iraqi Kurdish Democratic Party. Since he was a member of Shurish, Hamza Abd Allah's errand had to be taken seriously. Despite his left-wing credentials, it seems that he had been persuaded by Mulla Mustafa and the Soviet-backed Mahabad example that the participation of tribal notables was essential to success. Thus, 'all Kurdish organizations in Iraq should be dissolved and merged in the proposed party.'[20]

Mulla Mustafa's initiative created tension in Iraqi Kurdistan. He was now a national hero, defending the first ever Kurdish Republic. It was difficult to gainsay him, yet some could not agree with the proposal. Ibrahim Ahmad, by now KDPI's representative in Sulaymania, opposed it both because it fractured the idea of pan-Kurdish unity and because Mahabad required Mulla Mustafa's undivided allegiance.

The proposal raised particular difficulty for Shurish, since its own envoy was now advocating a novel tack which contradicted Shurish nostrums. At a meeting in early August Shurish dissolved itself. A majority favoured incorporation into the new proposed party, but several of the leadership preferred to join the ICP.

As for Rizgari, it was committed to Kurdish unity. The Barzani proposal for an Iraqi KDP seemed to endorse the legitimacy of the Iraq–Iran border. When it met in secret in Baghdad in early August, it splintered like Shurish, some opting for the new KDP, others going to the ICP, or to Hizb al Taharrur al Watani (the National Liberation Party). Possibly the Communist members of Rizgari wanted a party which would not attract such hostility from Baghdad. Many members disliked Mulla Mustafa's demand that his representatives in his absence should be Shaykh Latif and Ziyad Muhammad Agha, a demand justified on the grounds that the tribes were the only effective military force and that they would only support the nationalists if led by respected tribal and religious notables. It was a point of view destined to dog the maturation of the Kurdish movement in Iraq well into the 1970s.

The new Kurdish Democratic Party (KDP) held its first congress in Baghdad on 16 August. The 32 delegates elected a central committee with Hamza Abd Allah as secretary-general, Mulla Mustafa as president (in exile) and Shaykh Latif and Ziyad Agha as vice-presidents. It adopted a nationalist programme, to live in an Iraqi union to be attained through the free will of the Kurds but failed to give its programme either social or economic content – largely for fear of offending tribal chiefs and landlords. The influence of the chiefs and landlords, for example the Dizais of Arbil, hung like a cloud over the party and created a serious obstacle to social and economic change. It also made serious tension with the ICP almost inevitable. The KDP commenced a new official organ, *Rizgari* (Revolution), the following month.

After the collapse of Mahabad in early 1947, Ibrahim Ahmad joined the party and began to rally the leftists opposed to the bland nationalism on which the party had so far been built, but two years later he was arrested. In 1950 Hamza Abd Allah was also imprisoned. After a year of drifting, the leftists took the opportunity to convene a second congress in summer 1951 which elected Ibrahim Ahmad, himself just released from prison, as secretary-general. His first step was to sack Hamza Abd Allah.

In January 1953 the KDP's third congress took substantive steps to restructure the party. It changed its name, from Kurdish Democratic Party to Kurdistan Democratic Party, indicating that all people in Iraqi Kurdistan regardless of ethnic identity could participate. It was a gesture towards civic nationalism. It formally expelled Hamza Abd Allah for divisive tactics within the party. It replaced *Rizgari* with a new organ, *Khabat Kurdistan* (Battle of Kurdistan), and adopted a Leftist programme, calling for agricultural reform and the recognition of peasants' and workers' rights and the introduction of labour associations. In practice the party avoided open advocacy of class struggle because it had no roots among the peasant class and because the landowning class was so strong.

The Socio-economic Struggle

Ever since the 1920s the position of the notables class, which might otherwise have weakened, had been reinforced and incorporated more closely into the ruling establishment. This was not only on account of the early British decision to work through the notables, but because their economic position had become much stronger as a result of the Land Settlement Laws of 1932 and 1938 which, regardless of the intention, facilitated the transfer into their hands of great swathes of tribal and state lands. Of the 46 magnate families in Iraq owning over 30,000 dunums (7,500 hectares/18,600 acres), 11 were Kurdish. The most notable were the Begzada Jaf in Kirkuk and Sulaymaniya, who held 539,333 dunums most of which had been acquired by violence against peasants, by land seizures, and by the misappropriation of land provided for the settlement of tribesmen. The Begzadas found it more profitable to put hired labour rather than tribespeople on the land. Further north, the comparatively parvenu Dizais owed their land-holdings (52,350 dunums) to a successful moneylending business, taking land from defaulters. In Arbil district 45 out of 65 villages entirely populated by Kurds were owned almost exclusively by absentee Turkoman notables.

The regime had found itself increasingly dependent on landlords and tribal chiefs from the time of Faysal's death in 1933. This was partly because of the instability of government itself, but also because of the questionable loyalty of an army led increasingly by officers of middle or lower middle class origin with little affection for the monarchy. It was a trial of opposites, the ancien régime against the emergent middle class, the countryside against newly burgeoning towns. The growing collaboration between regime and tribal chiefs was evident in the composition of successive parliaments and establishment parties. Kurdish aghas were well represented in Nuri Said's Constitutional Union Party established in 1947. Chiefs of the Jafs, Dizais and Mir Mahmalis (another family with over 30,000 dunums) were all members of the party's Higher Committee.

It was the Communists, rather than the KDP, who first took on the aghas. They had already established themselves among the workers of Arbil, Kirkuk and Sulaymaniya. In 1946 they supported Kirkuk oil workers against the Iraq Petroleum Company. They had also begun to create a constituency among the peasants. In 1947 they supported a peasant rising in Arbat, near Sulaymaniya.[21] In Ottoman times Arbat had been owned largely by its peasant population, except for seven plots set aside to fund a Qadiri oratory in the village. After 1918 Shaykh Mahmud used his influence to acquire total possession of the village; when he distributed some of his enormous holdings to his sons in the 1940s, Shaykh Latif received Arbat. While Shaykh Mahmud had levied no more than one tenth of the yield, his son now sought to extract dues amounting to one third of the yield, and even tried to impose a corvée.

Once it was clear that the government would do nothing to protect the peasantry, the ICP decided to make Arbat the battleground for confronting the aghas. When the peasants refused to take Shaykh Latif's orders in November 1947, the latter brought 400 armed men into the village and flogged every adult male in front of their families. The incident provoked solidarity demonstrations in Sulaymaniya, but although the Land Settlement Committee found in the peasants' favour, Shaykh Latif felt free to flout the law. He continued to send armed men into the village to cut the water supplies and burn the crops. The ICP gave leadership and guidance to Arbat, helping the peasants defend the village. However, in 1948, following disclosures by a disgruntled ex-party member, the government was able to smash ICP cells all over the country. The peasants quickly submitted. Shaykh Latif was able to strike a compromise, recognizing their title but charging one eighth of the crop yield for his water.

Arbat was something of a watershed: for the first time in living memory, the peasantry had taken on the agha class, demonstrating that change was a real possibility. When the peasantry rose against the Dizais six years later the ICP was again involved, partly because the Kurds now constituted a substantial number of senior party members.[22]

These were exceptional events. The countryside was still relatively unpoliticized, the towns providing the stage for political change. This had been evident in 1948–49 when Sulaymaniya, Kirkuk and Arbil (like many other towns in Iraq in the wake of the unpopular Treaty of Portsmouth) (a revision of the Anglo-Iraqi treaty of 1930) had been disturbed by political demonstrations, while – Arbat apart – the countryside remained completely quiet. The peasants may have been routinely swindled by the agha and landlord class, yet it was still the latter that purported to represent them. Activists, be they Communist Party or KDP, still had a long way to go.

In 1953 it may still have been difficult for the KDP to use the class issue in canvassing support. Yet social change and growing discontent were already under way, and the increasingly socialist hue of party doctrine was in tune with the times. This was largely the result of changing economic circumstances. Since oil exports commenced in 1934 there was increased wealth in Iraq, though it became clear that this new wealth was not trickling down to the lower social echelons. An increasing number of people were leaving the land in search of work, either in the oil industry, or in one of the towns of Kurdistan or in Baghdad itself. In its 1953 programme, the KDP had included oil nationalization and Kurdistan's claim to a fair share of oil revenue and heavy industry

In some ways the economy of Kurdistan began to improve in the mid-1950s following the construction of the major dams (the Dukan and Darband-i Khan) with their substantial irrigation and power potential, and the construction of major cement and tobacco factories near Sulaymaniya. In 1954 came the appointment of a Kurdish Minister of the Interior, whose undeclared intention was to ensure that Kurdistan got its fair share of the national economy.[23]

Yet throughout the 1950s the clamour continued for development projects to soak up the surplus labour of Kurdistan, and for improvement in agricultural methods. The visible disparity in wealth, abject rural poverty and the drift to the towns were already undermining landlord–peasant relations. The trouble with the most obvious means of agricultural development, mechanization, was that it put more peasants out of work, and put the comparative wealth of the landlord class into yet higher relief. Some foresaw the possibility that unrest might well spread from town to rural hinterland.

In such changing circumstances it behove the KDP to attract a broader swathe of Kurds, as the ICP was already successfully doing. In 1954 the KDP and ICP collaborated to field candidates in primary elections in villages. Since the 1953 congress the KDP had moved significantly closer to the ICP, for it now advocated an alliance with the socialist camp and the replacement of the Iraqi monarchy with a popular democratic republic in which the Kurdish people could form an autonomous entity.

Both the KDP and ICP had increasing reason to rally their strength in the light of international developments. In February 1955 Iraq had signed a defence agreement with Turkey, as part of the 'Northern Tier' defence line against the Soviet threat. Iran, Britain and Pakistan joined this 'Baghdad Pact' shortly after. Kurdish government officials and aghas who had done so well under the Iraqi monarchy welcomed the increased stability the pact promised. The Turkomans in Kirkuk and other marginal zones of Kurdistan welcomed it too, since it forged fresh links with Turkey, their cultural patron.

The KDP central committee, on the other hand, saw the pact as yet another inter-state manoeuvre (like the 1937 tripartite Treaty of Saadabad) against Kurdish particularism, as well as an imperialist alliance against the forces of the Socialist Bloc. As events were to prove, the Baghdad Pact was a catastrophic miscalculation, unnecessarily heightening tension with pan-Arab nationalism abroad and within Iraq. Opposition to the pact by Arab nationalists, socialists and left-wing liberals, and even right-wing Islamic groups, reminded the Kurds of their separate identity.

In the light of such developments, Kurdish solidarity was more desirable than ever. In 1956 the KDP re-admitted Hamza Abd Allah (long since freed from prison) and his coterie known as the KDP–Progressive Front. Many of the Kurdish section of the ICP also joined the KDP in 1957 and for a while, to indicate these amalgamations, the KDP was known as the 'United' Kurdistan Democratic Party. Hamza Abd Allah and other notable figures were readmitted to the central committee and Politburo. The orientation of the party remained clearly socialist and friendly towards the Soviet Bloc, and sharply critical of the Baghdad Pact.

Meanwhile, changing social circumstances in Kurdistan, disturbingly leftist expressions of both Arab and Kurdish nationalism, and the enormous popularity of Nasser, persuaded some Kurdish aghas that the Hashimite monarchy was no longer to be relied upon. In December 1956, with the Suez campaign at its troubled climax, a wave of anxiety swept across the landlord and notable class of Kurdistan. Emissaries of a group of northern Kurdish aghas,[24] repeating similar approaches made in central and southern areas, called on the British consul in Mosul for arms, ammunition and finance to help establish an anti-Communist and independent Kurdistan in northern Iraq. Britain, they hoped, would support the venture. For good measure and as earnest of good faith, they undertook the liquidation of Mulla Mustafa in the Soviet Union. It indicated how isolated the agha class was beginning to feel.

By the beginning of 1958 the pace of events had quickened. The KDP was already in touch with the Free Officers who, modelled on their namesake in Egypt, sought the overthrow of the Hashimite monarchy and the establishment of a democratic republic, in line with the political objective set out at the KDP's 1953 congress.

Sources

Great Britain: Public Record Office: series FO 371 nos 18945, 24560, 34940, 40038, 40039, 40041, 40178, 45311, 45323, 45346, 52369, 68472, 82000, 82499, 128040, 128041.

Published: Ibrahim Ahmad, *Al Akrad wa'l Arab* (Baghdad, 1937); F. David Andrews, *The Lost Peoples of the Middle East* (Salisbury, N.C., 1982); Hanna Batatu, *The Old Social Classes and the Revolutionary Movements in Iraq* (Princeton, 1978); Dziegiel, *Rural Community of Contemporary Iraq; Iraq Directory* (Baghdad, 1936); Sa'ad Jawad, *Iraq and the Kurdish Question, 1958–70* (London, 1981); Majid Khadduri, *Independent Iraq* (London, 1951); Walter Laqueur, *Communism and Nationalism in the Middle East* (London, 1961); Sharif, *Al Jamiyat wa'l Manzimat;* Farouk-Sluglett and Sluglett, *Iraq Since 1958* (London, 1987).

Unpublished: Othman, 'Contribution historique'.

Interviews: Ibrahim Ahmad (London, 15 June 1988); Muhammad Rasul Hawar (London, 20 June 1993).

Notes

1. They were encouraged by Hikmat Sulayman, an opposition politician hoping to orchestrate Kurdish and Middle Euphrates tribal discontent.

2. These were Janesti Kurdistan in Baghdad, two Islamic charitable societies, and two clubs in Koi-Sanjaq, one devoted to science and education; *Iraq Directory 1936*, pp. 557–561.

3. Ibrahim Ahmad, private interview, 15 June 1988.

4. See Sharif, *Al Jamiyat wa'l Manzimat*, p. 92, for other members.

5. FO 371/24560 Edmonds, 'Russia and the Kurds', 15 February 1940.

6. FO 371/34940 CICI no 138, 4 October 1943.

7. FO 371/40039 Barzani to Cornwallis, 13 December 1943.

8. The terms were: (1) Mulla Mustafa to live temporarily outside Barzan area (to save the government's face); (2) Shaykh Ahmad and his family to return to Barzan immediately; (3) Kurdish army officers to be appointed to liaise during normalization; (4) grain supplies to devastated villages of Barzan area and relief work on roads; (5) withdrawal of the army from Mergasur; see FO 371/40041 Cornwallis to Eden, Baghdad, 23 March 1944.

9. FO 371/40039 Thompson to Eden, Baghdad, 23 August 1944.

10. FO 371/40039 Cornwallis to Eden, Baghdad, 10 December 1944.

11. For evidence of Mulla Mustafa's intentional provocations, see the list of incidents in FO 371/45311 Dawson Shepherd, 'Barzani situation', Baghdad, 15 August 1945; see also FO 371/45323 Thompson to Foreign Office, Baghdad, 7 August 1945.

12. Sharif, *Al Jamiyat wa'l Manzimat*, p. 121 which quotes from Muhammad Shirzad, *Nidal al Akrad* (Cairo 1946), pp. 27–28.

13. Rizgari was not alone in appealing to the international community. From 1943 the Allied Powers and then the UN and other international groupings were lobbied; see Jwaideh, 'The Kurdish nationalist movement', pp. 792–802 for a list of such diplomatic *démarches* 1943–58.

14. Al Qaida, November 1945, quoted by Sharif, *Al Jamiyat wa'l Manzimat*, p. 131.

15. FO 371/45346 Stonehewer Bird to Eden, Baghdad, 3 May 1945.

16. Shirzad, *Nidal al Akrad*, pp. 28–29, cited in Jwaideh, 'The Kurdish nationalist movement', p. 707.

17. FO 371/82499 Clarke to Mack, Kirkuk, 6 December 1949.

18. It had been described by British intelligence as 'the best literary review in the Middle East', FO 371/52369 CICI comments on FORD paper 'The Kurdish Problem', 1 May 1946.

19. Kutschera in *Le Mouvement National Kurde*, p. 190.

20. Salih al Haydari's memoirs quoted in Sa'ad Jawad, *Iraq and the Kurdish Question, 1958–70*, p. 19. See also Haydari *et al.* quoted in Sharif, *Al Jamiyat wa'l Manzimat*, pp. 141–152.

21. The following account is paraphrased from Batatu, *The Old Social Classes*, p. 612.

22. Between 1949–55 all the general secretaries were Kurds, and 31.3 per cent of the central committee was Kurdish, compared with only 4.5 per cent of the party leadership in the previous eight-year period, Batatu, *The Old Social Classes*, p. 664.

23. This was Said Qazzaz, executed after the 1958 revolution as a stooge of the ancien régime.

24. These included: Mahmud Agha Zibari, Divali Agha Duski, Abd Allah Sharafani, Salih Agha Abd al Aziz (Amadiya) Abd al Aziz Hajj Milu of Mizuri and two Yazidi shaykhs, FO 371/128040, Mosul Political Report, December 1956.

CHAPTER 15

THE KURDS IN
REVOLUTIONARY IRAQ

Introduction

The *coup d'état* by Brigadier Abd al Karim Qasim and his fellow Free Officers on 14 July 1958 promised a more hopeful era for the Kurds. When he took power Qasim pledged the establishment of a democratic republic and formed a cabinet composed of officers and members of the United National Front. Although the ICP and KDP were excluded, Shaykh Mahmud's son Baba Ali was invited to join. Qasim also formed a three-man 'Sovereignty Council', a Sunni, a Shi'i and a Kurd.[1] It was a gesture.

As KDP Secretary-General, Ibrahim Ahmad had immediately pledged the party's support for the new regime, issuing a declaration that hailed the new regime, and freedom and equality for the Kurdish and Arab peoples.[2] When the provisional constitution was published two weeks later, Article III read 'Arabs and Kurds are partners in the Homeland, and their national rights are recognized within the Iraqi entity'[3] – recognition at last. All seemed set fair for resolving the tensions existing between Baghdad and the Kurdish community since 1921.

In reality the scene was set for a series of interlocking struggles between various contenders for power in the new situation. At the most obvious level there was a clash of personalities. Foremost of these were Qasim and Mulla Mustafa. Qasim, paranoid concerning his own position and without a party organization of his own, soon found himself playing off one power group against another in order to neutralize potential challengers. Mulla Mustafa, invited back from exile by Qasim, was determined to assume the leadership of Iraq's Kurds. It was when these two fell out irretrievably, during the course of 1961, that the first Kurdish war in Iraq began.

However, behind the clash of personalities lay more complex problems, a conflict between rival nationalisms, between the civilian and military elements in Baghdad, and between tribalism and ideology in Kurdistan. These tensions undermined each side in its search for a successful resolution of the Kurdish question.

Thus the post-Hashimite stage was filled with a new array of leading players: the Arab nationalists, the KDP and its leading personalities, the ICP which hoped to play a major role in the formation of post-Hashimite Iraq and finally the Kurdish aghas who saw the overthrow of the monarchy (to which they had become so indispensable) as a catastrophe.

Dealing with the Arab Nationalists and the Communists

The first sign of trouble arose from the tension between Kurdish and Arab nationalists. Qasim was urged by KDP Secretary-General Ahmad to include Kurdish autonomy in the Provisional Constitution. But he was also under pressure from Abd al Salam Arif, his deputy, and other Arab nationalists who wanted to take Iraq into the United Arab Republic (UAR). They opposed Qasim's apparently pro-Kurdish attitude, especially his welcome to Mulla Mustafa. Qasim did not wish to bow to Arab nationalist pressure, and certainly had no intention of playing second fiddle to Nasser in an enlarged UAR. Nor did he wish to be stampeded into conceding too much too soon to the Kurds.

It is unlikely that Qasim had thought through the question of Kurdish autonomy, but his own character disposed him to deny power to any other party or body. So he asked Ahmad to be patient, promising that autonomy would be included in the permanent constitution.

In the meantime Ahmad, who believed Arab nationalism would be the prevailing force of the future, quietly tried to build relations with Arif. He was conscious of the huge acclamation for Nasser in the Arab world. He had himself been warmly received by Nasser in October and appreciated the Egyptian leader's friendly gestures towards the Kurds, including support for Kurdish radio broadcasts.

While Arif spurned Ahmad's advances, Qasim became convinced that the two were plotting behind his back. The Kurds were arguably the single greatest obstacle to unity with the UAR and Qasim wanted to keep this pretext up his sleeve. So he hardly wanted the KDP and the Arab nationalists to make common cause. Qasim quickly stripped Arif of his powers and imprisoned him, but his suspicion of Ahmad grew. By the end of the year he wanted Mulla Mustafa to remove him.

Mulla Mustafa had returned via Cairo to a tumultuous welcome in Baghdad in early October. He had cabled Qasim after the overthrow of the monarchy to pledge his devotion to Arab–Kurdish co-operation, and to seek Qasim's consent to his return.

Qasim decided that Mulla Mustafa was potentially a powerful counterweight to the Arab nationalists and that there was unlikely to be any love lost between them. So he named him Chairman of the KDP (a position Mulla Mustafa had theoretically held during his eleven years in exile), gave him one of Nuri Said's old residences in Baghdad, a car, and a handsome monthly stipend.[4]

In one light, Mulla Mustafa was almost Qasim's employee, in another he was anything but. Up in the fastnesses of Bahdinan, Mulla Mustafa was very much his own man, beholden neither to KDP urban intellectuals, like Ibrahim Ahmad and Jalal Talabani, nor to the Iraqi government. He held the core of the KDP's fighting force, had charismatic standing with the Kurdish people and, unlike the KDP Politburo, he had Qasim's ear.

It suited Mulla Mustafa to co-operate with Qasim, since he had been publicly confirmed by him as leader of the Kurds. He realized that Ahmad's flirtation with Arab nationalists was also dangerous for relations with Qasim. He had little difficulty in finding allies in the Politburo to help oust Ahmad and replace him with the pro-Communist Hamza Abd Allah in January 1959.

At the time it seemed a good idea. Hamza Abd Allah had always been close to the Communists, considering them to be the prevailing force of the future. In October the KDP and ICP had reached a compromise on their ideological conflict: the KDP abandoned its claim to an independent Kurdistan in return for ICP endorsement of administrative autonomy. There was no doubt that the ICP enjoyed better local organization and support than any other party. It was clear, too, that Qasim favoured the KDP and ICP as counterweights to the Arab nationalists and the Baath.

Mulla Mustafa's men soon proved their worth to Qasim, helping to suppress a serious rising in Mosul in March 1959. Superficially the rising was led by Arab Nationalist (and Baathist) officers disillusioned by Qasim's 'betrayal' of the revolution, and provoked by a major demonstration in the city of 250,000 armed 'Peace Partisans', widely seen as a Communist front organization. In practice it became a catalyst for ideological, class, tribal and ethnic tensions. It developed into a contest between Sunni pan-Arabism and the mainly Kurdish and Christian leftist elements in the city, but Muslawi peasants also took on their landlords, while Kurdish and Arab troops of the Fifth Brigade attacked their Arab officers,[5] and one tribe fought another.

At the behest of Mulla Mustafa, Kurds streamed into Mosul 'in self-defence against Arab chauvinism',[6] and even recalling the murder of Shaykh Mahmud's father 50 years earlier. The Communists, led by a Kurd,[7] and Barzani tribesmen played a major role in quelling the revolt and wreaking vengeance on Nationalists and Baathists. At least 200, and possibly as many as 2,500, died in four days of disorder. While the Communists and Kurds settled scores in Mosul, Qasim used the events as a pretext to purge Nationalists and Baathists from the armed forces and government.

Thus the Communists and the Kurds helped Qasim deal with his principal challengers. Although not yet in government, the Communists could reasonably hope to share power on account of their grassroots strength. No one else could rally the same numbers for political demonstrations. Furthermore, the ICP effectively controlled the People's Resistance Forces (a locally organized militia) which was in a process of rapid expansion, and could count on the KDP since Hamza

Abd Allah followed ICP's line. In fact the two parties had recently reached an understanding regarding their activities in Kurdistan. As a result the ICP was rapidly becoming the principal danger to Qasim's position.

In mid-July 1959 another serious disturbance occurred, this time in Kirkuk, a town waiting to explode. Once again, the spark was a rally by leftists. It will be recalled that the ICP in the north was preponderantly Kurdish. Tension had been growing for some time between Turkomans, the originally predominant element, and Kurds who had settled increasingly during the 1930s and 1940s, driven from the land by landlord rapacity and drawn by the chance for employment in the burgeoning oil industry. By 1959 half the population of 150,000 were Turkoman, rather less than half were Kurds and the balance Arabs, Assyrians and Armenians.

Kirkuk suffered high unemployment, exacerbated by the departure of European commercial ventures and a hiatus in development projects as a result of the revolution. Mulla Mustafa's triumphal visit to the town the previous October had nearly resulted in bloodletting. On this occasion, however, Kurdish Communists and Kurdish members of the Popular Resistance Force (PRF) attacked shops and their owners. Officially 31 Turkomans were killed, but the real figure was more like 50.

Qasim held the Communists rather than the Kurds responsible for these 'barbaric and inhumane'[8] events, and since they coincided with an ICP campaign to enter the government, he finally decided to act against them. At the end of the month he publicly stated his horror, and claimed that the Students Union (ICP dominated) had marked houses in Baghdad from which certain victims were to be dragged. These, significantly, included the Barzani house. Qasim had a willing ally in Mulla Mustafa who had claimed only a month earlier that Communists had tried to assassinate him near Rawanduz.

Mulla Mustafa's first task was to rescue the KDP from the ICP's embrace. He possibly already sensed Qasim's change of direction. In any case, he himself had begun to see the ICP as a nuisance in Kurdistan. There had been serious rivalry with ICP commanders in May during tribal fighting (see below). Then, ten days before the mayhem in Kirkuk, he had dismissed some of those in the KDP politburo he felt were too much in ICP's pocket. After Kirkuk, he invited Hamza Abd Allah to 'discuss' his pro-Communist policy, but the latter declined. So he sent a Barzani squad to storm the KDP headquarters and eject Abd Allah. The remaining members of the Politburo agreed to stay in line with Qasim's policy.

By late August there was open conflict between the KDP backed by Kurdish tribesmen and the ICP. During the next few months, Mulla Mustafa helped Qasim reduce the Communists. In January 1960 when Qasim's Law of Associations required registration of political parties and associations, technical reasons were produced to prevent the ICP from registering. Qasim had cleverly neutralized the ICP for the time being.

In the meantime Mulla Mustafa allowed the KDP Fourth Congress in October 1959 to re-elect Ibrahim Ahmad as secretary-general and re-instate Talabani as

Politburo member. Both had welcomed Mulla Mustafa's ousting of Abd Allah but Ahmad also wanted to minimize Barzani influence on the KDP. There was little love lost between the two men. Mulla Mustafa 'talked freely, with a bitterness amounting to hatred, against the alleged inertia, cowardice, inefficiency and intellectual presumptuousness of the KDP politicians, singling out Ibrahim Ahmad for his particular dislike.'[9] Ahmad complained of Mulla Mustafa's 'selfishness, arbitrariness, unfairness, tribal backwardness and even his dishonesty'.[10] But while he wanted to reduce his influence, he knew that Mulla Mustafa's leadership was indispensable.

In a new programme approved at the Fourth Congress, Ahmad declared that 'the party would struggle to widen the national rights of the Kurdish people on the basis of autonomy within the entity of Iraq and to include such an article in the permanent constitution.'[11] Ahmad was anxious to establish the KDP and Kurdish rights in a manner which would guarantee them against personal ambition, either from Mulla Mustafa or from Qasim. In fact Qasim refused to register the KDP in January along the lines of its programme. He took particularly strong exception to the idea of 'autonomy' which he said would be exploited by his enemies, and he forced the KDP to drop this article.[12]

Mulla Mustafa and the Tribes

The aghas and landlords had been appalled by the revolution. Under the Hashimites all the main tribes had been represented in government or parliament. Among the congratulatory telegrams that inundated the new regime there was not one from the Kurdish (or Euphrates) chiefs. Their great political and economic gains of the previous 37 years of monarchy suddenly seemed in jeopardy. Their worst premonitions were fulfilled in September with the Agrarian Reform Law, which proposed to limit landholdings to a maximum of 1,000 dunums of irrigated and 2,000 dunums of rainfed land – this implied redistribution of almost half the total cultivated area of Iraq (24 million dunums) to the peasantry.

The next blow was the return of Mulla Mustafa, very clearly Qasim's protégé. Those who had helped drive him out of Iraq in 1945, and those who had either been given or had exploited Barzani lands since 1945 felt especially apprehensive. When they learnt of Mulla Mustafa's first interview with Qasim, this apprehension must have turned to cold fear: when asked to forget old adversaries (the Harkis, Surchis, Baradustis and Zibaris), Mulla Mustafa refused since 'they were criminals.'[13] A few aghas even fled to Iran. Soon it became obvious that Mulla Mustafa was receiving substantial amounts of arms and equipment to strengthen his position in Kurdistan. This was disquieting to a broader swathe of tribal Kurds, including even southern tribes, like the Jaf, the Pizhdar, and even followers of the late Shaykh Mahmud.

In April and May 1959 the Baradust and then the Pizhdar rose in revolt against the Iraqi Republic and its hated agent, Mulla Mustafa.[14] It was a desperate gesture, and Barzani tribesmen, backed by the PRF, the army and the air force had little difficulty in driving the rebels either into Turkey or into Iran.

Once again Mulla Mustafa had rendered signal service to Baghdad. He had helped Qasim deal with most of his perceived threats, the Arab Nationalists and the Baath, the Communists and rebel Kurdish tribes. He was not only unassailable in Kurdistan, but held an ambiguous position in the republic. On the one hand, apart from the army, he was arguably Qasim's main prop and stay. On the other, he was now so strong as to threaten the paranoid president. It was probably for this reason that Qasim promptly pardoned the Baradust and Pizhdar rebels and invited them to return. By this time, however, Mulla Mustafa had begun to deal with his other enemies: in November he managed to kill Ahmad Muhammad Agha (Mahmud's brother), chief of the Zibaris, his men burning Zibari villages and crops and seizing livestock; then he attacked the Harkis, Surchis, Baradustis and others in the northern area.

The Road to Revolt

Qasim was displeased with Mulla Mustafa's increasingly undisputed grip on Kurdistan and he began to build relations with Mulla Mustafa's tribal enemies, for example the Surchis and Harkis. He also tried to restore Mahmud Zibari's position by convening a reconciliation, but the two leaders now hated each other so much they ended up cursing each other. Qasim then began to distance himself from Mulla Mustafa and the KDP. In a speech in early 1960 he publicly disparaged the Kurds and in particular the Barzanis, noting that apart from the Arab revolt of 1920, the Bakr Sidqi and Rashid Ali coups of 1936 and 1941 respectively, all other revolts before 1958 had been encouraged by the 'imperialists'.[15] Thus Qasim began to alienate Mulla Mustafa publicly. It was not long before he started sending arms and money to Mulla Mustafa's tribal rivals, for example Shaykh Rashid of Lawlan and the Baradustis.[16] While the KDP was holding its Fifth Congress in May 1960, Qasim received Surchi and Harki delegations and ensured this took precedence over the congress in press coverage the following day. It was a deliberate slight.

The KDP naturally shared Mulla Mustafa's dismay at the downturn in their relations with government. *Khabat* expressed frustration with the failure of the government to make progress on functional equality.[17] Mulla Mustafa formally signalled his disappointment by refusing to attend the 14 July celebrations commemorating the overthrow of the monarchy.

In the autumn fierce fighting broke out between Barzani and the Harki and Zibari tribes, the latter supported by Qasim. Ahmad in Baghdad was charged with 'stirring up national dissensions and instigating fanaticism'.[18] He was acquitted, but it was a warning and he went into hiding. At the turn of the year Qasim publicly denounced 'plotters' against the republic. Mulla Mustafa had no doubt as to whom Qasim was referring, for he found his privileges and stipend withheld and Qasim unwilling to receive him. He was now *persona non grata* in Baghdad.

For a while both sides avoided open conflict. In February Qasim cancelled the Kurdish Teachers' Convention in Shaqlawa, a testy response to demands for cultural rights. Then he spoke of treating Kurds as an indistinguishable as well as indivisible part of the Iraqi people, a proposition which contradicted thoughts of autonomy or equal status. It was redolent of the Ataturk approach. When in February *al Thawra* proposed that state policy should be to 'fuse' the Kurds and Arabs of Iraq, *Khabat* reacted angrily. But in an interview with the Beirut daily *al Nahda*, Mulla Mustafa emphasized his loyalty:

> the building of a genuine Iraqi unity upon complete equality between Arabs and Kurds in their rights and obligations.... No more is required than organisation, legislation and help from the government to enable the Kurds to practice these rights.[19]

In the meantime, however, inter-tribal conflict between pro-Qasim and pro-Barzani forces increased. At the end of February one of Mulla Mustafa's allies ambushed and killed a pro-government chief of the Khushnaw near his stronghold, Shaqlawa.[20] Ibrahim Ahmad was again arrested on an unsubstantiated charge of complicity.

Ibrahim Ahmad (who was soon released from custody) and Jalal Talabani were now openly hostile to Qasim. They felt increasing frustration that Qasim had taken virtually no steps towards autonomy, cultural rights or economic development in Kurdistan. In March *Khabat* published a strongly nationalist speech by Talabani, and was promptly closed down. By the end of the month no officially licensed Kurdish journal was still in print. Some KDP branches too had been closed down, and the Iraqi military presence in Kurdistan increased.

During the summer the KDP made demands, wearily familiar to those who remembered the events of 1930, for the introduction of Kurdish as an official language, the return of Kurdish officials from Arab areas, and progress on agricultural reform and industrial development, including nationalization of the oil industry. In addition, they asked for the removal of troop reinforcements, an end to martial law, an abandonment of the so-called 'transitional period', the restoration of democratic liberties and practical implementation of Article III of the Constitution.[21] Qasim ignored them. When the KDP called a strike on the anniversary of the September 1930 shootings, this too was ignored.

Revolt 1961–1963

The Kurdish revolt against Qasim occurred almost inadvertently and was conducted by three mutually suspicious groups. The first of these, and indeed the constituency which effectively precipitated the war, was composed of tribal aghas and their followers who sought to reverse the Agrarian Reform Law. Implementation had commenced in 1959, and was intended to provide a transitional period in which landlords and those who would receive land could rearrange their affairs. In fact it had led to a serious breakdown in agriculture with some landlords prematurely abandoning land they thought they would lose, some peasants trying to seize land, and a drift to towns where disorder led to the breakdown of share cropping arrangements and general damage to traditional landlord–peasant relations. Some aghas who held land either side of the border returned from exile in Iran as they sensed Qasim's authority begin to slip, and set up a right-wing party called Shurish. In June a tribal delegation travelled to Baghdad to seek abrogation of the new land tax that had been introduced with the agrarian reform, and an end to the tribal unrest engendered by Qasim's policy in the region. They were refused an audience and returned to Kurdistan empty-handed but resolved to resist payment of the tax. In effect they had rebelled.

Rebellion spread rapidly among landlords and aghas who now saw the chance to render the land reform measures void. They were encouraged by the example of their peers, by Qasim's fortuitous preoccupation with his claim on Kuwait and his dispute with Western oil companies. In striking testimony to the strength of tribal loyalties, their followers were insufficiently aware of the social and economic issues at stake to recognize that they were supporting the very class that exploited them, or that they stood to benefit from land reform.

Neither Mulla Mustafa nor Qasim yet sought direct conflict. Qasim hardly welcomed a war in Kurdistan when he needed troops to protect his own position in Baghdad and for his trumpeted takeover of Kuwait. In June he had summoned Shaykh Ahmad Barzani, whose good relations with him had somehow survived, to Baghdad. The British believed he wanted assurances that the KDP would not be used to rally opposition against him. He offered to release KDP detainees and reinstate Mulla Mustafa's stipend. Given that Shaykh Ahmad could hardly have gone to Baghdad without consent, one must conclude that Mulla Mustafa also preferred negotiation to war at this stage. However, no agreement was reached.

In any case, Qasim was taking no chances. He summoned friendly aghas to Baghdad, notably the Zibari. Apart from supplying the anti-Barzani coalition in the north with arms and money, it seems he was also trying to create an outer ring of friendly tribes along the Iranian border. On the eastern flank the Jaf of Halabja were so disunited as to offer no threat. Northwards, the Pizhdar, between Ranya and Qala Diza, had already rendered valuable service against the ICP. Qasim also tried to win over the Aku chief, Abbas Mamand, whose tribal lands lay in the border marches between Ranya and Rawanduz, but without success. Mamand had already decided in favour of the rebels.

As the government's authority became increasingly tenuous, Mulla Mustafa used the opportunity to hit those like Shaykh Rashid who had been receiving arms and money from Qasim. In July and August his men swept through their territories in the knowledge that Qasim was unable to protect them. Over 7,000 sought refuge in Turkey and Iran. By mid-August Mulla Mustafa had a firm grip on northern Kurdistan. He had not yet joined the rebels but it was only a question of time. He had assured Abbas Mamand, a longstanding friend and ally, that he would come to his help if he were attacked by the government.

Qasim now viewed Mulla Mustafa as part of the Kurdish rebellion. In July he had turned down a demand from Mulla Mustafa and the KDP for a substantial measure of autonomy for Kurdistan. In early August he asked Iran to confirm that, if aircraft were inadvertently to violate its airspace while operating against the Barzanis, it would take no action.

On 11 September Abbas Mamand's forces ambushed an army convoy near Bazyan and Qasim responded with indiscriminate air strikes on villages over a wide area, including Barzan. This brought not only Mulla Mustafa but also many other aghas into the war, and Zakho and Koi-Sanjaq fell briefly to the rebel forces. Qasim had, in effect, brought together two distinct Kurdish tribal groups, the old reactionary chiefs out essentially to protect their landed interests and Mulla Mustafa whose agenda was a blend of tribalism and nationalism. By December the army had dealt effectively with Abbas Mamand's disorganized forces, but Mulla Mustafa was quite another matter. He now took charge, using different tribes as irregulars intermittently to strike suddenly and swiftly at camps, outposts, convoys and communications, the essential ingredients of guerrilla warfare.

The economic reasons for revolt went beyond the narrow interests of the agha class. For at least a decade Kurdistan had been afflicted with growing unemployment. In part this was the natural result of a growing population and the drift to towns in search of jobs which did not exist. But it also resulted from a regime in which peasant indebtedness led to evictions. Many landlords looked forward to the removal of share-cropper or tenant farmers, since with the beginning of mechanization hired labour was a preferable means for production. The 1958 Revolution exacerbated the problem, for long-standing infrastructural programmes now ground to a halt; foreign companies abandoned a volatile and high risk environment, and the convulsion caused by the uncertainties of the land reform all led to unemployment and a pool from which fighters might easily be recruited.

On 24 September Qasim ordered the closure of the KDP, thus driving its membership into rebellion also. Throughout the summer a debate had raged within the party between a minority (led by Talabani) who urged that the KDP should take over leadership of the rebellion and use it for nationalist purposes, and the majority (led by Ahmad) who believed the aims of the KDP were wholly contrary to those of the rebels. As a party the KDP had condemned the rebellious aghas because their motive was to protect their class interests while the KDP was committed to social and economic progress.[22]

The KDP commenced operations against the government in December 1961. The decision was damaging, although passivity might well have led to the party's total demise. As it was, the KDP became an ally of Mulla Mustafa and the tribes he now controlled. The KDP was forbidden by Mulla Mustafa to operate in his own sphere of influence from Aku territory northwards, and its operations therefore barely stretched as far north as Arbil and Raniya. Even here it found itself reliant on tribes to bolster its own modest forces, and thereby lent them prestige. In the words of Sa'ad Jawad, 'Had the KDP remained true to its championship of Kurdish national aspirations, it would never have submitted to the tribal leadership and thus ruined its chances of leading the movement.'[23]

As it was, the fate of the rebellion lay in the hands of Mulla Mustafa and the chiefs, not the KDP, and their objectives were different from the party's. Indeed, Mulla Mustafa spoke seldom of Kurdish national rights. His main complaints like those of his associates concerned the Agrarian Reform Law and the inter-tribal conflicts promoted by Qasim. Furthermore, he still seemed to want a deal with the British,[24] a desire which revealed not only the enormous ideological gulf between himself and the KDP but also his failure to recognize that British intervention to protect Kuwait from an Iraqi takeover that summer had been exceptional. When approaches to the British came to nothing, Mulla Mustafa approached the other 'arch-imperialist', the United States.

Although within the area it controlled the KDP pushed ahead with the land reform,[25] its decision lost it influence among educated Kurds who were critical of an alliance with reactionaries. But the greater damage was to the KDP's reputation with the Iraqi opposition parties, particularly the ICP but also the Arab nationalists. It was now clear that the KDP preferred Kurdish reactionaries to progressive Iraqis. The ICP had already denounced the rebellion by reactionaries and the 'Anglo-American imperialists and oil companies' it said were behind them.[26] They suspected the KDP wanted separatism, not a democratic Arab–Kurdish Iraq. Not surprisingly, therefore, KDP appeals to the Iraqi opposition to join in the overthrow of Qasim fell upon deaf ears. Inside Kurdistan, however, many Kurdish members of the ICP deserted to the nationalist cause.

The war itself was a desultory affair, consisting of raids and ambushes by the rebels and reprisals largely in the form of air raids on villages. By January 1962 the rebels claimed that 500 villages, roughly one quarter of the total, had been attacked and it is possible that up to 80,000 had lost their homes. That spring Mulla Mustafa launched attacks on Zakhu and Dohuk, and on pro-government tribesmen whom he drove over the border. Those chiefs who seemed reluctant to support him soon found their villages plundered. In the south the KDP tried to forge a regular Kurdish fighting force, and those who enrolled became known as *peshmergas* (those who face death). Both the KDP and Mulla Mustafa benefited from the training provided by those Kurdish regular officers and men who deserted to the rebel cause.[27]

Qasim already realized how damaging this unnecessary war had become and in November 1961 and again in March 1962 he offered an amnesty and also an undertaking to make good the damage and to ensure Kurdistan received its full share of national economic development. By now the rebels felt sufficiently successful that the terms they might have accepted the previous summer were no longer enough. Mulla Mustafa raised his demands to a point that amounted to a public humiliation which Qasim could not endure.

The Kurdish rebels were not alone in recruiting from the pool of unemployed. Alongside the tribal chiefs (Zibari, Surchi, Harki, Baradusti and Khushnaw, etc)[28] who opted to support Qasim out of an almost ideological loathing of Mulla Mustafa, there were plenty of unemployed Kurds willing to take up arms if they were to be paid. Then there was a third category who took up arms under coercion, or who vacillated in order to avoid retribution from one side or the other. The latter included members of tribes on the nationalist side, even some from the Barzanis. Pro-government Kurdish forces, known as *fursan* (knights) by the government propagandists and more derisively as *jash* (little donkeys) by the rebels, amounted to about 10,000. This number declined as the war went increasingly against the government, and as the idea that it was dishonourable to fighting against the nationalists became more widespread.

The government also had large numbers of Kurds in its regular forces. The 2nd Infantry Division based at Kirkuk was predominantly Kurdish. In spite of desertions, there were probably as many Kurds ranged on the government as on the rebel side. But there was a qualitative difference between Mulla Mustafa's forces and the *jash*. Whereas Barzani forces were careful only to attack military targets, the *jash* and army tended to shell and loot indiscriminately, driving more young men into the rebel camp.

It was tempting for outside observers coloured by European nationalist values to treat the *jash* as shameful collaborators, and certainly this is how the rebels, particularly the KDP, came to treat them. But the reality was always more complex. This was partly because most tribesmen had few notions of nationalism and saw government as a legitimate and useful ally against an enemy tribe. But many among the *jash* were of unreliable loyalty. It was hardly accidental that Mulla Mustafa, acutely short of weapons, 'manages, on several occasions by strange coincidence, to cause the surrender of groups of pro-Government tribesmen just after they have been re-supplied with arms and ammunition'.[29] Running with the hares but hunting with the hounds has been an enduring feature of 'pro-government' Kurds.

By the end of 1962 Qasim was no closer to quelling the rebels than he had been a year earlier. On the contrary, the war had generally gone against him, in spite of his control of the air. His troops on the ground had little stomach for a savage war in the mountains. In the meantime it was clear that Qasim was becoming isolated politically, and that his downfall was a matter of time. In fact it was imminent.

The KDP had recognized the value of establishing ties with those who might seize power. At first they tried to interest the Communists in staging a coup, but they had demurred.[30] By December 1962 it was clear that the Arab Nationalists, the Nasserists and the Baath, were best placed. In December and January the KDP began negotiating with them. The latter wanted assurances that while the army was concentrated on the overthrow of Qasim in Baghdad, the Kurds would not exploit army weakness in the north. The KDP was happy to meet this requirement. It believed that in return it had received assurances regarding full Kurdish autonomy.

The Baath Government of 1963

Nothing could have been further from the truth. Following the overthrow of Qasim on 8 February, the Kurds found themselves trying to negotiate with the National Council of the Revolutionary Command (NCRC) and the government it formed under a Nasserist President Abd al Salam Arif and the Baathist Prime Minister Ahmad Hasan al Bakr. On 10 February the KDP formally welcomed the coup and sought a ceasefire, the release of prisoners of war, compensation for the injured, the removal and punishment of those responsible for torturing Kurds, and an official declaration of autonomy.

Kurdish negotiators suffered major handicaps. In Baghdad there was a widespread belief that foreign agencies, especially Iran and Western oil companies, were using the Kurds as a Trojan horse. The more extreme Arab nationalists considered Southern Kurdistan as Arab land inhabited by a non-Arab minority. But for the regime as a whole, the question of Kurdish autonomy was a side issue to the central preoccupation of both Nasserists and Baathists: the question of Arab unity.

The KDP was naturally extremely uneasy about the prospect of the Kurds becoming part of a larger Arab entity. They felt compelled publicly to welcome it but pointed out that the proposed union of Iraq with the UAR made the question of Kurdish autonomy that much more pressing. It was a moot point whether Jalal Talabani's inclusion in the Iraqi delegation that went to Cairo towards the end of the month was merely to demonstrate Kurdo-Arab amity or to define Kurdish rights as the KDP hoped. In fact Talabani found Nasser a good deal more forthcoming than his co-delegates on the question of autonomy. His anxieties were well founded, and he handed them a document setting out alternative Kurdish demands that depended on whether Iraq remained separate or sought a federal or integrated union with the other Arab states.[31] When Iraq, Egypt and Syria finally issued a formal agreement to form a Federal Arab Republic in mid-April, neither the Kurds nor their rights were mentioned.

The disparity of opinion in Baghdad, however, was not over whether to concede autonomy but over what method should be used to reduce the Kurds. The armed forces, which ascribed their poor showing to Qasim's inept direction of the war, favoured a military solution which would defeat the Kurds once and for all.

The civilian Baath had not forgiven the Kurds for their part in the events in

Mosul in March 1959. But it preferred to undermine the Kurds non-violently, by 'infiltrating or splitting the Kurdish movement',[32] perhaps making a few cultural concessions in the process. It was happy to stress the rights of Kurds as 'brothers and friends of the Arabs', an affirmation that fell far short of Kurdish *national* rights, let alone autonomy.

To show its goodwill, a delegation went to visit Mulla Mustafa in the stronghold from which he had been unwilling to descend in early March. Mulla Mustafa demanded an immediate and formal recognition of Kurdish autonomy, and that this should cover virtually the whole of the old vilayet of Mosul including the Kirkuk oilfields, excluding only the city of Mosul itself. Among his demands was an insistence on the creation of separate Kurdish armed forces, and that autonomous Kurdistan should receive two thirds of the national oil revenue, a proportion justified by the location of the oilfields in territories he claimed. Finally, he warned that fighting would recommence if the government did not accede to his demands within three days; in fact he had already ordered his guerrilla forces back to their battle positions. On 7 March the government persuaded Mulla Mustafa to compromise based on 'recognition of the national rights of the Kurdish people on the basis of self-administration'. But the next day he had once more raised his demands.

The government concluded that no agreement with Mulla Mustafa was possible but it needed time to prepare the army for another round. So a delegation was despatched which persuaded him to accept 'decentralization' rather than autonomy, with Kurdish and Arabic as official languages in the Kurdish province. It also regretted that Kirkuk was not negotiable since the government was committed to honour international oil contracts.

Dissatisfied, the KDP submitted a detailed autonomy plan in late April, one which would give the Kurds freedom over virtually all matters except foreign affairs, finance and national defence.[33] It also required inclusion of the Kirkuk, Khaniqin and north-west Mosul oilfields within the autonomous region, and a proportionate share of their revenues.[34]

Such demands went far beyond what the government was willing to accept. The key reason lay with the oilfields, but the government could also point to the 1947 census which indicated that Kurds comprised only 25 per cent of the population of Kirkuk town, and only 53 per cent of the province. By May it was clear not only that there was stalemate in the negotiations but that a resumption of hostilities was almost inevitable. Ever since March Mulla Mustafa had repeated threats of a renewal of war. Now Baghdad took up the challenge.

On 5 June Baathi troops surrounded Sulaymaniya, imposed a curfew and began rounding up wanted men. When martial law was lifted three days later the population found the streets littered with dead people and a mass grave containing 80 bodies. Many others had also disappeared. On 10 June Baghdad issued a communiqué accusing the Kurdish *peshmerga* forces of numerous violations of law and order since the coup.[35] It arrested Kurdish delegates in Baghdad and the same day launched a three-pronged offensive towards Amadiya, Rawanduz and Koi-Sanjaq.

Had the Kurds been united they might have fared better in the first round of war. But whatever trust had existed between Mulla Mustafa and the KDP had evaporated during the ceasefire. There was now little love lost between the northern and southern camps of Kurdish resistance. Mulla Mustafa, jealous of the standing of KDP and its leading negotiator, Jalal Talabani, had openly criticized the Kurdish trip to Cairo and had tried to undermine Talabani's position as 'the representative of the Kurds', since it clearly undermined his own position.

Thus government forces had little difficulty in capturing Barzan or in advancing beyond Koi-Sanjaq towards Raniya, nor of controlling the area around Sulaymaniya by September. At first it looked as if the Kurdish resistance might be crushed. But in fact the rebels bided their time beyond the reach of the Iraqi army. As army commanders slowly realized, only the easiest parts of Kurdistan had been captured. Then, in November the Baath government was overthrown.

Mulla Mustafa's Triumph over the KDP

The new regime was led by Abd al Salam Arif, assisted by a National Command of the Revolutionary Council (NCRC), weighted heavily in favour of senior army officers, Arab nationalists and Nasserists. Although the new regime was no better disposed towards the Kurdish question than its predecessor, it sought peace with the Kurds because the war had been unpopular, costly and, as the army belated had discovered, a military failure.

In fact Arif had contacted Mulla Mustafa before his coup in order to elicit his co-operation 'to resist the Army offensive until he could oust the Baathists'.[36] Arif may have offered Mulla Mustafa as *quid pro quo* the reduction of the KDP. At any rate that is precisely what happened.

Mulla Mustafa was more concerned to achieve unquestioned paramountcy over the whole Kurdish movement than to prosecute his war with Baghdad. The latter could wait. So he welcomed Arif's goodwill messages after the coup, and responded to appeals from Nasser and Ben Bella in January to settle the quarrel amicably.

Once again Mulla Mustafa demonstrated his poor political judgement. On 10 February he signed a peace agreement with Arif in his personal capacity rather than as KDP president. The key items of the agreement recognized the national rights of the Kurds within a unified Iraqi state; undertook the release of all prisoners of war and restoration of Kurdish property; accepted the reinstatement of government administration in the northern region and lifted the economic blockade.

As Ahmad and Talabani were quick to point out, Mulla Mustafa had put his name to an agreement that omitted any mention of self-administration let alone Kurdish autonomy, the centrepiece of the whole Kurdish position and what they had been fighting for. It also omitted mention of Kurdistan, employing the favoured Arab nationalist euphemism 'the Northern Region'. They criticized his poor judgement and his unilateral behaviour.

Arif threatened force against any opponent of Mulla Mustafa, while the latter warned that any resistance to government forces would constitute a declaration of war against himself. A few days later Mulla Mustafa, in a clear reference to the KDP, indicated he had no objection to the abolition of political parties, 'as long as it serves Iraq's interests'.[37] Mulla Mustafa began to receive arms and money from Arif.

Kurdistan was rent with schism. On one side, Ahmad, Talabani and the KDP intelligentsia asserted an ideological position evolved over the previous 20 years. On the other, Mulla Mustafa was able to rally the conservatives, the tribal and religious leaders of Kurdistan. For these it was a contest between the religious and the secular, the primordial and the nationalist, tradition versus atheistic Marxism.

Despite the ideological strength of their position, the Ahmad–Talabani group had no chance against Mulla Mustafa. Ever since 1961 the KDP had portrayed Mulla Mustafa as heroic leader of the nation. His portrait hung in public places and in many homes. He was the face of the Kurdish revolution. It was now that the KDP had reason to regret throwing in their lot with Mulla Mustafa and the tribal chiefs in 1961. The cause had miscarried.

Ahmad and Talabani found themselves a diminishing minority within the Kurdish movement as many KDP members voted with their feet. In March Ahmad and a few colleagues went to Mulla Mustafa's camp near Qala Diza to seek a rapprochement and to plead for the fundamental principle of Kurdish autonomy. Mulla Mustafa grew angry as he insisted he had given his word of honour that the 10 February Agreement was a final settlement. Fearing for their lives, Ahmad and his group slipped away at night, back to their own head-quarters in Mawat. They soon found that Mulla Mustafa had replaced virtually all the KDP commanders with people loyal to himself.

Ahmad now tried to rally supporters against Mulla Mustafa. He convened a Sixth KDP Congress at Mawat in April. Few turned up. Those who did passed a resolution condemning Mulla Mustafa's unilateral and unauthorized deal with Baghdad. Ahmad may have seized the moral high ground, but Mulla Mustafa had the support of most Kurds and also the government in Baghdad.

In June Mulla Mustafa sent a message via Abbas Mamand Agha of the Aku, inviting Ahmad and Talabani to meet him in Raniya. He proposed a neutral committee to prepare for a new congress, on the grounds that Ahmad's Mawat Congress had not enjoyed a quorum. Ahmad and Talabani agreed but found Mulla Mustafa had quietly left Raniya having unilaterally nominated a committee that excluded all of the Ahmad–Talabani group. Fearing arrest, they fled at night back to Mawat where Ahmad only then published the damning Mawat Congress resolution that he had not done previously.

Mulla Mustafa held *his* Sixth Congress at Qala Diza in July.[38] Representatives of the Ahmad–Talabani group who arrived to participate were promptly arrested. The Congress established a National Council for the Command of the Revolution, a consortium of the KDP, the *peshmerga* and tribal leaders, chaired by Mulla Mustafa. Predictably, the congress declared the Mawat meeting illegal and expelled most of the old KDP central committee. A few days later Mulla Mustafa sent his son, Idris, with a large force to drive Ahmad, Talabani and their 4,000 or so followers into Iran. Mulla Mustafa had won.

Once he was undisputed cock of the walk, Mulla Mustafa was able to don Ahmad's clothing. The Qala Diza Congress demanded autonomy, informing the government that a return of the civil administration was unacceptable – the very issues for which he had been condemned so vehemently by Ahmad and Talabani. Mulla Mustafa also reorganized the KDP, using the skills of Kurdish ex-ICP members to extend the influence of the KDP in Kurdish life.

A drift back to war was inevitable. In May Arif's new Provisional Constitution had referred only vaguely to the Kurds, true to the 10th February Agreement but contrary to what Kurds aspired to. In October Mulla Mustafa made the demands he had so signally failed to do in February, calling for autonomy, the inclusion of Kirkuk and Khaniqin oilfields within that autonomy, the use of Kurdish as an official language in Kurdistan and a fair share of the oil revenue. He also established three assemblies to administer Kurdish affairs: a Senate chaired by Shaykh Latif, a consultative assembly under the presidence of Mamand Abbas Agha, and an executive 'Revolutionary Council' under his own direction.

Arif told Mulla Mustafa that in his view the government had largely kept to the 10 February Agreement and that he, Mulla Mustafa, was the chief obstacle to progress. In fact Arif was under pressure on the Kurdish question from senior officers, whom he feared might overthrow his regime.

Both sides now prepared for war. In early March the 100,000-strong army commenced its offensive against 15,000 *peshmergas*. Most Kurds rallied to Mulla Mustafa, and even Ahmad, Talabani and their supporters were allowed back to support the national struggle. The re-opened war proved inconclusive, with the army holding many towns and villages, but losing large swathes of territory to the *peshmergas* by night. Contrary to expectation the army commenced an offensive despite the weather conditions during the winter of 1965–66. It planned a final assault on Mulla Mustafa in April. But before this could happen, President Arif was killed in a helicopter accident. As the struggle for power took place in Baghdad, the war ground to a halt in the north.

The death of Arif brought the latent conflict between the civilian and militarist elements in government into the open. Arif himself had favoured strengthening the civilian element in government and had appointed Abd al Rahman Bazzaz as Prime Minister in autumn 1965. Bazzaz had picked a largely civilian cabinet, and replaced the NCRC with a National Defence Council composed of civilians as well as soldiers

Bazzaz had already recognized the centrality of the Kurdish question to the country's progress and had wanted to negotiate a peaceful solution. He also had no difficulty recognizing Kurdish nationality. To this end his administration had declared:

> The new administrative law will affirm the reality of Kurdish nationalism and will enable our citizens in the north fully to preserve their language and cultural heritage. It will also enable them to carry on local activities which do not conflict with the unity of the country and which in no way paves the way for the loss of any part of our homeland.[39]

But his defence minister, General Uqayli, determined to bring Mulla Mustafa and his partisans to heel, had persuaded Arif to permit resumption of the war that winter.

When Abd al Salam Arif was killed, Mulla Mustafa announced a one-month ceasefire to allow the new regime 'to ponder upon the Kurds' demands'.[40] In fact both sides needed a breather. But it was not long before the new president, Abd al Salam's unambitious brother, Abd al Rahman, gave way to the militarists. 'No autonomy will ever be granted to the Kurds.... The government has never envisaged negotiations with the rebels.'[41]

So the army proceeded with its next offensive while Bazzaz, who had little belief that the army could win, bided his time. In May the army tried to seize the key stretch of road from Rawanduz to the Iranian border, the main route for rebel supplies from Iran and the location of the *peshmerga* headquarters. The air force used napalm and chemical weapons,[42] but the army suffered the worst defeat it had ever borne at the hands of the Kurds, losing hundreds of men.

Bazzaz moved quickly. By the end of June he had enticed a Kurdish delegation to Baghdad to meet Arif and himself. Both parties wanted a settlement before the army launched another assault. After a fortnight of negotiation, Bazzaz broadcast a 15-point offer to the Kurds, on 29 June. The following day Mulla Mustafa accepted it, for it fulfilled nearly all Kurdish demands. It recognized Kurdish nationality within Iraq, promised decentralization with freely elected administrative councils and proportional representation for Kurds in central government. It also recognized Kurdish as an official language, with all ancillary linguistic and cultural rights, and undertook to establish a parliamentary system of government within a year.[43]

The Bazzaz Declaration came close to the twin requirements whereby the Kurdish question in Iraq could be resolved, autonomy for the Kurds and an electoral parliamentary democracy for all Iraq. Three of the 15 articles were kept secret. One of these dealt with an old grievance, promising to detach the Kurdish parts of Mosul province and reform them as a Kurdish province based on Dohuk. The second promised to allow the KDP to function publicly, once elections had taken place. Finally Bazzaz promised a step-by-step general amnesty.[44]

The triumph of Bazzaz was shortlived. The following month he found his position undermined by Abd al Rahman Arif, egged on by officers who resented his disdain for the army, and he resigned. There is no reason to doubt that Bazzaz had taken a sincere and principled stand regarding the Kurds and the need to return to democratic politics. With his departure the best chance both for the Kurds and a democratic republican Iraq disappeared. His successor, an army general, showed no inclination to implement the Bazzaz Declaration, and in any case considered Mulla Mustafa to be unrepresentative of all Kurds. He had a point, in view of Mulla Mustafa's many tribal and ideological adversaries.

Ahmad and Talabani had not forgiven Mulla Mustafa, and the mix of personal dislike and ideological disagreement had by now developed into a bitter feud. Although they had assisted Mulla Mustafa in the first phase of the army assault on Kurdistan in April 1965, they broke with him in January 1966 and commenced hostilities against him, armed and financed by a government which hoped to use them as a counterweight to the Barzanis. They continued to claim to be the true KDP, and resumed publication of their own edition of *Khabat*.

Ahmad and Talabani took the position that they supported the government in the expectation it would implement the Bazzaz Declaration, but they also questioned whether autonomy could be realized before the landlord and agha classes had been defeated. Thus they found themselves fighting side by side with the despised *jash* as, in Mulla Mustafa's words, the 'new mercenaries'.[45] Mulla Mustafa could afford to denigrate, for Ahmad and Talabani's forces were far too weak to defeat him.

Breaking with his officers, however, President Arif decided to visit Kurdistan that autumn. He met Mulla Mustafa, an event that could only enhance the latter's standing among the Kurds and also in all Iraq. Mulla Mustafa knew the Kurds needed a breather. Around 750 villages had been destroyed and nearly 200,000 villagers displaced. Arif implicitly rebuked his subordinates, stating 'the Kurdish problem has been complicated by political errors and bad management.'[46] He made Mulla Mustafa all sorts of promises he could not keep, regarding the Bazzaz Declaration and the rehabilitation of Kurds into national life, and a truce was agreed. However, as he began to realize that the army was fighting a war it could not win, he also began to recognize that to implement the Bazzaz plan could well lead to an army coup.

While the war with the army had come to a standstill, Mulla Mustafa was able to consolidate his own position in Kurdistan, dealing with his tribal and ideological rivals. His Seventh KDP Congress formally accepted the Bazzaz Declaration in November 1966 in the interest of avoiding further bloodshed but added the proviso that 'it does not correspond with the revolution's objective of autonomy.'[47] It signalled to Baghdad that the Bazzaz Declaration was, as far as Mulla Mustafa and the KDP were concerned, a start rather than a conclusion to the Kurdish question. But it was predictably critical of Baghdad's 'malicious' failure to make progress on any of the declaration's points, and took the provocative liberty of publicizing the three secret clauses

Mulla Mustafa used the ensuing stalemate to maintain a desultory dialogue with Arif and to increase his demands. He obtained consent to publish a daily paper in Baghdad, *al Taakhi* (Fraternity), that was openly critical of the regime. The regime feared closing it down in case Mulla Mustafa resumed Kurdish radio transmissions, which had been suspended following the Bazzaz Declaration. The Mulla also used the hiatus to attack his rivals.

Mulla Mustafa obtained help from two of Iraq's main ideological enemies, Iran and Israel. Iran looked favourably towards Iraq's Kurds as a cat's paw against the pro-Soviet regime after the fall of the Hashimites. After Qasim's fall Iran began arming the Kurds with modern weaponry. By 1966 Iran was probably supplying 20 per cent or more of Mulla Mustafa's requirements and disregarded the Iraqi protests of early 1966. In return Mulla Mustafa undertook to deny Iraqi Kurdistan to Iranian Kurdish militants. By late 1966 Israel was assisting Mulla Mustafa.

After June 1967 both the government and the army were too weak to be much threat to Mulla Mustafa. This was partly because of the shock of the Six-Day War, but it was also because of a new factor. Baghdad could now only defeat the Kurds if it could seal the border with Iran. Otherwise the *peshmergas* could continue indefinitely, being both resupplied and if need be seeking temporary refuge from over the border. Baghdad's efforts to end Iranian assistance to the Kurds were unavailing. In the end the government's weakness, demonstrated by its inability to deal with the Kurds or to field a force against Israel, destroyed it. In July 1968 the Baath and the army carried out a successful coup.

Sources

Great Britain: Public Record Office, series FO 371: nos 133069, 133070, 133072, 134255, 140913, 140916, 140918, 140920, 140921, 140924, 141050, 149845, 157662, 157663, 157664, 157665, 157666, 157670, 157671, 157674, 164233, 164234, 164235.

Secondary sources: David Adamson, *The Kurdish War* (London, 1964); Arfa, *The Kurds*; Batatu, *The Old Social Classes*; Uriel Dann, *Iraq under Qassem: A Political Study 1958–63* (New York, 1969); Dziegiel, *Rural Community in Contemporary Iraq*; Mahmud al Durra, *Al Qadhiya al Kurdiya* (Beirut, 1966); Solomon Gershon, 'The Kurdish national struggle in Iraq' in *New Outlook*, no. 3, March–April 1967; Edmund Ghareeb, *The Kurdish Question in Iraq* (Syracuse, 1981); Sa'ad Jawad, *Iraq and the Kurdish Question, 1958–1970* (London, 1981); Majid Khaddouri, *Republican Iraq: a Study in Iraqi Politics since the Revolution of 1958* (London, 1969); Edgar O'Ballance, *The Kurdish Revolt, 1961–1970* (London, 1973); I.C. Vanly, *Le Kurdistan Irakien, Entité Nationale. Étude de la Révolution de 1961* (Neuchatel, 1970).

Periodicals: *Hawkar*, *The Times*.

Interviews: Ibrahim Ahmad (London, 28 May 1993), Husayn Agha Surchi (London, 18 February 1992).

Notes

1. The Kurd was Khalid Naqshbandi, a member of a religious (*murshid*) landed Arbili family. He was generally respected, but hardly an acknowledged political leader among the Kurds.

2. See Sa'ad Jawad, *Iraq and the Kurdish Question, 1958–1970* (London, 1981), p. 37 for the text.

3. Jawad, *Iraq and the Kurdish Question*, p. 38.

4. Mulla Mustafa received a monthly stipend of ID500. *In toto* the Barzani clan received allowances fluctuating between ID 1,000 and ID 2,000 monthly; Mahmud al Durra, *al Qadhiya al Kurdiya* (Beirut, 1966), p. 280.

5. Kurdish officers were almost invariably posted away from Kurdistan, a policy initiated by the Hashimites after the Barzani rebellion of 1943 and continued by Qasim.

6. Words ascribed to Ibrahim Ahmad, Dann, *Iraq under Qassem*, p. 174.

7. Mahdi Hamid, who had supported Mulla Mustafa in 1945 and was in the ICP from 1948; Batatu, *The Old Social Classes*, p. 884.

8. Jawad, *Iraq and the Kurdish Question*, p. 44.

9. Dann, *Iraq under Qassem*, p. 335.

10. Ibid.

11. Jawad, *Iraq and the Kurdish Question*, p. 48.

12. In fact the Fifth Congress reinstated the aim in May 1960, Jawad, *Iraq and the Kurdish Question*, p. 50.

13. *Radio Baghdad*, 8 October 1958, in Dann, *Iraq under Qassem*, p. 138.

14. The leaders were Shaykh Rashid of Lawlan, his son-in-law, Mahmud Khalifa Samad, an important agha of the Baradustis (both of whom had a bitter feud with Mulla Mustafa) and Shaykh Muhammad Sadiq, son of the late Shaykh Taha.

15. Jawad, *Iraq and the Kurdish Question*, p. 69.

16. Shaykh Rashid asked for an undertaking that the ICP would not be allowed to operate in Kurdistan, and that the Barzanis would be evicted from Baradusti villages; Karim Khan Baradusti, interview, London, 18 February 1992; FO 371/149845 Falle to Home, Baghdad, 27 September 1960.

17. These frustrations included (i) workers dismissed from government service for membership of the KDP; (ii) failure to get the directorate general of Kurdish studies functioning; (iii) the officially sponsored slogans for the 14 July celebrations ignored Kurdish nationhood; (iv) Kurdistan did not get its share of development projects; (v) the authorities neglected Kurd peasant needs; Dann, *Iraq under Qassem*, p. 332.

18. *The Iraq Times*, 17 November 1960, in Dann, *Iraq under Qassem*, p. 332.

19. *Al Nahda* (Beirut), 20 February 1961.

20. This was Sadiq Agha Miran. The assassin was Mahmud Kawani, possibly acting on the orders of Mulla Mustafa.

21. There were a least three petitions, see FO 371/157673 Chancery to FO, Baghdad, 25 May 1961; Jawad, *Iraq and the Kurdish Question*, p. 74; FO 371/157674 Chancery to FO, Baghdad, 10 July 1961.

22. For an analysis of the tensions between the KDP and its tribal allies, and the tensions within the KDP, see FO 371/164234 Stoakes, IPC Beirut, 27 August 1962.

23. Jawad, *Iraq and the Kurdish Question*, p. 82.

24. Mulla Mustafa wrote to the ambassador in Damascus, to discuss the means of destroying Communism and its hirelings in Iraq (and every part of Kurdistan) and to agree the line to be taken concerning international oil companies 'so that Great Britain can achieve what it wants for the benefit of the British people and the Kurdish people likewise.' FO 371/157671 Clarke to FO, Damascus, 15 December 1961.

25. Consequently some landowners there threw in their lot with Qasim; Jawad, *Iraq and the Kurdish Question*, p. 84.

26. FO 371/157674 pamphlets in Chancery to FO, Baghdad, 5 October 1961.

27. By October 1962 it was reckoned that there were about 600 army deserters in the rebel ranks; FO 371/164235 Allen to Hiller, Baghdad, 22 October 1962.

28. For a list of twenty tribes pledging support to the government, see FO 371/157670 Chancery to FO, Baghdad, 12 October 1961.

29. FO 371/157671 Burrows to FO, Ankara, 9 December 1961.

30. It was a decision ICP must bitterly have regretted. During the 1963 coup at least 5,000 Communists were killed in street fighting and extra-judicial killings by the triumphant Baath. In a subsequent purge another 150 were executed and 7,000 imprisoned. The party never recovered. Batatu, *The Old Social Classes*, pp. 972, 985, 988.

31. The text is in Durra, *al Qadhiya al Kurdiya*, pp. 316–17.

32. The words of Ali Salih al Saadi, the secretary-general of the Baath at the time, in Jawad, *Iraq and the Kurdish Question*, p. 130.

33. The text is in Durra, *al Qadhiya al Kurdiya*, pp. 318–324.

34. The formal government offer and Kurdish counter proposals are published verbatim in David Adamson, *The Kurdish War* (London, 1964), pp. 208–215.

35. The text is in Durra, *al Qadhiya al Kurdiya*, p. 235.

36. The view of the Baathi secretary-general, Ali Salih Saadi, Jawad, *Iraq and the Kurdish Question*, p. 155.

37. Jawad, *Iraq and the Kurdish Question*, p. 184, n. 34.

38. See Vanly, *Le Kurdistan Irakien*, pp. 231f. for a detailed account of this congress.

39. Quoted in Khadduri, *Republican Iraq*, p. 255.

40. G. Solomon, 'The Kurdish national struggle in Iraq', *New Outlook*, vol. x, March/April 1967, p. 10 quoted by Jawad, *Iraq and the Kurdish Question*, p. 195.

41. *The Guardian*, 28 April 1966, quoted by Jawad, *Iraq and the Kurdish Question*, p. 196.

42. This was not the first occasion chemical weapons had been used. Talabani protested their use on two occasions, see *The Times*, 21 May, 20 August 1965.

43. For a listing of the 12 public clauses, see Solomon, 'The Kurdish National Struggle', pp. 12–13.

44. The Bazzaz text is in Vanly, *Le Kurdistan Irakien*, pp. 379f.

45. Jawad, *Iraq and the Kurdish Question*, p. 219, n. 53.

46. *Baghdad Radio*, 1 November 1966, in Solomon, 'The Kurdish national struggle', p. 17.

47. KDP Communiqué, 25 November 1966 in Vanly, *Le Kurdistan Irakien*, p. 270.

CHAPTER 16

THE KURDS UNDER THE BAATH,
1968–1975

Introduction

In 1970 the KDP and the new Baath government reached an accord which reflected the government's own sense of insecurity and the Kurds' basic demands. The agreement failed for several reasons. Foremost of these was that the government's true instincts were to centralize. Autonomy was a temporary ploy while it gained enough strength to impose direct control. Within the Baath there was strong ideological disapproval of making major concessions to the Kurds. Within the KDP it was not appreciated how its alliances with Iran, Israel and the US appeared so treasonous in Baghdad. Because of its oil reserves, both sides focused on the fate of Kirkuk as the litmus test of the agreement, an issue on which neither side showed much flexibility. Mulla Mustafa committed the fundamental error of believing that the external players, the US and Iran would help him defeat Iraq, rather than use him for their own purposes. He also failed to appreciate that the Iraqi army was now strong enough to defeat him in the field. As a result the years 1968–75 led to bitter defeat, massive population transfer and the implementation of a sham autonomy in Kurdistan.

The Baath, Mulla Mustafa and the Ahmad–Talabani Group

The Baath and the Kurds were not, of course, strangers to each other. In theory, the Baath laid claim to Iraqi Kurdistan as an integral part of the Arab world, and therefore took the view that Kurdish self-determination was impossible since it contradicted this claim. Yet, in spite of the clash of nationalisms there was room for some optimism.

Michel Aflaq, the Baath's founding ideologue, had been aware of the danger of Arab nationalism excluding non-Arab minorities. For him the socialist dimension of Baathi belief tempered nationalist exclusivity. In 1955 he made his view clear regarding the Baath's approach to national or religious minorities:

When we call for economic equality and the offering of equal opportunity, we mean that we have delivered the nation's cause to its true owners, the people. They are in fact one with no distinction between Muslim and Christian, Arab or Kurd or Berber.... What does the Kurdish sector of the people want, and to what do they aspire (except for some leaders who have feudal interests) other than to live a happy and dignified life where they receive what others receive and give what others give. These individuals do not want more than what the Arabs want for themselves.[1]

Although the Baath, like other Arab nationalist groups, were too preoccupied with issues of the Arab world to give much thought to minority relations, it did attempt once or twice to explain its position to Kurds who were instinctively suspicious of it.

It was natural, too, that Baath leaders should approach those Kurds ideologically closest to them, those who justified their nationalism in a socialist context. Aflaq met with Ibrahim Ahmad, for example, shortly after the 1958 Revolution and the KDP decided to join the United Front of which the Baath was already a member. In 1962, when they began to plot the downfall of Qasim, the Baath had been able to approach the KDP to make sure it would not oppose them.

This had been the positive side, but there had been a less happy history too. The Baath did not forget the persecution they had endured at the hands of Kurds in Mosul and Kirkuk in March and July respectively of 1959, nor the frustration of dealing with Mulla Mustafa. It was not convinced that either Mulla Mustafa or the KDP were true representatives of the Kurds. Rather, they seemed 'separatist, feudalist and imperialist stooges', not 'loyal and true Iraqi Kurds'.[2]

The Kurds, for their part, had watched with alarm Baathi enthusiasm for Iraqi union with the UAR. They remembered that in 1963 the Baath had been a good deal more ferocious in war than Qasim had been. But their revolt had been a major factor in the downfall of the Baath in November.

During the years 1963–68, the Baath had time to reconsider the wisdom of fighting the Kurds, but largely neglected to do so. It bitterly noted that Mulla Mustafa accepted terms from Arif in 1964 that were less generous than those the Baath had offered him. However, as it planned a resumption of power it had made contact with both Mulla Mustafa and the Ahmad–Talabani faction. Mulla Mustafa had been frosty, Ahmad and Talabani a good deal more positive. Among the Baath's leading advocates of a more amenable approach to the Kurdish question was Saddam Husayn.

When the Baath recovered power in July 1968, 'The resolution of the Kurdish question in a peaceful manner' was among the party's goals.[3] This decision was not based on any commitment to Kurdish rights but upon the imperative to consolidate its own position. While it held effective power in the Revolutionary Command Council, the Baath wanted to create the illusion of a broader representation in government in order to neutralize the threats that might arise from the Kurds and the Communists, the two constituencies strong enough to threaten the Baath's position.

It was therefore anxious to co-opt both groups into government to prevent them making common cause against the Baath. The thought of Kurdistan's military prowess combined with the Communists' network across Iraq was a disturbing one. But it was initially unsuccessful with the Communists, who were unwilling to participate before civil liberties were guaranteed and the ICP legalized.

The Baath had more success with the Kurds. It nominated a number of them to the new cabinet,[4] and declared its intention to implement the Bazzaz Declaration. With this in mind, it naturally turned to the Talabani–Ahmad faction with its readiness to co-operate and its recognizable socialist ideology. It evidently thought it could eclipse Mulla Mustafa as a focal point for the Kurdish movement.

It was equally natural that Talabani and Ahmad should welcome the new regime. Ideologically they felt more at ease with the Baath than they had done with any previous regime, since they also believed in socialist as well as nationalist principles. It was also a wonderful opportunity to displace Mulla Mustafa as representative of Kurdish national aspirations. They received a government stipend for their troops, called 'Jash 66' by Mulla Mustafa's men. In Baghdad, they were allowed to publish a newspaper, al Nur, which carried their particular point of view. Talabani wrote fulsomely of the Baath as 'the first ruling Arab political party ... to extend its hand to the Kurdish people directly, sincerely, and hopefully',[5] and the first to 'recognize the national rights of the Kurdish people'. Talabani and Ahmad endorsed Baath policy, but in return they sought concessions in order to enhance their own credibility among the Kurds. In Mulla Mustafa's disparaging words, however, Talabani and Ahmad were 'agents for anyone who pays',[6] an observation full of irony in view of his own relations with Qasim and Arif. In reality both parties eagerly sought confirmation from government so as to strengthen their authority inside Kurdistan, just as their tribal predecessors had done for as long as anyone could remember.

Mulla Mustafa did not reject the Baath outright, but he insisted that co-operation was contingent on the Baath dumping Ahmad and Talabani. Since it would not comply, he withdrew his representative from the cabinet, dismissing them contemptuously, 'All they want today is to gain time to consolidate the basis of their regime.'[7] It proved a perceptive remark.

Mulla Mustafa chose other means to demonstrate that he was indispensable. From autumn a number of clashes took place between his troops and Ahmad–Talabani forces. On most of these occasions Mulla Mustafa demonstrated the greater skill as well as numerical strength. In essence Mulla Mustafa was repudiating the Baath on account of its association with his Kurdish enemies.

The Baath indicated its commitment to the Bazzaz Declaration almost immediately, issuing decrees for Kurdish to be taught in all Iraqi schools and universities; for a new university to be established in Sulaymaniya and for a general amnesty for those who had particpated in the Kurdish war. It also declared Nawruz, the Kurdish New Year, as an official holdiay, and recognized the Kurds' right to preserve their nationality. It even established a Bureau for Northern Affairs attached to the Revolutionary Command Council. It really hoped to undermine Mulla Mustafa.

Baath apprehension at another Kurdish war increased with the danger of Iranian involvement. It was apprehensive of Iran's growing regional domination, evidenced in January by its claim to Bahrain. It was well aware that Iran was supplying Mulla Mustafa with artillery and other sophisticated equipment. In the hope that it could erode popular support for Mulla Mustafa, it declared its intention to implement the outstanding articles of the Bazzaz Declaration in February 1969.

Ignoring such statements, Mulla Mustafa began attacking the government's troops in March, demonstrating his increased military capacities by shelling Kirkuk's oil installations, an act that embarrassed the Baath internationally, particularly with the British-owned Iraq Petroleum Company.[8] The Baath was acutely aware of the escalating cost of the war, remembering how its regime had been undermined by the Kurdish question in 1963.

The dangers for the Baath deepened further in April, with Iran's abrogation of the 1937 demarcation of the Shatt al Arab in favour of it being an international waterway. In Kurdistan both governments found themselves fighting by proxy, Iraqi forces giving close support to the Ahmad–Talabani group, against Mulla Mustafa armed with heavy weapons by Iran.[9] By midsummer it became clear that Iran was not acting alone when a former mayor of Baghdad, a self-confessed agent, stated that Mulla Mustafa had been armed by the CIA too.

By this time the Baath realized that the Kurds were unlikely to accept anything less than autonomy, and that this was the price for neutralizing Iran, as well as wooing the Communists. In June Michel Aflaq stated that 'The party has no objection to the right of the Kurds to some kind of autonomy'[10] and the government announced that a law would be promulgated on decentralization and that a Kurdish province of Dohuk would be constituted. There was another price to be paid also. In May the party journal had described Mulla Mustafa as a 'moderate', an indication that the leadership recognized that, given the Iranian dimension, it had little option but to talk with Mulla Mustafa. In October the party journal, al Thawra al Arabiya, declared that autonomy was the best solution to satisfy Kurdish national rights.

Mulla Mustafa welcomed the government's approaches. Although he had demonstrated his ability to see off government forces, albeit with foreign help, his followers were anxious for respite. Since 1961 there had been an estimated 60,000 casualties, over 3,000 (75 per cent of all) villages in Iraqi Kurdistan seriously damaged, and by 1969 there were 13,000 families dependent on the nationalist forces. There was also the attraction of outmanouevring the Ahmad–Talabani faction again.

When formal negotiations began in December each party soon found the other frustrating to deal with. The government could only get Mulla Mustafa to reveal the extent of his demands bit by bit. It was also exasperated by his preoccupation with his enemies rather than by the basic requirements of a political settlement; for he insisted that the government sever its relations with the Ahmad–Talabani faction and that it disband the Fursan Salah al Din, the *jash* force manned largely by Mulla Mustafa's tribal enemies. In the end it agreed.

However, the chief sticking point was Kirkuk. Despite the relatively recent arrival of most of the Kurds in Kirkuk town and its oilfields, the KDP felt passionately that it should be included in the autonomous area. It also claimed fringe Kurdish areas down to Khaniqin, areas in which oil was to be found. Some Iraqis feared ceding such areas would undermine Iraq's strategic security. As a result the government wanted to apply autonomy to people rather than land. It yielded to Mulla Mustafa on the principle of territoriality, but insisted that demarcation would depend on where there was a proven majority, and that this would be decided either by plebiscite or by census.

By early February an agreement was ready for signature, negotiated for the Kurds primarily by Dr Mahmud Uthman, the foremost figure after Mulla Mustafa in the KDP. This time it was the Kurds' turn to feel anger and frustration, for the document presented to them for signature bore little relation to the points agreed in the talks. This reflected the stress within Baath ranks, with the military wing unwilling to make such great concessions and the civilians led by Saddam Husayn wishing to make the compromises necessary for settlement.

Yet it is difficult to believe that Saddam Husayn was committed to such a settlement as a permanent solution. Rather, he was preoccupied with the instability of the regime. President Al Bakr and he needed time in which to consolidate, to achieve control over the military wing of the Baath, and hopefully to draw the Communists into co-operation until they could be discarded. In the event, Saddam himself travelled to Kurdistan to conclude an accord. He put a couple of blank sheets of paper in front of Mulla Mustafa and told him to write his demands, telling him he would not leave until they had both signed a mutually acceptable document. It worked. Saddam took back to Baghdad the agreement that led to a crucial declaration on 11 March 1970.

The 11 March 1970 Peace Accord and its Collapse

The accord reached and issued on 11 March as the government's policy on the Kurdish issue was not only the best deal the Kurds of Iraq had been offered, but it has remained the Kurds' favoured foundation stone for future relations with the rest of Iraq. The essential articles of the accord[11] were:

1. The Kurdish language shall be, alongside the Arabic language, the official language in areas with a Kurdish majority; and will be the language of instruction in those areas and taught throughout Iraq as a second language.
2. Kurds will participate fully in government, including senior and sensitive posts in the cabinet and the army.

3. Kurdish education and culture will be reinforced.

4. All officials in Kurdish majority areas shall be Kurds or at least Kurdish-speaking.

5. Kurds shall be free to establish student, youth, womens' and teachers' organizations of their own.

6. Funds will be set aside for the development of Kurdistan.

7. Pensions and assistance will be provided for the families of martyrs and others stricken by poverty, unemployment or homelessness.

8. Kurds and Arabs will be restored to their former place of habitation.

9. The Agrarian Reform will be implemented.

10. The Constitution will be amended to read 'the Iraqi people is made up of two nationalities, the Arab nationality and the Kurdish nationality.'

11. The broadcasting station and heavy weapons will be returned to the Government.

12. A Kurd shall be one of the vice-presidents.

13. The Governorates (Provincial) Law shall be amended in a manner conforming with the substance of this declaration.

14. Unification of areas with a Kurdish majority as a self-governing unit.

15. The Kurdish people shall share in the legislative power in a manner proportionate to its population in Iraq.

'History will bear witness,' the statement concluded, 'that you [Kurds] did not have and never will have as sincere a brother and dependable [an] ally as the Arab people.'

After the collapse of the accord and his defeat in 1975, Mulla Mustafa was to recall bitterly, 'At first they [the Baathis] came to us and said, "We will grant you self-rule." I said this was a ruse. I knew it even before I signed the agreement. But (our) people asked me, "How can you refuse self-rule for the Kurdish people?"'[12] It is easy, in the light of the crimes committed against the Kurdish people since then, to suppose the Baath acted wholly out of cynicism.

At the time, however, there were fewer grounds to suspect ill-faith. One may discount Tariq Aziz's retrospective statement, 'We were sincere when we announced the 11 March Manifesto. It wasn't propaganda. I say this because I was one of those who participated in the negotiations, and I know the sincerity of the leadership.'[13] But it was born out of necessity. As *The Times* commented in July, 'Ironically, apart from the Kurds the Baathist regime has no political friends inside Iraq. The Kurds have been watching with interest the lack of progress towards the desired national union of political forces and the creation of a National Assembly (promised by the regime).'[14] It was the regime's inability to form this more broadly based coalition, something the Kurds had demanded, which gave early cause for unease in Kurdish ranks.

Within the Baath, however, the leadership went to considerable lengths to explain the value of bringing the Kurds into fruitful partnership with the rest of Iraq, and that this could only be achieved through a full recognition of Kurdish national rights within Iraq. Its early measures indicated a sincerity of purpose.

Within a month of the signing of the accord, Saddam established a commission (four Kurds and four Arabs) to implement it. Mindful of Article 2, President al Bakr reshuffled the cabinet, appointing five leading Kurds, albeit to relatively junior posts. Articles 4 and 13 were implemented with the appointment of KDP members as governors of the provinces of Sulaymaniya, Arbil and Dohuk, as well as a mass of more junior appointments. By the end of April the Kurdish language was starting to be used in Kurdistan as required in Article 1, Kurdish journals had begun to appear and both a union of writers and a cultural society formed (Article 3), and student, youth, womens' and teachers' unions started (Article 5).

Money and energy were also invested in the reconstruction of villages, major infrastructural and economic projects were initiated, and implementation of the 1959 Agrarian Reform Law at long last commenced, with areas set aside for landless and refugee peasants (Articles 6, 8 and 9). In May the 'Fursan Salah al Din' were disarmed. In July the constitution was amended in accordance with Article 10. By the end of the year the government had agreed to pay for 6,000 *peshmergas* to act as a Border Guard, and provided Mulla Mustafa with a handsome monthly stipend of ID 35,000–50,000. It could also boast that 2,700 dwellings had been rebuilt, and over half the 100 destroyed villages in Arbil province had now been reconstructed.

The only cloud in the early honeymoon months was the Baath's refusal to approve the KDP nominee, Habib Karim, as Vice-President of the Republic (Article 12), on the grounds that he was of Iranian origin. Karim was a Faili Kurd, Shi'i by faith and Luri by origin. He was one of about 100,000 Fayli Kurds who had settled on the western side of the Zagros, many in Baghdad, during the Ottoman period. It was hardly a stumbling block.

By December 1970 Mulla Mustafa could even say 'For the moment we are optimistic. After ten years of fighting, the Iraqi Government offered us autonomy last March and so far they seem to be implementing the agreement.'[15] Yet it was the last such positive utterance. Before the month was out there had been an unsuccessful attempt on the life of his son, Idris, in Baghdad.

It now began to look as if the Baath were playing for time and the year 1971 brought a disintegration of trust between the two parties. The central issue was a demographic one. The census (Article 14) for disputed areas planned for December 1970 had been postponed till the spring by mutual agreement, but when spring came it was unilaterally postponed *sine die*. Mulla Mustafa accused the government of resettling Arabs in the contested areas, Kirkuk, Khaniqin and Sinjar,[16] and told the government he would not accept the census results if they indicated an Arab majority. He also dismissed the offer of the 1965 census, which he said was forged. When the government proposed to apply the 1957 census to Kirkuk, Mulla Mustafa refused it, since this was bound to show that the Turkomans, although outnumbered in the governorate as a whole, were still predominant in Kirkuk town. Given the residual animosity after the events of

July 1959, the Turkomans were likely to opt for Baathi rather than Kurdish rule. The Baath thought the Kurds might be packing disputed areas with Kurds from Iran and Turkey, but the real tensions surfaced over the Faili Kurds, resident in Iraq since Ottoman days and yet without Iraqi citizenship. The government argued they were Iranians, and now determined their fate by the simple expedient of expelling roughly 50,000 of them from September onwards.

By this time relations had already deteriorated to the point of armed clashes. Publicly Mulla Mustafa still spoke fair words of 'creating an atmosphere of trust and mutual confidence', but in private he told anyone who cared to listen, 'We have fought ten years for autonomy, we'll fight another five for Kirkuk if necessary.'[17] Given its network of informers, one must assume the Baath was well aware of Mulla Mustafa's real views. At any rate, it made an attempt on his life in September. A delegation of mullas went to visit him in his headquarters, unaware that the taperecorder they carried was packed with explosives. It detonated, killing them, but Mulla Mustafa and Mahmud Uthman were unscathed. Despite this assassination attempt, a public pretence was maintained on both sides that the conflict was ended 'for all time', and Mulla Mustafa accused the perpetrators of attempting to destroy 'the national unity of the Iraqi people'.[18] But the atmosphere of distrust was exacerbated by an acrimonious exchange in the press organs of the Baath and KDP.

Mulla Mustafa now raised the stakes by demanding concessions additional to those in the 11 March Accord. He wanted all army contingents to be withdrawn from Kurdistan, and Kurdish representatives to be admitted into the RCC and the army. This was a fair point, since the government was merely the executor of the decisions of the RCC. So far the Kurds had been offered a function in a central government bereft of power. When the Baath published its National Action Charter in November, designed to draw the Kurds and Communists into partnership with the Baath, the KDP remained sceptical. It was not convinced that the Baath genuinely desired wider participation.

The year 1972 proved a year of bad faith on both sides. Mulla Mustafa had not fulfilled his side of the bargain. He had refused to close the border with Iraq's adversary, Iran, and had continued to import arms and equipment. He had obstructed the free access, or return, of government officials to areas under his control. In August 1971 he had appealed to the United States for aid and had renewed this appeal in March 1972. Having survived an assassination attempt Mulla Mustafa may have felt justified in responding to the overtures of Baghdad's greatest enemies, but he was clearly cheating on the 'trust and mutual confidence' he advocated in public.

Following the signing of the Iraqi–Soviet Treaty of Friendship in April, Mulla Mustafa found the external support he had been seeking. Increased aid was provided by the Shah, who had been dismayed by the accord (since the Kurds were a principal instrument for weakening Baghdad) and alarmed by Baghdad's treaty with the Soviet Union.

In May 1972, the US decided it should support Iran in its opposition to growing Soviet involvement in the region. Previously the US had been chary of supporting the Iraqi Kurds on account of the spillover effect on the communities in Turkey and Iran, both US allies. Now it was acting 'in effect as guarantor that the insurgent group would not be summarily dropped by the foreign head of state (the Shah)'.[19]

On 1 June 1972 Iraq nationalized its oil facilities, thus gaining enormous financial power. For the Kurds this heightened apprehensions that Kirkuk's 'Kurdish' oil would be turned into 'Arab' oil. For the United States it provided a more important reason to undermine the Baath regime, for if it could be toppled, a 'new regime might let us back into the oilfields.'[20]

Mulla Mustafa showed the same naivety over his relations with the US that he had previously done with the British. 'We wanted American guarantees. We never trusted the Shah. Without American promises we wouldn't have acted the way we did.'[21] There is little evidence that he recognized that the US, like the Shah, would remain wholly opposed to Kurdish secession, because of its effect on Iraq's integrity and also on Iran and Turkey's Kurds. As subsequently became public knowledge, US policy ran thus:

> Both Iran and the US hope to benefit from an unresolvable situation in which Iraq is intrinsically weakened by the Kurds' refusal to give up their semi-autonomy. Neither Iran nor the US would like to see the situation resolved either way.[22]

It was a perfect summation of motive for almost every occasion when an external sponsor has supported Kurds.

Meanwhile the Soviet Union, unhappy at the prospect of the Kurds becoming a Trojan horse for Western interests sought to allay their concerns about its Treaty of Friendship with Iraq. The last thing the Soviet Union wanted was civil war in the country; but it was unable to give the assurances Mulla Mustafa required. Besides, Mulla Mustafa now saw far greater potential in his pro-Western alliance.

Mulla Mustafa also resumed his relations with Israel. He had had intermittent contacts since at least 1965, and had attacked government positions during the June 1967 war in order to distract Iraq from the Israeli front. By mid-September he was receiving a stipend of US$50,000 from Israel to distract and undermine the Baath.

Mulla Mustafa had already given Saddam Husayn every reason for alarm by working with Iraq's three cardinal enemies. In July two serious clashes occurred between Barzani and Iraqi forces at Kirkuk and Sinjar. The same month the KDP published an ambiguous statement about its aims, in which the one clear fact was that the 1970 Accord was a stepping-stone to something more:

> The central objective of our KDP and the liberation movement of our Kurdish people at the present phase is the realization and practice of self-rule.... Self-rule is not a

substitute for the Kurdish people's right to self-determination.... But the objective
realities ... necessitate raising the self-rule slogan so as to enforce the common struggle
against the two nationalities.[23]

In September the Baath sent the KDP a memorandum reviewing relations since
the 1970 Accord and emphasizing its aim to guarantee Kurdish national rights
and consolidate Iraqi unity. Regarding the latter it stated 'We do not part from
the truth when we say: you have not taken a single step along this path.'[24] It
accused the Kurdish leadership of fostering relations with Iran inimical to Iraqi
unity, listing 23 specific charges, and concluded with a list of requirements
regarding KDP conduct.

Now it was the Kurds' turn to talk of Baathi shortcomings. The KDP sent
its formal response at the end of November. As it pointed out 'all the important
positions in government and the armed forces have been monopolized by your
[the Baath] party.'[25] It had little difficulty in pointing the finger at Baathi bad
faith: Arabization policy in Kurdistan; exclusion of Kurds from legislative
authority and state planning; assassination attempts on Mulla Mustafa[26] and others;
obstruction and postponement of the census; expulsion of the Faili Kurds; the
bombing or razing of certain Kurdish villages. It gave credit where credit was
due. Certain clauses of the accord had indeed been implemented, but failure to
implement Articles 8 and 14 concerning the return of Kurdish villagers and
wrongful Arabization were tantamount to 'an undeclared war against the Kurdish
people'.

Thus the scene was set for the wholesale collapse of the accord. This did not
happen immediately, primarily because neither side was yet ready to take to the
battlefield. While Baghdad had to accept that its reluctance to implement the
spirit of the accord left Mulla Mustafa with the irresistible temptation of resuming
foreign friendships, the Kurds had to recognize that their outright association
with 'imperialist' enemies had cost them dear inside Iraq. Such an association
made an already highly conspiratorial regime even more paranoid concerning its
enemies; it alienated the KDP's traditional allies, the Communists and other
leftists who sympathized with Kurdish aspirations, but not at the price of alliances
with Iran, the US and Israel; ultimately it even drove some leading nationalists
out of Mulla Mustafa's camp.

As the months of 1973 passed the prospects for retrieving relations dimmed.
The Baath wanted Kurdish co-operation but was unwilling to share control. This
was clear not only from events so far but from the way it had enticed the
Communists into the 'National Front' proclaimed in 1972, but excluded them
from functional power. So the KDP responded to invitations to join the National
Front by insisting on agreement on the geographical extent of the Autonomy
Accord, upon functional control for the KDP in government, and free elections
for all Iraq within the year. Meanwhile they saw growing evidence of attempts
to change the ethnic balance when whole villages were forcibly evacuated in
Kirkuk, Aqra, Shaykhan and Khaniqin.

In any case, Mulla Mustafa can hardly have been attracted by the leftist label of the regime, given the foreign bedfellows he had chosen. By 1973, he was in a provocative mood, confident in the rash belief that the CIA and Iran would stick by him. Thus in June 1973 he boasted to *The Washington Post* that:

> We are ready to act according to US policy if the US will protect us from the wolves. In the event of sufficient support we should be able to control the Kirkuk oilfields and confer exploitation rights on an American company.[27]

It is difficult to imagine a statement more calculated to rile not only the Baath, but virtually the whole of Arab Iraq. At the end of the month Iraqi planes bombed Kurdish positions, while Mulla Mustafa mobilized his forces and warned of all-out war. Saddam pulled back from the brink.

Saddam had several reasons for restraint. Within the party the civilian wing was still not absolutely assured of its ascendancy, and war in Kurdistan might wreak the same disaster for it that the 1963 war had done. Saddam had another pressing reason for patience. The previous September he had been informed by Tehran that Iran would abandon the Kurds if Iraq abrogated the terms of Saadabad regarding the demarcation of the Shatt al Arab waterway. But his request that Masud Barzani come to Baghdad to resolve outstanding differences fell upon deaf ears; so he wrote to Mulla Mustafa pointing out the direct linkage between the Kurdish question and the Shatt al Arab dispute: *in extremis* Baghdad would have little choice but make the necessary border concessions in order to bring an end to the Kurdish problem.

Mulla Mustafa still refused to respond. His silence marked a turning point in relations. In the bitter post mortem following their defeat, Mahmud Uthman and his colleagues came to the conclusion that this was Mulla Mustafa's cardinal error of judgement. Instead of joining the National Front as he was exhorted to do, Mulla Mustafa and the KDP submitted new proposals for a form of self-rule that intended a federal solution. They sought self-rule for the Kurdish 'region', defined as those governorates where Kurds formed a majority. This definition would secure all the Kirkuk governorate including non-Kurdish villages and zones. Mulla Mustafa proposed Kirkuk as the 'capital' of Kurdistan.

Two other points indicated the way in which Mulla Mustafa had raised his demands. Instead of the autonomous region being an 'indivisible' part of the Iraqi state, there would now be a 'voluntary union' between the Kurdish and Arab parts of Iraq. Finally, in any legal dispute within the Kurdish region, local law was to have priority over central government laws. As one senior Baathi remarked 'The Kurds don't want self-rule but a state above a state', while for Saddam 'their draft is far removed from the concept of autonomy.'[28]

In October the Baath announced its decision to go ahead with a draft autonomy law and discussions were held with 600 independent and anti-Mulla Mustafa Kurds as well as with the KDP. It was a clear indication of the Baath's determination now to sweep the KDP aside if necessary. At the same time

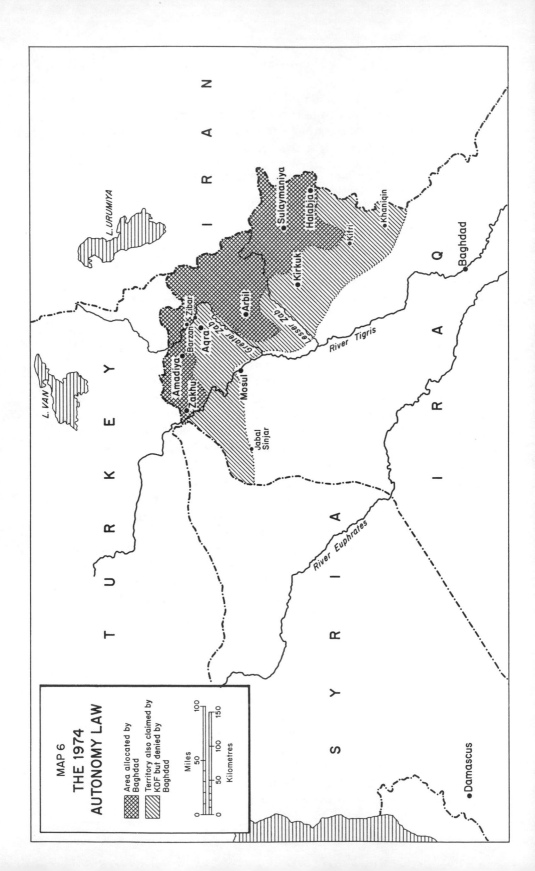

MAP 6
THE 1974
AUTONOMY LAW

Area allocated by
Baghdad

Territory also claimed by
KDF but denied by
Baghdad

Miles
0   50   100
0   50   100   150
Kilometres

TURKEY

IRAN

IRAQ

SYRIA

L. URUMIYA

L. VAN

•Sulaymaniya
Halabja•
•Kifri
•Khaniqin
•Kirkuk
•Arbil
Barzan•Zibar
Aqra•
Amadiya•
Zakhu•
•Mosul
•Jabal Sinjar

Greater Zab
Lesser Zab
River Tigris
River Euphrates

•Baghdad

•Damascus

Saddam broadcast his view that the KDP and the Kurdish people were by no means identical, and that the KDP had been infiltrated by counter-revolutionary forces. As if to confirm this impression, the KDP's Savak-trained security force, Parastin, began rounding up and killing Kurdish Communists, provoking great anger in the ICP which had spent the summer trying to achieve co-operation between the KDP and the National Front.

Mulla Mustafa, too, was preparing for war. But he had made the fatal error of predicating his campaign on Iranian backing. Thus he relied on a sophisticated anti-aircraft system provided by the Iranians to defend his headquarters at Hajj Umran, and reorganized his *peshmergas* to fight as a conventional force.

The Autonomy Law of 1974

In January and early March two last attempts were made at negotiation between senior KDP members and the Baath. Idris Barzani assured Saddam at the end of the first week in March that the Kurds would cut their ties with Iran if total agreement were reached.

Yet there could be no meeting of minds over the fate of Kirkuk. There was already a shabby history of government efforts since 1958 to remove Kurds from the city and environs. For both parties its value had been greatly enhanced by the nationalization of the oil industry. At the beginning of 1974 oil revenue was expected to be ten times higher than in 1972. A huge resource was now at stake. Kirkuk accounted for 70 per cent of the state's total oil output and Mulla Mustafa felt bound to claim both the town itself and a proportion of its oil revenue.

To the Baath, and its ICP partners in the National Front, this smacked of making Kurdistan an economically independent entity and also contradicted its belief in a centrally planned economy. In January its eighth regional congress had made economic development a priority. Kirkuk oil was central to that objective.

The government was still willing to go by the 1957 census, to allocate Chamchamal and Kalar divisions to the autonomous region, and allow a mixed administration for Kirkuk town answerable to Baghdad. Mulla Mustafa countered that such an administration should still be answerable to a Kurdish autonomous government. Neither side was willing to budge. Mulla Mustafa still claimed Kirkuk as the capital of the autonomous region. There were better candidates for the Kurdish capital. His own European representative, Ismet Sheriff Vanly, wrote subsequently 'Arbil and Suleymanieh are the two biggest entirely Kurdish towns in the country and the two most important centres of its national culture.'[29] The Kurds might claim Kirkuk as predominantly Kurdish but it was surely egregious to claim it as the capital.

The following day, 11 March 1974, Baghdad published its Autonomy Law and gave Mulla Mustafa a fortnight in which to accept it and join the National Front.[30] The terms of the Autonomy Law set out the Baath position, one that went further than any previous legislation, but which fell short of Kurdish demands regarding Kirkuk and regarding the real seat of power. The essential articles that caused unease or disagreement were:

1. Kurdistan, defined by the existence of a Kurdish majority according to the 1957 census, will enjoy autonomy as an integral unit within the framework of Iraq, according to the 11 March Accord, with Arbil designated as its metropolitan centre.

5/6. The area will be an autonomous financial unit within the financial integrity of the state. Its budget will be within the consolidated budget of the state.

13. The President of the Republic shall appoint a member of the (elected) Legislative Council to form an Executive Council. The President of the Republic may dismiss the chairman of the Executive Council at any time, in which case the Executive Council will be dissolved.

17. Police, security and nationality formations in the area shall be attached to their directorates general at the Ministry of the Interior, and their staff subject to the laws and instructions applied in the Republic of Iraq.

18. The offices of the central authority for the area shall fall under the ministries to which they are attached, and are subject to their general guidance.

19. Supervision of the legality of the decisions of the autonomous bodies shall be exercised by the Supreme Court of Appeal of Iraq.

It is clear that these articles allowed Baghdad to retain powers which, by judicious exercise, could effectively strip the autonomous region of any real self-control. This is what the Kurds feared and this is what actually happened.

Mulla Mustafa had staked everything on the support promised him by the USA and Iran. 'If you will give us arms to match those [Iraqi] arms, we will fight,' he told the Americans in March. 'Otherwise, we will make peace. We don't want to be massacred.'[31] 'Without American promises,' he said later, 'we would not have acted the way we did. Were it not for the American promises, we would never have become trapped and involved to such an extent.'[32] One must conclude that Mulla Mustafa, despite his experiences since 1943, remained an innocent abroad. He still had not fully recognized that neither patron actually welcomed Kurdish autonomy.

Perhaps he was unduly impressed by the military missions of the USA, Israel and Iran sent to assist him. No sooner had the fortnight's grace expired than Mulla Mustafa repeated his offer to allow Western oil companies to exploit the Kirkuk oilfield, betraying his own inflated notion of Kurdistan's strategic importance, adding 'Kurdistan has become an important factor in the military and political equation of the Middle East. It is the duty of the Western powers to advise us what role it should play.'[33] He also promised that he would prevent the Kurds in Iran and Turkey from agitating for independence, a promise he could not possibly fulfil, as must have been immediately apparent to US officials. That he made this undertaking in return for US aid suggests that he was only now beginning to realize that neither Iran nor the USA were backing him for any motives but their own.

While Mulla Mustafa and the KDP formally decided to reject the Autonomy Law, others felt they could no longer go along with him. Three prominent members, Hashim Aqrawi and Mulla Aziz of the central committee, and Aziz Aqrawi of the Politburo and a military commander, had all felt compromised by alliances with Iraq's imperialist enemies, and by the conflict with the ICP. When they had protested the previous December Mulla Mustafa had expelled them. They charged Mulla Mustafa with anti-democratic practices and condemned him for the kidnapping and in some cases execution of certain Kurdish leaders. They and others joined the National Front in Baghdad, arguing that the Autonomy Law was the best they could hope for and should be supported. Other Leftist Kurds believed that Saddam Husayn was no longer serious about an agreement. The Autonomy Law, for them, was by dictat.

The most bitter pill for Mulla Mustafa was the defection of his eldest son, Ubayd Allah, who claimed his father 'does not want self-rule to be implemented even if he was given Kirkuk and all of its oil. His acceptance of the [autonomy] law will take everything from him, and he wants to remain the absolute ruler,'[34] and he condemned his father for his failure to implement the agrarian reform.

The 1974–75 War

By April Mulla Mustafa probably had about 50,000 trained *peshmergas* and possibly another 50,000 irregulars. Kurds, including army deserters, had been flocking to his banner once war seemed inevitable. His forces were trained for conventional war but he was short of heavy weapons. Against such forces Baghdad could deploy about 90,000 troops, backed by 1,200 tanks, armoured vehicles, and 200 aircraft.

Mulla Mustafa had a two-fold strategy. He decided to hold the crescent of mountainous country along a line from Zakhu to Darbandikan. He also hoped to hold the Kirkuk oilfield in artillery range, thereby demonstrating to the US that Kirkuk was realistically within his reach. But he lacked the long-range artillery to make this objective feasible.

The Iraqi army soon showed its mettle, in tactics, training and discipline. It made a priority of relieving or withdrawing besieged garrisons from within the Kurdish controlled area. Then it drove up the main axes into Kurdistan, capturing Amadiya, Aqra, Rawanduz, Raniya and Qala Diza by the autumn. The government now held more of Kurdistan than at any time since 1961. Moreover, the army showed no sign of withdrawal, as it had on previous occasions, once its tactical positions became snowbound. For the Kurds that meant there would be no respite in which to rally in the spring. From their position in Rawanduz Iraqi forces threatened to capture the whole Shuman valley, the chief Kurdish supply route running up to the Iranian border.

Iran had hoped the Kurdish war might even lead to the overthrow of the Baath, as it had done in 1963, but instead it found itself having to back the

Kurdish forces overtly. Not only did it send Iranian Kurds to assist the *peshmergas*, but also deployed regular forces, dressed in Kurdish garb. It also provided light and medium field guns (75mm and 130mm) and long range (175mm) support from the Iranian side of the border that could easily reach Qala Diza. In the air Iran's US Hawk missiles effectively brought down Iraq's recently supplied MiG-23 warplanes.

The Iran–Iraq Agreement, March 1975

Such help did not alter the basic prognosis that Iran could not save the Kurds from eventual defeat. By mid-February Kurdish forces were giving way throughout Bahdinan. David Nabarro, a doctor with the Save the Children Fund, graphically reported meeting a legendary commander defending the Shaykhan front:

> We met him walking up the road towards Shillia, surrounded by a retinue of senior officers. A tall, thin man with a slight limp, aged about 60. Tears were pouring down his cheeks as he spoke to us of his despair. 'We had only ancient mortars and automatic rifles with little ammunition, insufficient to match the fire power of the Iraqi tanks and continued aerial bombardment from low-flying fighters.'[35]

To Nabarro it was clear that the Kurdish rebellion was finished.

Only the direct intervention of Iran, in other words a full-scale war was likely to change the outcome. It was an eventuality neither side welcomed. Indeed, up to December Iraq had been secretly offering to cede the Shatt al Arab demarcation if Iran would cut off its aid to the Kurds. At the time Iran still hoped to topple the Baath. Now it was happy to take the offer Iraq had already made. Thus the warning Saddam Husayn had given 18 months earlier finally came true. On 6 March 1975, at the OPEC Conference in Algiers, Saddam Husayn and the Shah agreed a formal settlement of outstanding border differences. Iraq ceded the *thalweg* (deepest point) demarcation of the Shatt al Arab, and both parties agreed to abide by the 1913 Constantinople Protocol, and the Frontier Demarcation Commission of 1914. Furthermore both parties agreed forthwith to maintain strict border security and prevent subversive infiltration from either side.

Within hours of the agreement Iranian forces were withdrawn and supplies to Mulla Mustafa suspended. Then Iraqi forces thrust up the Shuman valley, threatening Hajj Umran. By agreement with Iran, Baghdad offered Mulla Mustafa a ceasefire from 13 March to 1 April in order to allow his forces to retreat into Iran or surrender.

Mulla Mustafa and the KDP were shattered by the sudden turn of events. On 23 March they decided to abandon the fight. A few dissenters resolved to continue the struggle. Well over 100,000 Kurds, fighters, their families and others, crossed into Iran to join the 100,000 Kurdish refugees already there. Thousands of others surrendered to Iraqi forces, lured perhaps by generous payments for the surrender of weapons.

The cost of this wasteful war had been high. In financial terms it had eaten up US$2.5m per day on the Iraqi side, and about one eighth of that figure for the Kurds. Both sides gave wild figures for casualties, but one may accept the estimate of a Red Cross representative that Iraq lost 7,000 men with another 10,000 injured. The Kurdish figure was probably somewhat less.

In addition to the casualties of war, the cost to the civil population was particularly heavy. Thousands fled their homes before the Iraqi onslaught, and by the winter many were suffering from hunger and exposure. Undoubtedly it was in Bahdinan that the suffering was most serious, exacerbated by Turkey's refusal to open the border to allow a free flow of foodstuffs, and by acute overcrowding in such shelter as existed.

The Aftermath of the 1974–75 War

The Baath had moved quickly to implement the Autonomy Law and create an aura of progress in Kurdistan. On the outbreak of war it had removed Mulla Mustafa's five ministerial appointees, and replaced them with his leading Kurdish critics. Given the impossibility of conducting elections in war conditions, it selected 80 Kurds as members of the Legislative Council and appointed Hashim Aqrawi to select and chair the Executive Council. He had been a KDP Politburo member but had broken with Mulla Mustafa in late 1973. Another Kurd, Taha Muhi al Din Maaruf, was appointed Vice-President of the Republic.[36]

After its suppression of armed resistance, the regime moved quickly to strengthen its grip on the region. It was a profoundly bitter period for the Kurdish population, for the regime created a security belt along the Iranian and Turkish borders, which progressively widened from 5 km to eventually 30 km in places. This involved the razing of at least 500 villages in the first phase and may have reached 1,400 villages by 1978. At least 600,000 and probably very many more men, women and children were deported to *mujama'at*, 'collective' resettlement camps. These collective villages were drab townships located near major towns, with long wide avenues to permit control by armoured vehicles. Anyone caught returning to their ancestral homesteads was summarily executed, without regard for age or sex. It is difficult to believe that the regime did not intend to shatter the communities it transferred, and to strip them of their independence and dignity.

Others were sent to south Iraq, to Diwaniya, Nasiriya and Afak. These tended to be the families of recalcitrants or active supporters of Barzani, or of refugees who had failed to return during the period of amnesty (up to 20 May 1975). Of the 210,000 or so Kurds who sought refuge in Iran, only 140,000 had returned by the expiry date.

The government also used the opportunity to settle the demographic balance in disputed areas. According to Kurdish sources one million residents were removed from the disputed districts of Khaniqin, Kirkuk, Mandali, Shaykhan, Zakhu and Sinjar, but the scale was impossible to verify. Such deportees were replaced with Egyptian and Arab Iraqi settlers. These measures came to a halt in the summer of 1976, probably because Kurdish officials drew attention to the way such measures encouraged Kurds to return to guerrilla activity.

Besides making it difficult for Kurds in Kirkuk to hold title to their property, the governorate was rearranged to ensure an Arab majority. Towns with a heavy Kurdish majority, for example Kalar (30,000), Kifri (50,000), and Chamchamal (50,000), Tuz Khurmatu (80,000), were removed from Kirkuk and allocated to Sulaymaniya, Diwaniya or the new province of Salah al Din.

Other distasteful measures included financial rewards to Arabs who took Kurdish wives, a deliberate encouragement of ethnic assimilation, the transfer of Kurdish civil servants, soldiers and police out of Kurdistan, the removal of Kurdish faculty from the new university in Sulaymaniya and the Arabizing of some place names. Undoubtedly Baghdad also resorted to arrests, torture and executions to ensure its writ went unchallenged.

On his return to Britain, Nabarro reported the plight of the Kurds to the Foreign Office, where he was told, 'We depend on Iraq for £500,000,000 of contracts each year – no government would let us sacrifice these for the sake of a disadvantaged minority.'[37] Similar judgements were made in the foreign ministries of other parliamentary democracies. No government cared to make a stand.

Certainly, the Iraqi regime invested heavily in the area in order to provide a level of economic satisfaction to offset the political repression. Its collective village programme created over 30,000 dwellings, at a cost of almost 90 million dinars. It also allocated 336 million dinars on developing the region, building up industry, laying metalled roads, building schools and clinics. Schools increased fourfold between 1974 and 1979; hospitals were built in Arbil, Rawanduz, Sulaymaniya and Salah al Din and tourist facilities developed. Indeed, the Iraqi government probably spent more per head of population in Kurdistan than elsewhere in the country during the second half of the 1970s.

To mark his elevation to the presidency, in August 1979 Saddam Husayn offered a special amnesty to militants outside Iraq and some 10,000 returned. On 1 January 1980 the authority of the chairmen of the Legislative and Executive Councils was enhanced by granting them ministerial status; in June elections were held for the first Iraqi National Assembly since the 1958 Revolution; in September elections were held for the Legislative Council, fulfilling the electoral requirement of the Autonomy Law; all candidates were carefully screened. Everyone knew that any challenge to the regime's policy would be dealt with stringently. It was an appearance bereft of substance, a poor substitute for freedom from fear.

Sources

Published: Farouk Sluglett and Sluglett, *Iraq since 1958;* Mirella Galetti, 'Sviluppi del problema Curdo negli anni 1976–78' in *Oriente Moderno,* no. 58, 1978; Ghareeb, *The Kurdish Question in Iraq;* Human Rights Watch/Middle East Watch, *Genocide in Iraq: The Anfal Campaign Against the Kurds* (New York, 1993); Jawad, *Iraq and the Kurdish Question;* Chris Kutschera, 'Irak, une forte odeur de petrole' in *Jeune Afrique,* 13 July 1971 and 'Machiavel, le Baas, et les Kurdes' in *Jeune Afrique,* 21 July 1973; PUK, *Revolution in Kurdistan: the Essential Documents of the Patriotic Union of Kurdistan* (New York, January 1977); Martin Short and Anthony McDermott, *The Kurds* (London, 1975); Ismet Sheriff Vanly, 'Kurdistan in Iraq' in Chaliand, *People Without a Country.*

Unpublished: David Nabarro, 'Medical aid to the Kurds in Iraq: 1974–1975' (undated personal account of the Save the Children Fund Relief Expedition to Iraqi Kurdistan).

Notes

1. Michel Aflaq, Fi Sabil al Baath, (Beirut, 1974), pp. 168–78, quoted by Ghareeb, *The Kurdish Question,* p. 54.

2. *Nidhal al Baath,* vol. vii, pp. 145–147, and pp. 280–281 quoted in Jawad, *Iraq and the Kurdish Question,* p. 231.

3. Ghareeb, *The Kurdish Question,* p. 73.

4. The initial cabinet included four Kurds, one of whom, Muhsin Dizai, represented Mulla Mustafa. Two weeks after the coup there was a putsch which ousted the leading non-Baath conspirators. The new cabinet included three Kurds, two of whom representing Mulla Mustafa declined to take their posts. The third, Taha Muhi al Din Maruf, represented the Talabani faction; see Farouk-Sluglett and Sluglett, *Iraq Since 1958,* pp. 113, 116.

5. *Al Nur* (Baghdad), 19 November 1968, quoted in Ghareeb, *The Kurdish Question,* p. 71.

6. Mulla Mustafa interview, 28 September 1976, quoted in Ghareeb, *The Kurdish Question,* p. 75.

7. *Le Monde,* 12 October 1968, quoted in Kutschera, *Le Mouvement National Kurde,* p. 265.

8. The shelling caused some US$5 million in damage, and reduced pumping capacity by 70% for ten days. The cost in lost revenue may have been as much as US$10 million; Farouk-Sluglett and Sluglett, *Iraq Since 1958,* p. 129; Ghareeb, *The Kurdish Question,* p. 77.

9. By late 1969 Mulla Mustafa had received over 100 light anti-aircraft guns, twenty 25-pounder guns, and anti-tank guns; Ghareeb, *The Kurdish Question,* p. 77.

10. Michel Aflaq, *Nuqtat al Bidaya* (Beirut, 1971), pp. 105–108 quoted in Ghareeb, *The Kurdish Question,* p. 81.

11. The abbreviated paraphrase used here is based on the translation provided by the Iraqi Ministry of Culture and Information, quoted in Martin Short and Anthony McDermott, *The Kurds* (London, 1975), Appendix 1.

12. Mulla Mustafa to Ghareeb, 28 September 1976, *The Kurdish Question in Iraq,* p. 89.

13. Tariq Aziz to Ghareeb, 25 November 1976, *The Kurdish Question in Iraq,* p. 92.

14. *The Times,* 4 July 1970.

15. *The Washington Post,* 13 December 1971, quoted by Ghareeb, *The Kurdish Question,* p. 102.

16. These were tribesmen, mainly the Tay, Shammar and Ubayd, Ghareeb, *The Kurdish Question in Iraq,* p. 106, 107.

17. Kutschera, 'Irak, une forte odeur de petrole' in *Jeune Afrique,* 13 July 1971.

18. Iraqi News Agency, 2 October 1971 in Ghareeb, *The Kurdish Question in Iraq,* p. 108

19. *The Village Voice*, 11 February 1976 in Ghareeb, *The Kurdish Question in Iraq*, p. 140.

20. Aron Latham, *What Kissinger was Afraid of in the Pike Papers* (New York, 4 October 1976), p. 60, in Ghareeb, The Kurdish Question in Iraq, p. 141.

21. Mulla Mustafa to Ghareeb, 13 September 1976 in *The Kurdish Question in Iraq*, p. 141.

22. The Pike Commission Report to the House of Representatives (19 January 1976), quoted in *The Village Voice* (New York), 23 February 1976, reproduced in Vanly 'Kurdistan in Iraq' in Chaliand, *People without a Country*, p. 185.

23. *Al Kadir*, 14–15 (July–August 1972) as quoted in *Al Thawra al Arabiya*, 10 October 1972 and published in English in Ghareeb, *The Kurdish Question*, p. 134.

24. Ghareeb, *The Kurdish Question*, p. 116.

25. Quoted in Ghareeb, *The Kurdish Question*, p. 120.

26. There had been a second attempt on Mulla Mustafa's life in mid-July 1972, see Chris Kutschera, 'Machiavel, le Baas, et les Kurdes' in *Jeune Afrique*, 21 July 1973.

27. As quoted in Kutschera, *Le Mouvement National Kurde*, p. 286.

28. Saddam Husayn, *Khandiq am Khandiqani* (Baghdad, 1977), p. 21, quoted in Sluglett, *Iraq Since 1958*, p. 166; on the KDP federalist demands, see Ghareeb, *The Kurdish Question*, p. 148.

29. Vanly, 'Kurdistan in Iraq', p. 158.

30. Farouk-Sluglett and Sluglett, *Iraq Since 1958*, p. 168; see also Kutschera, *Le Mouvement National Kurde*, pp. 295–97.

31. Latham, 'What Kissinger was Afraid of', p. 68, in Ghareeb, *The Kurdish Question*, p. 159; Kutschera, *Le Mouvement National Kurde*, pp. 291–292; Vanly, 'Kurdistan in Iraq', pp. 184–185.

32. Mulla Mustafa to Ghareeb, 13 September 1976 in *The Kurdish Question*, p. 159.

33. *New York Times*, 1 April 1974, quoted in Ghareeb, *The Kurdish Question*, p. 161.

34. Ubayd Allah Barzani to Ghareeb, 19 July 1974 in *The Kurdish Question*, p. 155.

35. David Nabarro, 'Medical Aid to the Kurds in Iraq: 1974–1975' (undated personal account of the Save the Children Fund Relief Expedition to Iraqi Kurdistan), p. 33.

36. Maaruf, a one-time colleague of Talabani, who had become an independent. He was still in office in 1993.

37. Nabarro, 'Medical Aid to the Kurds', p. 41.

CHAPTER 17

THE ROAD TO GENOCIDE, 1975–1988

Fragmentation and Weakness

Mulla Mustafa's departure from the struggle, with his sons Idris and Masud, left the Kurdish movement in Iraq in disarray. The KDP itself seemed to have fallen apart. First into the vacuum was Mulla Mustafa's old adversary, Jalal Talabani. Talabani had been allowed to return to the KDP fold following the 1970 Accord, but had been posted as party representative in Beirut, a form of exile to prevent him working against Mulla Mustafa. From here he went to Damascus where the Syrian government encouraged him to renew the struggle against the hated Iraqi Baath.

On 1 June 1975 Talabani and certain colleagues[1] issued a statement in Damascus announcing the formation of the Patriotic Union of Kurdistan (PUK).[2] The PUK was an umbrella organization for two Iraqi groups: Komala, a clandestine Marxist–Leninist group led by Nawshirwan Mustafa Amin, and the Socialist Movement of Kurdistan (KSM), led by Ali Askari, a doughty fighter and old colleague of Talabani's since 1964, and Rasul Mamand. This communiqué ascribed the collapse of the revolt to 'the inability of the feudalist, tribalist, bourgeois rightist and capitulationist Kurdish leadership',[3] and proclaimed the PUK's commitment to autonomy for the Kurds and democracy for Iraq. So it also called on all progressive and leftist forces to assist in 'the overthrow of the bloodthirsty dictatorial regime'.

In 1976 the PUK began operations. Ali Askari had received word from Talabani while in enforced residence at Ramadi and succeeded in escaping with his colleagues[4] to the mountains. Askari and his colleagues operated in the north, out of Baradust, while Nawshirwan Mustafa operated in the Sulaymaniya area.

Meanwhile other elements of the old KDP were beginning to recover from the trauma of defeat. In August 1976 Idris and Masud Barzani,[5] together with Sami (Muhammad Mahmud) Abd al Rahman who had been Minister for the Northern Region, 1970–74, and certain others met in Europe to launch the KDP Provisional Leadership (KDP-PL). It had already carried out its first operation in May. Its programme was now formally leftist, chastened by its bitter experience of Iran and the US. It was severely circumscribed by restrictions imposed by the Iranians. Idris established himself in Iran, Sami (as secretary-general) in the area of operations, while Masud did not return to Kurdistan until after the death of his father in 1979.

The third group to take to the field was led by Dr Mahmud Uthman, once head of the Executive Bureau of the KDP and earmarked by some to succeed as party leader. Uthman had disagreed with the decision to abandon the struggle in March 1975. In its first communiqué towards the end of 1976, his KDP Preparatory Committee was critical of the trust previously put in external powers. Uthman did not exempt himself from blame.

Finally, Pasok, a shadowy party dating from 1959, reformed itself in September 1976 as the Kurdish Socialist Party. It wanted the independence of *all* Kurdistan, but was willing to work for autonomy in each country as an intermediate objective.

Ali Askari

Nothing, however, illustrated the fundamental and unresolved weaknesses of Kurdish politics and society more than the feud that rekindled between the Barzanis and Talabani. This feud finally came to a disastrous head in 1978.

Ali Askari knew that Talabani, still in Damascus, remained deeply hostile to the Barzanis. Askari himself had had direct contact with KDP–PL and wrote to Talabani reminding him there was only one enemy, Saddam Husayn, and that intra-Kurdish feuds must be abandoned. But Talabani was determined to eliminate KDP groups because they had ambushed and killed PUK fighters on three separate occasions: July 1976, January 1977 when almost 50 men were wiped out as they crossed the Turkish border into Iraq, and again a month later.

There were several reasons why these bloody encounters took place and why the KDP was not disposed to take prisoners. The KDP commander, Sami Abd al Rahman, knew of Talabani's general instructions to hit the KDP, since it was part of PUK propaganda emanating from Damascus. Sami was in no mood to deal softly with such enemies and was backed by Idris who bore a visceral hatred for Talabani. Sami knew PUK movements, being informed by tribes on the Turkish side of the border area, notably the Goyan, the Jirki and the Sulayvan (who were also in Iraq). These were mercenary, prepared to take money from either side in return for information. But it seems that Sami had the better relations with them, and therefore the better intelligence. Sami had three KDP–PL bases inside Turkey, in Hakkari, Uludere and Sirnakh. These were tolerated by the Turkish security forces, presumably to foster intra-Kurdish fighting.

Talabani came to Kurdistan in 1977, at Askari's insistence, because of the loss of morale with a permanently absent party leader. He set up his headquarters just inside the Iranian border, west of Sardasht at Nawkan. It was an ideal spot from which to direct Nawshirwan's operations west and southwards, and Askari's activities further north. In April 1978 he sent Askari and his deputy, Dr Khalid Said, at the head of 800 men on a major expedition northwards, the prime purpose being to pick up a major quantity of arms which had been shipped from Qamishli to certain Kurdish villages just inside the Turkish border. Talabani gave written instructions that Askari was to wipe out KDP–PL bases en route,[6] but Askari seems to have intended to ignore these. He had already established workable relations with the KDP–PL in the Baradust area. However, a copy of these orders fell into Sami's hands via a Turkish Kurdish party, and with solid evidence of Talabani's intentions, Sami decided to act with vigour.

Askari's force marched northwards, harried by both Iraqi and Iranian air and ground forces. By the time he reached Baradust he was short of ammunition. He and Khalid split their forces and decided to march independently to rendezvous inside Turkey. Askari made contact with the KDP–PL and had no expectation of hostility. However, as he marched on into Turkey at the beginning of June, his force was ambushed by KDP and tribal forces, perhaps 7,500 *in toto*. Some of his force fought its way southwards in confusion. Some returned to Nawkan; others, believing they had been deliberately sent into a trap, surrendered to Iraqi forces. The remainder under Askari surrendered, after heavy losses. A similar fate befell Dr Khalid Said's force. Both Askari and Khalid Said were executed on Sami's orders, leaving a legacy of acrimony between and within the opposing Kurdish factions.

Unaware of the final fate of Askari, Talabani sent a revealing letter to his office in Damascus. 'Iraq, Iran and the KDP–PL are all enemies for us,'[7] he wrote, criticizing Askari's failure to hit the KDP–PL at the first opportunity. His letter also revealed secret negotiations with Savak, contrary to the public posture of the PUK and its sharp criticism of the KDP–PL's dealings with Iran. It was ironic that while Savak wanted the KDP–PL and PUK to co-operate and thereby maximize their operations against Iraq, Talabani offered to co-operate only if Savak broke with Idris Barzani and the KDP–PL.

Further damage was inevitable. In the background lurked the Askari affair, one which cast doubt on Talabani's judgement.[8] More immediately, Rasul Mamand felt ignored in favour of Talabani's old cronies.[9] On the night of Nawruz (21 March) 1979 Mamand led his KSM men, the bulk of PUK's fighters, out of Talabani's camp and allied with Mahmud Uthman's KDP–PC, which was also sited near Nawkan. In August they formally declared a new party, the Kurdistan Socialist Party (KSP).

By this time the Islamic Revolution had occurred in Iran. With its secularist and leftist ideology, the PUK was unable to take advantage. Like the Shah, the ayatollahs felt safer with the Barzanis.

Kurdish Factionalism

However, the KDP–PL still had its problems. At its Ninth Congress in Iran in November 1979, the party renamed itself KDP. Several intellectuals led by Sami Abd al Rahman began to dissociate themselves from the party, dissatisfied with the traditionalism implicit in Barzani leadership and its supporters, by the close ties forged by Idris with the Khomeini regime and by the serious clashes with the KDPI which was seeking autonomy from Tehran. As a result of these ties the KDP was now largely engaged in defeating the KDPI inside Iran on Tehran's behalf. Furthermore, Idris ran the Parastin, the secret police who monitored everyone, including Sami and his Politburo colleagues. Sami knew that if he remained inside the KDP he was destined to remain the servant of the Barzanis. In due course he and fellow dissidents seceded, to form the Kurdistan Popular Democratic Party (KPDP) in 1981.

Thus, by September 1980 when Iraq attacked Iran, Iraqi opponents of the regime found they now had to choose allies among a plethora of fractious Kurdish groups. In mid-November various Damascus-based groups declared the establishment of an Iraqi Patriotic and Democratic Front, pledged to overthrow the Baath regime. The main signatories were the PUK, ICP, KSP and the pro-Syrian Baath.[10] The PUK was delighted to lead a front from which the KDP had been excluded.

One may therefore imagine Talabani's anger to learn that on 28 November, a rival and stronger part of ICP, and also the main part of the KSP (led by Rasul Mamand) and Pasok had established a Patriotic Democratic Front with the KDP in Kurdistan, in clear opposition to the PUK. Talabani bitterly condemned the ICP,[11] but there was little he could do to prevent the disintegration of his own front. Within the ICP and the KSP, rivalries existed between those in Damascus and those still in Iraq.[12] The pro-KDP faction of the ICP blamed PUK's allies, the pro-Syrian Baath and the KDPI for fomenting conflict, disregarding the fact that the KDP, under Mulla Mustafa and now under Idris, was busy harrying the KDPI as *quid pro quo* for Iran's support. This behaviour by the KDP had sickened many Kurds who felt that a cardinal principle of the Kurdish struggle was that Kurds should not betray each other.

On the other hand the PUK, while willing to undermine the KDP, gave KDPI its support, even assisting it defend Mahabad against Iranian forces. Thus, while Syria and Iran remained undeclared allies against Iraq, their PUK and KDP surrogates remained in bitter enmity.

In view of the struggle to be fought against Saddam, such feuds seemed a self-indulgence. During the course of 1980, the PUK re-armed with funding from Syria, Libya and latterly Iran, using its new-found strength in its war against the KDP. It sought to hold and expand its fiefdom in the Surani-speaking area, while the KDP did likewise from the Kurmanji area of Bahdinan. Predictably, such quarrels undermined the effectiveness of the guerrilla war against the regime.

While both parties claimed successes against government troops during the first two years of the Iran–Iraq war, Saddam Husayn was able 'to boast that the Kurdish organizations would never be able to achieve anything since they were hopelessly divided against each other and subservient to foreign powers'.[13] He also announced the reduction of the military presence in Kurdistan, leaving the region in the charge of pro-government Kurdish forces, the *jash*, which began to be greatly expanded.

Saddam had good reason to be contemptuous of his Kurdish opponents. In midsummer 1982 the two warring parties agreed to allow each other's *peshmerga* bands to move freely through any part of Kurdistan, but they stopped short of co-ordinating their efforts. It was an extraordinary commentary on the seriousness of their struggle against Baghdad. In February 1983 nineteen Iraqi opposition groups were persuaded by Syria and Libya to commit themselves to unity of purpose against Baghdad, but the pledge barely lasted the return journey from Tripoli to the scene of operations. Shi'i Islamic groups, Kurdish nationalists, Arab secularists and Iraqi nationalists had little in common except a loathing of Saddam and in certain cases a loathing of each other. Despite the rhetoric of 'giving Iraqi Kurdistan real autonomy' only the Communists apart from the Kurds recognized with any seriousness a Kurdish right to self-rule.

In any case, tensions between the PUK and its opponents were still running high. In April the ICP, KDP and KSP launched attacks on PUK positions in Arbil governorate. The following month the PUK launched surprise counter-attacks, inflicting particular damage on the Communists, killing 50 and capturing another 70. In some circles the PUK was suspected of working in tandem with Baghdad, and possibly even Ankara.

The External Threat

It was now that the Kurds received a sharp reminder that, for all the external sponsorship they received in order to discomfit Baghdad, the regional consensus on holding the Kurds down remained a critical constraint against success. At the end of May Turkey launched a massive incursion across the border, ostensibly to deal with its own Kurdish rebels. It entered Iraq with Baghdad's approval under terms of 'hot pursuit' agreed with Iraq in 1978, using airpower as well as ground forces. It took over 1,500 prisoners but most of these were probably local civilians, rather than rebels against Ankara. It also inflicted serious loss on Baghdad's enemies, destroying ICP and KDP bases, and killing possibly 300 *peshmergas*. In August Turkey attempted another incursion, but withdrew after a stiff engagement with the KDP.

Then Iran, having absorbed and repulsed Iraq's forces from its territory, began its counter-attack. Although its main focus was the Shi'i south of Iraq, it chose to open another front in Kurdistan. In July it seized the important border town of Hajj Umran, in conjunction with the KDP. Although the KDP was left in effective control, it suited Tehran's ideological posture to vest the Shi'i Iraqi Dawa Party with official responsibility for Hajj Umran. Further south it seized the high ground commanding Qala Diza, and then Panjwin in October.

Yet Iran's motives were ambiguous. On the one hand its incursion was aimed against Baghdad, on the other it was aimed against KDPI and those Iraqi Kurds, pre-eminently the PUK, who supported it. Thus, Iran's thrust created alarm in Baghdad, which feared it might be unable to withstand a combined Iranian–Kurdish offensive. It also posed a threat for the PUK which had never made much secret of its distaste for the Islamic Republic.

The immediate effect of the Iranian advance was to push the PUK headquarters out of the border area and nearer Iraqi forces. Protesting the effect of Iranian 'liberation' in Shuwarta and Panjwin, the PUK now faced the danger of being crushed between the millstones of Baghdad and Tehran. Quite apart from the losses incurred through internecine warfare with rival Kurdish parties or in attacks on government troops, it had also lost 1,400 members, captured and executed by the government since 1976. It desperately needed a break.

The PUK Parley with Baghdad

Saddam had already foreseen the dangers of Iranian co-operation with the Kurds. Even before the Iranian attack he had been obliged to deploy 50,000 troops in Kurdistan to stiffen the local *jash*. At the beginning of 1983 he had also admitted to 48,000 deserters, many of them Kurdish and now in the mountains. Thus the Kurdish danger had now become one of great magnitude.

Saddam's first task was to placate the Kurdish population. He had already allowed Kurds to serve in Kurdistan rather than be deployed against Iran on the dreaded southern front. He had also tried to stem the flow of Kurdish desertions by offering an amnesty to deserters and allowing Kurdish deportees to the south back home. He now took steps to ingratiate himself further with the local populace, arranging for fresh Legislative Council elections in August.

Saddam needed to drive a wedge between the Kurdish rebels and Iran. Foreseeing the danger, he had put out separate feelers to the Barzani brothers, Talabani and other party leaders as early as summer 1982, when the tide had clearly turned in favour of Iran.[14] He particularly feared a thrust along the Hamilton Road from Hajj Umran to Rawanduz and towards Shaqlawa. If Shaqlawa fell, Arbil and the plain would no longer be safe.

His negotiations with the Barzanis proved fruitless, because he was unwilling to provide the gestures of good faith the KDP demanded.[15] Saddam may have concluded the KDP was too closely involved with Tehran to be free to negotiate. KDP help in Iran's seizure of Hajj Umran was, in the words of one western diplomat, 'a stab in the back that Saddam will never forget'.[16] Saddam revenged himself on the Barzani clan. These had been deported from Barzan valley and dumped in south Iraq in 1975 but had been relocated at the *mujama'a* of Qushtapa, south of Arbil in 1980. Soldiers stormed the *mujamu'u* at dawn one morning, seizing all males over the age of thirteen. 'I tried to hold onto my youngest son, who was small and very sick,' one mother recalled.

> I pleaded with them, 'You took my other three, please let me have this one.' They just told me, 'If you say anything else, we'll shoot you, and then hit me in the chest with a rifle butt. They took the boy. He was in the fifth grade.[17]

Up to 8,000 Barzani males were removed from Qushtapa and other settlements, including *jash* and even Ubayd Allah who had supported the Baath. These were paraded through the streets of Baghdad before execution. In Saddam's own words, 'They went to hell',[18] a foretaste of the greater slaughter to come.

In the meantime Talabani had been persuaded by the KDPI leader, Qasimlu, whose own struggle depended on Iraqi support, of the benefits of an accommodation with Baghdad. The PUK already had influence in substantially more of Kurdistan than the KDP. If he could bring about a successful neogiation, Talabani would become undisputed representative of the Kurdish people. So he set about demonstrating his ascendancy in Kurdistan, first attacking the ICP and KSP in May, and then routing *jash* formations, a direct indication to Saddam of the PUK prowess.

In December the PUK and Baghdad announced a ceasefire. This would allow for negotiations to establish a government of national unity that would include the ICP and the PUK; for the introduction of a broader autonomy agreement including genuinely free and democratic elections; for the formation of a 40,000-strong Kurdish army to protect Iraqi Kurdistan from foreign (i.e. Iranian) enemies; and for the allocation of 30 per cent of the state budget towards the rehabilitation of the Kurdish region.

PUK's announcement brought bitter recrimination from its former allies, particularly from ICP which had neither forgiven the PUK its attack the previous May nor had any intention of joining a government of national unity. Yet from PUK's vantage point, a ceasefire offered crucial advantages: a breathing space in which to reorganize, the supply of Iraqi weaponry in order to defend the Surani-speaking region from Iranian advances, and the possibility of handing to the Kurdish people an acceptable improvement on the autonomy law of 1974. If the PUK could achieve this, Talabani might displace Barzani as the real champion of Kurdish nationalism. Yet it was a highly controversial road to take. Just as the KDP lost supporters through its assistance to Iran against the KDPI, now the PUK, too, lost support. As many as 3,000 of its fighters probably deserted to the KDP.

PUK's demands were primarily (i) an extension of the autonomous region to include Kirkuk, Khaniqin, Jabal Sinjar and Mandali; (ii) a halt to arabization of disputed areas and the unfettered return of displaced Kurds; (iii) the removal of the *cordon sanitaire* along the Iranian and Turkish borders; the allocation of 30 per cent of oil revenue to the development of Kurdistan; (iv) security to be the responsiblity of a formally constituted *peshmerga* force; (v) the release of political prisoners; (vi) the dissolution of the 20,000 or so *jash*. This final demand did not merely concern the existence of such a pro-government force. The *jash* were organized under local tribal chiefs and strongmen, for whom the maintenance of armed retainers (for this is what the *jash* in practice were) conferred considerable political power. Talabani had no wish to allow such men any political importance under a new autonomy arrangement. For the same reason Talabani insisted on the removal of two pro-Baath groups, Hashim Aqrawi's pro-government KDP, and Abd al Sattar Tahir Sharif's Kurdish Revolutionary Party.

Saddam dragged his feet, for there were issues on which he was not ready to compromise. One of these was the fate of the disputed areas, particularly Kirkuk. If Saddam yielded Kirkuk, then Talabani would indeed have outdone Mulla Mustafa. But Saddam could hardly cede the core of Iraq's productive wealth. 'Do not insist on Kirkuk being a Kurdish town and we shall not insist on it not being Kurdish,' Saddam reportedly told Talabani.[19] Nor could he allow the inclusion of Jabal Sinjar, Mandali and Khaniqin, their being dangerously close to Syria and Iran. Of Talabani's demands, he only accepted the inclusion of Aqra and Kifri in the autonomous region. Saddam was also disinclined to compromise on the question of pro-government Kurds. He would countenance neither the disbandment of the *jash* nor dissolution of the pro-government KDP.

The other major sticking point was more critical than either the fate of Kirkuk or the question of collaborationists. This was the extension of democratic elections to all Iraq which, the PUK argued, was fundamental to the formation of a government of national unity.[20] There was no possiblity that Saddam would accept this. In any free election his disastrous conduct of the war would have removed him from power. Moreover, the idea of sharing power was wholly contrary to his nature.

By now PUK co-operation no longer seemed as critical to Baghdad as it had done. In December 1983 Saddam had been visited by the US Middle East Special Envoy who informed him that the defeat of Iraq would be contrary to his government's regional interests. In the early months of 1984 this view was translated into the provision of substantial assistance by the US, and by other industrialized countries, notably the USSR and France, which also feared the destabilizing consequences of an Iranian victory. Thus assured of sufficient assistance to stave off defeat, Saddam no longer needed to make concessions to the Kurds. In March talks broke down following the execution of about 20 draft dodgers in Sulaymaniya, half of whom were PUK members, and the shooting of student protesters in Arbil. The PUK had already lost about 1,400 members by execution since 1975. Then Talabani's brother and two nieces were shot by *jash*. A period of stand-off ensued.

Both sides were reluctant to return to conflict. For a moment in October it even seemed to the PUK that an agreement was close. But that month the Turkish foreign minister visited Baghdad and, so the PUK believed, warned that any agreement between Baghdad and the PUK would lead to the closure of Iraq's sole oil outlet through Turkey.[21] At any rate, the ceasefire collapsed and the PUK returned to the battlefield in January 1985.[22] For Baghdad the ceasefire had been useful. While it lasted it had been able to transfer four of the six divisions from Kurdistan to the southern front.

Now the PUK faced severely straitened circumstances. It had already forfeited the support of Syria and Libya by its parley with Iraq. Its conflict with its rivals had deepened with its betrayal, as these rivals saw it, of the struggle against Saddam. Profoundly isolated it sought rapprochement with Iran, and thus also with the KDP. Constituent members of the Patriotic Democratic Front (the KDP–led opposition coalition) had little wish to admit so untrustworthy a group.

While the KDP and PUK continued to denounce the other,[23] there was a growing realization that they could hardly afford such internecine conflict. Even as Talabani had been negotiating with Baghdad at the end of 1983 in fact, some Kurdish intellectuals had started trying to bring about a reconciliation between the two major parties. This began a process of dialogue which, behind the public utterances of criticism, led to the eventual joint declaration of the KDP, PUK, KSP and ICP in 1986 calling for unity against the regime.

Talabani also made his peace with Ali Akbar Rafsanjani, then Iranian Parliamentary Speaker, undertaking to cease assisting the KDPI. By 1986 the PUK like the KDP was receiving weapons and financial support in order to draw Iraqi troops away from the southern front where Tehran still hoped to break through to Basra and bring the war to a triumphant conclusion.

In Kurdistan the consequence was the steady expansion of Kurdish operations. In the north the KDP controlled virtually the whole border from the Khabur eastwards, at some points to a depth of 75 kilometres southwards. In May 1986 it captured Manjish, an important communications centre between Zakhu and Amadiya, and laid siege to Dohuk. In the south the PUK controlled the mountains from the country near Rawanduz southwards virtually to Panjwin, and was engaged in major battles around Sulaymaniya.

The countryside remained in government hands only during daylight hours. From the late afternoon even major roads were unsafe, the rebels demonstrating their long reach by kidnapping foreign workers from cities like Sulaymaniya and Kirkuk, or carrying out attacks as far west as Altun Kupru, Kirkuk, Tuz Khurmatu and Kifri. Indeed, with Iranian-supplied guns the PUK shelled the Kirkuk oil refinery in October.

In November 1986 Masud Barzani and Jalal Talabani finally met in Tehran in order to form a coalition. It was ironic that Kurdish co-operation was achieved under the aegis of a regional government dedicated to the frustration of Kurdish national aspirations. A month later the KDP and PUK were represented in a major conference of Iraqi opposition groups in Tehran.

In February 1987 the KDP and PUK issued a joint statement announcing their intention to strive to form a Kurdistan National Front, and beyond that an

Iraqi National Opposition Front. In the military sphere they pledged themselves to unify the *peshmerga* forces. In May 1987 these intentions became reality with the formation of a Kurdistan Front composed of the five foremost Kurdish groups, the KDP, PUK, KSP, KPDP, Pasok, The Toilers' Party and also the ICP and the Assyrian Democratic Movement. A joint command was established to oversee political and military activities. If such developments were a measure of Iran's growing need for help from Iraq's dissidents, they were also a measure of the growing menace for Baghdad.

Prelude to Genocide

Nothing illustrated that sense of danger to Saddam's regime more than the increasingly savage repression now undertaken against the civilian population. Cases had already occurred of revenge massacres and summary executions,[24] but now the situation began to deteriorate more dramatically. Following the break-up of talks with the PUK, 78 villages near Sulaymaniya were razed. The purpose was clear, to create a free-fire zone in an area where Iran and the PUK wished to operate. By November 1985 this figure had increased to 199, rendering 55,000 people homeless. Far worse, in September troops had rounded up 500 or so children (aged 10–14) in Sulaymaniya; a substantial number were tortured and eventually killed. The motive for their seizure seems to have been to extort information about relatives in the *peshmerga* movement, to make such relatives give themselves up and to deter others from joining it. In January 1987, for example, 57 bodies of those abducted in 1985 were delivered to their next of kin; some had their eyes gouged out, or bore other marks of torture. In October 1985 a few hundred youths and young men (aged 15–30) were arrested in Arbil. They, too, were tortured and killed.

The military co-operation achieved between rebel groups in Tehran and the strong backing provided by Iran changed the nature of the war in Kurdistan. As in 1974, the enjoyment of strong external support, evident in the provision of heavy weapons including SAM-7 missiles to protect base camps, led to a qualitative change in Kurdish tactics. Hitherto the KDP and PUK, true to their guerrilla experience, had generally been loathe to capture, let alone hold, population centres.

Now heavy attacks were launched against military centres, in concert with Iranian formations. In April 1987, for example, Kurdish forces attacked troops defending Sulaymaniya, inflicting heavy casualties and capturing strategic heights around the city. In May they captured Rawanduz, and a week later Shaqlawa, and in June the town of Atrush, just north of Ayn Sifni. By August 1987 Iranian forces were penetrating virtually all the border areas held by Iraqi Kurds.

From Baghdad's perspective, Kurdish forces were now a Trojan horse for an Iranian victory, as enemy troops flooded into the area. That impression was compounded by the ill-chosen words of the PUK (Komala) leader Nawshirwan

Mustafa Amin who declared 'We are preparing the Kurdish movement to recognize the moment has come for independence.'[25] The Kurds could thus be portrayed as traitors to the state, not merely opponents of Saddam Husayn.

In March Saddam had appointed his cousin General Ali Hasan al Majid as governor of the North. Al Majid was vested with virtually absolute powers which he soon used. Within 24 hours of the PUK's capture of positions in the Dukan valley near Sulaymaniya in April, al Majid responded with chemical attacks on Kurdish villages in Balisan valley, where the PUK regional command was also located.[26] Following the muffled explosion of the gas canisters, white, grey and pinkish smoke drifted across the villages, accompanied by a smell of apples and garlic. In the words of one survivor,

'It was all dark, covered with darkness, we could not see anything.... It was like fog. And then everyone became blind.' Some vomited. Faces turned black; people experienced painful swellings under the arm, and women under their breasts. Later, a yellow watery discharge would ooze from the eyes and nose. Many of those who survived suffered severe vision disturbances, or total blindness for up to a month.... Some villagers ran into the mountains and died there. Others, who had been closer to the place of impact of the bombs, died where they stood.[27]

Survivors who sought medical attention in Arbil were seized, taken away and all males executed, a practice that became routine as the regime began to extirpate Kurdish village society.[28]

Al Majid made himself more feared than Saddam. In order to defeat the *peshmergas* he introduced a scorched earth policy, accompanied by mass executions and deportations. His decrees of June 1987 defined large swathes of Kurdistan as a prohibited area: 'Within their jurisdiction, the armed forces must kill any human being or animal present within these areas,'[29] even though many people were still living there. In fact implementation had already begun. Between April and September he razed 500 villages in order to deny the *peshmergas* food and shelter. He also approved reprisals against villages suspected of aiding the rebels, or those protesting deportations. On 12 May civilian drivers caught on the main road between Sulaymaniya and Sardasht were arbitrarily executed. Those families which evaded deportation were formally deemed to have joined the guerrillas, and were therefore to be exterminated. In Halabja governorate protesting deportees were subjected to artillery bombardment and two suburbs of Halabja town were razed. In late November, to cite another example, the village of Shiman near Kirkuk was surrounded and bombarded. Survivors were executed. In September al Majid had authorized the round-up and deportation of the families of 'saboteurs', in effect all those who did not have relatives in the army, or the *jash*. Yet his hands were tied until he had the troops available to occupy and pacify Kurdistan.

Not everyone in Baghdad favoured such tactics. The Iraqi parliament debated a law to give the Kurds greater autonomy, as a sweetener to the bitter deeds of the state. But the hardliners won. When Izzat Ibrahim al Duri, the Iraqi vice-president, advocated more humanitarian methods of dealing with the insurgency, he was retired. In Arbil the vice-president of the Legislative Assembly and ex-Mayor of Sulaymaniya, Shaqir Fattah, suggested that if the government were genuine in its concern for reconciliation in Kurdistan it could usefully negotiate with the Kurdish political parties. He disappeared without trace.

The pro-Government Kurds [30]

From the collapse of the PUK ceasefire talks Baghdad had also worked strenuously to build up the *jash* (or *fursan*) forces. By summer 1986 there may have been as many as 150,000 (and possibly nearer 250,000), at least three times as many men as the Kurdish movement could field. A relatively small number of these belonged to special groups (*mafariz khassa*) attached to General Security, or to the emergency forces (*quwat al tawari*) engaged in intelligence and counter-insurgency in towns. But the vast majority of Kurds belonged to the National Defence Battalions (*qiyada jahafil al difaa al watani*), a poorly equipped force which, by manning road blocks, etc, freed regular forces for the war against Iran.

The nature of the *jash* merits some discussion in order to discard the cruder assessment of them as merely shameful collaborators. In the words of Masud Barzani,

> Before 1975 one could talk of real *jash*, who genuinely supported the government against the nationalists. But by 1983 in the Ira—Iraq war the situation was very different. We simply could not give everyone a place in our ranks. So many joined the 'Light Brigades'. We pushed them to join these battalions. Many of the *jash* were secretly affiliated to us.[31]

Moreover, the enrolment figures for the *jash* were greatly inflated. The reason for this lies not in the government's deliberate inflation of figures but in the corrupt nature of the *jash* organization. The system relied on local leaders recruiting or organizing their following. In the mountains many chiefs were happy to provide fighters, since this renewed their traditional role of patronage which had been attenuated since 1958. In their own view they had protected their people. In 1960 probably 60 per cent of Kurds claimed a tribal affiliation. By the late 1980s this proportion had probably fallen to about 20 per cent, but even this was a substantial resource. In some cases – such as the Baradustis, Khushnaw, Surchis, Sulayvanis, Harkis and Zibaris – there were longstanding reasons for opposing the Barzanis. Other chiefs – from the Jaf, the Bilbas and the Pizhdar for example – had ensured their position and that of their followers against local opponents by taking a pro-government position. Others, under pressure of war, felt compelled to co-operate with the *jash* in order to avoid, for example, having their villages razed (although this was not necessarily a protection). All of them were tempted to exaggerate the number of men they could field in order to maximize the government stipend paid for their fighters. In the words of one chief:

> Our situation was not easy. We were three years with the *jash*. We wanted to keep our people safe. I had 1,500 men from the tribe. I was defending my people, 10,000 of whom were living in peace because of me. There was no work in Kurdistan and no way to get money. The government was bringing men from Sudan to work but would not take Kurds. By enrolling in the *jash* the Kurds did 15 days duty per month. Many had escaped from the army. They were all asking me for safety so as not to be killed in the Iran–Iraq war. So we defended them by putting them in the *jash*.... Most went to their houses and did nothing. I only took 50 men to do duty. My enrolment book says 1,500, so I took money for 1,500 but took only 50 people who I used full time on behalf of the others.[32]

Even the shaykhs, who had suffered such a rapid eclipse as a result of their displacement as arbitrators by local government, had used the opportunity to recover some of their dwindling fortunes. Their experiences since 1958 throw light on another aspect of government relations with Kurdish society. In 1958 most had emigrated to Iran to avoid Qasim's new broom but returned when he lost his grip on Kurdistan in 1961. Some of them still had followings of 10,000 or more. During the 1960s and early 1970s they had tended to drop out of political life and concentrated on building their *takiya* networks, which grew during this period. They were left alone by the government since, unlike the aghas, they no longer seemed a threat and there was no point in gratuitously driving them into the arms of Mulla Mustafa. Religious centres in Arbil, Koi-Sanjaq, Kirkuk and Sulaymaniya proliferated. Many ill-educated disaffected tribesmen or non-tribal labourers were attracted to one of the Qadiri or Naqshbandi *takiyas*, just as similar people had been attracted to the Barzani *takiya* a century earlier.

When the Baath returned to power in 1968, it realized the importance of keeping the Kurds divided so that a cohesive movement did not challenge its exploitation of Kirkuk oil. It therefore began to pay money into the *takiyas*, allowing shaykhs to wield power as 'fixers' with access to government. This process was made easier when Izzat Ibrahim al Duri, an Arab Qadiri who knew the networks personally, became interior minister in 1974.[33] After the Iranian revolution Saddam used the shaykhs as a shield against revolutionary Islam and as a Sunni 'bridgehead' into Iran. The most notable of them was Shaykh Uthman Naqshbandi of Biyara,[34] who had fled in 1958 and only returned to Iraq in 1980. He had already acquired the status of the most respected Naqshbandi shaykh of his day. He and his sons lent their religious authority to the idea of Sunni struggle versus the Shi'i threat.[35] Other shaykhs were active militarily, leading *jash* against the nationalists, particularly the PUK with its Marxist rhetoric. Thus, bankrolled with oil money, many shaykhs acquired new patron status locally.

In the towns and non-tribal countryside, many landlords or local strongmen, known as *mustishars* (or government 'advisers') also actively recruited *jash* retainers from villagers or local townspeople. Some were professionals, doctors for example, able to build their own patronage networks. Foremost among the motives of those who enrolled was the avoidance of conscription into the regular army and death on the southern front. Many were deserters who turned themselves in on the promise of amnesty if they served as *jash*. Those joining the *jash* were usually able to continue their economic activities and to live at home. Like any local volunteer force, they were normally required to serve periodically. Thus those recruited remained economically productive, as agricultural labourers, shopkeepers, etc. The *mustishars* who recruited them frequently pocketed their stipends, on the incontestable grounds that by recruiting them they saved them from the worse fate of army service. Most of those in the *jash* happily forewent their stipend in order to lead a quiet life.

As indicated above, there was a natural inclination among *mustishars* to maximize the government stipends passing through their hands by inflating the numbers of men they had recruited. Deals were struck with local army officers responsible for adminstering the *jash*. None of this should be surprising, for the corrupt inflation of recruitment figures must be one of the most universally practised and longest established gambits in time of war. Thus there was a system to serve large numbers of people, army officers, local Kurdish leaders and ordinary Kurds, anxious to avoid the penalties of war and if possible to benefit from it. On the whole the regime tolerated such corrupt practice, and regularly rotated *jash* from one location to another to minimize the help they might give to the *peshmergas*.

It should not be assumed that all *jash* acted in this way. Some, pre-eminently the Zibaris, had a real axe to grind against the nationalists. Latto and Arshad Zibari, whose father had been assassinated by Mulla Mustafa, carried out the destruction of Barzan. Others, as in any country, were willing to assist in any way that would ingratiate themselves with an oppressive regime. Certainly some of the anti-Barzani chiefs were richly rewarded for their services, receiving lucrative factory licences, or land grants, or export/import privileges. Some, for example, the leaders of the Surchi, Harki and Zibari tribes were already extremely wealthy. They now became wealthier still, in one case able to purchase property in Mayfair.

Yet the majority of *jash* were half-hearted. Some had considered the choice of fighting for the Kurdish forces, but were discouraged from joining. Both the KDP and the PUK were unable to meet the potential supply of recruits, for the simple reason that they would increase the administrative burden and undermine the effectiveness of the Kurdish forces.[36] As a result some *jash* acted as informers for their favoured party and others sheltered wounded *peshmergas*.[37] Some went further. In May 1986, for example, the KDP had captured Manjish because the local Duski chief switched allegiance from Baghdad to the KDP.

As things turned out the *jash* were not exempt from the massive resettlement programme. Many were moved after the rebels were defeated. Armed *jash* who threatened trouble were transferred until their families had been moved. This resettlement did not, in fact, undermine the tribal *jash* system. On the contrary, it strengthened it. Tribal groups were resettled together in the townships, where the absence of alternative employment reinforced their dependency on their chief and his dependency on government, and this began to replace territoriality as a defining basis for tribal solidarity.

The Anfal Operations[38]

By January 1988 the threat to Baghdad had deepened as Iranian troops seized the strategic heights overlooking Mawat and crossed the Qara Chulan river. The penetration of Kurdish and Iranian forces deeper into Kurdistan in the spring and a breakthrough onto the Mesopotamian plain down the Diyala river now became a serious danger. Saddam sent a secret message seeking a resumption of negotiations with the PUK, but Talabani dismissed the idea without a change of ruler.[39]

This was last attempt of Iran to defeat Iraq. Elsewhere its efforts had ground to a standstill. The challenge Iraq now faced in Kurdistan provided the opportunity and the troops that Ali Hasan al Majid needed finally to solve the Kurdish problem. In order to defeat the Kurdish forces he now initiated Operation Anfal (a blasphemous abuse of Quranic injunction)[40] – a series of major assaults on *peshmerga*-controlled areas, using chemical and high explosive air attacks – before ground forces occupied the area.

'Anfal I' was designed to disrupt PUK-Iranian plans to capture the Dukan dam. It began in early February with the indiscriminate bombardment of inhabitants of the Jafati valley near Sulaymaniya, including PUK forces. It took three weeks to capture the area. Heavy casualties were inflicted. Virtually all adult and teenage males who were arrested disappeared – in accordance with al Majid's instructions. Those who escaped suffered extreme privations as they tried to cross the snow-bound mountains to the east.

At the end of February Jalal Talabani formally accused the regime of genocide, with 1.5 million already deported, and 12 towns and over 3,000 villages razed.[41] Yet the West was generally inclined to dismiss Kurdish claims of genocide, either because they were politically inconvenient, or because it was suggested such reports were probably wild exaggerations. It was only in the aftermath of the Gulf War that evidence collated by Middle East Watch showed that previous Kurdish claims were not only incontrovertible but also in many cases an understatement of the ordeal through which Iraq's Kurds were then passing.

On 15 March 1988 PUK and Iranian forces captured the town of Halabja, strategically situated above Lake Darbandikan to the east, inflicting heavy casualties on Iraqi forces. They seemed likely to advance to the Darbandikan dam. The following day Iraqi forces retaliated, shelling the town for several hours. During the afternoon those in air-raid shelters began to smell apple and garlic. Unable to prevent the entry of the gas, they stumbled out into the streets:

> Dead bodies – human and animal – littered the streets, huddled in doorways, slumped over the steering wheels of their cars. Survivors stumbled around, laughing hysterically, before collapsing.... Those who had been directly exposed to the gas found that their symptoms worsened as the night wore on. Many children died along the way and were abandoned where they fell.[42]

Approximately 5,000 civilians died.

Baghdad's savagery at Halabja had a shattering effect on Kurdish morale. It was well known how lethal chemical weapons could be, but it was now internationally clear that Saddam Husayn would resort to killing on a scale previously unimaginable in order to destroy those who threatened him.

A week later al Majid initiated Anfal II, to destroy all Kurdish presence in Qara Dagh, south of Sulaymaniya, a mountain range already surrounded by Iraqi forces. Once again chemical attacks on one village after another preceded ground action. Soon the hills were thronged with fleeing people. The majority, moving north towards Sulaymaniya, were rounded up and taken to assembly areas where their names were recorded and their valuables and IDs removed. Male and female were segregated. The males were driven off to undisclosed locations and exterminated. On the southern side of Qara Dagh a more comprehensive policy prevailed: hundreds of women and children also disappeared without trace.

With Anfal III in mid-April the scene shifted to Garmiyan, the area south of Kirkuk and adjacent to the west side of Qara Dagh which had also been a stronghold of the PUK. Once again all adult or teenage males captured began their nightmare journey to the execution grounds. In southern Garmiyan, where PUK resistance was fiercest, thousands of women and children were also taken for execution.

In many cases the civilian population was rounded up by the *jash*. In some cases the *jash* allowed women or children to escape under cover of darkness. They had *carte blanche* to loot whatever they wished according to Quranic prescription: 'Give the men to us and you can have the property,'[43] as one Baathi put it. On the whole the *jash* were dutiful servants of the Anfal, probably unaware that their round-ups were not a prelude to confinement in *mujama'at* but rather to mass execution.

At the beginning of May the Anfal (IV) operation swung northwards to deal with the area between Kirkuk, Arbil and Koi-Sanjaq. Hundreds more died from chemical attack on the bank of the Lesser Zab. Out of sight, possibly 30,000 Kurds were taken away. In the areas of greatest resistance women and children too were taken to the execution grounds. During the summer months three more Anfal operations (V, VI and VII) were carried out to remove PUK forces in Balisan and the mountain recesses east of Shaqlawa. In certain cases the population was persuaded to turn themselves in on the spurious promise of pardon. It made no difference to their fate.

By now Iran was economically and militarily exhausted by its efforts to destroy a regime supported by the international community. In April its forces had been driven from Faw and the environs of Basra. In the first half of July it lost Sardasht, Zubaydat and Mawat, and withdrew from Halabja and Hajj Umran. On 22 July it announced it would accept UN Security Council Resolution 598, and on 20 August this ceasefire came into effect.

During the next four days troops were massed around Bahdinan. On 25 August Anfal VIII began with chemical and high explosive bombardments on the villages and valleys in which fleeing civilians and *peshmergas* were concentrated. Eight-year-old Agiza remembered what happened. She was tending the family livestock above her village when she saw the planes fly in, dropping bombs, one of which exploded close to her house.

> It made smoke, yellowish-white smoke. It had a bad smell like DDT, the powder they kill insects with. It had a bitter taste. After I smelled the gas, my nose began to run and my eyes became blurry and I could not see and my eyes started watering too.... I saw my parents fall down with my brother after the attack, and they told me they were dead. I looked at their skin and it was black and they weren't moving. And I was scared and crying and I did not know what to do. I saw their skin turn dark and blood coming out from their mouths and from their noses. I wanted to touch them but they stopped me and I started crying again.[44]

Thousands were asphyxiated in the precipitous valleys through which they fled. On 29 August in Bazi Gorge approximately 2,980 fugitives were gassed, and their bodies subsequently burnt by government troops.[45] Elsewhere all captured males were exterminaed. Amnesty International was inundated with reports of hundreds of civilians being deliberately killed.

We shall never know the exact number of those who perished in the Anfal operations, but they probably accounted for 150,000–200,000 lives. In a few cases villagers and *peshmergas* were shot without distinction on the spot. The vast majority of people, however, were sent to Topzawa, a large army base south-west of Kirkuk which housed a transient population of approximately 5,000. It was here that the registration and segregation took place with a brutality reminiscent of Nazi death camps. Teenage and adult males were lined up rank after rank, and stripped of everything but their clothes, and interrogated. Beatings were routine. 'We saw them taking off the men's shirts and beating them,' one old man recalled. 'They were handcuffed in pairs, and they took away their shoes. This was going on from 8.00 am until noon.'[46] After two or three days at Topzawa, all these males were loaded onto closed trucks. They were not seen again.

Through the testimonies of six survivors we know the end of the road for the men of the Anfal. Taken to the execution grounds at Ramadi, Hatra and elsewhere, they were tied up in long lines alongside deep trenches, and shot. When the trenches were full, they were covered in.

The elderly and a few women and children were bussed to a concentration camp in the south-west desert of Iraq, at Nuqra Salman. Routine punishment at Nuqra Salman included being made to squat without movement for two hours, or being tied to a metal post in the midday sun. From June onwards death by beatings, exposure and infection was commonplace in Nuqra Salman, running at a rate of four or five a day. One man kept a tally, 517 dead by the day of his release in September, but more died after his departure. Many were deliberately left to rot for days where they died before being thrown into pits, which took about 40 corpses each.

Most women were taken to Dibs camp, close to the Kirkuk–Mosul highway. Both these categories were held for four or five months until the end of *peshmerga*'s resistance at the beginning of September. Thousands however, did not survive. Many children died of malnutrition and dysentery at Dibs. Approximately half the women were taken to other terminals of the Anfal, for example the death pits of Samawa.

At first the regime answered all enquiries regarding its victims: 'They were arrested during the victorious Anfal operation and remain in detention', but as the number of relatives seeking the missing grew during the following two years, it changed its response to 'We do not have any information concerning their fate.'[47] So, despite the registration of his victims, Saddam Hussein massaged the truth into some vague misadventure of which his administration no longer had any knowledge.

By the end of the war almost 4,000 villages and hamlets were destroyed, and at least 1.5 million people had been forcibly resettled.[48] Yet the government had still not finished with its rearrangement of Kurdistan. In December it announced its intention to create 22 new towns, each to accommodate 10,000–15,000 resettled Kurds. First it razed Sangasar, a town of 12,000 inhabitants. Then in June 1989 it razed the town of Qala Diza, offering resettlement to its 100,000 inhabitants, and another estimated 100,000 people living in the town's environs. Raniya, a town of 25,000, was similarly threatened. By July 45,000 out of 75,000 square kilometres of Kurdistan had been cleared of Kurds, according to the Kurdistan Front. This was no longer about security but the atomization of Kurdish society, except for those groups in service to the government.

The Refugees

Before the end of August 1988 60,000 Kurds had found their way into Turkey, among them Agiza and thousands of other surviving casualties of the gas attacks. It was symptomatic of Western media attention that the refugee crisis in Turkey received more coverage than that in Iran, although the numbers involved were substantially lower. Iran already had 50,000 refugees from the 1975 war, and since then had received at least 50,000 Faili Kurds expelled in the late 1970s. By 1987 at least another 50,000 had crossed the border. By the end of August 1988, probably another 100,000 or so crossed bringing the total to something in the order of 250,000.[49]

Turkey initially refused entry to the refugees, warning that those who crossed the border would be returned. It feared the crisis would accelerate Kurdish national feeling inside the republic. However, such was the fear of renewed chemical attack or massacre by ground troops that Turkish forces could only have barred the refugees by shooting them. Besides, the Turkish prime minister, Turgut Ozal, had good reason to show humanity. He wanted to generate good will in south-east Anatolia for domestic as well as foreign relations reasons, most notably the desire to enter the European Community.[50] Thus, Ankara relented but refused refugee status to those that crossed,[51] and confined them to camps at Yuksekova, Mus, Diyarbakir and Mardin. It also denied non-Turkish agencies any access to the refugees.

Once international interest began to subside, Turkey took steps to reduce the refugee presence. When Iraq announced an amnesty on 6 September, neither the Kurds nor international organizations believed it trustworthy. Nevertheless, the Turkish authorities put pressure on some to return, and some of the thousand or so who did so disappeared. In fact the executions and torture continued in the Iraq death camps for months. Turkey also spirited some 20,000 refugees into Iran where, despite government protests they were settled in camps near Khoi, Urumiya and Ushnaviya.

The refugees led a drear and restricted existence, interrupted only by major outbreaks of food poisoning in June 1989 and again in January 1990. In both cases it was clear that the poisoning was deliberate, presumably an attempt by Baghdad to stampede refugees into returning. A month later Baghdad renewed its offer of amnesty for returnees. Again, few responded. The harsh conditions in Turkish camps remained preferable to the rule of terror in Iraq.

The International Response

Nothing more clearly illustrated the vulnerability of the Kurdish people than the international failure to take any substantive measure to restrain Iraq from its chemical attacks.

It was not as if the world did not know of these attacks. Within a week of Iraq's first use of gas against the Kurds, the PUK issued press statements, and formally appealed to the United Nations. Some victims came to Europe for treatment. The evidence was incontestable. Reports were also carried in the international press,[52] but no action was taken. The industrialized world was anxious that Iraq should prevail against Iran and was unwilling to jeopardize this objective by the application of international convention.

Then came Halabja, the worst single violation of the 1925 Geneva Protocol on the use of chemical weapons since Mussolini had invaded Abyssinia in 1935. As the *Financial Times* reported on 23 March, 'the international community's response to the Kurds' mounting cries of alarm has so far been a deafening silence.' On 26 March Iraq implicitly admitted using gas. In April a distinguished group of British scientists tried to send detectors and decontaminators to Kurdistan, but were forbidden by manufacturers acting on British government orders.[53]

In June, however, when it was clear that Iran could sustain war no longer, Britain called for an automatic international investigation whenever a state was accused of using such weapons, a warning to Iraq that now the danger was over it should stop its chemical warfare. Britain also took a leading role in drafting UN Security Council Resolution 620, passed on 26 August, condemning the use of such weapons and calling for 'proper and effective measures' in the case of such use. Only the day before, Masud Barzani had appealed to the UN to deter Iraq's chemical assault on Bahdinan, where it was already gassing thousands of Kurds, as it continued to do until October.

The international community soon demonstrated the measure of its commitment to UNSCR 620. As the world press reported chemical casualties, governments began to react. On 30 August the British government, for example, announced its 'dismay', and four days later spoke of its 'grave concern'. But as *The Independent* reported on 6 September, Britain denied receiving any firm evidence but 'was happy to make the running at the UN on chemical weapons, but did not want to "get out in front" over Iraq'. It did not favour its own investigation but asked for information from Turkey, which had already denied any evidence of the use of chemical weapons. *The Guardian* gave its own verdict:

> the bulldog still refuses to give even the softest bark against the most blatant use of chemical warfare for 50 years.... There was no condemnation. No censure. Officially HMG still awaits firm evidence. Even the FO's most seasoned diplomats should cringe at such humbug.... You don't often find it, even *in extremis*, but morality still has a place in international relations. And sometimes the failure to speak out against the indefensible, drenched in shuffling hypocrisy, betrays a supine immorality all of its own.[54]

In the United States the State Department accused Iraq of using chemical weapons, but a week later suddenly turned coy, refusing to produce the proof it had, and suggesting a UN investigation. As it probably knew, Turkey had already decided to refuse any UN investigative team access to Kurdish refugees in its territory.[55]

It was clear why neither Britain nor any other state wished to take a lead. Behind the expressed concern of governments not to jeopardize the Iran–Iraq peace talks by condemnation of Iraq, lay the real concern not to jeopardize the massive post-war reconstruction projects (estimated at $50,000 million) that Iraq was bound to put out to tender.

Bolder spirits sought to collect and publish evidence of what had happened. Two US bodies, the Senate Foreign Relations Committee and a private organization, Physicians for Human Rights, both published overwhelming evidence of the use of chemical weapons.[56] Apart from the physical evidence collected, the Senate report concluded that to dismiss eyewitness reports would require one to believe that 65,000 Kurdish refugees confined in five disparate locations were able to organize a conspiracy in 15 days to defame Iraq and that these refugees were able to keep their conspiracy a secret not only from us but from the world press.

Later, the journalist Gwynne Roberts brought back soil samples which revealed the actual substances used in these attacks.

In the face of such evidence most European Community countries reprimanded Iraq but did not allow this to interfere with their political and economic concerns.[57] Britain, for example, doubled its export credit facility to Iraq,[58] something that hardly squared with the Foreign Secretary's remark, 'We have been at the forefront of anxiety and grave concern about these [CW] allegations.'[59] During the Scott Enquiry in 1993 it was revealed that ministers decided to relax export restrictions to Iraq after the Iran–Iraq ceasefire in order to secure new orders, 'but Sir Geoffrey [Howe] felt it would be "too cynical" to announce the change while the FO was receiving thousands of letters protesting about Iraqi attacks on the Kurds.'[60]

In the US Senate a bill was introduced to impose tough sanctions and to cut off $800 million in US credit guarantees and exports of sensitive equipment. However, too much was at stake,[61] and the bill was opposed by the US government and so failed to reach the statute book. In Germany a voluntary agency accused twelve German pharmaceutical companies of providing materials and equipment for the manufacture of chemical weapons by Iraq, and accused its government of countenancing such activities, and dragging its feet on investigating breaches of its own restrictions.[62] In June 1988 Masud Barzani had also accused France, Italy and the Netherlands of assisting Iraq's chemical warfare programme.

It was clear that many states of the industrialized world were trading in sensitive materials with Iraq and had little intention of curtailing their arms sales on account of either UNSCR 620 or the 1925 Protocol. Barely a year after Halabja, Britain, France, Italy, Greece, Portugal, Turkey, as well as Eastern Bloc countries and Latin American states participated in the first Baghdad International Exhibition for Military Production. The US was already engaged in the sale of sensitive equipment to Baghdad. Such sales tended to be justified on the grounds of providing domestic employment and preserving regional stability, a concept which clearly excluded from its definition the physical safety of hundreds of thousands of ordinary people in the region.

Sources

Published: Dlawer Alaaldin, *Death Clouds: Saddam Hussein's Chemical War against the Kurds* (London, 1991); Martin van Bruinessen, 'The Kurds between Iran and Iraq' in *Middle East Report*, no. 141, July–August 1986; Shahram Chubin and Charles Tripp, *Iran and Iraq at War* (London, 1988); Galletti, 'Sviluppa del problema Curdo'; Gesellschaft für Bedrohte Völker,

Germany and Genocide in Iraq: Persecution and Extermination of Kurds and Assyrian Christians, 1968–1990 (Gottingen, 1991); Ghareeb, T*he Kurdish Question in Iraq*; Kamran Karadaghi, 'The two Gulf wars: the Kurds on the world stage' in Chaliand, *People without a Country* (London, 1993); Samir al Khalil, *Republic of Fear: The Politics of Modern Iraq* (Berkeley/Los Angeles, 1989); Middle East Watch/Human Rights Watch, *Genocide in Iraq: The Anfal Campaign against the Kurds* (New York, 1993) and *Bureaucracy of Repression: The Iraqi Government in its own Words* (New York/Washington, February 1994); Muhammad Malek, 'Kurdistan in the Middle East Conflict' in *New Left Review*, no. 175, May/June 1989; More, *Les Kurdes Aujourd'hui*; Pax Christi International, *Elections in Iraqi Kurdistan* (Brussels, August 1992); Physicians for Human Rights, 'Winds of Death: Iraq's use of poison gas against its Kurdish population' (Somerville, MA, February, 1991); PUK, *Revolution in Kurdistan*; Gwynne Roberts, 'Winds of Death' on *Despatches*, Channel 4 TV, 23 November 1988; United States Senate Foreign Relations Committee Staff Report, 'Chemical weapons use in Kurdistan: Iraq's final offensive' (Washington, 21 September 1988).

Newspapers, journals, etc. BBC, *Summary of World Broadcasts*, *The Financial Times*, *The Guardian*, *International Herald Tribune*, *The Kurdish Observer*, *Le Monde*, *Middle East International*, *The Morning Star*, *Observer Foreign News Service*, *Pesh Merga*, *The Times*.

Unpublished. Sami Shoresh, 'The contemporary religious situation among the Kurds of Iraq' (unpublished diss., London, 1993).

Press releases, statements. Iraqi Kurdistan Front, 'The chronology of chemical attacks in Kurdistan' (undated release, late 1988); KDP press statements; PUK press statements; Amnesty International statements.

Interviews. Dlawer Alaaldin (London, 8 August 1989); Karim Khan Baradosti (London, 18 February 1992); Masud Barzani (London, 21 July 1989 and Salah al Din, 10 October 1991); Adil Murad (London, 26, 29 July 1993); Omar Sheikhmuss (London, 15 March 1985); Sami Shoresh (London, 1 July 1993); Husayn and Jawhar Surchi (London, 18 February 1992); Jalal Talabani (London, 9 February 1990); Hoshyar Zibari (London, 18 July 1990); several *jash* leaders who asked not to be named (Sulaymaniya, 9–12 October 1991).

Notes

1. Adil Murad, Abd al Razzaq Aziz, Kamal Fuad, Fuad Masum, Nawshirwan Mustafa Amin and Umar Shaykhmus.
2. Its proper title was suffixed 'Provisional Committee'.
3. PUK, *Revolution in Kurdistan*, p. 1. This publication repeatedly denounces the 'tribal leadership' of the Kurdish national movement.
4. These included Umar 'Dabbaba' Mustafa, Dr Khalid Said, Said Kaka, and Saad Aziz, interview with Adil Murad, 26 July 1993.
5. Mulla Mustafa's previous heir apparent, his son Luqman, had been killed in action in May 1965.
6. These instructions were contained in a letter by Talabani, dated 14 April 1978. The main KDP base in Baradust was just east of the Hadan valley.
7. Talabani to PUK HQ (Damascus), Nawkan, 20 June 1978.
8. Some members of PUK wondered whether Talabani had deliberately sent Askari to his death.
9. Notably Umar Mustafa, and the now deceased Khalid Said and Ali Askari.
10. Al Jubha al Wataniya al Dimuqratiya al Iraqiya, established 14 November 1980. Other signatories included the Iraq Socialist Party, the Iraq Nationalist Movement

(Nassarists) and the Popular Army Organisation (Marxists).

11. The split within the ICP deepened, with one group supportive of the KDP, the other favouring the Arab nationalists.

12. Adil Murad and Mahmud Uthman were signatories in Damascus. Uthman reportedly felt that Mamand had intentionally undermined him within the party. At KSP's first conference, Mahmud Uthman refused to stand and Mamand became party leader (Adil Murad received the most votes but stood aside on account of his youth and limited experience); Adil Murad, interview with author, 29 July 1993.

13. Shahram Chubin and Charles Tripp, *Iran and Iraq at War* (London, 1988), p. 105, quoting BBC, *Summary of World Broadcasts* BBC/SWB/ME 27 February 1982.

14. Mahmud Uthman of the KSP secretly met Saddam but concluded that no agreement was possible partly because the KSP's influence in Kurdistan was so limited.

15. The KDP sought the return of all Kurds from resettlement camps and the release of political prisoners. Saddam refused to do either.

16. *International Herald Tribune*, 28 March 1984.

17. Middle East Watch, *Genocide in Iraq*, p. 40.

18. *Al Iraq*, 13 September, 1983 in Middle East Watch, *Genocide in Iraq*, p. 41. The Barzanis were presumably executed in south Iraq, like the majority of those liquidated by the regime.

19. *Le Monde*, 14/15 October 1984.

20. By now some members of the ICP had broken ranks to pursue the chimera of democracy, *The Guardian*, 3 February 1984.

21. Whatever the truth of this, on 17 October Turgat Ozal announced agreement on joint action against the rebels.

22. The inciting incident sparking renewed hostilities was the ambush and killing of Mama Risha, PUK commander for Kirkuk province. The previous September another senior commander, Sayyid Karim had been ambushed and killed by *jash*.

23. As late as 1986 Jalal Talabani could still disparage other groups in the following terms: 'All the other parties have very little influence in Kurdistan. The Barzanis are a very small group and dependent on Iran. If you take their tribe from them, and go to the cities and the countryside, you will find that they are a small minority mainly because they have committed lots of bad things against the people.' Cyclostyled PUK transcript of interview given to a French journalist in 1986.

24. For example, the execution of the entire population of Sharistan village, Raniya district, after a nearby clash with PUK fighters in December 1976, the summary execution of 300 draft dodgers, deserters and suspected *peshmerga*s in November and December, 1985.

25. *Le Monde*, 16 April 1987.

26. The main ingredients of these chemical attacks were mustard gas, tabun and sarin. Over 30 locations in Sulaymaniya and Arbil governorates were attacked, 15–19 April 1987.

27. Middle East Watch, *Genocide in Iraq*, p. 62.

28. In May 1987 386 gas casualties were assembled at Shaykh Wisanan (Arbil governorate) and executed. At the beginning of February 1988 426 gas casualties 'disappeared without trace' having sought medical attention; the following month another 400 casualties, including 150 children, were executed outside Sulaymaniya on 2 April. See *Germany and Genocide*, pp. 48–48 and Middle East Watch, *Genocide in Iraq*, pp. 62–69.

29. Art. 5 of decree of 3 June 1987. For genocidal directives, see Middle East Watch, *Genocide in Iraq*, pp. 79–84, and its Bureaucracy of Repression, pp. 70–72.

30. This section is drawn from interviews with *jash* leaders after they had gone over to the nationalist movement in March 1991. For obvious reasons most of them preferred to remain anonymous.

31. Masud Barzani interview with the author, Salah al Din, 10 October 1991.

32. Interview with a tribal chief (name withheld) in Sulaymaniya in October 1991.

33. Ibrahim was a regular visitor to *takiyas* in Kirkuk governorate. He was specially charged with responsibility for security in Kurdistan, and became Deputy Chairman of the RCC in 1979.

34. Shaykh Uthman ultimately settled near Istanbul and became the major focus for Kurdish Naqshbandis in Turkey, as well as for Naqshabandis from all over the world.

35. It should be noted that while in south Iraq, the government spread propaganda emphasizing the Arab–Ajami nature of the struggle (with its resonances of the Arab conquest of the Sassanian empire in the mid-seventh century CE), in Kurdistan it was the Sunni–Shi'i contest which received emphasis.

36. While operating as guerrillas it was important these groups were of manageable size. To fight a more conventional war, they needed heavy weapons as well as increased manpower.

37. Masud Barzani interview with author, Salah al Din, 10 October 1991.

38. The most authoritative sources are Middle East Watch, *Genocide in Iraq* and *Bureaucracy of Repression*.

39. In fact by now, in view of Halabja, no Kurdish leader could conceivably have parleyed without jeopardizing all Kurdish support.

40. *Surat al anfal* refers to the battle of Badr in 624CE, 'Allah revealed His will to the angels, saying: "I shall be with you. Give courage to the believers. I shall cast terror into the hearts of the infidels. Strike off their heads, maim them in every limb."' The Anfal Operation is meticulously described in Middle East Watch, *Genocide in Iraq*, pp. 93–207.

41. *Daily Telegraph*, 4 March 1988. The towns named were Agh Chalar, Basna, Barzinja, Kanarwa, Shuwarta, Karazah, Kharmal, Qala Chulan, Qaradagh, Sangaw, Suri Qulat, and the old section of Rawanduz. Chemical attacks had been in the Balisan and Jaffati valleys.

42. Middle East Watch, *Genocide in Iraq*, p. 106.

43. Testimony in Middle East Watch, *Genocide in Iraq*, p. 161.

44. Physicians for Human Rights, *Winds of Death*, p. 3.

45. Seventy-seven villages in Zakhu, Amadiya, Aqra, Dohuk, Sarsang, Margasur and Rawanduz districts were gassed, 25 August–1 September, listed in *Pesh Merga*, no. 18, March 1989; see also *The Independent*, 3 September 1988.

46. Middle East Watch, *Genocide in Iraq*, p. 217.

47. Middle East Watch, *The Bureaucracy of Repression*, p. 116.

48. The tally, according to the PUK was (i) Destroyed: villages 3839; schools 1757; mosques 2457; hospitals and medical centres 271. (ii) Deported families 219,828, approximately 1.5 million on an average of seven persons per family. The US averred it was unaware of this systematic destruction. In fact it knew from its satellite surveillance. On the maps it issued during the Gulf War, three quarters of the villages in Kurdistan were marked 'destroyed'.

49. Many lived in two large camps outside Karaj near Tehran, and at Jahrum near Shiraz. Further emergency camps were established along the border area as reception areas. Iran allowed UNHCR and ICRC limited access. Other foreign agencies were denied access.

50. He wanted support for a referendum on 25 September. He also wanted Kurdish support in order to reduce the power of the Kemalist influence in the army. Turkey applied for membership of the European Community in 1987.

51. As signatory of the Refugee Convention of 1951, Turkey had not acceded to the 1967 protocol which widened the original definition beyond Europe. It was therefore legally able to deny refugee status to those who had not arrived across its European frontier.

52. PUK appealed to the international community on 16, 17, 23 April, 15, 19 and 25 May, and again on 4 September 1987; press reports in most major Western newspapers, e.g.

The Daily Telegraph, 24 April 1987, *The Guardian*, 2 May 1987, *International Herald Tribune*, 12 May 1987.

53. These scientists belonged to the Working Party on Chemical and Biological Weapons. The government banned the export under the export ban on weapons or equipment for military use it claimed to implement against Iraq.

54. *The Guardian*, 7 September 1988.

55. The evidence was almost certainly intercepted Iraqi military communications, *The New York Times*, 15 September 1988. See also *The Financial Times*, 9 and 15 September, *International Herald Tribune*, 14 September, *The Guardian*, 15 September 1988.

56. Senate Foreign Relations Committee Staff Report, 'Chemical Weapons use in Kurdistan: Iraq's Final Offensive' (Washington, 21 September 1988); Physicians for Human Rights press release of 22 October 1988 and its substantive report 'Winds of Death: Iraq's Use of Poison gas against its Kurdish Population' (February 1991).

57. As one diplomat working on Iraq and the Gulf informed the author in November 1988, 'the Government had no intention of jeopardizing its political and economic prospects in Iraq and the Gulf for the sake of the Kurds.'

58. From £175 million for the financial year 1987/88 to £340 million for FY 1988/89.

59. *The Independent*, 10 September 1988.

60. *The Times*, 30 July 1993.

61. Apart from the $800 million in export credits, hard-pressed Iowa farmers needed to export wheat to Iraq.

62. Gesellschaft für Bedrohte Völker, *Germany and Genocide in Iraq*, pp. 3–4. The first intimations of such trade, it claimed, had been in 1984, but had continued since then. On 28 November 1987 *The Guardian* stated that a major German pharmaceutical firm was giving cover for the importation of raw materials for CW production in Baghdad, and reported a major accident in a Beirut laboratory involved in the programme. West Germany had a $167 million credit line in 1987, *The Independent*, 5 October 1988.

CHAPTER 18

UPRISING AND SELF-RULE

Psychologically, the defeat of 1988 was more devastating than that of 1975. The extent of genocide, symbolized by Halabja, slowly became apparent. Saddam had literally committed overkill.

In 1975 a genuinely liberal and generous policy towards Kurdish autonomy that gave KDP leaders functional responsibility might have brought Kurdish insurgency to an end. Neither the Kurds nor Baghdad were any longer in doubt concerning Baghdad's military powers. In such circumstances a magnanimous and generous offer by Baghdad might have brought the Kurdish community into a productive and fulfilling relationship with the rest of the country. But Saddam was incapable of it.

In the wake of state genocide in 1988, there was little left for Kurdish leaders to lose. In July 1988 when defeat already stared them in the face, the KDP Central Committee resolved to continue the struggle come what may, a decision confirmed when the party held its Tenth Congress in December 1989. The PUK clung to a miniscule border enclave from which it mounted attacks. Neither party had any difficulty in soliciting material support from the Iraqi Baath's arch enemy, Syria. Operations were thus undertaken as far into Iraq as the Arbil plain and even inside Kirkuk town. In one attack, for example, 22 airpilots were killed in the ambush of a government bus. But the strategy now was wholly different from that which prevailed during the Iran–Iraq war. With the threat of chemical weapons, and an almost universal absence of habitation, the Kurdistan Front now waged war by lightning raids and ambushes, without holding any territory at all. Both parties set up food and weapons caches in the mountains for the hundreds of guerrillas still willing to fight. Politically, it was crucial to national morale that guerrilla activity should be at a sufficient level to prevent Baghdad from hiding the fact of continued resistance. Talabani warned of escalating the struggle with attacks on a range of targets in Arab parts of Iraq. The natural inference was that such operations would tie up large numbers of government troops and have an attritional effect.

Yet would the Kurdistan Front parley with Saddam Husayn? This seemed implicit in Masud Barzani's verdict, 'The Kurdish question is a political question which cannot be solved by military means.'[1] Yet there was little evidence that such soundings made any real impression on Baghdad. The state was happy to make tentative and indirect efforts to parley but felt under no compulsion to do so. Indeed it had specifically excluded Talabani from its amnesties in 1988/89. Baghdad only needed to worry about the Kurdistan Front if some other major threat to the regime were to materialize.

By July 1990 outward appearances suggested nothing of the sort. On the contrary, it was the KDP which was filled with dark foreboding, for at the end of June Masud Barzani had met Iranian leaders and come away with the distinct impression that they intended to conclude a formal peace agreement with Iraq. This would inevitably include sealing the border to prevent guerrilla activity against either state.

The Gulf Crisis

In such circumstances, Saddam Husayn's misjudged invasion of Kuwait, the international decision to apply sanctions and to threaten force to compel an unconditional withdrawal, came as an almost miraculous respite for the Kurdistan Front.

Suddenly and quite unexpectedly events had conspired to give it a unique opportunity. Saddam, recognizing the enormous dangers he faced once Turkey had decided to comply with the international blockade against Iraq, withdrew his forces from much of Kurdistan with the exception of sensitive points, for example the Iran–Iraq–Turkey border 'triangle' and the Zakhu border crossing. He also sent Mukarram Talabani to make peace overtures to the PUK and ICP. But neither could afford to associate with Saddam while he defied the world community.

On the other hand nothing could be more dangerous than for the Kurds openly to side with the US-led coalition against an embattled Iraq, and both the KDP and the PUK sought to dispel speculation that they were willing to participate in a US-inspired campaign to overthrow Saddam. Like Iran, they longed for Saddam's discomfiture but feared open association with the West. Both inside Iraq but also in the Arab and Muslim worlds the Kurdistan Front had to avoid giving the impression of betrayal. In Damascus leading members of the Kurdistan Front declared a united front with Baath, Nasserist and Islamic opponents of Saddam. Yet suspicion was bound to grow, with Talabani's widely reported but politically fruitless visit to Washington in mid-August, and officially recognized visits by the PUK and KDP leaderships to France in September.

Saddam, busy clearing the decks for action in Kuwait, was sufficiently fearful of the Kurdish threat to offer the Front a peace deal in October. But the Front was unwilling to strike deals in circumstances of such uncertainty. It was substantially stronger, through the deployment of almost 5,000 *peshmergas*, and through the contacts it had established with the freshly mobilized *jash* forces and with Kurds in the regular forces. The Kurdish Front had been able to tap uncertainty as to the outcome of the crisis, with assurances that given *jash* co-operation it would forgive and forget the past. Thus it gained not only a wide and deep information network but also a Trojan horse within the towns and townships to which the Kurdish population was now confined. Indeed it could boast an ability to insinuate its fighters into virtually any town in Kurdistan.

Nevertheless, as the US-led Coalition forces assembled their full might in Saudi Arabia and the crisis moved towards open conflict, the Kurdistan Front continued to insist that the Kurds would stay neutral in a shooting war. It was fearful of attacking while Saddam still had the capacity to use chemical weapons. As Izzat Ibrahim al Duri, deputy chairman of the RCC, had warned the people of Sulaymaniya, 'If you have forgotten Halabja, I would like to remind you that we are ready to repeat the operation.'[2] It had received no indication from the Coalition leaders that it would receive any military support in the event of a rising against Saddam, even though it was tying down eight regular divisions and another 100,000 *jash*.

There were practical reasons why the Coalition was unwilling openly to support the Front. It feared the break up of Iraq, and the unleashing of both internal and external forces that might try to seize parts of the country. Within Iraq there was the fear that the Kurds and Shi'is might shake off Iraqi sovereignty in their respective lands.

Externally, there was the danger that Turkey and Iran would intervene in the event of internal collapse. Iran had historic and religious interests in southern Iraq. Turkey had an historic and economic interest in the old vilayet of Mosul. It will be recalled that it had conceded Mosul under League of Nations arbitration grudgingly, resenting the loss of an area it had claimed under the National Pact of 1923, and of its oil reserves, capable of fuelling Turkey's economic development. It also feared that the greater freedom that had always been allowed to the expression of Kurdish cultural identity in Iraq would excite its own Kurdish population. If it seized the vilayet it would be able to apply the same constraints on Iraq's Kurds.[3] During the Iran–Iraq war speculation had arisen again concerning Turkish intentions, particularly following its first cross-border operation in 1983 and more explicitly in 1986, when it reportedly notified the United States and Iran that it would demand the return of the vilayet in the event of Iraq's collapse.

With Saddam's seizure of Kuwait, Turkey saw the possibility of reviving its claim and the more immediate danger of Iraqi Kurdish independence. It had almost certainly, therefore, made its costly commitment to the Coalition cause,[4] including its provision of facilities at the Incirlik airbase, contingent on a cast-iron undertaking that the Coalition would not permit the emergence of an autonomous Iraqi Kurdistan.

As the crisis deepened, President Ozal publicly declared that Turkey, Iran and

Syria were in agreement that no Kurdish entity should be allowed to emerge from the Gulf crisis. Yet Ozal also now made the first serious steps towards public recognition of the Kurdish people since the foundation of the republic, responding to an approach from Talabani in mid-February which included assurances that Iraqi Kurds did not seek separation from Iraq. A few days later Talabani and Muhsin Dizai (KDP) travelled to Ankara to meet Ozal who responded to the frisson of horror inside Turkey with the remark 'There is nothing to be afraid of [in] talking. We must become friends with them. If we become enemies, others can use them against us.'[5] Ozal was hedging his bets, seeking to soften Ankara's standing with Turkey's own Kurds (see chapter 20), while preparing for the possible need to negotiate with Iraq's Kurds if Iraq collapsed.

Uprising

With the Coalition's wholesale defeat of Iraqi land forces on 28 February events inside Iraq began to move rapidly. Almost immediately much of Shi'ite southern Iraq rose in revolt, encouraged by mass desertions from the army. With most of Saddam's surviving forces committed to recovering the major towns of the south, unrest gathered pace in Kurdistan, amidst *peshmerga* attacks on army units.[6]

On 4 March this unrest exploded in a popular uprising in Raniya. Other locations rapidly followed suit, with most of Kurdistan including Dohuk, Arbil and Sulaymaniya in rebel hands by 10 March. On 13 March Zakhu fell. As Masud Barzani admitted, 'The uprising came from the people themselves. We didn't expect it.'[7] As a result, in the words of a spokesman, the Kurdistan Front 'merely followed the people onto the streets'.[8] It had been hesitant to enter towns in case of massive retribution. It now preferred these to remain under civil control, and for the civil authorities to negotiate with local army units.

It was now that the *jash* played a crucial role in the Kurdish struggle. On 29 January they had heard the Front's formal announcement of an amnesty for them. It is possible, as some claimed, that the Aku *jash* of Abbas Mamand[9] initiated the uprising in Raniya. Others claimed it was another *jash* tribal chief, Anwar Bitwarta. Be that as it may, almost everywhere it was the local *mustishars* who now wielded most power and who negotiated the departure of Iraqi forces unwilling to join the uprising. In Zakhu, for example, Umar Sindi, leading *mustishar* and tribal chief, offered all regular forces safe conduct to government lines if they laid down their arms. At Amadiya the *mustishar* advised the local army commander to withdraw his men to barracks to avoid provoking a popular uprising, leaving public order to the *jash*. Once his advice was taken, he obtained the troops' surrender. Not a shot had been fired. Only a few *jash* leaders opted to remain loyal to Saddam.[10]

The majority of *jash* leaders were thus transformed from embarrassed collaborators with Baghdad into champions of the uprising. Kurdish forces expanded from 15,000 to well over 100,000 men in the space of a few days. It was not long before the *mustishars* were assiduously recruited by member parties of the Front, each trying to enhance its strength on the battlefield and *vis-à-vis* other Front members. Anwar Bitwarta, for example, brought 10,000 men of the Khushnaw to the KSP. Umar Surchi Bikhmar took his 15,000 men to the KDP, pragmatically swallowing his reluctance to accept Barzani leadership. Karim Khan Baradust, mindful of his more bitter feud with the Barzanis, joined the PUK. Over the coming months many *jash* melted away, while *mustishars* sought the most attractive offer. Later on, certain tribal chiefs broke away to form their own party.

In the meantime the Kurds pressed forward, encouraged both by the apparent success of the rebel Shi'a, and by the warning issued by the United States to Iraq against the use of chemical weapons against its own citizens. The Front held a line parallel with the Kirkuk–Baghdad highway, including Kalar, Kifri, Tuz Khurmatu, Chamchamal and a foothold in Kirkuk. Now it launched a major assault on Kirkuk itself, the jewel in the Kurdish crown. On 19 March the town fell.

Mass Flight

The Kurdish triumph proved shortlived. Saddam had already proved his willingness to inflict massive civilian casualties in order to defeat the rebels. By 13 March 5,000 women and children had been taken hostage as the rebel threat to Kirkuk increased. Civilians in government-held parts of the town were rounded up and killed. With the rising in south Iraq now contained, Saddam rushed his best troops, the Republican Guards, northwards, supported by aircraft, heavy weapons and tanks. The rebels were ill-equipped to confront such technology.

It now appeared that the US-led Coalition did not wish Baghdad to lose control of the country or, rather, as indicated in unattributable briefings, it desired the defeat of the rebels before the overthrow of Saddam Husayn.[11] It was also clear that the US wished to assure Turkey and Saudi Arabia that it would help neither the Kurds or the Shi'is. While the United States had forbidden the use of fixed-wing aircraft under the ceasefire terms, it refused to forbid helicopters which were used with deadly effect against both combatants and civilians.

It was a bitter cup. Talabani and Barzani jointly accused President Bush: 'You personally called upon the Iraqi people to rise up against Saddam Hussein's brutal dictatorship.'[12] Bush had indeed announced just before the ground war began that 'there's another way for the bloodshed to stop, and that is for the Iraqi military and the Iraqi people to take matters into their own hands to force Saddam Hussein, the dictator, to step aside', a statement subsequently broadcast to Iraq by the Voice of America. Furthermore, the Saudi-controlled Voice of Free Iraq broadcast similar incitements to the population in Kurdish as well as Arabic. While Bush and his allies exonerated themselves, it was difficult to avoid the conclusion that the Coalition had indeed sought to incite dissident Iraqis but on a deniable basis.

On 28 March the Iraqi counter-offensive, using heavy weaponry and airpower, compelled the rebels to abandon Kirkuk, then the other foothill towns of Arbil, Dohuk and Zakhu. As they advanced, government forces seized up to 100,000 Kurds and Turkomans around Kirkuk, Dohuk and Tuz Khurmatu. Panic spread as stories of atrocities began to circulate. Perhaps as many as 20,000 Kurds and Turkomans perished in the Iraqi onslaught.

Mass panic and flight gripped all Kurdistan. Over 1.5 million Kurds abandoned their homes in a mad stampede to reach safety either in Turkey or Iran. All the roads and tracks to the border rapidly became clogged. On the road to Turkey one journalist said he had seen nearly 500 fugitives killed by phosphorous bombs dropped from helicopters: 'People are burned to death inside cars. Iraqi helicopters are bombing civilians without let up.'[13] Similar scenes occurred on the roads to Iran. The rebel forces largely disintegrated as fighters rushed to escort their families to safety.

Provide Comfort

As such images of cruelty and distress came to dominate news reports around the world, public criticism of a Coalition leadership which washed its hands of responsibility mounted. There was a distasteful contrast between the Coalition's readiness to fight to protect oil and reinstate an autocratic regime in Kuwait and its reluctance to protect Kurds and Shi'is. As one newspaper remarked:

> Mr Major, to his shame, says he cannot recall asking them [the Kurds] 'to mount this particular insurrection', as though the revolt were a freakish event which had nothing to do with us.... The man [Bush] who reportedly told the CIA in January to provoke the Kurds into insurrection and preached rebellion during the Gulf War, now acts like someone with a nasty bout of amnesia.[14]

Throughout the crisis the US administration, while likening Saddam to the most evil of dictators and encouraging the population in his overthrow, had nevertheless refused contact with opposition groups on the grounds of 'non-interference' in Iraq's internal affairs. Only on 28 March as Saddam's forces cut a swathe through his opponents did the USA finally decide on a dialogue with opposition leaders.

The failure to protect the Kurds now threatened to soil the reputation of the Gulf victors. On 5 April UN Security Council members passed Resolution 688 in order to restrain Baghdad. UNSCR 688 condemned 'the repression of the Iraqi civilian population in many parts of Iraq, including most recently in Kurdish populated areas' and demanded 'that Iraq, as a contribution to removing the threat to international peace and security in the region, immediately end this repression [and] that Iraq allow immediate access to international humanitarian

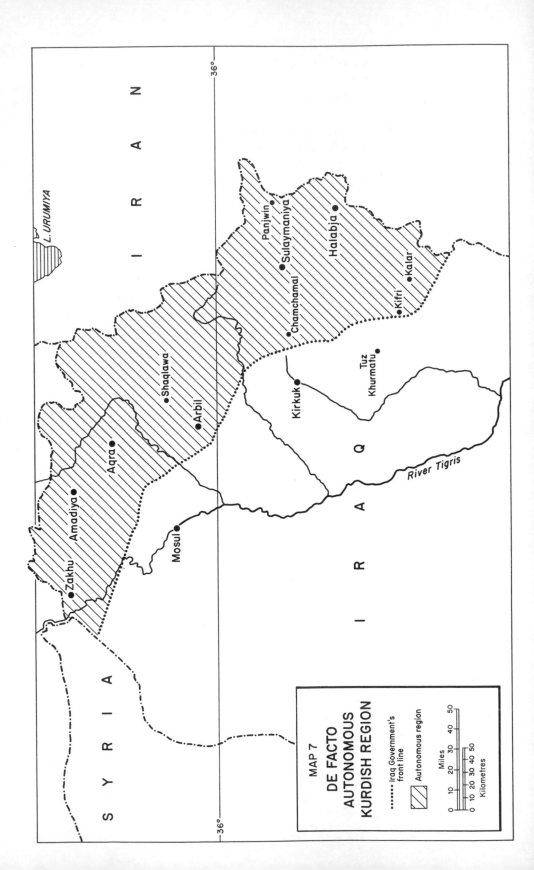

L. URUMIYA

I R A N

Panjwin
Sulaymaniya
Halabja
Chamchamal
Kifri
Kalar

Shaqlawa

Arbil

Tuz
Khurmatu

Kirkuk

Aqra

River Tigris

Amadiya

I R A Q

Mosul

Zakhu

36°

36°

S Y R I A

MAP 7
DE FACTO
AUTONOMOUS
KURDISH REGION

.... Iraq Government's
        front line

Autonomous region

Miles
0   10   20   30   40   50
0 10 20 30 40 50
Kilometres

organizations to all those in need of assistance in all parts of Iraq'. The resolution
was historic on two counts. It was the first (since the league's arbitration of the
Mosul vilayet in 1925/26) to mention the Kurds by name, thus lifting their status
internationally. It was also the first time the United Nations had insisted on the
right of interference in the internal affairs of a member state. Both precedents
suggested that the UN was beginning to re-assess its axiom of non-interference
in members' internal affairs, a fact that augured well for the future of the Kurds
and other endangered minorities. But the Security Council was careful not to
give its resolution force under Chapter 7 of the UN charter.

Meanwhile, the danger had not lessened on the ground. Had Baghad realized
how weak the resistance to their advance really was, it would undoubtedly have
pressed its attack. However, on the main Rawanduz road its troops ran into stiff
and skilful resistance that suggested a stronger force than the mere 150 men
Masud Barzani had at his disposal at Salah al Din. In view of that resistance, of
the need to regroup while containing both the Shi'i and Kurdish threats, and the
danger of renewed Coalition intervention, Baghdad decided against further
advances.

By the end of the first week of April over 250,000 Kurds had reached the
Turkish border, with an equal number still on their way. Many had fled without
preparation, hopelessly equipped for the winter snows. Yet despite the bitterly
cold conditions, Turkish troops denied them access to Turkey.

> Mothers carrying babies confronted Turkish troops ... begging to be allowed through
> to seek medical assistance.... Others brought grandparents on their backs or carried in
> makeshift stretchers of blankets. But anyone who tried to cross into Turkey was beaten
> back with rifle butts.[15]

Most made what shelter they could on the snowy mountain sides.

By contrast Iran opened its borders, allowing its own Kurds to open their
homes, schools and mosques to the fugitives. Piranshahr, for example, a town of
25,000 gave shelter to another 75,000 people. But there were far too many to be
accommodated in this way. Emergency camps were set up for almost one million
refugees. Both on the Turkish border and in Iran many of the very old and very
young fell sick and died, of exposure, respiratory infections, or dysentery.

The crisis on the Turkish border received much greater attention, however,
partly on account of the drama of refugees denied access to safety, but also
because Turkey was a member of the Coalition and of NATO. Ozal, anxious to
avoid the mounting international pressure began to allow some of the half million
refugees to cross the border[16] and called for the creation of a 'safe haven' on the
Iraqi side of the border. It was an idea adopted with enthusiasm first in London,
then in Washington, as a means to avoid further international odium.

In mid-April the Coalition announced the establishment of a 'safe haven'
inside Iraq, prohibiting Iraqi planes from flying north of the 36th parallel. On
28 April it began moving the first Kurds into this haven from the border area

under conditions close to coercion. This complemented the massive relief operation mounted by inter-governmental, governmental and non-governmental agencies that had begun, first unilaterally and then under the terms of a Memorandum of Understanding (MOU) agreed between the United Nations and the Iraqi government on 18 April 1991.

Renewed Autonomy Negotiations

Meanwhile, the absence of any Coalition intervention to prevent the defeat of Kurdish forces and the mass flight of the civil population compelled the Front to negotiate with Saddam, as it had warned on 1 April. The previous week, as Iraqi forces retook Kirkuk, it had received a proposal from Saddam for a settlement based on the principle of confederation.

Both sides desperately sought respite from the dire straits in which they found themselves, the Kurds from their flight into sub-zero conditions in the mountains, Saddam from barely tolerable internal and external political and military pressures.

Sceptical of the adequacy or reliability of the 'safe haven', Front leaders, including Talabani, arrived in Baghdad to discuss 'an Iraqi offer for expanded autonomy within the federated structure of Iraq promising democracy, pluralism, and constitutional rule in Baghdad'.[17] Masud Barzani emphasized that the Front did not seek the resignation of Saddam or political independence, just democracy for Iraq and autonomy for the Kurds. Yet nothing could more certainly lead to Saddam's overthrow than genuine democracy. Meanwhile Talabani shocked the world by publicly embracing Saddam who, he stated, had agreed to abolish the Revolutionary Command Council and hold free multi-party elections within six months. Shrewder minds recognized that Saddam could have no intention of carrying such measures through.

Yet, for two or three weeks the Front looked as if it might secure what it wanted, including the designation of Kirkuk as the administrative capital of the autonomous region.[18] On 9 May a second delegation, this time led by Masud Barzani, announced from Baghdad that the government would actually concede Kirkuk. This proved wishful thinking, as did the government's consent to the international guarantees the Front wanted for any agreement. On 17 May Barzani euphorically announced an imminent agreement. But it was now clear that Baghdad was no longer happy with ceding Kirkuk, Khaniqin or Mandali as the Front required.[19] In order to secure a deal the Front declared itself happy to cede control of oil in return for Kurdish adminstration of the city. However, Baghdad insisted the Kurds cut all foreign contacts, reflecting its fear of Kurdish co-operation with external enemies and its desire to ensure the Kurds had no resort but Baghdad.

Meanwhile, the Kurds' Iraqi allies were appalled by what they saw as a betrayal of the joint opposition of Kurds, leftists, Arab nationalists and Islamists, which had been forged in Damascus in December 1990. Fakhry Karim, an ICP leader whose brother Kurdish Communists were within the Kurdistan Front, argued that negotiation with Saddam could only strengthen his position. Democracy and Kurdish autonomy in any meaningful sense were wholly inimical to the nature of the regime.

However, apart from Kurds and Shi'is now fighting for their very existence, the Joint Opposition was weak. No rising of any consequence had taken place in the Sunni Arab parts of Iraq. The leftists and nationalists no longer had a credible power base in Arab Iraq. Nor were they in the desperate straits that now faced the Kurds. As for the Kurdish Communist section of the ICP, it reluctantly decided to remain within the Front, even though it shared ICP's scepticism and disapproval.

By mid-June it was clear that the negotiations were grinding to a halt. In Baghdad Saddam, finding Barzani an easier negotiating partner than Talabani, refused to discuss constitutional changes until an autonomy pact had been agreed.

In Kurdistan disagreement became evident in the leadership. Talabani, in his characteristically mercurial way, was now more sceptical of a deal than Barzani. Well-versed from 1984 in Saddam's foot-dragging style of negotiation, he warned that a deal without international guarantee and which left the borders of the autonomous region undefined[20] was unacceptable, and that he was willing to resume the conflict if necessary. He was supported in this view by Mahmud Uthman (KSP). Talabani believed he could persuade the Coalition to provide the guarantees and protection he wanted, since the US and also EC members had spoken favourably of an autonomy arrangement.[21]

Barzani, however, argued that it was better to accept a deal that re-established the Kurds in their homeland than risk further war. His scepticism about the duration of Coalition protection proved well founded as Coalition troops withdrew first from Iraq in mid-June,[22] and then from their rear position inside Turkey, leaving Coalition protection solely based on airpower at the Incirlik airbase, and subject to Turkish six-monthly agreements.

Yet, was he 'too soft' as Mahmud Uthman claimed?[23] Barzani had been deeply moved by the events he had experienced: the destruction of so many Barzanis (1983); the Anfal; the universal destruction of Kurdish villages; the mass flight of a whole people; the thousands of deaths in this latest round of the Kurdish struggle. He dreaded a return to war. He, too, may have been swayed by the self-justification of many *jash* leaders, like Husayn Surchi who had angrily told KDP leaders:

> My villages are still standing and are still wealthy, my people still dress as Kurds, speak Kurdish and have a good life. Look what your nationalism has done for you. Your villages are destroyed, your people have been forcibly re-settled, you live in exile and you have nothing left. Why call me a traitor?[24]

When Front leaders met towards the end of June, Baghdad had increased its demands to include the surrender of all heavy weapons, the closure of Front radio stations, and the severance of all Front foreign relations. Saddam also wanted Kurdish leaders to join his government.

Barzani accepted the majority view that these demands should be refused. 'We can agree to peace,' Mahmud Uthman remarked, 'but not to be partners with the Baath. He [Saddam] wants to isolate the Kurds and their friends and wait until they are weak before moving against them.'[25] The Front was fully supported by *jash* commanders who feared for themselves under any autonomy deal, keenly aware that Saddam did not forgive easily. In early July the Front formally stated that no agreement could be made outside the context of democracy for all Iraq, and that nothing short of a concrete timetable would suffice.

Frustration renewed the danger of war. Although formally in control, by June government forces found it impossible to deny a *peshmerga* presence in the cities of Arbil and Sulaymaniya. An uneasy situation persisted with troops ordered to kill 'any armed or unarmed Kurd who tries to insult military personnel'.[26] Coexistence finally broke down on 20 July as *peshmergas* took control of both cities. Under a new arrangement government troops deployed outside. Meanwhile, troops evicted Kurds and Turkomans from areas under government control, replacing them with Arab farmers and town-dwellers.

In September and October further serious fighting broke out first around Kirkuk, and in early October around Kifri, Kalar and Sulaymaniya, as both sides tested their respective defences and Coalition commitment. Saddam hoped the Coalition would prove supine while Talabani hoped to provoke its intervention. On the ground government forces retook Kifri and shelled Sulaymaniya, precipitating the flight of 100,000 Kurds to the border. Yet such government gains were dearly bought. On each occasion, in July and in October, it was estimated that it lost 5,000 men (a division in strength).[27]

It was now clear that an autonomy agreement was most unlikely. Only Barzani clung to the hope of a deal, perhaps more acutely aware than his colleagues of the enormous number of displaced and dependent people in the liberated zone and the way Saddam had reminded people of their continuing dependence by his provision of salaries to government employees and of free petrol and electricity. The others were opposed to a deal that fell substantially short of what they wanted.

Saddam placed Kurdistan under siege in late October, withdrawing his troops behind a defensive line, cutting off all salaries to Kurdish employees, and gradually imposing a blockade on the Kurdish region (gradual in order to avoid a moment of direct confrontation with the United Nations). Saddam did this not only to make life uncomfortable but to remind ordinary Kurds that, materially speaking, life would be much better without the Kurdistan Front. He wished to enforce autonomy on his own terms. More fighting took place around Arbil in early November and the number of newly displaced rose to 200,000.

As Saddam knew, winter was the best time to apply economic pressure. By January he was constructing a fortified line held by three army corps. Minefields, suggesting permanence, were laid. In most places the two front lines were a mile or two apart, but at Kalar barely 300 yards separated them. Those who entered Kurdistan were stripped of fuel and foodstuffs, reducing supplies in the region to barely a quarter of the previous level.

Provisions were unevenly available. The 1.2 million people of Sulaymaniya got only one tenth of its government allowance up to October.[28] It suffered because it was furthest from the Turkish supply route. It was impossible to withstand the cold without adequate food and shelter in the mountains, yet both were lacking on account of the blockade, and on account of the almost universal destruction of housing.

Doubtless Saddam also hoped the Front would be inadequate to the task and would rapidly lose popularity among a cold and starving population seeking respite from their ordeal. Indeed, his hope was partially fulfilled with demonstrations against the Front's inefficiency in Dohuk, Sulaymaniya, Panjwin and Halabja, and the eviction of Front officials from certain locations for inefficiency or corruption. People took to the streets chanting 'We want bread and butter, not Saddam and not the Kurdistan Front.'[29] As Masud Barzani admitted 'Our governing process is paralyzed ... there is a crisis within the Kurdistan Front.'[30]

Kurdistan's Elected Government

There was indeed a crisis. The Front recognized Saddam's intention to force their submission to his terms, but it decided that the blockade was an opportunity for the Kurds unilaterally to choose their own future and it gave up further thought of a deal with Saddam. However, it was also acutely aware that Saddam had, in the words of the KDP spokesman, Hoshyar Zibari, 'laid a trap'.[31] Someone had to adminster Kurdistan, but if the Front set up an independent administration because of government abdication, this would alarm Turkey, Iran, Syria and the West.

It was important to reassure all parties of Kurdish intentions to remain within the Iraqi state. In early January KDP and PUK representatives joined other Iraqi opposition representatives in Damascus to lay the groundwork for an Iraqi government in exile.

The Front now formally withdrew from the autonomy negotiation and declared its intention to replace the old Legislative Assembly (still full of Saddam's placemen) with a freely elected parliament and leader. An election was proposed for 3 April. It was generally hoped that such an election would produce a clear leadership, provide a form of government based on the choice of the people, and would eliminate the paralysis which had characterized much of Kurdistan since the uprising. The *modus operandi* of the Front to date had allowed each party to act independently, but had required all actions by the Front to enjoy unanimity

Even one of the tiny parties could veto a Front decision. Without telephones, government by the Front required endless journeys by party envoys to the headquarters at Khalifan, each point of dispute being referred by courier back to party headquarters. It was no way to run a liberated zone. It was also hoped that a proper government would be able to establish a unified *peshmerga* force of about 80,000 men, and a police force of 20,000 to replace the estimated 400,000 or so fighters at large on the streets of Kurdistan.

Like many elections elsewhere, the campaign was essentially a personality contest. It was about loyalty to leaders rather than matters of ideology. Barzani, anxious not to alarm Iraq's neighbours, emphasized the need for reaching agreement with Baghdad, and adopted the slogan 'autonomy for Kurdistan, democracy for Iraq'. Talabani proclaimed Kurdish self-determination within a federal Iraq, a slogan that clearly hinted at something closer to independence, despite assurances regarding Iraq's configuration.

Yet it is unlikely many were swayed by such considerations. The overwhelming majority voted according to their sense of personal loyalty. Many were the beneficiaries of patronage networks, either directly to a political leader, or via intermediaries through whom services or supplies were obtainable. Others had moved in order to be in the same party as the majority of their family, a new kind of communal solidarity pattern. Many *jash*, who could sell their services, had 'shopped around'. Some had been lured by money, for example into one of the Islamic parties funded by Iran or by Saudi Arabia, or by a better deal in another party. Others had become disenchanted. Many of the *jash* chiefs who had submitted to the KDP, PUK or KSP, had now withdrawn to form their own 'Society of Kurdish Tribes'.[32] They were anxious to defend tribalism, a form of identity to which perhaps 20 per cent of Kurds still subscribed, against what they perceived as the political and social transformation of Kurdistan, a process in which the political parties were the leading agents.

The election finally took place 19 May, on the basis of proportional representation, with a threshold of 7 per cent of the vote to qualify for seats. Smaller parties agreed to this, confident they could easily gain this minimum. The Front also agreed on the election of a leader. It was careful to ensure the electoral terms were consistent with the 1970 Autonomy Accord signed in Baghdad. Certain parties combined to improve their chance of seats, the Toilers Party joined the PUK list in return for an assured three seats and Pasok combined with the KSP. Various small Islamic groups[33] combined under the title of the Islamic Movement, led by Mulla Uthman Abd al Aziz of Halabja (see below). Others, notably the Society of Kurdish Tribes and the small, semi-clandestine pro-PKK Partiya Azadiya Kurdistan, chose not to participate.

An unspecified number of seats were allocated to the two main minorities, the Turkomans and the Assyrian Christians. There were probably about 300,000 Turkomans in Iraq.[34] They had suffered as much as the Kurds at Saddam's hands and had become militant during the 1980s after a decade of docility. They wanted

Kirkuk within the autonomy zone and were willing to argue its precise status with the Kurds later. Their relations with the Kurds were chequered, but had improved after Qasim's fall. Some, for example General Kemal Mustafa, had joined Mulla Mustafa. Relations deteriorated following the 1970 Autonomy Accord agreement, when the government deliberately played the two off by supporting the Turkomans. The only political group, the National Turkoman Party was not a member of the Front although its forces co-operated informally. It chose not to participate in the election because of the danger for the majority of Turkomans still under government control and to avoid offending Ankara, with which the party naturally had close relations.

The Assyrians voted separately from the Kurds. Assyrians had worked within the Kurdish national movement since the 1960s. One of the most famous *peshmerga* commanders was an Assyrian woman, Margaret George Malik, killed in 1966. Crudely, Assyrians tended to fall into two categories, those in the countryside who identified with the Kurdish movement, and the town-dwellers who tended to identify more with the Arab population. Saddam deliberately sought to co-opt Assyrians since they were vulnerable and therefore likely to be loyal. There were 2,000 Assyrian *jash* formed by a Zakhu merchant and based at Sirsank. These simply went home during the uprising. The only Assyrian party of note was the Assyrian Democratic Movement (ADM), founded in 1979. Its only challengers were small surrogate parties of the main Kurdish parties.[35]

The Kurdistan election was, for all the haste in its preparation and the occasional cases of fraud or malpractice, an historic moment. Externally, it demonstrated almost uniquely outside Israel and Turkey, the ability of a Middle Eastern electorate to conduct a peaceful, multi-party election. Its example was a symbolic threat not only to Saddam but to all un-elected regimes in the region.

The results demonstrated that only the KDP and PUK enjoyed a large following. The KDP and PUK received 45 per cent and 43.6 per cent of the vote respectively and, given some irregularities, it was judged a dead heat.[36] The other parties were devastated by their failure to gain anything like the 7 per cent threshold. Only the Islamic Movement achieved 5 per cent of the vote. The KSP and the ICP took only 2.6 and 2.2 per cent respectively, while the KPDP received only 1 per cent. For both Mahmud Uthman (widely regarded outside Kurdistan as its shrewdest politician) and Sami Abd al Rahman it was a bitter pill to swallow. The KPDP, KSP and Pasok disappeared, first combining in June as the Unity Party but breaking up in summer 1993, most joining the KDP but a KSP rump led by Rasul Mamand joining the PUK.

In the leadership election Barzani had gained 48 per cent, Talabani 45 per cent and Uthman only 2 per cent. It was decided to set the result aside and for Barzani and Talabani to lead the Front jointly.

It was less clear what to do with the results of the election. Abroad it provoked unease among Iraq's neighbours, none of which were willing to recognize either the assembly which convened on 4 June or the Kurdish Regional Government

(KRG) that was nominated a month later. Within Kurdistan the two-party democracy functioned with difficulty. Parliament was composed of 105 seats, 50 apiece to the PUK and KDP lists, and five reserved for the Assyrians of which four were taken by the Assyrian Democratic Movement and one by the KDP's Kurdistan Christian Unity Party. The government was composed of an equal balance of PUK and KDP members, but without the participation of either leader.

Economic War

Saddam's economic war ate progressively into Kurdish reserves. By August 1992 his blockade was virtually total, with a complete fuel ban introduced in July. By October the price of kerosene was two hundred times that in July 1990, rice eighty-fold. People began to part with their assets.

Whenever he came under international pressure Saddam would relent, allowing a new Memorandum of Understanding to be signed, and for relief trucks once more to drive into Kurdistan. But he usually found a fresh way to inhibit relief, for example by delays at newly established roadblocks. From July 1992 he initiated attacks on UN and expatriate voluntary agency staff involved in the relief operation, and bombed trucks, a campaign that continued into 1993. There were always hungry Kurds who could be hired to carry out such operations. By August 1992 Sulaymaniya was receiving only 20 per cent of its proper food ration, Arbil only 16 per cent. By January 1993 this had further reduced to less than 10 per cent, a figure that had not improved by the spring, 1994.[37]

Inevitably the Kurds also suffered from the decline in international commitment. In the first place the United Nations decision to provide relief under a Memorandum of Understanding with Baghdad allowed Saddam plenty of scope to undermine international relief efforts. This was compounded by severe underfunding of the rehabilitation operation and by the shortcomings of the various UN agencies involved, which exasperated both Kurdish and expatriate voluntary agencies.[38] Early in the crisis the UNDP had commissioned a report which set out a coherent strategy for medium and longer term rehabilitation of Kurdistan, beginning with the provision of security and the clearance of mines, and progressing to the resuscitation of the rural economy. Two years later the UNDP had failed to make any substantial progress on the report recommendations. The provision of capital for fertilizers, livestock, seed and equipment was simply not forthcoming. In the meantime UN assessments of food and fuel requirements were seriously underestimated, on the assumption that Saddam would provide two thirds of the requirement, despite evidence to the contrary.

After the Kurdish election, international and government agencies eschewed working through the official administration or related institutions for fear of implying their recognition of the KRG. Thus the KRG was by-passed on the most pressing issue it faced, the rehabilitation of Kurdistan. To deny the Kurds control over their own requirements contradicted the basic principles of relief and development; this was particularly so, given the enormity of the task of recovery. Much village agriculture had been destroyed over a decade earlier. In many cases return to the villages was made harder by the Anfal operation. A survey in Panjwin area revealed that up to 10 per cent of family heads were widows. Probably over 35,000 family (male) heads perished in the Anfal, let alone other males. In the Barzan region some ruined villages were populated only by women and children. In such circumstances it was not surprising that by the autumn of 1992 only an estimated 43 per cent of Kurdistan's arable land was actually under cultivation.

However, the Kurdish leadership too was responsible for certain shortcomings. Government attempts to raise revenue were based largely on the taxation of trade entering Kurdistan. These efforts were compromised by the political parties and local aghas attempting to boost their own revenues from the same source. They all sought to take a toll on relief supplies. As a result revenues were barely sufficient to pay salaries, with virtually nothing left for programme implementation.

Furthermore, it was widely believed that political parties and local strongmen connived at widespread asset-stripping. From the collapse of the uprising onwards, many Kurds removed plant and heavy equipment and sold it, largely in Iran, in order to boost their personal income. By August 1992, for example, of Arbil municipality's 700 vehicles, only 92 remained. The most notorious single incident was the stripping of equipment from the Bikhma dam project, near Rawanduz. Asset-stripping was frequently carried out by local landlords, aghas or erstwhile *mustishar*s. Political leaders were tempted to turn a blind eye in return for assurances of support. Thus, a weak and threatened government, albeit nationalist, found itself abetting the old patronage system.

Where prohibitions were enforced, smuggling took place which undermined the political and social cohesion of the liberated region. Perhaps the most damaging was the smuggling of the cereal harvest to the Iraqi government which offered a higher price than the Front could afford. In 1992 the liberated region produced approximately 200,000 metric tons of wheat. This was over half the requirement, but a substantial proportion was lost by smuggling. This happened again in 1993, when the Kurdish government needed $50 million to buy a bumper harvest of approximately 400,000 tons. Baghdad offered a higher price,[39] and the level of social discipline or political commitment was insufficient to deter aghas or black marketeers. In the end, as Saddam well understood, the detachment of the economy from KRG control would increase Kurdish dependence on Baghdad.

The Turkish Dimension

Talabani was soon convinced that Turkey was the key to the future of Iraqi Kurdistan. His logic was based upon simple premises: an autonomy deal with Saddam would not be worth the paper it was written on, since no external agent would act as guarantor and referee; Iraqi Kurdistan could only be sustained and protected via Turkey (given Iran's relations with West, there was no foreseeable prospect of Iran being the main conduit for aid or protection) and finally that President Ozal had already demonstrated he wished to abandon the Kemalist legacy regarding the Kurds (see chapter 20).

Such factors persuaded Talabani to develop the channel with Ankara. In external relations Barzani followed where Talabani led, and both parties soon had liaison offices in Ankara. Ever speculative, Talabani went further. With no guarantee of permanent and effective Coalition air protection,[40] Talabani visited Prime Minister Demirel in July 1992 and raised the question of Turkey's claim to Mosul vilayet. 'Mr Demirel only laughed,' he disclosed afterwards, 'but it must be discussed. Iraq has violated all its obligations made in 1926 and 1932.... I am not taking Turkey as an ideal. I am taking it as relative to Iraq and Iran. Here [in Turkey] there are newspapers that openly support the PKK. Here you can speak and shout. There is a democratic process.'[41] In effect, he was inviting Turkey to consider annexing Iraqi Kurdistan.

It is unlikely that Talabani had a mandate from Kurdistan's elected leaders for this initiative,[42] although if Turkey had responded favourably it could have had profound consequences for the region. Turkey would have acquired the Kirkuk oilfields and four million Kurds. Given the coherent and developed nature of Kurdish nationalism in Iraq, it is unlikely it could have annexed this territory without recognizing Kurdish autonomy. This would almost inevitably have led to accepting Turkish Kurdish rights, with a federal union of Turkey (a Turkish and a Kurdish republic) being a logical consequence.

The dangers – of alienating the West, of hostilities with Syria and Iran not to mention Iraq, and the explosive domestic consequences – all deterred Turkey from acting. In November Turkey confirmed with Syria and Iran their joint commitment to uphold the territorial integrity of Iraq, and implicitly opposed the Kurdish declaration of a federal state in Iraq in October.

Nevertheless Ankara used the Kurdish leaders' dependency to obtain their participation in a massive operation against the PKK in the border area during October and November 1992 (see chapter 20). Both the KDP and PUK had a longstanding, if difficult, relationship with PKK. Although the Front removed most of those it captured rather than surrender them to Turkish forces, the operation caused deep controversy within Kurdish society. Yet, while Ankara withheld *de jure* recognition of the Kurdish government, its reliance on Iraqi Kurds implied *de facto* acceptance of realities. As the editor of *Hurriyet* remarked, 'For Ankara, the Kurdish federal state is becoming more legal by the day.'[43] Indeed, in August 1993 the Turkish government gave the Kurdish government in Arbil US$13.5 million in aid, hardly the act of a government that did not recognize another.

Democracy or Neo-tribalism?

Meanwhile, inside liberated Kurdistan, the election of May 1992 and the formation of the KRG could not hide the fundamental longstanding or more recent divides that now existed. It was one thing to hold free elections but quite another to run a functional democracy, which demanded the creation of credible institutions. The dead heat between the KDP and PUK merely underlined the manifold and overlapping antagonisms between the two parties: personal between the two leaders, geographical between Bahdinan and Suran, linguistic between Kurmanji and Surani, and ideological between 'traditionist' and 'progressive' cultures. The geographical pattern had been confirmed in the vote, with the KDP's over-whelming sway in Dohuk, and the PUK's supremacy in Sulaymaniya and Kirkuk provinces.[44]

With the KRG denied international recognition, Barzani and Talabani agreed to stand outside government in order to pursue their international diplomacy. This exacerbated the problem. Abroad as well as inside Kurdistan they tended to compete not co-operate, travelling separately to the world's capitals. Washington was finally compelled to insist they could only visit in tandem. In the words of one veteran Kurdish politician

> They [Barzani and Talabani] do not trust each other. If you visit one all he can do is talk about the other. They are obsessed with their party rivalry ... they do not work out a common strategy. There is no strategy at all, except to get ahead of the other party.[45]

But the greatest damage was done to the KRG. Exercising power outside the electoral system hardly helped the development of democratic institutions. The KRG was left executing the decisions of leaders, with full responsibility but delegated authority. No one was in any doubt that regarding the exercise of coalition government, Kurdistan was now run by the two party headquarters. The PUK veteran Fuad Masum was appointed prime minister, but resigned in protest in March 1993:

> If the two leaders of PUK and KDP enter parliament, we will be rescued from considerable trouble. Every decision now needs a party decision. If the leaders join the government there will not be this uncertainty.[46]

In order to ensure parity between the two parties, governmental posts were shared equally. Where a minister belonged to one party, his deputy belonged to the other. It was an uneasy condominium, with two parallel administrations reaching down to the police on the street or the teaching staff in a school. Joining one or other party became the essential prerequisite to advancement. The patronage role of both political parties became disastrously entrenched in the fledgling administration undermining any chance of democratic institutional growth.

Thus, following the demise of traditional tribalism as the prime form of socio-political organization during the 1970s, the 1990s saw the emergence of neo-tribalism as two major 'confederations' competed for hegemony in Iraqi Kurdistan. At the centre of each party, as with traditional confederations, lay a core of those loyal to the paramount. Beyond this core lay a widening group of people who supported one confederation or the other less directly. Thus the system of patronage and power still reached down to the street through intermediaries who themselves acquired followings through local patronage. These new 'aghas' are the *peshmerga* or *jash* commanders who commanded their own following.

Changed circumstances may lead such chiefs to switch allegiance from one confederation to another, as in the past. Several did so following the demise of the lesser parties in the 1992 election. One of the most notable of these 'adventurers' was Muhammad Haj Mahmud, a formidable ex-KSP commander in Sulaymaniya with 20,000 *peshmergas*, who sought a new position for himself between the KDP, PUK and Iran.

In May 1994 the stress between the two confederations erupted in open fighting, sparked by a land dispute near Qala Diza between a KDP claimant and local non-tribal farmers supported by the PUK. This dispute also exposed older tensions in Kurdish society, between one tribe and another, between tribal and non-tribal, as well as between the KDP and PUK. It was symptomatic of the mutual antagonism that both sides were guilty of killing prisoners. Barzani and Talabani proved incapable of controlling their own forces, and battles raged intermittently in Rawanduz, Shaqlawa, Qala Diza and elsewhere until the end of August, leaving possibly over 1,000 dead, and causing more than 70,000 civilians to flee their homes. An uneasy stand-off ensued, with Kurdistan now politically and militarily partitioned.

The conflict was complicated by the intervention of the Islamic Movement of Kurdistan (IMK), the confederation of Islamic groups. The 1992 election had revealed Islamic sentiment to be weakest in the more conservative and tribal areas (Dohuk and Arbil governorates) and strongest in the more developed Sulaymaniya and Kirkuk, where it had attracted 8 and 6 per cent of the vote respectively. This indicated that the Qadiriya and Naqshbandiya tended to do well in areas where the conservative alternative, the KDP, was not dominant. Its leader, Mulla Uthman Abd al Aziz of Halabja, had stood in the 1992 election for the Kurdish presidency, taking 4 per cent of the vote. In view of his *jash* record, this was a significant achievement. His following grew rapidly following the election thanks mainly to financial support from Iran. As one politician remarked at the time, 'The ground in Kurdistan is ready for an Islamic revival. They see the mistakes and corruption of the KDP and PUK very clearly and Iran supports these groups with food and weapons.' In July 1993 Mulla Ali Abd al Aziz, Mulla Uthman's brother, travelled to Tehran accompanied by Muhammad Hajj al Mahmud, to meet Rafsanjani, Khamenei and Vilayati, in sharp contrast with Talabani and Barzani who had not been afforded this privilege in recent years.

The growth of IMK around Mulla Uthman's home town of Halabja had already led to fierce clashes with the PUK in December 1993, in part the result of animosity between 'obscurantists' and 'atheists', as each side was wont to view the other, but also the result of the IMK challenge to an area the PUK considered its own. On that occasion the PUK had prevailed on the battlefield but accepted the arbitration of the KDP, with which the IMK enjoyed friendly relations.[47]

With fighting raging between the KDP and PUK in May 1994, IMK seized the towns of Halabja, Panjwin and Khurmal, fiercely attacking PUK positions. By the time the fighting died down in autumn 1994, the IMK was still in possession of a large swathe of land around these three towns. It was also clear that the KDP and IMK had operated co-operatively to worst the PUK and that the IMK was receiving strong support from Iran.

1994–99: The contest for Iraqi Kurdistan

For the greater part of the 1990s it could be said that the fate of Iraq's Kurds was largely determined by particular interacting factors. These were:

(i) the state of the Kurdish economy under UN and Iraqi embargo; (ii) the rivalry between the KDP and PUK which resulted in the *de facto* partition of the liberated area for much of the decade; (iii) the American determination to use the region it was protecting as a springboard for the overthrow of Saddam Husayn, an objective with which it became increasingly obsessed, and as a lever in its policy of 'dual containment' (of Iraq and Iran); (iv) the PKK's use (or abuse) of Iraqi Kurdish territory to prosecute its war on Turkey; (v) Baghdad's concern to bring the Kurdish region back within its orbit and its fear that the US, Turkey, Iran and Syria were all seeking to co-opt part or all of the Kurdish population against it; (vi) the various concerns of Iraq's northern regional neighbours: Turkey, anxious to extirpate the PKK and to prevent the emergence of a vibrant Kurdish autonomous region on its south-eastern border; Iran and Syria anxious to thwart US dual containment, including its gambit to encircle the Fertile Crescent by informal military alliance between Israel, Turkey and itself.

These were unpromising circumstances in which internal Kurdish conflicts, essentially a struggle for ascendancy between the KDP and PUK, could be resolved. In December 1994 the KDP and PUK plunged again into open fighting, triggered by a tribal land dispute. The consequence was 500 dead, thousands displaced, the civil administration paralysed and Arbil in the hands of the PUK.

Anxious to re-establish sufficient stability for its twin strategic ambitions, and to deny a vacuum for its adversaries, Syria, Iraq or Iran, to exploit, the US brokered a fragile ceasefire in April 1995. However, this only held for three months. In July when fighting broke out again, Iran held mediation talks in Tehran. Like Syria, it wished to rival the US and Turkey as a major actor in the area and it was in a strong position since it controlled the PUK's only egress to the outside world.

Meanwhile it became common knowledge that the KDP was negotiating with Baghdad. From 1994 and possibly earlier, Barzani had resumed secret contacts with Baghdad. Armour and artillery began to appear in the KDP arsenal, reportedly provided by Baghdad. When the United States again sought to mediate during the July 1995 round of KDP–PUK fighting, the KDP was noticeably slow to respond to its invitation. In August and September the US secured a ceasefire at meetings in Drogheda and Dublin, but with no resolution of the fundamental disputes: the KDP's monopolisation of revenues on the Turkish border and the PUK's seizure of Arbil.

The internal conflict was made more volatile by the unstable nature of the contesting parties. In addition to the personal animosity between Barzani and Talabani, the peshmerga forces were characterized by mercurial and undisciplined behaviour particularly among the surrogate armed groups that had attached themselves to one side or the other. During the summer of 1996 tension between the KDP and PUK began to increase again, with the trigger to renewed conflict again being tribal.[48] Skirmishes followed almost daily between the two factions and each accused the other of initiating hostilities. In mid-August a locally raised brigade of KDP forces in Dargala, east of Rawanduz, defected to the PUK, precipitating a major struggle for the Shuman valley and Hajj Umran.

In August the KDP rapidly expanded the area of conflict to include the countryside around Arbil, using some of the heavy weaponry it had received from Baghdad. In London the KDP hastily withdrew from US mediation efforts. Having already reached a tactical understanding with Saddam Husayn, the KDP had formulated a battle-plan for the decisive defeat of the PUK. The build-up of provocations in July and August provided the pretext with which to carry it out. At the end of August the KDP moved rapidly, strongly supported by Iraqi armour and artillery, to capture Arbil, the Dagala heights east of Arbil, and also Koi Sanjaq. A week later, KDP forces entered Sulaymaniya uncontested, and the defeat of the PUK seemed complete. In and around Arbil, Iraqi forces rounded up and executed dozens of opponents of the regime. Others died resisting capture. Another 1,500 Arab and Kurdish opponents of the regime were taken away in captivity. Everyone assumed that the dreaded *mukhabarat* were now back in operation in the autonomous region. Nothing demonstrated more clearly the fragile credibility of US protection nor the deep terror inspired by the expectation of Iraqi involvement, than the flight of 80,000 from Sulaymaniya as the KDP made its rapid advance on the city in the first week of September.

In the immediate aftermath, Saddam removed the blockade imposed since 1991. It appeared to be a reward to Barzani, now apparently supreme.

However, contrary to expectation, the PUK made a dramatic recovery in mid-October when its regrouped forces, strongly aided by Iran, mounted surprise attacks and rapidly recovered most Surani-speaking territory, including Sulaymaniya. However, it failed to recapture Arbil.

Why had Baghdad and Tehran sponsored the Kurdish parties? They both wished to displace US influence in the Kurdish region and defeat this dimension of US containment. Baghdad obviously wished to reassert its influence and was able to remind the Kurdish contestants that, whatever the US hoped to achieve in the future, Baghdad remained the long term determinant of their future. Tehran likewise wanted an end to US influence in the area but it also wanted an end to KDPI use of Iraq. So it required PUK assistance against the KDPI as the price for its facilities and support against the KDP. Thus, increasingly, KDP-PUK rivalry drove each party into greater dependency on, and co-operation with the aims of, their respective external rival sponsors.

Meanwhile, the US was desperate to salvage its anti-Saddam programme predicated upon the stability of the liberated Kurdish region. In late October 1996 it persuaded both parties to agree a permanent ceasefire, with regular co-ordination meetings in Ankara.[49] The offer of $11 million helped the two parties accept US mediation. Many basic sticking points remained however, most notably the equitable distribution of customs revenues for the whole region. At the time the KDP was accused of hogging an estimated $250,000 in daily revenues at the Khabur crossing from Turkey. In fact its income was much more.

For the US the events of autumn 1996 had been a chastening lesson in the limitations of its influence and the flimsy nature of the opposition coalition it had nurtured. It duly withdrew its military mission from Zakhu, and evacuated 7,000 locally-employed personnel at risk from Iraqi reprisals. These evacuees, representing some of the best educated people of the region, were the core of a growing emigration of more sophisticated Kurds, Assyrians and Turkomans who saw no future in the internally riven region.

Barzani now sought to outmanoeuvre Talabani politically. At the end of October he demonstrated his continuing intimacy with Baghdad by receiving Ali Hasan al Majid, architect and perpetrator of the Anfal, at his headquarters in Salah al Din. In addition to his continuing flirtation with Baghdad, in November he also reached an agreement with Iran to open the Hajj Umran border, worth $100,000 daily to the KDP. Essentially he was seeking to build relations with the key regional players.

The ceasefire was not destined to last. In March 1997 Barzani temporarily withdrew from the Ankara process, accusing the PUK of assassinating three of his officials. Then there was a major clash of forces near Arbil. In May a fresh outbreak of conflict occurred between the PUK and the IMK in its Halabja enclave. Tehran mediated between the two, having possibly provoked the conflict in the first place in order to establish its own role as mediator and arbiter in the south.

Turkey was clearly establishing a similar position for itself in the north. The US withdrawal from Zakhu gave it a much freer hand to intervene against the PKK, and to co-opt the KDP in this process. In May 1997, Turkish forces invaded north Iraq for the third time during the 1990s, this time, however, in close co-operation with the KDP.

The PKK had grown into a serious danger for the KDP. At an ideological level its pan-Kurdish independence ideology struck some Iraqi Kurds as more attractive than the KDP's position of autonomy within Iraq. On the ground, it destabilized the area, compromised the KDP in its relations with Turkey and provided the PUK with a handy cat's-paw in the north. So when Turkey crossed the border, the KDP also attacked PKK-associated organisations in Arbil, killing those it captured.

Under duress from both Turkey and the US, the PUK also undertook to 'prevent terrorist elements, the PKK in particular, from having a presence or activities in northern Iraq'.[50] The strategic importance of the US, Turkey and Iran to its own future left the PUK with little option but to comply in the cases of both the PKK and the KDPI. Losing use of the PKK may have increased the PUK's sense that it was losing the struggle for ascendancy to the KDP, especially since Turkey's growing alliance with Israel was particularly threatening to the PUK's two patrons, Syria and Iran. At the same time Saddam, Barzani's recent ally, was demonstrably and steadily recovering from the defeat of 1991.

However the PUK's overwhelming problem was money, for economic power determined how many peshmergas could be engaged and therefore the potential for the defeat of one's adversary. It shared this problem with the INC, from which the US had withdrawn support in early 1997. In the summer of 1997 both accused the much better financed KDP of illegally profiting from the cross-border trade with Turkey. They accused the KDP of taking $800,000 daily in dues on Iraqi oil sold to Turkish truckers in contravention of UN sanctions, and a further $270,000 in daily charges on 'traffic' across the Khabur. Such figures were substantially in excess of previous estimates and were not convincingly contradicted. If the true figures were only half these, they still dramatically indicated the KDP's financial ascendancy.

By the autumn of 1997 the PUK decided its economic vulnerability could no longer permit the 'neither peace nor war' situation with the KDP. In October it launched a massive assault on the KDP, retaking positions along the Iranian border and pushing towards the strategic Hamilton Road. But its positions came under assault from Turkish warplanes and land forces, which no longer pretended neutrality between the KDP and PUK and the PUK was forced back to its previous ceasefire line, and a new ceasefire agreed.

It was not until September 1998 that the US was able to persuade both parties into a formal agreement. Beyond the usual verbiage concerning pluralism, democracy and human rights, both parties undertook to ensure that an interim Assembly and administration would reconvene by spring 1999, with a view to holding fresh elections (postponed from 1995) on 1 July 1999. Furthermore, the KDP undertook 'to extend appropriate financial assistance on a monthly basis to the public service ministries in PUK areas.' Apart from a single KDP payment, by mid-June 1999 none of these objectives had been met. The KDP demanded replacement of the ill-starred 50:50 arrangement of 1992 with a 51:49 arrange-ment reflecting, it claimed, the real 1992 electoral result, something to which the PUK could not possibly accede. It also accused the PUK of providing support for the PKK. As a result, no meaningful agreement was reached between the two factions in summer 1999.

In the meantime, the US did what it could to bolster the Kurdish region as the springboard for its own wider plans. It undertook gradually to widen the northern

and southern 'no-fly' zones, and to designate 'armour-free' zones to prevent the
Iraqi army from advancing. Furthermore, at the beginning of 1999 it named seven
Iraqi opposition groups eligible for US$97 million earmarked for the overthrow of
Saddam. Of the Kurdish groups so named, the KDP rejected any involvement,
while the PUK equivocated. Both were too frightened of Baghdad's retribution. But
they had little option but to host other opposition groups. Wanting continued
protection they found themselves hostage to the US policy to overthrow Saddam.
Knowing that in due course they would have to treat with Baghdad, they were
equally anxious not to antagonise Saddam.

Indeed, Baghdad had made its displeasure over the September 1998 Agreement
clear. In particular, it reminded the KDP of its vulnerability by reducing the quantity of oil and diesel it allowed to pass by truck to the Khabur crossing. In 1997 it
allowed 10 million litres of fuel to cross daily. In October 1998 it reduced to the
amount to 6 million litres and, as the US sought to establish the Iraqi opposition in
the Kurdish region, it reduced this further, to 1 million litres daily in April 1999. It
also switched the export route into PUK territory, for export to Iran. In mid-April it
also massed armour on the fringes of the Kurdish region, a clear reminder of the
dangers the Kurds would run if they sided too openly with the US.

Continuing dependence

At a material level considerable reconstruction took place during the 1990s as ordinary Kurds rebuilt their lives under Coalition protection. This included the
reconstruction of approximately 3000 villages and the clearance of mines in order to
recover agricultural land. By the end of the decade, however, as many as 20 per cent
of Kurds were still in the dispiriting *mujamma'at*, Saddam's settlement towns, and
only 20 per cent of Kurds were living in the countryside. This was partly because of
various obstacles in returning to their villages, but it was also because of the high
degree of dependence on the outside assistance. Indeed, the most vulnerable were
those without direct access to rural food production. It was also due to the severely
impaired economy and the difficulty of rebuilding it.

Certain categories were particularly vulnerable. The Anfal had left as many as
100,000 widows, and an even greater number of orphans, many of them seriously
disturbed by their experiences. Without traditional support structures many of these
felt unable to return to their villages. In addition there were large numbers of internally displaced persons. Every conflict between the KDP and PUK generated more
displaced people in addition to over 100,000 people expelled for their political
loyalties from one fiefdom or the other. On its borders, too, Baghdad resumed
arabisation of the Kirkuk region in the late 1990s. Well over a thousand Kurdish
and Turkoman families, perhaps as many as 10,000 people, crossed into the autonomous region during 1998–99. Turkey's forays did not help either. In October 1997,
for example, 10,000 were displaced when troops crossed the border.

The prime effects of the KDP-PUK confrontations were to leave the region politically and economically partitioned with two separate capitals, Arbil and Sulaymaniya, tolls imposed on traffic by the rival forces, and both 'official' and freelance tax extortion and levies. By 1996 unregulated or black-market business was a more important component of the economy than formal activity. Both parties struggled to dominate trade. This adverse situation also led to emigration by those with the resources to escape, mainly the better qualified within the population.

Reconstruction was also complicated by food aid. With the food-for-oil programme, the Kurdish region began to receive about 13 per cent of food imports to Iraq. This was less than its proportionate due but its effect damaged agricultural revival. Anticipating a consequent drop in market prices, many farmers reduced crop production.

In fact, by 1999 the economic situation had indeed substantially improved. Nevertheless, Iraqi Kurdistan continued to suffer major malaise. The population had largely lost confidence in the warring political leaderships upon which it depended, and it was only able to contemplate the future with foreboding, since this would inevitably involve settling with Baghdad.

Sources

Published: Michael Gunter, *The Kurds of Iraq: Tragedy and Hope* (New York, 1992); David Keen, *The Kurds in Iraq: How Safe is Their Haven Now?* (London, 1993); Michael Meadowcroft and Martin Lunn, 'Kurdistan elections for Iraqi Kurdish national Assembly and Leader of the Kurdistan Liberation Movement, Tuesday 19 May – Monitoring Report' (London, June 1992); Middle East Watch, *Endless Torment: The 1991 Uprising in Iraq and its Aftermath* (New York, 1992); Pax Christi International, 'Elections in Iraqi Kurdistan' (Brussels, 1992); Sarah Graham-Brown, *Sanctioning Saddam: The Politics of Intervention in Iraq* (London, 1999); Jonathan Randal, *After Such Knowledge, What Forgiveness? My encounters with Kurdistan encounters with Kurdistan* (New York, 1997); Nederland-Koerdistan Stichting, *Iraqi Kurdistan 1991–96: Political Crisis and Humanitarian Aid* (Amsterdam, 1996)

Newspapers, etc. Institut Kurde de Paris, *Bulletin de liaison and d'information, Christian Science Monitor, The Financial Times, The Guardian, The Independent, International Herald Tribune, Liberation, Middle East Journal, Le Monde, New York Times, The Observer, Pesh Merga, The Turkish News, Wall Street Journal,* Washington Kurdish Institute, daily press bulletins.

Unpublished: Kurdistan Front 'Mashru al jubha al Kurdistaniya al Iraqiya li'l hukm al dhad li'l iqulim Kurdistan' (n.p. 12 May 1991); John Rogge. 'Report on the medium and longer term resettlement and reintegration of displaced persons and returning refugees in the proposed Kurdish autonomous region of Iraq' (Report for UNDP, Manitoba University, Winnipeg, July 1991); Mansur Sajjadi, 'State of economy in Kurdistan' (SOAS, London, April 1991); Patriotic Union of Kurdistan, 'Memorandum on the recent developments in Iraqi Kurdistan' (n.p., 29 May 1994), Kurdistan Democratic Party, 'What happened in Iraqi Kurdistan?' (n.p., June 1994).

Interviews: Sami Abd al Rahman (London, 21 January 1991 and Rawanduz, 12 October 1991); Siyamand Banna (Zakho, 1 October 1991); Massad Barzani (London, 21July 1989, Salah al Din, 10 October 1991); Karim Khan Baradusti (London, 18 February 1992); Tom Hardie-Forsyth (Cranleigh, 10 October 1993); Fuad Masum (Shaqlawa, 10 October 1991); Adnan

Mufti (Shaqlawa/Sulaymaniya, 3–9 October 1991); Adil Murad (London, 26, 29 July, 2 August 1993); Nawshirwan Mustafa Amin (London, 1 July 1993); Husayn Surchi (London, 18 February, 1992); Dr Mahmud Uthman (London, 11 November 1992); Hoshyar Zibari (London, 18 July and 30 August 1990, 13 July 1993).

Notes

1. Interview with Masud Barzani, London 21 July 1989.
2. *International Herald Tribune*, 25 January 1991.
3. Britain had feared this during the 1998 Iraqi revolution, FO 371/134255 Chancery to FO, Istanbul, 18 July 1998.
4. Turkey lost substantial revenue from its transit trade (Iraqi oil to its Mediterranean outlet, and a heavy road haulage business).
5. Christian Science Monitor, 15 March 1991.
6. Between 27 February and 4 March KF forces launched 50 attacks on army positions or targets, Agence France Press (AFP) 4 March 1991.
7. *The Independent*, 24 April 1991.
8. Burhan Jaf to AFP, 4 March 1991.
9. Interview with Husayn Surchi and Karim Khan Baradusti, London, 18 Feruary 1992. It will be recalled that Abbas Marmand was closely involved in the 1961 rebellion. By now he was an old man, but younger members of his family presumably took a lead.
10. These are most notably Lattu and Arshad Zibari. Others who fled to Baghdad included Qasim Agha of Koi-Sanjaq, responsible for the deaths of many peshmergas and therefore unwilling to trust the Kurdish amnesty.
11. *Wall Street Journal*, 14 March and *The Financial Times*, 3 April 1991.
12. *International Herald Tribune*, 30 March 1991.
13. Rafet Balli of Milliyet, in *The Independent*, 3 April 1993.
14. *The Independent*, 7 April 1991.
15. *The Independent*, 11 April 1991.
16. Up to 100,000, *The Independent*, 5 April 1991.
17. Barham Sulih, *The Observer*, 21 April 1991.
18. For the Kurdistan Front's demands, see its 'Mashru al jubha al Kurdistaniya al Iraqiya li'l hukm al dhati li'l iqlim Kurdistan', 12 May 1991.
19. It was the PUK which laid heaviest emphasis on the claim to Kirkuk, Khaniqin and Mandali because they fell within its perceived political orbit. Sinjar was of greater interest to the KDP particularly the KFDP of Sami Abd al Rahman, himself a native of Sinjar
20. The fate of Sinjar, Aqra, Shaykhan, Khaniqin and Kirkuk still remained unresolved.
21. The Foreign Secretary, Douglas Hurd, had called for 'a decent autonomy for the Kurds within the borders of Iraq but would not assist that process. *The Times*, 3 May 1991. See also the reported US memorandum on a 'permanent, secure, autonomous Kurdish region' in *The Independent* 4 May 1991, on the EC's position see *The Independent*, 30 April, 11, 20 and 24 June 1991; *The Observer*, 30 June 1991.
22. At a planning meeting on 9 May, as Kurds were only beginning to enter into the 'safe haven', General Shalikashvili announced the US intention of leaving the area at the beginning of June. This caused consternation to British officers who managed to secure a postponement of three weeks during which time they set up a mobile support team. Interview with Tom Hardie-Forsyth, Cranleigh, 10 October 1993.
23. *The Independent*, 26 June 1991.
24. Interview with Siyamand Banna, Zakhu, 1 October 1993.
25. *The Independent*, 25 June 1991.
26. Middle East Watch, *Dictionary of Repression*, p. 125.

27. See *The Independent*, 13, 20 and 24 September, 9 October 1991 and 25 January 1992; The Observer, 29 October 1991.

28. 1,000 tons of wheat flour compared with a monthly allowance prior to October of 9,600 tons, The Independent, 19 and 25 January 1992.

29. Interview with Husayn Surchi, London, 18 February 1992.

30. Al Huyat, 22 December 1991, quoted by Gunter, *The Kurds of Iraq*, p. 89.

31. *The Independent*, 25 January 1992.

32. For example, Husayn Surchi, Karim Khan Baradusti, Muhammad Asad Fattah Agha Harki and Farhan Hajji Agha Shamdin Sulayvani, whose careers had been shaped by feuds with the Barzanis.

33. Including Kurdish Hizb Allah led by Shaykh Muhammad Khalid Barzani (son of Shaykh Ahmad, Masud's uncle) and the Kurdistan Union of Clergy led by Mulla Hamid of Sirsank.

34. The Iraqi National Turkoman Party claims there are 2.5 million Turkomans in Iraq, of whom 50,000 are currently in exile.

35. Kurdistan Christian Unity (KDP), Democratic Christians (PUK), Kaldo-Ashur Democratic List (ICP).

36. After the re-allocation of votes for parties under the 7 per cent threshold, the KDP had 50.8 per cent and the PUK 49.2 per cent. Some irregularities were found on both sides, but it was also recognised that hall all Kirkuk been included, then the PUK would probably have polled virtually the same number of votes as the KDP.

37. Keen, The Kurds in Iraq, p. 33 and statement of Mr Maz van der Stoel, Special Rapporteur on Iraq, 50th Session of the Commission of Human Rights, 28 February 1994.

38. See Keen, *The Kurds in Iraq*, pp. 34–53.

39. Baghdad badly needed th crop itself, not only on account of the international blockade but also because the Kurdish region produced approximately half Iraq's wheat crop and one third of its barley.

40. For example, in April 1992 when Iraqi forces had shelled villages and towns along the Greater Zab, triggering the flight of 40,000 people, turkey was unwilling to allow the Coalition to strike back to protect the Kurdish civilians.

41. *The Independent*, 25 July 1992.

42. Sami Abd al Rahman, for example, had been very hostile to the idea of Turkish annexation at the height of the Gulf crisis, interview with the author, London, 21 January 1991.

43. Quoted by The Independent, 16 November 1992.

44. The KDP took 86 per cent of the Dohuk vote while the PUK took Sulaymania and Kirkuk with 60 per cent in both governorates, compared with KDP's 27 per cent. Arbil governorate was evenly divided. The KSP attracted most votes in Sulaymania and very few elsewhere. The KPDP only polled significantly in Dohuk. The ICP mangaged 3 per cent in Arbil and Kirkuk, but less than 1 per cent in conservative Duhuk.

45. Mahmud Uthman, interview, London, 11 November 1992.

46. Hawker, no. 8, May 1993.

47. Shaykh Muhammad Khalid, leader of Kurdish Hizb Allah, is Masud Barzani's uncle.

48. The KDP suspected the leaders of the hitherto neutral Surchi tribe of secret alliance with the PUK. This was something the KDP could not afford since the Surchi controlled a section of the strategic Hamilton road to Rawanduz. It therefore attacked the principal Surchi village, killing its chief, Husayn Agha.

49. It established a 2,000-strong force, composed mainly of Turkomans and Assyrians, to monitor an agreed ceasefire line between the two parties.

50. *Middle East International*, No. 551, 30 May 1997.

BOOK V

ETHNO-NATIONALISM
IN TURKEY

CHAPTER 19

THE KURDISH NATIONAL REVIVAL IN TURKEY, 1946–1979

The Revival of Shaykhs and Aghas

Although Turkish Kurdistan had been so totally and brutally subdued during the 1930s, successive governments in Ankara remained curiously sensitive to the Kurdish question. With an almost complete news blackout in Kurdistan it was difficult to know how far Kurdish irredentism survived the Kemalist bulldozer. Rumours of Bolshevik-encouraged risings in eastern Anatolia filtered out in late summer 1940, but more substantive reports would undoubtedly have reached Iran or Iraq had they been of any significance. In spring 1945 there were, apparently, Kurdish meetings in Diyarbakir and Giavar at which troops made arrests and hanged 120 chiefs. But if such events testified to the durability of Kurdish sentiment, they testified even more to the firmness of the government's grip.

However, Ankara remained nervous. Nothing illustrated its anxieties more clearly than its almost hysterical concern expressed at the Soviet decision to invite a hanatul of Iranian Kurds to Baku in November 1941. In summer 1946 the government was again transferring Kurds westwards and even northwards to Kars and Ardahan. Denial was still the order of the day. An article in *Son Posta* dated 11 April 1946 echoed the establishment view, 'In Turkey no Kurdish minority ever existed either nomadic or settled, with national consciousness or without it.'

Yet, in struggling with the political, social and economic problems which beset it from 1945, the Turkish state created the very conditions in which a combustion of national and social ideas could eventually take place in Kurdistan.

Until 1946 the single party system bequeathed by Mustafa Kemal, and the indirect electoral system whereby a college of electors chose the representatives for the Grand National Assembly, allowed the Republican People's Party (RPP) and a chosen local elite to maintain power. By 1945, however, this authoritarian system was in crisis, under increasing challenge from within the party.

In January 1946, a group of RPP schismatics were allowed to form an opposition, the Democratic Party. With the creation of political pluralism the floodgates were opened to many pent-up feelings repressed under the Kemalist system, and it was inevitable that the new Democratic Party should become in part a vehicle for those who wanted revenge.

With their sights set on the elections scheduled for 1950, the Democrats wooed votes on the idea of greater civic freedom. Above all, they knew that there was a potent reservoir of pent-up resentment over the Kemalist religious reforms, especially in the countryside where over 80 per cent of the population lived. A generation after the abolition of the caliphate and the suppression of the *tariqas*, formal 'official' Islam seemed in retreat, but the same could not be said of folk Islam. It was well known, for example, that the Sufi brotherhoods operated underground, and nowhere more so than in Kurdistan.

Well aware of how many votes the shaykhs and their followers could deliver, the Democrats were quick to exploit this feeling and openly advocate religious freedom. In January 1947, fearing that it would be outflanked on the religious question, the RPP allowed religious instruction in schools and gave permission for Muslim schools to be established alongside state schools. But such concessions did little to offset its reputation as the party that had dismantled the Sunni state, and the shaykhs instructed their followers accordingly. Said Nursi, for example, exhorted his followers to support the Democrats in 1950. He was not alone: the Mawlana Khalid Naqshbandi movement around Bitlis and Khizan with which, of course, Said Nursi had close links, also supported the Democrats, as did many Qadiris. The Democrats had tapped into a network which criss-crossed Anatolia, and nowhere more thickly than in the east.

After its victory, the Democrat Party was careful to maintain a position consistent with the accepted values of the Kemalist state, but allowing a degree of freedom. Able to portray itself as champion of a Turkish nationalism which had 'rediscovered' its historical and religious roots,[1] the party rewarded the faithful among its supporters with moves to bring Islam back into the heart of national identity. Almost immediately after its victory Article 526 of the penal code was amended to allow muezzins to recite the call to prayer in Arabic. A few days later religious radio broadcasts were permitted and for the first time the Quran could be heard on Turkish radio. In October 1950 religious instruction in school was made virtually compulsory; by 1960 the construction of 5,000 mosques had been financed.

Undeniably the Democrat Party was stringent with zealots who tried to take more in the way of concessions to religious feeling than the government had offered. It dealt severely with members of the Ticani, Naqshbandi and Qadiri orders in 1951 after several of the ubiquitous Ataturk statues and busts that adorned each town in Turkey had been defaced. It closed down a Muslim Democrat Party in 1952 as illegal, and it restrained the activities of Said Nursi's Nurculuk throughout the 1950s.

Yet its strategy undoubtedly assisted the revival of traditional Islamic values at the heart of the state. Apart from the lands around Afion–Isparta–Eskischir, it was in Kurdistan that the axis between religious and political solidarities revived most strongly. Thus the Kurdish countryside became once more the stronghold of Islam, an environment hostile to, and dangerous for, radicals of the secular left. The only major exception was Dersim where Alevis feared Sunni revivalism. It is ironic that while in Iraq and Iran, the religious networks of Kurdistan were much reduced by the 1950s and received virtually no encouragement from the state, in secular Turkey the state assisted their political as well as religious revival, giving the Kurdish shaykhs both material and moral support. The majority of Sunni Kurds felt closer to Sunni Turks than they did to Alevi Kurds, a factor reassuring to many of the Turkish establishment.

The other strand pursued by the Democrat Party in its quest for power between 1946 and 1950 similarly reached deep into the countryside. Anxious to exploit the sense of grievance against the RPP, the Democrat Party decided to co-opt the old agha class which had suffered so heavily since 1923. Even those aghas in exile still held title to lands in Kurdistan, for in 1926 the republic confirmed private land from the Ottoman period and also vested aghas and peasants with the title to lands they customarily controlled and used.

The agha was still intermediary between illiterate villagers and the outside world. It was irrelevent that the state had abolished the class distinctions of 'agha', 'beg' or 'shaykh'. These families still operated the village guesthouse, the focus of rural life, and still mediated individual or collective village difficulties with local officials. Not much had changed since Ziya Gokalp's description half a century earlier (page 95).

It was not as if the RPP had wholly eschewed the aghas. It may have exiled large numbers, but it also kept its own stable of notables, ones who would serve the regime against its enemies. Those families that supported the regime tended to do so not for any ideological reason, but to acquire material advantage or worst a local rival. In the critical period, 1920–22, for example, the Perincoglu of Diyarbakir were quick to ingratiate themselves with the Kemalists in order to destroy the more powerful Cemioglu whose Kurdish national sentiments made them reluctant to co-operate with Mustafa Kemal.[2] With the emergence of an opposition party in 1946, the RPP had recognized the dangers of leaving a large notable class in exile. In 1947 it allowed 2,000 exiled agha families to return to their former lands. As the RPP may have forseen, the Democrats exploited the profoundly bitter feelings of the exiles and specifically wooed those with significant tribal or peasant retinues. When it was swept to power in 1950, a substantial proportion of its vote came from this constituency, lately exiled aghas forming a significant element in the new Grand National Assembly (GNA).[3]

There was one further dimension to the co-optation of the agha class. Large numbers of them were closely connected with the shaykhs, either because they were shaykh-landlords themselves or because they were linked by marriage or by discipleship to shaykhly families. Kamran Inan, for example, who became a Democrat deputy in 1954 was the son of Shaykh Salah al Din of Khizan, who was exiled after the Shaykh Said rebellion.[4] Kinyas Kartal, to cite another example, was a tribal agha who became a disciple of Said Nursi during years of exile and was elected deputy for Van in the 1960s.[5]

The Democrats based their appeal not only on greater civic freedom but also on economic liberalism, an area in which they directly challenged the etatism of the Kemalist era. Until 1945 the countryside had largely escaped state interventionism and, particularly in the war years, many large landlords had made fortunes out of their cereal-producing estates. That year the RPP turned its attention to the land question, and introduced a Land Reform Bill. Its purpose was to achieve the full and effective use of arable land by allocating adequate amounts to peasants who either had too little or none at all. In fact most land for reallocation was state or old *waqf* land and properties over 50 hectares, but there were a good number of such landlords in the south-east. Such was its unpopularity among a largely landed Assembly that only strict party discipline ensured that the bill was passed, and the RPP retreated from its implementation, amending it in 1950 under the pressure of multi-party politics, in order not to lose landlords who controlled the rural votes.

However, the land reform debate had been a critical episode in the split of the future Democrat nucleus from the RPP. From 1946 onwards the Democrats presented themselves as the party of private property, and made agriculture the cornerstone of their electoral appeal, arguing that large estates would be most productive and profitable. They were able to point not only to the half-hearted RPP land reform but also to its weaknesses. For example, they argued that most state land distributed to peasants, 1945–50, had previously been village communal grazing land and that the newly landed peasantry often acquired soil barely adequate for arable purposes, while many others found themselves deprived of grazing facilities.

It was not difficult to win people over. The Democrats got *fatwas* from shaykhs indicating the sanctity of private property in Islam. It was a mess which the Democrats exploited, but with the aghas firmly in mind. These represented a coherent and small target group. The province of Diyarbakir, for example, was electorally controlled by fewer than twenty landlords. In the 1954 election the Democrats captured 34 out of the 40 seats in Kurdistan.

Had there been an educated peasantry, an informed public debate could have taken place in which the Democrat appeal to the sanctity of private property, conveniently confirmed by Muslim clerics across the country, might have been countered by the potential social and economic benefits of smaller scale farming. But the peasantry were deeply subservient to their landlords in Kurdistan. Indeed, it was natural for the Kurdish peasantry to view land reform as proposed by the Kemalist party at best with suspicion, at worst as yet another ploy to destroy the old solidarities of Kurdistan. So when the Democrat Party promised to protect

THE KURDISH NATIONAL REVIVAL IN TURKEY 399

the big landlords, the Kurdish peasantry who had most to gain from an intelligent land reform voted for it as instructed by their agha landlords.

The Democrat government enthusiastically supported agricultural development, but for them this meant land reclamation, large 'efficient' estates and mechanization. It was the introduction of tractors which provided the next step in a process which laid the socio-economic groundwork for the explosion of Kurdish nationalism in the 1980s. Post-war Marshall Aid allowed the government to import tractors regardless of the social consequences. In 1948 the country had only 1,750 tractors. In 1950 the floodgates opened and twelve months later there were 10,000. The US-based International Bank reckoned any more tractors would dislocate small farmers and tenants. But more did come: by 1953 there were 30,000 and a year later 40,000.

Nowhere was mechanization so extensively used as in Kurdistan. Small and tenant farmers, with plots that could not justify ownership of a tractor, found themselves having to hire tractors against a proportion of the crop from local large landowners. In practice, as the Kurdish novelist Yasar Kemal observed, 'The peasant is again share-cropping on the lands distributed by the Government: *he provides the land, the agha provides the tractor* [his emphasis].'[6] Those that managed a living as share-croppers but retained their land were arguably the more fortunate. Many small farmers and landholders ended up selling off their land to the tractor-owning magnates *and* being put out of work. The relatively lucky ones remained as agricultural labourers or mechanics for the infernal machinery that had impoverished them.

However, the aghas held back from maximizing the use of agricultural machinery and tended to maintain a larger retinue of share-croppers than strictly necessary. In many cases the recently landless were provided with small plots, just large enough to dissuade them from migrating to the employment uncertainties of urban life. The reason was simple. The aghas still needed voting power in order to remain attractive to the political parties that arranged easy credits, technology, fertilizers, improved seed strains, agricultural access roads and so forth. It was easy for them to remind their peasants of the dangers of defying their electoral instructions, but sweeteners such as the promise of a school, piped water or electrification were also used from time to time. By the early 1960s rural 'employment' in fact disguised heavy seasonal unemployment, for 80 per cent of the population had no activity during the quietest time of year, January, compared with only 10 per cent unemployment at the peak period in July.

With the economic downturn in the mid-1950s, the RPP and other smaller parties ate into the Democrats' rural Kurdish constituency, wooing some aghas and their captive electorate away. The Democratic Party lost over a quarter of a million votes in Kurdistan between 1957 and 1961. Its rivals made their inroads, just as the Democrats had done, by promising each loyal locality roads, tractors, electrification, the construction of schools, and in the case of the more clericalist and right-wing Republican Peasants Nation Party, mosques

It was inevitable that the parties based in Ankara should seek to exploit the tensions and rivalries in different districts. If one family supported the Democrats, its rival would support the other. In fact party competition had such a divisive impact that following the military intervention of 27 May 1960, the National Unity Committee (NUC) closed down local party branches because they had so polarized villages and small towns that tea houses and other communal areas became the fiefdoms of particular 'political tribes', places of physical danger to supporters of their rivals.

The National Unity Committee was also alarmed by the process of land accumulation in the hands of the Kurdish aghas and the political power that accompanied it. In 1960 they banished 55 aghas from Kurdistan, and announced they would distribute their lands to the peasantry.[7] Had the NUC expropriated a larger number of aghas and implemented a full land redistribution, it might have broken the aghas' political power and restructured the rural economy of Kurdistan. But the aghas resorted to delaying tactics and enlisted the help of their political friends to soften the terms of exile and expropriation. Shortly after the NUC handed government back to a coalition civil administration in 1961, these aghas were allowed to return to Kurdistan where their estates were restored to them virtually untouched. It was a telling commentary on the powerful axis of mutual dependence that now existed between the political parties in Ankara and the aghas of Kurdistan. Indeed, the aghas ceased to be Kurdish in two vital senses: they quietly disowned their Kurdish origin, and they exploited their relationship with the peasantry not as a means to semi-independence from the centre as in the old days, but in order to become more closely integrated members of the ruling Turkish establishment.

During the next two decades the aghas and shaykhs continued to play an active role in the political and economic life of the region. After the return to civil administration, those who had previously supported the Democrats now tended to support the Justice Party, although a few opted for more right-wing groups, like the Turkish Nation Party. As before, the parties competed heavily for the more influential landlord families, and once again towns and rural areas were divided in their loyalties. In Siverek, for example, the Bucaks supported the Justice Party, the rival Kirvars the RPP. In Hilvan (near Urfa) the Sulaymans supported the Justice Party, and the Paydar the RPP.

For the peasantry things got progressively worse. Per capita income and literacy in Kurdistan were substantially lower than elsewhere. On the whole the country people lived in comparatively small villages which reflected the decentralized nature of society. According to one count there were 36,000 settlements in Kurdistan with fewer than 2,000 people. In 1973 a Guardian journalist visited one such settlement outside Siverek, and sketched his vignette:

Annazo's 20 families are landless. They receive free homes and half the earnings of the harvest in return for cultivating cotton, wheat, fruit trees and other crops. The real power in the region is held by big landowners.... They function as unelected justices of the peace, mayors and social workers in villages that lack any other governmental authority. Also they are often the only link between the village and the Government institutions in towns nearby.[8]

The Bucaks were the local landlord clan, reportedly owning a total of 60 villages. While the Bucak owner of Annazo, Yuksel Erdal Oral,

looks after family interests in Siverek, his father looks after the interests of the region and the Bucaks as a Senator in Ankara.... Landowners like Yuksel are the [Justice] party's link with the villages that would otherwise be well beyond its reach.... On election day headmen and landlords round up villagers and take them voting. Bucaks boast they can deliver 8,000 votes at the polls. With that kind of influence, the family virtually picks its own district representative in Ankara.

By the late 1980s many share-croppers, for example on the large cotton estates, found themselves earning less than half what they could earn a decade earlier for a ten-hour day.

On the whole, most aghas drifted away from their villages, leaving them in the hands of local agents while they enjoyed life either in a local town or possibly in Ankara. With an adequate income from their fiefdoms, most neglected their estates. The sons of aghas tended to acquire a taste for the cosmopolitan pleasures of Ankara or Istanbul. Sometimes one son would remain to manage the estate, while others qualified as doctors, lawyers or engineers.

Migration and Demography

Hundreds of thousands of Kurds abandoned the land as a result of the massive mechanization of Turkish Kurdistan in the 1950s, joining those who had been resettled during the revolts of the 1920s and 1930s, and those whose pastoralism had been deliberately disrupted by the state during the 1930s. Most of these, for example, the deportees from Dersim, had been integrated into the industrial proletariat of Malatya, Adana, Sivas and Kaysari. Many Kurdish conscripts also sought their fortune in western Anatolia to which they were routinely posted, after their discharge. Indeed, although military service was generally unpopular and evaded, some Kurds enlisted in order to learn Turkish and thus be equipped to live in the West where jobs could more easily be found.

Most of those leaving rural areas in the 1950s and after sought employment in a local town, and only moved beyond Kurdistan subsequently. Thus by the mid-1960s they were converging mainly on Diyarbakir (25 per cent of migrants), Elazig (16 per cent), Siirt (15 per cent) and Urfa (8 per cent).[9] The population of Diyarbakir grew prodigiously over the years, from 30,000 in the 1930s to about 65,000 by 1956, 140,000 in 1970 and 400,000 by 1990. Of those migrants who moved beyond Kurdistan, approximately 41 per cent went to Istanbul, 18 per cent to Ankara, 15 per cent to Adana and 4 per cent to Izmir. Over the years the number of migrants greatly increased, and the fact that they tended to live in close proximity with each other established permament strongholds of Kurdish identity across the republic. In due course the existence of these communities was to make the Kurdish question a visible reality even for the citizens of Istanbul, 800 miles away from Kurdistan.

It might be thought that the beginning of major emigration from Turkish Kurdistan would have led to a measurable decline in population growth in the east. However the statistics indicate that the Kurdish community had a significantly higher birthrate than Turks. This had first become noticeable by a comparison of the republic's first two census figures, for 1927 and 1935.[10] Between 1940 and 1965 the Kurdish population of those provinces where they constituted a majority doubled, while the Turkish minority increased by barely 80 per cent. Government statistics for the latter year indicated that while 41 per cent of the republic's population were under the age of 15, in Kurdistan the figure was 48 per cent.

Here, for a state determined to stamp out Kurdish communal identity, were real grounds for apprehension. So, in spite of the inherent problems of Turkey's population growth, the state blocked the introduction of family plannning except in a very limited way, because it would more probably be adopted in the Turkish west of the country, and thus accelerate the changing demographic balance in favour of the Kurds.

The Nationalist Revival

These were the socio-economic changes which were eventually to play a key role in the burgeoning national movement in the 1980s. This movement was borne by economic deprivation, social injustice and physical displacement as well as ideas of ethnic identity, all of which combined in the late 1970s to create the conditions for revolt.

In the oppressive circumstances of the mid-1950s, however, when a deeply ignorant peasantry was held in thrall by its aghas, it is hardly surprising there was barely a glimmer of national feeling. As a young diplomat, Anthony Parsons spent three weeks touring Turkish Kurdistan in the autumn of 1956, meeting Kurds and travelling widely. 'I did not catch the faintest breath of Kurdish nationalism which the most casual observer in Iraq cannot fail to notice,' he reported.[11]

However, national revival was already beginning in the cities of Kurdish migration. The first to raise the question of their Kurdishness were those whose assimilation had been deliberately intended. Musa Anter, for example, had been sent from Mardin to boarding school in Adana. As the only Kurd in his class he had learnt his identity through mockery, an experience repeated among many exiles who went to local schools. Mahmut Altunakar of the True Path Party recalled a similar experience:

Until I arrived in Kutahya I did not know I was Kurdish. We used to throw stones at those calling us Kurds in Diyarbakir. We came to Kutahya and they called us Kurds. They baited us with 'Where is your tail?' Going to school was an ordeal. Then we understood our villagers were right, we were Kurds.[12]

Anter was sent to study law in Istanbul in 1941, one of several of the brightest, handpicked by the First Inspectorate General (covering most of Kurdistan) to be turned into good Turkish citizens. He was lodged in a special hostel for students from the east, where he made contact with fifty or so other young intellectuals from different parts of Kurdistan. Among these were Tarik Ziya Ekinci, subsequently secretary-general of the Turkish Workers Party, Yusif Azizoglu, Democrat deputy and founder of the Turkish Nation Party, and Faik Bucak, founder of the Democratic Party of Turkish Kurdistan (KDPT). Thus in Ankara and Istanbul, alongside migrant workers, small but highly articulate groups of educated Kurds gathered to form the intellectual spearhead of Kurdish identity.

At the end of the 1950s this small body of intellectuals began to be encouraged by external developments. From Cairo and Yerevan Kurdish language broadcasts were beamed across the region, the former aimed at unsettling Baghdad, the latter at unsettling Ankara and Tehran also. But easily the most critical impetus to Kurdish feeling came from the Iraqi Revolution in July 1958 and the return from exile of Mulla Mustafa. It was not lost on many Turkish Kurds that he was a Kurmanji like themselves.

Earlier that year Musa Anter and others had begun publishing *Ileri Yurt* (Forward Country) in Diyarbakir. It marked the beginning of almost a decade of Kurdish publications, and the first Kurdish self-expression in Turkey since the Dersim revolt. It was the beginning of *Doguculuk* ('Eastism'), the campaign to develop Turkey's woefully neglected Kurdish provinces. On the whole the Eastists, including several deputies, were careful to avoid open reference to Kurds or Kurdistan, but no one with any knowledge of the region could doubt what was in their minds.

Events in Iraq now began to affect Turkish–Kurdish relations. Following the massacre of Turkomans by Kurds in Kirkuk in March 1959 Arsim Erin, the deputy for Nigde, openly exhorted revenge: 'Kurds killed our brothers, come let us kill as many Kurds as they killed Turkomans. Are you not going to repay with interest?'[13] Over 80 Kurdish students, organized by a young law-yer, Meded Serhat, demonstrated in protest and this in turn led to the arrest of 49 leading Kurdish intellectuals. *Ileri Yurt* was closed down, Anter and his colleagues were among those arrested.[14] President Bayar and Prime Minister Menderes, as well as the security police, wanted the 49 hanged. It was the likelihood of adverse international reaction which discouraged them.[15] The '49' episode dramatically raised national awareness among literate Kurds, especially when Sait Elci, one of the 49, defended the individual and collective rights of Kurds in court

The state authorities were extremely disturbed by growing Kurdish defiance in Iraq and the expression it seemed to encourage in Turkey. In May 1960 certain aghas had led their peasantry in protest against government neglect during a deepening period of drought. How far it had genuinely nationalist overtones is difficult to say, but the authorities took fright and accused them of agitating for a free Kurdistan. Those deemed leaders of the unrest, 248 individuals in all, were taken to a camp in Sivas. In November most were released under the National Unity Committee's amnesty, except for the celebrated 55 aghas and shaykhs exiled to Afion, Isparta, Antalya and Izmir under a new law of exile passed in October. Publicly the NUC spoke of breaking the feudal system, but since only six of those exiled were large landowners, it remained doubtful whether this was the real motive.

The Democrat Party was widely blamed for allowing the Kurds to get out of hand. *Cumhuriyet* preposterously claimed 'The late Government permitted Shaykh Said's son to go around the east in a Russian military jeep making his propaganda. The purpose was a new Kurdistan.'[16] Certainly this is what the NUC feared, little recognizing that the agha class was bound to become increasingly peripheral to the Kurdish movement.

The Turkish state under the NUC adopted a much more doctrinaire policy of denial towards the Kurds. When the quarrel between Qasim and Mulla Mustafa in autumn 1960 brought the prospect of war close to Turkey's border, President Gursel (who had led the military coup) warned against unrest, 'The army will not hesitate to bombard towns and villages: there will be such a bloodbath that they [any rebels] will be swallowed up in their country.'[17]

It was with feelings excited on both sides, that events built up to the greatest demonstration of Kurdish identity for a generation. By Law No. 1587 the NUC had already started systematically to change Kurdish place names into Turkish ones, 'names which hurt public opinion and are not suitable for our national culture, moral values, traditions and customs'. In January 1961 it enacted another law providing for the establishment of regional boarding schools with the specific intention of assimilating Kurds, just as had been recommended back in 1935.[18] President Gursel had just written a foreword to the second edition of M. Sherif Firat's *Dogu Illeri ve Varto Tarihi* (Ankara, 1948, 1961). This argued that the Kurds were in fact of Turkish origin and that there was no such thing as the Kurdish nation. Firat's book was convincing to the public because, besides the book's sentiments being endorsed by the president, Firat was himself a Kurd.[19] President Gursel now declared that no nation exists with a personality of its own, calling itself Kurdish, and noted that the Kurds were not only compatriots, but also racial brothers of the Turks.

On 8 May, within a few days of this denial of Kurdish national identity, major protest demonstrations took place in Mardin, Diyarbakir, Siverek, Bitlis and Van. Young Kurds held banners aloft proclaiming 'We are not Turks, We are Kurds.... The Turkish Government must recognize our national rights.'[20] According to

Kurdish sources, 315 demonstrators were shot dead, and another 754 wounded.[21] Only the most blinkered observer could fail to recognize the growing antiphony between state denial and national expression.

Yet the National Unity Committee was not of one mind. Within it there was a struggle between hardliners and moderates. Despite his attitude to the Kurds, Gursel supported a return to civilian rule and showed his readiness to allow Turkey to become a liberal democracy. He handed the task of drafting a new constitution to a group of intellectuals, a remarkable act for any general. On 27 May 1961, only 19 days after the bloody events in Kurdistan, the NUC enacted the most liberal constitution in the republic's history, which permitted freedom of thought, expression, association and publication, promised social and economic rights, and even granted trade unions limited rights to strike.

Naturally enough, Kurdish intellectuals tested the new dispensation. Although significantly more liberal than before, they soon found it fell short of its promise. In Istanbul Musa Anter, now free again, wrote for a new monthly bi-lingual (Turkish/Kurdish) journal, *Dicle–Firat* (Tigris–Euphrates) which ran to eight issues during 1962–63 before being stopped. Another intellectual, Yasha Kayar, together with Meded Serhat, both 'Forty-niners' like Anter, published *Deng* (Voice). Serhat was arrested after the second issue, and *Deng* itself closed down after its third issue. Serhat was, predictably, charged with separatism, the standard accusation of those who suggested Kurds also live in Turkey. Other journals had similarly brief lives,[22] and in summer 1963 their editors and leading contributors were arrested, and denounced as 'communists and separatists'.[23]

Of greater significance, however, was the debate now carried into the mainstream of Turkish intellectual life by a liberal Turk, Ahmet Hamdi Bashar in his journal *Barish Dunyasi* (World of Peace).[24] In its second issue in May 1962 *Barish Dunyasi* included an article which argued that no real development could take place in 'the East', while certain subjects are forbidden, or in a context of prohibition and violence. It argued that how people felt was crucial, and that therefore social mechanisms and spiritual outlets were important for local people, a coded plea for tolerance of the aghas and shaykhs until a more modern social system evolved. *Barish Dunyasi* threw the issue open in its ensuing editions, encouraging debate between state officials and Kurdish intellectuals. It attracted denunciation from both Left and Right for the views to which it allowed expression. In the end its willingness to permit a free debate led to its demise after its sixteenth issue in September 1963. But no one could pretend the 'Kurdish question' did not exist.

As in Iraq and Iran, politically-minded Kurds were faced with the dilemma of whether to work within the political framework of the country, or to oppose it. Among the former category Kurds were to be found across the political spectrum. Ismet Inonu, president from Ataturk's death in 1938 until the Democrat victory in 1950, was said to be a Kurd. So too were Admiral Fehmi Koruturk who became president following the 1971 military intervention, and General Semih

Sancar, chief of staff in the mid-1970s. Others deviated from strict Kemalism either to the Left or the Right, for example Yusif Azizoglu (Diyarbakir) who was one of the exiled aghas brought back by the Democrats in the 1940s, Ekrem Alican (Erzerum) and Shaykh Kasim Kufrevi (Kars), all of whom left the Democrats to found the Freedom Party (1955–58) taking many Kurds with them.

After the dissolution of the Democrat Party in 1960, the Right fragmented until the mid-1960s. Azizoglu and Alican led the New Turkey Party, founded after the 1960 coup, until its demise following the general election of 1965. Azizoglu inclined to the Right but, like leaders of the Justice Party, he played for the return of the 55 aghas in 1962 in order to attract their vote. He already enjoyed a substantial following in Kurdistan. Azizoglu expressed his 'Eastism' as Minister of Health in the shortlived second coalition of 1961–62. During that period he built more hospitals and dispensaries in Kurdistan than all previous administrations put together. He was soon accused of 'regionalism', in spite of Kurdistan's manifest backwardness, and forced to resign. In the 1965 election the few votes the NTP obtained were almost exclusively in Kurdistan.

The agha class on the whole tended towards the Justice Party, which had inherited the democratic mantle. During the early 1960s, however, the RPP clawed back a following among the great families of the region in spite of its increasingly centrist, according to some, leftist, character. It was the most plausible challenger to the Justice Party.

The first specifically Kurdish party, the Democratic Party of Turkish Kurdistan (KDPT) was born within this conservative ambience. Naturally it was an underground organization, since a Kurdish party by definition was illegal. KDPT was the ideological equivalent of Mulla Mustafa's KDP, purely nationalist and unwilling to examine the inherent tensions between ethnic nationalism, social traditionalism and social development. Yet, unlike Iraq's KDP, KDPT was destined to disappear virtually without trace. At face value this was because its founding secretary, Faik Bucak (from the great agha family of Siverek), was assassinated in July 1966, eight months after the party's foundation and his close colleague and successor, Sait Elci, was executed by a leftist schismatic in 1971.[25]

Yet beyond these setbacks lay the fact that from 1965 to 1971 the KDPT failed to put down strong roots where its cells existed. Probably the reason lay in the very conservatism of its ideology. Bucak and Elci had previously subscribed to the rightist values of mainstream Turkish politics. Consequently they appealed to a conservative society, one loyal to the aghas who 'looked after their interests' in Ankara. In such a context KDPT had little to offer.

The 1961 constitution allowed, for the first time in the republic's history, for the establishment of a socialist party, the Turkish Workers' Party. The TWP became important under its leader Mehmet Ali Aybar and took 3 per cent of the vote in 1965. Predictably the TWP attracted police obstruction and disruption. The TWP was highly attractive to many Kurds as the political atmosphere acquired a more strongly rightist flavour. The closure of one Kurdish or leftist journal after another was a symptom which thoughful Kurds could hardly ignore. While the state denied that Kurds were anything but Turks, many Turks denied even this fiction by repudiating them. To be Kurdish was, as being Turkish had been a century earlier, to be a primitive rustic or, worse, a Caliban. 'Where is your tail?' Kutahya school children had teased Mehmet Altunakar at secondary school in the 1930s. Such taunts were commonplace for every exiled Kurd. By the 1960s racism was still overt and undiminished, those living east of Malatya 'being regarded in all but official circles as foreigners'.[26] One journal, *Otuken*, stated 'Kurds do not have the faces of human beings' and advocated their migration to Africa to join the half-human half-animals who lived there. It went on to warn 'They can learn by asking their racial fellows, the Armenians, that the Turks are very patient, but when angry no one can stand in their way.'[27] Others made their hints at genocide more forthright, 'We need a solution [to the Kurdish question] as sharp as a sword. Bring the Cossacks or Kirghiz immigrants with their weapons. This will solve the problem once and for all.'[28] It was only with the Left that Kurds felt they were treated more or less as equals.

However, TWP was also attractive because it offered a means of organizational power for ordinary people, through the party and affiliated unions. The party itself was loathe to embrace the Kurdish question publicly, but many Kurds joined it nevertheless, since it was more willing to listen than any of the parties to the right of it. Some of Anter's old comrades from the Istanbul hostel days of 1941–42 became TWP activists, among them Tarik Ziya Ekinci. In 1965 he was one of four Kurds out of the 15 TWP candidates elected to the Grand National Assembly. Kurds and Alevis became the backbone of the TWP during the late 1960s. Many were attracted to TWP on account of the land ownership question and the grip of the agha class. Others had been attracted by its leftist ideas.

Frustrated with TWP's reticence over the Kurdish question, Ekinci and other colleagues formed autonomous cells within the party from 1966. After he had become party secretary-general in 1968, and a fellow Kurd, Mehmet Ali Aslan, had become party president the following year, a major effort was made to persuade the party to address the Kurdish question head on. Aslan had made a reputation for himself as the editor of *Yeni Akis* which openly advocated recognition of national rights for the Kurds. At TWP's Fourth Congress in October 1970 the party affirmed:

> There is a Kurdish people in the East of Turkey.... The fascist authorities representing the ruling classes have subjected the Kurdish people to a policy of assimilation and intimidation which has often become a bloody repression.[29]

In so doing TWP sounded its own death knell. Following military intervention the following year TWP was declared an illegal organization. However, as far as Kurds were concerned, it had been an effective vehicle for awakening a growing number of young Kurdish students, particularly in Ankara and Istanbul, who in their turn were to provide crucial leadership for the national movement.

The leftist movement had already proliferated, before the demise of TWP. In 1967 certain trade unionists broke away from the government-controlled Turk Is trade union congress to form the Confederation of Revolutionary Workers Unions (DISK). Leftist clubs and societies multiplied in the universities, most of them loosely associated with The Federation of Revolutionary Youth, Dev Genc, founded in 1969 and the cradle from which most of the revolutionary movements of the 1970s were born. (Dev Genc itself was closed down following the coup, but its adherents regrouped.)

In 1967 certain Kurds in DISK, in TWP, Dev Genc or in student associations organized mass meetings, crowds of 10,000 in Silvan and 25,000 in Diyarbakir, protesting against oppression of the Kurds and demanding democratic rights. This was the first real defiance of the state since 1938, but more significantly, it was the first mass *urban* Kurdish challenge to the republic. It signalled the critical shift in social mobilization away from the aghas and semi-tribal peasantry, towards urban-based, modestly educated students and young professionals, including a growing number who were themselves the scions of agha families but who rejected the values they had inherited. These formed the basis of a bourgeois intellectual leadership, largely of mildly leftist inclination, for growing Kurdish national feeling.

In spite of the spate of closures in the early 1960s, Kurds still tried to disseminate material in Kurdish, or in Turkish about Kurdish culture. Educated Kurds understood, just as the state had done, that Kurdish literature was essential to national formation. In response to imported materials the government decreed in 1967 'it is illegal and forbidden to introduce to, or distribute in, the country, materials in the Kurdish language of foreign origin in any form published, recorded, taped or material in similar form.'[30] One or two continued to produce material. Musa Anter produced a Turco–Kurdish dictionary later that year. In 1969 Mehmet Emin Bozarslan was arrested and charged for publishing a Kurdish elementary textbook and also for translating into Turkish and preparing for publication Ahmad Khani's great Kurdish epic *Mem-u-Zin*.

Despite such signs of intellectual unrest, however, it was still possible for those who knew the East intimately to dismiss them as the concern of a small and unrepresentative minority compared with the religious impulse which pervaded Kurdistan. As late as 1969 the sociologist Nur Yalman was able to write:

> It is a matter of considerable good fortune for Turkey that religious affiliations remain more important than linguistic affiliations. If the religious affiliation were weakened, they would have given way possibly to Turkish–Kurdish opposition of a more divisive kind. As it is, this latent structural cleavage is bridged by numerous institutions, among which religious ties play a cardinal role.[31]

Yet during 1969–71 Turkey entered a phase of deep unrest. Turkish and Kurdish trainees returned from Fatah camps in Lebanon to take a lead in the leftist struggle. The increasingly national flavour of leftist rallies in the East was unmistakable. In 1969 a network of cultural clubs were established across Kurdistan, as well as Ankara and Istanbul. These were known as Revolutionary Eastern Cultural Hearths, the DDKO.[32] Most of those belonging to DDKO were either members of TWP or close to it. DDKO stood for civil liberties and national awareness of the neglected state of the East, and sought to establish education programmes for peasants and women, which laid emphasis on political, civil and economic rights. That in turn implied social reform, particularly in the countryside to which they took their message. Above all, as was rapidly realized, DDKO implicitly stood for the Kurdish national movement in Turkey, and it soon became a target for right-wing activists who seemed to operate with the connivance of the state.

In January Ankara despatched commandos to the region to begin searching villages for separatists or signs of separatist activity. Its security operations rapidly became associated with the arbitrary brutality and torture that had marked the suppression of Kurdistan four decades earlier. One commando report actually ran along the following lines:

> Since the end of January special military units have undertaken a land war in the regions of Diyarbakir, Mardin, Siirt and Hakkari under the guise of hunting bandits. Every village is surrounded at a certain hour, its inhabitants rounded up. Troops assemble men and women separately, and demand the men to surrender their weapons. They beat those who deny possessing any or make other villagers jump on them. They strip men and women naked and violate the latter. Many have died in these operations, some have committed suicide. Naked men and women have cold water thrown over them, and they are whipped. Sometimes women are forced to tie a rope around the penis of their husband and then to lead him around the village. Women are likewise made to parade naked around the village. Troops demand villagers to provide women for their pleasure and the entire village is beaten if the request is met with refusal.[33]

The Baath–Barzani Accord in March 1970 heightened Ankara's apprehensions concerning its own Kurds, and this may have partly accounted for the new wave of brutality. For many the commando crackdown was regrettable but necessary. *Yeni Istanbul* ran a series of articles in October and November entitled 'What is happening behind the Mountains' which advocated education and economic improvement but only in conjunction with cultural imperialism, destruction of the tribal system and massive settlement of Turks to alter the character of the East.

In October 1970 DDKO leaders were arrested and major trials took place in Istanbul and Diyarbakir. Among those imprisoned were Musa Anter, Tarik Ziya Ekinci, Sait Elci and a young Turkish sociologist, Ismail Besikci, whose espousal of the Kurdish cause brought him repeated imprisonment at the hands of a government unable to abide a public discussion of its minority question. Under

Besikci's leadership those arrested produced a 150-page defence of Kurdish identity and rights, covering Kurdish history, language and society, the first major statement of its kind. Naturally they lost their case, and several received sentences in excess of ten years. DDKO was closed down.

While the situation in Kurdistan continued to deteriorate, two new leftist groups, the Turkish Popular Liberation Army (TPLA) and the Popular Liberation Front (TPLF) brought matters to a head at the beginning of 1971, raiding banks and abducting US servicemen. On 12 March the army intervened and took over control of the country. Martial law was introduced in twelve of the 67 provinces of the republic, including the major university or industrial cities, and also in Diyarbakir and Siirt. Thousands were rounded up in Kurdistan and detained in Diyarbakir and other prisons. What was interesting was that 75 per cent of those arrested came from the countryside, an indication of how far the rural population now seemed politicized, thanks presumably to the effectiveness of DDKO and local branches of the TWP.

The interior minister gave three reasons for military intervention: the rise of the extreme leftists and urban guerrillas; the response of the extreme rightists and 'those wanting dictatorship'; and finally, the separatist question in the East where he said a large number of weapons had been found. He accused Mulla Mustafa of assisting the separatists, and the latter of forming a Kurdish Independence Party.

In 1973, with relative tranquillity restored but none of the causes of unrest resolved, the army allowed a fresh general election and a return to unsupervised civil administration. The RPP won this election under its charismatic and mildly leftist leader, Bulent Ecevit. Ecevit attracted much of the politicized Kurdish vote, particularly since his rival, Demirel, had made his position on the Kurds abundantly clear, 'Anybody who does not feel Turkish, or who feels unhappy in Turkey, is free to go elsewhere.'[34] But Ecevit's leftist image also lost the party about one third its pre-1969 Kurdish notables.

Kurdistan became divided between town, predominantly RPP, and country, where the aghas and shaykhs instructed their constituencies to support the Justice Party or the National Salvation Party. The latter was openly Islamic revivalist and its leader, Dr Necmettin Erbakan, a Naqshbandi. Ecevit failed to achieve a majority and formed a coalition with the National Salvation Party. It was the first of ten administrations, only five of which enjoyed even *coalitional* majorities in the Assembly, before the army intervened again in 1980.

The 1971 coup, and the crackdown in Kurdistan had provoked deep dismay in leftist and Kurdish nationalist circles, partly because they were driven underground, partly because mainstream groups were fragmenting, and partly because the Soviet Union had done nothing to help them. During the 1970s a number of factors led to rapid proliferation of the Left, and the emergence of a Kurdish movement closely associated with it.

In July 1974 Ecevit amnestied thousands of young militants arrested during the period of military intervention. Others came back from self-imposed exile. Out of Dev Genc myriad new groups soon appeared, some Marxist–Leninist, but many Maoist in character. Some were the youth organizations of legal groups like DISK. Others were front organizations for illegal parties.

Their ranks were swollen by the expanding number of discontented young people. Rapid university student growth, from 100,000 to 150,000 between 1965 and 1969 alone, began to provide the leftists with a ready pool of young idealistic (or naive) recruits. More significantly, however, the number of university places available each year was wholly inadequate for the number of applicants. By 1977, for example, there were only 60,000 places for 360,000 candidates. Disconsolate and unsuccessful candidates who now faced the prospect of either unemployment or poorly paid jobs were easy prey to revolutionary ideas. For many who had arrived from small and backward Kurdish towns – as late as 1979 horse-drawn vehicles still outnumbered cars even in a city like Diyarbakir – life in Ankara or Istanbul was inevitably a heady experience. Unemployment rose officially from 600,000 in 1967 to 1.5 million in 1977. The unofficial figure was much higher. Each year only 40 per cent of new entrants to the labour market could find employment. Those university applicants who were successful soon learnt the indifferent quality of the education that lay in wait for them and so were highly susceptible to the utopian ideologies set before them. Those Kurds who joined the leftists tended to make no distinction regarding religious affiliation. Secular nationalism in their view had no place for backbiting between Sunni and Alevi.

By no means all joined the Left. Substantial numbers were attracted to far right groups, for example the 'Idealists' (*Ulkucular*), also known as 'Grey Wolves', (*Bozkurtular*), who were associated with the National Action Party of Alparslan Turkes. The Idealists were extremely hostile to Kurds and Communists, believing in the words of their ideologue, Nihal Atsiz, 'One who does not have Turkish blood is not Turkish even though he does not speak any other language except Turkish,' while Communists were 'people who are racially degenerate, villains, whose origins are not known and who are not Turkish'.[35] The Greywolves believed it their duty to expunge 'the enemy within'.

Most rightists accepted the Kemalist secular tradition, but not all. From 1965 to 1969 the religious *imam-hatip* school enrolment quintupled from 10,000 to 50,000. Many students lived in dormitories specially constructed for those too far from home, and inevitably such dormitories helped mobilize mass Sunni consciousness. A large number joined the National Salvation Party, or its local branches or affiliates. During the 1970s the Greywolves gained many Islamic adherents as the rightist and Islamic tendencies began to converge, particularly in Kurdistan.

Rightist groups were significantly different from the leftist ones in three vital respects. They were more united, more disciplined and most vital of all, being anti-Communist and anti-Kurd, they were perceived as useful by the state.

It was not long before Left and Right groups clashed, with fights on campus leading to fights elsewhere as ideological feuds spread across Turkey. In a number of cases these overlaid older clan or religious ones which students had brought with them to university. Thus Left–Right ideology, dangerous as it intrinsically was, also constituted both a vehicle and camouflage for other contests: Turk versus Kurd, Sunni versus Alevi, Sunni versus secularist, artisan/trader class versus rural migrant and urban proletariat. Between autumn 1973 and summer 1977 no fewer that 447 students were killed in such clashes, and in the latter year the two-month period leading up to the general election in June a further 70 died.

In late 1974 Ecevit was compelled to resign following a serious political miscalculation,[36] and was succeeded by Sulayman Demirel of the Justice Party who formed a National Front, a coalition with the National Salvation Party and the National Action Party, which openly expressed 'the need to Turkicize these [Kurdish] inalienable regions of the Turkish nation'.[37]

During the second half of the 1970s an increasing number of Kurdish leftists became dissatisfied with the way their problem was handled at the national level. Those of mildly leftist disposition could not fail to note that while the RPP pledged that 'appropriate measures would be taken to develop the East economically and to make up for the backwardness that has built up ... over the years',[38] it studiously avoided any reference to Kurds. On the whole the more militant Turkish leftists recognized but played down the Kurdish question as something that could wait until the triumph of the socialist revolution.

As a consequence small underground Kurdish parties began to form. The late Dr Shivan's leftist branch of the KDPT continued to operate,[39] while Kurdish members of the old TWP created a clandestine Socialist Party of Kurdistan in 1974 (KSPT). KSPT mobilized both the 'intellectual' class and the masses, the former with its bilingual *Riya Azadi/Ozgurluk Yolu* (Road of Liberty) which sought to awaken intellectual awareness of the Kurdish question among Kurdish and Turkish leftists, and the masses with *Roja Welat* (Sun of the Homeland), a more populist organ by which the party became widely known during *Roja Welat*'s short life, 1977–78. Like a number of Turkish groups, Dr Shivan's group and KSPT operated through legal youth front organizations, DDKD and DHKD.[40] These began to spread leftist ideas of Kurdish identity into the countryside as well as urban areas, where they clashed with traditionalist tribal and Islamic values.

During the second half of the 1970s urban and rural violence steadily increased as rightist groups, notably the Greywolves, clashed with leftists. Apart from university campuses and the shanties of Istanbul and Ankara, Kurdistan was the focus for these conflicts, in the areas of ethnic mix, like Sivas, Erzerum, Maras, Malatya, and also deep in Kurdistan where Sunnis and aghas feared the social and economic challenge of leftists.

State security forces also renewed their operations in Kurdistan, ostensibly to curb the violence but in practice turning a blind eye to rightist activities. It was the Left the army was after. By the end of 1978 20 to 30 were being killed daily in the East.

Yet to describe the struggle as one between Left and Right, or even simply between Turk and Kurd fails to take account of the complex tensions at play, particularly on the fringes of Kurdistan. There was a serious outbreak of violence in Malatya in April 1978.[41] In late December mayhem occurred in Maras. According to the official report, 109 were killed, 176 seriously wounded and 500 shops and homes destroyed. The prime perpetrators were Greywolves, the victims mainly Alevi Kurdish slum-dwellers. It was an attack by rightists on leftists, Turks on Kurds, Sunnis (probably Kurdish as well as Turkish) on Alevis. Finally it was an assault by city-dwellers on economic migrants (from Dersim and Alevi lowland areas) who now inhabited shanties and competed with the mainly Turkish citizens for employment in this notoriously Sunni town. Thus the victims at Maras were also representative of the growing class of migrant workers living in the slums of the industrial centres of Turkey.

Ecevit, briefly prime minister again from January 1978, responded to the Maras massacre by putting the whole of Kurdistan under martial law, but this did not halt the disorder elsewhere. In April 1979 the army uncovered a cache of over 370 firearms in Van. Although these were destined for Iranian Kurds, the discovery and the Kurdish fighting in Iraq greatly exacerbated army fears for the region. Ecevit spoke of 'foreign provocations for a separatist movement'.[42]

The same month a Kurdish minister, Serefettin Elci, had stated publicly 'There are Kurds in Turkey, I too am a Kurd.' This unleashed a furore in the Cabinet only resolved after a 17-hour crisis meeting.[43] In July a bomb exploded near a mosque in Corum during the main Friday prayer. A rumour that 'Communists' were responsible rapidly seized the town. By sunset a pogrom against Alevi and RPP supporters was under way, and 18 were killed. By now many slum quarters, be they Kurdish, or Alevi, had their own vigilante groups to protect against attack.

Finally, in the first week of September a major Islamic rally in Konya openly attacked the Ataturk legacy of secularism and westernization. By 12 September, it was reckoned that no fewer than 3,856 had died in the 8½ months since the Maras massacre.

On that day certain generals, led by General Evren, intervened for the third time, suspending civil government and imposing direct rule. They were galvanized by what they perceived as the imminent disintegration of certain core values of the Ataturk legacy: national unity, ethnic Turkism, populism and secularism, all of which were now under assault from the war between leftist and rightist groups, from Kurdish nationalists, Marxists and from Islamic revivalists.

They acted with great stringency during the period of direct rule to restore government authority. Officially only 592 persons died up to the moment when they returned responsiblity to civilian government in April 1983. But this was achieved at enormous cost. During their period of office, according to their own statistics over 60,000 people were arrested. Of these 54 per cent were leftists, 14 per cent rightists and only 7 per cent Kurdish separatists.

While such figures bore out the incontestable fact that like all Turkish administrations, the generals were much more harsh on the Left than the Right, it was difficult to believe the statistics on the Kurds. It was important for Ankara on the one hand to warn of the danger of Kurdish separatism but on the other to deny the actual extent of it. So the number officially arrested was limited to less than 4,500. The International League of Human Rights had a very different story. It claimed no fewer than 81,000 Kurds had been detained between September 1980 and September 1982. This suggested the problem of Kurdish dissidence was much more widespread than the generals cared to admit. The fact that two thirds of the Turkish army was deployed in Kurdistan in order to guarantee its tranquillity was not advertised.

When the generals returned the republic to civilian rule it was with a new constitution which stripped away most of the liberties which had escaped the revision of 1971. The 1961 Constitution had been about pluralism and civil liberties, the 1982 one was about control. It strengthened the power of the executive president, giving him the right to dissolve the Assembly and to rule by decree. It reduced the Assembly to one chamber from the bi-cameral system of 1961, and reduced the role of political parties. Above all, it included a 'catch-all provision, Article 14, which restricted the freedoms of individuals and organizations and prohibited political struggle based upon class, sect, language or race'.[44] It was a clear warning against Islamists, Marxists and Kurdish nationalists.

The vast majority of the electorate, 87 per cent (92 per cent of the 95 per cent who voted), approved such steps. It was a powerful reminder of the Turkish consensus on national authority and discipline. DISK and many trade unions were closed down, the old parties were dissolved and the new parties that participated in the election of 1983 were forbidden youth or women's associations or affiliates, and village or sub-district branches. Furthermore, parties were required to have an organization in at least 34 of the republic's 67 provinces. These were clear attempts to deny the chance for local feuding or for political participation by localist groups.

The election of November 1983, however, demonstrated the limits of the generals' influence. In disregard of General Evren's wishes the electorate chose the new Motherland Party (ANAP) to govern, under its leader Turgut Ozal. Ozal, unlike his predecessors, was a technocrat who had run the economy under the generals as deputy prime minister. But he embodied certain qualities which the generals feared. He was sceptical of etatism (the economic principle of Kemalism) and had worrying connections with the Islamic right. He had briefly been an unsuccessful National Salvation Party candidate during the 1970s and was closely connected with the Naqshbandiya.[45]

Thus, Turkey embarked into unchartered waters under a prime minister who clearly intended to restructure the country's economy. What few had bargained for, however, was the emergence of the Kurdish question over the next decade as Turkey's single greatest domestic challenge.

Sources

Great Britain, unpublished: Public Record Office: FO 195/2589, FO 248/1405; series FO 371 nos 24560, 27245, 31388, 45503, 52369, 67299, 72540, 130176, 153093, 163861, 523369.

Secondary sources, published: Feroz Ahmad, *The Turkish Experiment in Democracy* (London, 1977); Zulkuf Aydın, 'Household production and capitalism: a case study in south eastern Turkey' in Kathy and Pandeli Glavanis, *The Rural Middle East: Peasant Lives and Modes of Production* (London, 1990); Ismail Besikci, *Kurdistan: An Interstate Colony* (mimeograph, Australian Kurdish Association, 1991); Mehmet Ali Birand, *The General's Coup in Turkey* (London, 1987); Bozarslan, *Entre la umma et le nationalisme*; Ayse Neviye Caglar, 'The Greywolves as metaphor' in Andrew Finkel and Nukhet Sirman (eds.), *Turkish State, Turkish Society* (London and New York, 1990); Michael Gunter, *The Kurds in Turkey: A Political Dilemma* (Boulder, San Fransisco and Oxford, 1990); William Hale, *The Political and Economic Development of Modern Turkey* (London and New York, 1981); Infor-Turk, *Black Book of the Military 'Democracy' in Turkey* (Brussels, 1986); Majeed Jafar, *Under-Underdevelopment: A Regional Case Study of the Kurdish Area of Turkey* (Helsinki, 1976); Kemal Karpat, *Turkey's Politics: the Transition to a Multi-party System* (Princeton, 1959); Kendal, 'Kurdistan in Turkey'; Derk Kinnane, *The Kurds and Kurdistan*; Serif Mardin, 'Youth and violence in Turkey', *Archives Européenes de Sociologie*, vol. 19, 1978, 'Culture and religion: towards the year 2000' (mimeograph, June 1987), *Religion and Social Change* and 'The Naqshbandi Order in Turkish History' in Richard Tapper (ed.), *Islam in Modern Turkey* (London, 1991); Christiane More, *Les Kurdes Aujourd'hui*; Robert Olson, 'Al Fatah in Turkey: its influence on the March 12 Coup', *Middle Eastern Studies*, no. 9, 1973; Lucille Pevsner, *Turkey's Political Crisis* (New York, 1984); *Sosyalizm ve Toplumsal Mucadeleler Ansiklopedisi* (Istanbul, 1990); I.S. Vanly, *Survey of the National Question in Turkey* (Rome, 1971); Walter Weiker, *The Turkish Revolution, 1960–61* (Washington, 1963); Nur Yalman, 'On land disputes in eastern Turkey' in G.L. Tikku (ed.), *Islam and its Cultural Divergence* (Ann Arbor, 1977) and 'Islamic reform and the mystic tradition in eastern Turkey', *Archives Européenes de Sociologie*, vol. x, 1969.

Newspapers: *Ikibine Dogru*, *The Financial Times*, *The Guardian*, *The Daily Telegraph*, *International Herald Tribune*, *The New York Times*, *Observer Foreign News Service*.

Notes

1. The 'new nationalism' was pioneered from 1946 by a disciple of Ziya Gokalp, Hamdullah Suphi Tanriover, who emphasized the Ottoman and Islamic aspects of Turkish identity.

2. Fevzi Pirincoglu was so successful, he was appointed as Minister of Public Works in the Fethi Okyar cabinet of 1924. The feud between the two families continued into the 1930s, even though the Cemioglus were forced to live in Syria; *Ikibine Dogru*, vol. 4, no. 19, 20 May 1990.

3. The more notable of these were Dr Yusif Azizoglu, who later became a government minister; Mustafa Ekinci (Lice), Edip Altunakar (Diyarbakir), Mehmet Tevfik Bucak (Siverek), and Najat Cemioglu (Diyarbakir); see *Ikibine Dogru*, vol. 4, no. 19, 20 May 1990.

4. Inan was born in a cattle truck on an exile train. His local standing in Bitlis derived both from his spiritual pedigree and his landholdings. He subsequently became a Justice

Party deputy, senator for Bitlis and even challenged Demirel for the party leadership in 1978. But being Kurdish counted against him, as did his marriage to a Swiss. He joined the Motherland Party in the 1980s, became Minister for the South East Development Project (GAP) and unsuccessfully challenged Demirel for the presidency on the death of Ozal in 1993.

5. Kartal subsequently became speaker of the Grand National Assembly.

6. *Cumhuriyet*, 23 June 1955, quoted by Ahmad, *The Turkish Experiment*, p. 134.

7. These included Shaykh Said's son, Ali Reza Firat, and grandson Melik Firat; Kamran Inan's brother Zayn al Abidin Gaydali; Kinyas Kartal; Hamit Kartal, and several members of the Bucak family.

8. *The Guardian*, 12 March 1973.

9. Majeed Jafar, *Under-Underdevelopment* (Helsinki, 1976), p. 88.

10. See FO 371/52369 Research Department, 'The Kurds of Turkey', 5 May 1946 which noted that, since Turkish official figures minimized the number of Kurds, the actual growing disparity was greater than the statistics indicated.

11. FO 371/130176 A.D. Parsons, 'Report of a tour of south east Turkey, 29 September-19 October 1956'.

12. *Ikibine Dogru*, vol. iv, no. 19, 20 May 1990.

13. Arsim Eren, MP for Nigde, *Sosyalizm ve Toplumsal*, p. 2111.

14. *Ileri Yurt* lasted over eighteen months. It was only closed down in September 1961 after protests in the Turkish press over publication of Musa Anter's collection of nationalist poems entitled 'Kimil'.

15. Foreign Minister Fatin Rustu Zorlu apparently warned them that the international community had forgotten neither the Armenian genocide nor the Istanbul pogrom against Greek premises in 1956; *Sosyalizm ve Toplumsal*, p. 2111.

16. *Cumhuriyet*, 31 May 1960, quoted in *Sosyalizm ve Toplumsal Mucadeleler Ansiklopedisi* (Istanbul, 1990), p. 2110.

17. *Dagens Nyheter*, 11 November 1960, quoted in I.S. Vanly, *Survey of the National Question in Turkey*, p. 41.

18. By 1970 70 such schools had been established, 60 in Kurdistan, and the remainder where sizeable Kurdish communities existed outside Kurdistan.

19. Sherif Firat, of the Alevi Khurmak tribe, was a confirmed Kemalist; van Bruinessen, *Agha, Shaikh and State*, p. 300.

20. *Kurdish Facts*, quoted by Kinnane, *The Kurds and Kurdistan* (Oxford, 1964), p. 33.

21. Such figures were impossible to verify. Most of eastern Anatolia remained a military restricted area until 1966, inaccessible to foreigners without a special permit.

22. For example *Riya Newe* (New Path) edited by Dogan Kilic Shihhesenanli, Genel Yayin, Hasan Kilckaya, Yazi Isleri; Ziya Sherefhanoglu's *Reya Rast*, and *Voice of Silvan*.

23. *Sosyalizm ve Toplumsal*, p. 2126.

24. Established in April 1962.

25. The story of the KDPT is hardly central to the struggle of Turkey's Kurds, but merits a brief resumé. Faik Bucak founded the party in December 1965. It was explicitly separatist. The security forces got wind of his activities and he was shot by police agents in July 1966. He was succeeded by Sait Elci, a conservative nationalist who had been a Democrat activist in his home town of Bingol. For two years he built up a party following in Silvan, Diyarbakir, Batman and Siverek but was caught in 1968. While in prison Elci had become friends with Sait Kirmizitoprak, a leftist Dersim Kurd. After his release in 1969 Kirmizitoprak went to Iraq to support the KDP, where he was known by his *nom de guerre*, Dr Shivan. Following the KDP–Baath ceasefire of March 1970 he established his own leftist KDPT base in Zakhu. Elci and Shivan now represented opposing wings. When Elci crossed into Iraq in May 1971, Shivan captured and executed him. Shivan in turn was

caught and executed by Mulla Mustafa. Effectively it brought about the end of KDPT. Shivan's branch re-emerged as the Kurdistan Progressive Workers' Party (PPKK).

26. FO 371/163861 Burrows to Home, Ankara, 14 December 1962.

27. *Otuken*, no. 40, April 1967, quoted in Vanly, *National Aspects*, pp. 43–44, and in *Sosyalizm ve Toplumsal*, p. 2129.

28. *Milli Yol*, no. 14, 20 April 1967, quoted in *Sosyalizm ve Toplumsal*, p. 2129.

29. Kendal, 'Kurdistan in Turkey', p. 97.

30. *Official Gazette*, no. 12577 of 14 February 1967.

31. Yalman, 'Islamic reform and the mystic tradition', p. 59.

32. *Devrimci Dogu Kultur Ocaklari*. Its main 'hearths' were Diyarbakir, Ergani, Silvan, Kozluk and Batman.

33. This is not an exact verbatim translation, *Devrim*, no. 36, 23 June 1970, quoted in *Sosyalizm ve Toplumsal*, p. 2131.

34. Kendal, 'Kurdistan in Turkey', p. 93.

35. From Nihal Atsiz' works quoted by Ayse Neviye Caglar, 'The Greywolves as metaphor' in Andrew Finkel and Nukhet Sirman (eds) *Turkish State, Turkish Society* (London and New York, 1990), pp. 89, 93.

36. He had acquired such popularity as a result of his military intervention in Cyprus that he decided to dissolve his coalition and go to the country for a more decisive mandate. However, without the approval of the Assembly the constitution prevented an early election, and the majority in the Assembly, belonging to parties other than the RPP, decided to thwart his intentions. He was compelled to resign.

37. Kendal, 'Kurdistan in Turkey', p. 96.

38. *Ak Gunler* (Radiant Days) RPP election manifesto, quoted in Kendal, 'Kurdistan in Turkey', p. 95.

39. It renamed itself the Workers Party of Kurdistan in 1977. After the Apocular took this name, it revised its title in 1983 to the Progressive Workers Party of Kurdistan or *Partiya Pesenga Karkaren Kurdistan* (PPKK); More, *Les Kurdes Aujourd'hui*, p. 193.

40. The Democratic Revolutionary Cultural Association (*Devrimci Demokratik Kultur Dernegi*) and The People's Revolutionary Cultural Association (*Devrimci Halk Kultur Dernegi*), More, *Les Kurdes Aujourd'hui*, pp. 182, 194.

41. The mayor of Malatya, his daughter-in-law and two grandchildren were killed by a parcel bomb. Kurds poured into town and attacked government buildings. They were joined by rightists who attacked leftists and the local RPP headquarters. Nine were killed and 500 buildings destroyed. Kurd–Turk, Left–Right and Sunni–Shi'i tensions all played a part.

42. To some extent this was true, for Kurds were getting training from Fatah and ASALA.

43. Elci was eventually condemned to two years and four months' hard labour for claiming to be a Kurd.

44. As quoted by Pevsner, *Turkey's Political Crisis*, p. 98.

45. Ozal's brother, Korkut, had been a leading disciple of the Naqshbandi revivalist, Shaykh Mehmet Zahid Kotku (d. 1980), and this probably attracted votes in Kurdistan.

CHAPTER 20

THE P.K.K. AND THE
MASS MOVEMENT

By 1983 it was widely believed that armed dissidence in Turkey had been crushed. In 1981 the number of political killings had been reduced to 456, and the following year to 124. The quiet, however, was entirely illusory. In August 1984 a hitherto largely unknown party, Partiya Karkari Kurdistan (PKK – the Kurdistan Workers' Party) launched a series of attacks and ambushes on Turkish forces in the Kurdish region. During the next decade its activities resulted in the deaths of an estimated 12,000 people, and showed no sign of abating. Meanwhile, the Turkish state, which had briefly shown signs of seeking to accommodate Kurdish identity formally within the republic in 1990–93, retreated into a position of denial from which it had no obvious escape.

The PKK's rise had been a quiet one. It was born out of the vision essentially of one man, Abd Allah Ocalan, widely known by his nickname 'Apo'. Ocalan had been a student in Ankara at the time of the 1970 coup, involved with Devrimci Genc and with another leftist group, the Ankara Higher Education Association (AYOD). He drew inspiration from his friend Mahir Cayan, a leader of the Turkish revolutionary Left in the early 1970s. His home region was Hilvan-Siverek, but like many other urban Kurds he spoke Turkish, not Kurdish. Following the amnesty of 1974, Ocalan gathered six political colleagues to initiate a specifically Kurdish national liberation movement based on Marxism–Leninism. It was decided to sever all connection with Turkish Left groups. In 1975 Ocalan and his first followers withdrew from Turkish territory into the Kurdish marches, concentrating on building up a following in those areas from which they came: Urfa, Elazig, Tunceli, Gaziantep and Maras.

At first this small group, which began to recruit adherents in the Kurdish provinces, was simply known as the 'Apocular', or followers of Apo. The Apocular were unlike all previous Kurdish groups in Turkey (or elsewhere) in that they were drawn almost exclusively from Turkey's growing proletariat. They were filled with anger at the exploitation of both the rural and urban proletariat at the hands of aghas, merchants and the ruling establishment. More strongly than either the PUK in Iraq or Komala in Iran, the Apocular imbued Kurdish nationalism with the idea of class war.

It is also possible that the PKK's nationalism was all the more virulent because its founders sought to recreate an identity they felt they had lost. They were not alone: across the Middle East religious and ethnic groups that felt the loss of traditional identity through modernization or state attempts to homogenize society, sought to rediscover it through a revivalism that invoked an imaginary past. For the PKK the intensity of Kurdish national feeling was accentuated by the loss of spoken Kurdish among its founding members.

In 1977 the Apocular identified the enemies of the Kurdish people as the fascists (Greywolves and similar groups); agents of the state and those who supported them; the Turkish Left which subordinated the Kurdish question to the leftist revolution and finally the exploitative Kurdish landlord class.

In practice the PKK (as the Apocular called themselves from 1978) focussed on the last category. A good idea of the level of exploitation can be gleaned from Le Monde's description of a hamlet in Mardin province. Each family had a few chickens and possibly five or six goats. The agha would visit occasionally to reaffirm his authority and assign work. This consisted mainly of labour on the cotton plantations of the Mesopotamian plain two hundred metres below. All except the very old or very young would descend to the plain daily, to work an eleven-hour day. For this the rates of pay were US$1 for a child, $1.50 for a woman and $2 for a man. Villagers reckoned they had a 30 per cent mortality rate among the children. This was in 1983.[1]

Rather than assaulting the agha class as a whole, the PKK operated with fine calculation, exploiting blood feuds where these existed, helping to create them where they did not and, according to Western intelligence, becoming 'involved in local politics by offering their services to local politicians and influential families in the Urfa region'.[2] As one close associate of Ocalan later remarked 'whenever we managed to win one person from a family or tribe at that time [1978], the whole family or tribe came to our side.'[3] They also attacked other leftist groups, driving them from Urfa province, irrespective of whether they were Kurdish or Turkish. The Apocular were, above all, an exclusivist group of true believers.

In this early phase Ocalan directed his energies towards his own home area, and targeted the local agha and neo-fascists. In August 1979 his men unsuccessfully tried to assassinate Mehmet Celal Bucak, local landlord and Justice Party deputy for Siverek, beginning a long-running feud with his clan. Bucak controlled 20 villages and Siverek itself, according to one villager, sending retainers to 'burn our crops at night if we break the old patterns'.[4] After Demirel took office as prime minister in November 1979 it was natural that his administration should undertake a drive against a group threatening one of the party's more important vote-agents. This merely heightened the tension in Siverek, with the town divided into a number of areas effectively 'held' by one group or the other. The PKK, it seems, was increasingly popular in its stance against a hated local magnate, 'making its chief appeal to a new generation which resents deference and servility'.[5]

Following the 1980 coup 1,790 suspected PKK members were captured, substantially more than from any other single Kurdish group. Several were members of the central committee. But the PKK's key leaders slipped over the border into Syria, from where with official blessing,[6] they prepared for a return to the field.

During the period of military rule, 1980–83, the PKK lay low, making only occasional raids to kill soldiers on the border. At its first congress in July 1981 it regretted its conflict with other Kurdish groups, for example the pro-Soviet KUK.[7] It also decided on the need for relations with Iraqi Kurds to establish safe bases in northern Iraq where the border crossing was much easier. This required an understanding with the KDP, despite its political conservatism and its 'defeatist' aim of autonomy rather than independence. In May 1983 Turkish forces launched a major reprisal for attacks in the border area, but the heaviest casualties were among Iraqi Kurds. At a time when Ankara and Baghdad seemed allied against the Kurds, Barzani had little hesitation in agreeing a protocol with the PKK in July, allowing the PKK the use of northern Iraqi territory, with the proviso that neither party harmed the other. Northern Iraq and the border marches with Syria and Iran now became the main field of PKK activity. The PKK was fortunate in its timing, for it caught the growing Kurdish mood of defiance against the state both in Iraq and Iran at a time when Turkey was openly supporting Baghdad and Tehran against the Kurds.[8]

The PKK prepared to return to Turkey. At its second congress in 1982 it formulated a strategy of three broad phases: defence, balance and offence. Through a process starting with guerrilla activity but ending in conventional battle, it seems that it hoped to drive Turkish forces from Kurdistan. Such a formulation may seem crude, but within its context the PKK evolved and carried out a skilful first phase to put the state, despite its overwhelming conventional strength, on the defensive in Kurdistan. It predicated its efforts on the avoidance of direct confrontation with the security forces and on demonstrating the limits of state control.

It was a shrewd move that caught the changing social mood in the countryside. For a number of years there had been growing disaffection with the aghas who controlled so many facets of country life and still acted as mediators with local and central government. The system so assiduously cultivated by the Democrats and the Justice Party was now in decay. Yet a narrow class of landlords still had enormous power. Fewer than 3 per cent of the rural population, almost all absentee, owned 33 per cent of the arable land. In Hakkari province a landlord who could deliver over 3 per cent of the total provincial vote was not unusual. In the November 1983 election one landlord instructed his 500 villagers to support ANAP (the Motherland Party), and by influence through his villagers he probably garnered more like 5,000 votes, 9 per cent of the provincial vote. Only 11 defied his will for, as he pointed out, the peasants knew that those elected had the region's interests at heart, road repairs, clinics, schools and so forth.

The peasantry were increasingly disaffected yet often diffident about confronting their aghas. For example, in 1979 one nationalist group, Ala Rizgari,[9] was campaigning in Bucak territory around Siverek; in one village it finally organized a mass protest against the landlord. As several hundred protesters marched through his lands one hot summer day, a big Mercedes drove up to the head of the column, and out stepped the landlord. 'Where are your leaders?' he asked. A handful of peasants shuffled forwards. The Bucak landlord pointed to one of his houses. 'Why don't you take that house over there as your office and meeting place? I'll fix it up with a refrigerator and furniture so that you can meet and have cold drinks available. You have your meetings there. There's no need to block the roads with marches, especially on such a hot day. Just meet there and let me know what else you need for the house.' With that he drove away. The demonstrators meekly complied with his instructions, as they had always done.

The PKK changed all that by shooting landlords. In this way it showed that there was another method of dealing with the enemy class, and cruelly demonstrated the inability of the state to protect its own. Furthermore, it began to stage some spectacular ambushes against the security forces. In October 1984 it followed up its initial August attack first by killing three members of a unit responsible for guarding President Evren at Yuksekova, and then ambushing and killing eight soldiers in Cukurca, Hakkari. In spring 1985 the PKK came to national attention again with a major battle in Siverek in which over 60 guerrillas, troops and civilians died. By August 1985 almost 200 had died in about 70 armed incidents. Compared with the disorders of the late 1970s it was still minor stuff, and the chiefs of operations and intelligence divisions of the General Staff were able to claim that they had, effectively, crushed the separatists. But while they could claim success in the encounters that came to national attention, it was the constant challenge to state authority by the occasional killing of soldiers or landlords which began to have a serious psychological effect in the area.

The PKK created a climate of fear. It struck ruthlessly in the heartlands of conservatism in Kurdistan, and seemed to preach an irreligious creed of atheism and social revolution. It created great ambivalence among ordinary Kurds. Most feared it, some loathed it for it threatened their secure position within the system or within their traditional world view, others secretly (or not so secretly) admired its daring. These feelings, fear, loathing and admiration began to have serious impact during the years 1987–88 when the PKK began to strike against those villagers armed by the state to resist its progress.

The Village Guards

Because of PKK attacks on its local supporters, the government decided to arm villagers so that they could protect themselves. In April 1985 the Village Law was amended to allow for the maintenance, at government expense, of 'temporary village guards'. These village guards were reminiscent of the Hamidiya, the local militia system used in the early days of the republic and the contemporary Iraqi *jash*. The first clans to offer manpower for the guards tended to be those identified with the Right and far Right political parties, or already in conflict either with the PKK directly, or with local clans which enjoyed PKK support. Among the more notable tribes involved were the Jirki, Pinyanish, Goyan and the Mamkhuran. As with the Hamidiya, the government was quite willing to use tribes which it normally viewed as criminal or delinquent. Of these the most notorious was the Jirki in Hakkari, whose chief, Tahir Adiyaman, was still wanted for the killing of six gendarmes in 1975. Adiyaman struck a bargain with state officials, and after a token court appearance, raised a force of Jirkis as village guards around Beytussebap. Another Hakkari chief demanded the release of his son from prison before providing village guards. Recruitment grew apace. By 1990 there were approximately 20,000 village guards, by 1993, 35,000.

Whereas in Iraq the enrolment had been primarily to avoid service against Iran, in Turkey the incentive was economic. With high unemployment or underemployment, and extremely low average incomes, the official village guard salary offered an income several-fold above the average per capita income in the area. By 1992 the monthly stipend of a village guard was approximately US$230 in impoverished areas where the annual per capita income was little more than $400. Individual village guards did not necessarily receive their full salary. As in Iraq, the aghas collected the money for those on their payroll and, according to custom, provided the bounty and hospitality expected of them. In autumn 1992 Sadun Seylan, chief of the Alan tribe in Van, who owned 26 villages, fielded 500 village guards, a force he could increase six-fold if necessary. For these 500 men, Seylan received $115,000 monthly.

The intrinsic venality of the system led to corrupt gambits. As in Iraq, some local officials worked with local aghas to create false enrolment lists. This was sometimes in addition to longstanding informal arrangements between official and agha regarding smuggling and other profitable but illegal activities. Some village guards justified their existence by phoney battles, seeking government compensation for damage inflicted by themselves. Some village guards and local officials, it was rumoured, even handed a percentage of their income over to the PKK to buy them off.

Like Hamidiya chiefs, certain aghas exploited their position to dispossess the vulnerable. Invoking Islam, some drove Assyrian and Yazidi villagers from their land near Mardin, others did the same to Alevi villagers near Maras. The victims knew it would be foolish to take their case to court. The aghas also used their weapons to settle local scores. In 1992, for example, eight civilians travelling by minibus in Mardin province were stopped and shot. As intended it was assumed to be the work of the PKK, until an unusually painstaking prosecutor demonstrated the perpetrators were village guards.

The aghas also used their close relationship with the security forces to their own economic advantage, for example to obtain local construction contracts. Tahir Adiyaman was awarded the contract to build a local police housing complex, and district elementary school. His was one of several cases that came to public attention. Thus the village guard system became profitable in its own right, and those who participated had every reason to perpetuate the impression that they were indispensable to state security. Thus, too, the government found itself financing tribal revival and racketeering contrary to the Ataturk legacy and also contrary to the economic and social necessities for peace and stability.

Those tribes refusing a government invitation to join the village guards risked retribution. Some were expelled from their villages, which were then razed. In the case of one chief, the security forces persuaded him to reconsider his position by executing his brother in front of his villagers. Several tribes migrated to avoid coming under either government or PKK pressure.

The PKK Response

By 1985 the government had constructed a wire mesh fence along its border with Syria. The Iraqi border, running through precipitous mountains, was impossible to fence. The village guards were therefore all the more important as a means of blocking PKK access and supply routes.

It was therefore important to the PKK to prevent this network from materializing. At the beginning of 1987 the PKK launched a ferocious assault on the system. During the next two years it deliberately wiped out village guard and agha families, men, women and children, without compunction, in Mardin, Siirt and Hakkari provinces.[10] Such massacres had a seriously intimidating effect, but also led to counter reprisals on PKK 'supply villages', in which the village guards demonstrated they were no less ruthless than the PKK.

The PKK was able to demonstrate the inherent weakness of the village guard system. Most village guard contingents were only about half a dozen strong. Lacking telephone or radio, they were easy victims to surprise attacks. As a result the security forces found themselves having to provide protection to the village guards and during 1987 it seemed the PKK would destroy the system as enrolment dropped from 20,000 to 6,000. But more tribes were persuaded to join. In September 1989 the PKK named thirteen tribes it threatened to attack.[11] In some cases it hit tribal leaderships hard. In Van it killed the son and two cousins of Sadun Seylan, chief of the Alan. Some village guards became fearful, but surrender of their weapons was no guarantee against PKK reprisals. In other cases a whole village would arm in order to be strong enough to resist attack by 30 or more PKK fighters.

The PKK paid a price for its ruthlessness. Masud Barzani decided to abrogate the KDP agreement with the PKK, 'The PKK is earning the hatred and disgust of all the Kurdish people,' he remarked. But this was only partially true. Whatever the methods of the PKK, the population rapidly discovered that there was little it did which was not matched by the ruthlessness of the security forces. A major migration to town began of those caught in the crossfire of the conflict.

The PKK also paid a penalty for 'overkill'. At a time when their campaign seemed to be working, the PKK made the mistake of killing envoys of Tahir Adiyaman seeking a PKK amnesty while the Jirkis resigned from the village guards. Such actions drove tribesmen back into the guard system. When the PKK finally changed its policy to offer an amnesty in January 1991, the damage was already done. Few were inclined to trust it, and village guards continued to grow.

Another aspect of the PKK struggle was brought into focus by tightened security along the border. In 1985 it formed the Kurdistan Popular Liberation Front (ERNK), intended to be the nucleus inside Kurdistan, to provide civil networks for supply routes, bases, urban warfare and intelligence, and finally the kernel to mobilize the masses. In a land of such deep impoverishment and state oppression, ERNK rapidly expanded. It was this burgeoning mass support that made the PKK so dangerous to the state.

Government Counter-measures

The government sought to outdo PKK intimidation, matching terror for terror, in an apparent belief that if only the Kurds were more fearful of Ankara than they were of the PKK, it would be able to stifle the insurgency. In a prosperous society that stood to lose much by civil conflict such a doctrine might have worked. But in the impoverished circumstances of Kurdistan, where the mass of population had such meagre economic expectations and where traditional methods of co-optation through landlords was in advanced decay, such methods merely fuelled the conflict.

The military coup of 1980 had already brought a more stringent regime to Kurdistan. The army had had relatively little to do with the struggle between Left and Right on university campuses and in the slums and, apart from Korea (1950–52), Cyprus (1974) and its role within NATO, its prime experience and justification over half a century had been in holding the Kurds down. It was natural therefore for the army to focus on Kurdistan but by its methods it helped fulfil its own worst fears.

First, it tried to stifle Kurdish culture. In October 1983 it introduced Law 2932 prohibiting the use of Kurdish. Already the term 'Kurdish' was such a bogey that the law found a form of words to make its prohibition explicit without mentioning the offending word.[12] Such a prohibition primarily affected the literate and activist classes. But the administration went further to remind the illiterates too that all trace of Kurdish identity was to be banned. In December 1982 the minister for education reminded all provincial governors that folk songs in east and south-east Anatolia might be used for ethnic or separatist purposes and must only be sung in Turkish. Although such instructions were routinely ignored, periodically exemplary sentences were handed to offenders. Those who gave their children Kurdish names found that (under Law 1587) names which 'contradict the national culture, morality and traditions and insult the public cannot be legally registered on birth certificates'. A number of cases arose in which children were renamed. It was easier to change place names. By 1986, 2,842 out of 3,524 villages in Adiyaman, Gaziantep, Urfa, Mardin, Siirt and Diyarbakir had been renamed to expunge Kurdish identity. No Kurd could be unaware of what was happening. Inevitably, however, the army saw its prime role as ensuring physical control. During the 1980s the number of troops allocated to the control of Kurdistan steadily increased to reach 200,000 by the early 1990s.

In 1987 a governor-general was appointed over the eight Kurdish provinces in which a state of emergency was declared. His powers were extensive, including the evacuation of villages and pasturage where this was deemed necessary. He was expected to bring much needed co-ordination to the various bodies fighting the guerrillas, the police, gendarmerie, army and village guards, and the separate intelligence networks each operated.

State oppression was most overwhelming and pervasive in the field of physical abuse and torture. Only pro-government villages were inexperienced in the routine of security sweeps in which hundreds were arbitrarily arrested and beaten to confess to assisting the PKK. Doubtless many had, either by conviction or intimidation, assisted the PKK with food, shelter or merely by looking the other way as they passed through. But the manner in which the security forces sought evidence from those it detained was calculated to be the most potent nutrient to the PKK's own recruitment activities.

Few escaped the trauma or frequency of security operations. In some cases 'capture and kill' orders were issued. In the words of one asylum seeker, 'The children became so fearful that whenever a policeman came to the house they would immediately put their hands on their heads as a gesture of surrender.'[13] Those detained were kept in inhumane conditions and frequently received bastinado (falaka), electric shocks or sexual abuse. In the words of one peasant, 'I was ready to confess that I had killed one hundred men, because they brought my wife and sister, stripped and threatened to rape them right there.'[14] In Diyarbakir prison 32 were officially acknowledged to have died in custody between 1981 and 1984. Unofficial sources estimated twice this number, including four prisoners who immolated themselves to escape their tormentors.

Thus every Kurdish village learnt what the state meant by law and order. One loyalist Kurdish deputy of the Assembly, asked his opinion in 1987, reckoned that 'When the military took over in 1980, the Kurds were happy. But then the military started getting worse than the terrorists, so now about 40 per cent of the villagers in the border areas support the terrorists.'[15]

Conditions of life continued to deteriorate as the conflict intensified. At the beginning of 1989 reports were published in Turkey of deepening army brutality and of mass graves in Siirt and elsewhere, thought to be where detainees who were unaccounted for had been buried.[16] In July 1987 Decree 285 had widened the governor-general's powers not only to evacuate villages at his discretion but also to deport the population from the region. The number of evacuated hamlets and villages, mainly along the border, reached 400 by the end of 1989, climbing inexorably during the next three years, as evacuations and destruction happened elsewhere, to exceed 2,000 villages destroyed by the end of 1994, with over 750,000 rendered homeless.

Regular troops replaced the gendarmerie on the Syrian border because of the latter's inefficiency and suspected corruption. It was well-known that local authorities routinely turned a blind eye to massive smuggling, and benefited from it. It was now becoming increasingly clear that smuggling and PKK activity were tightly entwined. Sheep might be herded out of Turkey, and weapons brought on back on the return journey.

The International Dimension

Turkey's borders compelled the protagonists to seek external cooperation. Turkey unsuccessfully sought the co-operation of its neighbours; Syria would agree to Turkish requests but then fail to uphold them.[17] In April 1988 the PKK was able to hold a convention lasting a fortnight in Latakiya, attended by over 300 Kurds. Iran seemed less willing to give the PKK free rein but refused to provide Turkey with any assurances. It disliked its attacks on Iran's ally, the KDP, and its proffering of asylum to opponents of the Islamic republic.

Turkey assumed it enjoyed the support of Iraq, since the latter had given it the right of hot pursuit. It was probably unaware that the PKK was providing Baghdad with intelligence concerning KDP movements and Turkish troop dispositions. It also had to endure two major waves of Kurdish refugees, 60,000 in August 1988 and approximately half a million in April 1991. Both gave powerful impetus to national feeling and solidarity among Turkey's Kurds, and compelled Ankara to reconsider and modify its traditional policy.

The PKK sought to offset the loss of KDP support by an alliance with the PUK in May 1988. It was easy for the PUK to offer an alliance, since its own fiefdom lay too far south to face Turkish reprisals. PUK's support was also less useful to the PKK, since it could offer no bases in Bahdinan. As Turkey tightened security along the Syrian border, the PKK also began to seek greater facilities from Tehran. It began purchasing arms from the Pasdaran. In February 1988 Prime Minister Ozal sought Iranian co-operation regarding border security, a tacit admission the PKK were crossing the eastern frontier too.

The Political Arena

Regardless of its methods, the conflict between the PKK and the state progressively radicalized the Kurdish population. While the government could still count on many rightist or religious families to support it, there was a steady drain of younger members of such families because of the economically depressed con ditions, or because younger family members acquired sufficient education to question their subservience to the authority of aghas or shaykhs, or finally because they had spent time away from the village and seen how society functioned away from the traditional bonds which held village society together.

These processes of transformation had taken place largely unnoticed by the Turkish public until 1990 when the qualitative change in the struggle for Turkish Kurdistan could no longer be ignored. In March that year the PKK offensive was eclipsed by the burgeoning civil resistance to the security forces. For the first time, families of PKK martyrs dared collect the corpses for burial from the authorities and arranged public funerals which rapidly became opportunities for mass protest. On 20 March 10,000 Kurds demonstrated in Cizre and security forces imposed a curfew on 11 towns in Mardin and Siirt provinces; a growing number of civilians were shot by the security forces. The death toll for March exceeded 100, compared with only 16 recorded deaths for the first three months of 1989. The mayor of Nusaybin caused a sensation (and lost his job) by telling the Reuters correspondent that about 95 per cent of his townspeople were happy to support the PKK. The PKK, for its part, abandoned its attacks on civilians at the end of 1990 to emphasize the state itself as the principal cause of human rights violations. It announced an amnesty for those village guards who turned their weapons in, but there were lapses in its own respect of it.

For the first time a public debate took place in Turkish circles concerning the Kurdish insurgency. The popular view was that the only language the Kurds understood was that delivered by the security forces, and that even tougher action was required. But there was growing recognition among politicians that the military had no answer to the progressive loss of 'hearts and minds' in the south-east, and had yet to demonstrate they could even deal with the military challenge.

The state therefore adopted an increasingly schizophrenic attitude. On the one hand draconian measures were introduced to support the military. In April, following an emergency cabinet meeting, the government introduced Kararname 413, giving the governor-general sweeping powers to recommend the closure of any publishing house anywhere in Turkey that 'falsely reflects events in the region or engages in untruthful reporting or commentary'. This was censorship to ensure people remained ignorant of developments. It outraged the press, and psychologically implied that the state was losing the information war and that the security forces wished to hide what they were doing. Circulation of the PKK's underground paper, *Serxwebun*, increased. Everyone wanted to know what was going on. Kararname 413 also indicated the much tougher conditions Kurds could now expect, for the governor-general was given wider powers forcibly to resettle 'those persons whom it is deemed necessary ... in places which the Ministry of the Interior shall determine'.[19] During the next few months the number of villages razed and people deported soared: 19 villages in Dersim were razed in April 27 villages and 81 hamlets in Sirnak were evacuated and razed in August–September, rendering over 30,000 homeless; in Buhtan alone 300 villages and hamlets were evacuated in the period up to November, with the displacement of 50,000. Many victims had simply refused to join the village guards.

Kararname 413 was probably drafted by army generals; but in order to appear in control President Ozal assumed it as his own,. In the words of one commentator, 'When the chips are down, no Turkish politician ever calls for a softer policy towards the Kurds.'[19] But protests were made across the political spectrum. When the Social Democrats (SHP) sought to challenge the legality in the Constitutional Court, the government redrafted and combined it with another one, renumbered as Kararname 424.[20] Even ANAP deputies protested, aware of the damage it would do them in their Kurdish constituencies.[21]

The SHP had tried to be all things to all men. In 1986 it had claimed that the whole south-east was 'a sort of concentration camp, where every citizen was treated as a suspect, and oppression, torture and insult the rule'.[22] Yet in 1988 it had purged certain Kurdish party members for expressing concern about state policy towards Kurdistan. It had suspended one deputy who had raised the Kurdish question in the Assembly. In late 1989 seven others[23] were expelled for attending an international conference on the Kurdish question in Paris. Other Kurdish deputies quit in protest. Now, with such mass feeling in the south-east, the SHP sensed the danger of losing its constituency there. It was, in fact, undergoing precisely the same strains felt by Ecevit's RPP a decade earlier.

In July 1990 the SHP published a lengthy report on conditions in the southeast and made startling recommendations to ease the situation: free expression of identity and linguistic freedom of expression, abolition of the village guards, the governorate-general and state of emergency, and a major programme of regional development. In Kurdistan the report was received sceptically as a ploy to attract the Kurdish vote. It was well known that the SHP chairman in Van, for example, was also one of the more important village guard commanders.[24] Nevertheless, it marked the beginning of visible stress within the heart of Turkish party politics. The report was largely written by the Diyarbakir deputy, Hikmet Cetin, a close confidant of the party secretary, Deniz Baykal. A Kurdish viewpoint was beginning to find a voice. Nor was this voice confined to the Left.

A stunning sequence of public and private utterances came from the Right. At the outset of 1991 Mesut Yilmaz, shortly before his appointment as prime minister, opined that Kurdish should become Turkey's second official language, a sure cause for apoplexy among certain party colleagues. At the same time President Ozal announced his acceptance of the idea of an autonomous Kurdish region in northern Iraq.

It was not only the Turkish establishment that was exploring the political landscape. A few days before the proclamation of Kararname 413, Ocalan had warned of greater bloodshed but also declared, 'There is no question of separating from Turkey. My people need Turkey. We can't split for at least 40 years.'[25] It was the first indication that Ocalan welcomed a move from the military to the political arena. Such, however, was the climate in Ankara that no leading statesman could respond and expect to survive politically. The rest of 1990 was marked by deepening savagery on the battlefield, and the apparent ascendancy of government forces over the insurgents.

Yet such appearances were deceptive, for the struggle out on the mountains was firmly secondary to the process of mass psychological detachment taking place in Kurdistan. No one now doubted that the Kurdish question was the most serious domestic challenge the republic faced. It was only two years since the term 'Kurdish question' had first appeared in the press. President Ozal was now caught between the military imperative of defeating the PKK and the need to reconcile the disaffected among the republic's 12 million or so Kurds. A confidential report on the year 1990 indicated that the PKK now enjoyed widespread support in several towns in Buhtan and Diyarbakir provinces, though it was less popular in Van and Agri, where the army had been less repressive.

Spring 1991 saw a succession of steps that indicated the tumult in which Ankara now tried to handle the Kurdish question. In February Ozal introduced a draft bill into the Assembly to repeal Law 2932 and thereby allow the use of Kurdish except in broadcasts, publications and education. This legalized what was already happening on the streets of Istanbul, let alone in Kurdistan, where Kurdish was freely spoken and Kurdish music cassettes openly available. Yet the Turkish outcry forced Ozal to delay. In spite of its own recommendations only seven months earlier, the SHP was among those that denounced Ozal for departing from the Kemalist tradition.

By now the Kurdish issue had acquired more serious dimensions. Approximately 2,500 had died since 1984. A furore in establishment circles followed Ozal's casual admission he had met the Iraqi Kurdish leadership a few days earlier, thereby breaking another Kemalist shibboleth. This, of course, had done nothing to discourage thousands of Kurds taking to the streets for Nawruz in Sirnak, Idil, Cizre, Midyat, Adana, Izmir and Istanbul. If anything, the political imperative to parley with Iraq's Kurds and the row it created in Ankara had accelerated Kurdish feeling north of the border. On 12 April Ozal persuaded the Assembly to allow Law 2932 to be repealed. He sweetened the pill by introducing the same day a draconian new anti-terrorism law which defined terrorism as 'any kind of action ... with the aim of changing the characteristics of the Republic', a definition which covered any democratic attempt, for example by demonstration, rally or publication, to moderate the stringent character of the state.[26]

Then, in December 1991, the first Kurdish language newspaper, *Rojname*, was permitted to start publishing. Other Kurdish organs followed suit but they were constantly harassed by state authorities. *Yeni Ülke* for example, and its proprietor, Serhat Bucak, faced 44 charges within months of starting publication. Most of its issues were confiscated or banned.

In the meantime, however, half a million Kurdish fugitives from Saddam's forces had pressed against Turkey's south-eastern frontier, and the state found itself pursuing two contradictory and inimical policies. On the one hand its anti-terror law opened the floodgates to yet greater repression of Kurds. On the other, the government found itself moving from open dialogue to regular formal relations with Iraq's two main Kurdish parties, the KDP and PUK, both of which opened liaison offices in Ankara.

The PKK itself now took its modest hints at a political compromise further. In March, at the height of the Iraqi Kurdish uprising, a spokesman indicated that the PKK might welcome a federalist solution within Turkey. Six months later, in November 1991, by which time the total death toll exceeded 3,000, the journalist Ismet Imset asked Ocalan whether he might accept a federal solution to which the latter replied, 'Unquestionably this is what we see.'[27] From a leader hitherto adamant about the imperative to create an independent state by force of arms, such a response indicated a desire for a negotiated compromise. Ozal shocked Ankara by saying he would be willing to talk about a federal system if only to oppose it. A month later Ocalan offered Ankara a ceasefire and negotiations if the latter released all PKK prisoners, ceased its 'secret war' in Kurdistan, permitted free political activity in Turkey and announced its own adherence to a cease-fire. Ocalan referred not only to the military contest in the countryside, but to the 'disappearances' or unaccounted for deaths following police arrest, where victims tended to be Kurdish activists. For example, in July Vedat Aydin, chairman of the new pro-Kurdish People's Labour Party (HEP), had been arrested by police and his tortured body found a few days later on an Elazig refuse tip.

These were demands no Turkish political leader could possibly entertain, particularly since the PKK now seemed to be creeping into the Turkish political system by stealth. The HEP had been formed by Kurdish MPs expelled from the SHP two years previously, with the clear intention of advancing Kurdish political, cultural and human rights. It was viewed by the Turkish Right as the political arm of the PKK. In the November general election, the True Path Party (DYP) had emerged with the largest number of seats and its leader, Suleyman Demirel, was able to form a coalition with the SHP. But in the south-east the general election had demonstrated PKK power. In Sirnakh, for example, 70 per cent of the vote went to the HEP, following PKK instructions. The DYP and SHP leaders, Demirel and Erdal Inonu, rushed to the south-east straight after the election, promising to uphold human rights, and revise the anti-terror law, state emergency and village guard system.

Any early optimism following the 1991 election was soon dashed. In the south-east the SHP had made an electoral alliance with the HEP which had returned 22 deputies to the Assembly. It was natural that the SHP should welcome the HEP under its umbrella in order to wield power in the Assembly. However, two of the new deputies[28] took their oath with a plea for Turko-Kurdish brotherhood in *Kurdish*. Thus, while Kurds may have rejoiced at so bold a statement of

Kurdish identity in the very heart of the republic, Turks felt outraged by this brazen challenge. Both deputies were forced out of the SHP but the damage had been done, and the alliance with HEP foundered. The more liberal Turks in the Assembly, natural allies for Kurds anxious to see the beginning of a political process, had now been thoroughly frightened off.

While Kurds looked up to their new champions in the Assembly, many Turks, probably a majority, began to see the HEP as an agent of the 'terrorists'. It was no wonder, therefore, that the Turkish establishment felt extremely reluctant to engage in dialogue, even within the Assembly, let alone with Ocalan and his colleagues.

Although now on the periphery of business in the Assembly, the Kurdish presence was a painful reminder at the heart of the state of the failure of Turkish nationalism to absorb its growing minority. On the ground it was clear that the security forces were rapidly losing control of the population.

To the jeremiahs of the Kurdish cause it was easy to be cynical about what was offered with one hand only to be withheld with the other. Yet the political landscape had indeed irreversibly changed. In March 1987 it had still been possible for a senior government minister to ask 'Is there such a thing as a Kurd? ... The only people prepared to call themselves Kurds are militants, tools of foreign ideologies.'[29] By 1992 Ozal was arguing for a change of approach: an amnesty for the guerrillas and recognition of the PKK as a participant in Turkey's political system. Ozal represented the radical school of thought. The conservatives, led by Demirel, had no intention of allowing any such thing, not because Kurds did not exist but because the concessions Ozal had in mind were 'unconstitutional'. Indeed, on becoming prime minister Demirel himself had uttered the fateful words 'Turkey has recognized the Kurdish reality.'[30] That, in itself, was arguably 'unconstitutional'.

The Religious Dimension

At the end of the 1980s Kurdish nationalists had found themselves facing growing danger ostensibly from the religious constituency of Kurdistan, and its tendency to the Right. The religious impulse had always been a complex issue. Observant Sunni Kurds felt drawn into the wider orbit of Sunni Islam in Turkey and had responded to the liberalization introduced by parties of the Right in the 1950s. During most of the 1980s the religious impulse in Kurdistan had seemed in abeyance. The religiously inclined tended to vote for ANAP or the True Path Party,[31] while most town-dwellers supported SHP.

In fact Islamic sentiment flourished in the 1980s not only in Kurdistan but all over Turkey. State funds for religious purposes were increased during the decade, and in 1990 the religious budget more than doubled. At the state level an affinity between the Naqshbandiya – easily the largest collection of *tariqas* in Kurdistan – and ANAP rapidly developed in the early 1980s, partly because of

Ozal's Naqshbandi relatives. Islam had its value. The Hanafi school, the formal law school of Ottoman Turkey, had always emphasized the duty of obedience to the state.

Yet the Islamic movement was also feared among Kemalists for its political ambition. Although there had been fewer that 200 religious foundations in the country before 1980, their rapid burgeoning in the 1980s – 350 in 1983, 850 in 1985 and 1128 in 1987 – testified both to the multiplicity of networks and the total growth in Muslim sentiment. In 1990 secularists were shocked by the attendance of 20,000 worshippers at a Nurculuk ceremony in Ankara.

The revivalist process had been accelerated by Saudi and Iranian support for the construction of mosques and student hostels, for religious education and for certain *tariqa*s. Religious education in Kurdistan had a value even for the Kemalists in government, for it would slow down the spread of secular nationalism. The Islamic movement also began to permeate the executive structures of state. Certain religious networks sought to infiltrate key sectors of state, for example the armed forces, police and the education network. Indeed, in 1990 the armed forces, the most committed guardian of the republic's secular ideals, expelled hundreds of servicemen for their links with Islamic organizations. Under Prime Minister Ozal and his Interior Minister, Abdulkadir Aksu, both of whom were well known for their religious sympathies, the ranks of the police and gendarmerie forces in Kurdistan were filled by officers of Sunni revivalist persuasion, making religious observance in the police force common where 20 years earlier it had been rare.

During the mid-1980s an overtly anti-ethnic and anti-secular Islamic movement, Hizb Allah Yumruki (The Fist of God Party), began to grow out of the Islamic revival in Diyarbakir. Its rise followed closely on the mid-1991 appointment of a pro-Islamic police chief to the area. Some of these Hizb Allahis had been to Iran for theological training. They subordinated Sunni–Shi'i tensions to the greater goal of defeating atheism. Hizb Allah Yumruki was almost certainly in alliance with other Islamic groups across Turkey. It did not challenge the secular republic directly, but began to identify secularist victims for assassination.[32]

It focussed its attention on Kurdistan, where it saw the secular nationalist movement as prime enemy, because of its close association with atheistic Communism and because it challenged the Turkish Right with which the Islamic tendency was so closely associated. In 1991, in response to the surge in PKK success, Hizb Allah Yumruki, or 'Hizb Contra' as it was also known, embarked upon a damaging programme of assassinations and bombings. Journalists, pro-PKK activists, trade unionists and professionals, identified with the secular nationalist Left, became targets for Hizb Allah. By the end of 1993 over 500 activists had been killed, among whom the most noteworthy was Musa Anter, shot down during a visit to Diyarbakir in September 1992. Journalists writing for *Ikibine Dogru, Yeni Ulke, Ozgur Gundem,* or other leftist journals sympathetic to the Kurdish cause began to live in acute fear as colleagues were abducted, tortured and murdered. Even news vendors for such journals became targets.

Yet government security forces proved unable to solve any of these crimes. On the contrary, Prime Minister Demirel remarked after Musa Anter's death, 'Those killed were not real journalists. They were militants ... they kill each other.'[33] Furthermore, the state itself embarked upon a campaign of closures and harassment which, combined with the assassination of its journalists, forced *Ozgur Gundem* to close despite its large readership. By the end of 1993 no suspects had been arrested, let alone charged. Kurdish nationalists drew the inescapable conclusion that Hizb Allah worked hand-in-glove with government at the local level and possibly at the centre also. The death squads created a new climate of fear in Kurdistan.

By the late 1980s the PKK had found its progress damaged by the government's use of religious feeling against it, and the suggestion that the PKK intended to suppress Islam. While the majority of observant Sunni Kurds tended to the Right, the PKK and its sympathizers hoped to appeal to some of the complex strands in Kurdish Islam, stressing areas of dissonance with the Turkish Right. For example, it began to emphasize the imperatives of social liberation within the context of Islam, and found mullahs willing to follow ideas similar to those embraced by Shaykh Izz al Din al Husayni in Iran, and established a small group led by an elderly Bitlis cleric.[34] These clerics took the view that Islamic universalism and Kurdish national identity were not mutually exclusive. At a formal level they could appeal to the Quranic acknowledgement of ethnic and solidarity groups, 'We have made you nations and tribes',[35] and remind their followers of their qualitative distinctiveness, for example, that the Shafi'i school in Kurdistan was less deferential to authority than the Hanafi tradition of the state. And they could point to the qualitative and cultural superiority of the Kurdish *turuq* which had kept the faith alive while the formal structures of urban Islam had largely surrendered to Kemalism. Here was a source of pride for the autonomous and neglected periphery against the authoritarian centre. Since 1923 that centre had been secular and inimical to the institutions on which Sunni Islam had traditionally focussed. Kurds, they argued, could and should draw *religious* pride from Shaykh Said's revolt.

Shadowy groups associated with the PKK came into being. The Partiya Islami Kurdistan (PIK), for example, came to public attention with a wave of bomb attacks in Istanbul, Ankara and Malatya in March 1990. Its organ, *Cudi*, went so far as to give ethnic opposition to the Turks' Islamic justification, and drew a distinction between the unacceptable use of nationalism as a creed and a God-given identity to be cherished. On these grounds, too, PIK demanded Kurdish civil rights.[36] Another group, Islami Harekat (Islamic Movement) appeared in Van in 1991.

The PKK's immediate objective in fostering such groups was to counter government efforts to portray the PKK as a Satanic evil, and if possible to claw back the initiative with an illiterate rural population. In some areas it was reckoned that up to 50 per cent of the vote was influenced by local shaykhs, and it paid the PKK to seek to woo young shaykhs and mullas to its cause.

However, the PKK was also moved by strategic considerations. It wanted to operate more freely from Iran. While it knew Iran had pragmatic reasons for creating a nuisance in Turkey, it also recognized that it should present itself as well-disposed to Islam. In 1989 Ocalan's brother Osman had established a liaison office in Iran, and the following year negotiated the establishment of 20 operational bases from which to strike at targets in Van, Agri and Kars provinces. In his Nawruz speech in 1990 Ocalan played up the positive aspects of the Islamic revolution.

GAP and the Absence of an Economic Solution

It was well understood among more thoughtful Turks that the key to the conflict was partly political but possibly primarily economic. It was well known that the per capita income in the south-east was barely 42 per cent of the national average and barely a quarter of per capita income in Turkey's richest Aegean/ Marmara region. It was equally well known that no government had ever taken the serious steps required to reverse the growing economic disparities between western and eastern Turkey. The Kurdish provinces, unquestionably the poorest, received less than 10 per cent of the national development budget.

It was therefore with a good deal of fanfare, that Ozal had begun to implement the South East Anatolia Development Project (GAP). This ambitious project proposed to harness the power of the Euphrates and Tigris rivers to produce the hydro-electricity that would fuel Turkey's industrial expansion in the early years of the twenty-first century and to irrigate adjacent lands leading to a major expansion of agriculture and related agro-industries. Those living in the region, it was claimed, would enjoy substantial economic benefit. The planners proposed to raise per capita income in the region to 55 per cent of the national average, an increase of ten percentage points.

In reality GAP revealed that government either failed to understand the economic dimension of the Kurdish question, or that its intentions were primarily to do with wringing whatever wealth it could from the south-east for the benefit of the rest of the country. For, as the GAP master plan itself admitted, within the region 8 per cent of farming families owned over 50 per cent of the land, while 41 per cent held between 10 and 50 dunums and another 38 per cent held no land at all. Of the large landowning families, a substantial portion were absentee, content to allow inefficient farming as long as they obtained an adequate income from their lands. Without a fundamental land reform it was inconceivable that the majority of the farming population could benefit from GAP. The last attempt at land reform, in 1978, was abortive thanks mainly to the fear of the main parties in Ankara that it would destroy the system that delivered their votes. Plans to create state-run enterprises and smallholder co-operatives seemed more likely to drive large numbers off the land.

Furthermore, it was difficult to see how a largely illiterate population would be able to benefit from capital-intensive agriculture or agro-industry, let alone the ancillary sector that would grow up to service it. The Kurds had neither capital nor education. Capital would come from western Turkey, or from abroad, given secure conditions. The notoriously poor education provision of Kurdistan, with overcrowded classrooms and unsympathetic Turkish teachers, told its own story. By 1990 average literacy in Mardin province, by no means the worst affected province, was 48 per cent compared with a national average of 77 per cent. This was hardly surprising since all education was in a language foreign to the majority of rural inhabitants. The enrolment figures spoke for themselves. Only 70 per cent of children ever appeared at school, and of these only 18 per cent went on to secondary education, of whom only 9 per cent completed the secondary cycle.

Thus the two essential prerequisites for the region's economic progress, the final removal of the landowning agha class and the introduction of Kurdish-medium primary education could not be implemented because both measures contradicted state policy regarding the control of Kurdistan. By 1994 Ankara remained locked in contradictions of its own making and Kurdistan in the poverty borne of state neglect and paranoia.

The Failure to Find a Modus Vivendi

Meanwhile in the political arena, spring 1992 had begun ominously with about 100 civilians killed by security forces during Nawruz, now unmistakably the annual focus for Kurdish national expression. With strident calls from the Right to stop the shilly-shallying and to deal with the PKK once and for all, Ozal now effectively surrendered responsibility for the south-east to the military, retreating from the liberal gestures made at the outset of the year. Ozal was under pressure because a quarter of the 4,000 dead since the start of the PKK campaign in 1984 had perished in the previous year. The Turkish establishment would not allow the army to appear weak.

In August 1992 security forces assaulted the town of Sirnak, following unsubstantiated reports of PKK activity there. The entire population, roughly 20,000, fled *en masse*, and many buildings were damaged irreparably. Similar occurrences took place elsewhere, at Dargecit and Cukurca. Almost 2,000 died in 1992. The PKK soon demonstrated its ability to destroy the illusion of government authority. At the end of September it wiped out 40 members of a village guard clan near Van, most of them women and children. The following day it ambushed and killed 29 troops. It also provoked fear among the Kurds of Iraq. At the end of July it imposed a blockade on Iraqi Kurdistan as a reprisal for restrictions on its own activities. It did so simply by warning truck drivers of retribution if they back the initiative with an illiterate population. In some areas it was reckoned that up to 50 per cent of the vote was influenced by local shaykhs, and it paid the PKK to seek to woo young shaykhs and mullas to its cause.

However, the PKK was also moved by strategic considerations. It wanted to operate more freely from Iran. While it knew Iran had pragmatic reasons for creating a nuisance in Turkey, it also recognized that it should present itself as well-disposed to Islam. In 1989 Ocalan's brother Osman had established a liaison office in Iran, and the following year negotiated the establishment of twenty operational bases from which to strike at targets in Van, Agri and Kars provinces. In his Nawruz speech in 1990 Ocalan played up the positive aspects of the Islamic revolution.

The Failure to Find a Modus Vivendi

Meanwhile in the political arena, spring 1992 had begun ominously with about 100 civilians killed by security forces during Nawruz, now unmistakably the annual focus for Kurdish national expression. With stride it calls from the Right to stop the shilly-shallying and to deal with the PKK once and for all, Ozal now effectively surrendered responsibility for the south-east to the military, retreating from the liberal gestures made at the outset of the year. Ozal was under pressure because a quarter of the 4,000 dead since the start of the PKK campaign in 1984 had perished in the previous year. The Turkish establishment would not allow the army to appear weak.

In August 1992 security forces assaulted the town of Sirnak, following unsubstantiated reports of PKK activity there. The entire population, roughly 20,000, fled *en masse*, and many buildings were damaged irreparably. Similar occurrences took place elsewhere, at Dargecit and Cukurca. Almost 2,000 died in 1992. The PKK soon demonstrated its ability to destroy the illusion of government authority. At the end of September it wiped out 40 members of a village guard clan near Van, most of them women and children. The following day it ambushed and killed 29 troops. It also provoked fear among the Kurds of Iraq. At the end of July it imposed a blockade on Iraqi Kurdistan as a reprisal for restrictions on its own activities. It did so simply by warning truck drivers of retribution if they crossed the border. This was sufficient to strike fear in the hearts of those supplying Iraq's Kurds.

Given Iraqi Kurdish anger at such an act and Iraqi Kurdish dependence on Ankara for survival, it was easy for Turkey's general staff to persuade the Kurdish Regional Government in Arbil to assist in a massive offensive against the estimated 5,000 or so PKK guerillas hidden in the ravines of Bahdinan. In an operation during October and November which involved thousands of Turkish troops driving southwards towards Iraqi Kurdish forces sweeping the mountains fastnesses of northern Iraq, hundreds of PKK fighters were killed.[37] The vast majority fled, to surrender either to Iraqi Kurdish forces or to escape into Iran.

In the aftermath rumours emerged of bitter disagreement within the PKK concerning Ocalan's leadership and strategy. For it was clear that the massing of 5,000 fighters against Turkish targets marked a disastrous change in PKK strategy, away from guerilla operations that tied down the maximum number of troops for the minimum effort, into direct conventional confrontation aimed at driving Turkish forces out of parts of Turkish Kurdistan. This strategy was faulty on two counts. The PKK had no reasonable chance of defeating Turkish forces in a conventional war, since the latter enjoyed superior mobility and firepower through helicopter transport and gunships, artillery and armour. Furthermore, Ankara was almost certainly in receipt of satellite intelligence from the United States. Its other flaw was to move the focus of conflict away from mass mobilization of the civil population, where the potential for wresting control of the region from the state truly lay.

During the winter there was considerable speculation that the backbone of the PKK had now been broken. Even before Turkey's October offensive, the PKK was under considerable pressure on account of Syria's closure of its training facilities in the Biqaa valley in September. Ocalan himself was moved to Lataqiya. Following the defeat in Bahdinan, Ocalan had come under bitter criticism, notably from his brother Osman, and PKK units were rumoured to be deserting him. Then, the 13 March 1993 edition of *Sabah* carried an article in which Talabani indicated that following his own meeting with him in February, Ocalan was now ready to abandon the armed struggle. His offer seemed more modest than previous ones, and included a PKK condemnation of terrorism and an offer to abandon hostilities: a declaration in favour of a negotiated solution and a willingness to allow Kurdish deputies, rather than the PKK, to negotiate with Ankara on behalf of the Kurdish people; a commitment to the unity of Turkey and the rejection of separatism and a commitment to the legal democratic process.

Sure enough, on 17 March 1993 Ocalan himself announced a unilateral ceasefire to run from Nawruz (21 March) until 15 April, during which time his forces would only defend themselves if attacked. If the Turkish government were responsive, Ocalan stated, 'There is no reason why we should not extend our ceasefire... I personally would like to be able to return unarmed to the south east in order to engage in political activity.'[38] In Turkey it was taken as a sign that Ocalan had undergone military defeat and now sought whatever he could gain politically. On 16 April he renewed the ceasefire indefinitely. It seemed he had lost his stomach for the fight. His demands were no more than had been mooted by leading Turkish politicians, 'We should be given our cultural freedoms and the right to broadcast in Kurdish. The village guard system should be abolished and the Emergency legislation lifted. The Turkish authorities should take the necessary measures to prevent unsolved murders and should recognize the political rights of Kurdish organization.'[39] Significantly, Ocalan made no mention of self-determination.

By a cruel irony, President Ozal died of a heart attack the following day. In February Ozal had written a six-page letter to Prime Minister Demirel about the progressive alienation of the Kurdish community and the PKK's pervasive and growing authority, and of the long-term threat to Turkey's territorial integrity.[40] His solution, however, combined advocacy of an open debate with the mass deportation of up to 100,000 Kurds to deny the PKK a sympathetic population in their areas of operation. In fact roughly that number had already been deported, but without the desired effect. It had merely spread the networks of PKK support.

It is fruitless to speculate on whether history might have been different had Ozal survived. However, Turkey and Ocalan had lost the only statesman who had proved capable of imaginative if modest gestures towards the Kurds. Ozal was succeeded as president by Demirel, who defeated his nearest rival, the Kurd Kamran Inan, by a substantial margin. Demirel, despite placatory remarks on his assumption of the premiership in 1991, had demonstrated no serious concern to resolve the Kurdish question by political means. He now sat on his hands and allowed the army to take Ocalan's ceasefire as a sign as weakness. On the ground it renewed its efforts to round up some of the 7,000 fighters Ocalan claimed were still at large in Turkey. During the next six weeks troops killed about 100 guerillas and civilians, arrested hundreds of others, and renewed house demolitions. Demirel and the army made it clear that no negotiations nor any other concessions were in prospect. They would crush the PKK utterly before reassessing state policy towards the Kurds.

On 24 May a group of PKK guerillas stopped a bus near Bingol and killed the 35 off-duty troops aboard. This was probably the work of a rogue PKK commander intent upon sabotaging the ceasefire. Although he had not authorized the attack, Ocalan now had little alternative but formally to declare the ceasefire over, which he did in June. The PKK resumed the fight because Turkey had failed either to make a gesture, such as allowing Kurdish-medium television or radio broadcasts, or suspending military action. Indeed, had the state suspended security activity, this in itself would probably have convinced the majority of Kurds that the state was ready to abandon its traditional implacability.

Once again Turkish Kurdistan was plunged into bitter fighting. the new prime minister, Tansu Ciller (Turkey's first woman prime minister), was insufficiently assured of her own position to gainsay the General Staff's decision to renew its offensive, which included destructive assaults on the towns of Kulp and Lice. On one July day 75 civilians, soldiers and guerillas died. That month the death toll (since 1984) rose to an estimated 6,500.

Both protagonists now sought to widen the compass of the conflict to affect the rest of Turkey. In Ankara the Kurdish party, HEP, was banned in July as a symbolic gesture against Kurdish national feeling. Some ex-HEP deputies had already formed a new group, the Democratic Labour Party (DEP), signalling the futility of the state's action. In a further demonstration of rage against Kurds, the State Constitutional Court also ordered one of the most moderate Kurds in the Assembly to be stripped of his parliamentary immunity.[41]

The PKK too was willing to carry its struggle into Turkish Turkey, deploying new weapons in its armoury. In mid-June it launched a series of attacks against tourist sites on Turkey's south coast, and warned against foreign tourists visiting Turkey.[42] It also started taking European tourists in Kurdistan hostage. On 24 June it attacked the Turkish embassy in Berne, a forerunner to co-ordinated attacks on other Turkish targets in West European cities in November. These led to the banning of the PKK and its affiliates in Germany, and the detention of a number of PKK supporters in France, steps which threatened the PKK's financial resources, reportedly raised through extortion and intimidation among emigrant Kurds.

The PKK also demonstrated its grip on the south-east. If Hizb Allah Yumruki could intimidate the press, so could the PKK. On 18 October it banned all Turkish and foreign reporters from 'Northern Kurdistan', and successfully closed down all Turkish newspaper representations in the region. Obedience to this closure was a remarkable demonstration of the PKK challenge to state authority in the region. By the end of 1993 the overall death toll exceeded 10,000 and the state faced the prospect of its south eastern provinces slowly sliding out of civil control.

By 1993 the PPK had been waging its guerrilla war for almost a decade. It had every reason to be satisfied with its progress. Since 1984 it had successfully expanded its field of operations, and had become the most serious challenge ever posed against the Republic. It had had two prime objectives: to create a coherent national movement and to persuade the Turkish state to parley. On the first count it had, by 1993, been hugely successful. It had driven from the field any serious competitors for the Kurdish national mantle. The PKK happily shouted down any other Kurdish voices. There was no room for views other than those of its leader. It had also galvanized a great swathe of Kurds. This was most discernible at Nawruz, when thousands took to the streets, both in Kurdistan and in the cities of migration. Here the ordinary people of Kurdistan could demonstrate their identity in public. In 1992 no less that 70 people had died in Nawruz demonstrations. Furthermore, a very substantial number of Kurds seemed to have a relative or friend actively supporting the revolt. In short, it had indeed created a coherent national movement that was unlikely to disappear even with its own demise.

Bringing the Turkish state to the negotiating table, however, was much harder to achieve. By 1993 it was already becoming apparent to the PKK leadership that a plateau had been reached in terms of what guerrilla operations could achieve on the ground. This was the reason for its unilateral ceasefire in the spring of that year. It no longer wished to fight. It wanted to talk.

The State response to the Kurdish challenge

There is no doubt that President Ozal had been acutely aware of the seriousness of the challenge. Shortly before his death he had written to his prime minister, Suleyman Demirel in the starkest terms, 'The Turkish Republic is facing its gravest threat yet. A social earthquake could cut one part of Turkey from the rest, and we could all be buried beneath it.'[43] Ozal saw the wider ramifications. His successors were denied that freedom by the National Security Council which ensured that dealing with the Kurdish question remained firmly within its own remit.

The National Security Council resolutely continued to seek a purely military solution. Three hundred thousand army and gendarmerie troops were deployed in the area. They were supported with assault helicopters, and almost certainly by satellite information on guerrilla movement from the United States. Under Decree 285 of July 1987 which had established the State of Emergency Region, the governor general had been empowered to evacuate villages on a temporary or permanent basis. By 1990, according to press reports, about 326 villages had been evacuated, primarily in Siirt, Hakkari and Van. As the conflict spread to Diyarbakir and Tunceli, so evacuations were carried out there also. Shortly after becoming prime minister in October 1991, Demirel was informed 'The [counter-insurgency] operation will involve area cleansing and evacuation on a systematic basis.'[44] This soon started to happen. In February 1993 Ozal called for: 'A planned, balanced migration, including members of all segments of [Kurdish] society, to predetermined settlements in the West is essential.'[45] However, the evacuations were anything but orderly and migration was wholly unplanned, chaotic and leading to great human tragedy and widespread environmental destruction. The government, shy of admitting what it was up to, blamed the PKK. By the end of 1994 at least 2,000 villages had been emptied. In July 1995 a government minister admitted that no less than 2,664 villages had been evacuated, with well over two million rendered homeless. Moreover, he acknowledged that these evacuations were at the hands of the security forces and not the PKK as the State usually alleged.[46] By mid-1996 the toll was in the order of 3,000 villages and three million homeless. By summer 1999 the evictions had exceeded 3,500 and still had not finished. The security forces simply went wider afield, to empty villages in Sivas, Erzincan and Erzerum, in order to eradicate potential havens for the guerrillas.

Accounts of victims and eyewitnesses, among them conscripts disturbed by what they had witnessed, testified to the extreme brutality with which evacuations were carried out. This included deliberately degrading behaviour, arbitrary arrest, violence, torture, extra-judicial killings, sexual violence or threats of violence and the wanton destruction (or plunder) of moveable property, livestock and food stocks.[47] In 1995 the Turkish Human Rights Association (IHD) published a major survey regarding those displaced by these evictions. Overall, over 90 per cent confirmed they had come under direct state pressure to leave and 88.7 per cent believed they had been targeted simply because they were Kurds.[48] In 1994 alone, the agricultural loss was estimated at US$350 million. In Diyarbakir province, for example, it was estimated that livestock were reduced by 50 per cent, stock rearing by 30 per cent and forested areas by 60 per cent.

The majority of the displaced remained for the time being in the region, seeking shelter in the nearest major town or city. One may gauge the stressful impact by comparing certain town populations in 1991 with the estimated population by 1996:

Town	Population 1991	Estimated pop. 1996
Hakkari	35,000	80,000
Batman	150,000	250,000
Van	153,000	500,000
Diyarbakir	380,000	1.3 million[49]

It was not long, however, before some of these involuntary migrants began to move to the larger cities of migration outside the Kurdish region. Most favoured destinations where there were already relatives or fellow villagers. Favourite destinations were Adana, Mersin, Iskanderun and other coastal towns, or the large cities in the west, most notably Istanbul, Ankara and Izmir. By August 1994, barely two years since wholesale evacuations were started, it was estimated that the population of Adana had grown from 900,000 to 1.5 million, and that of Mersin from 550,000 to about one million. Most evacuees found themselves living in shanty areas on the edge of town.

While the number of assassinations of perceived opponents of state policy on the street declined, the number of 'disappearances' and abductions increased substantially. Many took place in broad daylight by members of the Special Teams (Özel Tim) or intelligence (JITEM) organs of the gendarmerie. Plain clothes police were unabashed to declare their identity. Sometimes bodies of the disappeared would be found on refuse tips or by a lonely roadside. It was not unusual for such bodies to bear the marks of torture. Other bodies were never recovered.

Pro-Kurdish political parties were a particular target for harassment. In the run-up to the local elections of March 1994, the Democratic Labour Party (DEP) formally withdrew after the assassination of party members, bomb attacks on its headquarters and branch offices and the arrest of many members. When a PKK bomb killed six army cadets in Istanbul, the state arrested six Kurdish DEP deputies, removed their parliamentary immunity and charged them with separatism. The two most notable were Leyla Zana and Hatip Dicle, both of whom received 15-year jail sentences for belonging to and assisting an illegal armed group (the PKK). The evidence was flimsy, but the state was convinced that HEP and DEP were merely the PKK in political clothing. Other DEP leaders fled to Europe. In June 1994 DEP was closed down. Although a new party, the People's Democratic Party (HADEP) was formed, it was clear that the state remained determined to stifle any discussion of the Kurdish question by Kurds themselves. In the December 1995 national elections, HADEP received more than 1.2 million votes, despite widespread intimidation of candidates and supporters, several of whom suffered arrest, torture or murder. Three HADEP officials were killed in Elbistan (Maras province) alone. But HADEP's appeal was almost completely confined to the south-east. While in Diyarbakir over 50 per cent of the electorate chose HADEP, very few Kurds in Istanbul voted for it.

At its second party congress in June 1996 a young militant tore down the Turkish flag and replaced it with a PKK one. Although the organisers quickly removed the PKK banner, it provided the pretext on which the newly elected 32-member leadership council could be arrested. Three other delegates were shot dead on their way home. Murat Bozlak, the Chairman, was among those arrested, tried and imprisoned. A year earlier he had survived an assassination attempt on his own doorstep.

None of this was remotely surprising. Turkey viewed HADEP no differently from its predecessors, and decided to place it under overt and covert pressure.[10] At the beginning of 1999, with another general election in prospect for April, the chief prosecutor presented an indictment for the closure of HADEP to the Constitutional Court. But it was not merely parties sympathetic to the PKK that it could not endure. The state was determined to stifle any Kurdish voice. In February the pro-Kurdish Democratic Mass Party (DKP) was closed. This had been led by Serafettin Elci, a veteran noted for his moderation. The DKP had called for political, civil and cultural rights *within* the Republic and had never suggested secession. Nevertheless it and its leader were accused of making 'separatist' propaganda. The DKP was the fifteenth political party closed by the Constitutional Court since Turkey returned to civilian rule in 1983.

Meanwhile, on the battlefield, the security forces continued to pursue PKK guerrilla groups. It was a sign of their apparent ascendancy that in 1997–98 the state lifted the State of Emergency in four of the ten provinces to which this regime had been applied throughout the 1990s. From 1997 incursions into northern Iraq had become a regular feature of these operations. Some of these involved the movement of 30,000 or more troops over the border. The KDP became an eager assistant in these Turkish operations. This partly resulted from the stranglehold Turkey could apply at the Khabur crossing, Ibrahim Khalil. But the KDP also greatly resented PKK guerrillas in Bahdinan who did their best to recruit Iraqi villages the KDP viewed as its own constituency, into its doctrinaire ranks. Yet however many guerrillas Turkey claimed to have killed, Bahdinan always seemed to harbour more. Moreover, just as tranquillity seemed slowly to be re-established in parts of the south-east, the PKK would launch attacks elsewhere, for example the Black Sea region.

However, from 1996 the PKK found itself increasingly on the defensive, losing access to food and shelter because of the evictions and suffering an increasing level of casualties. By 1996 the estimated number of deaths was 20,000. By 1999 they were thought to exceed 35,000. The area dominated by the PKK was unmistakably contracting. It was clear that guerrilla tactics were failing. Thus, for the third time, Ocalan offered a unilateral ceasefire in September 1998 in the hope that Turkey would respond. Turkey, however, had other plans in mind.

Dealing with Ocalan

In October 1998 Turkey suddenly massed 10,000 troops on Syria's northern border and demanded that it expel the PKK and hand over Abdullah Ocalan forthwith. Syria and Lebanon had been the home-base of the PKK ever since the 1980 coup. Turkey's collusion with Israel in this ploy was unmistakable. Even since 1994 Turkey and Israel had been working closely together on security matters. By 1996 Israeli pilots were flying warplanes inside Turkey's airspace and providing advice on counter-insurgency methods. This formed part of the United States' strategy for the region, a strategy welcomed by Turkey's generals but viewed with caution by its diplomats who did not welcome polarisation of the region. With Syria vulnerable to

Israeli air attack, and the prospect of invasion by the unquestionably stronger Turkish armed forces, Syria rapidly brought PKK activity to a halt and signed an undertaking with Turkey on 'mutual security', essentially the prevention of PKK activity across their joint border.

However, Ocalan was not handed over. He quietly left Syria for Moscow. In mid-November he flew to Rome, where he sought asylum but was arrested. Italy hoped Germany would seek his extradition having issued an international arrest warrant for him, but the latter declined, fearful of the domestic reaction among its resident half million Kurds. Italy refused Turkey's extradition request, unwilling to extradite him to a state where the death penalty was still in force. In mid-January Ocalan left for Russia. He hoped he would be able to reach the Hague, but the Netherlands refused to admit him. At the end of the month he flew to Athens. There can be little doubt that the Greek Foreign Ministry came under intense US pressure. On 1 February Ocalan arrived in Nairobi, the CIA's African intelligence base. On 15 February he was abducted on his way to the airport to fly to South Africa, and handed to Turkish special forces waiting at the airport.

Turkey put Ocalan on Imrali island, 35 km from Istanbul. He was held incommunicado for ten days, after which he was afforded very limited access to two lawyers, never in private and never with case papers. Predictably, therefore, when Ocalan appeared in court on 31 May, his defence was in disarray. The case was transacted with speed. Ocalan himself made a placatory and apologetic defence, describing PKK militancy as 'a mistake', and stating in perverse disregard of the facts that the human rights situation since 1990 was much improved, whereas in reality it had reached its worst since Dersim in 1938. He said nothing of the thousands killed, the mysterious murders and deaths in police custody, nor of the millions rendered homeless. The prosecution raised the emotional temperature by bringing mothers of fallen soldiers to the witness stand. Much play was also made of the thousands of Kurds and their families who had suffered intimidation and worse at the hands of the PKK. But Kurds who had been tortured and killed by the state, many of them non-combatants, were barely mentioned. Thus, far from being a shop window for Kurdish grievances, the trial focussed on the challenge the PKK had posed to a law-abiding society. There can be little doubt that Ocalan, either of his own free will or subject to Turkish psychological pressure, missed a unique opportunity to state the Kurdish case.

On 29 June Ocalan was found guilty of treason and sentenced to death. Yet there was no certainty he would die although this is what Turkish public opinion definitely sought. A Court of Appeal, Parliament and the President had, sequentially, to approve the sentence. In the meantime, the defence lawyers had taken Ocalan's case to the European court in Strasbourg.[51] President Demirel assured the international community that Turkey would abide by Strasbourg's ruling, but many doubted it.

In the meantime, following Syria's expulsion of Ocalan, Turkey had stepped up its drive against Kurdish expression. When HADEP organized countrywide protests against Ocalan's temporary detention in Rome, in November 1998, more than 3,000 supporters were detained by the authorities. One detainee died from police torture in Diyarbakir, while in Istanbul another died at the hands of an angry Turkish crowd. Following Ocalan's capture, the security forces clamped down further. Nawruz 1999 was very tightly controlled. The greatly feared gendarmerie 'Special Teams' were deployed for the first time in Kurdish shanty areas of Turkey's western cities. Roughly 8,000 were detained during Nawruz, of whom no less than 1,700 were detained in Istanbul.

The crisis for the PKK

Ever since Ocalan had been compelled to leave Syria, the PKK leadership had been in deep crisis, and this deepened with his capture in Nairobi. The PKK military wing blamed the European wing for showing too much faith in obtaining asylum for Ocalan in Europe. It was clear that Europe had little inclination to confront both the United States and Turkey. While the guerrillas continued their struggle in the mountains, a small spate of bombings reminded Turkey's civilian population and also tourists that the PKK could, if it so wished, bring mayhem and destruction to the Turkish part of Turkey. But it was a dangerous game to play, as the PKK had always been aware. Bomb attacks in the west could transform the conflict from one between the Kurdish people and the state into an inter-communal struggle. While the PKK leadership struggled with what to do, in early August Ocalan called from his cell on Imrali island, for a complete cessation of PKK military activity. Within a couple of days, the PKK announced that it would indeed abandon the military struggle. Yet this left a dilemma. With no sign of a break in Turkish obduracy, how could the PKK prosecute its struggle by other means?

The cost of repressing the Kurds

It seemed as if the generals had won, but had they? No one could doubt the uniquely damaging impact of the war since 1984. By 1999 it was costing the state US$10 billion annually in military terms alone. The loss in terms of damage to the environment, to agriculture and human productivity, even if it were in the most impoverished part of the country was still enormous. It had also cost Turkey hugely in terms of international investment. Tourism, for example, by the late 1990s was worth US$8 billion annually, double its value only seven years earlier. But in 1999 tourism was over 30 per cent down. An opinion poll in Germany to establish the reason indicated that more people had been dissuaded from holidaying in Turkey by its poor human rights record than from fear of bombs.

Furthermore, Turkey's treatment of its Kurds during the conflict had brought Turkey into growing conflict with Europe. By the mid-1990s it was well known in informed circles that Turkey routinely broke the European Convention on Human Rights particularly with regard to the right to life, the right to fair trial, freedom from torture, freedom of assembly and of expression. Amnesty International regularly published searing cases of violations of the grossest kind.

This record notwithstanding, the European Union entered into customs union with Turkey in December 1995, and Turkey undertook to clean up its human rights record. No such improvement took place, and in 1997 to its utter fury, Turkey found itself not even on the waiting list for entry into the Union. It had been overtaken by recent East European applicants. Furthermore the Union strongly criticized Turkey's record. Worse was to come. A trickle of individual plaintiffs to the European Court turned into a stream. From 1996 onwards Strasbourg began finding against Turkey on an almost routine basis, and found Turkey guilty of persistent and serious violations with regard to village destruction, torture and unlawful killings. In October that year Turkey's own lawyer resigned remarking 'Turkey always promises, but never fulfils... defending Turkey is impossible in current circumstances.'[52] It was therefore no great surprise that in June 1999 the Council of Europe's 41-member ministerial committee publicly rebuked Turkey for repeated and serious human rights violations.[53] No member of the Council of Europe had been censured in this way before. Ever since it joined NATO half a century earlier, Turkey had relied on the importance of its strategic alliance with the West to outweigh Western misgivings over its human rights record. Yet, by 1999, however much countries like Britain and Germany wished to overlook such matters in favour of their economic and strategic interests, a growing body of parliamentarians and human rights activists prevented them from doing so.

Internally Turkey also paid a heavy price. There can be little doubt that the Kurdish challenge was used as a pretext by the National Security Council to maintain its own ascendancy, and thereby dangerously diminish the process of civil government and democracy. As self appointed guardian of the Kemalist legacy, the National Security Council tried to freeze any organic evolution of the Turkish republic. No civil government could survive without the approval of the NSC. This led to serious decline in the political process. Apart from the rightist Turgut Ozal, no political leader emerged with the stature and skill to challenge the NSC and to win.

Having taken charge of the Kurdish question following Ozal's death, the armed services chiefs allowed the emergence of a profoundly corrupt state of affairs at the heart of the state. This corruption was starkly revealed in the Susurluk incident[54] which demonstrated that some of the highest officials of the state were closely involved in criminal activities: in major drug smuggling;[55] in the funding and facilitation of death squads recruited from past and present members of the National Intelligence Agency (MiT) and also from members or supporters of the extreme right National Action Party. These had been responsible for the assassination of Kurdish activists and human rights workers.

Furthermore, the Kurdish question has placed great pressure on Turkey's political structure which, since the 1950s has been in a process of fragmentation and diminishment. Part of this was the natural result of the three military interventions, which had weakened the authority of the electorate. It was also the result of the ideological doctrine introduced by the 1980 regime of 'Turkish-Islamic' synthesis, intended to reconcile the Turkish, Ottoman and westernising factors in society by giving emphasis to the centrality of Turkish-Sunni identity. The Kurdish revolt demonstrated the strong challenge faced by the 'Turkish' part of that synthesis. The rise of the Welfare (Refah) Party to become senior partner in elected government in 1996 challenged the state definition of the Islamic dimension, which the NSC could only address by removing Refah from office and banning it in 1997. The Virtue (Fazilet) Party replaced it, a continuing challenge to the secular-modernising ethic of Kemalism. Finally, in response to the Turkish-Islamic synthesis, the Alevi community, probably 15 million in number of whom up to one third is Kurdish, began to loosen its identity with the political left in favour of establishing political Alevism.

Thus, at the beginning of the twenty first century, Turkey finds itself in a profound dilemma concerning conflicting identities which must be resolved if it is to flourish socially and economically as well as democratically. These are formidable challenges for which the National Security Council is manifestly inadequate. Apparently incapable of managing political change, the NSC and bureaucracy has reacted very negatively to the growing frustration of important institutions of civil society that question the conduct of the Kurdish problem. In 1995 the Turkish Union of Chambers of Commerce published the results of a survey which revealed two overriding and uncomfortable factors about the Kurdish problem: that Kurdish cultural identity and support for the PKK were both more extensive that had previously been appreciated in government circles; and that approximately two-thirds of those Kurds polled wanted a measure of self administration within the Republic, and barely 11 per cent favoured secession, giving the lie to the much-parroted Turkish cry of separatism.[56] Publication of the report caused a furore, and its distinguished Turkish author, Professor Dogu Ergil, came under police scrutiny. Eighteen months later the NSC reacted with even greater fury towards a report commissioned by the Turkish Industrialists and Businessmen's Association (TUSIAD).[57] This one called, *inter alia*, for cultural freedom with regard to the place and personal names of Kurdish society, for the removal of any barriers on the Kurdish language, for freedom of Kurdish expression including the freedom to form political parties that could explicitly represent Kurdish concerns. Yet it was the call for an end to the NSC in its present form and strength which provoked intense anger in the armed forces. Although carefully worded, the report indicated that the wealth producing sector believed Turkey was in serious political crisis, with serious gulfs between conflicting identities: military-civil, religious-secular, Turkish-Kurdish and Sunni-Alevi.

GAP and the Absence of an Economic Solution

Meanwhile, Turkey still faced a massive economic challenge. It was well understood among more thoughtful Turks that the key to resolving the conflict was partly political but possibly primarily economic. By the beginning of the 1990s it was well known that the per capita income in the south-east was barely 42 per cent of the national average and barely a quarter of per capita income in Turkey's Aegean/ Marmara region. It was equally well known that no government had ever taken the serious steps required to reverse the growing economic disparities between western and eastern Turkey. The Kurdish provinces, unquestionably the poorest, received less that 10 per cent of the national development budget.

It was therefore with a good deal of fanfare, that Ozal had begun to implement the South East Anatolia Project (GAP). This ambitious project proposed to harness the power of the Euphrates and Tigris rivers to produce the hydro-electricity that would fuel Turkey's industrial expansion in the early years of the twenty-first century and would irrigate adjacent lands leading to a major expansion of agriculture and related agro-industries. Those living in the region, it was claimed, would enjoy substantial economic benefits. The planners proposed to raise per capita income in the region to 53 per cent of the national average, an increase of ten percentage points.

In reality GAP revealed that government either failed to understand the economic dimension of the Kurdish question, or that its intentions were primarily to do with wringing whatever wealth it could from the south-east for the benefit of the rest of the country. For, as GAP master plan itself admitted, within the region, 8 per cent of farming families owned over 50 per cent of the land, while 41 per cent held between 10 and 50 dunums and 38 per cent held no land at all. Of the large landowner families, a substantial proportion were absentee, content to allow inefficient farming as long as they obtained an adequate income from their lands. Without a fundamental reform it was inconceivable that the majority of the farming population could benefit from GAP. The last attempt at land reform, in 1978, was abortive thanks mainly to the fear of the main parties in Ankara that it would destroy the patronage system that delivered their votes. Plans to create state run enterprises and smallholder co-operatives seem more likely to drive large numbers off the land.

Furthermore, it was difficult to see how a largely illiterate population would be able to benefit from capital-intensive agriculture or agro-industry, let alone the ancillary sector that would grow up to service it. The Kurds had neither capital nor education. Capital would come from western Turkey or abroad, given secure conditions. The notoriously poor education provision of Kurdistan, with overcrowded classrooms and unsympathetic Turkish teachers, told its own story. By 1990 the average literacy in Mardin province, by no means the worst affected province, was 48 per cent compared with a national average of 77 per cent. This was hardly surprising since all education was in a language foreign to the majority of rural inhabitants. The enrolment figures spoke for themselves. Only 70 per cent of children ever appeared at school, and of these only 18 per cent went on to secondary education, of whom only 9 per cent completed the secondary cycle.[8] Dicle University in Diyarbakir, intended to serve the region was actually full of students from other parts of Turkey for whom Dicle University was a last resort.

Thus the two essential prerequisites for the region's economic progress, the final removal of the landowning agha class and the introduction of Kurdish-medium primary education could not be implemented because both measures contradicted state policy regarding the control of Kurdistan.

Government officials made much of GAP's benefits for the local population. But the few local people who had benefited by the end of the decade were greatly outnumbered by those who had lost their land. The Ataturk dam had displaced at least 50,000 villagers in the early 1990s, and the Ilisu dam on the Tigris promised to displace another 20,000. As elsewhere in the world, large dams had a tendency to cause environmental and ecological damage and to displace large numbers of people. Far from being a panacea for the ills of the region, by 1998 only 42 per cent of local people were aware that GAP was a development project, and over 10 per cent thought it was merely a TV channel.[59] Only 11 per cent of those polled had either short or long term expectations of GAP.[60]

In fact the economic gulf between western and eastern Turkey widened during the 1990s. One reason was the war, but another was the decline in per capita spending by the government in the east and south east during the decade. By the mid-1990s the Eastern and South-eastern regions combined was producing less than a quarter of what Turkey's richest region, Marmara, produced. In the words of a Virtue (Fazilet) Party report in the summer of 1999, 'in western regions of Turkey the per capita income is $4,000–$5,000, while in the east and south east it is only $600–$900.'[61]

One reason was that the single most important activity of this impoverished region, stock-rearing, had taken such a battering in recent years. For centuries eastern Anatolia had been known for stock-rearing, with large herds driven to the west for slaughter. In 1970 livestock still accounted for 12.3 per cent of Turkey's GNP. By 1997 it had dwindled to 2.2 per cent. In 1979 livestock still accounted for 30 per cent of agriculture, but as a proportion had, by the end of the century, almost halved. Much of the decline was attributable to the war. Village evictions and stringent prohibitions on grazing in the summer pastures was one crucial factor. The other, which was a result of these strictures but also the whole distortion of the economy affected by the military presence, was smuggling. By 1999, 80,000 tonnes (approximately 5 per cent of Turkey's annual meat requirement) was smuggled, largely from Iran. The local livestock economy of Hakkari sharply portrayed the change: in 1984 the province held an estimated 5 million livestock. Fifteen years later it was barely one tenth of this figure.

In March 1999, following Ocalan's capture, Prime Minister Ecevit announced a plan to boost economic activity in the 26 provinces of the East and South-eastern regions. But he allocated US$108 million, sufficient to create employment opportunities for 8,200 jobs in the region. With 80 per cent unemployment among the millions of displaced, Ecevit's pledge was merely the last in a succession of worthless yearly commitments by Turkey's political leaders to address the economic challenge in the east. In reality the region needed the kind of money being spent on defeating

the PKK. Turkey's 1999 draft defence budget earmarked US$3.4 billion on procure-
ment, with the aim of spending US$31 billion over 8 years. That was the kind of
finance that might in due course render the existence of both an army and a large
gendarmerie force in the south-east unnecessary. As one expert remarked, 'The
economic conditions in the area... are hardly different from those in Turkey in the
early days of the Republic.'[62] But by the end of the century no such spending was in
prospect, just as there was no indication that with the apparent end to PKK hostilities, there was an intention to address the fundamental political, economic and
social reasons for Kurdish discontent.

Living together

One of the more remarkable features of the conflict was that after fifteen years of
bitter and savage war, the conflict had not descended into an inter-communal one.
The danger of this eventuality had been greatly increased by the progressive outflow
from the Kurdish region of both economic migrants and dispossessed fugitives from
military operations. The apparent end of PKK armed action gave hope that such a
long expected development would be averted. Yet the danger remained that this
nightmare might still emerge. Many towns and cities on the south coast and in the
Hatay faced a major influx of migrants. So, too, did Istanbul and Izmir. Here, too,
displaced people faced police surveillance and harassment. Indeed, these slum areas
became extensions of Kurdistan, where active nationalists, passive 'assimilationists'
and willing adherents of the Turkish Republic all jostled together. By mid-1996 the
Turkish human rights association, Mazlum-Der, claimed that Adana, Mersin and
Antalya, hitherto predominantly Turkish towns, now had a Kurdish majority.
Indeed, its president told a parliamentary commission the following year:

> 'In cities like Adana, Mersin and Antalya, Turkish and Kurdish districts are emerging.
> Turks cannot enter the Kurdish district and *vice versa*. One should realise that with a little
> provocation this will lead to very serious social clashes. These people [the evicted] have
> lost not only their flour and bread but their honour as well. One cannot ignore thousands
> of families who make their kids beg. In other words, the incident [village evacuations] has
> a very serious socio-psychological dimension.'[63]

It was undeniable that polarization between migrant communities and their
neighbours had increased during the conflict. A poll conducted by the mass circulation *Sabah* in spring 1992, when the Kurdish challenge had not reached its climax,
indicated that only 25 per cent of Turks felt they could live with Kurds in a 'brotherly
way'. It also revealed a profound distrust regarding Kurdish political ambitions.
While 70 per cent of Kurds insisted they did not want an independent state, no fewer
than 89 per cent of Turks were convinced that they did.[64] From time to time migrant
Kurdish labour was driven away by angry local people, reacting to the latest Turkish
losses. Migrant Kurds learnt to keep their own counsel, avoid speaking Kurdish in
public and blame the PKK for actions that had patently been perpetrated by the

security forces. However, the danger was that while Kurds might suppress the truth in their daily contact with Turks, migration would feed the kind of transformation that had happened in Beirut where, during the 1960s and 1970s recently urbanized villagers lost their *unpoliticized* traditional culture in favour of a highly politicized one. A warning sign of increasing polarization came in the April 1999 election, with the greatly increased vote for the extreme right National Action Party by Turks (establishing it as second strongest party), and the capture by HADEP of six Kurdish cities in the concurrent local elections. By its own draconian policy the state had spread the cancer, as it saw it, to other parts of the body of the Republic and fostered the political extremes. Yet it seemed oblivious to the long-term legacy of anger, bitterness and communal danger its daily acts of humiliation were bound to leave.

Psychological or physical separation of the two major communities of the Republic was complemented by a continuing Turkish anxiety at Kurdish population increase. In 1989, according to the official statistics, the average gross reproduction rate in Turkish Kurdistan was 2.75 per cent, compared with one for Turkish regions of the Republic of 1.49 per cent. Roughly 50 per cent of the Kurdish population was under fifteen compared with less than 35 per cent of the Turkish population. The implications of such statistics were abundantly clear. A minority that was approximately 23 per cent of the population today would grow as a proportion of the total population at an accelerating rate, unless the Kurdish birthrate dropped dramatically. Admittedly, large numbers of Kurds married Turks, or simply assimilated into Turkish culture, but there was little likelihood that Kurdish identity would do anything but grow. Of the three million so brutally displaced during the 1990s, half statistically must have been under the age of 15. They had seen their parents shamefully humiliated by the security forces and felt the fear. In all likelihood the state had sown dragon's teeth for the future.

If so, then the state was wasting its time chasing guerrillas either inside Turkey or in northern Iraq. Somehow it had to find the means to bring its Kurds into productive relationship with the rest of the country. With its intensified drive against all non-violent national expression or discussion, by HADEP and by Turkish human rights organisations and by journalists, it was difficult to detect any ability or willingness of the state to address the underlying issues. The progressive diminishment of Turkish political life, the weakness of democracy and the widespread acceptance of the necessity for human rights violations by the state in order to maintain order, all make it difficult to be optimistic. Yet the state cannot deny the contradictions lying at the heart of the Republic forever. Social conflict, growing economic frustration and under-performance, and the near certainty of renewed political violence with a thwarted and oppressed minority are likely to lead to a more serious crisis in the future.

Sources

Official: Turkey, Prime Ministry State Planning Organization, *The South East Anatolia Project (GAP): Final Master Plan Report*, vol. 1 (Ankara, 1989); State Institute for Statistics, *1991 Statistical Yearbook of Turkey* (Ankara, 1992).

Published: Bozarslan, *Entre la umma et le nationalisme*; Helsinki Watch, *Destroying Ethnic Identity* (Washington, 1983, 1990) and *Nothing Unusual: The Torture of Children in Turkey* (New York and Washington, 1991); Ismet Imset, 'PKK: the Deception of Terror' in *Briefing* (Ankaara, January 1987–May 1988) and *The PKK: A Report on Separatist Violence (1973–1992)* (Ankara, 1992); More, *Les Kurdes Aujourd'hui*; Philip Robins, *Turkey and the Middle East* (London 1991) and 'The overload state: Turkish policy and the Kurdish issue', *International Affairs*, vol. 69, no. 4, October 1993; Lale Yalcin-Heckmann, *Tribe and Kinship among the Kurds* (Frankfurt, 1991) and 'Kurdish tribal organization and local political processes', in Andrew Finkel and Nukhet Sirman (eds), *Turkish State, Turkish Society* (London and New York, 1990); Amnesty International, *Turkey: No Security without Human Rights* (London, October 1996); Human Rights Watch, *Weapons Transfers and Violations of the Laws of War in Turkey* (New York and Washington, 1995); Medical Foundation for the Care of Victims of Torture, *Staying Alive by Accident: Torture Survivors from Turkey in the UK* (London, February 1999); Pope, Nicole and Hugh *Turkey Unveiled: Ataturk and After* (John Murray, 1996); Robert, Olsen (ed.), *The Kurdish Nationalist Movement in the 1990s* (Lexington, Kentucky, 1996); Sauar, Erik *Turkey's Struggle with Democracy and Kurds* (Trondheim, 1996).

Newspapers and Magazines: Briefing, *The Daily Telegraph*, *The Egyptian Gazette*, *The Financial Times*, *Al Hayat*, *The Independent*, *International Herald Tribune*, *Kurdish News and Comment*, *Kurdistan Report*, *Middle East International*, *Le Monde*, *New York Times*, *Observer Foreign News Service*, *The Times*, *Turkey Briefing*, *Turkish Daily News*, *Turkish Probe*, *Voice of Kurdistan*, Helsinki Watch and Amnesty International briefings and press releases, IMK (International Association for Human Rights of the Kurds) Weekly Information Service; Kurdish Information Bulletin; Washington Kurdish Institute daily press briefings.

Interviews: Only the following may safely be named: Musa Anter (Istanbul, 18 September 1990); Sedat Aybar (London, summer 1993); Ismail Besikci (Ankara, 24 September 1990); Serhat Bucak (Istanbul, 17 September 1990); Hatip Dicle (Diyarbakir, 2 October 1990); Jane Howard (Ankara, 26 September 1990); Ismet Imset (Ankara, 25 September 1990); Kamran Inan (Ankara, 25 September 1990); Meded Serhat (Istanbul, 20 September 1990); Professor Aydin Yalcin (Ankara, 24 September 1990).

Notes

1. *Le Monde*, 16 June 1983.
2. Quoted in Imset, The PKK, p. 24.
3. Sahin Donnez, quoted by Imset, *The PKK*, p. 18. The deliberate fostering of inter-tribal conflicts was confirmed by Baki Karer, and original Apocu who defected in 1985.
4. *Financial Times*, 21 January and 1 October 1980; Imset, *The PKK*, p. 19; the Times, 12 May 1980.
5. *International Herald Tribune*, 25 June 1980.
6. Syria had longstanding grounds for unhappiness with Turkey. In 1921, the French had lost substantial territory Syrian Arabs had hoped would fall within the new state's borders. In 1939 France ceded the Sanjaq of Alexandretta (Hatay) to Turkey, a sop to dissuade Ankara from an alliance with Nazi Germany. The port of Alexandretta had been Syria's principal Mediterranean outlet.
7. Kurdistan Ulusal Kurtulusculari (KUK), formed in 1978 out of the Marxist wing of the KDPT, was very hostile to the PKK, Imset, *The PKK*, p. 31.
8. In March 1984 Turkish warplanes entered Iranian airspace to attack Iranian Kurds in Mahabad and Sardasht, *Le Monde*, 13 March 1984.

9. Ala Rizgari (Flag of Freedom), was a splinter from Rizgari, sceptical about Rizgari's belief that only an independent Communist group could secure Kurdistan's independence, and in favour of working with other groups.

10. For example, 10 killed on 23 January 1987 at Basyurt Efeler, Mardin; 17 killed on 20 June 1987 at Pinarcik, 11 killed on 22 July 1987 at Tasdelen, Hakkari; 9 killed on 28 March 1988 at Findik Yazioymak, Siirt.

11. These were (a) Van province: the Artushi, the Milan, the Mukri, the Shamsikani, the Takuranli, and the Buruki (led by Kinyas Kartal); (b) Siirt province: the Batuyan, the Tatar, the Aktung; (c) Hakkari province: the Kirki, the Fuyan, the Pinyanish and the Harki, Imset, *The PKK*, p. 113.

12. Law 2932 of 19 October is enacted 'in order to protect the indivisible unity of the state, with its land and nation; the national sovereignty, the national security, and public publication of ideas other than the first official language of each country which recognizes the Republic of Turkey' (Art. 2). [The authors had recalled that Kurdish was the second official language of Iraq.] 'The mother tongue of the Turkish citizen is Turkish. It is forbidden: (a) to develop any form in activity in which a language other than Turkish. It is used and disseminated as the mother tongue; (b) at gatherings, or demonstration to carry posters, banners, signs or other such objects written in another language ... or to broadcast in another records, tapes or video-cassettes, or other objects of the media in another language, without the consent of the highest official in the region' (Art. 3).

13. Unsworn affidavit by asylum seeker, quoted in McDowall, *The Kurds: A Nation Denied*, p. 61

14. Helsinki Watch, *Destroying Ethnic Identity* (1988), p. 12.

15. Helsinki Watch, *Destroying Ethnic Identity* (1988) p. 21.

16. See reports in *The Independent*, 24 and 31 January and 6 June 1989.

17. There were repeated attempts by Ankara to obtain Syrian cooperation against the PKK from March 1985 onwards. Syria was by now incensed by Turkey's Euphrates dam programme.

18. Quoted from the translation in *Turkey Briefing*, vol. 4, no. 3, June 1990. For a discussion of Kararname 413 see also Helsinki Watch, Destroying Ethnic Identity (1990).

19. Ken MacKenzie, *Middle East International*, no. 374, 27 April 1990.

20. In December 1990 it was renumbered yet again (as No. 430) to pre-empt the Constitutional Court.

21. For example, Nurettin Dilek, deputy and ex-mayor of Diyarbakir, repeatedly warned Ozal of the implicit dangers.

22. *Cumhuriyet*, 12 February 1986, quoted by Martin van Bruinssen, 'Between guerilla war and political murder: the Workers' Party of Kurdistan', *Middle East Report*, no. 153, July–August 1988, p. 42.

23. These were Mehmet Ali Eren, Kenan Sonmez, Ahmet Turk, Salih Sumer, Mehmet Adnan Ekmen, Ismail Hakki Onal, Mehmet Alinak.

24. This was Aabdurrahman Ozbek, commander of the Ezdinan tribe.

25. *The Independent*, 7 April 1990.

26. For the full text see Helsinki Watch, 'Turkey: new restrictive anti-terror law', 10 June 1991.

27. Imset, *The PKK*, p. 342.

28. Leyla Zana and Hatip Dicle.

29. Yilderim Akbulut, ANAP Interior Minister, *Middle East International*, no. 296, 20 March 1987.

30. *Middle East International*, nos. 414, 415, 6 and 12 December 1991.

31. Many Naqshbandis and Qandiris supported *Anap*. Most of the Nurculuk tended towards the True Path Party, though the more militant supported Alpaslan Turkes' National Action Party.

32. More or less the first of these was Professor Muammer Aksoy, President of the Turkish Law Foundation, a Kemalist organization, who was murdered in January 1990.

33. *Middle East International*, no. 433, 11 September 1992.

34. The group was called Yurtsever Dinadamlari Birligi (The Patriotic Men of Religion), see Imset, *The PKK*, p. 141.

35. Sura, XLIX, verse 13.

36. *Cudi*, no. 4, 1990, quoted a *hadith* of the Prophet: 'At the end of time, the Turks, sons of Turan, with small eyes and large faces, will come down to the banks of the Tigirs. The people living there [according to *Cudi*, today's Kurds] will divide into three categories. One group will think only of the spoils and will perish [for abandoning the *jihad*]. Another group will take refuge under Turkish power [i.e. the regime], thus falling into unbelief. A final group, with their women and children, will wage *jihad*. These will be the martyrs.' Quoted by Hamit Bozarslan, *Entre la umma et le nationalisme*, p. 1. See also p. 3.

37. There is a large discrepancy between Turkish General Staff figure of 1,056 and Kurdish estimates of between 150 and 200.

38. *Turkey Briefing*, vol. 7, no. 1, April 1993.

39. *Turkey Briefing*, vol. 7, no. 2, Summer 1993.

40. *The Independent*, 13 November 1993.

41. This was Fehmi Isiklar.

42. Bomb attacks took place in Antalya on 27 June and 17 July, Istanbul on 25 July and Kusadasi on 30 July.

43. *The Independent*, 13 November 1993.

44. Medico International and the Kurdish Human Rights Project, *The Destruction of Villages in South East Turkey* (London, June 1996) p. 8.

45. This letter was published in extensive excerpts in mid-November 1993, in *Turkish Probe* and *Turkish Daily News*.

46. These admissions cost him his job, *Milliyet* (Ankara) 19 November 1994 and 25 July 1995. In a remarkable denial, all four governors-general for the period of 1987–1997 denied ordering a single village evacuation, 'Report of the Parliamentary Committee on Migration from Villages of the East and South-east', (n.d. probably autumn 1997).

47. For an overview, monitoring, and specific case studies see Kurdish Human Rights Project, *The Destruction of Villages in South-East Turkey* (London, June 1996); Stiching Nederland-Koerdistan, *Forced Evictions and Destruction of Villages in Dersim (Tunceli) and the Western part of Bingol, Turkish Kurdistan, September–November 1994* (Amsterdam, March 1995); Human Rights Watch/Helsinki Watch *Turkey: Forced Displacement of Ethnic Kurds from South East Turkey* (New York and Washington, October 1994) and *Weapons Transfers and Violations of the Laws of War in Turkey* (New York, Washington, Los Angeles, London and Brussels, November 1995). See also, Lustgarten, McDowall and Nolan, *A Fearful Land*, pp. 16–24 for evidence regarding the ambush and murder of civilians at Guclukonak, Siirt province.

48. IHD, *Yasadiklari Topraklardan Metropoliere qoc Eden Kurt Ailelere Yonelik Arastirma* (Istanbul January 1995), quoted in Ismet Imset, 'Village Evacuations' unpublished paper, March 1996.

49. Medico International and Kurdish Human Rights Project, *The Destruction of Villages*, p. 19.

50. This became public knowledge when a document 'Proposals for Solutions [to the Kurdish conflict]' submitted to the National Security Council on 27 January 1997 was leaked to the press.

51. The case was based upon unlawful abduction (Article 5), and inadequate facilities for the preparation of a defence (Article 6). For a critique of the unfair nature of the trial, see Amnesty International, 'Turkey. Death sentence after unfair trial: the case of Abdullah Ocalan', August 1999.

52. Professor Bakir Caglar, quoted in *Middle East International*, no. 537, 8 November 1996.

53. By this time out of a total of 9,979 individual complaints brought to the European Court, 2,115 came from citizens of Turkey.

54. In November 1996 a car crash occurred at Susurluk. The only survivor was a conservative Kurdish landlord, tribal chief, and DYP MP for Urfa, Sedat Bucak. He commanded a 10,000 contingent of the Village Guard. Those killed were Abdullah Catli, a Turkish 'mafia godfather' in possession of a false diplomatic passport and false ID, wanted by Interpol; Huseyin Kocadag, ex deputy chief of police in Istanbul and ex-co-ordintor of the gendarmerie contra-guerrilla 'Special Teams' and a former beauty queen turned mafia hit woman.

55. Valued, possibly into exaggeration by one member of the government inquiry into Susurluk, at US$70 billion annually.

56. Turkiye Odaler ve Borsaler Birligi, *Dogu Sonunu* (Ankara, July 1995). The survey carried out by Professor Dogu Ergil, interviewed 1,256 people in three eastern provinces where the PKK was active, and three southern provinces to which Kurds migrated. In brief, the following facts emerged: 82.6 per cent of Kurds could still speak Kurdish; 35 per cent admitted to a friend or relative in the PKK, but the remaining 65 per cent of interviewees significantly refused to answer this question; 11 per cent wanted an independent Kurdistan; 36 per cent wanted a Turkish–Kurdish federation; 17 per cent wanted local administration reforms; and 11 per cent wanted autonomy. With regard to these different forms of self-administration, the survey concluded that interviewees had only a vague idea of what those options might imply.

57. TUSIAD, *Perspectives on Democratisation in Turkey* (Istanbul, January 1997). Its author was the distinguished constitutional lawyer, Bulent Tanor.

58. This policy, incidentally, was self-defeating and actually encouraged the perpetration of Kurdish speakers. For it was the next generation of mothers who dropped out of school first, thus ensuring they would lull their babies to sleep in Kurdish, not Turkish.

59. GAP television was an attempt to provide a TV service for the south-east.

60. Chamber of Architects and Engineers, 'A Study in Diyarbakir of social problems resulting from forced displacement of people in the region,' quoted in *Kurdish News Bulletin*, 9–15 June 1998.

61. *Turkish Daily News*, 4 June 1999.

62. Hikmet Ulubay, quoted by *Turkish Probe*, 11 April 1999.

63. Yilmaz Ensaroglu, 'Report of parliamentary enquiry into problems of migrants from village evacuations in the east and south-east', (n.d. probably autumn 1997).

64. *Middle East International*, no. 423, 19 April 1992.

CHAPTER 21

THE KURDS IN EXILE: BUILDING THE NATION

Introduction

The first edition omitted discussion of Kurdish exile, an increasingly important dimension of Kurdish history and particularly of the advance of Kurdish national solidarity. It will be recalled that the early advances of national ideas took place largely outside Kurdistan, either in Istanbul, 1908–22, or beyond the reach of the Ottoman authorities. The first publication that was culturally if not politically nationalist was *Kurdistan*, a Kirmanji-medium paper that itself reflected the precarious nature of exile life. The first five issues were published in Cairo in 1898, but after pressure from Istanbul, it moved to Geneva, London and even Folkestone. Thirty-one issues appeared before it closed in 1902. During that period copies reached a narrow intellectual elite in some of the towns of Kurdistan. Obviously, exile offered safety from Ottoman, Turkish, Arab or Iranian suppression, but it also offered arenas of intellectual stimulus that did not really exist inside Kurdistan. When the Kemalists occupied Istanbul in 1922, many of those who had formed the coterie of Kurds interested in ethnic nationalism fled abroad.

Following the establishment of the Turkish Republic it was natural for the Khoybun to establish itself in Syria, where it could be close to Kurdistan across a virtually unpoliced border, could operate under the benign tolerance of the French mandate authorities and might, even though it might not wish to admit it, learn from the Arab nationalist movement in Syria. It was in Syria, too, that Jaladat Badr Khan started the journal *Hawar* in the early 1930s and developed Latin script Kirmanji, thereby making Kirmanji available to the new generation of Kurds inside Turkey.

By the end of the twentieth century, the pattern and importance of exile had been transformed. The Kurdish diaspora had become a key instrument for the advancement of Kurdish national identity, and for its internationalisation. By this time the Kurdish question had ceased to be an internal question to each country in which a Kurdish community found itself, and was ceasing to be a purely regional question. It was certainly firmly a European question, and arguably an international one.

The first post-1945 exiles

The rise of Arab nationalism rendered the Arab world a less tolerant environment for exile Kurds, and some drifted to Europe. More importantly, in the 1960s a growing number of young Kurdish intellectuals came to Europe for their education. Most came from Iraq, but others were from Iran, Syria or Turkey. The most notable exile was Abd al Rahman Qasimlu, who studied in France and Czechoslovakia before becoming leader of the KDPI in Iran. It was not long before Kurds were forming student associations in western European countries, exchanging experiences from different parts of Kurdistan. Some represented Kurdish political parties, most notably Barzani's KDP. Others became interested in propagating discussion of Kurdish political and cultural matters, for example developing Kurdish language and literature.[1] These early journals attracted the work of important writers and poets unable to publish in Turkey or Syria.

Economic Migrants

During the 1970s the balance changed with a growing influx of migrant workers from Turkey, responding to the demand for unskilled labour in the rapidly expanding European economy. At first most were from western or central Turkey and were Turkish, but that soon changed. From the later 1970s significant numbers from eastern Turkey started to arrive, not only attracted by the prospect of gainful employment but also pushed by the growing disorder and repression in eastern Turkey. Wherever they settled they also created elements of community life: shops, mosques, cafes and restaurants and various kinds of clubs and associations mainly concerned with mutual assistance. Those from eastern Turkey had at first described themselves as Turkish, according to their Kemalist education. The first Kurdish workers association was Komkar, which in due course became a federal umbrella for dozens of local organisations.

Under the influence of politicized Kurdish students already in European cities, and also increasingly conscious of the political nature of state treatment of 'the east', many started to describe themselves as Kurds. That 'reawakening' was a continuing process. In campaigning (with partial success) to ensure that host countries recognized Kurdish linguistic identity, Komkar did much to advance cultural consciousness among the Kurdish workforce.

Significantly, as with other migrant communities from Asia, Africa and the Caribbean, it was the second generation which showed stronger interest in its origins than the migrant parents. By the late 1970s Kurdish literacy classes were organized in different European centres. Many Kurds only learnt Kirmanji once in Europe. The existence of a written as well as spoken language had a profound and growing psychological effect on expatriate Kurds. The desire to discover 'who I am' led to a significant surge of interest in political and linguistic identity among younger Kurds during the 1980s and 1990s.

The refugee decades, 1980–2000

It will be recalled that the Kurdish communities in Iran, Iraq and Turkey endured more severe conflict with the state from 1980 than ever before. In each case thousands, tens of thousands or even hundreds of thousands of Kurds were compelled to abandon their homes. The numbers involved made the proportion fleeing Saddam in 1975 seem modest. By the mid-1980s it was reckoned that possibly 500,000 Kurds were living in Europe. By 1999 the number probably exceeded 750,000. Many Iraqi Kurds continued to be drawn to Britain, while most from Turkey went to Germany, in both cases for linguistic and historic reasons that reached back into the early years of the century. Many Iranian Kurds went to France. Many Iraqi and Iranian fugitives tended to be well-educated. Among those from Turkey were many farmers and peasants, with a low literacy level but a sense of profound injustice at the brutality meted out to their communities in the Kurdish countryside. Others, particularly intellectuals, were drawn to Sweden which offered a particularly benign environment for research and publishing. Sweden became something of an intellectual engine room for the Kurdish diaspora, where numerous publications in Kirmanji and Surani appeared from 1956 onwards.

It was inevitable that refugees, with their essentially political baggage, should have a dramatic effect on the Kurdish migrant scene. Whether they came from Iraq, Iran or Turkey, they all were either themselves the direct victims of state brutality or had close friends or relatives who were. On the whole it was the PKK rather than other Turkish or Iraqi movements, which mobilized these refugees and their migrant predecessors. It organized student and workers unions, information offices and publishing ventures all over Europe. Unlike Komkar with its primary concern to help Kurds make something of their lives in Europe, the PKK made sure the struggle for Kurdistan was always at the forefront of Kurdish thinking: 'to especially marginalized members of the second generation growing up in Germany, involvement in PKK activities offered a sense of meaning and self-respect. Numerous young men and women devote their lives entirely to the party, to an extent not much encountered in other political organisations.'[2] Some disliked the PKK's ideology and methods and chose to support the Socialist Party of Turkish Kurdistan, or some other group. The majority of those from Turkey, however, were impressed by the PKK's ability to challenge the Turkish State as no Kurdish group had ever done before, and willingly gave it their support. Such was its military success in Turkey that in the early 1990s the PKK 'captured' a large number of community associations in Europe. One by one, these associations elected known supporters or sympathisers with the PKK as its officers. By 1990 there could have been hardly a single European Union country without at least one and possibly dozens of Kurdish organisations. In London, for example, 25 such associations were in existence in the mid-1990s. Ten of these were community associations, the two largest of which, the Kurdish Workers Association and Halkevi, were strongly sympathetic to the PKK in the 1990s. Illustrative of the psychological journey of such organisations, Halkevi had been established in 1984 essentially as a Turkish organisation but by the 1990s emphasized its Kurdishness. Many of the exile communities gave very generously to their party or association. The PKK in particular received massive contributions, but it was not alone. It was rumoured that extortion rackets took place on a widespread scale. That may have been so, but many gave willingly.

Unlike Kurdistan, where kinship and religion remained important components of identity, the same could not be said for the diaspora community. Political outlook dominated all other considerations, and the Alevi-Sunni distinction, for example, which remained important in Turkey was of little consequence in Europe.

As in Kurdistan itself, the celebration of Nawruz became particularly important. This Spring, or New Year, Festival on 21 March had first been adopted in Iraqi Kurdistan as a national day among Kurds. (For Iranian Kurds the festival had no such political significance because it is also celebrated as Iran's New Year by Iran's entire population, Kurds and non-Kurds alike. The festival derives from pre-Islamic traditions in Iran.) From modest parties in private houses across Europe in the 1970s, by the 1990s Nawruz had become an opportunity in exile to demonstrate Kurdish identity on the streets or in public assembly halls. It offered young and otherwise marginalized refugees a chance to affirm their identity and national struggle.

Other institutions provided a public voice in other spheres. A Kurdish Institute in Paris was established in 1983 for the advancement of Kurdish academic and cultural studies. Two other important organisations came into existence: the International Association for Human Rights of the Kurds, based in Bonn, and the Kurdish Human Rights Project, based in London. Both brought Turkey's serious violations of human rights to national and international attention, through the cases brought to the European Court in Strasbourg, through publications and through co-operative projects with European and international organisations. The 1980s saw a proliferation of Kurdish publications, a clear response to the ordeal Kurds had experienced in Iran, Iraq and Turkey.

Meanwhile, more overt developments had taken place. Thanks to the initiative of Mme Danielle Mitterand, a major international Kurdish conference took place in Paris in 1989. Among those who attended, but expressly forbidden to, were seven Turkish Social Democrat (SHP) MPs. On their expulsion from the SHP, they had formed the HEP and this on its demise had given birth to the DEP. It was six DEP senior officers fleeing to Brussels in 1994 who established the Kurdistan Parliament-in-Exile, where Kurdish concerns could be discussed. Although dominated by Kurds from the Turkish parliament, this parliament tried to incorporate a cross section of politicians, writers, members of youth and religious organisations (Assyrians, Yazidis and Alevis). It held its first assembly in the Hague, in April 1995, a symbolic location with connotations of international justice. Further meetings were held in Vienna, Moscow and Rome. The Parliament rapidly became a PKK-dominated organisation. With a permanent office in Brussels, the working capital of the European Union, the Parliament met in different European locations. In the autumn of 1998 it met in Italy's parliament buildings where it enjoyed the endorsement of most of Italy's political parties. More widely, the parliament received recognition from several European governments and was able to establish information offices in several European cities. Despite the influence of the PKK, the parliament stuck to the idea of a negotiated solution to the conflict in Turkey.

With modern technology, the Kurds of Europe rapidly discovered they need not be wholly cut off from their fellows in Kurdistan. In the 1970s transistor radio and cassette tapes provided an important channel for political action and cultural communication. These developments, however, were as nothing compared with the information revolution of the 1990s. Communication by mobile/cellular phone, by fax and by e-mail rendered state borders highly permeable. The proliferation of websites on the internet also provided 'notice-boards' for the Kurdish people and those interested in them. In 1995, with money raised within the expatriate community, a pro-PKK satellite television service, MED-TV was established in London and Brussels. It had an electrifying effect on Kurds inside Turkey, exciting their sense of national solidarity and giving them heart at a time when Turkey's destruction of the Kurdish habitat had reached a climax. As one villager remarked, 'sometimes the only electricity in the village will be reserved for watching this channel.'[3] However, MED-TV found itself unable to conform to the disciplines demanded of it by British broadcasting regulations, and after several warnings its licence was withdrawn in April 1999, when it was found guilty of 'inciting violence'.[4] Three months later, however, a new service, MEDIA-TV was announced. Although politically motivated Kurds may find they are unable to respect the restraints required of them operating out of parliamentary democracies, the medium is bound to become easier and cheaper to operate. In other words, Turkey, Iraq and Iran will be unable to repel the information offensive. Furthermore, they will find that this form of assault on their centralized and ideological battlements much more threatening than guerrilla operations.

As increasing numbers of Kurds sought asylum in the European Union during the 1990s, its member states found they could no longer ignore the growing militancy of their Kurdish communities. Tensions came to a head in 1993–94, mainly in Germany. A number of bomb attacks were launched on Turkish targets in 1993, thought to be inspired by the PKK. Germany proscribed the PKK and some 30 affiliated organisations. At Nawruz, 1994 Kurds blockaded the Cologne ring-road, and elsewhere two or three Kurds immolated themselves. Chancellor Kohl was reported exclaiming 'The terror has reached a new dimension!'[5]

Turkish Kurds were widely thought of as potential terrorists. An arrest warrant was issued for Abdullah Ocalan. But such Kurdish demonstrations of anger with

Turkey and also with Germany dramatically reminded Germany and other EU states of the growing incompatibility of hosting large refugee communities while continuing to supply Turkey with war materièl for its war on the Kurdish people.

Britain, too, took the anti-terror line. In 1994 it arrested the PKK European representative as he was about to address a meeting at the House of Commons, and detained him pending his extradition to Germany in connection with the 1993 bombings. Britain and Belgium also treated MED-TV with great suspicion, in 1997 raiding its premises and removing its financial accounts and other items. Both countries clearly sought proof of PKK funding. Nothing demonstrated the growing importance of the Kurdish question in Europe more than the final odyssey of Abdullah Ocalan. His journey to Italy, its refusal to offer him asylum, and Germany's refusal to activate its arrest warrant, all demonstrated that EU states found the Kurdish issue now very hot to handle.

Predictably, however, it was Turkey above all that sought to stifle Kurdish nationalism in exile. It monitored Kurdish demonstrations across Europe and established networks of informers. Apart from jamming transmissions, it also made strong diplomatic representations in London for the closure of MED-TV, so much so that when MED-TV was finally closed it was widely believed in the Kurdish community that it was the result of pressure from Turkey. Meanwhile, in Kurdistan Turkish security forces had for some years been smashing satellite dishes.

Back in Europe, Kurdish asylum seekers demonstrated their ability to attract attention. This reached a climax with the abduction of Ocalan from Nairobi, when major demonstrations took place in 20 European cities, diplomatic premises were occupied and three Kurds were shot dead by Israeli security guards in Berlin. Turkey's Kurdish question thus became front page news in Europe's press. A growing proportion of Europe's better informed population became aware that many Kurdish asylum seekers in their midst bore the scars of Turkish torture.

During 1999, therefore, the Kurdish question became a European issue, and that in order to resolve this growing issue inside the Union, Europe would have to address Turkey's conflict with its Kurds more clearly than hitherto. Turkey also was beginning to discover that to have unhappy Kurds in Europe might in the long run prove more dangerous to its internal ideological order than offering them a liberalized environment within the borders of the Republic. Launching raids into Iraqi Kurdistan was easy enough. Staunching the flow of Kurdish nationalist ideas and culture from Europe into Turkish Kurdistan and the growing communities of cities like Istanbul, Izmir and Adana was likely to be impossible. Furthermore, with every violation of human rights inside Turkey, the Kurdish people were increasingly able to trouble the conscience of the outside world. Having thus almost won the military campaign in the south-east, Turkey was slowly waking up to the fact that it had catastrophically lost the information war.

Sources

Martin van Bruinessen, 'Kurds in Europe: exile, politics and cultural renaissance', paper given at Kurdistan photographic exhibition, Rotterdam, 1997; Martin van Bruinessen, 'Kurds in movement: migrations, mobilisations, communications and globalisation of the Kurdish question', Working Paper No. 14, Islamic Area Studies Project of Tokyo (Japan 1999); Ralf Goldak, 'Thinking the Kurdish Diaspora in Germany' PhD Diss, University of Aberystwyth, 1997; Östen Wahlbeck, *Kurdish Diasporas: A Comparative Study of Kurdish Refugee Communities* (London, 1999).

Notes

1. Their titles express the political and cultural concerns: *Çiya* (Mountain); *Çiray Kurdistan* (Light of Kurdistan); *Denge Kurdistan* (Voice of Kurdistan); *Heviye Welêt* (Hope of Homeland); *Pirsing* (Ray); *Xôndkari Kurd* (Kurdish Student), Hassanpour, *Nationalism and Language in Kurdistan*, p. 270.

2. Bruinessen, van, 'Kurds in movement', p. 19,

3. *The Independent*, 19 February 1999.

4. MED-TV had already been fined £90,000 for three separate breaches of the broadcasting impartiality requirement in 1998.

5. *Suddeutsche*, 24 March 1994.

AFTERWORD

The twentieth century has drawn to a close for the Kurdish people with the capture of arguably their greatest leader of the century. For Abdullah Ocalan sustained an armed revolt against the state for longer than any other Kurd over the preceding 200 years. He also did more than any other leader to forge a mass movement among the Kurdish people. In some ways he was similar to Mulla Mustafa. Like him, he ruthlessly cut down rivals and groups, and inspired fear and hatred as well as devotion in Kurdish ranks. But he did more than Mulla Mustafa to build a movement based on national solidarity. No other Kurd succeeded in provoking mass demonstrations as far afield as Armenia, Iran and the capitals of the Europe Union.

Yet the advance of the Kurdish national movement has been marked also by significant setbacks. Urbanisation, land reform and the transformation of peasantry into a landless proletariat all assisted the process of national formation. Yet tribalism and patronage remain powerful impediments, arguably more powerful in 1999 than they had been two decades earlier. In places this is because society has continued to function along traditional lines. More widely, however, it is because of two crucial factors. Both Ankara and Baghdad have assiduously cultivated tribal and neo-tribal networks as a means for extending the fell influence of patronage against Kurdish national leaders. Both the Village Guards in Turkey and the Jash in Iraq are evidence of the extensive nature of that patronage network. Physical danger and economic straits resulting from conflict have also dramatically increased popular dependence for protection and employment on those best placed to give it.

Inevitably, Kurdish political leaders have been unable to resist the simple means of patronage to enlarge their constituency. It has been true in both Turkey and Iraq. In particular it is very hard to distinguish the dynamic of power for today's KDP and PUK from that of, say, eighteenth century tribal confederations. Fostering client networks rather than patriotic commitment to a national ideal is what really determines the behaviour of the KDP and PUK. This must be considered a serious erosion of national development. Indeed, rather as Arab nationalism turned out to be the empty rhetoric whereby authoritarian regimes could obtain popular acquiescence in much of the Arab world, so Kurdish nationalism has been used in Iraq to reinforce neo-tribal networks of control and competition. Both the KDP and PUK demonstrated during the 1990s that defeat of the other was more important to them than the dangers implicit in seeking outside patrons, just as their eighteenth and nineteenth century predecessors had done.

At the same time there has been a retreat in what one might describe as prescriptive national ideology. Not only has a lot of Marxist rhetoric been quietly junked, but also a more pluralist idea of what the nation might be seems to be emerging. This is particularly true in the case of the PKK which in the early 1990s still embraced a monoculture comparable to that of the Turkish state. In the late 1990s the PKK seemed much more willing to listen to other Kurdish points of view, and even to accommodate them within a broadening movement. That can only be taken as evidence of growing maturity, and the realisation that mass mobilisation requires more rather than less tolerance of national debate.

One senses also that the age of the peshmerga may be drawing to a close. In Iran guerrilla war has been notably unsuccessful, except in tying down large numbers of troops. In Iraq government forces have demonstrated that guerrilla warfare can lead to the destruction of the very people on whose behalf the struggle has been waged. That, too, might be the lesson drawn from the war waged by the PKK which has also witnessed massive destruction of the rural habitat. The one great achievement in all three countries which the peshmergas can claim is that they captured the imagination of the Kurdish people. But this achievement is now in the past. In any case, this kind of violence aroused vehement hostility among the majority communities of the states in question. In that respect the peshmerga struggle proved ultimately counterproductive. The challenge now is to find new means to advance Kurdish national feeling. The use of new methods, for example using cyberspace and satellite to advance forbidden ideas, may prove more effective in the future.

The other conclusion to be drawn is that in all three states Kurdish autonomists have prevailed over the secessionists (the assimilationists were never much competition). A diminishing number of Kurds are persuaded of the wisdom of secession. Albeit an enticingly prospect, it appears unattainable but also less desirable. Kurds are increasingly dependent on social and economic life beyond Kurdistan. However much they may resent Arab or Turkish rule, an impoverished and confined Kurdish state holds less appeal.

Whether Kurds are able to attain genuine autonomy must remain an open question. In all three countries the answer to that question may lie with the economic prospects. Two important processes are likely to happen with increased prosperity. First, the grip of patronage, whether in favour of the state, the tribe or a political party is likely to diminish as individuals enjoy greater security of person and the means of gainful employment without the mediation of a patron. Second, economic prosperity will drag in its wake political liberalisation. For such things to happen, however, Iraq must be free to rebuild its economic life and all three countries encouraged by the outside world to accompany economic growth with progressive democratic and pluralistic freedoms.

THE TREATY OF SÈVRES

10 AUGUST 1920: ARTICLES RELATING
TO KURDISTAN

Article 62

A Commission sitting at Constantinople and composed of three members appointed by the British, French and Italian Governments respectively shall draft within six months from the coming into force of the present Treaty a scheme of local autonomy for the predominantly Kurdish areas lying east of the Euphrates, south of the southern boundary of Armenia as it may be hereafter determined, and north of the frontier of Turkey with Syria and Mesopotamia, as defined in Article 27, II. (2) and (3). If unanimity cannot be secured on any question, it will be referred by the members of the Commission to their respective Governments. The scheme shall contain full safeguards for the protection of the Assyro-Chaldeans and other racial or religious minorities within these areas, and with this object a Commission composed of British, French, Italian, Persian and Kurdish representatives shall visit the spot to examine and decide what rectifications, if any, should be made to the Turkish frontier where, under the provisions of the present Treaty, that frontier coincides with that of Persia.

Article 63

The Turkish Government hereby agrees to accept and execute the decisions of both the Commissions mentioned in Article 62 within three months from their communication to the said Government.

Article 64

If within one year from the coming into force of the present Treaty the Kurdish peoples within the areas defined in Article 62 shall address themselves to the Council of the League of Nations in such a manner as to show that a majority of the population of these areas desires independence from Turkey, and if the Council then considers that these peoples are capable of such independence and recommends that it should be granted to them, Turkey hereby agrees to execute such a recommendation, and to renounce all rights and title over these areas.

The detailed provisions for such renunciation will form the subject of a separate agreement between the Principal Allied Powers and Turkey.

If and when such renunciation takes place, no objection will be raised by the Principal Allied Powers to the voluntary adhesion to such an independent Kurdish State of the Kurds inhabiting that part of Kurdistan which has been hitherto been included in the Mosul Vilayet.

THE KURDS OF SYRIA

Introduction

Kurds probably constitute between 8 and 10 per cent of the population of modern Syria, probably between 1.2 and 1.5 million out of a total population of an estimated 15.3 million in 1998. They are located in three principal areas in northern Syria: (i) Kurd Dagh and 'Afrin, a mountainous area in the far north western part of Syria area, on the north-eastern side of the Turkish Hatay (the Sanjaq of Alexandretta), a southern outcrop of the Anatolian plateau; (ii) in the border area with Turkey in the north western extremity of the Jazira, around the town of Jarablus; (iii) the north-eastern corner of the Jazira, in the governorate of al-Hasaka, particularly from Ras al 'Ayn through Qamishli to Dayrik in the 'pan handle' of Syria.

These Kurdish communities have different origins. Those of Kurd Dagh are the southern extremity of the larger indigenous Kurdish community in Turkey, and have inhabited this mountainous region for centuries. The northern Jazira was largely a desert zone except for Kurdish and Arab pastoralist tribes and a handful of villages until settlement began in the latter half of the nineteenth century. The largest influx of settlers occurred during the 1920s, fugitives from Turkish repression (see p. 198f).

Damascus also has a large and longstanding Kurdish community, dating back to the middle ages when Kurdish armed bands fought both as regular and irregular forces of the Muslim armies. Saladin was the most famous of these soldiers. The Kurds settled in their own cantonments outside the city, a usual pattern for troops stationed permanently near a city. Of these cantonments, the two most notable became the quarters of al-Salhiyya and Hayy al-Akrad (the Kurdish Quarter), both on the north east side of the city on the slopes of Jabal Qasyun. Leading Kurds acquired a degree of authority through their command of Kurdish auxiliary janissary forces. By the seventeenth century these forces had declined into local paramilitary formations, giving their leaders considerable independent power locally. Hayy al-Akrad at that time acquired a reputation for disorderly behaviour. In the nineteenth century Kurdish immigrants, mainly from south-eastern Anatolia, chose to live in Hayy al-Akrad because they were not welcome within Damascus proper. While the Damascus Kurdish community retained its distinctive clannishness, it also became Arabic-speaking, with probably about 40 per cent entirely Arabicized by 1920. There are probably about 300,000 Kurds in Damascus today. There are a similar number living in Aleppo, mostly migrants both from 'Afrin and from the Jazira.

Almost all Kurds in Syria are Sunni, with the exception of two small communities of Yezidis. One of these is the western-most portion the Yazidis of Jabal Sinjar, which straddles the Syria-Iraq border in the Jazira. The other community is in Jabal Sim'an and the 'Afrin valley close to Kurd Dagh. In all, the Syrian Yazidis probably do not number more than about 10,000.

Kurds in the Jazira and in Kurd Dagh speak Kirmanji, the main northern Kurdish dialect spoken widely through Turkey and in the northern part of Iraqi and Iranian Kurdistan. Many Kurds are bilingual, and those families living for more than one generation in the Arab cities of Syria tend to speak Arabic.

Damascus and the Politics of Notables

From about 1900 onwards political developments conspired to create first unease and then enmity between the Kurdish minority and the majority of inhabitants in Syria who, as Arabs, began to embrace Arab nationalist ideas. The rift happened in a variety of ways. A divergence grew among the elite Ottoman families in the first two decades of the twentieth century, between those who wished to shore up the Empire by renewing the vigour and authority of Istanbul and those, primarily living in the provinces, who sought to introduce administrative decentralisation, with local authority in the hands of the dominant ethnic communities.

The al-Yusufs and the Shamdins were the two leading Kurdish *agha* families controlling al-Salhiyya and Hayy al-Akrad. By a number of shrewd moves, including domination of the grain and livestock trades they had became two of the most powerful families of Syria.[1] Having become closely engaged with the Ottoman establishment, and being dependent on a traditional ethnic and kinship power base, the al-Yusufs – the more important of the two families – did not share the growing Arab or Syrian nationalist enthusiasm of many of the younger urban elite. Nationalism threatened to erode their traditional power based on local kinship and patronage and, beyond that, promised unforeseen consequences in which political transformation seemed inevitable and with it, equally inevitably, a diminution of al-Yusuf power. As a consequence, the al-Yusufs strongly identified with the Ottoman authorities in Istanbul and with the authoritarian Committee of Union and Progress from 1908 onwards, against those nationalist groupings which wanted to decentralise the empire.

It is no surprise, therefore, that the Kurdish *agha* class generally did not welcome the Arab Revolt of 1916 nor the arrival of the Amir Faysal as the new ruler of Syria in 1918. As a member of the Syrian Congress of 1919 Abd al Rahman al-Yusuf,[2] the undisputed leader of the Damascus Kurdish community, quietly opposed Syrian independence, wanted to recognise the establishment of a Jewish national home in Palestine and strengthened contacts with the French before the latter actually overthrew the Kingdom of Syria in the summer of 1920. It would be difficult to imagine an agenda at this juncture more inimical to Arab aspirations.

The impression that even Arabized Kurds were hostile to Arab nationalism was reinforced under French rule. When France acquired the League of Nations mandate for Syria after the First World War, it adopted a policy of fostering minority identity in order to weaken the Sunni Arab majority. When Arab nationalists and the Druzes of south Syria staged a major revolt against French rule in 1925, France used auxiliaries recruited from the minorities to assist in crushing it. Among these were Kurdish (as well as Armenian and Circassian) forces, some of whom were recent immigrants from Turkey while others were residents of the Kurdish quarter in Damascus, enrolled by their local patron, 'Umar Agha Shamdin. France also deliberately recruited the minorities into its regular local force, Les Troupes Spéciales du Levant, with important consequences for Syria's future as an independent state.

When Khoybun was founded in 1927 it assured France and Britain that it would give no encouragement to Kurdish nationalism in either Syria or Iraq. Initially it enjoyed encouragement from France, but it caused Arab nationalists disquiet, a fact recognized by some Kurds as potentially compromising their position in Syria. A number of professional class Kurds in the Kurdish quarter – doctors, lawyers, journalists and teachers – became interested in Kurdish nationalism through Khoybun. France restricted the activities of Khoybun in the summer of 1928 following sharp protests from Ankara concerning its anti-Turkish activities, and it was closed shortly after. It was also in Damascus that the leading figure in Khoybun, Prince Jaladat Badr Khan, an exile from the princely family that once ruled Bohtan (the area centred on Cizre/Jazira-bin-Umar just inside Turkey), published *Hawar* (a Kirmanji-medium journal), and developed the use of Latin script as better suited to an Indo-European language like Kurdish.

Kurdish national consciousness in Syria found its first real expression in the submission of a petition to the Constituent Assembly of Syria in June 1928 seeking official use of the Kurdish language alongside other languages and in education in the three Kurdish regions, and also the appointment of Kurdish government administrators in these regions. These demands echoed the requirements of the League of Nations when it awarded the vilayet of Mosul to British-controlled Iraq in 1926, but they were not acceded to.

Yet it would be misleading to suppose that all, or necessarily most, Kurds embraced the Kurdish nationalist agenda. Several leading Kurds worked within the broad ranks of Syrian nationalism, but inevitably it was those who waved the banner of Kurdish particularism that attracted Arab notice.

The Jazira, 1920–1946

The primary area of Arab-Kurdish tension was destined to be in the Jazira. Before the First World War the Jazira was largely empty and life there insecure. There had been seasonal Kurdish pastoralist tribes for centuries, most notably the Milli and Miran confederations. These wintered on the Jazira plain before ascending into the foothills of Anatolia for summer grazing. These northern lands of the Jazira were occupied during the summer months by certain bedouin tribes, notably the Shammar (to whom the Milli were tributaries), and also the Tayy, driven north by the intense heat of the desert. Thus the area was one shared by two essentially seasonal pastoralist systems, that happened to be either Kurd or Arab. This picture was already changing towards the end of the nineteenth century with the decline of lawlessness for which the region had been notorious.[5] Some Kurdish tribes began moving southward off the Anatolian plateau, abandoning their pastoralism in favour of farming.

By 1918 Kurds probably slightly outnumbered Arabs in the Jazira. From 1920 onwards, however, many more Kurdish tribespeople arrived, fleeing from the Turkish armed forces particularly during the pacification of the tribes, 1925–28. Although the precise number crossing the new international border is unknown, it was probably in the order of about 25,000. Christians also arrived in even larger numbers, mainly Armenians but also Kaldani, Suryani and even Greek Orthodox.[6] In 1933 8,000 Assyrians sought asylum from Iraq, some of whom were settled in the Khabur valley in the 'pan handle' of the Jazira.

There were now several factors which made the Jazira a turbulent and complex region. Its remoteness, its composite ethnic content, its largely non-Arab character and its almost complete lack of interest in or engagement with the new states of Greater Syria, as constituted by the French,[7] made integration difficult. Several Kurdish tribes continued to cross and recross the border with Turkey, largely to try to revenge themselves on the Turks.

The newly arrived tribes jostled uncomfortably with the existing ones. They quickly settled down to a sedentary existence which Arab tribes began to imitate. There was a feeling that the newly arrived tribes had stolen a march on local Arab tribes, expressed in increasing competition for water. But there was competition with longer-standing Kurdish tribes also. The most powerful Kurdish chief to emerge from this period was himself a very recent arrival, Haju Agha of the Havarkan, a confederation once of 24 tribes (see p. 199).[8] Having helped the French secure north-eastern Syria, he predictably became a political favourite of theirs. But he was also Khoybun's leading advocate in the region, helping to awaken nationalist feeling among tribal Kurds.[9] Over the next decade or so, Hajo Agha progressively shifted from being a traditional tribal chief into a feudal landlord with many villages to his name.

A major economic transformation now occurred in the Jazira. Traditionally Diyarbakir had been the northern Jazira's commercial outlet. This suddenly ended with the new international border. Qamishli, created by the French on the railway line opposite Nusaybin (Turkey), became an important new market centre, as did al-Hasaka – another French creation – destined to become the provincial capital. In the absence of Mosul, also now separated by an international border, Aleppo became the nearest major city. Christian migrants of southern Turkey and northern Mesopotamia tended to settle in towns, of which Qamishli was the most important. Some Kurds settled in towns but the majority established villages in what were relatively unsettled but highly fertile rural areas. Previously pastoralist tribes, whether local or newly arrived turned increasingly to cultivation, and it soon became clear that the Jazira could become the granary of the new state of Syria.

The 1937 French *Rapport Annuel* to the League of Nations listed the main population of the Jazira as follows:

> 42,000 Muslim Arabs, who were mainly pastoralist with a growing minority village-based;
> 82,000 Kurds, almost entirely villagers;
> 32,000 Christians, mainly town dwellers engaged in different forms of trade and business, in Qamishli, al-Hasaka and smaller centres.

None of these groups formed a coherent whole. In the words of Albert Hourani a decade later:

> 'split up between a large number of sects and peoples, none of which dominates the rest, and lacking the elements of stability which would be furnished by a long settled population, the Jazirah presents a complex problem which is intensified by a number of factors: tension between Christians and Muslims and between Arabs and Kurds; the eternal enmity between Beduin and settled folk; the influence of the clergy and particularly French missionaries; and the interference of Turkey from just across the frontier.'[10]

The majority of each of these groups shared a suspicion of the Arab nationalists in Damascus with their centralizing ambitions. Until the mid-1930s Arab nationalists were too pre-occupied with other matters to be concerned with the Jazira. Local French officials had a free hand to pander to, and foster, localism. Local autonomist inclinations were deliberately encouraged when a separate *sanjaq* of the Jazira was established in 1932, two years after a special regime was established for the Sanjaq of Alexandretta (subsequently handed to Turkey in 1939 and renamed the Hatay).

By this time the nationalist ambition to re-unite all Syria was beginning to worry people in the Jazira. In 1933 the Christian population of al-Hasaka began to agitate for greater autonomy. In 1936 local fears were realized when the French reluctantly allowed the growing Syrian Arab nationalist movement to form a government over all Syria. A new autonomist movement led by the Christian mayor of Qamishli and by two Kurdish tribal chiefs, Haju of the Havarkan and Mahmud of the Milli, opposed government from Damascus. Remarkably, in view of Turkey's comprehensive opposition to pluralism, these autonomists even agitated briefly for annexation to Turkey in 1937. Violent clashes occurred between government authorities and the local Christian population, and then between Christians and Kurds.[11] In September 1938 a General Conference of the Jazira, chaired by Haju,[12] appealed to France for full self-government. The French High Commissioner promised a special regime for the Jazira, and the following year, 1939, the predominantly Kurdish Jazira (as also Jabal Druze in south Syria and Latakiya with its Alawite hinterland), was detached from the Sunni Arab heartlands of Syria and brought back under direct French control.

3 Syrian independence and the triumph of Arab nationalism

Under British duress, France withdrew from Syria in 1946. Syria became truly independent and united under an elected Arab nationalist government. Many Damascene and Aleppine Kurds eagerly supported the new nationalist government, but certain communities were restive, most notably the Druze and Kurdish communities in the extreme south and north east of the country respectively.[13] Apparently the Badr Khans continued to hanker after Kurdish independence. When Arab Syria became embroiled in the first Arab-Israeli war of 1948, Kamuran Ali Badr Khan, Jaladat's brother, was already in Paris as the European representative of the Kurdish national movement, but also on the payroll of Israeli intelligence. In July 1948 the Israelis sent him to Transjordan, Syria, and Lebanon with a view to examining how the Arab states' war effort could be interrupted. He reported back, proposing that Israel should help organise a rising by discontented minorities, including the Kurds. These proposals came to nothing as Israel was too preoccupied to have resources to devote to Badr Khan's schemes,[14] but Syrian intelligence may have got wind of his approach to the Israelis. This would certainly help explain Syria's growing fear that the Kurdish community was untrustworthy and might prove a Trojan Horse.

In the meantime, in early 1949 the first in a rapid succession of military coups brought army officers with a partly Kurdish background to power. These dictators relied on officers of similar ethnic background.[16] It was not surprising that some Arab nationalists saw such behaviour as a reprehensible carry-over from Kurdish participation in Les Troupes Spéciales and some condemned the 'Kurdo-military regime' in Syria.

The third of these dictators, Adib Shishakli was, despite his part-Kurdish origin, determined to create an homogeneous Arab-Muslim state. Kurds, Assyrians and Armenians soon felt the alienating effects of a string of decrees requiring for example that hotels, cafes and cinemas be given purely Arab names, that only Arabic might be spoken at any public meetings, festivals or celebrations, and that Muslims must sit in equal numbers with non-Muslims on all committees of minority organisations.

After Shishakli's overthrow in 1954 a more specifically anti-Kurdish backlash slowly began. High- and middle-ranking officers of Kurdish descent began to be purged from the armed forces.[17] Gramophone records of Kurdish music, and Kurdish publications were seized and destroyed, and their owners imprisoned. Yet this backlash was not systematic, nor did it happen overnight. For example, 'Abd al Baqi Nizam al-Din, a Kurd from al-Hasaka, held ministerial posts from 1949 until 1957, and was closely associated with mainstream Syrian parties and politicians; but then there had been no hint of Kurdish particularism in his politics. Likewise, his brother Tawfiq, 'a colourless, politically unambitious soldier',[18] became Chief of Staff in 1956, and was removed from office a year later not because he was Kurdish but because radicals progressively displaced the moderates as the country slid within the orbit of the Soviet Bloc.

In the second half of the 1950s Arab nationalist fervour swept across the Arab world, inspired largely by the rise of Nasser in Egypt, the discomfiture of Britain, France and Israel in the Suez and Sinai campaigns of 1956, followed by the over-throw of the Hashemite monarchy in Iraq in 1958. Arab nationalist feeling, and the excitement engendered by the idea of strength through pan-Arab unity left little room for non-Arab minority groups within the political order. In 1957, in an event that seems to have been inspired by ethnic hatred, 250 Kurdish schoolboys perished in an arson attack on a cinema in 'Amuda. Having been largely tolerated since 1946, Kurdish publications were formally forbidden in 1958. That year Syria formed a union with Egypt as the United Arab Republic (UAR). Egypt's monopoly of power drove Syria to secede in 1961, but the union ushered in a period of intense Arab nationalism which led to heightened discrimination against the Kurds.

Quite by chance, the UAR had been established a few months after the founda-tion of the Kurdistan Democratic Party of Syria (KDPS), in July 1957. In its programme the KDPS called for recognition of the Kurds as a distinct ethnic group with cultural rights, and for democratic government in Damascus. It also drew attention to the lack of economic development for Kurdish areas, and also to the fact that the police and military academies were closed to Kurdish applicants, and that Kurdish military and civil officials had been discharged. Furthermore, the KDPS vehemently opposed the formation of the UAR. In 1960 the leaders of KDPS were rounded up and imprisoned.[19]

In the provisional constitution drafted after the collapse of the UAR in 1961, Syria was formally described for the first time as the Syrian Arab Republic (SAR), a warning of the ethnic exclusion that Kurds were now to face. The Ba'ath took power in March 1963, a month after the Ba'ath had similarly seized power in Iraq.

Arab nationalism left little room for Kurdish identity either in Iraq or Syria. In both countries Kurdish intellectuals had been attracted to political ideologies which subordinated feelings of ethnic nationalism to class struggle. It was no accident that the Communist parties in both countries had a disproportionately large representa-tion of Kurds, particularly in the senior echelons. The Communist Party of Syria (CPS) became widely thought of as 'the Kurdish Party', because of its close associa-tion with the Kurdish community, and because it was led by the politically astute Kurd, Khalid Bakdash. In both Iraq and Syria the Ba'th and the CP became bitter opponents in this period. The Syrian Ba'th never committed the wholesale slaughter committed by the Iraqi Ba'th against the Communists in 1963. It did not have to. The CPS was too closely identified with the Kurdish community to command wider support. The Syrian Ba'th merely continued the repression of the CPS by predecessor regimes but later co-opted it into the National Progressive Front.

Almost immediately, the Ba'th embarked upon a campaign to contain the Kurdish population of the Jazira, with the slogan of 'save the Jazira from becoming a second Israel', to Western ears an absurd slogan, but one that was believable in the siege psychology of Syria at the time. It also sent troops to assist Iraq in its war against Barzani's rebel forces.

Dealing with the Jazira

Arab nationalists had good reason to be paranoid about internal and external enemies.[20] Nowhere was the Syrian Arab cause less assured than in the north where so many non-Arab communities lived, particularly in al-Hasaka governorate. The population had grown rapidly, and it was the growth since 1945 that gave cause for Arab concern. In its own words, the government believed that

> 'At the beginning of 1945, the Kurds began to infiltrate into al-Hasakeh governorate. They came singly and in groups from neighbouring countries, especially Turkey, crossing illegally along the border from Ras al 'Ain to al-Malikiyya. Gradually and illegally, they settled down in the region along the border in major population centres such as Dirbasiyya, Amuda, and Malikiyya. Many of these Kurds were able to register themselves illegally in the Syrian civil registers. They were also able to obtain Syrian identity cards through a variety of means, with the help of their relatives and members of their tribes. They did so with the intent of settling down and acquiring property, especially after the issue of the agricultural reform law, so as to benefit from land redistribution.'[21]

Official figures available in 1961 showed that in a mere seven year period, between 1954 and 1961, the population of al-Hasaka governorate had increased from 240,000 to 305,000, an increase of 27 per cent which could not possibly be explained merely by natural increase. The government was sufficiently worried by the apparent influx that it carried out a sample census in June 1962 which indicated the real population was probably closer to 340,000.[22] Although all these figures may have been exaggerated, they were credible given the actual circumstances. From being lawless and virtually empty prior to 1914, the Jazira had proved to be astonishingly fertile once order was imposed by the French Mandate and farming undertaken by the largely Kurdish population. By the early 1960s al-Hasaka governorate had the second highest density of rural population in Syria per unit of *cultivated* land but remained easily the lowest per unit of *cultivable* land. In other words, al-Hasaka still had plenty of exploitable land and was consequently intensely attractive to poor and unemployed people in surrounding areas, and was likely to draw people in. Inside Syria Arab tribes from neighbouring provinces were likely to be attracted to al-Hasaka's agricultural potential. A strong suspicion that many migrants were entering Syria was inevitable. In Turkey the rapid mechanisation of farming had created huge unemployment and massive labour migration from the early 1950s onwards. The fertile but not yet cultivated lands of northern Jazira must have been a strong enticement and the affected frontier was too long feasibly to police it. The government in Damascus felt it had good grounds to fear that many of those entering al-Hasaka governorate were neither Syrian nor Arab, and that this presented a security problem. Indeed, in the view of the British Embassy,

'It seems doubtful if the Damascus government could easily control the area if Kurdish dissidence from within Syria's borders, or an irruption by Kurdish tribesmen from without, should disturb the uneasy tranquillity.'[23]

Whatever the truth of the matter, the government in Damascus decided to ensure Arab control. On 23 August 1962 it promulgated a special decree (No. 93) authorising an exceptional population census in the governorate of al-Hasaka. The stated purpose was to establish who had entered the country illegally from Turkey, and it was carried out a few weeks later during the course of one day, 5 October. All non-Arab inhabitants, in practice only Kurds, had to prove by documentation that they had been resident in Syria prior to 1945. Many were unable to do so and as a result, it seems that approximately 120,000 Kurds were stripped of their citizenship as were their descendants and the descendants of the progeny of male non-citizens even when the mother was an attested citizen of Syria.

The Syrian government took the view that all these were illegal infiltrators, largely from Turkey, who were changing the demographic balance of the region. A few who moved fast enough were able to produce documentation to prove their pre-1945 residence, and were reinstated as Syrian citizens. The Syrian government later admitted many mistakes had been made. Among those stripped of their citizenship were Osman Sabri, a well-known Damascus-based nationalist and poet who had been born in al-Hasaka province in 1906, and more significantly, the nationally eminent Nizam al-Din brothers: 'Abd al-Baqi who had been a mainstream politician and cabinet minister between 1949 and 1957; and Tawfiq who had been the armed forces' Chief of Staff, 1956–57. The idea that either of the latter, who had risen to the very top of public life, could possibly have been infiltrators brought the whole exercise into disrepute.

A popular programme of anti-Kurdish sentiment was launched which invoked Arabism against the Kurdish threat, and hinted at a connection between Kurdish nationalism, Zionism and Western machinations, connections that were certainly true in the case of Kamuran Ali Badr Khan, who continue to act for Israel in the 1950s and 1960s.[24]

In November 1963 a confidential report was produced by the head of the internal security for al-Hasaka, a Lt Muhammad Talab Hilal. This report cast the problem in stark racist terms:

'the bells of Jazira sound the alarm and call on the Arab conscience to save this region, to purify it of all this scum, the dregs of history until, as befits its geographical situation, it can offer up its revenues and riches, along with those of the other provinces of this Arab territory... The Kurdish question, now that the Kurds are organizing themselves, is simply a malignant tumour which has developed and been developed in a part of the body of the Arab nation. The only remedy which we can properly apply thereto is excision.'[25]

Hilal proposed a twelve point plan to destroy the coherence of the Kurdish community: (i) displacement of the Kurds from their lands; (ii) denial of education; (iii) return of 'wanted' Kurds to Turkey; (iv) denial of employment opportunities; (v) an anti-Kurdish propaganda campaign; (vi) replacement of local Kurdish 'ulama [religious clerics] with Arab ones; (vii) 'divide and rule' policy within the Kurdish community; (viii) Arab settlement of Kurdish areas; (ix) establishment of an Arab cordon sanitaire along the border with Turkey; (x) the establishment of collective farms for Arab settlers; (xi) the denial of the right to vote or hold office to anyone lacking Arabic; (xii) denial of Syrian citizenship to non-Arabs wishing to live in the area.

Although decided upon in 1965, it was only in 1973 that the government implemented Hilal's plan for the creation of 'the Arab belt', al-hizam al-'arabi, a 10–15km wide strip 375 km in length, from 10 km west of Ras al-'Ain along the Turkish border as far as Iraq, and then southwards around the 'pan handle', along the Iraqi border to Tal Kuchik. The plan proposed the deportation of about 140,000 Kurds living in 332 villages, and their replacement with Arabs from the Euphrates bedouin tribes displaced by the creation of Lake Asad, following the creation of the Tabqa Dam. Town dwellers were excepted.

By the mid-1950s Al-Hasaka along with other peripheral areas, Dayr al-Zur, Dar'a and Suwayda', still lagged behind the rest of Syria in the completion of a cadastral survey to delimit and determine land titles. Al-Hasaka was noteworthy as one of the few parts of Syria where very large estates, some of 100,000 ha in size, existed.[26] Possibly because the survey was incomplete, al-Hasaka had been excepted from the land reform that took place at that time, and the break-up of large Kurdish estates was now described as a land redistribution. Tellingly, however, the Kurdish peasants who worked these lands now lost their access to them as Arabs displaced by Lake Asad moved in. However, when government forces arrived to evict the Kurdish inhabitants from their villages, the latter refused to move from their homes and it was decided not to force them. In 1976 the government abandoned the resettlement of more Arabs in Kurdish areas. But it did not remove those Arabs already settled in 41 specially constructed new villages in the hizam al-'arabi, nor did it lead to the re-instatement of Kurds on their previous land holdings.

As outlined above, relations between the Arabs and Kurds of Syria had been characterized by mutual suspicion regarding their respective nationalisms and by Arab fears of foreign infiltration and also of foreign powers or groups making fell use of Kurdish national feeling in Syria. Israel, possibly regretful that it had not exploited Kurdish nationalism in 1948, had a well-attested policy of fomenting unrest among the religious and ethnic minorities of neighbouring states. To the east, the Kurds had been running rings around the Iraqi army from 1961 onwards and it was during the 1960s that Israel began giving Barzani active support. To the north, in Turkey, there were the first stirrings of Kurdish national expression after decades of suppression. (see p. 406). Damascus wanted to create a *cordon sanitaire* between its own Kurds and those of its neighbours.

There was also an economic dimension. The Jazira had replaced the Hawran as the prime granary and cotton region of Syria. The discovery and exploitation of oil at Qarachuk and Rumaylan in the Jazira may have started to attract Kurdish workers. The Syrian government may have feared Kurdish demographic dominance of its newly found oil-fields, as had happened in Kirkuk.

A major socio-economic consequence of dispossession in the Arab Belt was increased Kurdish labour migration mainly to Damascus and Aleppo in search of work.

Kurds in Syria today

Today, the Kurds of Syria remain victims of discrimination and oppression but not nearly on the scale endured in Iraq, Turkey or Iran. The most obvious act of discrimination arises from the failure to abrogate the settlement of Arabs on Kurdish farmlands in *al-hizam al-'arabi*, or find alternative lands for dispossessed Kurds, and the failure to reinstate tens of thousands of stateless Kurds with citizenship. Following the census of 1962, approximately 200,000 remain stripped of their citizenship either as *ajanib* (resident foreigners), or as unregistered *maktumin* (literally 'concealed').[27] Since probably over 80 per cent were born after 1962 it is an absurdity, intended to maintain the 'paper' preponderance of Arabs in al-Hasaka. *Ajanib* and *maktumin* depend on the goodwill of officials for basic access to state services, which provides the security system with an easy way of co-opting Kurds as informers on other members of their community.

As in Turkey, Kurdish has never been recognized as an official language and from 1986 its use was forbidden in the workplace. In 1988 another decree reportedly prohibited the singing of non-Arabic songs at weddings and festivals. That such measures are not fully observed is evident in the renewed attempts to prohibit Kurdish in 1989, and again in 1996. Kurds are unable to study, publish, speak officially or write in Kurdish. Since 1958 Kurds have not been allowed to publish materials in Kurdish and therefore find themselves paying exorbitant sums to printers to produce materials clandestinely. Books are printed in Beirut and then imported and distributed in Syria. Possession of books in Kurdish is tolerated. Private schools to teach Kurdish may not be established.[28] Teaching occurs informally in private homes. As in other parts of Syria, there has been a policy of Arabising place names. In the Kurdish region the intention is clearly to expunge Kurdish or Aramean names in favour of Arabic ones. Both the Jazira and Kurd Dagh have been affected. During the 1970s many village and town names were changed. The effort to expunge Kurdish place names continues apparently unabated.[29] From 1992, apparently, the Hasaka governorate refused to register children with Kurdish names. It would appear that this was a response to a growing fashion for giving children Kurdish names. One may surmise that this fashion was part of the resurgence in Kurdish national feeling in response to Kurdish popular mobilisation in south-east Turkey at this time. In February 1994 the governor of Hasaka directed that all businesses that did not have Arabic names should have one week in which to rename their establishments in Arabic.[30] Furthermore, Nawruz is an annual moment of tension between the community and the Syrian authorities, when numerous arrests are normally made.

Kurds suffer discrimination in employment opportunities. It is ironic that the shortage of employment opportunities has led to young Kurdish male citizens volunteering for continued service in the armed forces. Many have been used in the Special Units attached to the Ministry of Defence and at the direct disposal of the President. It seems that the inherent economic weakness of the Kurdish community in Syria has made these Kurds highly dependent on and therefore loyal to the inner regime. Kurdish units, part of the so-called Defence Companies under the command of Hafiz al-Asad's brother, Rif'at, acted brutally to crush the major Sunni Muslim revolt in Hama in February–March 1982. Because of this, the Kurds as a community have remained compromised in the eyes of many ordinary Sunni Arabs, fulfilling in their eyes the role of military agent of whichever regime is in power: Ottoman, French and now Ba'thist.[31] After the banishment of Rif'at from Syria in 1984, the Defence Companies were re-integrated into the army. Virtually no Kurds now have officer status, in striking contrast with the 1940s and 1950s, and those that do are confined to non-combat or administrative branches of the services.

By the 1990s some members of ethnic minorities had achieved membership of the Syrian parliament. To that extent it could be said that they have access to Syria's highly straitened form of political participation. No political party is allowed – apart from the Ba'th – to represent an ethnic group or aspiration. Kurdish members of parliament consequently belong primarily to the Syrian Communist Party (CPS), with which they have had traditional ethnic links. In recent years, certainly since the early 1990s, however, young Kurds have become progressively better educated, more politically aware and have consequently progressively distanced themselves from the CPS. The CPS itself has fragmented in recent years into three or four groups.

Kurdish political parties

There are at least 15 unrecognized political parties seeking to represent Kurdish interest in Syria.[32] Almost all of these trace their origin to the Kurdistan Democratic Party of Syria. All share the same basic political philosophy: democracy for all Syria and equality between Kurdish and Arab citizens with full cultural and social rights for Kurds.

As mentioned above, the Kurdistan Democratic Party of Syria (KDPS) was established in mid-1957, illegally and clandestinely. The KDPS' first president was Dr Nureddin Zaza, and its first journal entitled *al Parti*. In due course it called for the liberation and unification of Kurdistan by revolutionary means, so it was hardly surprising its leaders were arrested. Yet it was the call for an end to the Nasser regime in Syria which actually provoked the round-up. In 1962 KDPS split informally into two factions, one under Dr Zaza which wanted to concentrate on social and cultural rights within Syria, and the other, led by Osman Sabri, which wanted to continue the struggle along revolutionary lines for the liberation and unification of all parts of Kurdistan. The party split formally in 1965, the moderate one retaining the KDPS title under Hamid Darwish (Dr Zaza having been imprisoned), and Osman Sabri's group calling itself the Left Syrian Kurdish Party (Hizb al-Yisari al-Kurdi al-Suriyyi). In 1970 an attempt was made to reconcile the two groups under the auspices of Mulla Mustafa Barzani in Iraqi Kurdistan. The two factions refused Barzani's appointment of a Provisional Leadership with the consequence that the conference ended with the creation of a third party, KDPS-PL, effectively a Syrian branch of the Iraqi KDP.

In 1975 the Left Syrian Kurdish Party split into two factions, one of which under Salah Badreddin was vehemently pro-KDP and anti-PUK, and the other pro-PUK. It was an indication of the way that Iraqi Kurdish parties tended to pull Kurdish parties from elsewhere into their orbit. In 1977 an entirely new party joined the fray, 'al-Hizb al-Ishtaraki al-Suriyyi' ('the Socialist Kurdish Party of Syria'), but it was finally dissolved in 1988. In 1978 the KDPS-PL split into two, one calling itself 'KDPS' and the other 'KDPS – al-Parti'. In 1979 Hamid Darwish renamed the KDPS 'The Progessive KDPS'. By now it was already confusing, but worse was to come. In 1980 the faction of the Left KDPS led by Salah Badreddin which had called itself Yeketiya Gel', now renamed itself 'Hizb al-Ittihad al-Sha'bi fi Suriya' (the Popular Union Party of Syria). It split in 1991. In 1985 the new Left KDPS split, one party giving itself the new name of 'Hizb al-Shaghila al Kurdiya' ('the Kurdish Worker Party'). During the 1990s further schisms and efforts at re-unification occurred, and the listing at footnote 32 is thought to be reasonably current. Although sometimes reflecting an ideological difference, factionalism more often reflects a personality clash over the distribution of power. The leader of a schismatic group will normally surround himself with relatives.[33] The consequence is that particular families are identified with particular parties, as are those families' villages; and that political leadership tends to depend on family relationship quite as much as on political skill. This kind of pattern condemns Kurdish politics to fragmentation and ordinary Kurds who hope for political strength to constant frustration. The fractious nature of Kurdish politics means that individual parties are unlikely to present the authorities with the kind of challenge that might be taken seriously.

Since 1970 all these parties have tended to drop the term 'Kurdistan' and used the term 'Kurdish' instead, an attempt to indicate to the Syrian government that they make no claims for a united Kurdistan, and wish to work for cultural and political rights within the framework of the Syrian Arab Republic. Although not formally recognized, these parties tend to be tolerated. After 1978 the regime gave some of them informal recognition. In 1990 three Kurdish leaders were elected to the Syrian parliament; Hamid Darwish (Progressive Kurdish Democratic Party); the late Kamal Ahmad of KDPS, and Fuad Aliko of the Kurdish Popular Union Party. These parties, incidentally, have strongly encouraged young Kurds to pursue education and training despite the discriminatory situation. There is a growing recognition that only through education will the Kurdish community gain economic or political strength.

In August 1998 the formation of a new party was announced, rendering other Kurdish parties 'unnecessary': Hizb al-Tajammu 'al-Dimuqrati al-Suriyyi. (The Collective Syrian Democratic Party) under the reported leadership of an alleged ex-PKK apparatchik, Agha Mohammad Marwan al-Zarki. Since al-Zarki has enjoyed freedom to announce the new party, the logical inference is that it enjoys tacit government sponsorship. In character with the ideological jargon of the Syrian Ba'th, al-Zarki spoke of 'the struggle against suspect external initiatives and groups linked to Israeli imperialist agencies, which seek to break the steadfastness of our (Kurdish) people and disturb the amity with their brother Arabs' and the aim to 'close every rift in front of misguided people who aim to create internal disruption and schism with Kurdish material to destroy national cohesion.'[34] Al-Zarki's reported statement also referred to the threat from the Israeli-Turkish-US alliance. The implication is that while it will be merely a cypher of the state, it will also provide greater pretext for the suppression of unauthorized Kurdish parties.

The PKK

The PKK leadership fled to Syria following the military coup in Turkey in 1980 when the security forces launched a massive round-up of suspected members of illegal organisations. Syria offered Ocalan training facilities inside Lebanon with diplomatic offices in Syria. Syrian help was crucial to the initial success of the PKK. By 1987 the PKK had offices in Damascus and in the north at Qamishli, Rasuliya, Darbasiya, Dayrik, 'Ayn al-'Arab, Afrin, Aleppo and al-Hasaka. Initially, with its slogan of an independent Kurdistan, the PKK enjoyed almost unanimous sympathy within the Kurdish community in Syria, and was able to recruit young Syrian Kurds with little difficulty. It did so in an atmosphere charged with nationalist fervour and high unemployment. Seven thousand Syrian Kurdish recruited into the PKK remain unaccounted for from the 1980s, and it is assumed they were killed either in training or in battle. It is also claimed that the families of the disappeared never received military call-up papers for these young men, with the clear implication that the government either quietly accepted enrolment in the PKK in lieu of military service, or alternatively that it was informed by the PKK of Syrian casualties.

During the 1990s anger grew at the way the PKK was riding roughshod over local sensibilities. In particular, there was growing resentment with the PKK's levy of money, goods and services from the Kurdish population. The PKK also adopted the line that Syria had no Kurds of its own and that those living there were all refugees from Turkey. In stating this in an interview in 1996,[35] Ocalan suggested that Syria as well as Kurds would be pleased to see the movement of Kurds back northwards, a line that chimed nicely with the Syrian government's apparent desire to minimise Kurdish citizenship in Syria. Even if this assertion was partially true in the sense that a substantial number of Kurds had indeed arrived across the new international border during the 1920s, Syria's Kurds did not regard themselves as refugees and did not aspire to 'return'. After 75 years or more living in Syria, the Kurds had firmly become part of Syrian society. Given Syria's own discrimination against Kurds and its Arab ethnocentricity, this line of argument probably enjoyed official sanction. Official blessing to the PKK compared with the second class status of Syrian Kurds also generated resentment, particularly regarding such things as the celebration of Nawruz, and the way PKK *wasta* (influence) opened doors that remain firmly closed to ordinary Syrian Kurds.

In October 1998 the PKK presence in Syria came to a rapid and dramatic end when Turkey suddenly concentrated troops along the border and threatened military intervention unless Syria closed PKK training camps and expelled Ocalan. Significantly weaker than Turkey militarily and fearful of Israel to its rear, Syria complied and negotiated a new security agreement with Turkey.

Syria, the Kurds and regional relations

Syria's sponsorship of the PKK was a consequence of the serious grievances it has continued to have against Turkey: (i) the loss of the Sanjaq of Alexandretta in 1939, the legitimacy of which it does not accept; (ii) Turkey's unilateral harnessing and damming of the Euphrates, adversely affecting the quantity of water let down into Syria. A new cause for Syrian concern lay with Turkey's growing alliance with Israel since 1996. This alliance, which enjoyed US support, was threatening since it clearly had as its aim the containment of Syria and the defeat of the PKK. From Syria's perspective this alliance constituted an attempt at strategic encirclement.

Internal Security: Syria and its Kurds

It was inevitable that the PKK's struggle against Turkey should help excite national pride among Syria's Kurds. Yet it did not lead to separatism.

It is possible to argue that the possibility of Kurdish irredentism within Syria was a real worry roughly between the years 1920 and 1970. Successive Syrian regimes, but most notably the Ba'th, evolved a policy of rigid and ruthless control to meet this danger. They were prepared to brook no wavering from the official line. The present regime still ensures firm and close control. There seems to be a dislocation between its recent and apparent moves towards liberalisation, evidenced in the release of some political prisoners, and the perpetuation of policies that deny and exclude Kurds. In part this may reflect Syria's apparent inability to abandon old habits of thinking and practice, a characteristic of its innate conservatism and its reluctance to depart from the rhetoric and value system of the preceding generation when Arab nationalism and the Cold War were the dominant themes of the new Syrian state. Today the borders with Turkey and Iraq can be relatively easily policed, particularly since Turkey has established a fence along the Syria border. The terrain of northern Syria makes the idea of a guerrilla war unsustainable.

More than that, as in Turkey and Iran (and Iraq in normative times), a large proportion of Kurds seek their education or their living outside the predominantly Kurdish area, settling in the large cities of each state: Istanbul, Izmir, Tehran, Tabriz, Mosul, Baghdad and in Syria, Damascus or Aleppo. Many of those who do not leave Kurdistan remain dependent on remittances from migrant workers. Thus many Kurds, regardless of romantic sentiment, recognize that economically and culturally they are not only Kurdish but also belong to the wider community of the country in which they live.

Sources

Abdallah Ocalan, *Qa'id wa Sha'b: sab'at ayyam ma'a Abu* (Athens, 1996); Amnesty International, *Annual Reports*, 1995–1998; Amnesty International, 'Syria: Repression and impunity: the Forgotten Victims' April 1995; Ian and Morris Black, Benny, *Israel's Secret Wars* (Hamish Hamilton, 1991); Nikolaos van Dam, *The Struggle for Power in Syria: Sectarianism, Regionalism and Tribalism in Politics, 1961–78* (Croom Helm, 1979); Nikolaos van Dam, *The Struggle for Power in Syria: Politics and Society under the Asad and the Ba'th Party* (IBTauris, 1996); Nelida Fuccaro, 'The Kurds of Damascus under the French Mandate' unpublished paper given at Kurds and the City Conference, Sevres, September 1996; Nelida Fuccaro, 'Kurds and Kurdish nationalism in mandatory Syria: politics, culture and identity' English version of paper published in German in C. Bork, E. Salversberg, S. Hajo (edr.), *Ethnizat, Nationalismus, Religion und Politik in Kurdistan* (Munster: Lit.Verlag, 1997) pp. 301–326; Albert, Hourani, *Syria and Lebanon: A Political Essay* (Oxford University Press, 1946); Albert Hourani, *Minorities in the Arab World*, (Oxford University Press, 1947); Human Rights Watch, *Syria: The Price of Dissent* (Washington and New York, July, 1995); Human Rights Watch, *Syria: The Silenced Kurds* (Washington and New York, 1996).; IBRD, *The Economic Development of Syria* (John Hopkins, Baltimore, 1955); al-Ittihad al-Sha'bi al-Kurdi fir Suriya, *al-Ittihad/Hevgirtin* (organ of the external department of al-Ittihad al-Sha'bi al-Kurdi fi Suriya, bi-lingual Arabic/Kirmanji, published quarterly in Bonn, Germany); Philip S. Khoury, *Urban Notables and Arab Nationalism: The Politics of Damascus 1860–1920* (Cambridge University Press, 1983); Philip S. Khoury, *Syria and the French Mandate: The Politics of Arab Nationalism, 1920–1945* (Princeton University Press, 1987); Stephen Hemsley Longrigg, *Syria and Lebanon under the French Mandate* (Oxford University Press, 1958); Jonathan Randal, *After Such Knowledge, What Forgiveness? My Encounters with Kurdistan* (Farrar, Strauss and Giroux, 1997); Patrick Seale, *The Struggle for Syria: A Study of Post-War Arab Politics, 1945–58* (Oxford University Press, 1965); Patrick Seale, *Asad: The Struggle for the Middle East* (IBTauris, 1988); United States, Department of State 'Syria Country Report on Human Rights Practices for 1997' (Bureau of Democracy, Human Rights and Labor, January 1998); Ismet Cheriff Vanly, 'The Kurds in Syria and Lebanon', in Philip Kreyenbroek and Stefan Sperl, *The Kurds: A Contemporary Overview* (Routledge, 1992).

Notes

1. The four leading Kurdish agha families were the al Yusuf, Shamdin, Agribuz and Buzu. By 1900 Abd al Rahman al Yusuf, himself the fruit of a strategic union between the

al Yusuf and Shamdin families, acquired extensive estates in the Hawran, a series of provincial administrative posts, and the lucrative post of Amir al Hajj, responsible for the safe conduct of the annual pilgrimage caravan from Damascus to Mecca.

2. Ironically, given his political intentions, Abd al Rahman al Yusuf became first Prime Minister of the Kingdom of Syria).

3. Fuccaro, 'The Kurds of Damascus under the French Mandate'.

4. It is worth noting that both Kurdish and Arab confederations often included dependent tribes or groups of different ethnicity or religion: Arab or Kurdish, Muslim, Christian or Yazidi. Such differences were seldom an issue in the world of tribal politics.

5. The Yazidi tribes of Jabal Sinjar had a particularly long history of pillaging caravans passing through the apex of the Fertile Crescent.

6. Following the Franco-Turkish treaty of Ankara of October 1921 whereby France ceded Cilicia to the Turkish nationalist forces, 30,000 Armenians crossed into Syria. There was another influx in late 1922, and another 30,000 Christians entered Syria in mid-1923. By the end of 1923 some 120,000 Christians had entered Syria. Although most settled elsewhere, by 1930 there were about 30,000 Christians in Jazira.

7. Apart from constituting Greater Lebanon by annexing parts of historic Syria to Mount Lebanon, France also established a state of Latakiyya (for the Alawi minority in the mountains behind that port), a state of Jabal Druze for the Druzes of southern Syria; a state of Aleppo and another of Damascus, essentially to break up the Sunni Arab majority, and also separate administrative status for the Sanjaq of Alexandretta.

8. Haju had arrived almost penniless, but had been given a small patch of land by much longer established Duriki, and on it he eventually built the town of Tirbe Spi. Unlike most Kurdish chiefs he did not spend time on agriculture. Haju gained power by two traditional methods: prowess in raiding, and ingratiating himself with government, in this case the French. He also embraced Kurdish nationalism, and became the most influential Syrian Kurd in Khoybun.

9. Further west, Mustafa and Bozan bin Shahin Barazi, both chiefs of the Barazi tribe of the Jarablus region were similarly active.

10. A.H. Hourani, *Minorities in the Arab World* (Oxford University Press, 1947) p. 81.

11. For an account of these disorders, see Fuccaro, 'Kurds and Kurdish Nationalism'.

12. During the previous two years Haju had apparently swung like a weather vane between support for Damascus and for localism.

13. This was the subject of secret discussion between the Amir Abdullah of Transjordan, who hoped to gain control of Syria, and the Jewish Agency, August 1947, Avi Shlaim, *Collusion Across the Jordan* (Oxford, 1988) p. 95.

14. Badr Khan proposed recruiting Druzes, Circassians, Maronites and Kurds in his schemes, Israel State Archives, Foreign Ministry file 3749/1 as cited in Ian Black and Benny Morris, *Israel's Secret Wars* (Hamish Hamilton, London 1991) p.65 and Jonathan Randal, *After Such Knowledge, What Forgiveness? My Encounters with Kurdistan* (Farrar, Strauss and Giroux, New York, 1997), p. 188. In fact the Druzes were already in contact with the Jewish Agency, and Druze envoys visited the British political resident in Amman, offering to thwart the Syrian army's entry into Palestine on condition that Jabal Druze would be incorporated into Transjordan. In the event, neither the Druzes nor the Kurds did anything. Such was the weakness of the Syrian forces immediately after independence, that the Druze threat was perfectly credible. The Maronites of Lebanon had had direct contact with the Jewish Agency from the 1930s.

15. Kamuran's brother Jaladet died in mysterious circumstances on his Golan farm in 1951, killed it was believed, by Syrian intelligence. Information from Western Kurdistan Association, 7 August 1998.

16. The first, Husni Za'im, relied on an exclusively Circassian corps of bodyguards.

17. J.C. Hurewitz, *Middle Eastern Politics: The Military Dimension*, (1969), p.133.

18. Patrick Seale, *The Struggle for Syria*, p. 260.

19. Later, after the Syrian Ba'th had broken with its sibling party in Iraq, the Syrian regime co-opted elements of the party as the Syrian part of Barzani's KDP, with the intention of assisting the Kurdish insurgency in Iraq. The KDPS never really recovered from the initial round-up of its leaders, and remained fragmented.

20. France and Britain had both used minority groups as tools of their policy during the Mandate period; France had done its best to destroy Syrian unity ever since 1920; Britain had occupied Egypt in the nineteenth century and had withdrawn only to invade Suez in 1956; it had handed Palestine to Zionist settlers who usurped the land and drove half its inhabitants out; the United States was implicated in the overthrow of the elected government of Syria in 1948; it had rebuffed the development plans of both Egypt and Syria and clearly favoured Israel; Israel had sown discord wherever possible between the different ethnic and confessional communities in neighbouring countries.

21. Syrian Embassy to Human Rights Watch, 12 July 1996, in Human Rights Watch, *Syria: The Silenced Kurds* (Washington 1996).

22. Public Record Office (PRO) FO 371/164413 Report on the Census taken in the Province of al Hassakah, 8 November 1962.

23. FO 371/164413 Report on the Census in the Province of al Hassakah.

24. Black and Morris, *Israel's Secret Wars*, p. 184. The British mission in Damascus reported 'Some newspapers are now making sly references to the tour made by the United States Ambassador in the north-eastern provinces as recently as last month [October 1962]. In fact the Syrian public is being dramatically invited to see the Jazirah as potentially 'another Israel'.' FO 371/164413 Report on the Census taken in the Province of Hassakeh.

25. *Study of the National, Social and Political Aspects of the Province of Jazira (Dirasat 'an Muhafizat al- Jazira min al-Nawahi al-Qawmiyya wa-l-Ijtima'iyya wa'l-Siyasiyya)* pp. 2, 6 translated by Ismet Cheriff Vanly, 'The Kurds in Syria and Lebanon', Philip G. Kreyenbroek and Stefan Sperl, *The Kurds: A contemporary overview* (London 1992), pp. 153, 154.

26. IBRD, *The Economic Development of Syria*, (Johns Hopkins, Baltimore, 1955) pp. 354, 355.

27. *Maktumin*, numbering about 75,000, are composed of (i) Children born of a male Syrian-born 'foreigner' who marries a Syrian citizen; (ii) Children born of the union of a Syrian-born 'foreigner' and a *maktum/maktuma*; (iii) Children born of *maktumayn* parents.

It is thus possible for a Kurdish household to be composed of a father who is an *ajnabi* (foreigner), a mother who is a Syrian citizen, and children who are unregistered *maktumin*. Parents of such children have substantial difficulty obtaining any form of written documentation at all, and such children may not be admitted to school without approval from political security.

28. Yet Armenians and Assyrians are freely allowed to run their own schools teaching their own languages. Needless to say, there is no objection to the teaching of English, French or German. Kurdish alone seems to be unacceptable.

29. A circular was sent to all relevant offices and departments in al-Hasaka governorate in January 1998 notifying them to observe only the new names of 55 villages and 49 farmsteads in Ras al 'Ayn and Darbasiya districts. These new names were issued by the Minster for Local Administration the previous month. Subhi Harb, Chief of the Executive Office of al-Hasaka Governorate, Circular No. 14875 of 6 January 1998 to all relevent departments, enclosing the letter from Yahya Abu 'Ali, Minister for Local Administration, dated 20 December 1997 which refers to Ordinance No 36 of 11 August 1971 and Law No 56 of 15 July 1980, and the decision of the Executive Office of the Council of al-Hasaka governorate, No. 541 of 28 October 1998, as published in *al Ittihad*, No. 27, July 1998.

30. Order No. 932, 24 February 1994, al-Hasaka governorate.

31. Shortly after the Islamists were crushed in 1982, a graffito appeared on a wall in the Kurdish quarter of Aleppo that probably sums up popular Arab Muslim antipathy: 'al-akrad kilab al 'alawiyyin' ('the Kurds are the dogs of the 'Alawis') – the 'Alawis being the dominant confession in Syria.

32. It does not seem worth burdening the text with a listing of current party groups, since many of these seem transient. The most recent spate of schisms is readily discernable from the repetitive nomenclature:

1. al-Hizb al-Dimuqrati al-Kurdi al-Suriyyi (KDPS), led by Shaikh Baqi.
2. al-Hizb al-Dimuqrati al-Kurdi al-Suriyyi(KDPS) also known as 'al-Parti' led by the late Kamal Ahmad, d. 1997.
3. Hizb al-Ittihad al-Sha'bi al-Kurdi al-Suriyyi, also known as Yeketi (The Kurdish Popular Union Party of Syria), led by Salah Badreddin.
4. Hizb al-Ittihad al-Sha'bi al-Kurdi al Suriyyi, apparently recently seceded from Yeketi (the Kurdish Popular Union Party of Syria) under the leadership of Fu'ad Aliko.
5. al-Hizb al-Yisari al-Kurdi al-Suriyyi (The Kurdish Leftist Party of Syria), led by Ismat Fathallah.
6. al-Hizb al-Yisari al-Kurdi al-Suriyyi (The Kurdish Leftist Party of Syria), led by Yusif Dibu.
7. Hizb al-Shaghila al Kurdi (The Kurdish Worker Party), led by Abd al Basit.
8. Hizb al-Shaghila al Kurdi (The Kurdish Worker Party), operates by committee, without any leadership since this would be ideologically anti-democratic.
9. al-Hizb al-Ishtiraki al-Kurdi al-Suriyyi (the Kurdish Socialist Party of Syria) (led by Sabah Kado).
10. al-Hizb al-Dimuqrati al-Taqaddami al Kurdi al Suriyyi (the Progressive Kurdish Democratic Party), led by Hamid Darwish.
11. al-Hizb al-Dimuqrati al-Taqaddami al Suriyyi (the Progressive Democratic Party) (led by Rashid Hamo).
12. al-Hizb al-Dimuqrati al-Kurdi (led by Isma'il 'Amu, and now allied with KPUPS aka Yeketi).
13. Hizb al-Shaikh Ali (also now allied with Yeketi.)
14. Hizb al-Wahda al-Dimuqrati led by Isma'il 'Umar.

33. This is as true for Leftist organisations as it is for traditionalist ones.

34. 'Al-Tajamma 'al-Watani al-Dimuqrati badil "al-ahzab" al-Kurdiyya al-Suriyya?', *al-Hayat*, 20 September 1998.

35. See his remarks in Abdallah Ocalan, *Qa'id wa Sha'b: sab'at ayyam ma'a Abu [Leader and People: Seven Days with Apo]* (Athens, 1996) p. 169. Ocalan holds a garbled view of the region's history, including the erroneous but widely believed idea that the 'Alawiyyin of Syria are of the same origin as the Alevis of central Anatolia.

THE KURDS IN LEBANON[1]

Introduction

There is a close connection between the Kurds of Syria and Lebanon since virtually all those in Lebanon came either from or via Syria, and their fortunes are conditioned by the fact that Lebanon has become a satrapy of Syria since Syrian forces entered Lebanon in 1976 during the Civil War. Syria will watch the Kurds of Lebanon carefully and is likely to thwart any effort to advance the Kurdish cause in any way which might, in its own view, adversely affect Syrian interests.

Historical Background

The present community of at least 100,000 Kurds is the product of several waves of immigrants. The first major wave was in the period 1925–50, when thousands of Kurds fled the violence and poverty that characterized Kurdish life in the Republic of Turkey. Most came from the Tur Abdin/Mardin region. All of these immigrants travelled through Syria, some sojourning there before finally arriving in Lebanon. The second significant wave took place during the 1950s and 1960s, when at least 50,000 are thought to have arrived in Lebanon. Many of these came a result of the 1962 census in al-Hasaka province (see p. 474). Many of those thus stripped of their Syrian citizenship moved into Lebanon. Others, like many Syrian Arabs, were drawn to Lebanon by the comparative dynamism and prosperity of the Lebanese economy. These Kurds moved into slum areas, most notably those quarters that formed part of the 'Belt of Misery' that surrounded affluent Beirut.[2] Excluding the 200,000 or so Palestine refugees, the Kurds probably comprised some 35 per cent of the remaining slum dwellers. Some Kurds also settled in poor downtown areas, like Basta and, following the Jewish emigration after the 1967 war, into the old quarters where many Jews had lived: Bab Idris, Wadi Abi Jamil and Mina al Husn.

Most of Lebanon's Kurdish communities eked out a living as day labourers in the construction industry, benefiting from the massive building boom of the 1950s and 1960s. Others were sharecroppers, mainly on the fruit and market garden estates of the coastal plain, while others became street peddlers, a significant sector of the retail economy. They competed with the other two large constituencies of unskilled casual day labour: the large Palestine refugee population (by 1970 over 300,000) and Shi'i peasants abandoning their lands in south Lebanon, either for economic reasons or because of Israeli reprisals in the region. Other Kurdish communities settled in the coastal cities of Tripoli, Sidon and Tyre, and also in the inland city of Baalbek in the Biqa' valley. As with other rural migrant families, Kurds tended to settle in urban locations according either to tribal or village identity. Thus, the solidarities of pre-urban existence were reinforced but also politicized in the often alien as well as alien-ating culture of city life.

The Civil War and After

On the whole, the Kurds had little reason to take sides in Lebanon's civil war. For the most part denied citizenship, there seemed little reason to get involved. That to some extent changed with the sack of al-Karantina/al-Maslakh in January 1976 by the Maronite Phalange forces. The inhabitants, Kurds, Palestinians and Lebanese Muslims (mainly Shi'is) were either shot or driven out and their hovels levelled. Survivors fled to south Beirut. Other Kurdish areas in Maronite-dominated East Beirut were also eliminated. As the Maronites pressed their advance into West Beirut, some Kurds joined the Progressive Socialist Party, led by Kemal Junblat and otherwise composed almost exclusively of Druzes. The fact that the Junbalat family, which enjoyed undisputed leadership of the formidable Druze community, was of Kurdish origin may have played some part. Perhaps another reason was that Kurds found they lived more happily in proximity with the Druzes than with other Leba-nese communities. Some Kurds joined the Sunni Murabitun, only to discover they were treated as second class members of this militia, not being Arab.

Following Israel's invasion of Lebanon in June 1982, many Kurds became subject to further expulsions. Most moved to the Biqa' valley. Following the establishment of a pro-Israeli/pro-US Phalange-dominated regime under Amin Gemayel, Chris-tian-dominated government forces began to harass the unwanted people of the southern suburbs, mainly Palestinians and Shi'is but also Kurds, rounding up, detaining or expelling those without proper papers. Barely a year later Druze and Shi'i militia forces, backed by Syria ousted Israel's Maronite surrogates from predominantly Muslim areas.

In late 1983, Amal, the main Shi'i militia, began to exert its hitherto untested power to achieve ascendancy in South and West Beirut on behalf of Syria. Although its main focus was the suppression of the Palestinian population, it also rooted many Kurdish families out of their homes. After the rapid elimination of the Murabitun, Kurds and Druzes once more stood together to resist Amal's encroachments into vital areas of West Beirut. During this conflict, which lasted until 1987, the Kurdish population in Lebanon dropped by almost a half, to about 60,000. Following the negotiated withdrawal of all militias however, and the handover of public order and security to Syrian forces, the Druze Progressive

Socialist Party retreated to its heartland in the Shuf mountains. This left the Kurds vulnerable to Syrian surveillance and harassment.

Altogether nearly 20 per cent of Lebanon's total population was displaced by civil war and Israel's invasion and occupation of southern Lebanon. Many Kurds fled to Europe to avoid the brutal vicissitudes of life in Lebanon. Apart from the Palestinians, the Kurds probably suffered most during the civil war. They still feel relatively friendless. They have found few in Lebanon really willing to fight their corner, or represent their interests. The Kurds mistrust the political elite, almost without exception.[3]

Political Parties

National feeling among Kurds in Lebanon grew in response to the exploits of Mulla Mustafa Barzani in Iraq. The Kurdistan Democratic Party of Lebanon, better known as al-Parti, became a legally recognized party in 1970. But it has already existed clandestinely for a decade under the name Munazzama al-Shabiba al-Kurdiyya (The Organisation of Kurdish Youth). Its founder and driving force was Jamil Mihhu who had been befriended by Mulla Mustafa. KDPL was intended by Mulla Mustafa to act as a counterweight to the activities of Salah Badreddin of the KDPS, who opposed Barzani. In fact Mihhu fell out with Barzani who imprisoned him in Iraq, 1971–74. On his release Mihhu became a supporter of Baghdad's autonomy plan for Iraq's Kurds. KDPL ceased to function with the death of Mihhu in 1982, by which time KDPL was, like so many other Kurdish ventures, little more than a vehicle for a particular family's political ambition, in rivalry more with other Kurdish groups than grappling with the issues that faced the community. All that survives today from different Kurdish political parties is the Broad Kurdish National Front (al-Jabha al-Wataniyya al-Kurdiyya al-Arida). It wisely welcomed Syria's intervention in Lebanon in 1976. The weakness of the Kurdish movement in Lebanon (and arguably in Syria) is its failure to mobilize mass support. In his study of the Kurds in Lebanon, Lokman Meho argues that this failure resulted from an almost complete failure to address community concerns. Rather than creating community solidarity in the fields of economic and social concerns, which clearly were (and still are) pressing for an impoverished, largely slum-dwelling community, those that formed parties did so on the basis of political concepts and ideologies which had precious little to do with the Kurdish experience in Lebanon.

Citizenship

The major issue for Kurds in Lebanon is the question of citizenship. The balance of confessional and ethnic communities has been critical ever since the establishment of Greater Lebanon by France in 1920. At that time Christians probably slightly outnumbered Muslims. A census in 1932 showed that Christians outnumbered Muslims by a ratio of 6:5. The knowledge that Muslims tended to have a higher birth rate and the failure to shift popular identities from confessional or ethnic basis to a Lebanese national one meant that at no time did the authorities dare authorize a new population census. Furthermore, it meant that the Christian Maronite-dominated state was unwilling to accept Muslim immigrants as citizens lest it upset 'the balance', in fact the imbalance of Christian political predominance. Until 1940 it remained possible to acquire Lebanese citizenship after five years residence, but many, including Kurdish migrants, failed to recognize the value of acquiring citizenship. Legislation in 1940 made Lebanese naturalization theoretically impossible. It was only following this legislation, and with the introduction of war-time rationing in 1941 that non-citizen Kurds began to recognize the functional usefulness of citizenship.

In the post-1945 era, following Lebanon's formal independence, the question of citizenship affected two major (mainly or wholly) Muslim ethnic categories: the Palestine refugees (who having been expelled from Palestine in 1948 amounted to no less than 10 per cent of the population inside Lebanon), and the Kurds, who by the 1960s possibly represented almost 3 per cent of the population in Lebanon.

No Lebanese leader was willing to campaign for the Kurds to obtain citizenship, the internal confessional balance in Lebanon being too explosive an issue.[4] A handful of Kurds successfully obtained Lebanese citizenship, usually through the influence they could bring to bear through money or contacts. By 1982 fewer than 20 per cent had obtained citizenship. Approximately 10 per cent were without any form of identity, or were registered as Syrians or even Palestinians. The balance, over 70 per cent, held ID cards marked *'qaid al-dars'* ('under consideration'). These proportions probably changed as a result of the Shi'ite onslaught on West Beirut, in which the poorest Kurds, i.e. those without citizenship, suffered the most. As a consequence, the remaining population reduced from about 100,000 to 60,000 of whom 30 per cent probably held citizenship, 5 per cent remained without any papers, and 65 per cent were in the *qaid al-dars* category.

In 1994, in an attempt to resolve some of the outstanding demographic problems, the government issued a citizenship decree, whereby those without citizenship were invited to file applications. Even though many Kurds either could not afford the cost of application or simply did not believe in it, the processing of large numbers of Syrian and Kurdish applicants took two years. Since 1996 it is believed that approximately 60 per cent of Lebanon's Kurds hold Lebanese citizenship.

Source

Lokman Meho, '*The Dilemma of Social and Political Integration of Ethnoclass Groups within Pluralistic Societies: The Case of the Kurds in Lebanon*' (unpublished master's dissertation, American University of Beirut, 1995).

Notes

1. I am indebted to Dr Lokman Meho for kindly furnishing me with a copy of his Master's dissertation, cited at the end of this appendix. This is essentially a brief summary of his work.

2. For those familiar with Beirut, these were most notably (from north east to southwest) al-Karantina/al-Maslakh just east of the port area, Burj Hammoud, Furn al-Shabbak, Jnah and further south, by the airport, Burj al-Barajna.

3. The exceptions are (i) Kemal Junbalat, Druze chief, maverick politician and leader of the leftist Arab nationalist forces during the civil war, assassinated by Syria in 1977, (ii) Sami al-Sulh, Sunni Prime Mininster in the 1950s, and the two Sunni Prime Ministers Salim al-Hoss in the 1980s and Rafiq al-Hariri in the 1990s.

4. In 1961 Kemal Junbalat, then Interior Minister, sought a solution by granting Kurds 'non-specified' citizenship whereby the children born in Lebanon of such parents would acquire Lebanese citizenship. The measure was soon abandoned following opposition, presumably from Christian politicians concerned about the changing confessional balance.

APPENDIX 4:

THE KURDS OF THE CAUCASUS

Demography

Although there are no recognized Kurdish territories in the former Soviet Union, there are possibly approximately 500,000 Kurds, mainly in the Caucasus, but with some in Turkmenistan and other Central Asian republics. However, the number and distribution of Kurds must be extremely tentative. The following, based on Kurdish claims, may only be described as a very approximate estimate[1]:

Republic/territory Kurds		Percentage of population
Azerbaijan	200,000	2.8
Armenia	75,000	1.8
Georgia	40,000	0.9
Turkmenistan	50,000	1.3
Kazakhstan	30,000	
Kirghizia	20,000	
Uzbekistan	10,000	
Tajikistan	3,000	
Siberia	35,000 (of whom 30,000 are in Vladivostock)	
Krasnodar	30,000	
Other	12,000	

Much depends upon one's definition of a Kurd. In Armenia the vast majority of Kurds are Yezidi, many of whom prefer this rather than 'Kurd' as their primary identity.

In Azerbaijan virtually all Kurds are Sunni Muslim and either by choice or by compulsion the majority became assimilated into the Azeri population. Generally, Azerbaijani Kurds are ambivalent about their ethnic origin, and the term 'Kurdish' is more often a geographical expression, referring to the inhabitants of what was once known as 'Red Kurdistan' (see below), where the majority are indeed of Kurdish ethnic origin. Some, however, have been 'rediscovering' their Kurdish identity since *glasnost* in the 1980s. While Sunni Muslims may marry any other Sunni

Muslims, thus allowing for assimilation, Yazidis may not marry outside their religion which confines them since all Yazidis by definition are of Kurdish culture.

Brief history up to 1918

There have been Kurds in the Caucasus for possibly a thousand years. It is possible that Kurdish tribes assisted in halting the Arab Muslim northward advance at the Araxes or Aras river in the seventh century. The first real evidence of a Kurdish presence is the Shaddadid dynasty in the Caucasus from the tenth to eleventh century. They were probably few in number and on the very periphery of Kurdish expansion from the Zagros region. Some would have been nomadic tribes, others soldiers and warlords that settled the region during phases of Muslim expansion. There is no evidence to suggest that these groups were self-consciously Kurdish. More probably they were self-consciously Muslim, on the marches between Muslim and unconquered lands. Following the Mongol invasion and devastation of the whole region in the thirteenth century (see pp. 23–24), Kurdish tribes moved into previously Armenian lands in the southern parts of Karabagh.

At the end of the sixteenth century Shah Abbas forcibly settled thousands of modern Iran, as a bulwark against the Turkoman tribes to the north. In the eighteenth century Nadir Shah did likewise. It is from these frontier settlements that, apart from a Kurdish population still extant in north eastern Iran, a few small communities of Kurds exist north of the Atrek river, just inside Turkmenistan, mainly in Ashkabad.

The greater proportion of Kurds inside the former Soviet Union's borders result from four processes. In the eighteenth century there was a migration of tribes northwards into the Caucasus region, particularly onto the Yerevan plain. Secondly, progressive Russian conquest of the Caucasus region brought Georgia finally under its rule in 1813. The rest of the Caucasus down as far as the Araxes river, the present international border, was incorporated into the Czarist empire, together with its various peoples in 1827. Then, in the second half of the nineteenth century and the early part of the twentieth century, Ottoman and Sunni Muslim persecution of the Yazidis in northern Mesopotamia and eastern Anatolia prompted a substantial migration to the comparative safety of Christian Armenia and Georgia. Finally, Muslim Kurds, less comfortable in Christian Armenia, not least because of Kurdish complicity in the Armenian genocides of 1895 and 1915, tended to migrate to Muslim Azerbaijan. The last Kurds to become Soviet citizens were members of the Bruk group of Kurdish tribes fleeing Reza Shah's pacification in Iran.

The Soviet Period

How many Kurds were incorporated into the Bolshevik republics remains uncertain, but it was probably in the order of 200,000–300,000, and they formed one of over 100 recognized nationalities in the new Soviet polity. They found themselves isolated from other Kurdish communities for the first time by the relatively imper-meable borders established by the Bolsheviks. In Azerbaijan many assimilated into the dominant Azeri culture. Whether this was as a result of duress or the natural result of similarity of culture and lifestyle and common Sunni beliefs is unclear. At any rate, by 1926 only 17 per cent of the 41,000 Kurds supposedly in Azerbaijan identified Kurdish as their mother tongue.

Part of the territory awarded to Azerbaijan had a predominantly Kurdish popula-tion. This was the area sandwiched between Nagorny-Karabakh and the Soviet Republic of Armenia, and comprised the south-western districts of Kelbajar, Lachin, Zengelan and Kubatly. But it is a moot point how long the Kurds had predomi-nated. In 1919–20 the substantial minority Armenian poplation was driven out by Azeri and Kurdish forces under the leadership of Khosrov Bey Sultanov, a local Kurdish warlord who was appointed governor of Karabagh by the Azeri administra-tion in Baku. In 1923 these districts were unified as the Kurdish Autonomous Province, more colloquially known as 'Red Kurdistan'. It comprised an area about half the size of Lebanon. Its capital was first at Lachin but later at Susha, a previ-ously Armenian town. In accordance with Soviet policy, the education and culture of this small indigenous people was encouraged, with Kurdish-medium schools, its own newspaper, *Sovyet Kurdustan* (which existed until 1961), and a Kurdish broad-casting service.

The Bolshevik policy of collectivisation led to widespread uprisings among many peasant communities, not least among the Kurds of the Autonomous Province. Given the major rising taking place with Armenian support in Agri Dagh (pp. 203–207), the Bolsheviks may well have feared an infection of national feeling. Possibly in order to forestall the danger of this, the Province was reduced to district status in 1929 and reincorporated into Azerbaijan the following year.

Like other small communities the Kurds became victims of forced migrations and purges, in their case probably because of their proximity to international borders beyond which lay larger numbers of Kurds. In 1937 thousands of Kurds were forcibly removed from Armenia and Azerbaijan to Kazakhstan, other Central Asian republics, and Siberia. In 1944 a similar fate overtook some of the Kurds of Georgia. One of those transported as a child, NK Nadirov, recalls being deported from Nakhichevan in 1937:

'All grown-up men were gathered together and taken away by train, no one knows where to this day. Nobody has returned. Following [after the] men, women and children were forced to leave their property, homes and cattle and were taken in an unknown direction in goods vans not fit for transportation of people. The most terrible thing was that nobody knew why and where they were taken. It took several years for survivors to find the location of their relatives.'[2]

In many resettlement locations Kurds remained under curfew, unable to leave their town or village without permission, with the risk of 25 years in prison for those who disobeyed.

Developments since the demise of the Soviet Union

Glasnost contributed to a resurgence of identity and expression, and also to a recognition of the repression of the Stalinist years. In 1988 some 10,00 Kurds in Azerbaijan returned their Azeri identity papers to Moscow with the explicit request that their identity be changed from Azeri to Kurd. At the 28th Congress of the Communist Party in September 1989 a resolution promised: 'to take every measure in order to solve the problems of the Crimean Tartars, Soviet Germans, Greeks, Kurds, Meshtekian Turks and others.'[3] In fact no measures seem to have been taken. Instead, the Kurdish communities were overtaken by the Nagorny Karabagh conflict between the republics of Armenia and Azerbaijan, which they were unable to avoid. In 1990 the dispute erupted into full scale warfare, and both sides applied pressure on their Kurdish minority. At least 18,000 Muslim Kurds fled from Armenia and from the autonomous enclave of Nakhichevan. Of these it is believed that 11,000 found refuge in Azerbaijan, while 7,000 or so went to Krasnodar, just east of Crimea. In Azerbaijan 2,000 fled to avoid harassment or forced conscription.

Following the defeat of the Azeris in Nagorny-Karabakh by the Armenians, the Kurdish Liberation Movement declared the re-establishment of the Kurdish Autonomous Region, in early 1992. This was almost certainly an Armenian-inspired political ploy to wrest the land, old 'Red Kurdistan', from Azerbaijani control. Those Azerbaijani Kurds still in the area refused to participate in the enterprise. In any event, any Kurdish hopes were short-lived. In May 1992 Karabagh and Armenian forces drove a corridor through the Kurdish populated area of Lachin in order to connect the freshly captured region of Nagorny-Karabagh with the Republic of Armenia. They burnt and looted as they went, displacing its predominantly Kurdish population of 25,000. Lachin was renamed Kashatag. In April 1993 Armenian forces widened the corridor to include the district of Kelbajar, where 60,000, mainly Kurds were also displaced. In the words of the US Department of State Human Rights country report:

> 'They [the Armenian forces] drove out the inhabitants and looted and burned the provincial capitals and most of the villages of these regions. The UN Security Council condemned these offensive actions, including the looting and burning.'[4]

Kelbajar was renamed Karvajar by the Armenians. By the end of 1993 Kubatly and Zengelan had also been occupied. The majority of the displaced moved to the traditional Kurdish winter pasturages of the hot dry central Azerbaijani lowlands. In May 1994 a ceasefire was brokered between Azerbaijan and Armenia. Efforts to negotiate a peace by the Organisation for Security and Co-operation in Europe and by its inner caucus, the Minsk group, established specifically to deal with the Karabagh question, failed. Azerbaijan seeks total restitution of occupied territory, promising a generous autonomy to Karabakh. Armenia, while prepared to consider this insisted on retaining the Lachin corridor, while Karabaghis insisted on maintaining a second corridor through Kelbajar. By 1999 no compromise had been possible and the indigenous Kurdish inhabitants remained displaced mainly in central Azerbaijan.

In Armenia, following the collapse of the former Soviet Union and the loss of automatic minority representation and the revival of strong ethnic identity, politically-minded Yazidis have become divided. Some affirm loyalty to the Armenian republic and tend to play down their Kurdish identity while others assert their Yazidi Kurdish identity and complain of Armenian discrimination.[5] In addition there has been growing interest in and support for the PKK, whose representatives have been allowed freedom of movement in Armenia. Armenia is understandably alive to the travails of Kurds in Turkey. Following Ocalan's eviction from Syria 2,000 Kurds demonstrated in Yerevan. Following his capture, about 100 Kurds occupied the UN mission building, while two tried to immolate themselves outside the Greek embassy.

Sources

Julie Flint, *The Kurds of Azerbaijan and Armenia*, Kurdish Human Rights Project, London, December 1998; Jemshid Heydari, 'The Kurds of the USSR', unpublished mimeograph, February 1991; Kendal, 'The Kurds in the Soviet Union', in G. Chaliand, *People without a Country* (London 1980); Kurdish Human Rights Project, *Kurds in the Former Soviet Union: a preliminary Report on the Situation of the Kurdish Community in the Republics of the former Soviet Union* (London, November 1996); *Middle East International*; NK Nadirov, 'The Position of the Kurds in the USSR', unpublished mimeograph, June 1991; Ismet Cherif Vanly, 'The Kurds in the Soviet Union', in Kreyenbroek and Sperl, *The Kurds: A contemporary overview* (Routledge, London and New York, 1992).

Notes

1. This estimate is based upon information in Minority Rights Publications, *The World Directory of Minorities* (London. 1997), Ismet Cheriff Vanly, 'the Kurds in the Soviet Union' in Kreyenbroek and Sperl, *The Kurds: A Contemporary Overview* (London, 1992); Jemshid Heyderi, 'The Kurds of the USSR', unpublished mimeograph, February 1991; Tim Potier, 'The Kurds and Other Minorities of the Caucasus Republics' unpublished mimeograph, August 1996.

2. N. Nadirov, 'Position of the Kurds in the USSR', unpublished mimeograph presented to Kurdish symposium, Pantheion University, June 1991, p. 5.

3.Quoted in Nadirov, 'Position of the Kurds', p. 6.

4. US Department of State, *Country Reports on Human Rights Practices for 1994* (Washington 1995) p. 741.

5. These complain that some Kurdish intellectuals who asserted 'Yazidis are Kurds' were put on trial. They also claim that various Kurdish intellectuals have been assassinated, for example, Dr Sihide Ibo, Dr Dewreshian and Hesen Abbasian, and that other intellectuals have consequently fled, see www.yezidi.org.

INDEX